Communities of Discourse
The Rhetoric of Disciplines

Editors

GARY D. SCHMIDT
Calvin College

WILLIAM J. VANDE KOPPLE
Calvin College

Prentice Hall, Englewood Cliffs, New Jersey 07632

Library of Congress Cataloging-in-Publication Data

Communities of discourse : the rhetoric of disciplines / editors,
   Gary D. Schmidt, William J. Vande Kopple.
      p.   cm.
   Includes bibliographical references and index.
   ISBN 0-13-151515-2 :
      1. College readers.   2. Interdisciplinary approach in education.
   3. English language—Rhetoric.   I. Schmidt, Gary D.   II. Vande
Kopple, William J.
   PE1417.C63757   1993
   808′.0427—dc20   92-25108

Acquisitions editor: *Philip Miller*
Editorial/production supervisor: *Edie Riker*
Cover design: *Bruce Kenselaar*
Prepress buyer: *Herb Klein*
Manufacturing buyers: *Patrice Fraccio and Bob Anderson*
Editorial assistant: *Kara Hado*
Credits and copyright acknowledgments appear at the back of the book
on pages 729–730 which constitutes an extension of the copyright page.

Printed in the United States of America

10   9   8   7   6   5   4   3   2   1

ISBN   0-13-151515-2

For
David, Rebecca, Kathleen and James
GS

For
Jonathan, Joel, and Jason
BVK

CONTENTS

PREFACE   *xi*

PART I RHETORIC

DISCOURSE COMMUNITIES   *1*

RHETORIC   *6*

**READING WITHIN DISCOURSE
COMMUNITIES**   *21*

**WRITING WITHIN DISCOURSE
COMMUNITIES**   *35*

PART II READINGS

**DISCOURSE COMMUNITIES IN
HISTORICAL STUDIES**   *47*

Introduction 47

Thucydides 50

  BOOK II *51*

Bede 62

  A HISTORY OF THE ENGLISH CHURCH AND
    PEOPLE 63

William Bradford 72

  HISTORY OF PLYMOUTH PLANTATION 73

  NEW ENGLISH CANAAN 79

Edward Gibbon *85*

ROME IN POWER AND DECAY *86*

Robert Graves *93*

WAS BENEDICT ARNOLD A TRAITOR? *94*

Fernand Braudel *109*

THE MEDITERRANEAN AS A PHYSICAL UNIT:
CLIMATE AND HISTORY *110*

Robert G. L. Waite *128*

HITLER'S "PRIMAL SCENE TRAUMA" *129*

Gerda Lerner *137*

THE CREATION OF PATRIARCHY *138*

Eugene D. Genovese *155*

TIME AND WORK RHYTHMS *156*

Robert Hughes *167*

A HORSE FOALED BY AN ACORN *168*

Interconnections: Questions for Writing *176*

DISCOURSE COMMUNITIES IN THE ARTS

180

Introduction *180*

Aristotle *183*

ARISTOTLE'S POETICS *184*

Sir Philip Sidney *194*

AN APOLOGIE FOR POETRY *195*

Charles Lamb *207*

ON THE ARTIFICIAL COMEDY OF THE LAST
CENTURY *208*

Roger Fry *216*

AN ESSAY IN AESTHETICS *217*

Paul Rosenfeld *230*

CHARLES IVES *231*

Mao Zedong *239*

TALKS AT THE YENAN FORUM ON ART AND
LITERATURE *239*

Bruno Bettelheim *254*

   JACK AND THE BEANSTALK *255*

   THE ELF *266*

Tzvetan Todorov *270*

   THE TYPOLOGY OF DETECTIVE FICTION *271*

Tania Modleski *281*

   THE MASTER'S DOLLHOUSE: *REAR WINDOW* *282*

Gail (Luttmann) Damerow and Rick Luttmann *298*

   AESTHETICS OF ESKIMO DANCE: A COMPARISON
   METHODOLOGY *299*

Interconnections: Questions for Writing *310*

DISCOURSE COMMUNITIES IN PHILOSOPHY *313*

Introduction *313*

Plato *316*

   THE ALLEGORY OF THE CAVE *317*

Augustine *322*

   BOOK II *323*

Julian of Norwich *333*

   REVELATIONS OF DIVINE LOVE *334*

Rene Descartes *342*

   MEDITATIONS ON FIRST PHILOSOPHY *343*

John Locke *355*

   BOOK II: CHAPTER I *356*

Benjamin Lee Whorf *369*

   AN AMERICAN INDIAN MODEL OF THE
   UNIVERSE *370*

Jean-Paul Sartre *378*

   EXISTENTIALISM *379*

Thomas Merton *390*

   ZEN BUDDHIST MONASTICISM *391*

Thomas S. Kuhn *408*

THE ROUTE TO NORMAL SCIENCE *409*

Virginia Essene *420*

WHY YOU CAME TO PLANET EARTH *420*

Interconnections: Questions for Writing *428*

DISCOURSE COMMUNITIES IN THE SOCIAL SCIENCES

431

Introduction *431*

Adam Smith *434*

OF THE DIVISION OF LABOUR *435*

Karl Marx and Friedrich Engels *444*

THE COMMUNIST MANIFESTO *445*

Sigmund Freud *457*

CASE 4: KATHARINA *458*

Émile Durkheim *469*

THE DUALISM OF HUMAN NATURE AND ITS
SOCIAL CONDITIONS *470*

Bronislaw Malinowski *483*

CORAL GARDENS AND THEIR MAGIC *484*

Harold Dwight Lasswell *501*

THE DEVELOPING SCIENCE OF DEMOCRACY *502*

B. F. Skinner *514*

THE STEEP AND THORNY WAY TO A SCIENCE OF
BEHAVIOR *515*

Carol Gilligan *529*

WOMAN'S PLACE IN MAN'S LIFE CYCLE *529*

William G. Ouchi *548*

THE WORKINGS OF A JAPANESE
CORPORATION *549*

Suzanne J. Kessler and Wendy McKenna *563*

TOWARD A THEORY OF GENDER *564*

Interconnections: Questions for Writing *577*

DISCOURSE COMMUNITIES IN SCIENCE   *581*

Introduction *581*

Aristotle *585*

  HISTORY OF ANIMALS *586*

The Book of Secrets *593*

  THE FIRST BOOK OF THE VIRTUES OF CERTAIN
    HERBS *594*

Galileo Galilei *600*

  ON MOTION *601*

Charles Darwin *611*

  "KEELING ISLANDS: CORAL FORMATIONS" *612*

Albert Einstein *627*

  E = MC^2 *627*

Rita Levi-Montalcini *633*

  A PRIVATE LABORATORY *á la* ROBINSON
    CRUSOE *633*

Fritjof Capra *645*

  THE NEW PHYSICS *645*

Stephen Jay Gould *669*

  ONLY HIS WINGS REMAINED *670*

Wayne Frair and Percival Davis *684*

  EVOLUTION AND SCIENCE *684*

James Crutchfield, J. Doyne Farmer, Norman H. Packard, and
  Robert Shaw *698*

  CHAOS *699*

Interconnections: Questions for Writing *723*

Interconnections: Questions for Discussion and Writing About
  and from Within the Represented Disciplines *725*

COPYRIGHT ACKNOWLEDGMENTS   729

INDEX   733

PREFACE

To put together a collection of readings is to set out, implicitly if not explicitly, our assumptions about the act of writing. We assume that writers write to communicate, whether that communication be to another person, a group, or even to oneself. We assume that such things as the writer's understanding of the audience, the writer's attitude toward the subject, the rhetorical mode the writer chooses to structure his or her ideas, the levels of diction, the strategic structuring of paragraphs and sentences to best convey the ideas—all of these—are involved in the writer's attempt to communicate.

We contend that all of these elements are affected, at least in part, by the communities of discourse within which a writer lives and works. Each community has its own perceptions about how the act of writing ought to be performed. While many of these perceptions overlap—all of the discourse communities represented in this book, for example, agree on basic principles of good rhetoric—many other perceptions may clash. Such clashes may be brought about by a community's culture, its point in history, its philosophical assumptions about the nature of the world and how to understand that world, or its academic disciplines. For example, the medieval scientist who authored *Book of Secrets* was part of a discourse community that approached subjects in very different ways than the community of twentieth-century Darwinian naturalists of which Stephen Jay Gould is a member.

We have drawn the essays from five different areas of study: history, the arts, philosophy, science, and the social sciences. We have chosen each essay because its author represents one or more very specific discourse communities, and because the essay illustrates both the clashes and agreements within discourse communities about the nature of effective writing. We chose them because they illustrate the kinds of writing that have characterized each discourse community. And we chose them because they are good reads. For in the end, a written piece may be judged to be effective or ineffective depending upon whether it can hold the attention of its intended audience.

And these essays have been selected because they challenge certain ways of thinking by articulating forcefully and persuasively points of view held by specific communities. Perhaps you have never before encountered psychoanalytic explanations for historical events, articulate expressions of Darwinism and creationism, feminist claims of patriarchalism, New Age theories of human existence. It is our hope that these essays will confront you with ideas that are being debated in contemporary North America—as well as ideas that have been debated throughout the world for the last two-and-a-half millenia.

We could have organized these essays in many different ways. Among the possibilities for instance, we could have grouped them by cultures they are products of, by the periods in history they represent, by the religious stances implicit or explicit in them, or by the political ideologies that inform them. In other words, we could have presented essays in clusters corresponding to cultural, historical, religious, or political discourse communities.

We have chosen to present the essays according to the discourse communities associated with different academic disciplines. The first cluster, for example, contains essays dealing with history, and within that and the other clusters we move from the oldest to the most recent essays.

We present the essays according to academic disciplines because, first, in a book intended primarily for college students, an organizational scheme based on the discourse communities of different disciplines is easier to grasp than one based on the discourse communities of culture, religion, or political ideology. In addition, many students today make it their goal to learn to think and write as those in one or another particular discipline do. We believe that our organizational scheme will help them see more clearly how writers in various disciplines proceed. Why do we move from oldest to most recent essays in each disciplinary section? Primarily because writers in a discipline always work within a historical context. What was written before them will affect what they do and how they do it. Moving through the disciplines historically will allow us to see specific signs of this. It will also give us an idea of what it means to make progress in a discipline.

We introduce each selection with information about its author and about the rhetorical situation that the author faced. This information will help you understand the selection more fully and see how valuable the kind of pre-reading activities we recommend in Chapter 3 can be. After each selection we include two sets of questions for discussion. The first set centers on the discourse community as reflected in the selection. The second set of questions centers on the rhetorical strategies that the author of the selection employs. Following the two sets of questions are some suggestions for writing. Some of these will suggest that you try to write *as a member* of the discourse community represented by a selection. Others will suggest that you write *about* the discourse community represented by a selection. After all of the selections associated with a discipline, we list some additional topics for writing which ask you to pursue connections between two or more of the selections from that discipline. At the end of the collection we pose several writing questions that ask you to make connections between the five different academic areas represented in this book.

One of our overarching goals is to sensitize you to different ways in which different discourse communities communicate meanings. But we also hope that you come to agree with us that communication across the boundaries between different discourse communities is possible, and that finely honed rhetorical abilities do much to enable such communication. Ultimately, of course, we hope that you will expand your reading and writing abilities, and that you will use them to move into larger and larger communities of discourse as long as you read.

Putting together a collection like this also shows some of our assumptions about reading. A quick glance at the table of contents suggests that you will not be able to speed read these essays. Because they are written with specific audiences in mind, the essays are challenging, particularly for those who might be unfamiliar with these communities. But because the authors of these essays share many perceptions about rhetorical skills, the essays are also accessible. In most cases you will not find these quick reads, but you will find them to be engrossing.

And this is how we assume reading should be. Reading for content alone means reading on only one level. It is true that certain forms of writing call for such a form of reading: the mystery that you buy at the supermarket to while away a lazy August afternoon probably calls for a reading that focuses only upon content. But these essays call for more. They ask you to examine the rhetorical patterns and strategies that enable the writer to communuicate the content. They ask for a careful analysis of how those strategies and patterns are affected by the writer's discourse community.

We assume that successful reading involves understanding a writer's attempts to communicate his or her ideas. To this end, we have chosen to anthologize full essays, or longer selections from important texts which are complete in themselves. Full communication does not come through abbreviated messages. The texts that we have included, consequently, are texts that the authors themselves would recognize as having an internal consistency, a fully developed argument. And for the most part we have tried to keep the essays in a format exactly as the authors envisioned them. Unless otherwise noted, the illustrations accompanying the texts are taken from the original essays. The footnotes are often original with the pieces; we have added notes only for purposes of clarification, generally not to supplement what the writers themselves are doing.

We acknowledge with gratitude the debts we owe to our editors at Prentice Hall. Most especially we thank J. Philip Miller, who has remained constant through the vicissitudes of time, and Kate Morgan. She, together with Tracy Augustine, contributed much to the final format of the manuscript. Our thanks also to Robert Vande Kopple who helped in particular on the Stephen Jay Gould essay and who gave us direction for the entire science section. For that section we are also indebted to Del Ratzsch, David Van Baak, and Randall Van Dragt. For advice concerning the discourse communities of psychology we gratefully acknowledge Martin Bolt; for those in the arena of history we thank James Bratt and David Diephouse.

That the manuscript ever moved from the shadowy meta-world of green light to the realm of hard copy is due entirely to Alma Walhout, secretary of the English Department of Calvin College, and a host of student assistants, namely Michelle De Rose, Keri Bruggink, Laura Vander Hart, Rebecca Warren, Kathy Struck, and Alicia Holton. We acknowledge most especially the efforts of our research assistant, Heather Bouwman, who cheerfully tramped back and forth to the library, managed files, checked footnotes and bibliographic references, researched many of the writers, and typed. The book might have been finished without her, but it would have been less of the happy project that it became.

To thank our spouses for their support during the writing and editing of this book is really to thank them for being themselves. And that we do with joy.

DISCOURSE COMMUNITIES

Most of you are probably at or near the point when, after considering the many different academic programs available at your college or university, you must decide which program or progams to major in. For a few of our own students each year, this decision is easy. One of our current students, for example, has known since before she was in high school that she wanted to major in cultural anthropology in college.

But for some of our current students, the time when they review academic programs is one of great uncertainty. Writing in her journal, one of our students described her uncertainty this way: "All the possible fields to study and you must choose one. How in the world are you supposed to know?"

A few of these students actually find this time of uncertainty exciting. One wrote in his journal that "there are so many areas that interest me." He added that he would probably graduate with a "double major in biology and English with a minor in sociology with an emphasis in engineering."

For most of our undecided students, however, sooner or later this time of uncertainty leads to anxiety. One wrote that "I am terrified of continuing in college and not knowing what to major in." Another admitted that "in some bizarre way I wish I lived in a country where someone would just tell me what to specialize in."

What makes choosing a field to major in particularly frightening for some students is that as they read assignments and listen to lectures in various disciplines, they have difficulty understanding what people are writing and talking about. Some of our students have described to us how they have attended lectures in various disciplines, struggled to find anything like threads in the arguments, and left with barely a suspicion as to what the lectures were about.

Our basic claim in this book is that, as you survey the various academic programs available to you, what you are seeing are the products of many different discourse communities at work. In fact, at this point in your lives, quite possibly you are being exposed to a larger number of various discourse communities than you ever will be again. The work of some or many of these communities might not make sense to you now. But now you are probably not a full member of any of these communities; you must choose which one or ones you want to learn the ways of and then work your way into full membership. Our goals are to introduce you to many different discourse com-munities, to help you read and write successfully within several discourse communities, and to aid you in understanding and evaluating the work of many communities you do not become a full member of, both while you are in college and throughout the rest of your lives.

What is a discourse community? In general terms, it is a group of people who share ways to claim, organize, communicate, and evaluate meanings. More specifically, if you and a friend have one or more discourse communi-ties in common, the two of you will probably spend a significant amount of time focusing your attention on the same issues and things. And both of you will probably have a firm sense of why you focus on those issues and things. Moreover, the two of you will share many ways to think and communicate about those issues and things, as well as many ways to evaluate your thinking and communicating. Finally, the two of you will agree about many kinds of actions that your thinking and communicating can and should lead to. In great measure, then, the systems of meaning associated with the discourse communities that you belong to will be at the center of how you interact with others and the world.

To further clarify the nature of discourse communities, we should look at some of the ways they can differ from each other. In the first place, we see that people from different discourse communities often differ in their funda-mental beliefs about reality. For example, one writer whose work we anthol-ogize, the Venerable Bede (see 62), writes out of the discourse community of medieval Christianity. Within that system of meaning he sees what many modern people would regard as coincidences or accidents as miracles caused by God. On the other hand, Jean-Paul Sartre (see 378) writes out of the discourse community of modern existentialism, and within that system of meaning he calls readers to face the consequences of admitting to themselves that God is dead.

People working within different discourse communities also often differ in what they study and in what they are concerned about. Sometimes they study altogether different objects or phenomena. For example, Mao Zedong (see 239), writing within the tradition of Marxist art criticism, focuses on how artists in Red China should construct works of art to elevate and educate the masses and thereby to strengthen the country's commitment to Marxism. Fer-nand Braudel (see 109), working within the community of scholars practicing what is often called "total history," examines how several aspects of life in the Mediterranean world affected events in the age of Phillip II of Spain. And Benjamin Lee Whorf (see 369), working as a linguistic anthropologist, studies whether the structures of Native-Americans' languages lead them to see the world differently from the ways that speakers of other languages, especially European languages, do.

Sometimes people from different discourse communities focus on differ-ent aspects of the same object or general phenomenon. Both Gerda Lerner (see 137) and Carol Gilligan (see 529) focus generally on the place of women in the modern world. But Lerner, who works as a feminist historian, tries to trace how, throughout the history of Western culture, men have institutionalized a subordinate position for women. And Gilligan, who works within the discourse community of feminist developmental psychologists, studies how women's overall systems of morality are different from those of men and how women develop these systems.

As you have probably guessed, members of one discourse community often employ methods in their work that differ from those that members of other discourse communities use. Among the different methods described in the essays that we include in this book are all of the following: probing one's own memory, channeling voices from powers beyond this world, speculating about people's basic motivations, examining accounts of the lives of slaves in the American South, reading several novels of a particular kind and thinking about what structures they have in common, interviewing subjects of different ages and backgrounds, sending opinion surveys to other people, observing the actions of a tribe of people and then asking a native informant what those actions signify, examining and measuring objects and animals in the natural world, and analyzing sections of nerve tissue under a microscope in a laboratory. Some of these methods are occasionally used by members of more than one discourse community; others are used only by members of one particular discourse community.

Of course, different methods lead to different kinds of evidence. To consider a few examples, in the essays we include, the probing of one's memory leads to personal testimonies or accounts. The reading of novels and thinking about what their structures have in common leads to a classification of probable structures for that kind of novel. And the laboratory analysis of sections of nerve tissue leads to precise measurements of how cells grow and become specialized for different functions.

Different methods, then, produce different kinds of evidence. And these kinds of evidence are often so clearly different from each other that one of the better ways for you to increase your skill in distinguishing one discourse community from another is to ask, "What kinds of evidence does this one group of people accept? What kinds does this other group accept?" If both groups accept the same kinds of evidence, they are probably parts of an overarching discourse community. If one group rejects the kinds of evidence that the other group values, then the two groups are probably included in different discourse communities.

If one discourse community depends on evidence of a different kind from that which another discourse community depends on, you would expect that these two groups would use different terms in communicating about their work. And that is exactly what happens. As you read writers from the various discourse communities represented here, it might occasionally seem to you that one writer is using a different dialect of English from another writer. For example, Robert G. L. Waite (see 128), who represents a discourse community that has come to be called psychohistory, uses terms such as *primal scene trauma*, *castration anxieties*, and *Oedipal fantasies*. Roger Fry (see 216), who helped to found the discourse community of formalist art criticism, writes about "disinterested intensity of contemplation," "rhythm of line," and the "balancing of the attraction to the eye about the central line of the picture." Finally, Thomas S. Kuhn (see 408), who writes within the discourse community of the philosophy of science, writes about "normal science," the "emergence of a paradigm," and the "genesis and continuation of a particular research tradition."

Once a discourse community agrees about what counts as valid evidence, it also has to reach agreement about how much of that evidence to use and about how to present that evidence. Here again, discourse communities can differ radically from each other. Some demand that their members present all possible evidence. Others require only a representative sampling of evidence. Some hold that their members ought always to proceed in a straight line, step by logical step, incrementally. Others encourage their members to circle around from one bit of evidence to the next, hinting at logical connections, gradually weaving the evidence into an appealing texture.

Additionally, different discourse communities make progress toward addressing their concerns in different ways. Some make progress in small steps along the same line of inquiry. Others encourage some of their members to work along different lines. Still other communities operate along one line for a while and then abandon it entirely and pursue a different one.

Finally, and perhaps most importantly, members of different discourse communities usually work to achieve different ultimate purposes. In "Keeling Islands: Coral Formations" (see 611), Charles Darwin, one of the earliest evolutionary biologists, aims to describe three classes of coral reefs and then to argue for his own hypothesis about how they originate and change. Gerda Lerner, a feminist historian, has a very different ultimate purpose. In "The Creation of Patriarchy" (see 137), she summarizes the steps in the historical development of the system of patriarchy and then argues that both women and men need to step outside patriarchal thought and develop a feminist worldview. And Virginia Essene pursues yet a different overall goal. Working within the community of New Age thinkers and writers, she seeks in "Why You Came to Planet Earth" (see 420) to move young adults to recognize that they are bodies of light similar to angels and that they chose to come to earth long ago to rescue the planet from such evils as war, violence, and negative thinking.

In view of the many specific ways in which one discourse community can differ from another, it is easy to see why those unfamiliar with a particular community could be shocked or baffled by what and how those in that community talk and write. Discovering that one's way of claiming and communicating meaning is not the only way can be devastating. The whole process of maturing reflects how people either learn or fail to learn how to encounter and respond to the discourse of communities that are new to them. Some people regard each encounter with a new discourse community as unsettling and intimidating. Others view each such encounter as an exciting adventure. They look forward to encounters with systems of meaning that are different from their own.

As you move through your college career, you might be surprised at how many systems of meaning there are and at how different some of these are from your own. To this point we might have given you the impression that the only different discourse communities in the world are the various academic disciplines. That is not the case. The different academic disciplines do constitute different discourse communities, but other groups of people do too. For example, people from different cultures usually make up different discourse communities. So do people with different religious beliefs. And people holding different economic theories also usually make up different discourse communities.

In this light, it is easier to see that not all members of one particular discourse community will have overall systems of meaning identical in all respects. It is possible for those who have one discourse community in common (for example, the discourse community of quantum physics) to have others not in common (for example, the discourse communities of different religions). And it is also possible for people to move in and out of discourse communities, changing their systems of meaning as they grow older.

In view of all the ways in which members of one discourse community can differ from members of another discourse community, you might wonder how the members of one would ever be able to communicate with the members of another. Unfortunately, too often people from different discourse communities do not communicate well at all. You might have had the experience of reading essays written by members of different discourse communities. With each essay addressing the same issue or problem, perhaps you discovered that the writers seemed to write past each other, never seeming to find common ground. Or worse, you might have read people who missed understanding each other so completely that they gave up trying and literally had a fight using words on a page.

But is all speaking and writing between discourse communities just a babble of voices, a war of words? No. Often people from different discourse communities do communicate well with each other. These people are usually those who have worked hard to bring their differences into the open, to see the nature of these differences clearly, to seek the reasons for these differences, and to react to them with humility. These people are also usually skilled in the art of rhetoric, an art that enhances communication both within and between discourse communities. We believe that those who are skilled in rhetoric are those who will be able to continue enlarging the number of discourse communities they can communicate within. In so doing, they may actually succeed in bringing several different discourse communities together in one much larger, overarching discourse community. We will examine some key aspects of the art of rhetoric in the next chapter.

RHETORIC

The claim we made for rhetoric at the end of the first chapter perhaps surprised you, particularly because the word *rhetoric* has some very negative associations for many people today. Candidates for public office give long speeches on the campaign trail, which many commentators then dismiss as "mere rhetoric." Elected officials make promises to their constituents, and many of these constituents dismiss the promises as the "usual rhetoric." In these contexts, *rhetoric* is associated with hot air, emptiness, even intentional deception.

Such associations are unfair to the origins of the word *rhetoric* in ancient Greece. From the beginning, rhetoric was linked to persuasive skill, to the ability of people to move others to see things as they did. This skill was especially valued in the practices of advising political assemblies, arguing cases in law courts, and praising or blaming others in public ceremonies.

In this book, we use *rhetoric* to refer to the art of using language to have desired effects on people. Usually we will focus on using written language. Rhetoric is essentially a matter of choice at all stages of the writing process— from the time when writers decide how to organize an essay to the time when they select individual words. These choices are usually not either totally right or totally wrong. With each choice, writers may gain something, but they may lose something too. Such choices are inescapable. A writer cannot say, "I'll avoid deciding how to develop this paragraph." or "I'll skip finding a way to phrase this sentence." Writers always end up making choices, some of which may be far better than others. Their goal is consistently to make choices that win more than they lose.

In the following text, we examine some of the major rhetorical considerations that writers must keep in mind as they make choices about their writing. As you become familiar with these considerations, you will be better prepared to analyze and evaluate choices in others' writing and to make wise choices for your own.

CONTEXT

Skilled rhetoricians know that they never write in a vacuum; they write in a complex social context. They cannot be aware of all aspects of that context, but they are usually very much aware of many variables and the implications that these variables have for their writing. Some of these considerations can be described as follows: Writers always write in a certain place, at a certain time, for particular readers (whom we will call their audience), for a specific purpose, with various kinds of evidence, and with various consequences. We will examine several of these aspects in more detail, starting with the matter of audience.

AUDIENCE

When people write, they almost always write to or for others. Occasionally they might write pieces without a clear audience in mind and send these pieces into the world hoping that they will find or create their own audience. Occasionally they might write for themselves. Most of the time, however, they write for other people, who are probably fairly clearly identified in their own minds. To analyze the writing of people from within and outside your own discourse communities, and to communicate effectively with members of your own and other discourse communities, you must understand audiences and what it will take to have particular effects on them.

Certain subjects might be appealing to some people and offensive to others. One organizational strategy might be exactly right for some readers and exactly wrong for others. A piece might seem overdeveloped to some readers, underdeveloped to others. Sentences that impress some readers might leave others cold.

Writers who want to affect readers in a particular way must analyze those readers carefully. Sometimes they might write to people with whom they have several discourse communities in common. At other times they might write to people from discourse communities entirely different from their own. And at still other times they might write to a very diverse set of readers. They might have several discourse communities in common with some of these readers, only one or two discourse communities in common with others, and no discourse communities in common with still others.

Starting by analyzing what discourse communities their readers belong to should help writers as they ask how numerous those readers are, how old they are, what their social standing is, and how well they know them. Answers to questions about these matters will help writers determine such things as what kinds of words to choose, what tone to adopt, and what stylistic level to write on.

For example, imagine that you had to write a note about some fairly routine matter, say an upcoming round of golf, to only a few people, all of whom are about your age and your social standing, and all of whom you know well. You would probably have some unusual effects on them if you wrote the note in a highly formal and wordy style:

> Arrangements which will allow and facilitate our beginning a round of golf on this coming Saturday, the twenty-third day of October in the year Nineteen

Hundred and Ninety-Three, have been formalized. Commencement of the aforementioned round of golf will be at nine o'clock in the morning at the Meadowbrook Country Club, located one-half mile north of the intersection of Negaunee Road and Post Avenue. Failure to comply with all of the arrangements as dutifully specified herein will have serious and dire consequences.

If you wrote to friends in this way, at first they would probably think you were joking. If you made it clear that you were serious, they might start to suspect that you have a weird quirk in your character that they did not know about before. And if you remained serious about this note and wrote more notes like this to them, it would probably not take them too long to start looking for a new golf partner.

Successful writers also analyze how much their audience knows about their subject. How much they know will affect several moves the writers make. For one thing, it will affect how much background information they need to convey. If you were to write about Philip II (see 109) for seventh graders, you might write a sentence like this:

Philip II, the powerful king of Spain in the sixteenth century, frequently had to worry about crop failures.

If you were writing to a team of professors teaching a college seminar on the history of Spain, however, the information about Philip II as a powerful king in the sixteenth century would be unnecessary and even unwise to include. These professors would probably be insulted by being told what they already know very well.

How much an audience knows about a subject will also affect how many terms writers need to define as well as how extensively they need to define them. Someone who takes a psychological approach to history and who is writing to people who take the same approach can use a phrase such as *primal scene trauma* (see 457); such readers will understand this phrase without any trouble. However, the moment the historian writes to people without specialized knowledge, he or she will have to explain that *primal scene trauma* is the trauma that sometimes results when children first see their parents having sexual intercourse. And the researcher may have to go on to describe some of the possible effects of that trauma.

How much readers know will even affect how many connectives or transition words writers should use. If readers know little about a subject, writers will probably want to make many relationships of logic or time explicit, using words like *furthermore, similarly,* and *after that.* If they know almost as much as the writers do about the subject, the writers would probably choose to use fewer connecting words, being confident that their readers will follow the logic of the presentation with just a little help. In fact, it may be wise to use fewer connectives, since such readers may feel patronized if each connection is explicitly marked for them.

A similar point is that writers will have to estimate readers' knowledge before they decide how much information to repeat from sentence to sentence. Many grammatical structures, especially subordinate clauses, allow writers to take information that they have expressed in one sentence and express it again, usually in slightly abbreviated form, in a subsequent sentence. Sometimes this works very well. It works, for example, in directions to people assembling things that they know little or nothing about:

> Take the rear assembly (marked number 1 on the diagram) and, using a quarter-inch socket wrench, loosen nuts A and B so that the short axle can be inserted into slot C. Once you have the short axle inserted into slot C, tighten nuts A and B.

In the second sentence of these directions, the writer repeats information about the short axle and slot C. Does he or she need to do this? Not if the reader is someone who does this kind of assembling all day long, five days a week. But for those who know little about this operation, the repeated information can be a sign of encouragement:

> You've made it through step 1. Don't panic. Soon even you will have assembled the new robotic rug cleaner.

As writers analyze their audience, they must also try to learn how those readers expect certain kinds of essays to be organized. This is particularly true when they write to readers from cultures other than their own. Several of our students have spent either a summer or a full academic year teaching English in China. One difficulty almost all of them complain about centers on organizational patterns for essays. They try to teach the Chinese students to organize essays as many North Americans often do: with the evidence arranged point by point in a straight line either leading from or to an explicit main point. Their students often resist this in their writing, since they have cultural experiences that lead them to prefer a more circular or recursive organizational pattern. They approach their point from one angle, never being explicit about it, and then they circle around and approach the point from another angle. The pattern our students were trying to teach them was almost offensive to them.

Finally, writers should try to discover what their audience believes, values, or feels about their subject matter. Doing so will help them decide what they can take for granted and what they must debate at length. If writers claim, as Wayne Frair and Percival Davis do (see 684), that a scientific account of the history of the earth can be compatible with religious belief, they cannot assume that all readers will see science as a subjective endeavor, one that is affected by scientists' beliefs and assumptions. In fact, that may be one of the key points they will have to argue, as Frair and Davis do at length.

Similarly, analyzing the beliefs, values, and feelings of an audience helps writers decide what kinds of evidence to use and how to use it. Much of the evidence that Virginia Essene uses comes from voices that she says she has channeled from beyond this world (see 420). New Age thinkers accept such evidence without question. Other people would wonder how anyone could ever accept such voices as legitimate evidence.

Sometimes, it is true, audiences can seem distant to writers, and then writers are not able to carry out all of the analyses described here. Often, however, they can carry most of them out. The skill that you display in carrying them out should help you greatly as you evaluate others' writing and communicate in writing within and beyond your own discourse communities.

PURPOSE

Once people actually write to others, they do things to them, they act on them. Perhaps you have not thought of your own writing as doing something, as acting on readers. This is probably because the writing you have to do in many school situations is artificial. You are supposed to invent readers and write a persuasive essay for them. Or you are to write a descriptive essay for an audience of your own imagining. In fact, however, you know that in most cases your one and only reader will be your teacher or professor. In some cases you also know that the instructor does not really expect to learn anything from your writing or to be affected by it. Outside school, however, you usually write to specific people whom you affect in various ways. In the process, you often affect or change yourself as well. What you aim to do to readers we will call your *purpose*.

Different people have different ways of classifying possible purposes in writing. In ancient Greece, Aristotle classified the kinds of public communication as having one of three possible purposes: advising political assemblies, arguing cases in law courts, and praising or blaming public officials. Others agree that there are three general purposes for writing, but they disagree with Aristotle about what they are. They say that writers can move people, teach them, or delight them. Many current teachers of composition depend on a four-part classification of purpose. They say that writers can describe, narrate, explain, or argue. Some of them subdivide argument into two processes: one that appeals to readers' reason and seeks their assent, and another that appeals to readers' emotions and seeks to move them to action.

Each of these classifications has its good points. Often it is necessary to talk of purpose in writing in such general terms. Yet we believe that you will learn most about writing if you think about your own and others' purposes very specifically. The more specific your thinking is, the more likely you are to be successful both in evaluating whether other writers have achieved their aims and in deciding what you have to do to achieve yours. Michael Stubbs points out that people can use language for all of the following purposes: "promising, asserting, describing, impressing, intimidating, persuading, comforting, gossiping, arguing, complaining, reciting, swearing, protesting, betting, and so on indefinitely."

A good way to get a more concrete idea about purposes in writing is to consider the many different things writers do in a typical daily newspaper. We looked through the October 10, 1988, issue of our local newspaper, *The Grand Rapids Press*, and found writers trying to achieve many different specific purposes.

The purpose that most people would say is primary for newspapers is reporting the news as clearly and objectively as possible. Such reporting was plentiful. One writer reported on Kirk Gibson's home run in the twelfth inning to lift the Dodgers over the Mets in the fourth game of the 1988 National League Championship Series. Another reported on the killing of three Palestinians by Israeli troops who were searching for agitators.

Related to reporting is the act of alerting people to changes and upcoming events. An optometrist alerted current and prospective patients to a change in the location of his office. An item in the Date Book section announced a course entitled "How to Be an Effective Father." A special column announced several upcoming cultural events. A similar column alerted readers to all the movies playing in town and added a short summary of each of them. Someone also presented information on what the television shows for that day would be about.

Many writers tried to buy or sell things. One wanted to sell a garden-sized, like-new, almond-colored bathtub. One offered a service: "You call—I haul." One wanted to buy "all Oriental rugs." A firm wanted to hire "assertive people for advertising sales positions."

Many different writers gave various kinds of advice. Ann Landers gave advice about how to cope with sharing a name with a famous person (a reader named Ann had married a man with the surname Landers). Heloise passed on advice from a reader who works out often and consequently has to wash her workout clothing frequently; she tells readers that she hooks all her sports bras closed before washing them so that they won't snag her leotards. Dr. Paul Donohue recorded the symptoms a reader complained about, offered his own tentative diagnosis that the symptoms are not associated with chronic mono, and advised the reader what to do next.

Closely related to giving advice is answering questions. A minister who had lectured in Grand Rapids responded to five questions about the evils of rock music. Lou Holtz responded to questions about how well prepared the Fighting Irish would be to face Miami in a football game.

Many writers gave their opinions about various matters. The writer of a letter to the Public Pulse gave her opinion that teachers do an enormous amount of hard work for paltry wages. The Reformed Baptist Church provided a short advertisement giving its opinion on the "gospel truth of evolution."

Opinion moved into the realm of satire as Erma Bombeck poked light fun at the parental practice of always telling children that they are too young for some things, too old for others. Mark Russell satirized George Bush and

Michael Dukakis for the kinds of promotional pictures their advisors posed them in. Oliphant added pictures to writing to satirize Dukakis, showing him telling others not to leave home without an ACLU card.

Opinion became critical review as a writer evaluated a program of music from Czechoslovakia performed by the New World String Quartet, as another summed up and evaluated "Soldier, Child, Tortured Man," and as others provided short evaluative statements about movies then playing.

Many papers also include a section in which grieving friends and relatives mourn and commemorate those who are deceased: "Not a day do we forget you, thoughts of you are always near. We who love you, sadly miss you, as it dawns another year."

Finally, there were many examples of writers doing one thing in order to do another. Members of the Mormon church asked, "What do you know about the Mormon Church?" They wanted more than an answer; they wanted readers to find out more about their church and join it. Finally, Pine Rest Christian Hospital asked readers to take a short quiz about stress in their lives. Representatives of the hospital were hoping that increased awareness about stress and its effects would lead readers to attend one of their seminars on stress management.

In this light, it is clear that purposes for writing are usually very specific indeed. If we were to ask Mark Russell what the purpose of his piece in *The Grand Rapids Press* was, in which he described poses he would like to see presidential candidates Bush and Dukakis photographed in, he would probably say that his point starts with satire of two candidates whose managers pose them in all sorts of superficial ways. He might add that his point extends to a concern that the American people demand that they be given less superficiality and more substance during a political campaign. Russell would probably be able to be this specific and more. He would probably not use terms as general as some people do when they discuss purpose. He would probably not say that his purpose was general persuasion or the blaming of public officials, although his purpose is certainly related to both of these.

The clearer and more specific you are in thinking about purposes, the more able you should be to recognize and evaluate others' purposes and to achieve your own. You will be more likely to avoid purposeless prose, such as the following short piece:

> I took a different way to work this morning. The bricklayers had made good progress on the office building being built across from campus. Two cars were already in the faculty parking lot. As I walked to my office, I glanced into the departmental conference room. The janitor had vacuumed the carpet in the hallway. Soon the maintenance workers would have to come and repaint the walls. The heat was obviously already turned on in the building.

All the sentences in this piece have something to do with the writer's arriving at the office in the morning. But together they serve no higher purpose. The reader is tempted to ask, "So what? What's all this coming to?" When people first encounter prose like this, they get edgy and restless. Later they become frustrated and stop reading.

Before leaving the topic of purpose, we should touch on a subject that has arisen over and over in the history of studying rhetoric. The subject has to do with ethics. Writers can become very skilled at achieving their particular purposes on particular audiences. However, some of these purposes in themselves might be unethical. Additionally, it might be unethical for some writers to have certain purposes because of their motives. And some of the methods writers employ might be unethical. Finally, it might be unethical to try to have certain effects on certain audiences. In all these cases, rhetorical skill counts for less than ethical integrity.

Prior to and during World War II, Adolf Hitler and other Nazi officials used speeches and pamphlets very effectively. One of their purposes was to move the German people to see the Jews as less than fully human, as a kind of disease. Hitler referred to them, in fact, as "Jewish bacilli." The result of all this was that some Germans were more ready to tolerate the atrocities committed against the Jews. On the one hand, we have to say that such men as Hitler and Goebbels were marvelously talented rhetoricians. One only has to watch films of them delivering speeches at Nuremburg rallies to stand in awe of the power they exercised over people's minds with language. On the other hand, we would have to say that the purposes they used rhetoric for were grossly unethical.

THESIS

The most explicit encapsulation of a writer's purpose in an essay is the thesis. The thesis is usually expressed in one sentence, and hence writers often refer to their thesis sentences. But the thesis can be distributed across several sentences, particularly if it is complex and highly qualified. And sometimes the thesis may be implied, not directly stated.

Some people assume that only essays that are generally argumentative in purpose have theses. They associate the words *thesis sentence* with argumentative or even combative sentences such as "The curriculum of the modern American university is being destroyed by liberals." We stress, however, that most kinds of writing have a thesis, although people do not customarily talk in such terms. A writer's perspective is always evident. There is always a selector of details, an arranger of evidence, an interpreter of events, a teller of the tale.

Consider essays considered descriptive. Some people assume that such essays have no theses since they are, in effect, direct reflections of reality. But descriptive essays can never be direct reflections of reality. Someone decides which details to include and which details to omit; in fact, no one could ever notice all the details of a slice of reality, let alone record them all. Moreover, someone decides how to characterize the selected details and how to present them to readers. Reality does not force one and only one organizational scheme on writers. Each writer has to decide. And as they decide, they usually try to convey a dominant mood or impression, an expression of which would constitute their thesis: "The ferry surged off into the mist, leaving us hushed, wondering how far we had to go to reach the other shore."

Or consider essays considered explanatory. Again, some say that such essays have no theses because, after all, nothing in them is really being contested. But someone decides what to explain and how to explain it. One writer may explain in one way why female praying mantises sometimes eat their mates, while another writer may explain this phenomenon in an entirely different way (see Gould 669). Explanations, too, are usually interpretations.

We hold, therefore, that most pieces of writing (perhaps such pieces as grocery lists are exceptions) reveal a perspective, reveal a writer asking others, as Joan Didion puts it, to "listen to me, see it my way, change your mind." Usually, as we noted in the first chapter, the writer's perspective is molded by and reflects the perspectives of the discourse communities he or she is a part of. Whatever these perspectives are, we claim that most essays are essentially forms of persuasion.

As we noted, the thesis is usually expressed in one sentence. Some characteristics of good thesis sentences are as follows. First, they are complete sentences. More accurately, they are predications; they both announce a topic of concern in the subject and comment on that topic in the predicate. We stress this point because many students view their thesis sentences as mere indicators of topics. They write fragments such as "The whole matter of racism on college campuses." This presents a topic (the matter of racism on college campuses), but it does not say anything about it. To do this, a writer would have to add a predicate: "Racism on college campuses is caused by insecurity."

Similarly, the thesis is more than a statement of intention. Many composition teachers penalize students if they write sentences such as "In this essay I intend to examine three systems of animal communication." Skilled writers, however, sometimes include such sentences in their essays, often at the very beginning. Charles Darwin begins "Keeling Islands: Coral Formations" (see 611) by writing "I will now give a very brief account of the three great classes of coral-reefs; namely, Atolls, Barrier, and Fringing-reefs, and will explain my views on their formation." But these writers are usually developing longer essays than students typically write, or they are, like Darwin, working on a book with several subsections, and they use statements of intention to show what direction they will take. Moreover, they include a thesis sentence in addition to the statement of intention. Many students include only a statement of intention and not a thesis sentence. This is the main reason, we think, why teachers react negatively to statements of intention in students' essays.

A closely related point is that a thesis sentence should make a point that is not self-evident. One assumption underlying writing is that it ought to convey something that is new or not obvious. People usually read to make connections and to grow, not to go over what they already know. Thus they will probably pay little attention to an essay with a thesis sentence such as "Many students leave home to attend college." They all know that. But a thesis sentence such as "Moving away from home to attend college is the greatest shock to those who were most eager to move" would probably catch many readers' attention.

Many writers have success developing thesis sentences to which some people are opposed. The close association between thesis sentences and argument shows that throughout history many people have attempted to defend theses that have stirred up heated debate. Not all writing is appropriate for this, but some pieces lend themselves well to controversial theses. Too many of our students think they can produce good essays by trying to write safe ones; they try to develop positions that everyone will agree with. In doing this they forget that the diversity of discourse communities in the world makes total agreement possible only about a limited number of things. They also forget that if everyone agrees with their thesis, they are probably developing a rather inconsequential idea. In some areas, the more opponents you have, the more confident you can be that you are working on something important.

Good thesis sentences also state positions that can be handled effectively in the space available. Some of our students often make large claims that they think they can defend in five hundred words. They assert that "anabolic steroids ought to be banned" or that "given the nature of American society, rising rates of teenage suicide are inevitable." Both of these are predications, but they are predications that will probably demand more elaborate treatment than two pages of writing will allow. The opposite problem, of course, is that some students make claims that they can adequately defend in two pages but try to defend in ten. They display great ingenuity in finding several different ways to say the same thing.

Finally, we should add a note about words in thesis sentences. One problem we commonly see involves vague words. Students argue that a particular string quartet is "touching" or "moving," or that a certain approach to debt in the Third World is "remarkable." When they use words such as "moving," they might have a definite meaning in mind. Readers, however, might not. How was the writer moved? To what extent? Is being moved good or bad? Are *good* and *bad* even the right terms to use in asking about being moved?

In sum, as you read other writers, one of the more important things you can do is to identify and evaluate their thesis sentences. And as you develop your own essays, one of the more important things you can do is to try to ensure that you are working with good thesis sentences.

EVIDENCE

Very few readers ever accept a thesis simply because they see it in print. Most readers will not accept a thesis unless the writer supports it with enough of the right kind of evidence. As you read more and more material originating both within and outside the discourse communities that you are a member of, you might well be amazed at all the different kinds of evidence that come into play. Some communities admit many different kinds of evidence and value them all about equally. Others admit just as many kinds of evidence, but value some more highly than others. Still other communities admit far fewer kinds of evidence, with some of these communities valuing all the kinds equally and others valuing some more highly than others.

In this section, we will describe many kinds of evidence that writers can use, even if few writers use all of these kinds together in one essay. We hope that as you become more aware of the various kinds of evidence, you will develop greater sensitivity to the kinds of evidence that various discourse communities respond to and value highly. As you develop greater sensitivity, you will be both better able to evaluate how well other writers have made their cases, and you will become more skilled in making your own.

Before we describe several kinds of evidence, however, we must issue two notes of caution: First, you must remember that sometimes people make claims that rest only on personal belief. As we noted in the first chapter, the Venerable Bede (see 62) claims that several different events are miracles. Others may read this selection and label the events pure coincidences, nothing more. Since this disagreement rests on differences in personal belief, it cannot be resolved. In fact, when people try to resolve such disagreements, they often end up only losing patience with one another.

Second, we hasten to add that sometimes people have unexamined and unjustified beliefs, in which cases valid evidence can be brought to bear and disagreements can be resolved. But both sides in such disagreements have to be humble about their own views and patient with each other as they work to see what kinds of evidence are most applicable to their disagreements.

Several kinds of evidence are available to writers. We believe that these kinds fall into one group related to the natural world and into another group related to human nature, actions, and institutions.

Evidence about the natural world is usually associated with discourse communities within the physical sciences. Some of this evidence comes from focusing on a part of the world and then observing and recording how that part changes over time. For example, Charles Darwin (see 611) focuses on different kinds of coral reefs and records how they change as time passes and conditions in the ocean vary.

Or people introduce elements into a natural setting and observe what changes. Stephen Jay Gould (see 669) writes about scientists who placed male black widow spiders on the webs of female black widow spiders and watched carefully to see whether the larger and stronger females would eat the males or allow the males to mate with them.

Such evidence can be very compelling, but much of it applies only to the natural world apart from human beings. When it does apply to human beings, it often is related to how the human body and mind work or become diseased. Some people who work with such evidence, however, would say that the human mind and body remain healthy or become diseased according to whether they are in or out of rhythm with the forces of the natural world (see Capra, 645).

Writers who seek evidence about human nature, actions, and institutions sometimes use their own opinions, intuitions, and experiences. They are observers of human life as well as their readers are, and they have views about and experiences of life that they sometimes wish to focus on in their writing. Several of the writers that we include in the sections on philosophy and the arts describe such views and experiences. Much of the material that we include from St. Augustine (see 322) is a record of his personal experiences, particularly his experiences as a disobedient and wild young man. Recording personal opinions, intuitions, and experiences can make writing vivid and emotionally compelling. But writers' personal experiences will not apply to everything they write about. And their intuitions and personal opinions will not count for much with some discourse communities. Some communities within the social sciences, for example, might demand a tabulation of the opinions of dozens of people.

Even though some writers do not interview or read about dozens of people, in many cases they use the opinions, intuitions, and experiences of others as evidence. In their work on gender attribution in Western culture, Suzanne Kessler and Wendy McKenna (see 563) interviewed many men who dressed as women and many women who dressed as men to try to discover what aspects of a person's appearance people pay most attention to as they decide whether a person is male or female. The opinions, intuitions, and experiences of other people have the same general advantages and disadvantages as one's own opinions, intuitions, and experiences do. They can be very vivid and compelling. But they will not apply to all cases, and they will not count for much in some discourse communities. No matter what hundreds of people say about their experience of modern art, members of a community of art critics and historians are not likely to change their opinions about that art.

While a writer's and others' opinions may not count for much in some communities, those of experts in the appropriate field might. As Robert G.

L. Waite (see 128) builds his case that Adolf Hitler was what psychiatrists call a "borderline personality," he quotes several experts in the field of personality disorders to show that many of Hitler's actions and beliefs were perfectly consistent with those of other people with borderline personalities. The better the credentials of the experts and the more clearly they are associated with the subject area in question, the more persuasive they are likely to be.

Some writers also use anecdotes. These are little stories or recountings of events; usually they have a clear point. Anecdotes can be very vivid. Those of you who read Rita Levi-Montalcini (see 633) will probably remember for a long time her anecdotes about how, during World War II, she experimented on nerve tissues in a small house in the hills of Italy while cities in the valleys were being bombed and shelled. But anecdotes carry an aura of informality, and if a rhetorical situation is very formal, anecdotes might not be appropriate for it. If they appear to be appropriate, they usually work better the more typical they are. An anecdote that presents an atypical person in an atypical situation will be convincing to few people, no matter what discourse community they belong to.

Closely related to anecdotes are analogies. These involve comparing one thing to another, often in a rather extended fashion. These are frequently used to make other kinds of evidence clearer and more understandable. In "Keeling Islands: Coral Formations" (see 611), Charles Darwin draws an analogy between details about a castle and an island with an encircling coral reef: "We see an island, which may be compared to a castle situated on the summit of a lofty submarine mountain, protected by a great wall of coral-rock, always steep externally and sometimes internally, with a broad level summit, here and there breached by narrow gateways, through which the larger ships can enter the wide and deep encircling moat." Of course, such analogies work only if there are many revealing similarities between the items or activities compared. If the analogy gets readers thinking about differences between the items or activities, it will fail as a piece of evidence.

When writing about human nature, actions, and institutions, many people, most notably those working within discourse communities in history and the arts, use historical events as evidence. Fernand Braudel (see 109) cites details about how monarchs in the Mediterranean world before the time of Phillip II of Spain reacted to droughts in planning their military campaigns. He goes on to use these details to explain why Phillip and other monarchs contemporary with him made the decisions that they did. This kind of evidence can be extremely persuasive, especially if writers can show that the circumstances of events at one point in the past are similar to those of the events at a point in the more recent past, in the present, or in the projected future. If readers can spot significant differences between two different events or eras, they will be less inclined to accept historical evidence.

Some evidence about human nature, actions, and institutions, especially evidence often used within discourse communities in the social sciences, moves in the direction of the scientific. For example, some researchers can take vast opinion surveys, can correlate opinions with such variables as age, gender, religion, social class, and political party, and can predict what certain kinds of people will think and do in the future. Of course, those who gather such data must be unbiased, they must work with a proper sample of people, and they must not overstate their conclusions and predictions.

Other researchers observe people interacting and draw conclusions from carefully recorded aspects of the interactions. For instance, Carol Gilligan (see 529) observed males and females talking about moral dilemmas and found that the males appeared to appeal to different moral standards from the ones that the females appealed to. The males usually appealed to a set code, a statement of a person's general and absolute rights. The females usually thought in terms of responsibilities; facing a difficult moral issue, they usually asked how they could act so that they would be treating all the individuals involved most responsibly. Findings such as these can be very striking, but they always need to be interpreted. Where do these differences come from? Do they interact with other aspects of males' and females' behavior? How do they affect the ways that males and females interact with each other? How do they affect the course of human events? Writers who use such evidence have to be careful that the findings they record are valid and that they interpret them carefully. Readers might accept their findings but not their interpretations of them. And as you can guess, members of some discourse communities within the physical sciences would consider both the recording and the interpreting of such details entirely too subjective.

Finally, other researchers introduce changes into social situations and record how those changes affect those interacting in those situations. They might want to learn how a group of men changes its conversational patterns when a woman joins them, or how various women react to interruptions by men. Here again, the results of such experiments persuade readers only if the situations of the experiments are typical of many others and if the interpretations of the results appear valid.

When skilled writers have assembled their evidence, they often try to think of all the reasons others might not accept it and the way they use it. If they come up with some good objections to their presentation, they face an important decision. Should they try to ignore the objections? This is most unwise. Whenever people write, particularly to members of discourse communities other than their own, they can encounter objections. Pretending that these do not exist can lead their readers to think that the writers either do not know the subject well or have not really tried to meet other minds.

It is wiser to admit that there are objections and to respond to them. Sometimes writers respond by admitting that there is an objection that they have little to say about. Even this is more effective than ignoring the objection. But sometimes they are able to show how the objection is flawed, irrelevant to their main point, or really not very damaging to their case. And sometimes they can even refute the objection. When that is possible, and when they do so in a reasonable tone and do not gloat about it, they impress readers as having great control over a position.

SUMMARY

In this chapter we have not addressed all the rhetorical considerations that writers should keep in mind as they make choices about their writing. But we have addressed some of the more important considerations, the ones that should be most helpful to you as you analyze and evaluate choices in others' writing and make choices in your own.

READING WITHIN DISCOURSE COMMUNITIES

In the second chapter, we examined some of the major aspects of the art of rhetoric. In this chapter we develop the claim that you should keep those same and some additional aspects in mind as you analyze and evaluate what you read. We did not describe all the possible aspects of rhetoric. Nor will we detail everything that you should keep in mind as you read. That would be impossible, partially because each of you will probably employ some unique reading strategies. But we hope to pass on enough advice to help you read material from your own and other discourse communities with increasing insight and pleasure.

We especially hope that you will always avoid two immature responses to written material—in people young and old. Some people accept everything they read without any hesitation whatsoever. Writers can have just about whatever effects on them that they might care to. Some of these readers almost revere whatever appears in print, and what they have read most recently they revere the most.

On the other hand, some people refuse to admit that any views different from their own could be valid. Their views have been set since they were very young, and they refuse to acknowledge any ideas that clash with their own. We occasionally meet students like this, students who start arguments in every class they speak up in and then absolutely refuse to listen to evidence counter to their own.

You can understand why we called both of these responses immature. The first is unstable, and the second allows no growth. How can people maintain a relatively stable core of being and yet learn from others? We hold that people can do so by being critical readers, being fair-minded and receptive to the ideas of others, but also being discerning about those ideas. If people become skilled critical readers, they will continually learn about others and their views of the world. At the same time, they will be testing and refining their own views of the world.

PREREADING

To develop more skill as a critical reader, you should do several things before reading. You should find out as much as you can about the authors. When did they live? What careers did they pursue, and what were their credentials like? Someone who worked for a tobacco company will probably not be the most unbiased writer about smoking. Someone who was criticized by his or her peers for distorting the findings of experiments will probably not be a good source of information about interpretation in science, unless, of course, the person is making a full confession. You should also try to learn which discourse communities your authors belonged to. And it would be helpful to discover what specific causes they supported. In this connection, knowing who your authors' frequent opponents were can help you clarify your pre-reading expectations.

To find the kinds of information described above, you can check works such as *The International Who's Who, Current Biography, Biographical Index, The Dictionary of American Biography,* and *The McGraw-Hill Encyclopedia of World Biography*. If your authors are somewhat famous, chances are good that general encyclopedias will also devote some space to them. We checked on Bronislaw Malinowski (see 483) in the *Britannica Micropaedia,* and we learned that after earning one Ph.D. in philosophy, he went on to earn another for anthropological study in New Guinea. After earning these degrees, he continued his work in anthropology, the best known of which was with the Trobriand Islanders. Within anthropology and related disciplines, Malinowski helped to found a discourse community of functionalists, people who believed that in a culture each custom or object fulfilled an important function and was intricately related to all other customs or objects in that culture. Only by investigating all these functions and their interrelations, Malinowski would say, can an anthropologist ever understand a culture. Such information would prepare us well for reading material by Malinowski and by other functionalists.

Some scholarly areas have their own biographical aids. For writers in science, for example, you can check works such as *American Men and Women of Science,* the *Dictionary of Scientific Biography,* and the *World Who's Who in Science*. Different works include different amounts of information about scientists and focus on scientists from different periods of history.

Besides checking on the authors you read, you should seek as much information as you can about the contexts in which they wrote. When did they write the pieces you will read? Were those pieces addressed to special audiences? If so, how did the authors shape their pieces to suit those audiences? And what can you find out about the effects of the pieces on their respective audiences?

If you are reading whole books, you will be able to find the answers to many of these questions in their prefaces. Too many readers skip prefaces and thereby make an unfortunate mistake, since prefaces can reveal many important things.

They can reveal why a book was written and for whom it was written. For example, Wayne Frair and Percival Davis, authors of *A Case for Creation* (see 684), note in their preface that they are writing "for the informed layman and the student in his early years of scientific training." They hope to help such readers "set forth a case for creation with all the care and skill that a lawyer would use to convince a skeptical jury."

Prefaces often reveal what theoretical frameworks authors are working within. In the prologue to *The Flamingo's Smile* (see 669), Stephen Jay Gould writes that his book owes its "reputation to coherence supplied by the common theme of evolutionary theory."

Prefaces can show how a book is organized. In *Gender* (see 563), Suzanne J. Kessler and Wendy McKenna conclude their preface by briefly describing each of their six chapters.

And prefaces can even reveal what the thesis of a book is. In his preface to *The Turning Point* (see 645), Fritjof Capra mentions the crises that modern physics has undergone. He also mentions crises that our society as a whole faces: high inflation and unemployment, shortages of energy, disasters in health care, dangers from pollution, and a rising rate of crime. Then he states that "The basic thesis of this book is that these are all different facets of one and the same crisis, and that this crisis is essentially a crisis of perception. Like the crisis in physics in the 1920s, it derives from the fact that we are trying to apply the concepts of an outdated world view—the mechanistic world view of Cartesian-Newtonian science—to a reality that can no longer be understood in terms of these concepts."

If you are reading articles, you should note where they orginally appeared. Different journals have different orientations, and these will affect the nature of the articles that appear in them. Take *The Nation* and *National Review* for examples. Their titles are similar, and you might expect the articles that appear in them to be similar too. In fact, the articles are similar in that they often focus on the same things. But that is where the similarity usually ends.

We examined the issue of each journal that appeared just before the 1988 presidential election. Here is part of an editorial from *The Nation*:

> Reaganism has been a moral nightmare and a political disaster for all but a greedy few and their fawning friends, and Bushism, if it should come to pass, will be no better in kind. We expect that *Nation* readers will want to cast their votes this week against this national blight. Dukakis in the White House could provide the margin of hope and even survival for the victims of Republican neglect or hostility: the poor, minorities, Central Americans, people with AIDS, women seeking abortions.

You can see that *The Nation* adopts a perspective on the left of the political continuum.

Now here is part of a column from the *National Review* on the same subject:

> But as between the presidential choices there can be no serious question. Not everything about George Bush gives grounds for hope. But his selection of undeniably conservative themes for his campaign should banish any lingering

doubts about his central standing in the broad Church of Reaganism. And everything about Mr. Dukakis does give grounds for distress. He has failed to exorcise the ghost of liberal ideology that has clung all too convincingly to his campaign. That being so, his claim to competence offers no solace. To coin a phrase: Competence in the pursuit of liberalism is no virtue.

The *National Review*, clearly, adopts a perspective much more to the right of the political continuum than *The Nation* does. You should try to get a good idea about the orientation of each journal that you read in.

While working with journals, you should also attend to how much credibility they have. If you were to write a long paper to fulfill the research requirements for a seminar in the social sciences and used only the news magazines that you find at the checkout counter of your local convenience store, magazines that usually contain stories about Elvis Presley being alive and well and living in South Dakota, you will cause your peers and professor to question at least your ability to select credible evidence.

Whether you are working with books or articles, one thing you should do before moving from prereading into reading is to review the purpose you have for your reading. Have you been asked to summarize the results of an experiment described in a research report? Have you been given the task of checking whether an article or chapter presents data that you and other members of a research team are unaware of? Have you been told that an article or chapter presents evidence that runs counter to a position that you are formulating? If you have a purpose such as one of these, it will certainly affect how you approach your reading. But even if your purpose is closer to the analyzing and evaluating that you will often do in college, it is wise to remind yourself of it before you start to read.

Finally, you should try to make sure that your own beliefs and assumptions do not prevent you from reading material fairly. You might be asked to read Frair and Davis as they set forth a case for creation (see 684). Some of you might assume that such a case cannot be made, that it is nonsense, the product of religious raving. But if you skip their chapter or read it only superficially because of this assumption, you never give them a fair chance. It would be better to let them make the best case they can and then evaluate it. You might still end up evaluating their case negatively, but to do so after letting them make it is a far better thing than not to let them make it at all.

A QUICK OVERVIEW

When you are asked to read, analyze, and evaluate a piece of writing, we recommend that you give it two different readings. The first of these is a quick overview. Doing a quick overview is not the same thing as skimming. When readers skim, they usually scan very rapidly, looking only for a few choice kernels of information. When they do a quick overview, they seek a global view of the assumptions, purpose, and procedures of a piece. In essence, readers are trying to learn what action the author is attempting to perform with the work and how he or she is trying to perform it. A quick overview works well with all but book-length documents, which usually demand more time even for an overview than you can give them.

As you start a quick overview, you should ask what the genre of a piece is. If Stephen Jay Gould is the author, for example, you should ask whether he is writing a formal research report for fellow paleontologists or a more informal essay for the relatively diverse audience of *Natural History*. The genre of a piece will affect what is done in it and how it is done.

You should then examine the title. Does it indicate what the subject of the piece is? Does it give clues about the writer's position on that subject? The title might set you up to think that the writer's position is of one nature when it turns out to be of another, but at least you will have a start in moving to the heart of the piece.

If the piece has an abstract, you should examine it closely. If you had a question about whether the writer was ironic with the title, the abstract will answer it. It is intended to give you a brief account of the substance of the article. We have never seen an abstract that an author used ironically or intentionally made ambiguous. Authors know that some readers decide whether or not to read their articles solely on the basis of their abstracts. Authors therefore try to keep their abstracts from starting games of interpretation.

Next you should read the first paragraph or two carefully. Doing so will often show you what context the author is working within, and it may give you the author's thesis.

After this you should read the first sentence or two in each paragraph, trying to piece together how the author is structuring the work. You will also often get an indication of the kinds of evidence the author is using. Seeing what kinds of evidence the author uses should help you toward an idea of the nature of the overall case.

Finally, read the last paragraph or two. What technique does the author use to conclude? What information does the author convey at the end? Does the conclusion, even on the basis of this quick overview, seem satisfying to you?

Doing an overview should not take you long, and it will leave you with some important information. You should have a good idea of the author's purpose, the subject, the thesis, the method of development, the kinds of evidence, and perhaps some of the implications of the piece. With this information, you can build a basic interpretive framework to use as you start the second reading. This framework should increase your ability to comprehend the piece, and the feeling of potential control as you read should increase your pleasure.

ACTIVE READING, ANALYSIS, AND EVALUATION

Your second reading of a piece should be an in-depth reading. You should be active, seeking the author's meanings section by section, responding to those meanings, and predicting what meanings will follow. Whenever you own the essay or book you are reading, you should read with pen or marker in hand, underlining or highlighting and making notes as you go along, taking care not to defeat your purpose by underlining or highlighting everything. Sometimes you will ask questions of the material, note connections between that material and other pieces on the same subject, jot notes about what the author is basing his or her overall approach on, predict the implications of accepting the author's claims, show how words resonate in ambiguities and ironies, and even congratulate yourself on predicting correctly how the author will develop the piece.

During this active reading, you should attend to all the aspects of rhetoric that we discussed in the second chapter. Try to determine whether the author is writing to a specialized audience or not. One good way to do this is to see whether the author makes assumptions about what the audience believes. For example, does the author assume, as Marx and Engels do (see ???), that history is the record of struggles between economic classes, or does the author bring this claim out into the open and argue it? Another good way to determine whether your author is addressing a specialized audience is to ask what he or she assumes readers know. Does the author assume that readers know about the law of the equivalence of energy and mass, or does the author do as Einstein does (see 627) and explain this law in detail? Finally, what kinds of words does the author use? Does he or she use such technical terms as *primal scene trauma* (see 457) without defining them? If the author does, you can assume that he or she probably intended the piece for readers with specialized knowledge. It is important to learn whether an author intended a piece for readers with specialized knowledge or not, because if he or she did, you might have to do some background work to become the kind of reader the piece demands. Whenever this is the case with essays that we include here, we try to provide enough footnotes to help you become the right kind of reader.

Your quick overview probably gave you a fairly good idea about the author's purpose. Now you can try to identify that purpose even more precisely. Remembering that different purposes are possible within different discourse communities, you should pay close attention to the words the authors use in their introductions and—if they include such—in their statements of intention. Are they going to analyze? That is, are they going to break something down into parts? Are they also going to classify? That is, are they going to put these parts in certain kinds of categories? Gerda Lerner (see 137) writes that she is going to explain and then argue. If you pay close attention to such words, you should be able to identify authors' overall purposes very precisely.

Your general overview probably led you to focus on a sentence as the author's thesis sentence. Now you can determine whether that sentence by itself expresses the thesis or whether some other sentences also express parts of the thesis. You should also consider whether these sentences are ironic or not. Sometimes authors boldly maintain one position while, in fact, they hold the opposite position. Some elements that will help you determine whether your author is ironic are words like *fortunately* and *alarmingly*. When such words appear in moderation, they usually provide a clear and direct link to the author's position. When they appear with unusual frequency, they can signal that the author's thesis is really the opposite of that which appears in print. An author who loads a thesis sentence up with words such as *sadly* or *unfortunately* signals that he or she is not to be taken at face value.

The quick overview also should have given you a good idea of the main points your author uses to develop and support the thesis. As you read more closely, you should recheck the main points and be sure that you know what all of the terms in them mean. If you do not know what some of the terms mean, use their context to guess at their meanings. Then see how accurate your guesses are by using a good dictionary. Later you should add these words to a list of words whose meanings you have recently learned. This is something of a chore, but making a habit of it can increase your power and pleasure as a reader later on.

As you move through the main points of the essay, use your overall mental framework for the piece to predict which point follows the one you are attending to. Then make sure that your framework was accurate, that you did not miss or misinterpret a point. Also, pay close attention to the logical connections between main points. First find out what they are, and then evaluate whether they are valid or not. Some writers introduce sentences with a *therefore*, when in fact they conclude nothing in them. If you do not spot such examples of shoddy logic where they exist, you can be led well along an incorrect interpretive path.

While you attend to the logical connections between main points, it should be fairly easy also to note major turning points in the piece. A piece might have ten main points, but three of them might underlie a section focusing on the positions of those opposed to the thesis, four of them might underlie a section developing the thesis, and three of them might underlie a section showing how the thesis should be applied. You should spot the individual points and the three major subsections that the points underlie.

As some students do this kind of work, they like to write short summaries of each paragraph, adding to them indications of how each paragraph is connected to its neighbors. Others prefer to construct a brief outline showing major subsections and main points. Still others use the margins to diagram how subsections and main points are related. We think that some such method will help you see and remember how what you read is structured.

Once you have a good idea about major subsections and the main points underlying them, you should begin evaluating how the author develops the work. As you do so, pay some attention to the author's assumptions. What does he or she take for granted? Discovering these assumptions can be important, for many debates about writing center not on the evidence that is presented but on that which is assumed. Some authors indicate explicitly what they have assumed. Robert G. L. Waite prefaces his book on Adolf Hitler (see 128) by stating how he believes a "psychohistorian" should proceed. Other authors, however, give no explicit indication about their assumptions. It is up to you to detect them.

After you have considered your author's assumptions, you should examine more closely the evidence that he or she uses. What kind of evidence is it? Is the evidence all of the same nature? Beyond that, you should evaluate whether it was gathered correctly and whether it fits the case at hand and the discourse community it is used in. As we noted in the second chapter, some kinds of evidence, such as analogies, can be less than fully appropriate in some cases. Is that true of any of the evidence that you are examining? Finally, does the author use enough evidence to make his or her case well?

One question that we think is particularly important for you to ask is whether authors acknowledge that there are sides other than their own on issues. You should look for what other positions authors mention and ask why they disagree with them. Seeing how authors react to positions different from their own can tell you much about the strength of the authors' cases. Just as important, you should try to determine whether there are sides of an issue that authors are trying to ignore or obscure. When authors do this, they generally feel vulnerable to attacks from those sides, so it is important to learn what they are. You will not want to accept authors' positions until you are confident that those positions are defended well against all other reasonable positions. And if you cannot accept a particular position, you should force yourself to be as clear and specific as you can about why you cannot.

After reading an essay or a chapter and before deciding how successful it is, some students like to set it aside for a day or two. When they come back to it, they find that they are in a good position to evaluate whether the essay worked on them as it was supposed to. And if it did not, the time between the reading and the final evaluation usually helps them be specific about why it did not.

It might be helpful for you to see an example of how someone else, keeping these reading strategies in mind, actually goes through part of an essay and makes notes about it. We reprint here the first eleven paragraphs of Carol Gilligan's "Woman's Place in Man's Life Cycle" (the complete chapter appears on 529), annotated by one of us while doing a close analytical and evaluative reading. You will see that the reader underlines some phrases and sentences and make notes to himself in the margins. He also connects some of these notes with arrows. Because all the reading strategies that we recommended to you hardly ever apply to a single piece of writing, not all of those strategies will be reflected in the notes and underlinings here. But you will see many of them reflected in these notes and underlinings.

In the second act of *The Cherry Orchard*, Lopahin, a young merchant, describes his life of hard work and success. Failing to convince Madame Ranevskaya to cut down the cherry orchard to save her estate, he will go on in the next act to buy it himself. He is the self-made man who, in purchasing the estate where his father and grandfather were slaves, seeks to eradicate the "awkward, unhappy life" of the past, replacing the cherry orchard with summer cottages where coming generations "will see a new life." In elaborating this developmental vision, he reveals the image of man that underlies and supports his activity: "At times when I can't go to sleep, I think: Lord, thou gavest us immense forests, unbounded fields and the widest horizons, <u>and living in the midst of them we should indeed be giants</u>"—at which point, Madame Ranevskaya interrupts him, saying <u>"You feel the need for giants—They are good only in fairy tales, anywhere else they only frighten us."</u>

[margin notes: 1 introductory reference to The Cherry Orchard — how fit her purpose?; his view; her view; her overall subject]

Conceptions of the human life cycle represent attempts to order and make coherent the unfolding experiences and perceptions, the changing wishes and realities of everyday life. <u>But the nature of such conceptions depends in part on the position of the observer. The brief excerpt from Chekhov's play suggests that when the observer is a woman, the perspective may be of a different sort. Different judgments of the image of man as giant imply different ideas about human development, different ways of imagining the human condition, different notions of what is of value in life.</u>

[margin notes: 2; her thesis?; men and women have different perspectives on life cycle? different life cycles?]

At a time when efforts are being made to eradicate discrimination between the sexes in the search for social equality and justice, the differences between the sexes are being rediscovered in the social sciences. This discovery occurs when <u>theories</u> formerly considered to be sexually neutral in their scientific objectivity are found instead to <u>reflect a consistent observational and evaluative bias.</u> Then the presumed neutrality of sci-

[margin note: 3]

ence, like that of language itself, gives way to the recognition that the categories of knowledge are human constructions. The fascination with point of view that has informed the fiction of the twentieth century and the corresponding recognition of the relativity of judgment infuse our scientific understanding as well when we begin to notice how accustomed we have become to seeing life through men's eyes.

A recent discovery of this sort pertains to the apparently innocent classic *The Elements of Style* by William Strunk and E. B. White. A Supreme Court ruling on the subject of sex discrimination led one teacher of English to notice that the elementary rules of English usage were being taught through examples which counterposed the birth of Napoleon, the writings of Coleridge, and statements such as "He was an interesting talker. A man who had traveled all over the world and lived in half a dozen countries," with "Well, Susan, this is a fine mess you are in" or, less drastically, "He saw a woman, accompanied by two children, walking slowly down the road."

Psychological theorists have fallen as innocently as Strunk and White into the same observational bias. Implicitly adopting the male life as the norm, they have tried to fashion women out of a masculine cloth. It all goes back, of course, to Adam and Eve—a story which shows, among other things, that if you make a woman out of a man, you are bound to get into trouble. In the life cycle, as in the Garden of Eden, the woman has been the deviant.

The penchant of developmental theorists to project a masculine image, and one that appears frightening to women, goes back at least to Freud (1905), who built his theory of psychosexual development around the experiences of the male child that culminate in the Oedipus complex. In the 1920s, Freud struggled to resolve the contradictions posed for his theory by the differences in female anatomy and the different configuration of the young girl's early family relationships. After trying to fit women into his masculine conception, seeing them as envying that which they missed, he came instead to acknowledge, in the strength and persistence of women's pre-Oedipal attachments to their mothers, a developmental difference. He consid-

[margin annotations:]
male perspective dominates

All of them? Is this possible (see Kessler + McKenna: Soc Construction)

one bit of evidence: bias in Elements of Style

turns to psychological theories — same bias

Oedipus: killed father married mother

reud saw fferences in male development causing their developmental failure [handwritten margin note]

ered this difference in women's development to be responsible for what he saw as women's developmental failure.

Having tied the formation of the superego or conscience to castration anxiety, Freud considered women to be deprived by nature of the impetus for a clear-cut Oedipal resolution. Consequently, women's superego—the heir to the Oedipus complex—was compromised: it was never "so inexorable, so impersonal, so independent of its emotional origins as we require it to be in men." From this observation of difference, that "for women the level of what is ethically normal is different from what it is in men," Freud concluded that women "show less sense of justice than men, that they are less ready to submit to the great exigencies of life, that they are more often influenced in their judgements by feelings of affection or hostility" (1925, pp. 257–258). 7

the conclusion [handwritten margin note]

Thus a problem in theory became cast as a problem in women's development, and the problem in women's development was located in their experience of relationships. Nancy Chodorow (1974), attempting to account for "the reproduction within each generation of certain general and nearly universal differences that characterize masculine and feminine personality and roles," attributes these differences between the sexes not to anatomy but rather to "the fact that women, universally, are largely responsible for early child care." Because this early social environment differs for and is experienced differently by male and female children, basic sex differences recur in personality development. As a result, "in any given society, feminine personality comes to define itself in relation and connection to other people more than masculine personality does" (pp. 43–44). 8

odorow's view: nen more than n define nselves in ation to others [handwritten margin note]

In her analysis, Chodorow relies primarily on Robert Stoller's studies which indicate that gender identity, the unchanging core of personality formation, is "with rare exception firmly and irreversibly established for both sexes by the time a child is around three." Given that for both sexes the primary caretaker in the first three years of life is typically female, the interpersonal dynamics of gender identity formation are different for boys and girls. Female identity for- 9

If this changes, how will the changes affect children's personality development? [handwritten margin note]

Source of girls' gender identity — like their mothers

mation takes place in a context of ongoing relationship since "mothers tend to experience their daughters as more like, and continuous with, themselves." Correspondingly, girls, in identifying themselves as female, experience themselves as like their mothers, thus fusing the experience of attachment with the process of identity formation. In contrast, "mothers experience their sons as a male opposite," and boys, in defining themselves as masculine, separate their mothers from themselves, thus curtailing "their primary love and sense of empathic tie." Consequently, male development entails a "more emphatic individuation and a more defensive firming of experienced ego boundaries." For boys, but not girls, "issues of differentiation have become intertwined with sexual issues" (1978, pp. 150, 166–167).

Source of boys' gender identity — separation from mothers

Writing against the masculine bias of psychoanalytic theory, Chodorow argues that the existence of sex differences in the early experiences of individuation and relationship "does not mean that women have 'weaker' ego boundaries than men or are more prone to psychosis." It means instead that "girls emerge from this period with a basis for 'empathy' built into their primary definition of self in a way that boys do not." Chodorow thus replaces Freud's negative and derivative description of female psychology with a positive and direct account of her own: "Girls emerge with a stronger basis for experiencing another's needs or feelings as one's own (or of thinking that one is so experiencing another's needs and feelings). Furthermore, girls do not define themselves in terms of the denial of preoedipal relational modes to the same extent as do boys. Therefore, regression to these modes tends not to feel as much a basic threat to their ego. From very early, then, because they are parented by a person of the same gender . . . girls come to experience themselves as less differentiated than boys, as more continuous with and related to the external object-world, and as differently oriented to their inner object-world as well" (p. 167).

Chodorow's positive interpretation of differences between girls' and boys' development

Consequently, relationships, and particularly issues of dependency, are experienced differently by women and men. For boys and men, separation and individuation are critically tied to gender identity since separation from the mother is essential for the development of masculinity. For girls and women, issues of feminity or feminine identity do not depend on the achievement of separation from the mother or on the progress of individuation. Since masculinity is defined through separation while feminity is defined through attachment, male gender identity is threatened by intimacy while female gender identity is threatened by separation. Thus males tend to have difficulty with relationships, while females tend to have problems with individuation. The quality of embeddedness in social interaction and personal relationships that characterizes women's lives in contrast to men's, however, becomes not only a descriptive difference but also a developmental liability when the milestones of childhood and adolescent development in the psychological literature are markers of increasing separation. Women's failure to separate then becomes by definition a failure to develop.

men and women experience relationships and individuation differently

As we noted before the selection from Gilligan, some of the reading strategies we recommended to you are not reflected in the notes and underlinings the reader makes, and some are not reflected very frequently. For example, the reader makes very few notes distinguishing one kind of evidence from another, mainly because Gilligan depends almost exclusively on references to psychologists' theories and observations.

But many of the strategies we recommended are reflected in notes and underlinings here, and these notes and underlinings draw attention to important bits of information in the essay. The reader's notes do not always take the form of complete sentences, but they really do not need to. They are meant to help him analyze and evaluate the selection, and as long as they fulfill that function, they are acceptable regardless of the form they take.

Even though many of these notes are not complete sentences, if you were to read only the notes, you would learn many significant things about the selection from Gilligan. You would have a very good idea that she is working from within a discourse community that brings feminist perspectives to bear on developmental psychology. You would know that her subject is the different views of the human life cycle. You could be quite confident that her purpose is to correct the observational bias she sees in past work on the human life cycle. You could be equally confident that the sentences at the end of her second paragraph express her thesis. And you would be able to summarize her early main points, those drawing on the work of Chodorow and Stoller to correct some mistaken interpretations going all the way back to Freud.

Not all of the notes summarize or reinforce points from this selection. A few notes ask questions. One note asks whether all categories of human knowledge could possibly be constructed. Another asks whether boys and girls will begin to go through different processes of personality development if fathers begin to take as much responsibility for child rearing as mothers do. Gilligan does not answer these questions in these paragraphs or in the paragraphs that follow. But that does not mean that the questions are wasted. The reader can use them as stimuli for research and writing in the future.

If, in your own reading, you use the strategies we recommend in this chapter, we are confident that you will be able to avoid the two immature responses to reading that we described earlier. We are confident that you will be able to read critically, receiving others' ideas fairly but testing them rigorously. Through these processes you should be able to learn more about others' views of the world and test and refine your own. Moreover, you should be able to work your way into membership in more and more discourse communities.

WRITING WITHIN
DISCOURSE
COMMUNITIES

Throughout your academic career, after you have read material produced in various discourse communities, you will often choose to respond to that material in writing. Your responses to various materials can be very different from one another, particularly if the materials originate in different discourse communities. After reading the selections we include here, for example, you will be asked to produce a wide variety of responses.

After the selection by Robert G. L. Waite (see 128), who represents the discourse community of psychohistorians, one writing assignment asks you to analyze the appeal that the music of Richard Wagner had for Adolf Hitler. After the selection by Thomas S. Kuhn (see 408), who represents the discourse community of philosophers of science, one of the writing assignments asks you to interview several scientists and then generalize about how they view the nature of work in their fields. After the selection by Bruno Bettelheim (see 254), who represents scholars taking a psychological approach to works of art, a writing assignment asks you to produce a Marxist interpretation of a fairy tale as a contrast to Bettelheim's psychological interpretation. After the selection by Galileo (see 600), who represents the discourse community of Renaissance scientists, a writing assignment directs you to perform one of the experiments Galileo describes and to write up your findings in a standardized laboratory report. And after the selection by B. F. Skinner (see 514), who represents the community of behavioral psychologists, one writing assignment asks you to write a book review of Skinner's *Walden II*.

These five assignments call for written responses that are very different from each other. If you focus on what they ask you to do, you will see that they call for five different actions: analyzing, generalizing, interpreting, reporting, and reviewing. During your academic career, you will probably be asked to perform such actions frequently. In addition, you will probably often be asked to perform actions such as describing, explaining, classifying, comparing, and arguing.

We think that you will have the best chance of performing all of these and other actions successfully if you keep the points that we made in the second chapter about rhetoric firmly in mind. That is, whatever a writing assignment asks you to do, you will respond to it best if you think carefully about your audience, purpose, thesis, and evidence. More specifically, you will respond best if you consider questions such as the following: Who are your readers likely to be, and what do they know and believe about your subject? What is your precise purpose for writing? What kind of thesis does that purpose call for, and will you need more than one sentence to express the thesis adequately? Finally, what kinds of evidence are most appropriate in your writing situation, and how much of these kinds should you use?

One of the better ways that we can think of to help you answer such questions as you prepare to write is to show you how we would respond to them if we were to complete some of the writing assignments that we include in this book. We will describe some of the thinking about rhetoric that we would do if we were asked to respond to two of the writing assignments that follow the selection we included in the third chapter from Gilligan's "Woman's Place in Man's Life Cycle." These two assignments are very different from each other.

THE FIRST WRITING ASSIGNMENT

The first of the two writing assignments is worded as follows: "A national news magazine has issued a call for 500-word opinion pieces on 'How Feminism Has Affected My Campus.' You decide to respond to this call."

After beginning to think about our response, we realize that we will probably be writing to a large and diverse audience. Our readers will probably range widely in age from the late teens on up. And they will probably be members of many different discourse communities, some of which we are also members of, and some of which we know little about. But we will never be able to tell for certain how many discourse communities we have in common with most of them, since they will always remain unknown to us. For the most part, we will be writing to strangers.

In such a situation, we will have to avoid intimate or quite casual word choices. We judge that it will be appropriate for us to use personal pronouns such as *we* and *I*. But we will have to avoid slang expressions and words closely linked to casual conversations. And if we use any words that are common on our campus but may not be common on many others (such as *Weltanschauung*, or view of the world or reality) or any words that might carry unique meanings on our campus (such as *cultural mandate*, which we use to refer to responsibilities for affecting culture), we will have to define them.

On the other hand, the assignment does not seem to call for a heavy and formal response. We do not need to feel pressure to show off; we are not writing as bureaucrats to a group of superiors. So we have no reason to be tempted to use phrases such as *effect an alteration* in place of words such as *change* and *alter*.

What kinds of information are readers such as ours likely to bring to our essay? We judge that they will probably know a good deal about feminism and its overarching effects on our culture. So we will probably only try their patience if we go through a long review of the nature and history of the feminist movement. And we may use up too many of our five hundred words in telling readers what they already know. Therefore, we decide that we will need no review of feminism in North America; we should be able simply to refer to it at the appropriate time.

However, our readers will probably not know very much about our college. And they will need to know some things about it in order fully to understand our comments about the effects of feminism here. Thus we will write that we are focusing on Calvin College, which is located in Grand Rapids, Michigan. People associated with Calvin have always thought of it as a liberal arts college, but recently more and more professional and pre-professional programs have won a place in the curriculum. Calvin currently enrolls about four thousand students. Most of them come from the Midwest, and most have ties to one Protestant denomination or another. Thus our student body is probably more homogeneous than those of many other colleges. In general, our students are comparatively conservative, not among the first to be affected by new movements and ideologies. Most faculty members, too, have ties to one Protestant denomination or another. But there is not as much conservatism among the faculty as there is among students.

This is all background information, and we would probably allot to it only a paragraph, probably the first paragraph. The primary function of this paragraph would be to acquaint readers with the institution that we will be focusing on.

After this background information, we judge that we will need a transition to the heart of the piece, and the best way to formulate one is to think about our purpose. To help in this, we look at the key words in the assignment. Those words are *your opinion*. What we are asked to do is to give our personal views on the effects of feminism on our college. And as we think of the call for manuscripts that we are responding to, we begin to suspect that the editors of the news magazine probably intend to gather several opinion pieces together in a section with a title such as "Opinions on College Campuses about Feminism." We ultimately decide that a question would work well to move into the body of our piece. After a paragraph introducing readers to Calvin College, we will start a new paragraph with a question such as "How has feminism, which has had pervasive effects on our culture, affected us at Calvin College?"

The best way to answer this question, we decide, is with our thesis. Our thesis will appear early, and we think that such an early appearance will be appropriate in this context. In most articles in news magazines, the thesis or main point does appear early, and readers are not accustomed to working their way through long discussions in order to discover the thesis at the end. So the second sentence of our second paragraph will be our thesis sentence, and in order to draw attention to our thesis, we decide to end the second paragraph immediately after it.

As an expression of our personal opinion, our thesis will have an argumentative edge to it. Our thesis is as follows: "Although the feminist movement has achieved some long-overdue reforms at Calvin College, the work of the movement is not complete, since many people still have self-conscious questions and festering wounds."

In an essay of only five hundred words, we will not be able to marshall a large array of several kinds of evidence to support our thesis. Nor will our readers expect such an array of evidence. But they will expect us to give reasons for our opinion, and most of our reasons will come in the form of personal observations and anecdotes. These would not be appropriate in some rhetorical situations, but we think that they are entirely appropriate here, especially because personal opinions often are formed on the basis of personal observations and the experiences that anecdotes grow out of.

What are our reasons to write that the feminist movement has achieved some long-overdue reforms at Calvin College? We think most immediately of some reports in the past of sexist comments that male professors have made to female students: "That's right, honey." "Oh, you wouldn't need to know that to raise a family." "Don't worry your pretty little head over it." The more recent reports we have heard indicate that the number of such comments is diminishing.

We also think of a report by a team of examiners from the North Central Association after they visited our campus recently to decide whether we deserved to be reaccredited. One thing they mentioned—and with some suprise—was that on this campus, where in many ways people show great concern for fairness and equality, issues concerning women and women's rights have been sorely neglected, especially in formal curricular settings. After receiving that report, the college got busy, and now in connection with women's issues we have many more books in the library, many more courses on those subjects in the curriculum, many more pertinent entries on the calendar of special events, and many more discussion groups among student and faculty organizations than we had even five years ago. We decide to allot one paragraph to the details of the sexist comments and the accreditation report and one longer paragraph to details about recent reforms.

But as we noted in our thesis sentence, the work of the feminist movement on our campus is not complete; all around us we see people with self-conscious questions and festering wounds. We decide to move from details about the questions to details about the wounds, and whenever we have a choice, we will include less serious details before more serious details.

Many of the self-conscious questions we see people wrestling with have to do with who may extend courtesies to, or accept courtesies from, whom. To illustrate such questions, we would probably include in a short paragraph an anecdote about the hyperkinetic dancing before doorways that we often see. A group including one or more men and women approaches a door, and then the shuffle begins: "I'll get the door. No, I'll get the door. It's all right; I'll get the door myself." Such dances are almost comical—unless, of course, you are in the group doing the dance.

We would probably allot another paragraph to an anecdote about more serious questions. About three years ago a student whom we know had become very uneasy with some of the comments she had been hearing in a class taught by a young woman known as a feminist. The comments were perfectly consistent with the views many feminists held. They were comments about not wasting one's education, about not sacrificing control over one's life and body by becoming pregnant and agreeing, if only tacitly, to be a child's primary caretaker in the early years of the child's life. The young woman's words were poignant: "But I love my fiancé and can hardly wait to get married. And I've always wanted to have children and to be with them practically all the time until they start school. I never thought of that as a burden or as being exploited. Who am I—the biggest fool on earth? Am I supposed to feel guilty about all my dreams?" Her questions left us with unsettling emotions that we still have not found the right name for.

The final observations we would include have to do with questions that the feminist movement has left people on our campus asking, but they also have to do with the wounds that people have suffered in arguments in response to those questions. On our campus we have students called "presem." They intend to go on to a seminary after college, hoping to serve someday as ministers in various Protestant denominations. You can probably guess that as the feminist movement gained momentum in recent years, more and more of these students have been young women. They feel a clear and urgent call from God to serve as ministers.

You may respond, "Excellent. Churches need many more women in such positions." The tension on our campus arises because there are many other people here—both men and women—who interpret some verses in the Bible as directly forbidding women from serving as ministers. And thus the battles begin: On one side are those who feel a clear call from God to pursue a course of action, and on the other side are those who believe that pursuing such a course of action is nothing short of heresy and a direct undermining of the foundation of churches. When the stakes are as high as these, the wounds suffered by those on both sides are deep and not easily healed.

As we indicated, these comments would be our final bits of support for our thesis. To this point, our essay would include seven paragraphs: one to give some background information on Calvin College, one to present our thesis, one to give the details of the sexist comments and the North Central accreditation report, one to describe recent reforms, and three to describe various questions and wounds. Now we have to decide how to conclude. In some ways it would make good sense to conclude with the comments about the wounds that people on both sides of the women-in-ministry issue have suffered. But ultimately we decide that doing so would cast a pall over the whole piece. Thus we decide to conclude with the following short paragraph, which would directly follow the comments about people's wounds:

> In this light, it is clear that the work of the feminist movement at Calvin College is not complete. But the reforms that we have seen in the past give us hope for the work in the future. We hope for the time when men and women, their questions answered and their wounds healed, interact with one another and participate in the life of this institution on equal terms.

THE SECOND WRITING ASSIGNMENT

The second of the two writing assignments that we will respond to also appears after Gilligan's "Woman's Place in Man's Life Cycle." This assignment is worded as follows: "Use the methods and materials devised by Matina Horner (described in Gilligan's essay) to test for success anxiety among students on your campus. Then write up the results of your test in a standardized research report to be submitted for credit to your instructor in an introductory psychology class." This assignment obviously is intended to lead students who are relatively new to experimental psychology to learn about it by performing an experiment.

The first thing that we do is to read over the sections of Gilligan's chapter in which she describes Horner's work. There we learn that Horner discovered that a significantly greater percentage of women than men felt anxiety about competitive achievement. Horner gave approximately the same number of men and women a sentence, told them to regard the sentence as the first line of a story, and asked them to complete the story. When she analyzed the content of these stories, she found that many more women than men wrote stories in which, if characters faced success in some competitive arena, they became anxious and stifled their competitive striving. Horner postulated that the women who wrote such stories have a motive to avoid success, a motive they have developed because they think that success for women will lead to social rejection and a loss of femininity.

After reviewing Gilligan's report on Horner's work, we decide that to be as clear as possible about the details of Horner's experiment, we should read her original research report. Checking the list of references in Gilligan's book shows us that Horner's original report appeared in volume twenty-eight of *The Journal of Social Issues*. In that report we find that Horner presents the results of several different but closely related experiments. The one we will be able to replicate most satisfactorily is the one in which she used college freshmen and sophomores as subjects. She asked eighty-eight males and ninety females from a large midwestern university to write a story to follow a lead sentence that she provided for them. The females received this lead sentence: "After first term finals, Anne finds herself at the top of her medical school class." The males received this sentence: "After first term finals, John finds himself at the top of his medical school class."

To score the stories the subjects wrote, Horner used a "present-absent system" that was sensitive to words and images showing writers' reactions to success. She classified a writer as having the motive to avoid success if that writer made statements in the story showing conflicts over success, anticipating negative consequences of success, denying any responsibility for achieving success, or rejecting the lead sentence altogether.

Horner found that fifty-nine of the ninety women wrote stories containing evidence of the motive to avoid success. As Horner puts it, the women's stories "were filled with negative consequences and affect, righteous indignation, withdrawl rather than enhanced striving, concern, or even an inability to accept the information presented in the cue." On the other hand, only eight of the eighty-eight men wrote stories in which there was evidence of the motive to avoid success. In Horner's words, statements in their stories "showed strong positive feelings, indicated increased striving, confidence in the future, and a belief that this success would be instrumental to fulfilling other goals— such as providing a secure and happy home for some girl." When Horner analyzed her experimental results (using a statistical measure called the chi-square test), she found that the difference between the percentage of women exhibiting success anxiety and the percentage of men exhibiting success anxiety was highly significant.

The question we decide to use to guide our preparations, then, is whether subjects on our campus will react as Horner's subjects did. Our first prepartory step is to produce the materials we will give to subjects. We decide that we should give each subject two sheets of regular-sized paper stapled together. On the top of the first we will include a title. But we do not want to reveal too much about what we are testing for, so we decide to use the fairly vague title "Story Completion."

Below the title we will ask subjects to give us some information about themselves. We would like to know each subject's name, age, gender, class level in college (freshmen? sophomore?), marital status, and race. Providing such bits of information is a standardized routine in many experiments. We decide to have subjects provide this information before starting the actual experiment so that they can become comfortable in the experimental setting.

After the section in which we ask subjects to provide information about themselves, we will give them directions about how to complete our experimental task. We will say that when they flip over to the second page, they will see a sentence. We will use the same sentences as leads that Horner did. We will inform our subjects that they should regard the sentence they see as the first one in a story that they should write. We will add that they need not use more than thirty minutes or one side of the second piece of paper for their stories. At the bottom of the first page, we will thank them for their willingness to help us with this project.

Horner had a large number of male and female subjects, eighty-eight and ninety, respectively. But her study was part of her doctoral work, work on a level much higher than ours. We decide that an instructor in an introductory psychology course would not expect us to have such a large number of subjects. Besides, we will not have time to analyze stories from dozens and dozens of subjects. But we realize that we cannot settle for two or three male and female subjects, since it would be possible in such a situation for one or two exceptional cases to throw off the results. We ultimately decide to use twenty male and twenty female subjects. To facilitate comparing our results with Horner's, we would like to have freshmen and sophomores as our subjects.

Fortunately for us, the psychology department at our college requires that all students in introductory psychology courses participate in at least two experiments conducted by fellow students. And the department has a bulletin board on which students can advertise their experiments and ask for other students to volunteer to serve as subjects. We decide to advertise our experiment there, and we issue a call for twenty freshmen or sophomore males as well as twenty freshmen or sophomore females. Our last bit of preparatory work is to reserve a room in which to conduct the experiment. We have decided that we can run all our subjects through the experiment at the same time, so if we have a fairly large room, one of us can meet the subjects, hand out the experimental packets, go over the directions, and collect the packets at the end.

After we have conducted the experiment, we must analyze the results and write up our report. To make sure that our biases and wishes do not affect the analysis, we decide that we should not score the stories ourselves. Therefore, we ask three of our friends if they will score the stories for the presence or absence of words and images related to success anxiety. They agree, and we show them the paragraphs in which Horner describes what counts as evidence of success anxiety. Then we put the stories in random order and let our friends work on them. If they disagree about whether or not a story shows evidence of success anxiety, we ask them to confer and to try to reach a consensus. If they cannot reach a consensus, then we will accept the judgment of the two scorers who do agree. When our scorers are finished with the stories, we should be able to calculate a percentage of women and of men who wrote stories showing evidence of success anxiety. Since we have little training in statistics, and since our college does not have an office offering help with statistical analysis, we decide to ask the instructor in the introductory psychology course to do the statistical analysis of our results. This should take only a modest amount of time.

After our experimental data are analyzed, we begin writing up our research report. At this stage of our work, rhetorical considerations again come to the fore. We know that the instructor in the introductory psychology course will be our primary reader. But we also know that this assignment is designed to help us take our first steps into the discourse community of experimental psychologists and perhaps into more specific discourse communities within the group of experimental psychologists. So we should write our report thinking of members of such communities as potential readers. If our report is good enough, the psychology professor will help us find an audience for it among practicing experimental psychologists.

Such readers will bring much information to our report. They will know about experimental work in general, and they will probably know about the work on success anxiety. They might even be familiar with Horner's work. Therefore, we will be able to use a somewhat specialized vocabulary. We will not want to use words that unnecessarily limit the number of people who can understand our report. But we can certainly use the names of statistical tests without explaining those tests, and we can use terms such as *success anxiety* and *a present-absent system of scoring* without having to define them. Moreover, we need not repeat a lot of information from sentence to sentence. Experimental psychologists are very much used to following the descriptions of detailed experiments. And with all the pressures on their time, they want these reports to be as concise as possible.

Such readers are professionals, and they will expect us to write as professionals. We will have to maintain a fairly formal style, taking care not to slip into chattiness or slang expressions. And we should largely avoid references to ourselves as experimenters and writers. In writing about experiments, authors traditionally use passive verbs and omit references to themselves. For example, many scientists would write "Thirty subjects were gathered" rather than "We gathered thirty subjects," their operating assumption being that if the experiment is well designed and executed, the identities of the experimenters are not important. However, in recent years some writers have begun to question the practice of always using passive verbs, and some articles with active verbs and references to experimenters have appeared. In such a changing situation, we decide to be cautious. In the main we will use passive verbs and omit references to ourselves. But we will include active verbs and the pronoun *we* when it would be awkward or strained not to. For instance, we will write "We decided that" rather than "A decision was made to."

An important thing for us to realize about our readers is that they will have firm expectations about how our report is organized. We will have to adhere to the format recommended by the American Psychological Association, a format that calls for dividing research reports into sections.

We must start with a title, one that is clear and informative. In some of your writing, you might wish to use clever or allusive titles, but that would not be a wise strategy in this situation. We know that we have the best chance of luring those who are doing research on success anxiety into reading our article if they are able to discern, perhaps from just a brief reference in an index, what our article is about. Thus we will not try to be cute with our title; we will call our article "Success Anxiety Among Male and Female Underclass Students at Calvin College."

Immediately after the title we must include an abstract, which is a summary of what we tried to find out, how we proceeded, and what we actually found. In an abstract our main concerns are conciseness and clarity. Conventionally, abstracts are only 100 or 150 words long. Our abstract must be utterly clear and unambiguous because many researchers decide whether or not to read a report on the basis of the abstract alone.

After the abstract, we move into the first section of the paper. The first section is titled the "Introduction." Here we tell that in our work we are trying to answer the question of whether underclass students at Calvin College display patterns of success anxiety similar to those displayed by Horner's subjects. We must also provide some background about previous work on success anxiety. We will refer to Horner's work, of course, but we will also include references to some of the studies Horner cites in her report. Some checking in the library shows us that in the time since Horner ran her tests, others have continued in this line of work. We read these more recent reports and refer to them, adding brief notes about the details of the experiments. Included here will be references to Kearney's "A Comparison of Motivation to Avoid Success in Males and Females" (1984), Ray's "Fear of Success and Level of Aspiration" (1985), and Ishiyama et al.'s "Adolescents' Fear of Social Consequences of Academic Success as a Function of Age and Sex" (1985).

In the Introduction, we also must tell what we will add to the body of scientific information about success anxiety and how, in general, we will do so. The sentence or sentences that we use here are really statements of our purpose in the report. Since our study represents our first step into the discourse community of experimental psychologists, our contribution to existing knowledge will be quite modest. We are adding nothing to the knowledge of how to test for success anxiety since we are using methods and materials used in the past by Horner. We do make some contribution to what is known about success anxiety, though, since we are learning whether Horner's results are replicable. And it is worth remembering that our subjects are different from Horner's and that we are testing several years after Horner did. Between the time of Horner's report (1972) and ours, the feminist movement might well have affected both men's and women's attitudes toward competitive achievement.

The next section of an experimental report is called the "Methods" section. This often has several subsections. In the first, we must provide some identification of our subjects, tell how numerous they were, and indicate how they were selected. The second subsection deals with our experimental materials. We must describe what materials we used and how we prepared them. The last subsection focuses on our experimental procedure. We must describe where and how we conducted the test. We should reproduce exactly whatever we said to subjects before, during, and after the test.

Then we move on to a section called "Results." Here we inform our readers about what data we came up with and how we analyzed them. We will report the percentages of men and women showing success anxiety in the stories they wrote, and we will give the figures derived from the statistical analysis of these percentages. Often readers such as ours welcome seeing the results of studies laid out in one or more tables, so we will construct a simple table to show the percentages of men and women exhibiting success anxiety and the data indicating whether or not the difference between these percentages is statistically significant.

The final part of our report is entitled the "Discussion" section. Here is where we will come closest to expressing what would traditionally be viewed as a thesis. For here we must try to explain our results. Horner found that a significantly greater percentage of women than men exhibited success anxiety in story-completion tasks; she explained this result by saying that her women subjects feared success anxiety because they thought it would make them seem less feminine and would lead to social rejection. It is possible that our test would turn out just as Horner's did and that we would explain our results the same way that she did.

But our test might turn out differently. We can imagine, for example, that we would have an even greater percentage of women fearing success in competitive achievement, primarily because many women on our campus come from homes in which the mother has a very traditional role. Or we can imagine that many of our male subjects as well as many of our female subjects might show anxiety about competitive achievement, largely because students on our campus hear a great deal about cooperation, altruism, and service to others. But whatever way our test turns out, the discussion section is the place for offering an explanation of the results and for estimating how much of a contribution to the work on success anxiety these results make, however modest that contribution might be.

The discussion section is also the place to connect our work to related work in experimental psychology as well as to list some questions raised by our work that we would like to pursue in the future. After reading and thinking about the work on success anxiety, we would like someday to study subjects who show signs of success anxiety. We would like to learn whether a significant number of them come from certain kinds of families, from certain levels on the economic scale, and from certain kinds of religious orientations. In another line of work, we would like to investigate those who at one time had success anxiety and decided to try to fight it off. We would like to learn what made them decide to fight this anxiety and what methods they used to fight it.

After the discussion section, we close our report by listing all the references we have cited. We list them alphabetically, according to the format recommended by the American Psychological Association and described in most handbooks for college writing.

As you can tell, our experimental report differs greatly from our essay about the effects of feminism on our campus. The differences are probably most evident when you contrast the statistical data in the report to the personal anecdotes in the essay. Our main point in this chapter is that if our responses to the two writing assignments approach success, they do so primarily because we applied rhetorical considerations to both of them.

A NOTE ON REVISION

We would try to finish both of the essays we have described in this chapter well ahead of the time when we have to submit them. Doing this gives us time to set the essays aside for a day or two, and it gives us some distance from them. When we come back to them, we will be able to examine them with fresh eyes to see if they should be changed.

We urge you to be brave enough to change drafts of essays. Too many of our students finish composing an essay, heave a huge sigh of relief, and then copy it over or have it typed, never suspecting that they could improve it further. They do not take seriously the witness of almost every writer who has ever talked about the craft of writing: The best results come from revising.

If possible, ask some of your friends to read your drafts over for you. Before they read, let them know as much as possible about the appropriate rhetorical situations. With that knowledge, they can often help you see places where you have not gone as far as you could toward engaging the minds of your readers.

In addition, it is a good idea to read your essays aloud to others. They can alert you to points where you hesitate or stumble as well as to places where the rhythm of the prose is rough or monotonous. Afterwards, you can make any necessary revisions.

The last thing you should do is proofread and carefully edit your essay. Some of our students do not worry about leaving misspellings and the like in their essays. But at best these are signs of carelessness, and at worst they can really get in a reader's way. Such errors are your responsibility to catch and correct; you should not depend on a typist to correct them for you. In whatever community or communities of discourse you use essays, be sure that nothing you can control impedes the success of your message.

DISCOURSE COMMUNITIES IN HISTORICAL STUDIES

INTRODUCTION

As the Trojans gathered around the great wooden horse that stood proudly and perhaps arrogantly on their beach, they must have rejoiced to stand on a spot that had just the day before been occupied by the Greek army that had besieged Troy for a decade. The horse, they reasoned, would become an emblem of their victory, and they set about tearing down the city gates in order to bring the thing inside, ignoring the prophecy that Troy would fall once those gates were breached, as well as the strident cries of the seer Cassandra, doomed always to utter the truth and never to be believed.

While ignoring the voices of those who could look forward in time, the Trojans also ignored the voices of their own past. For ten years they had struggled against the wiles and strategems of the Greeks. For ten years they had known of the subtle trickery of Ulysses. But in the midst of the celebrations, they forgot all of this. The gates were torn down, Cassandra was ignored, and the horse carrying the Greek army brought gladly into the city. The next evening Troy would be a smoking ruin.

What is the purpose of history? This is a question often ignored by those who feel there is no need for a historical perspective. The experience of the French in Vietnam was ignored by American presidents during the late 1950s and early 1960s, with the result that America fell into the same endless cycles that the French had experienced. The defeat of Napoleon was ignored by Hitler as he opened a third front and marched into the Soviet Union, only to meet the same end as his predecessor.

On one level, history establishes patterns, so that we who live in the present can learn from those who lived in the past. History allows us to see the enormous harm done to an entire society when one part of that society is not allowed to exercise its full rights. It points out the merits of peaceful cooperation between neighboring countries. It points out the follies of a limitless arms race. These facts do not ensure that a society will always act according to the patterns established by history. But the patterns are there for those willing to profit from them.

As we write these words, Native Americans in Quebec have barricaded several roads that lead into what they see as ancestral homelands. Developers are anxious to turn those lands into a golf course with attendant condominiums; local authorities acknowledge the legitimacy of Native American rights to this land according to provincial law. Many of the local white inhabitants, who will not share in the profits from the golf course and who have no stake in the ancestral lands, are annoyed at the inconvenience of the blockade; many must now drive two hours to work, instead of a few minutes.

No matter which side of this issue you are on, it is important to recognize that this event does not exist as an isolated incident apart from anything else. It is a point in history, and it has historical precedent. Behind the blockade stands a people whose rights have been ignored, whose treaties have been violated, whose lands have been grabbed up by those who have no reverence for the earth. Before the blockade stands a group who live within a North American tradition: Land is something to be used and exploited; it is an economic entity. This issue can be resolved only with a mutual recognition of these historical patterns. To ignore them is to repeat the errors of the past.

Gerda Lerner argues that history empowers us. It allows us to establish links with our past, and it gives us a sense of our own traditions. From this continuity comes a sense of how we might act in the future, of what we might accomplish. Lerner suggests that, without a history, a group is without power—the position that many women in contemporary North America find themselves in. But she could also go on to show that other contemporary North American groups lack this history, in the sense that their contributions are ignored in mainstream American history texts. Native American and African American and American Chinese contributions come to mind here, but in the last decade other large ethnic groups have established themselves in North America; their history too will need to be told for them to have power in the contemporary society. History, as it chronicles a tradition, establishes a vision for future action.

But history is a slippery thing. In the nineteenth century, and even into the twentieth, many historians believed that history was an objective science. The historian need only find facts, arrange them in an appropriate sequence, and—most importantly—refrain from including the personal biases that could lead to interpretation. Such a historian would argue that any interpretation actually clouds the facts and hinders the meaning that is intrinsically part of a fact. Some modern historians have called this the "cult of facts" or "scientific history," terms that suggest the dominance of sheer fact over speculative interpretation.

But for most contemporary historians, such an approach to history is inappropriate, for it belies the notion that history is essentially a narrative that can be understood only as the historian shapes and gives meaning to the facts. Fact alone, from this perspective, cannot give meaning; fact has no meaning without attendant interpretation. For these historians, the fact is the mere beginning, the frame on which the most important and significant part of the historian's task is built. These historians would argue that the fact of the Quebec blockade is mere chronology; the interpretation of that block-ade, the motives for it, the influence of it—that is history.

But other historians have wondered if seeing the entire meaning of history in fact alone is merely inappropriate. Perhaps it is not even possible. All history is chronicled by writers who bring to their material certain percep-tions, by writers who take a specific stance toward their material that inev-itably affects the manner in which they understand and present that mate-rial. Would the history of the Quebec blockade as written by a Native American differ from an account of the same incident as written by a white writer, even if both believed they were being objective? And suppose they come to their writing with different preconceptions about how a writer ap-proaches an event? Or even about the nature of history itself? The following selections reflect the diversity of stances that historians take. For writers like Bede and Bradford, history is theologically centered, and their accounts cor-respondingly center on the role of the church. Writers such as Graves regard history as the acts of prominent figures, and they focus on how those figures affected the course of events. Waite examines a single prominent figure, but he examines him psychologically; he looks not so much at action but at the motivation for action.

Other historians reject the great-figure approach. Braudel finds that events are motivated not by prominent actors but by physical forces that have little to do with the presence of humanity. Durant and Genovese regard his-tory as the story of social forces. And Lerner sees history as establishing an artificial dichotomy between the roles of men and women. Each of these stances—Christian, psychoanalytical, Marxist, feminist among them—influ-ences the way the historian writes his or her works.

And this raises a larger question: Is it possible for history to be proven? Many historians argue that proof comes through establishing the validity of facts, and certainly it is possible to prove the validity of most facts. But other historians question whether it is possible to prove the meanings of facts. Is history a science that has no constant? If history is something that is perceived and interpreted by a writer and then judged by a reader who brings certain perceptions and beliefs to bear on it, then perhaps it might be argued that history is not an inviolable statement of fact. Similarly, if the historian is at liberty to select and arrange facts, leaving out what others have included, inserting what others believe to be insignificant, arranging for a given effect, interpreting according to one's discourse community, then it seems that his-tory and its meaning must be completely subjective.

This is one of the basic issues with which the following essays and selec-tions grapple.

Thucydides

(471?–400 B.C.)

The greatest Greek historian, Thucydides, was a contemporary of most of the events he chronicled. A wealthy Athenian, he was also a great admirer of Pericles, who brought Athens to the peak of its Golden Age. A nobleman by birth, he became one of the strategists of the Peloponnesian War against Sparta, a rival city-state. But as a soldier, he was disgraced. Ordered to relieve the city of Amphipolis from a siege, he departed instantly but found upon his arrival that the citizens had capitulated. The Athenians did not countenance failure. Thucydides was condemned and forced into exile, where he remained for twenty years, until just four years before his death. It was from this vantage point of exile that he was to write his great history, The History of the Peloponnesian War.*

A man wrongfully condemned and exiled might be expected to write with a strong bias, but Thucydides does not; he favors neither Sparta nor Athens in his history but remains impartial. Throughout the work, he is an objective historian who restrains himself from commenting upon the morality or ethics of the situation and instead merely recounts what happened. His methods are scientific, in that he deals only with that which is observable.

While this is generally true, it does not mean that Thucydides is completely unbiased. H.D.F. Kitto argues in The Greeks *(1951) that "Thucydides, like most Greek artists, is constructional, not representational, expressing his deepest thoughts in the architectural disposition of his material" (152). Those deepest thoughts center on the nature of war itself: "The cause of all these evils," Thucydides writes in Book III of* The Peloponnesian War, *"was the desire for power which greed and ambition inspire" (III, 83). All of his material works towards that one truth. The book thus becomes not only a history of a war between two city-states; it is also a plea against the meaninglessness of war and a cry against the repeating patterns that lead to war.*

In this selection, Thucydides writes of the Theban invasion of Platæa. The Thebans, allies of Sparta, are clearly in the wrong because they invade before war is declared. But Thucydides the Athenian does not show any moral outrage. Nor does he show outrage when the citizens of Platæa, allies of Athens, murder their hostages. Nevertheless, Thucydides has in mind a time when retribution comes upon both Thebes and Platæa, in particular the latter. Eventually the city would fall to the Spartan allies, and all the men who could not show some tangible evidence of loyalty to Sparta were killed; the women were sold as slaves. Thucydides has shaped the material so that it provides its own commentary upon events.

The following selection is the opening of Book II of Thucydides' The History of the Peloponnesian War, *translated by Henry Dale.*

BOOK II

The war between the Athenians and Peloponnesians and their respective allies 1
now begins from this period, at which they ceased from further intercourse
with each other without a herald, and having once proceeded to hostilities,
carried them on continuously; and the history of it is written in order, as the
several events happened, by summers and winters.

For the thirty years' truce which was made after the reduction of Eubœa 2
lasted fourteen years; but in the fifteenth year, when Chrysis was in the forty-
eighth year of her priesthood at Argos, and Ænesias was ephor at Sparta, and
Pythodorus had still two months to be archon at Athens; in the sixth month
after the battle at Potidæa, and in the beginning of spring, rather more than
three hundred men of the Thebans, (led by Pythangelus, son of Phylidas, and
Diemporus, son of Onetorides, Bœotarchs) about the first watch entered with
their arms into Platæa, a town of Bœotia, which was in alliance with the
Athenians. There were certain men of the Platæans who called them in, and
opened the gates to them, namely, Nauclides and his party, who wished, for
the sake of their own power, to put to death those of the citizens who were
opposed to them, and to put the city into the hands of the Thebans. They
carried on these negotiations through Eurymachus, the son of Leontiades, a
very influential person at Thebes. For the Thebans, foreseeing that the war
would take place, wished to surprise Platæa, which had always been at variance with them, while it was still time of peace, and the war had not openly
broken out. And on this account, too, they entered the more easily without
being observed, as no guard had been set before [the gates]. After piling their
arms in the market-place, they did not comply with the wish of those who
called them in by immediately setting to work, and going to the houses of
their adversaries; but determined to make a proclamation in friendly terms,
and to bring the city to an agreement rather, and to friendship; and the
herald proclaimed, that whoever wished to make alliance according to the
hereditary principles of all the Bœotians, should come and pile his arms with
them, supposing that the city would easily come over to them by this method.

The Platæans, on finding that the Thebans were within their walls, and 3
that their city was unexpectedly taken, being very much alarmed, and thinking that far more had entered than really had, (for they did not see them in
the night) came to an agreement, and having accepted the terms, remained
quiet; especially since they were proceeding to no violent measures against
any one. But by some means or other while making these negotiations, they
observed that the Thebans were not numerous, and thought that by attacking
them they might easily overpower them; for it was not the wish of the great
body of the Platæans to revolt from the Athenians. They determined therefore to make the attempt; and proceeded to join each other by digging through

the partition-walls [of their houses], that they might not be seen going through the streets; and set wagons without the cattle in the streets, to serve for a barricade; and got everything else ready, as each seemed likely to be of service for the business in hand. When things were in readiness, as far as they could make them so, having watched for the time when it was still night and just about day-break, they began to go out of their houses against them; that they might not attack them by day-light, when they would be more bold, and on equal terms with themselves, but in the night, when they would be more timid, and fight at a disadvantage through their own acquaintance with the city. So they assailed them immediately, and came to close quarters with them as quickly as they could.

The Thebans, on finding themselves outwitted, proceeded to close their 4 ranks, and repel their attacks, wherever they might fall upon them. And twice or thrice they beat them off; but afterwards, when the men were assailing them with a great clamour, and the women and slaves were raising a loud shouting and screaming from the houses, and pelting them with stones and tiles, and a violent rain also had come on in the night, they were frightened, and turned and fled through the city, the greater part of them, through the dark and dirt, (for the event happened at the end of the month,) being unacquainted with the ways out, by which they were to save themselves; while they had pursuers who were acquainted with them, to prevent their escaping: so that many were put to death. Moreover, one of the Platæans had shut the gate by which they had entered, and which was the only one opened, by driving the spike of a spear into the bar, instead of a bolt; so that there was no longer any way out even by that. As they were chased up and down the city, some of them mounted the wall and threw themselves over, and perished most of them: others came to a lone gate, and, a woman having given them an axe, cut through the bar without being observed, and went out, but in no great numbers, for it was quickly discovered; while others met their fate scattered about in different parts of the city. But the largest and most united body of them rushed into a spacious building which joined on to the wall, and the near door of which happened to be open, thinking that the door of the building was a gate [of the city], and that there was a passage straight through to the outside. When the Platæans saw them cut off, they consulted whether they should burn them where they were, by setting fire to the building, or treat them in any other way. At last, both those and all the rest of the Thebans that were yet alive, and wandering up and down the city, agreed to deliver up themselves and their arms to the Platæans, to do with them as they pleased. Thus then fared the party who were in Platæa.

The rest of the Thebans, who were to have joined them with all their 5 forces while it was still night, in case those who had entered should be at all unsuccessful, on receiving on their march the tidings of what had happened, advanced to their succour. Now Platæa is seventy stades* distant from

---

* A stade was about 200 yards. A day's journey for an army was about 150 stades.

Thebes, and the rain which had fallen in the night made them proceed the slower; for the river Asopus was flowing with a full stream, and was not to be crossed easily. So by marching through the rain, and having passed the river with difficulty, they arrived too late; as some of the men had been by this time slain, and others of them were kept alive as prisoners. When the Thebans learned what had happened, they formed a design against those of the Platæans who were outside the city, (for there were both men and stock in the fields, inasmuch as the evil had happened unexpectedly in time of peace) for they wished to have all they could take to exchange for their own men within, should any happen to have been taken alive. Such were their plans. But the Platæans, while they were still deliberating, having suspected that there would be something of this kind, and being alarmed for those outside, sent out a herald to the Thebans, saying that they had not acted justly in what had been done, by endeavouring to seize their city in time of treaty; and told them not to injure what was without; else *they* also would put to death the men whom they had alive in their hands; but if they withdrew again from the territory, they would give the men back to them. The Thebans give this account of the matter, and say that they swore to it. But the Platæans do not acknowledge that they promised to give back the men *immediately*, but when proposals had first been made, in case of their coming to any agreement: and they deny that they swore to it. At any rate the Thebans retired from the territory without having done any injury; but the Platæans, after getting in as quickly as possible whatever they had in the country, immediately put the men to death. Those who had been taken were one hundred and eighty, and Eurymachus, with whom the traitors had negotiated, was one of them.

When they had done this, they sent a messenger to Athens, and gave 6 back the dead to the Thebans under a truce, and arranged matters in the city to suit their present circumstances, as seemed best to them.—Now news had immediately been taken to the Athenians of what had been done with respect to the Platæans; and they straightway seized as many of the Bœotians as were in Attica, and sent a herald to Platæa, with orders to forbid their proceeding to extremities, in the case of the Thebans whom they had in their hands, till *they* also should take counsel about them: for tidings of their being dead had not yet reached them. For the first messenger [of the Platæans] had gone out at the very time of the entering of the Thebans; and the second, when they had just been conquered and taken: so that of the subsequent events they knew nothing. Thus then the Athenians were in ignorance when they sent their order; and the herald, on his arrival, found the men slain. After this the Athenians marched to Platæa, and brought in provisions, and left a garrison in it, and took out the least efficient of the men with the women and children.

When the business at Platæa had occurred, and the treaty had been 7 clearly broken, the Athenians began to prepare for going to war; and so did the Lacedæmonians and their allies, both intending to send embassies to the king, and to the barbarians in other parts, from whatever quarter either party hoped to gain any assistance, and bringing into alliance with them such states as were not in their power. And on the side of the Lacedæmonians, in addition to the ships already on the spot in Sicily and Italy, belonging to those who had espoused their cause, they were ordered to build more according to the greatness of the cities, so that in the whole number they should amount to five hundred; and to get ready a certain sum of money which was mentioned, while they remained quiet in other respects, and received the Athenians coming with a single ship, till these preparations should be made. The Athenians, on the other hand, were inspecting their present confederacy, and sending ambassadors to the countries more immediately around the Peloponnese, as Corcyra, Cephallenia, Acarnania, and Zacynthus; seeing that if these were firm friends to them, they would successfully carry on the war round the Peloponnese.

Indeed both parties had no small designs, but put forth their strength 8 to the war: and not unnaturally; for all men at the beginning apply themselves to it more eagerly; and at that time the young men, being numerous in the Peloponnese, and also at Athens, were, through their inexperience, not unwilling to engage in the war. And the rest of Greece was all in excitement at the conflict of the principal states. And many prophecies were repeated, and reciters of oracles were singing many of them, both amongst those who were going to war and in the other states. Moreover, Delos had been visited by an earthquake a short time before this, though it had never had a shock before in the memory of the Greeks; and it was said and thought to have been ominous of what was about to take place. And whatever else of this kind had happened to occur was all searched up. The good wishes of men made greatly for the Lacedæmonians, especially as they gave out that they were the liberators of Greece. And every individual, as well as state, put forth his strength to help them in whatever he could, both by word and deed; and each thought that the cause was impeded at that point at which he himself would not be present. So angry were the generality with the Athenians; some from a wish to be released from their dominion, others from a fear of being brought under it. With such preparations and feelings then did they enter on the contest.

Each party had the following states in alliance when they set to the war. 9 The allies of the Lacedæmonians were these: all the Peloponnesians within the Isthmus, except the Argives and Achæans (these were in friendship with both parties; and the Pellenians were the only people of the Achæans that joined in the war at first, though afterwards all of them did); and without the Peloponnese, the Megareans, Locrians, Bœotians, Phocians, Ambraciots, Leucadians, and Anactorians. Of these, the states which furnished a navy were the Corinthians, Megareans, Sicyonians, Pellenians, Eleans, Ambraciots, and Leucadians. Those that supplied cavalry were the Bœotians, Phocians, and Locrians. The rest of them sent infantry. This then was the Lacedæmonian confederacy. That of the Athenians comprehended the Chians, Lesbians, Platæans, the Messenians at Naupactus, the greater part of the

Acarnanians, the Corcyreans, the Zacynthians: also some other states which were tributary amongst the following nations; as the maritime parts of Caria, and Doris adjacent to it, Ionia, the Hellespont, the Greek towns Thraceward; the islands, which were situated between the Peloponnese and Crete, towards the east, and all the rest of the Cyclades except Melos and Thera. Of these, the Chians, Lesbians, and Corcyreans furnished a naval force, the rest of them infantry and money. Such was the confederacy on each side, and their resources for the war.

The Lacedæmonians, immediately after what had happened at Platæa, 10 sent round orders through the Peloponnese and the rest of their confederacy, for the states to prepare an army and such provisions as it was proper to have for a foreign expedition, with a view to invading Attica. When they had each got ready by the appointed time, two thirds from every state assembled at the Isthmus. And after the whole army was mustered, Archidamus, the king of the Lacedæmonians, who led this expedition, summoned to his presence the generals of all the states, and those highest in office and of most importance, and spoke to the following purport:

"Men of the Peloponnese and allies, both our fathers made many expe- 11 ditions, as well in the Peloponnese as out of it, and the elder part of ourselves are not without experience in wars. Never yet, however, have we marched out with a greater force than this; but we are now going against a most powerful state, and with a most numerous and most excellently equipped army on our own side. We ought then to show ourselves neither inferior to our fathers, nor degenerated from our own character. For the whole of Greece has its expectation raised, and is paying attention to this attack, with good wishes that we may succeed in our designs, through their hatred of the Athenians. Though, then, some may think that we are making the attack with superior numbers, and that it is very certain our adversaries will not meet us in battle, we must not, for this reason, go at all less carefully prepared; but both the general and soldier of each state should, as far as concerns himself, be always expecting to come into danger. For the events of war are uncertain, and attacks are generally made in it with short notice, and under the impulse of passion; frequently, too, has the less number, through being afraid, more successfully repelled the more numerous forces, through their being unprepared in consequence of their contempt. In the enemy's country indeed men ought always to march with boldness of feeling, but at the same time to make their actual preparations with a degree of fear; for in this way they would be at once most full of courage for attacking their adversaries, and most secure against being attacked. But in our own case, we are not going against a state that is so powerless to defend itself, but against one most excellently provided with every thing; so that we must fully expect that they will meet us in battle; and if they have not already set out before we are there, yet [that they will do so], when they see us in their territory wasting and destroying their property. For all are angry, when suffering any unwonted evil, to see it done before their eyes, and in their very presence: and those who [on such provocation] reflect the least, set to work with the greatest passion [to avenge themselves]. And it is natural that the Athenians should do so even to a greater extent than others, since they presume to rule the rest of the world, and to go against and ravage their neighbours' land, rather than see their own ravaged. As then we are marching against a state of this description, and shall gain for our forefathers, as well as for ourselves, the most decided character, one way or the other, from the results; follow where any one may lead you, valuing order and caution above every thing, and with quickness receiving your commands. For this is the finest and the safest thing that can be seen, for a large body of men to show themselves maintaining uniform discipline."

Having thus spoken, and dismissed the assembly, Archidamus first sent 12 Melesippus, son of Diacritus, a Spartan, to Athens; in case the Athenians might be more disposed to submit, when they saw that the Peloponnesians were now on their march. But they did not admit him into the city, nor to their assembly; for the opinion of Pericles had previously been adopted, not to admit any herald with an embassy from the Lacedæmonians, when they had once marched out from their frontiers. They sent him back therefore before hearing him, and ordered him to go beyond the borders that same day, and [to tell those who sent him] that in future, if they wished to propose any thing, they should send ambassadors after they had retired to their own territories. And they sent an escort with Melesippus, to prevent his holding communication with any one. When he was on the frontiers, and was about to be dismissed, he spoke these words and departed, "This day will be the beginning of great evils to Greece." When he arrived at the camp, and Archidamus found that the Athenians would not yet submit at all, he then set out and advanced with his army into their territory. At the same time, the Bœotians, while they furnished their contingent and their cavalry to join the Peloponnesians in their expedition, went to Platæa with the remainder of their force, and laid waste their land.

While the Peloponnesians were still assembling at the Isthmus, and were 13 on their march, before they invaded Attica, Pericles, son of Xanthippus, who was general of the Athenians with nine colleagues, when he found that the invasion would take place, suspected that either Archidamus, because he happened to be his friend, might frequently pass over his lands, and not ravage them, from a personal wish to oblige him; or that this might be done at the command of the Lacedæmonians for the purpose of raising a slander against him—as it was also with reference to *him* that they had charged them to drive out the accursed; and therefore he publicly declared to the Athenians in the assembly, that though Archidamus was his friend, he had not been admitted into his friendship for any harm to the state; should, then, the enemy not lay waste his lands and houses, like those of the rest, he gave them up to be public property, and that no suspicion might arise against him on these grounds. He gave them advice also on their present affairs, the same as he had before given; namely, to prepare for the war, and bring in their property from the country, and not go out against them to battle, but to come in and guard the city, and get ready their fleet, in which they were so strong, and keep the allies tight in hand; reminding them that their main strength was derived from the returns of the money paid by these, and that most of the advantages in war were gained by counsel and abundance of money. And [on this head] he told them to be of good courage, as the state had, on an average, six hundred talents coming in yearly as tribute from the allies, not reckoning its other sources of income; while there were still at that time in the Acropolis 6000 talents of coined silver; (for the greatest sum there had ever been was 9700 talents, from which had been taken what was spent on the propylæa of the citadel, and the other buildings, and on Potidæa;) and besides, of uncoined gold and silver in private and public offerings, and all the sacred utensils for the processions and games, and the Median spoils, and everything else of the kind, there was not less than 500 talents. Moreover, he added the treasures in the other temples, to no small amount, which they would use; and, in case of their being absolutely excluded from all resources, even the golden appendages of the goddess herself; explaining to them that the statue contained 40 talents of pure gold, and that it was all removable; and after using it for their preservation they must, he said, restore it to the same amount. With regard to money, then, he thus encouraged them. And as for heavy-armed troops, he told them that they had thirteen thousand, besides those in garrisons and on the ramparts to the number of sixteen thousand. For this was the number that kept guard at first, whenever the enemy made an incursion, drawn from the oldest and the youngest, and such of the resident aliens as were heavy-armed. For of the Phaleric wall there were five and thirty stades to the circuit of the city wall; and of that circuit itself the guarded part was three and forty stades; a certain part of it being unguarded, viz. that between the long wall and the Phaleric. There were also the long walls to the Piræus, a distance of forty stades, of which the outer one was manned; while the whole circumference of Piræus with Munychia was sixty stades, though the guarded part was only half that extent. Of cavalry, again, he showed them that they had twelve hundred, including mounted bowmen; with sixteen hundred bowmen [on foot], and three hundred triremes fit for service. These resources, and no fewer than these in their several kinds, had the Athenians, when the invasion of the Peloponnesians was first going to be made, and when they were setting to the war. Other statements also did Pericles make to them, as he was accustomed, to prove that they would have the superiority in the war.

The Athenians were persuaded by what they heard from him; and pro- 14 ceeded to bring in from the country their children and wives, and all the furniture which they used in their houses, pulling down even the wood-work of their residences; while they sent their sheep and cattle over to Eubœa and the adjacent islands. But the removal was made by them with reluctance, from the greater part having always been accustomed to live in the country.

This had, from the very earliest times, been the case with the Athenians 15 more than with others. For under Cecrops, and the first kings, down to the reign of Theseus, the population of Athens had always inhabited independent cities, with their own guild-halls and magistrates; and at such times as they were not in fear of any danger, they did not meet the king to consult with him, but themselves severally conducted their own government, and took their own counsel; and there were instances in which some of them even waged war [against him], as the Eleusinians with Eumolpus did against Erectheus. But when Theseus had come to the throne, who along with wisdom had power also, he both regulated the country in other respects, and having abolished the council-houses and magistracies of the other cities, he brought them all into union with the present city, assigning them one guild-hall and one council-house; and compelled them all, while they enjoyed each their own property as before, to use this one city only; which, since all were counted as belonging to it, became great, and was so bequeathed by Theseus to those who came after him. And from that time even to this the Athenians keep, at the public expense, a festival to the goddess, called *Synæcia*. Before that time, what is now the citadel was the city, with the district which lies under it, looking chiefly towards the south. And this is a proof of it; the temples of the other gods as well [as of Minerva] are in the citadel itself, and those that are out of it are situated chiefly in this part of the city; as that of the Olympian Jupiter, of the Pythian Apollo, of Terra and of Bacchus in Limnæ, in whose honour the more ancient festival of Bacchus is held on the twelfth day of the month Anthesterion; as the Ionians also, who are descended from the Athenians, even to this day observe it. And there are other ancient temples also situated in this quarter. The conduit too, which is now called Enneacrunus, [or, nine-pipes] from the tyrants having so constituted it, but which had formerly the name of Calirrhoe, when the springs were open, the men of that day used, as it was near, on the most important occasions; and even at the present time they are accustomed, from the old fashion, to use the water before marriages, and for other sacred purposes. Moreover, from their living of old in this quarter ,the citadel even to this day is called by the Athenians the city.

For a long time then the Athenians enjoyed their independent life in the   16
country; and after they were united, still, from the force of habit, the generality of them at that early period, and even afterwards, down to the time of this war, having with all their families settled and lived in the country, did not remove without reluctance, (especially as they had but lately recovered their establishments after the Median war) but were distressed and grieved to leave their houses, and the temples which, according to the spirit of the ancient constitution, had always been regarded by them as the places of their hereditary worship; going, as they now were, to change their mode of life, and each of them doing what was equivalent to leaving his native city.

When they came into the city, some few indeed had residences, and a   17 place of refuge with some of their friends or relations; but the great bulk of them dwelt in the unoccupied parts of the city, and in all the temples and hero-chapels, except the Acropolis, and the temple of the Elensinian Ceres, and any other that was kept constantly locked up. The Pelasgium also, as it is called, under the Acropolis, which it was even forbidden by a curse to inhabit, and prohibited by the end of a Pythian oracle, to this effect, "the Pelasgium is better unoccupied," was, nevertheless, built over, from the immediate necessity of the case. And, in my opinion, the oracle proved true in the contrary way to what was expected. For it was not, I think, because of their unlawfully inhabiting this spot, that such misfortunes befell the city; but it was owing to the war that the necessity of inhabiting it arose; which war though the god did not mention, he foreknew that [owing to it] the Pelasgium would hereafter be inhabited for no good. Many, too, quartered themselves in the towers of the walls, and in whatever way each could: for the city did not hold them when they were come all together; but subsequently they occupied the long walls, partitioning them out amongst them, and the greater part of the Piræus. At the same time they also applied themselves to matters connected with the war; mustering their allies, and equipping an armament of a hundred ships for the Peloponnese. The Athenians then were in this state of preparation.

QUESTIONS ABOUT THUCYDIDES' DISCOURSE COMMUNITY AND HIS CONCERNS IN THIS ESSAY

1. Although there obviously were earlier troubles between Athens and Sparta, the Plataean affair can be viewed as the triggering incident for the entire war. Reread closely the description of this incident. What was its ultimate cause? Do you think Thucydides is making a general statement about causes of wars?

2. How wise do you think it is for invaders or conquerors to try to make a "friendly arrangement" with the invaded or conquered? Can this ever be a wise general policy?

3. Thucydides does not chronicle the end of Plataea at the conclusion of this section, nor does he hint at the destruction of the city and the execution or enslavement of its people. Why does he withhold this information?

4. Why does Thucydides stress the aspects of time in paragraph 2? Is it important that the historian ground events in chronological time?

5. Thucydides comments that oracles were consulted as the war preparations were being made. He makes no further comment about oracles, but later in *The Peloponnesian War* he suggests that they are trivial and unimportant. Why, then, would he mention oracles at this point? What does this suggest about his attitude towards the Athenians?

6. What is humorous about the line that "each thought that the cause was impeded at that point at which he himself would not be present" (paragraph 8)? Or is this not really funny?

7. One could make a good case that the entire war resulted from poor communi-

cation. Review the selection to pinpoint incidents in which communication is thwarted, blocked, or distorted. Describe how each incident is significant.

8. Based on your reading of this selection, how would you characterize the Greeks of that era? What were their values? How did they operate? Do you detect any significant differences between the Athenians and the Spartans? Do you find yourself favoring either the Athenians or the Spartans? If so, which group, and why?

QUESTIONS ABOUT THUCYDIDES' RHETORICAL STRATEGIES

1. At the beginning of this selection, Thucydides writes that "the history of it is written in order, as the several events happened, by summers and winters." What does he mean by the words "by summers and winters"? Is he speaking of the entire year or just of two seasons? Why did he find it necessary to make this claim? What does the use of this phrase suggest about his stance in relation to the material?

2. Thucydides shows some hesitation as he describes the conflicting stories about the incidents that led to the execution of the hostages in Plataea. How does he resolve the conflict represented by the two stories? How do you judge the effectiveness of the resolution?

3. Thucydides never describes his perceptions about the character of the Plataeans, yet the reader has a clear sense of his strong disapproval of them. How does Thucydides convey his disapproval?

4. Many things occur simultaneously in this selection, and Thucydides is confronted with the task of ordering them. How does he control the sense of time in this selection? Is the sense of time always strictly chronological?

5. Contrast the substance of the address by Archidamus to the Spartans with that of Pericles to the Athenians. What are some of the striking contrasts? Is Thucydides using these addresses to characterize both sides?

6. Why does Thucydides diverge from his material to include a long section on the history of the Athenian city-state? Why is this material placed in this context? Does it interrupt the flow of the piece? Is it in any way related to the war?

7. The Athenians warn Plataea against "proceeding to extremities" with the Theban hostages. Does this seem to be working as a euphemism here? Why would the Athenians use such a phrase? Is Thucydides commenting on the Athenians when he recounts this language?

8. Thucydides provides a good example of litotes, understatement, when he writes that in Athens there were great numbers of young men who "were not unwilling to engage in the war." Why does he write "not unwilling" and not just "willing"? What does his choice of words suggest?

WRITING FROM WITHIN AND ABOUT HISTORY AND ITS STUDY

Writing for Yourself

1. In your journal, speculate about why Thucydides named his history *The Peloponnesian War* rather than *The Attican War*. Do you think the title suggests any bias?

2. After reflecting on wars in which North Americans have been involved, list in your journal what you believe some of the ultimate causes of warfare are.
3. In your journal, write about what you might be willing to fight and perhaps die for.

Writing for Nonacademic Audiences

1. You have been asked by your former middle-school history teacher to give a lecture to her class about the United States's entry into the Spanish-American War. After researching the basic facts, you find that you need some angle by which to interpret these facts; you decide that you will focus on the lessons that that war has to teach us about armed aggression. Write up the lecture and the discussion questions that you will use during this forty-five minute class.
2. For a popular journal such as *Reader's Digest*, write a 500-word essay on the connotations that the word *Spartan* carries in contemporary American culture.

Writing for Academic Audiences

1. Your instructor in an introductory history class asks you to write a 500-word essay on the ways in which the bias of a historian may or may not influence the way that historian constructs a historical account. Using Thucydides and this selection as your principal example, write that essay.
2. After researching the 1968 conflict at Kent State University between National Guardsmen and students, write a historical account of the afternoon when several unarmed students were shot and killed. Like Thucydides, you will have to balance two sides and perhaps not depend completely upon a chronological approach to actions. Aim this 1,500-word essay at your peers in a rhetoric class.

   After writing this essay, speculate in your journal about how your stance might have differed if
   a. you had been writing in 1968.
   b. you had been a student at Kent State during the shootings.
   c. your brother had been drafted and was fighting in Vietnam.
   d. you were one of the students who, in the late 1980s, tried to erect a monument to the dead students on the Kent State campus but confronted enormous difficulties in raising the money for that monument.
   e. you might be eligible for the draft yourself.
3. Do some research to discover an incident in a battle or a war in which an error or a breakdown in communication proved to be disastrous to one side's fortunes. In a 750-word essay, analyze what caused the error or breakdown, and speculate about what could have prevented the error or breakdown.

Bede

(c. 673–735)

The Venerable Bede was one of the least traveled historians of his age—or of subsequent ages. When he was only seven years old he entered the monastery of Wearmouth in Durham, Britain; ten years later he moved to the monastery at Jarrow at its founding. Though he visited Lindisfarne and York in the north, he spent most of his time at Jarrow and probably never traveled beyond the boundaries of Northumbria. It was as a monk at Jarrow that Bede prepared for and wrote all of his texts, and at least partially through his writings Jarrow became an enormously influential monastery, contributing a great deal to the civilization of Britain. Soon after Bede's death, though, the monastery suffered three pillagings by the Danes (evidence of mass burials from these raids still exists in the ruins of the monastery) and was eventually burned by William I.

Bede observed that while he kept the regular disciplines and sang the choir offices daily, his principal interest lay in his study and writing. He composed treatises on the Old and New Testaments, on the nature of music, on grammar, on the tides, on the sciences, on the six ages of the world, on the lives of the saints and of the abbots in his order, and on the growth of the Christian church in England and Ireland. This final work, A History of the English Church and People, *was completed shortly before his death and helped to earn him the title of "Father of English History." The following selection contains chapters 17 to 21 of this work.*

A History of the English Church and People *is marked by a scrupulous attempt to separate what Bede regarded as historical fact from mere tradition and folktale. He examined ancient records. He carefully listed his authorities and validated them by showing their closeness to the incidents he relates. He drew on his personal knowledge. All the material is carefully organized and ordered to chart the progress of the church.*

Writing in the eighth century, Bede works from within an Anglo-Saxon culture that had been dominant in Britain for several hundred years. By this time the Saxons had driven the Britons west into Cornwall, Wales, and other fringes of the island. They had also established a strong church, perhaps the wealthiest and most learned of its time. Though Bede does attempt to stand back from this culture and judge it with a critical eye, he cannot help but see the Anglos and Saxons as a people sent by God to settle a fertile land and to drive out the worthless, sometimes idolatrous Britons; the Anglo-Saxon success, he would argue, was proof of that culture's destiny. The material he focuses on is closely tied to his belief in the immanence of God; nothing occurs in his world that does not bear witness to the fact of God's presence. For Bede, the story of the world is the story of God's continued intervention and presence.

When Bede turned to history, he maintained this sense of God's immanence. History was the story of the spread of God's kingdom, with its attendant victories over both physical and spiritual adversaries. History then becomes a moral stage on which the players act out roles that place them on one side or the other of divine providence. There is no middle ground. So when Bede deals with the Pelagians in this excerpt—or with any other group that hindered the growth of God's kingdom—his stance prohibits him from being objective. The Pelagians, who argued that the initial steps toward salvation do not need to be prompted by divine grace, become in Bede's hands a pernicious group that deserves to be stamped out, and actually Germanus has little trouble doing this. The miracles he performs—and which Bede chooses to include—attest to the rightness of his cause.

In writing his history, Bede is highly selective in the incidents he chronicles. For Bede, this is a history of God's kingdom, not man's, and so the matter that he deals with is the matter of the church. He recognized his role as a preserver of the literature, the arts, the knowledge, the history of the past. But he was not only a preserver; as a Benedictine monk he would see the past as a way to interpret and judge the present. The monk, then, provided the context within which the world might understand itself.

A HISTORY OF THE ENGLISH CHURCH AND PEOPLE

CHAPTER 17: *Bishop Germanus sails to Britain with Lupus: with God's help he quells two storms, one of the sea, the other of the Pelagians* [A.D. 429]

A few years before their arrival, the Pelagian heresy introduced by Agricola, 1 son of Severianus, a Pelagian prelate, had seriously infected the faith of the British Church. Although the British rejected this perverse teaching, so blasphemous against the grace of Christ, they were unable to refute its plausible arguments by controversial* methods, and wisely decided to ask help from the bishops of Gaul in this spiritual conflict. These summoned a great synod, and consulted together as to whom they should send to support the Faith. Their unanimous choice fell upon the apostolic bishops Germanus of Auxerre and Lupus of Troyes, whom they appointed to visit the Britons and to confirm their belief in God's grace. The two bishops readily accepted the commands and decisions of Holy Church, and put to sea. They had safely sailed half-way on their voyage from Gaul with a favourable wind when they were suddenly subjected to the hostile power of devils, who were furious that such men as they should dare to recall the Britons to the way of salvation. They

---

* *Controversial* used in the sense of rhetorical persuasion.

raised violent storms and turned day into night with black clouds. The sails were torn to shreds by the gale, the skill of the sailors was defeated, and the safety of the ship depended on prayer rather than on seamanship. Germanus, their leader and bishop, spent and exhausted, had fallen asleep, when the storm reached a fresh pitch of violence, as though relieved of its opponent, and seemed about to overwhelm the vessel in the surging waves. At this juncture, Lupus and his companions roused their leader, and anxiously begged him to oppose the fury of the elements. More resolute than they in the face of imminent disaster, he called upon Christ and cast a few drops of holy water on the waves in the Name of the Sacred Trinity, encouraging his companions and directing them all to join him in prayer. God heard their cry and their adversaries were put to flight; the storm was stilled, the wind veered round to help them on their course and, after a swift and peaceful passage, they arrived safely at their destination. Here great crowds gathered from all quarters to greet the bishops, whose arrival had been foretold even by the predictions of their opponents. For when the evil spirits had been expelled by the bishops from the persons of those whom they had possessed, they disclosed their fears and revealed the origin of the storms and perils they had raised, acknowledging themselves overcome by the merits and power of the saints.

Meanwhile, the island of Britain was rapidly influenced by the reason- 2 ing, preaching, and virtues of these apostolic bishops, and the word of God was preached daily not only in the churches, but in streets and fields, so that Catholics everywhere were strengthened and heretics corrected. Theirs was the honour and authority of apostles by their holy witness, the truth by their learning, the virtue by their merits. So the majority of the people readily accepted their teaching, while the authors of false doctrines made themselves scarce, grieving like evil spirits over the people who were snatched from their grasp. At length, after due deliberation, they dared to challenge the saints and appeared with rich ornaments and magnificent robes, supported by crowds of flattering followers. For they preferred to hazard a trial of strength rather than submit in shameful silence before the people whom they had subverted, lest they should appear to admit defeat. An immense gathering had assembled there with their wives and children to watch and judge, but the contestants were greatly dissimilar in bearing. On one side human presumption, on the other divine faith; on one side pride, on the other piety; on one side Pelagius, on the other Christ. The holy bishops gave their adversaries the advantage of speaking first, which they did at great length, filling the time, and the ears of their audience, with empty words. The venerable bishops then fed the torrents of their eloquence from the springs of the Apostles and evangelists, confirming their own words by the word of God, and supporting their principal statements by quotation from the scriptures. The conceit of the Pelagians was pricked, their lies exposed, and unable to defend any of their arguments, they admitted their errors. The people, who were acting as their judges, were hardly restrained from violence, and confirmed their verdict with acclamation.

CHAPTER 18: *Germanus gives sight to the blind daughter of a tribune. He takes some relics from the tomb of Saint Alban, and deposits relics of the Apostles and other Martyrs*

Immediately after this, a man who held the status of a tribune came forward 3 with his wife and asked the bishops to cure his blind daughter, a child of ten. They directed him to take her to their opponents, but the latter, smitten by guilty consciences, joined their entreaties to those of the girl's parents and begged the bishops to heal her. Seeing their opponents yield, they offered a short prayer; then Germanus, being filled with the Holy Ghost, called on the Trinity, and taking into his hands a casket containing relics of the saints that hung around his neck, he applied it to the girl's eyes in the sight of them all. To the joy of the parents and the amazement of the crowd, the child's sight was emptied of darkness and filled with the light of truth. Thenceforward all erroneous arguments were expunged from the minds of the people, who eagerly accepted the teaching of the bishops.

Once this abominable heresy had been put down, its authors refuted, 4 and the people established in the pure faith of Christ, the bishops paid a visit to the tomb of the blessed martyr Alban* to return thanks to God through him. Germanus, who had with him relics of all the Apostles and several martyrs, first offered prayer, and then directed the tomb to be opened, so that he could deposit these precious gifts within it. For he thought it fitting that, as the equal merits of the saints had won them a place in heaven, so their relics should be gathered together from different lands into a common resting-place. And when he had reverently deposited these relics, Germanus took away with him a portion of earth from the place where the blessed martyr's blood had been shed. This earth was seen to have retained the martyr's blood, which had reddened the shrine where his persecutor had grown pale with fear. As a result of these events, a great number of people were converted to our Lord on the same day.

CHAPTER 19: *Germanus is detained by illness. He puts out a fire among houses by his prayer, and is healed of his sickness by a vision*

While they were returning from this place, the ever-watchful Devil, having 5 set his snares, contrived that Germanus should fall and break a leg, not knowing that his merits, like those of the blessed Job,† would be enhanced by bodily affliction. While he was thus detained by illness, fire broke out in a cottage near his lodging, and after destroying the adjoining dwellings which at that place were thatched with reeds from the marshes, it was carried by the wind to the cottage where he lay. The people ran to pick up the bishop and carry him to a place of safety; but, full of trust in God, he reproved them and would not allow them to do so. In despair, the people ran off to fight the fire; but to afford clearer evidence of God's power, whatever the crowd en-

---

* The first English saint.
† A Biblical figure whose great afflictions led to great faith.

deavoured to save was destroyed. Meanwhile the flames leaped over the house where the saint lay disabled and helpless; but, although they raged all around it, the place that sheltered him stood untouched amid a sea of fire. The crowd was overjoyed at the miracle and praised God for this proof of his power, while innumerable poor folk kept vigil outside his cottage day and night hoping for healing of soul or body.

It is impossible to relate all that Christ effected through his servant, and 6 what wonders the sick saint performed. And while he refused any treatment for his own illness, he saw beside him one night a being in shining robes, who seemed to reach out his hand and raise him up, ordering him to stand on his feet. From that moment his pain ceased, his former health was restored, and when dawn came he continued on his journey undaunted.

Chapter 20: *The two bishops obtain God's help in battle, and return home* [a.d. 429]

Meanwhile the Saxons and Picts joined forces and made war on the Britons, 7 whom necessity had compelled to arm; and since the latter feared that their strength was unequal to the challenge, they called on the saintly bishops for help. They came at once as they had promised, and put such heart into the timid people that their presence was worth a large army. Under these apostolic leaders, Christ himself commanded in the camp. It also happened that the holy season of Lent was beginning, and was so reverently kept under the bishops' direction that the people came each day for instruction and flocked to receive the grace of Baptism. Most of the army sought Holy Baptism, and in readiness for the Feast of our Lord's Resurrection a church was constructed of interlaced boughs and set up in that armed camp as though it were a city. Strong in faith and fresh from the waters of Baptism, the army advanced; and whereas they had formerly despaired of human strength, all now trusted in the power of God. The preparation and disposition of the British forces was reported to the enemy, who, anticipating an easy victory over an ill-equipped army, advanced rapidly, closely observed by the British scouts.

After the Feast of Easter, when the greater part of the British forces, 8 fresh from the font, were preparing to arm and embark on the struggle, Germanus promised to direct the battle in person. He picked out the most active men and, having surveyed the surrounding country, observed a valley among the hills lying in the direction from which he expected the enemy to approach. Here he stationed the untried forces under his own orders. By now the main body of their remorseless enemies was approaching, watched by those whom he had placed in ambush. Suddenly Germanus, raising the standard, called upon them all to join him in a mighty shout. While the enemy advanced confidently, expecting to take the Britons unawares, the bishops three times shouted, "Alleluia!" The whole army joined in this shout, until the surrounding hills echoed with the sound. The enemy column panicked, thinking that the very rocks and sky were falling on them, and were so terrified that they could not run fast enough. Throwing away their weapons in headlong flight, they were well content to escape naked, while many in their hasty flight were drowned in a river which they tried to cross. So the innocent British army saw its defeats avenged, and became an inactive spectator of the victory granted to it. The scattered spoils were collected, and the Christian forces rejoiced in the triumph of heaven. So the bishops overcame the enemy without bloodshed, winning a victory by faith and not by force.

Having restored peace to the island and overcome all its enemies, both 9 visible and invisible, the bishops prepared to return home. Their own merits and the prayers of the blessed martyr Alban obtained them a peaceful voyage, and a propitious vessel restored them to their own welcoming people.

CHAPTER 21: *The Pelagian heresy revives, and Germanus returns to Britain with Severus. He heals a lame youth, and after denouncing or converting the heretics, restores the British Church to the Catholic Faith* [?A.D. 435–44]

After no great interval, news came from Britain that certain people were 10 again promulgating the Pelagian heresy. Once again all the clergy requested blessed Germanus to defend God's cause as before. Promptly assenting, he took ship and made a peaceful crossing to Britain with a favouring wind, taking with him a man of great holiness named Severus. Severus had been a disciple of the most blessed father Lupus, Bishop of Troyes; he subsequently became Bishop of Trier, and preached the Word in western Germany.

Meanwhile evil spirits throughout the land had been reluctantly compelled to foretell Germanus' coming, so that a local chieftain named Elaphius 11 hurried to meet the saints before receiving any definite news. He brought with him his son, who in the very flower of his youth was crippled by a painful disease of the leg, whose muscles had so contracted that the limb was entirely useless. Accompanying Elaphius was the whole population of his province. The bishops on arrival were met by the ignorant folk, to whom they spoke and gave their blessing. And having assured themselves that the people as a whole remained loyal to the Faith as they had left them, and that the error was restricted to a minority, they sought out its adherents and rebuked them. Suddenly Elaphius threw himself at the bishops' feet, and presented to them his son, the sight of whose infirmity proclaimed his need louder than words. All were moved to pity at the spectacle, especially the bishops, who earnestly prayed God to show mercy. Blessed Germanus then asked the youth to sit down, and drawing out the leg bent with disease, he passed his healing hand over the afflicted area, and at his touch health swiftly returned. The withered limb filled, the muscles regained their power, and in the presence of them all the lad was restored healed to his parents. The people were amazed at this miracle, and the Catholic Faith was firmly implanted in all their hearts. Germanus then warned them to live better and to shun all error. And the false teachers, who by common consent had been condemned to banishment, were brought before the bishops to be taken to the Continent, so that the country might be rid of them and they themselves brought to recognize their error. Henceforward, the Faith was maintained uncorrupted in Britain for a long time.

Having settled all these matters, the blessed bishops returned home as 12 successfully as they had come.

Germanus subsequently visited Ravenna to obtain peace for the people 13 of Armorica. There he was received with honour by the Emperor Valentinian and his mother Placidia, and while still in this city he departed to Christ. His body was carried back with a splendid escort to his own city and many signs of his holiness were shown. Not long afterwards, in the fifth year of Marcian's reign, Valentinian was murdered by supporters of the patrician Aëtius, whom he had executed, and with him fell the Empire of the West.

QUESTIONS ABOUT BEDE'S DISCOURSE
COMMUNITY AND HIS CONCERNS IN THIS ESSAY

1. Since Bede envisions history as the charting of moral growth of a people, he might be expected to relegate events that do not deal directly with that kind of development to the background. Not until the end of this selection does he hint at the momentous changes occurring elsewhere in Europe, changes that would have profound effects upon England. When Valentinian was assassinated, Bede writes, the empire of the West fell. But this is presented almost as a footnote, for from Bede's perspective, it is not central to the real history in which human beings participate. Where else in this selection does Bede relegate events to the background, events that might be deemed important in the history of western civilization? Does this relegation mean that Bede is narrowing his sights too much? Or that his history is distorted?

2. Bede writes that a storm was caused by demons, a broken leg by the devil. He writes of miraculous healings, powerful prayers, and angelic visions. What do these passages suggest about Bede's understanding of the world? Do these passages discredit Bede as a historian? How do these passages affect the reader's perception of Germanus? Do you think that these miracles actually occurred? If you think they did not, what would you say these accounts are based on?

3. Bede begins almost all of his paragraphs in this section with a reference to time. Examine these references closely. Are the references to fixed points in time or to other events recorded in the chronicle? What effect does this have? On the basis of these references, could you begin to speculate about Bede's view of time?

4. Toward the end of this section, Bede writes that once the false teachers were out of Britain, "the Faith was maintained uncorrupted in Britain for a long time." Would a similar cause–effect relationship be as likely today? Why or why not?

5. On the basis of this passage, how would you describe and evaluate the faith of the common believers in Britain? How does Bede evaluate it?

6. In chapter 20, Bede writes that "It also happened that the holy season of Lent was beginning" as the Britons were ready to fight the Picts and the Saxons. Does

Bede mean the phrase "it also happened" as we would, to suggest a coincidence? If so, did he slip up here?

QUESTIONS ABOUT BEDE'S RHETORICAL STRATEGIES

1. Certainly Bede—and any other historian—selects events and facts, but the historian also orders those facts, and that ordering can influence the reader in the same manner that the selecting does. For example, prior to the material on Germanus, Bede tells the story of Ambrosius, who helped the somewhat cowardly Britons to a number of victories over the Saxons. Bede then moves from the military aid of Ambrosius to the spiritual aid of Germanus. However, chronologically these were reversed; Germanus was in Britain before Ambrosius succoured the Britons. What has Bede gained by reversing this order? Is this a legitimate practice, or must the historian be bound by strict chronology?
2. Bede based much of his material on Constantius's *Life of St. Germanus*, whose text is not as detailed as that of Bede. Constantius describes the victory of the Britons quite tersely:

   But also at that time [the bishops] beat back by divine power the attack undertaken by the joint forces of the Saxons and the Picts against the Britons. When Germanus himself had been made the commander of the battle, he drove into flight a huge enemy force, not by the sound of trumpets, but by the voices of his entire army, raised to heaven in shouts of "alleluia."

   Compare this treatment to that of Bede. What elements has Bede added or specified? What does the inclusion of these elements suggest about his overall vision of history? About his perceived role as a historian?
3. In some ways, Germanus takes on the roles of Biblical figures; Bede suggests this through the use of analogues. Compare the calming of the English Channel with Christ's calming of the Sea of Galilee (Luke 8.22–25); the battle against the Pelagians with that of Elijah against the prophets of Baal (1 Kings 18.16–40); the victory of the Britons with that of the Hebrew army at Jericho (Joshua 6.1–21) and that of Gideon (Judges 7). What rhetorical purposes do these analogues serve? What does their inclusion suggest about Bede's vision of history?
4. How does Bede refer to Germanus and Lupus when he describes the confrontation with the Pelagians? Why does he do so? Is this a fair tactic?
5. *A History of the English Church and People* was first written in Latin, the scholarly language of the Middle Ages. This selection, though a translation, is still marked by Latin stylistic forms, one of which is the accumulation of parallel clauses in a single sentence: "Their sails were torn to shreds by the gale, the skill of the sailors was defeated, and the safety of the ship depended on prayer rather than seamanship." What does Bede gain rhetorically by the use of these balanced sentences? What effects do they have when Bede uses them to record the results of conflicts or struggles? (For example: "The conceit of the Pelagians was pricked, their lies exposed, and unable to defend any of their arguments, they admitted their errors.")
6. Bede provides several good examples of water imagery. Find these examples,

and then speculate about whether they are mere coincidences in his tale or carriers of important meanings.

7. Bede describes the bishops as "venerable" (paragraph 2). What are the connotations of this word? Do they suggest why Bede has deliberately chosen this adjective?

8. Within two sentences, Bede refers to the "untried" forces of Germanus and his "remorseless" enemies (paragraph 8). Would you say that these words are antonyms?

WRITING FROM WITHIN AND ABOUT HISTORY AND ITS STUDY

Writing for Yourself

1. Explore in your journal your understanding of a miracle.

2. In "Why I Am an Agnostic," Clarence Darrow, the well-known twentieth-century lawyer, argued that a supposed miracle would not point to divine intervention, but would suggest instead that we are not yet aware of all physical laws and properties. Explore in your journal your reaction to Darrow's comments.

Writing for Nonacademic Audiences

1. You are asked to participate in a book club made up of your peers. You will present to the club a discussion of the early cultural history of Britain, and your specific task is to deal with how the early church contributed to the civilizing of an anarchistic culture. Using Bede as a major source, write up a detailed outline for that fifteen-minute presentation.

2. Using *The Reader's Guide to Periodical Literature* or *The New York Times Index*, find instances in the last decade when miracles such as miraculous appearances, or weeping or bloodied icons have been claimed. Write a 500-word essay on how these perceived miracles have affected a local population; this article is to appear in a popular magazine.

3. Write a 750-word feature for your school newspaper on how religious you judge current college students to be.

4. Consider the following two accounts of the same incident, both written for the July 25, 1990, issue of *The Budget*, the journal of the Amish and Mennonite communities of the Western Hemisphere.

Fredericksburg, Ohio—Late Friday afternoon, an out-of-state draft horse got loose that was tied in a trailer in front of Yoder blacksmith shop. Since the door was unlatched the horse got out and was hit by a Berlin Mineral truck on S.R. 241, pitching him in the air and landing him right in front of the phone booth where he was killed almost instantly. The truck then hit a parked car owned by Mark Byler which he totaled and from there he hit the big tree in Cecil Yoder's front yard, overturning the truck with twenty tons of gravel. Mark Byler was making a phone call. Mrs. Levi B. Weaver was in the other phone booth and when she came out she was almost speechless. Nobody was hurt, but the driver was treated for shock.

Winesburg, Ohio—Last week a man from West Virginia had a draft horse at Ashery blacksmith shop to shoe and was tied on outside but got loose and went on Rt. 241 and a gravel truck hit it. A car was also hit but no one hurt.

Though both passages record the same incident, they record it in substantially different ways. Blend these two passages into one account to be published in *The Budget*.

Writing for Academic Audiences

1. For a course in historiography, write a 750-word essay in which you examine the differences between the two accounts of the horse accident published in *The Budget* (printed above) and how those differences affect a reader's perception of that event.
2. For a course in modern American history, write a 750-word essay on your views of the role that evangelical Christianity is playing in modern American culture. What is its role, and how do you react to that?
3. Interview a person who you think is devoutly religious. Try to learn whether he or she has progressed through stages of faith. Write up your findings in a 1,000-word essay for a course on the contemporary religious scene.
4. Write a 1,000-word essay for a history of religion class on the way historians have chronicled the history of the spring at Lourdes, France. In your essay, focus on how historians differ in the way they approach this story, and speculate on why those differences exist.
5. It is sometimes the case that a single person can affect a nation so strongly that the nation's course is changed for many years. In a 2,000-word essay, examine how one of the following figures changed a nation's course:
   Peter the Great—Russia
   Mao Zedong —China
   Ghandi—India
   Elizabeth I—Great Britain
   Corazon Aquino—the Philippines
   Martin Luther King Jr.—the United States
   Simon Bolivar—Brazil
   Fidel Castro—Cuba
   John A. MacDonald—Canada

William Bradford

(1590–1657)

Born in Yorkshire, England, William Bradford was brought up to be a farmer until, at age sixteen and against family convictions, he became a separatist, a member of a religious group that rejected attendance at England's established church. An active proponent of the immigration of the separatists to the New World, he sailed on the Mayflower, was part of the first group to explore what would become known as Cape Cod, and eventually landed at Plymouth. He was a prominent member of the settlement, and when John Carver died within a year of the landing, he succeeded to the post of governor, a position to which he was reelected thirty times.

Bradford's well-known History of Plymouth Plantation *follows the years 1620 to 1647. The history was kept only in manuscript form for two centuries, and its whereabouts were unknown for at least half that time. It was discovered in 1855 in the library of the Bishop of London and was printed in its entirety for the first time in the following year. In 1897, the manuscript was returned to Massachusetts.*

For Bradford, history bore the same kind of importance that it bore for Bede. His History of Plymouth Plantation *is not merely a journal recording the attempts to colonize a stretch of land; it is a religious history as well, written not just for himself, but as an explanation and declaration to the world of the purposes of this colony. Like Bede, Bradford recounts the planting of Christianity in the New World, and from that perspective this account is as much a religious history as it is a social history. Such a perspective might, in Bradford's own mind, justify his attitude toward the "Indeans." It might also explain the reaction of the Plymouth colony to Thomas Morton, for perhaps they saw in him not just a rival colony, but a threat to the religion being established on the shores of Massachusetts.*

Bradford, as one of the original settlers, is a historian writing from the inside. He has experienced the very things he is recording. While this brought him the advantage of firsthand knowledge, it also brought at least two disadvantages. First, the modern reader might have cause to wonder if Bradford is able to be objective in any sense, or if he will slant his perceptions of events. Second, the writer is very close to the events, so that a historian writing from within might not have the kind of distance that affords a wide and dispassionate perspective on the meaning of events.

Though Bradford was more tolerant of others' religious beliefs than other pilgrim leaders were, the following selection from his History of Plymouth Plantation *suggests that his tolerance had limits.*

HISTORY OF PLYMOUTH PLANTATION

Aboute some 3. or 4. years before this time,* ther came over one Captaine 1
Wolastone, (a man of pretie parts,) and with him 3. or 4. more of some
eminencie, who brought with them a great many servants, with provissions
and other implments for to begine a plantation; and pitched them selves in a
place within the Massachusets, which they called, after their Captains name,
Mount-Wollaston. Amongst whom was one Mr. Morton,† who, it should
seeme, had some small adventure (of his owne or other mens) amongst them;
but had litle respecte amongst them, and was sleghted by the meanest servants. Haveing continued ther some time, and not finding things to answer
their expectations, nor profite to arise as they looked for, Captaine Wollaston
takes a great part of the sarvants, and transports them to Virginia, wher he
puts them of at good rates, selling their time to other men; and writs back to
one Mr. Rassdall, one of his cheefe partners, and accounted their marchant,
to bring another parte of them to Verginia likewise, intending to put them of
ther as he had done the rest. And he, with the consente of the said Rasdall,
appoynted one Fitcher to be his Livetenante, and governe the remaines of
the plantation, till he or Rasdall returned to take further order theraboute.
But this Morton abovesaid, haveing more craft then honestie, (who had been
a kind of petie-fogger, of Furnefells Inne,)‡ in the others absence, watches
an oppertunitie, (commons being but hard amongst them,) and gott some
strong drinck and other junkats, and made them a feast; and after they were
merie, he begane to tell them, he would give them good counsell. You see
(saith he) that many of your fellows are carried to Virginia; and if you stay
till this Rasdall returne, you will also be carried away and sould for slaves
with the rest. Therfore I would advise you to thruste out this Levetenant
Fitcher; and I, having a parte in the plantation, will receive you as my partners and consociats; so may you be free from service, and we will converse,
trad, plante, and live togeather as equalls, and supporte and protecte one
another, or to like effecte. This counsell was easily received; so they tooke
oppertunitie, and thrust Levetenante Fitcher out a dores, and would suffer
him to come no more amongst them, but forct him to seeke bread to eate,
and other releefe from his neigbours, till he could gett passage for England.
After this they fell to great licenciousnes, and led a dissolute life, powering
out them selves into all profanenes. And Morton became lord of misrule, and

---

* 1628.
† Morton was not a Puritan, but an Anglican. He came to found a plantation and to trade—
　　illegitimate reasons for establishing a colony, according to the Puritans.
‡ A lawyer of small account. Furnivall's Inn was frequented by lawyers.

maintained (as it were) a schoole of Athisme. And after they had gott some good into their hands, and gott much by trading with the Indeans, they spent it as vainly, in quaffing and drinking both wine and strong waters in great exsess, and, as some reported, 10*li*. worth in a morning. They allso set up a May-pole, drinking and dancing aboute it many days togeather, inviting the Indean women, for their consorts, dancing and frisking togither, (like so many fairies, or furies rather,) and worse practises. As if they had anew revived and celebrated the feasts of the Roman Goddes Flora, or the beasly practieses of the madd Bacchinalians. Morton likwise (to shew his poetrie) composed sundry rimes and verses, some tending to lasciviousnes, and others to the detraction and scandall of some persons, which he affixed to this idle or idoll May-polle. They chainged allso the name of their place, and in stead of calling it Mounte Wollaston, they call it Meriemounte, as if this joylity would have lasted ever. But this continued not long, for after Morton was sent for England, (as follows to be declared,) shortly after came over that worthy gentlman, Mr. John Indecott,* who brought over a patent under the broad seall, for the govermente of the Massachusets, who visiting those parts caused that May-polle to be cutt downe, and rebuked them for their profannes, and admonished them to looke ther should be better walking; so they now, or others, changed the name of their place againe, and called it Mounte-Dagon.

Now to maintaine this riotous prodigallitie and profuse excess, Morton, 2 thinking him selfe lawless, and hearing what gaine the French and fishermen made by trading of peeces, powder, and shotte to the Indeans, he, as the head of this consortship, begane the practise of the same in these parts; and first he taught them how to use them, to charge, and discharg, and what proportion of powder to give the peece, according to the sise or bignes of the same; and what shotte to use for foule, and what for deare. And having thus instructed them, he imployed some of them to hunte and fowle for him, so as they became farr more active in that imploymente then any of the English, by reason of ther swiftnes of foote, and nimblnes of body, being also quicksighted, and by continuall exercise well knowing the hants of all sorts of game. So as when they saw the execution that a peece would doe, and the benefite that might come by the same, they became madd, as it were, after them, and would not stick to give any prise they could attaine too for them; accounting their bowes and arrowes but bables in comparison of them.

And here I may take occasion to bewaile the mischefe that this wicked 3 man began in these parts, and which since base covetousnes prevailing in men that should know better, has now at length gott the upper hand, and made this thing commone, notwithstanding any laws to the contrary; so as the Indeans are full of peeces all over, both fouling peeces, muskets, pistols, etc. They have also their moulds to make shotte, of all sorts, as muskett bulletts, pistoll bullets, swane and gose shote, and of smaler sorts; yea, some

---

* John Endecott became the governor of the Massachusetts Bay Colony.

have seen them have their scruplats to make scrupins* them selves, when
they wante them, with sundery other implements, wherwith they are ordinarily better fited and furnished then the English them selves. Yea, it is well
knowne that they will have powder and shot, when the English want it, nor
cannot gett it; and that in a time of warr or danger, as experience hath manifested, that when lead hath been scarce, and men for their owne defence
would gladly have given a groat a *li.*, which is dear enoughe, yet hath it bene
bought up and sent to other places, and sould to shuch as trade it with the
Indeans, at 12. pence the *li.*; and it is like they give 3. or 4.*s.* the pound, for
they will have it at any rate. And these things have been done in the same
times, when some of their neigbours and freinds are daly killed by the Indeans, or are in deanger therof, and live but at the Indeans mercie. Yea, some
(as they have aquainted them with all other things) have tould them how
gunpowder is made, and all the materialls in it, and that they are to be had
in their owne land; and I am confidente, could they attaine to make saltpeter,
they would teach them to make powder. O the horiblnes of this vilanie! how
many both Dutch and English have been latly slaine by those Indeans, thus
furnished; and no remedie provided, nay, the evill more increased, and the
blood of their brethren sould for gaine, as is to be feared; and in what danger
all these colonies are in is too well known. Oh! that princes and parlements
would take some timly order to prevente this mischeefe, and at length to
suppress it, by some exemplerie punishmente upon some of these gaine thir-
stie murderers, (for they deserve no better title,) before their collonies in these
parts be over throwne by these barbarous savages, thus armed with their
owne weapons, by these evill instruments, and traytors to their neigbors and
cuntrie. But I have forgott my selfe, and have been to longe in this digression;
but now to returne. This Morton having thus taught them the use of peeces,
he sould them all he could spare; and he and his consorts detirmined to send
for many out of England, and had by some of the ships sente for above a
score. The which being knowne, and his neigbours meeting the Indeans in
the woods armed with guns in this sorte, it was a terrour unto them, who
lived straglingly, and were of no strenght in any place. And other places
(though more remote) saw this mischeefe would quictly spread over all, if
not prevented. Besides, they saw they should keep no servants, for Morton
would entertaine any, how vile soever, and all the scume of the countrie, or
any discontents, would flock to him from all places, if this nest was not broken; and they should stand in more fear of their lives and goods (in short
time) from this wicked and deboste † crue, then from the salvages them selves.

So sundrie of the cheefe of the stragling plantations, meeting togither, 4
agreed by mutuall consente to sollissite those of Plimoth (who were then of
more strength then them all) to joyne with them, to prevente the further

---

* Screw-plates, screw-pins.
† Debased.

grouth of this mischeefe, and suppress Morton and his consortes before they grewe to further head and strength. Those that joyned in this acction (and after contributed to the charge of sending him for England) were from Pascataway, Namkeake, Winisimett, Weesagascusett, Natasco, and other places wher any English were seated. Those of Plimoth being thus sought too by their messengers and letters, and waying both their reasons, and the commone danger, were willing to afford them their help; though them selves had least cause of fear or hurte. So, to be short, they first resolved joyntly to write to him, and in a freindly and neigborly way to admonish him to forbear these courses, and sent a messenger with their letters to bring his answer. But he was so highe as he scorned all advise, and asked who had to doe with him; he had and would trade peeces with the Indeans in dispite of all, with many other scurillous termes full of disdaine. They sente to him a second time, and bad him be better advised, and more temperate in his termes, for the countrie could not beare the injure he did; it was against their comone saftie, and against the king's proclamation. He answerd in high terms as before, and that the kings proclaimation was no law; demanding what penaltie was upon it. It was answered, more then he could bear, his majesties displeasure. But insolently he persisted, and said the king was dead and his displeasure with him, and many the like things; and threatened withall that if any came to molest him, let them looke to them selves, for he would prepare for them. Upon which they saw ther was no way but to take him by force; and having so farr proceeded, now to give over would make him farr more hautie and insolente. So they mutually resolved to proceed, and obtained of the Govr of Plimoth to send Captaine Standish, and some other aide with him, to take Morton by force. The which accordingly was done; but they found him to stand stifly in his defence, having made fast his dors, armed his consorts, set diverse dishes of powder and bullets ready on the table; and if they had not been over armed with drinke, more hurt might have been done. They sommaned him to yeeld, but he kept his house, and they could gett nothing but scofes and scorns from him; but at length, fearing they would doe some violence to the house, he and some of his crue came out, but not to yeeld, but to shoote; but they were so steeld with drinke as their peeces were to heavie for them; him selfe with a carbine (over charged and allmost halfe fild with powder and shote, as was after found) had thought to have shot Captaine Standish; but he stept to him, and put by his peece, and tooke him. Neither was ther any hurte done to any of either side, save that one was so drunke that he rane his owne nose upon the pointe of a sword that one held before him as he entred the house; but he lost but a litle of his hott blood. Morton they brought away to Plimoth, wher he was kepte, till a ship went from the Ile of Shols for England, with which he was sente to the Counsell of New-England; and letters writen to give them information of his course and cariage; and also one was sent at their commone charge to informe their Ho^{rs} more perticulerly, and to prosecute against him. But he foold of the messenger, after he was gone from hence, and though he wente for England, yet nothing was done to him, not so much as rebukte, for ought was heard; but returned the nexte year. Some of the worst of the company were disperst, and some of the more modest kepte the house till he should be heard from. But I have been too long aboute so unworthy a person, and bad a cause.

QUESTIONS ABOUT BRADFORD'S DISCOURSE COMMUNITY AND HIS CONCERNS IN THIS SELECTION

1. What, in general, would be a motive for beginning a colony in the New World? What motives does Thomas Morton have in founding a colony?
2. Early in this selection Bradford writes that Morton "was sleghted by the meanest servants." What view of personal character seems to lie behind this statement?
3. Examine the description of life in Morton's colony. What characteristics of that life would be particularly repellant to the Puritans? Bradford notes that the name of the colony was changed to Merrymount, "as if this joylity would have lasted ever." Why does Bradford show such disdain?
4. How does Bradford depict the "Indeans"? Is this a stance you would anticipate a European of this time period taking? Why or why not? What distinctions does Bradford make between the English and the "Indeans"?
5. What specific dangers did Morton represent to the other colonists, according to Bradford? Are these dangers real, or merely rationalizations for the eventual takeover of Merrymount? Do these dangers in any way justify the takeover of Merrymount?
6. Why does Bradford take pains to show that no significant injury was done to either side when Miles Standish took over Merrymount?
7. Review the steps in the procedure the colonists used to exercise their grievance with Morton. Where do you think these steps came from—the colonists' knowledge of political procedure, of human psychology, of Biblical injunctions, or of something else?
8. What might be Bradford's reasons for writing this history?

QUESTIONS ABOUT BRADFORD'S RHETORICAL STRATEGIES

1. What rhetorical means does Bradford employ to cast Thomas Morton in a bad light? Does it seem to you that he is being objective, or would objectivity have been unimportant to Bradford? Is objectivity a desirable trait in any historian? Is it even possible for a historian to be objective?
2. Bradford at times uses sentence fragments in his work: "As if they had anew revived and celebrated the feasts of the Roman Goddes Flora, or the beastly practicses of the madd Bachinalians." Where does he use such fragments and to what purpose does he put them?
3. Does Bradford's description of the licentiousness at Merrymount call to mind

any Biblical story? How many parallels between Merrymount and the Biblical story do you think Bradford intends his readers to draw?

4. How does Bradford use allusions to the classical world? What does that world seem to mean to him?

5. When describing what Morton's followers did around the Maypole, Bradford doesn't detail all their practices. Instead, he writes that they danced, frisked, and engaged in "worse practises." Is writing "worse practises" as effective for Bradford as detailing what these practices would be? Consider first his Puritan friends as readers. Then consider modern readers. In both cases, is there any wisdom in leaving some things to the imagination?

6. At times Bradford steps out of the narrative of events to comment about them. "And here I may take occasion to bewaile the mischefe that this wicked man began in these parts. . . ." Why does he include such a comment? What might this suggest about his intended audience?

7. At least twice in this selection Bradford seems to reconsider what he has written. "But I have forgott my selfe, and have been to longe in this digression; but now to returne," he writes in one place. And he concludes with the observation that "I have been too long aboute so unworthy a person, and bad a cause." Are we to take these claims at face value, or do they serve another purpose? If they are true, why didn't he simply revise his manuscript?

8. Are there any places in this selection where you might suspect that Bradford is hedging, or perhaps slanting his perception of events? If there are such instances, what kinds of rhetorical strategies does he employ in them? Would you say that the use of such strategies involves an ethical decision on the part of the writer?

WRITING FROM WITHIN AND ABOUT HISTORY AND ITS STUDY

Writing for Yourself

1. In your journal, reflect on the connotations of the word *pilgrim*. In what senses is that word currently used?

2. In your journal, reflect on whether Americans do or do not truly know how to celebrate things.

Writing for Nonacademic Audiences

1. You are writing an application for a summer position at the Pilgrim Hall Museum in Plymouth, Massachusetts, which houses, among other pilgrim relics, the sword of Miles Standish. The essay on the application form asks you to state what you find to be particularly interesting about the pilgrims and their settling of the New World. Write that 200-word essay.

2. Many scholars say the United States has been profoundly influenced by the Pilgrim tradition. Do you think that influence is still evident? In a paper for a special Thanksgiving Day issue of a local magazine, write your 750-word response.

3. A friend of yours has asked you to speak to his sixth-grade history club on the

development of the spelling system for English. List and briefly describe the five to seven most significant events in this development. You should be able to cover these events with the class in a half hour.

4. As a tour guide for Plymouth Plantation, you have been asked to write a short accounting of the plantation's reaction to Thomas Morton. You will deliver this speech to tourists who visit the plantation during the summer. Write up that seven- or eight-minute account.

Writing for Academic Audiences

1. For a class in rhetorical strategies, write a 750-word essay in which you analyze all the techniques that Bradford uses to cast Morton in a bad light.
2. Read Nathaniel Hawthorne's short story "The Maypole of Merrymount." For a class in American literature, write a 500-word essay in which you discuss the ways in which Hawthorne uses the actual events of the Merrymount episode.
3. Write a 750-word essay for an introduction to political science class in which you discuss the legitimate conditions, if any, that would allow one group of people to take up arms against another group. Use specific examples to support your case.
4. Read over the following passage from Thomas Morton's *New English Canaan* (1637), which recounts the same events that Bradford recounts, though this time from Morton's perspective. Write a 750-word essay for a class in American history in which you examine the discrepancies in these accounts and suggest which might be the more reliable witness.
5. After reading the following selection from Morton's *New English Canaan* (1637), write a 750-word essay for a class in historiography in which you discuss how a historian weighs evidence and makes decisions in the face of contradictions.

NEW ENGLISH CANAAN

[*Of the Diversions at Merry Mount*]

The Inhabitants of Pasonagessit (having translated the name of their habita- 1
tion from that ancient Salvage name to Ma-re Mount; and being resolved to have the new name confirmed for a memorial to after ages) did devise amongst themselves to have it performed in a solemne manner with Revels, & merriment after the old English custome: prepared to sett up a Maypole upon the festivall day of Philip and Jacob; & therefore brewed a barrell of excellent beare, & provided a case of bottles to be spent, with other good cheare, for all commers of that day. And because they would have it in a compleat forme, they had prepared a song fitting to the time and present

occasion. And upon May-day they brought the Maypole to the place appointed, with drumes, gunnes, pistols, and other fitting instruments, for that purpose; and there erected it with the help of Salvages, that came thether of purpose to see the manner of our Revels. A goodly pine tree of 80. foote longe, was reared up, with a peare of buckshorns nayled one, somewhat neare unto the top of it: where it stood as a faire sea marke for directions; how to finde out the way to mine Hoste of Ma-re Mount.***

The setting up of this Maypole was a lamentable spectacle to the precise 2 seperatists: that lived at new Plimmouth. They termed it an Idoll; yea they called it the Calfe of Horeb: and stood at defiance with the place, naming it Mount Dagon; threatning to make it a woefull mount and not a merry mount.***

There was likewise a merry song made, which (to make their Revells 3 more fashionable) was sung with a Corus, every man bearing his part; which they performed in a daunce, hand in hand about the Maypole, whiles one of the Company sung, and filled out the good liquor like gammedes and Jupiter.

THE SONGE   4

      Cor. Drinke and be merry, merry, merry boyes,
Let all your delight be in Hymens joyes,
ô to Hymen now the day is come,
About the merry Maypole take a Roome.
      Make greene garlons, bring bottles out;
      And fill sweet Nectar, freely about,
      Uncover thy head, and feare no harme,
      For hers good liquor to keepe it warme.
Then drinke and be merry, &c.
ô to Hymen, &c.
      Nectar is a thing assign'd,
      By the Deities owne minde,
      To cure the hart opprest with greife,
      And of good liquors is the cheife,
Then drinke, &c.
Iô to Hymen, &c.
      Give the Mellancolly man,
      A cup or two of 't now and than;
      This physick' will soone revive his bloud,
      And make him be of a merrier moode.
Then drinke &c.
Iô to Hymen &c.
      Give to the Nymphe thats free from scorne,
      No Irish stuff nor Scotch overworne,
      Lasses in beaver coats come away,
      Yee shall be welcome to us night and day.
To drinke and be merry &c.
Iô to Hymen, &c.

This harmeles mirth made by younge men (that lived in hope to have 5 wifes brought over to them, that would save them a laboure to make a voyage to fetch any over) was much distated, of the precise Seperatists: that keepe much a doe, about the tyth of Muit and Cummin*; troubling their braines more then reason would require about things that are indifferent: and from that time sought occasion against my honest Host of Ma-re Mount to overthrow his ondertakings, and to destroy his plantation quite and cleane.

[Of a Great Monster Supposed to be at Merry Mount]

The Seperatists, envying the prosperity and hope of the Plantation at 6 Ma-re Mount, (which they perceaved beganne to come forward, and to be in a good way for gaine in the Beaver trade,) conspired together against mine Host especially, (who was the owner of that Plantation,) and made up a party against him; and mustred up what aide they could, accounting of him as of a great Monster.

Many threatening speeches were given out both against his person and 7 his Habitation, which they divulged should be consumed with fire: And taking advantage of the time when his company, (which seemed little to regard theire threats,) were gone up into the Inlands to trade with the Salvages for Beaver, they set upon my honest host at a place called Wessaguscus, where, by accident, they found him. The inhabitants there were in good hope of the subvertion of the plantation at Mare Mount, (which they principally aymed at;) and the rather because mine host was a man that indeavoured to advaunce the dignity of the Church of England; which they, (on the contrary part,) would laboure to vilifie with uncivile termes: enveying against the sacred booke of common prayer, and mine host that used it in a laudable manner amongst his family, as a practise of piety.

There hee would be a meanes to bring sacks to their mill, (such is the 8 thirst after Beaver,) and helped the conspiratores to surprise mine host, (who was there all alone;) and they chargded him, (because they would seeme to have some reasonable cause against him to sett a glosse upon their mallice,) with criminall things; which indeede had beene done by such a person, but was of their conspiracy; mine host demaunded of the conspirators who it was that was author of that information, that seemed to be their ground for what they now intended. And because they answered they would not tell him, hee as peremptorily replyed, that hee would not say whether he had, or he had not done as they had bin informed.

The answere made no matter, (as it seemed,) whether it had bin nega- 9 tively or affirmatively made; for they had resolved that hee should suffer, because, (as they boasted,) they were now become the greater number: they had shaked of their shackles of servitude, and were become Masters, and masterles people.

It appeares they were like beares whelpes in former time, when mine 10

---

* Morton refers here to the fastidious precision of Bradford and his company by linking them to the Pharisees that Christ condemns. See Matthew 23:23.

hosts plantation was of as much strength as theirs, but now, (theirs being stronger,) they, (like overgrowne beares,) seemed monsterous. In'-breife, mine host must indure to be their prisoner untill they could contrive it so that they might send him for England, (as they said,) there to suffer according to the merrit of the fact which they intended to father upon him; supposing, (belike,) it would proove a hainous crime.

Much rejoycing was made that they had gotten their capitall enemy, 11 (as they concluded him;) whome they purposed to hamper in such sort that hee should not be able to uphold his plantation at Ma-re Mount.

The Conspirators sported themselves at my honest host, that meant them 12 no hurt, and were so joccund that they feasted their bodies, and fell to tip-peling as if they had obtained a great prize; like the Trojans when they had the custody of Hippeus pinetree horse.

Mine host fained greefe, and could not be perswaded either to eate or 13 drinke; because hee knew emptines would be a meanes to make him as watchfull as the Geese kept in the Roman Cappitall: whereon, the contrary part, the conspirators would be so drowsy that hee might have an opportu-nity to give them a slip, insteade of a tester. Six persons of the conspiracy were set to watch him at Wessaguscus: But hee kept waking; and in the dead of night, (one lying on the bed for further suerty,) up gets mine Host and got to the second dore that hee was to passe, which, notwithstanding the lock, hee got open, and shut it after him with such violence that it affrighted some of the conspirators.

The word, which was given with an alarme, was, ô he's gon, he's gon, 14 what shall wee doe, he's gon! The rest, (halfe a sleepe,) start up in a maze, and, like rames, ran theire heads one at another full butt in the darke.

Theire grande leader, Captaine Shrimp [Miles Standish], tooke on most 15 furiously and tore his clothes for anger, to see the empty nest, and their bird gone.

The rest were eager to have torne theire haire from theire heads; but it 16 was so short that it would give them no hold. Now Captaine Shrimp thought in the losse of this prize, (which hee accoumpted his Master peece,) all his honor would be lost for ever.

In the meane time mine Host was got home to Ma-re Mount through 17 the woods, eight miles round about the head of the river Monatoquit that parted the two Plantations, finding his way by the helpe of the lightening, (for it thundred as hee went terribly;) and there hee prepared powther, three pounds dried, for his present imployement, and foure good gunnes for him and the two assistants left at his howse, with bullets of severall sizes, three houndred or thereabouts, to be used if the conspirators should pursue him thether: and these two persons promised theire aides in the quarrell, and confirmed that promise with health in good rosa solis.

Now Captaine Shrimp, the first Captaine in the Land, (as hee sup- 18 posed,) must doe some new act to repaire this losse, and, to vindicate his reputation, who had sustained blemish by this oversight, begins now to study, how to repaire or survive his honor: in this manner, callinge of Councell, they conclude.

Hee takes eight persons more to him, and, (like the nine Worthies of 19 New Canaan,) they imbarque with preparation against Ma-re Mount, where this Monster of a man, as theire phrase was, had his denne; the whole number, had the rest not bin from home, being but seaven, would have given Captaine Shrimpe, (a quondam Drummer,) such a wellcome as would have made him wish for a Drume as bigg as Diogenes tubb, that hee might have crept into it out of sight.

Now the nine Worthies are approached and mine Host prepared: hav- 20 ing intelligence by a Salvage, that hastened in love from Wessaguscus to give him notice of their intent.

One of mine Hosts men prooved a craven: the other had prooved his 21 wits to purchase a little valoure, before mine Host had observed his posture.

The nine worthies comming before the Denne of this supposed Monster, 22 (this seaven headed hydra, as they termed him,) and began, like Don Quixote against the Windmill, to beate a parly, and to offer quarter, if mine Host would yeald; for they resolved to send him for England; and bad him lay by his armes.

But hee, (who was the Sonne of a Souldier,) having taken up armes in 23 his just defence, replyed that hee would not lay by those armes, because they were so needefull at Sea, if hee should be sent over. Yet, to save the effusion of so much worty bloud, as would have issued out of the vaynes of these 9. worthies of New Canaan, if mine Host should have played upon them out at his port holes, (for they came within danger like a flocke of wild geese, as if they had bin tayled one to another, as coults to be sold at a faier,) mine Host was content to yeelde upon quarter; and did capitulate with them in what manner it should be for more certainety, because hee knew what Captaine Shrimpe was.

Hee expressed that no violence should be offered to his person, none to 24 his goods, nor any of his Howsehold: but that hee should have his armes, and what els was requisit for the voyage: which theire herald retornes, it was agreed upon, and should be performed.

But mine Host no sooner had set open the dore, and issued out, but 25 instantly Captaine Shrimpe and the rest of the worthies stepped to him, layd hold of his armes, and had him downe: and so eagerly was every man bent against him, (not regarding any agreement made with such a carnall man,) that they fell upon him as if they would have eaten him: some of them were so violent that they would have a slice with scabbert, and all for haste; untill an old Souldier, (of the Queenes, as the Proverbe is,) that was there by accident, clapt his gunne under the weapons, and sharply rebuked these worthies for their unworthy practises. So the matter was taken into more deliberate consideration.

Captaine Shrimp, and the rest of the nine worthies, made themselves, 26 (by this outragious riot,) Masters of mine Host of Ma-re Mount, and disposed of what hee had at his plantation.

This they knew, (in the eye of the Salvages,) would add to their glory, 27 and diminish the reputation of mine honest Host; whome they practised to be ridd of upon any termes, as willingly as if hee had bin the very Hidra of the time.

[*How the Nine Worthies Put Mine Host of Merry Mount into the Enchanted Castle*]

The nine worthies of New Canaan having now the Law in their owne 28 hands, (there being no generall Governour in the Land; nor none of the Seperation that regarded the duety they owe their Soveraigne, whose naturall borne subjects they were, though translated out of Holland, from whence they had learned to worke all to their owne ends, and make a great shewe of Religion, but no humanity,) for they were now to sit in Counsell on the cause.

And much it stood mine honest Host upon to be very circumspect, and 29 to take Eacus to taske; for that his voyce was more allowed of then both the other: and had not mine Host confounded all the arguments that Eacus could make in their defence, and confuted him that swaied the rest, they would have made him unable to drinke in such manner of merriment any more. So that following this private counsell, given him by one that knew who ruled the rost, the Hiracano ceased that els would split his pinace.

A conclusion was made and sentence given that mine Host should be 30 sent to England a prisoner. But when hee was brought to the shipps for that purpose, no man durst be so foole hardy as to undertake carry him. So these Worthies set mine Host upon an Island, without gunne, powther, or shot or dogge or so much as a knife to get any thinge to feede upon, or any other cloathes to shelter him with at winter then a thinne suite which hee had one at that time. Home hee could not get to Ma-re Mount. Upon this Island hee stayed a moneth at least, and was releeved by Salvages that tooke notice that mine Host was a Sachem of Passonagessit, and would bringe bottles of strong liquor to him, and unite themselves into a league of brother hood with mine Host; so full of humanity are these infidels before those Christians.

From this place for England sailed mine Host in a Plimmouth shipp, 31 (that came into the Land to fish upon the Coast,) that landed him safe in England at Plimmouth: and hee stayed in England untill the ordinary time for shipping to set forth for these parts, and then retorned: Noe man being able to taxe him of any thinge.

But the Worthies, (in the meane time,) hoped they had bin ridd of him. 32

Edward Gibbon

(1737–1794)

In writing about Edward Gibbon, Lytton Strachey suggested that Gibbon was a great historian because, and only because, he was a great artist. "Facts relating to the past," Strachey writes, "when they are collected without art, are compilations; and compilations, no doubt, may be useful, but they are no more History than butter, eggs, salt, and herbs are an omelette. . . . Gibbon's History is chiefly remarkable as one of the supreme monuments of Classic Art in European literature." This comes about, Strachey argues, from the balance and order and precision of his work, which is mirrored not only in the larger elements of selection, but also in the prose style itself.

In writing his six-volume The Decline and Fall of the Roman Empire (1776–1788), Gibbon chronicled a thousand years of history, and though his work is five volumes long, of necessity he had to be highly selective with his facts and succinct in his style. To achieve this he wrote his first chapter over three times, and the next two twice. The style he worked out in these opening chapters was highly balanced, patterned, and structured. There is a sense of deep control as Gibbon moves from phrase to phrase and from sentence to sentence. Part of this sense comes from the extraordinarily careful documentation (he was one of the first historians to include specific sources). But another part comes from his insistent presence, the "I" that frequently asserts itself as Gibbon goes through his history.

Much of this sense of control comes out of Gibbon's discourse community in the eighteenth century. This was a period that stressed the role of rational thought, that argued that humanity did not need to let the world act upon it; instead humanity could exercise its ability to think, to control, to re-form, and to understand the world. By extension, a writer, in using his or her rationality, could give order to such things as the past, or to a series of observations about the nature of light, or to the way in which one comes to understand a literary text.

Gibbon's passage on the decadence of the upper classes, excerpted here, is not developed with expository declamations against the evil of this class; Gibbon holds direct commentary to a minimum. Instead, he uses specific descriptions to depict a class that was deeply rooted in the demands of the self. At points he uses comparison to recall an earlier age when duty and honor and physical hardship for the sake of country were the dominant traits; the latter ages of Roman history, he suggests, suffer in comparison. So the meaning of the passage comes through the descriptive details Gibbon selects, orders, and arranges.

ROME IN POWER AND DECAY

The greatness of Rome (such is the language of the historian) was founded on   1
the rare and almost incredible alliance of virtue and of fortune. The long
period of her infancy was employed in a laborious struggle against the tribes
of Italy, the neighbours and enemies of the rising city. In the strength and
ardour of youth she sustained the storms of war, carried her victorious arms
beyond the seas and the mountains, and brought home triumphal laurels
from every country of the globe. At length, verging towards old age, and
sometimes conquering by the terror only of her name, she sought the blessings
of ease and tranquillity. The VENERABLE CITY, which had trampled on the
necks of the fiercest nations, and established a system of laws, the perpetual
guardians of justice and freedom, was content, like a wise and wealthy parent, to devolve on the Cæsars, her favourite sons, the care of governing her
ample patrimony. A secure and profound peace, such as had been once enjoyed in the reign of Numa,* succeeded to the tumults of a republic; while
Rome was still adored as the queen of the earth, and the subject nations still
reverenced the name of the people and the majesty of the senate. But this
native splendour (continues Ammianus†) is degraded and sullied by the conduct of some nobles, who, unmindful of their own dignity and of that of their
country, assume an unbounded licence of vice and folly. They contend with
each other in the empty vanity of titles and surnames, and curiously select or
invent the most lofty and sonorous appellations—Reburrus or Fabunius,
Pagonius or Tarrasius—which may impress the ears of the vulgar with astonishment and respect. From a vain ambition of perpetuating their memory,
they affect to multiply their likeness in statues of bronze and marble; nor are
they satisfied unless those statues are covered with plates of gold; an honour-
able distinction, first granted to Acilius the consul, after he had subdued by
his arms and counsels the power of king Antiochus. The ostentation of displaying, of magnifying perhaps, the rent-roll of the estates which they possess
in all the provinces, from the rising to the setting sun, provokes the just resentment of every man who recollects that their poor and invincible ancestors
were not distinguished from the meanest of the soldiers by the delicacy of
their food or the splendour of their apparel. But the modern nobles measure
their rank and consequence according to the loftiness of their chariots, and
the weighty magnificence of their dress. Their long robes of silk and purple
float in the wind; and as they are agitated, by art or accident, they occasionally discover the under garments, the rich tunics, embroidered with the figures of various animals. Followed by a train of fifty servants, and tearing up

---

*Numa was a legendary emperor of Rome, following Romulus and Remus.
†Ammianus Marcellinus (c. 330–400) was a Roman historian who wrote about the second
    through the fourth centuries A.D.

the pavement, they move along the streets with the same impetuous speed as if they travelled with post-horses; and the example of the senators is boldly imitated by the matrons and ladies, whose covered carriages are continually driving round the immense space of the city and suburbs. Whenever these persons of high distinction condescend to visit the public baths, they assume, on their entrance, a tone of loud and insolent command, and appropriate to their own use the conveniences which were designed for the Roman people. If, in these places of mixed and general resort, they meet any of the infamous ministers of their pleasures, they express their affection by a tender embrace, while they proudly decline the salutations of their fellow-citizens, who are not permitted to aspire above the honour of kissing their hands or their knees. As soon as they have indulged themselves in the refreshment of the bath, they resume their rings and the other ensigns of their dignity, select from their private wardrobe of the finest linen, such as might suffice for a dozen persons, the garments the most agreeable to their fancy, and maintain till their departure the same haughty demeanour, which perhaps might have been excused in the great Marcellus after the conquest of Syracuse. Sometimes indeed these heroes undertake more arduous achievements: they visit their estates in Italy, and procure themselves, by the toil of servile hands, the amusements of the chase. If at any time, but more especially on a hot day, they have courage to sail in their painted galleys from the Lucrine lake to their elegant villas on the sea-coast of Puteoli and Caieta, they compare their own expeditions to the marches of Cæsar and Alexander. Yet should a fly presume to settle on the silken folds of their gilded umbrellas, should a sunbeam penetrate through some unguarded and imperceptible chink, they deplore their intolerable hardships, and lament in affected language that they were not born in the land of the Cimmerians, the regions of eternal darkness. In these journeys into the country the whole body of the household marches with their master. In the same manner as the cavalry and infantry, the heavy and the light armed troops, the advanced guard and the rear, are marshalled by the skill of their military leaders, so the domestic officers, who bear a rod as an ensign of authority, distribute and arrange the numerous train of slaves and attendants. The baggage and wardrobe move in the front, and are immediately followed by a multitude of cooks and inferior ministers employed in the service of the kitchens and of the table. The main body is composed of a promiscuous crowd of slaves, increased by the accidental concourse of idle or dependent plebeians. The rear is closed by the favourite band of eunuchs, distributed from age to youth, according to the order of seniority. Their numbers and their deformity excite the horror of the indignant spectators, who are ready to execrate the memory of Semiramis* for the cruel art which she invented of frustrating the purposes of nature, and of blasting in the bud the hopes of future generations. In the exercise of domestic jurisdiction the nobles

---

* The legendary founder of Babylon who invented castration.

of Rome express an exquisite sensibility for any personal injury, and a contemptuous indifference for the rest of the human species. When they have called for warm water, if a slave has been tardy in his obedience, he is instantly chastised with three hundred lashes; but should the same slave commit a wilful murder, the master will mildly observe that he is a worthless fellow, but that if he repeats the offence he shall not escape punishment. Hospitality was formerly the virtue of the Romans; and every stranger who could plead either merit or misfortune was relieved or rewarded by their generosity. At present, if a foreigner, perhaps of no contemptible rank, is introduced to one of the proud and wealthy senators, he is welcomed indeed in the first audience with such warm professions and such kind inquiries, that he retires enchanted with the affability of his illustrious friend, and full of regret that he had so long delayed his journey to Rome, the native seat of manners as well as of empire. Secure of a favourable reception, he repeats his visit the ensuing day, and is mortified by the discovery that his person, his name, and his country are already forgotten. If he still has resolution to persevere, he is gradually numbered in the train of dependents, and obtains the permission to pay his assiduous and unprofitable court to a haughty patron, incapable of gratitude or friendship, who scarcely deigns to remark his presence, his departure, or his return. Whenever the rich prepare a solemn and popular entertainment, whenever they celebrate with profuse and pernicious luxury their private banquets, the choice of the guests is the subject of anxious deliberation. The modest, the sober, and the learned are seldom preferred; and the nomenclators, who are commonly swayed by interested motives, have the address to insert in the list of invitations the obscure names of the most worthless of mankind. But the frequent and familiar companions of the great are those parasites who practise the most useful of all arts, the art of flattery; who eagerly applaud each word and every action of their immortal patron; gaze with rapture on his marble columns and variegated pavements, and strenuously praise the pomp and elegance which he is taught to consider as a part of his personal merit. At the Roman tables the birds, the squirrels, or the fish, which appear of an uncommon size, are contemplated with curious attention; a pair of scales is accurately applied to ascertain their real weight; and, while the more rational guests are disgusted by the vain and tedious repetition, notaries are summoned to attest by an authentic record the truth of such a marvellous event. Another method of introduction into the houses and society of the great is derived from the profession of gaming, or, as it is more politely styled, of play. The confederates are united by a strict and indissoluble bond of friendship, or rather of conspiracy; a superior degree of skill in the *Tesserarian* art (which may be interpreted the game of dice and tables) is a sure road to wealth and reputation. A master of that sublime science, who in a supper or assembly is placed below a magistrate, displays in his countenance the surprise and indignation which Cato might be supposed to feel when he was refused the prætorship by the votes of a capricious people. The acquisition of knowledge seldom engages the curiosity of the nobles, who abhor the fatigue and disdain the advantages of study; and the only books which they peruse are the Satires of Juvenal, and the verbose and fabulous histories of Marius Maximus. The libraries which they have inherited from their fathers are secluded, like dreary sepulchres, from the light of day. But the costly instruments of the theatre, flutes, and enormous lyres, and hydraulic organs, are constructed for their use; and the harmony of vocal and instrumental music is incessantly repeated in the palaces of Rome. In those palaces sound is preferred to sense, and the care of the body to that of the mind. It is allowed as a salutary maxim, that the light and frivolous suspicion of a contagious malady is of sufficient weight to excuse the visits of the most intimate friends; and even the servants who are despatched to make the decent inquiries are not suffered to return home till they have undergone the ceremony of a previous ablution. Yet this selfish and unmanly delicacy occasionally yields to the more imperious passion of avarice. The prospect of gain will urge a rich and gouty senator as far as Spoleto; every sentiment of arrogance and dignity is subdued by the hopes of an inheritance, or even of a legacy; and a wealthy childless citizen is the most powerful of the Romans. The art of obtaining the signature of a favourable testament, and sometimes of hastening the moment of its execution, is perfectly understood; and it has happened that in the same house, though in different apartments, a husband and a wife with the laudable design of overreaching each other, have summoned their respective lawyers, to declare at the same time their mutual but contradictory intentions. The distress which follows and chastises extravagant luxury often reduces the great to the use of the most humiliating expedients. When they desire to borrow, they employ the base and supplicating style of the slave in the comedy; but when they are called upon to pay, they assume the royal and tragic declamation of the grandsons of Hercules. If the demand is repeated, they readily procure some trusty sycophant, instructed to maintain a charge of poison, or magic, against the insolent creditor, who is seldom released from prison till he has signed a discharge of the whole debt. These vices, which degrade the moral character of the Romans, are mixed with a puerile superstition that disgraces their understanding. They listen with confidence to the predictions of haruspices, who pretend to read in the entrails of victims the signs of future greatness and prosperity; and there are many who do not presume either to bathe or to die, or to appear in public, till they have diligently consulted, according to the rules of astrology, the situation of Mercury and the aspect of the moon. It is singular enough that this vain credulity may often be discovered among the profane sceptics who impiously doubt or deny the existence of a celestial power.

QUESTIONS ABOUT GIBBON'S DISCOURSE COMMUNITY AND HIS CONCERNS IN THIS SELECTION

1. In his *Narrative Form in History and Fiction* (Princeton, 1970), Leo Braudy argues that the pattern of *The Decline and Fall of the Roman Empire*, the

structure and order of the work, do not come out of the historical events themselves, but out of the literary structures Gibbon imposes on those events. How would you describe the stance of Edward Gibbon as portrayed in the above selection? How does he, as an artist, select and arrange his material so as to give a distinct impression of the last years of the Roman Empire?

2. Given the enormous range of material to be dealt with, Gibbon was forced to generalize at times, to take one incident from a number of incidents and suggest that it was typical of the period. Where do you see this process of selection and generalization at work in this passage? Is this a legitimate procedure for the historian, or does it distort history?

3. As Gibbon portrays the Roman nobles, what were they essentially striving for in their lives? Money? Pleasure? What? How likely are people striving for such goals to achieve them?

4. At several points Gibbon shows the Roman nobles going places, moving about. Characterize their moving about (to what places? why?). With these depictions, is Gibbon making a general point about the nobles?

5. Examine closely how Gibbon criticizes the Roman nobles. In terms of what values does he criticize them? What values seem to be important to him? Do you think that it is inevitable for the upper classes of any economically successful nation to become the kind of people that Gibbon says the Roman nobles were? Why or why not?

6. For several lines Gibbon comments on the eunuchs in the nobles' entourages. Why does he do so? Is he making claims that apply to more than the eunuchs?

7. Gibbon concludes this section by writing about Romans who consult astrologers. He concludes that "it is singular enough that this vain credulity may often be discovered among the profane sceptics who impiously doubt or deny the existence of a celestial power." How would you describe Gibbon's stance here? Is he criticizing the Romans from his own religious perspective?

QUESTIONS ABOUT GIBBON'S RHETORICAL STRATEGIES

1. In the headnote to Gibbon, we indicate that much of his art stems from the balance, order, and precision of his work. What other characteristics of his presentation would you consider artistic?

2. Gibbon calls some of the Roman nobles such things as "persons of high distinction" and "heroes." Is he being sincere? If not, why does he use such titles? Gibbon also compares the Roman nobles to earlier Roman soldiers and politicians. Why does he do so?

3. Early in this selection Gibbon writes about Rome's "infancy," her "strength and ardour of youth," and her "old age." What is this technique called? Why do you think Gibbon uses this technique where he does? Do you think he uses it successfully?

4. This passage is written as a single, long paragraph, and it is typical of Gibbon's approach to paragraphing. What is its unifying principle? Or would you argue that it is too diffuse, not unified at all? Why would Gibbon wish to use such a lengthy paragraph? Does he gain any rhetorical effects by its length? A modern writer might break this paragraph into several smaller units. Where might this

paragraph be divided? Should it be divided in more than one place? What would you gain and lose by such a division?

5. Gibbon's sentences are often lengthy and balanced. Many of the sentences begin with subordinate clauses, or with the object rather than the subject of the sentence, or even with a conjunction. Find sentences that fit these patterns. Generalize about the way Gibbon uses these patterns to affect the reader's understanding of the information being imparted.

6. Except for the verbs in the first few sentences, the verbs in this selection are all in the present tense. What is different about the information in the early sentences that leads Gibbon to put them in the past tense? Why does he choose to use the present tense in his description of the corrupt nobility? How does this affect the reader's perceptions of that class?

7. In this selection Gibbon uses several passive verbs. Identify the specific function such verbs fulfill. Are the verbs justified? Could some verbs be said to make his claims against the Roman nobles more general, more widely applicable?

8. What does Gibbon mean by "pernicious luxury"? How is it possible for luxury to be pernicious?

WRITING FROM WITHIN AND ABOUT HISTORY AND ITS STUDY

Writing for Yourself

1. Explore in your journal whether you think it is the case that all powerful societies will have an upper class like the one Gibbon describes in this selection.

2. Explore in your journal what you are striving for. What is the source of your deepest motivation?

Writing for Nonacademic Audiences

1. You have been asked to give a twenty-minute talk to a ninth-grade history class on the ultimate cause for Rome's fall. Write up that talk.

2. A debate over the current state of the United States has sprung up in the letters-to-the-editor section of your college newspaper. Write a letter to the editor yourself, in which you give your views on the issue.

Writing for Academic Audiences

1. Research the life of the historian Ammianus, whom Gibbon cites as a major source in this selection. For a history of civilization course, write a 500-word essay that explores those forces and tendencies that might have influenced Ammianus in his depiction of the Roman nobles.

2. Use *The Reader's Guide to Periodical Literature*, *The New York Times Index*, and historical texts to find articles about a wealthy North American of the twentieth century. After reading about this person, write a 500-word essay for an economics class on whether or not that person benefited North American society as a whole. You might deal with such figures as J. P. Morgan, Andrew Carnegie, Henry Ford, E. P. Taylor, a member of the Vanderbilt or Rockefel-

ler or Kennedy families, Donald Trump, or Mary Kay (of Mary Kay Cosmetics).

3. Write a 750-word essay for an ancient history course on some of the more startling diversions of the Roman nobles near the end of the Roman Empire.

4. Write a 1,000-word essay for a seminar in historiography on whether or not historians should try to be artistic in their presentations.

Robert Graves

(1895–1986)

Benedict Arnold has a great deal of rather unpleasant associations attached to him, so that even if one does not know any of the details of his life, one certainly knows that he is an archetypal traitor. It is somewhat ironic that this brave, dominating, resourceful, and powerful man is today remembered principally as a cliché. But in the following essay, the British writer Robert Graves seeks to reconsider Arnold's reputation, suggesting that the perception of Benedict Arnold as a traitor has come about because of a faulty, ethnocentric perception of his actions. In taking on this task, Graves becomes a revisionist historian, one who seeks to challenge accepted interpretations.

Graves's principal question is stated in the title, and the answer comes within the first two pages: He asserts that Arnold was indeed not a traitor. He begins his defense of this assertion by definition, which implies that a traitor becomes a traitor only if personal profit is involved (so Judas, for example, cannot be a traitor in this sense, since his act of betrayal came about for idealistic purposes). Graves then goes on to support the assertion through recounting historical facts, selecting those that suggest that Arnold was a man of courage and honor who fought nobly for the American Revolution until he perceived that the leaders of the Revolution were being dishonorable and that the Revolution would probably fail. His act, seen as a betrayal by the American side, was instead an act which, Arnold hoped, would end the war without further bloodshed.

Graves, perhaps best known for the historical novels I, Claudius *(1934) and* Claudius the God *(1934), arranges his facts to support the central assertion of the piece. His assertion is essentially an interpretive one, even as, he would argue, the claim that Arnold is a traitor is an interpretive claim. Had the war gone another way, it would have been illegitimate to label Arnold a traitor, in the same way that it is illegitimate today to label George Washington a traitor.*

But the implication of this approach is even more far-reaching, for it suggests that every historical act is necessarily interpreted in vastly different ways given the social and cultural perspectives of the historian. Similarly, a reader's judgment and evaluation of any historian's view must necessarily be shaped by the reader's social and cultural perspectives on the figure or event with which the historian deals. This perspective on history belies the value and permanence of fact, or at least calls that permanence into question.

Yet certainly it is a fact that Benedict Arnold conspired to turn over a key defensive position of the American army to the British army. It is also a fact that he was to be paid by the British for this service. Regardless of who won the war, it seems as if he must then be considered a traitor to the American cause. All of the other facts

*that Graves selects and arranges are not nearly as significant as this one. It is interest-
ing that Arnold was a capable soldier and leader. It is intriguing that much of the
American army was made up of mercenaries and British deserters. It is ironic that
the American Congress gave away its own honor. But are not these facts tangential?*

*Graves would argue that they are not. And the end result of his carefully con-
trolled and structured narrative is to suggest that it is these issues which must really
be considered if we are to interpret the meaning of Benedict Arnold's actions.*

WAS BENEDICT ARNOLD A TRAITOR?

The American Revolution brought into being a new way of life which, after 1
nearly two centuries of refinement, can now be confidently offered as a model
to the civilized world; if only because the United States has at last succeeded
Great Britain, which similarly succeeded France at the close of the Napo-
leonic Wars, as the richest, most progressive, most envied of all nations. We
British accept this change calmly enough, recognizing it as a natural consequence of the United States' energy, size, unity, and geographical separation
from the storm-centres of Europe; and feel grateful that armed American
intervention saved us, in two wars, from conquest by Germany. Then, since
nobody with a sense of realism would suggest that the United States should
re-enter the British Commonwealth, or that Great Britain should apply for
membership of the United States, and since the two countries have become
close allies, it is surely high time to revise the irreconcilable accounts of the
Revolutionary War commonly presented to British and American schoolchil-
dren. Nothing but good could come of discarding ancient historical propaganda which continues to embitter Anglo-American relations, and particularly of settling once and for all the crucial question: "Was General Benedict
Arnold a traitor to his country?"

The first sense of "traitor" in English is "a man who for base personal 2
motives plots to deliver a master, or liege, into the power of his enemies."
The best-known popular example is Judas; though his happens not to be a
very convincing case. One can hardly exculpate Judas of presumption and
officiousness; yet the New Testament evidence, examined in the light of contemporary history, suggests that he foresaw an abortive Messianic revolt
against the Romans, and arranged to have his Master placed in protective
custody. Thus Judas's kiss seems to have conveyed a friendly reassurance: "I
have done this for your own good!" When, however, he realized that his plan
had miscarried: that the High Priests had handed over Jesus to the Romans

instead of waiting until the Feast of Passover ended and then bringing him before the Jewish Supreme Court (which would doubtless have adjourned the case *sine die*), Judas tried to pay back the thirty pieces of silver, and committed suicide. I mention Judas because the second meaning of "traitor" is "a man who for base personal motives plots to deliver his native country into the power of its enemies;" and because "Judas" was a favourite insult cast at Benedict Arnold after his defection. Yet if Judas had been a traitor in the agreed sense, he could have demanded at least thirty thousand pieces of silver for his betrayal. The very fact that, when asked to name his reward, he chose precisely thirty (an ironical reference to the Temple Treasurers in Zechariah XI, who insulted a prophet of God by valuing him at the lowest legal sum) proves that he was not a traitor. A dishonest treasurer, as Judas is represented as being, would not have sold out at that petty price. He could have continued to amass large sums by quietly pocketing the donations which came flowing in from rich sympathizers, among them the wife of King Herod Antipas's finance minister (Luke XIII:3). Precisely the same argument holds good for Benedict Arnold. He may have been wrong-headed or presumptuous, but his motives seem to have been far from base, and his financial honesty beyond question. Like Judas, he accepted a mere token payment for an act which he hoped would save his nation from disaster.

Traitors are to be closely distinguished from rebels. Oliver Cromwell, 3 though rebelliously taking arms against King Charles I, did not call in the Dutch to win his battles, and cannot therefore be called a traitor to England. General Lee, who took arms against the Federal Government in the Civil War, was a rebel, no traitor; because Jefferson Davis and his Congress did not apply to the British for aid. It is indeed difficult to find, in modern history, traitors comparable with the Spartan king who went over to Xerxes during the Persian War, or Alcibiades, the Athenian general who went over to Sparta during the Peloponnesian War. True, the British hanged Sir Roger Casement as a traitor for his clandestine dealings with Germany in World War I, but Casement was an Irish patriot rather than a British traitor. They also hanged William Joyce ("Lord Haw-Haw") for treasonably broadcasting German propaganda in World War II; but Joyce did not regard himself as a British subject and, except on a doubtful technicality, was not one. Joyce can in fact be considered hardly more of a traitor to King George VI than Napoleon, whose native island had for a short period of his youth been a British possession, was a traitor to King George III. A stronger case might be made out against Goethe for traitorously eulogizing Napoleon, the invader of Germany; though it is usual to regard Goethe as a collaborationist who prudently kept his own small region from the depredations of the French "army of enlightenment." Or, yet more kindly, as an internationalist; a title, however, which should then in justice be conferred on Burgess and Maclean, the British Foreign Office officials who deserted to Russia during the Cold War: with the avowed, if foolish, intention of improving Anglo-Soviet relations.

Between 1775 and 1783, every native American was confronted with   4
the alternatives of being called a rebel for his disloyalty to King George, and
being called a rebel for his objection to the Revolution. The sides were pretty
evenly divided in this earlier Civil War, several "Loyalist" regiments assisting
the British throughout the struggle. A man might then obey the dictates of
his political conscience and, should he not at first possess such a thing, it was
soon forced on him. Probably three out of every four colonists would have
declared in 1775 that, little as they felt themselves bound by the laws of a
far-distant London Parliament, and loth as they were to be taxed for the
upkeep of British armed forces, even as protective garrisons against possible
attack by the French and Indians, they had no intention of going beyond
civil disobedience in their attempt to secure independence of the Crown. But
the Revolutionary Committees organized a newspaper and pamphlet propaganda campaign of the most inventive and sensational sort, as a means of
inciting the luke-warms and the don't-cares into active rebellion. It was a
technique carefully studied by the Sinn Feiners during the "Troubles" a century and a half later, and finally perfected by Hitler and Goebbels when they
set themselves to impose their Nazi creed on all Germans everywhere.

At the close of the Revolution, Samuel Adams had written: 5

> Here in my retreat, like another Catiline,* the collar around my neck, in dan-   6
> ger of the severest punishment, I laid down the plan of revolt: I endeavoured
> to persuade my timid accomplices that a most glorious revolution might be the
> result of our efforts, but I scarcely dared to hope it; and what I have seen
> realized appears to me like a dream. You know by what obscure intrigues, by
> what unfaithfulness to the mother-country a powerful party was formed; how
> the minds of the people were irritated before we could provoke the insurrec-
> tion.

Yet, though fear of having their houses burned down or their ships scut-   7
tled, or being given "a Marblehead Ride" in a coat of tar and feathers, obliged
even the most peace-loving colonists to join the local militia, companies that
would face a British command of equal numbers were few. Had it not been
for Washington's capture at Trenton of a thousand elderly, homesick, forcibly enlisted Hessians, and his subsequent surprise and repulse of a small British column at Princeton, no standing army would have been left him by
February 1777. Yet, as Lord Chatham pointed out, sensibly enough, one
could not conquer a map. The British Government must in the end have
granted the colonists their independence—even if this meant approving Congress's summary sequestration of royal and noble estates, to the value of forty
million dollars, for the benefit of land-hungry settlers. As it happened, however, things had to get far worse before they could get better.

Benedict Arnold was a native American: the great-grandson, and fourth   8

---

* Catiline (108 B.C.–62 B.C.) rebelled against the Roman counsuls and was eventually killed in
battle.

in direct descent, of his seventeenth-century namesake, three times Royal Governor of Rhode Island. Why he joined the Revolutionary forces, despite his Tory background, is no mystery. As a wide-awake merchant, he realized that Royal Governorships and an Established Church were anachronisms; so also were the immense estates of the Phillips, Pepperell, Morris, Penn, and Fairfax families; and the royal ban on free settlement of the lands beyond the Alleghenies. Only an all-American Parliament could solve outstanding problems of trade, revenue, defence, public works; and recent British commercial policy in Northern Ireland suggested that overseas interests were, as a rule, subordinated to those of the mother country. Arnold's decision to fight was coloured perhaps by a feeling that the British had undervalued him during his early service against the French in a New York company (1758–1759)—he deserted them in a huff and went home—and an ambition to prove himself a real soldier after all, despite thirteen years spent in trade. No one, indeed, understood better than he how to handle American volunteers: namely by leading them rather than by giving them directives. His phenomenal courage and energy shamed the least bellicose into heroism; and if he held a high opinion of himself, why, so did almost every man who served under him. Yet his successes, though approved by Washington, always caused jealousy, hatred and back-biting among senior officers whose military uselessness could not escape the shrewd censure of their free-spoken troops.

Washington's decision to fight the British was based on similarly common-sense grounds. He agreed with a view afterwards expressed by Tom Paine that the Colonists were morally entitled to break their allegiance as soon as it proved a burden, and held that Virginia's prosperity, threatened by a steep fall in tobacco prices at the close of the Seven Years' War, and the dumping of British goods, could be ensured only by secession. True, he bore a private grudge against the British: they had made light of his services in the French War and declined to give him a regular commission. At that time American militia officers, however exalted, ranked junior to the youngest ensign of a British line-regiment. Washington wrote to a Colonial official in 1754: "If you think me capable of holding a commission that has neither rank nor emoluments, you must entertain a very contemptible opinion of my weakness, and believe me to be more empty than the commission itself." 9

A personal grudge does not necessarily imply faulty political judgement; it merely spurs a man to action. Washington, however, consistently misunderstood the kind of war which he had been called upon to fight. American militiamen could not hope to beat trained European troops in pitched battles. The frontiermen, the best fighting material available, were adept at Indian warfare, sniping from behind trees at troops on the march, or picking off stragglers, but did not take kindly to volley-firing or "push of bayonet." It never dawned on Washington, as a would-be British regular, that there was no real reason why his men should fight any pitched battles at all. They could best wear the enemy down by guerrilla tactics: swift, well-planned raids; a 10 scorched-earth policy; harassing of vulnerable supply lines—the British could not transport everything by sea or river. When, in July 1776, five hundred Connecticut men volunteered to form an irregular cavalry commando, which was what Washington needed most, he replied that owing to a lack of forage he could use them only as infantry. When they would not give up their horses, he dismissed them; and it was years before the commandos led by Sumter, Marion and Pickens on the Revolutionary side, and on the British by Tarleton's Greens, a Loyalist force, proved how foolish he had been. Washington, in fact, shared the military creed of his generals, Horatio Gates and Charles Lee, who had held regular commissions respectively as major and lieutenant in the British Army. As a Virginian gentleman, not a populist, he believed in a system of command based on social differences rather than capacity for leadership, and supported by the savage old-world punishments of lashes, riding the wooden horse, and running the gauntlet. His difficulties in recruiting convinced patriots were largely due to their natural resentment at this most un-American way of soldiering. Those who did volunteer considered themselves the equals of their officers, whom they "valued no higher than broomsticks."

Arnold's first important assignment was to assist in the invasion of Can- 11 ada, and there raise a revolt of the French peasantry. A hopeless task, since the *habitants* were perfectly content with the liberties granted them after the British conquest of Canada: such as the abolition of *corvée*, a forced-labour system which had so irked them under French rule. Besides, Congress had unwisely protested to London against the British toleration of Catholicism in Canada; and religious freedom had been among the most welcome benefits bestowed on the *habitants*. Arnold reached the Canadian border after a two-months' march with 1,100 men through the woods of Maine in conditions of fearful privation and hardship, and made straight for Quebec. There he found the British on the alert, and had to call a halt until his colleague Montgomery arrived with 2,000 men from Montreal. The assault, delivered on the last day of 1775, failed. Montgomery lost his life; Arnold was severely wounded in the leg. The ravages of smallpox, lack of hard money to buy food, the expiration of numerous enlistments, and desperately cold weather, forced the Americans to retreat; reinforcements sent by Congress caught the smallpox too, and gave way before the British advance. Of an original 9,000 American invaders only 3,000 left Canada; the last man to cross the frontier being Arnold, who had ridden back to reconnoitre and narrowly escaped capture by the British vanguard.

The naval battle fought on Lake Champlain in October 1776 was the 12 most spectacular event of the war. Arnold, who had strengthened the American fleet of schooners by building four new galleys and eight gondolas, could outgun the British; but General Carleton, his opponent, fetched sailors from the Royal Navy to man another extemporized flotilla and, with their help, would have gained an absolute victory at Valcour Island but for Arnold's

fantastic courage. When his flagship, *The Royal Savage*, was clumsily handled and came under fire from the *Inflexible* frigate, the largest vessel engaged, he decided to abandon her while he could, and transfer to the *Congress* galley. Most of his officers on the *Congress* were soon killed or wounded
and, for want of trained gunners, he pointed and discharged every gun himself, stepping from one to the other "like a man touching off fireworks for the
King's birthday." That night he brought his shattered fleet away under cover
of mist and darkness, and the next day fought a desperate battle at Split
Rock. He beached the *Congress* only after she caught fire, and was the last
man to climb along her bowsprit to safety. He had even succeeded in saving
a small part of his fleet.

In April 1777, Arnold was in the forefront of a vigorous attack on Gov- 13
ernor Tryon's force which had raided Danbury; and chased them back to
their ships. For this, Washington recommended Congress to appoint Arnold
a major-general; but meanwhile Arnold's personal enemies charged him with
wrongfully commandeering goods from Montreal merchants for the use of
his troops. In May these charges were investigated by the Board of War. The
verdict, confirmed by Congress, was that his character and conduct had been
"cruelly and groundlessly aspersed."

In August, Arnold, now serving under General Philip Schuyler, 14
marched up the Mohawk Valley and raised the siege of Fort Stanwix; but
Schuyler was soon superseded by the egregious General Gates. When Burgoyne moved his army down the Hudson from Lake Champlain and, in September, came upon Gates at Bemis Heights, he could count himself unlucky
not to have defeated him at the first encounter by seizing a hill a short distance away and cutting his communications. Arnold, realizing danger, had
asked Gate's permission to take out part of his division and prevent this man-
oeuvre, which would have forced the Americans either to surrender or to
swim the river. Gates told Arnold to mind his own business, but Arnold won
the support of another born soldier—Colonel Dan Morgan, of the Virginian
Rifles, who had come very close to storming Quebec two years previously.
Together they raised such a storm at Headquarters, clapping hands to pistols
and swearing terribly, that Gates gave way in alarm: he let Arnold lead forward half a brigade of New England militia, stiffened by Morgan's riflemen.
These riflemen, now mostly Pennsylvanians of Northern Irish stock, were the
best troops in America. They could march forty miles a day, subsist on jerked
beef and corn porridge and, for mere sport, would take turns to shoot apples
off one another's heads at sixty paces. Arnold's command broke the resistance
of the Canadians and American Loyalists on the British flank and, though
repulsed with heavy loss by British regulars, quickly switched their attack to
the centre. There they would have got through, had Gates supplied the reinforcements demanded of him. When Arnold's horse fell dead, he fought on
foot, urging the weary men to a final effort. His exploits, which saved Bemis
Heights and kept Burgoyne from breaking through to Albany, provoked an-

ger and jealousy at Headquarters. Gates's chief of staff even circulated a story
that Arnold had stayed out of the battle and spent the whole day at Camp
drinking! In disgust, he resigned his command, which Gates accepted, allowing him to remain with the army only as a private person.

The second and decisive battle of Saratoga took place on October 7th, 15
1777. Arnold, forbidden by Gates to leave Camp, drew his sword and
wounded the officer ordered to detain him, then galloped into the thick of
the melee, bareheaded and in undress. The New England militia followed,
cheering enthusiastically; he managed to carry three regiments of Massachusetts infantry against Burgoyne's centre. These scattered the German troops,
forcing the British to fight a stiff rearguard action and abandon all their guns.
Later, Arnold attacked the enemy camp with a brigade of Continental troops,
but came up against British regulars, as in the previous battle, and was repulsed. Again switching his attack, he advanced in fading light towards a
redoubt which protected the right of the camp, scattered a force of Canadians, and captured the entire garrison of Brunswickers. As Arnold entered the
sally-port he had another horse shot under him, and a wounded German,
firing at point-blank range, shattered his thigh-bone.

Here he was finally overtaken by the aide-de-camp who, pursuing him 16
all day with an order from Gates to return at once, had been led into some
very hot spots. Arnold paid him no attention and summoned a surgeon. The
surgeon recommended amputation, but Arnold cried: "Goddam it, sir, if that
is all you can do with me, I shall see the battle out on another horse." The
battle, however, was already won; but by no action of Gate's, who, it is said,
had spent the greater part of the day preaching to a dying prisoner, Sir Francis Clark, the righteousness of the American cause. Sir Francis, unconvinced,
reproached him for spoiling the last hours of his life. Gates then turned to
one of his aides: "Did you ever hear such an impudent son of a bitch?"

Burgoyne, outnumbered, cut off from Canada, and dangerously short 17
of provisions and ammunition, chose to capitulate. Gates could have insisted
on an unconditional surrender, but was scared by news of Clinton's move up
the Hudson and had so little trust in his subordinates that he readily signed
the proposals put forward by Burgoyne. These allowed the British to march
away with the honours of war, on condition that the whole force engaged—
only 2,000 British troops were left alive—would abandon their arms and
agree never to serve in America again.

One Sergeant Downing, a New England militiaman, wrote after the 18
battle:

> Arnold was our fighting general and a bloody fellow he was. He didn't 19
> care for nothing. He'd ride right in. He's as brave a man as ever lived and they
> didn't treat him right. *He* ought to have Burgoyne's sword.

Washington persuaded Congress to thank Arnold for his services, and 20
gave him the Governorship of Philadelphia, which the British had recently

evacuated. A dangerous honour, since it did not carry with it the entertainment allowance which he would need to uphold the dignity of his office in that elegant town. There he married Margaret Shippen, daughter of a moderate Loyalist, and necessarily lived beyond his means. In February 1779, the Executive Council of Pennsylvania, under the presidency of Joseph Reed, an enemy of Arnold's, laid before Congress eight charges of misconduct, all of them trifling. A Congressional Committee exonerated Arnold, but in April, Reed obtained a reconsideration. Congress threw out four charges and referred the others to a court martial, which was left hanging over Arnold's head for eight months longer. In January 1780, the Court absolved him of all wrongful intent—the two main charges being those of giving a pass to a trading vessel on the Delaware River without first consulting General Washington, and using certain Army wagons, then lying idle, to move the property of private citizens beyond the reach of enemy foragers. To save Reed's face, the Court directed Washington to reprimand Arnold for his impudence. Washington did so, using the phrases "peculiarly reprehensible, imprudent and improper."

Arnold had originally taken arms against the British because this seemed 21 the only way to obtain redress of American grievances. Three public events now combined to alter his opinion. The first was the decision of Congress not to ratify the Capitulation articles signed by General Gates at Saratoga; thus the British troops, though granted the honours of war, found themselves placed in prison camps instead of being repatriated. There they were starved, ill-treated, and constantly offered bribes to desert. So open a breach of faith seemed to Arnold and other men of honour most disgraceful—especially since Congress still employed Gates.

The second event was Congress's rejection of the peace offer conveyed 22 by the King's Commissioners. Arnold thought these terms highly generous: a native American Parliament of two houses, to settle all domestic affairs of the colonies; free trade; and the assistance of the British fleet and army in time of need, without any obligation to pay for their upkeep.

The third event was the French alliance, which in so far as it involved 23 the despatch of French troops to America, Arnold thought plain treason. Military convention permitted the hiring of mercenaries to serve under a national flag—the present French and Spanish "Foreign Legions" are a relic of this—but it was a very different matter to sign a military pact with Britain's hereditary foe: an enemy against whom Washington, Schuyler, Gates and Arnold himself had all fought, and with whom most Americans had nothing in common, either politically, religiously or culturally. The French were, indeed, despised as the tools of a tyranny far more absolute than King George's. If Congress had treated men like Arnold and Dan Morgan generously, and let them conduct the war in true American fashion, rather than rely on foreigners who forced inappropriate Continental strategy, tactics and discipline on the revolutionaries, there would have been no need to call in the French. (Dan Morgan, consistently overpassed for promotion, remained a mere "bird-colonel," despite his remarkable victory at Cowpens, which he won when crippled by arthritis. He continued to be snubbed by the Board of War, and finally retired to his farm in disgust.)

These three events, combined with the misery and destitution that were 24 now afflicting his native country, and the general war-weariness that surrounded him, decided Arnold to "do a General Monk"—Monk being, of course, the Cromwellian who brought over the British Commonwealth Army bloodlessly to King Charles II's side at the Restoration and won great acclaim in consequence. The war had long ceased to be an American popular revolution. Joseph Galloway, a Pennsylvanian Congressman who had gone over to the British, reported that not one soldier in four of Washington's Continental Army, the only force continuously under arms, was a native-born American. Records show that most of them were Irishmen, the remainder British, with some German deserters and an average quota of fifty-eight freed Negroes to each battalion. Nathaniel Greene, the ablest American general after Arnold and (as Washington handsomely admitted) the true victor of Trenton, said that at the close of the war his army consisted largely of British deserters.

Arnold obtained from Washington the command of West Point, the 25 Gibraltar of America, and in a secret correspondence with General Sir Henry Clinton, then at New York, offered to surrender it; an act which, he believed, would end the war at a blow, and bloodlessly. He had initialled this correspondence signing himself "Monk" in May 1779, while commanding in Philadelphia; with the full approval, even perhaps at the instigation, of his wife. The first overture to Arnold is extant, so far as I can discover, only in a French version:

> . . . Render then, brave general, this important service to your country. 26
> The colonies cannot sustain much longer the unequal strife. Your troops are
> perishing in misery. They are badly armed, half naked, and crying for bread.
> The efforts of Congress are futile against the languor of the people. Your fields
> are untilled, trade languishes, learning dies. The neglected education of a whole
> generation is an irreparable loss to society. Your youth, torn by thousands from
> their rustic pursuits or useful employments, are mown down by war. Such as
> survive have lost the vigour of their prime, or are maimed in battle: the greater
> part bring back to their families the idleness and the corrupt manners of the
> camp. Let us put an end to so many calamities; you and ourselves have the
> same origin, the same language, the same laws. We are inaccessible in our
> island; and you, the masters of a vast and fertile territory, have no other neigh-
> bours than the people of our loyal colonies . . . From the northern to the south-
> ern pole, from the east to the west, our vessels find everywhere a neighbouring
> harbour belonging to Great Britain. So many islands, so many countries ac-
> knowledging our sway, are all ruled by a uniform system that bears on every
> feature the stamp of liberty, yet is as well adapted to the genius of different
> nations and of various climes. . . .
>
> Beware of breaking forever the links and ties of a friendship whose ben- 27
> efits are proven by the experience of a hundred and fifty years. Time gives to

human institutions a strength which what is new can only attain, in its turn, by the lapse of ages. . . .

United in equality we will rule the universe: we will hold it bound, not 28 by arms and violence, but by the ties of commerce; the lightest and most gentle bands that humankind can wear.

Arnold had at first demanded as his recompense no more than the value 29 of the private property which he would forfeit by the action, namely £10,000; and the same substantive rank in the British forces as he held in the American. This was routine procedure: in 1775, General Charles Lee had stipulated that Congress should grant him a similar compensation when he transferred from the British to the American Army. Later, when Arnold found himself commanding this critical fortress, he raised his demand to £20,000. The increase is perhaps a measure not so much of greed, as of increased resentment at what he believed to be the dishonesty of Congress in delaying payment of moneys due to him, while the Continental currency steadily declined in value. In effect, he accepted £6,319. But had he asked a couple of million dollars for the surrender of West Point, it would have been cheap at the price. Benjamin Franklin scoffed:

Judas sold only one man, Arnold three millions. Judas got for his one man 30 thirty pieces of silver, Arnold not a halfpenny a head.

It happened that Major André, the British agent sent to meet Arnold 31 between the lines and secretly arrange for the surrender of the fortress, was captured by a group of marauding "Skinners" who coveted his fine riding boots. In the heel of one of them they found the incriminating correspondence, and marched André off to American Headquarters for examination. Arnold escaped to the British lines before his fellow-officers could arrest him; André was convicted as a spy and sentenced to death by a court martial of French and American generals.

Sir Henry Clinton tried to exchange six captured American colonels 32 against André, but without success. Arnold thereupon offered to present himself at Washington's headquarters as a willing sacrifice, on condition that André's life would be spared. According to a letter published by Captain James Battersby of the 29th Foot, Clinton refused to let him go: "Your proposal, sir, does you great honour; but were Major André my own brother I would not consent to such a transaction." Washington dared not intervene to save André, for fear of being charged with complicity in the plot—Congress knew that he had planned to visit West Point at the time of its proposed surrender. André was therefore hanged. The British comment, voiced by Clinton himself, was: "The horrid deed is done. Washington has committed premeditated murder and must answer for the consequences." The fierce indignation which a discovery of treason always excites among luke-warm patriots revived the flagging cause of American liberty. Arnold was everywhere burned in effigy, and any man unfortunate enough to have the same surname, whether related to him or not, must needs adopt another. A plan was sponsored by Washington for Arnold's kidnapping by one Sergeant Champe, who was persuaded to desert and enter the British service with that main object, though incidentally to investigate the supposed treason of another American general. Washington promised Champe 100 guineas, five hundred acres of land, and three slaves. Jefferson believed that a bribe of 5,000 guineas would tempt a partisan unit to raid Arnold's camp and carry him off. An official order was issued denying Arnold the rights due to a prisoner of war if captured. All attempts to abduct him proved fruitless, however.

In command of Loyalists forces under the Earl of Cornwallis, Arnold 33 showed his grasp of strategic principles by raids on Richmond, Norfolk and Petersburgh, where he burned most of the tobacco which Congress had offered the French in payment for their services; but in vain. By the cynical incompetence of the Earl of Sandwich, First Lord of the Admiralty, the British fleet had been allowed to fall far below safety level. The Spanish, Dutch and French, joining in arms against Britain, began to prey on her inadequately protected merchant convoys. Three thousand vessels were captured or sunk before she regained command of the sea. Meanwhile, the French landed large forces in America. Washington re-equipped and paid his poor tattered Continental Army, now long immobilized at Valley Forge, and in May 1781 led his new allies southward to Yorktown, where Cornwallis with some six thousand sick and hungry British were cornered by the French. Encouraged by this unexpected turn of fortune, American patriots who had retired from active warfare some years previously, flocked up to the kill. This put 30,000 men at Washington's disposal: 20,000 being French soldiers and sailors. Cornwallis presently surrendered for lack of food and ammunition; the war ended.

In December 1781, Arnold had been invited to visit England and advise 34 King George on American affairs. He was never afterwards employed as a soldier. Twenty years later he died; not, like Judas, by his own hand, but of melancholia, assisted by gout, dropsy and asthma.

It would be unjust for an American to call Benedict Arnold a traitor; as 35 it would be discourteous for an Englishman to call George Washington a traitor. Washington erased the stigma of treason in 1783, when the Peace Treaty conceded the colonists all their demands, and he became the Father of his Country. In 1791, moreover, he sternly rebuffed Genêt, the French Revolutionary envoy, who came pleading for a renewed American alliance against Britain. As the proverb says:

Treason doth never prosper; what's the reason?   36
If treason prospers, 'tis no longer treason!

Washington's coat-of-arms, by the way, the stars and stripes (or *bars* and 37 *mullets*) of which appear in the United States flag, bore the motto: *Exitus Acta Probat*—which can mean either "the result is a test of the means employed" or, in a more cynical sense, "the end justifies the means." His obduracy in keeping the war going has since allowed the United States to develop a classless republican society, now their chief distinction; for it freed them from the incubus of a hereditary nobility with which the British intended to endow them. Not that Washington hankered after a classless society. Like John Adams, he believed in government by an aristocracy of wealth and talents. In fact, he hated the Republicans so bitterly that he tried to exclude them from the American armed forces; and it took a second Civil War to break the power of the Southern slave-owning gentry whose champion he had been.

QUESTIONS ABOUT GRAVES'S DISCOURSE COMMUNITY AND HIS CONCERNS IN THIS ESSAY

1. Robert Graves considered himself to be something of an iconoclast historian who rejected what many in his discourse community would consider to be givens. His *Claudius* novels represent a substantial reinterpretation of that figure's importance, and his *King Jesus* (1946) and *Homer's Daughter* (1955) reevaluate the central characters of those stories in a similar manner. Does this role as iconoclast affect Graves's interpretation of Benedict Arnold? How does it affect the ostensible purpose of the essay: to reconcile differing perceptions of Benedict Arnold based upon social, cultural, and national evaluations? If it is true that all history is affected by cultural biases, is it possible to ever arrive at the objective truth of the event?

2. Is it helpful for a discourse community to have iconoclasts within its ranks? Why or why not?

3. In general, how do differing viewpoints about historical incidents and characters originate? How significant a role does ethnocentrism play in the development of these differing perceptions? Is Graves, a British writer, free of them? Is any reader?

4. Fairly early in the essay, Graves writes that "It never dawned on Washington . . . that there was no real reason why his men should fight any pitched battles at all." How could Graves know this? On what basis does he write this? In general, how does Graves show that he knows what he is writing about? What kinds of evidence does he use in the essay?

5. In trying to recast the reader's perceptions of Benedict Arnold, Graves refocuses the reader's view of other Revolutionary War leaders, notably Samuel Adams and George Washington. How is Washington characterized in this essay? How does Graves generally go about describing a character? What does this process say about Graves's own view of the historian's task?

6. How much loyalty do we owe to our country? What could justify rebellion against the state?

7. At one point Graves writes that if Congress had let certain men conduct the war as they wished to, the colonists would not have had to call in the French. This statement is reminiscent of several statements made in connection with the Korean and Vietnam wars. Do you think it is inevitable that politicians will get

in the way of fighting men's good instincts? Is there any sense in which they should?

8. Do you believe that Arnold and others probably fought the Revolutionary War primarily for economic reasons, and not for enduring principles of liberty and justice? Do you believe that what you learned about the war in history classes was American "propaganda"? How do you react to such possibilities?

QUESTIONS ABOUT GRAVES'S RHETORICAL STRATEGIES

1. Graves takes some time at the beginning of the essay to define what he means by the term *traitor*. How does this definition work in terms of Graves's rhetorical strategy? Would it be possible to undermine his *entire* argument by disagreeing with this definition? What distinction does he make between a traitor and a rebel?
2. At one point Graves classifies Arnold with "men of honor." Is it fair for him to do this? Is he simply assuming what he must prove?
3. Graves refers to Arnold as a "wide-awake merchant." What does this suggest about Arnold and his motivations? Is Graves implying something about the other revolutionaries?
4. In writing about a character or an event, historians often make comparisons to establish meaning. Consider the following statements about the American revolutionaries:

   . . . the Revolutionary Committees organized a newspaper and pamphlet propaganda campaign of the most inventive and sensational sort, as a means of inciting the luke-warms and don't cares into active rebellion. It was a technique . . . finally perfected by Hitler and Goebbels when they set themselves to impose their Nazi creed on all Germans everywhere.

   What is the rhetorical effect of this statement? Is this a fair comparison for a historian to make?
5. In this essay Graves deals with a number of battles. He mentions "Washington's capture at Trenton of a thousand elderly, homesick, forcibly enlisted Hessians" and later, his trapping of "six thousand sick and hungry British" who were already virtually captured by French troops. Compare his treatment of Arnold's career as a soldier. What differences do you see in terms of the details Graves selects? How do these differences affect the validity of Graves's argument? How do they affect the validity of the history that Graves presents? Is this a legitimate rhetorical technique for a historian?
6. Several times Graves uses words like *perhaps* and *might*. For example, at one point he writes that "the increase [in money as recompense] is perhaps a measure not so much of greed, as of increased resentment of what he [Arnold] believed to be the dishonesty of Congress in delaying payment of moneys due him. . . ." How do words like this, which show some uncertainty on Graves's part, affect a reader? Is a historian wise to use hedging words like *perhaps*?
7. At the conclusion of the essay, Graves writes of "the incubus of a hereditary nobility." What is an incubus, and how is it appropriate in this context? Do

you find it strange that Graves, who was a British subject, should write of the nobility in this manner?

8. Why does Graves gloss so quickly over the end of Arnold's life? Is it simply because he feels that he has presented his argument and that the rest of Arnold's life is irrelevant?

WRITING FROM WITHIN AND ABOUT HISTORY AND ITS STUDY

Writing for Yourself

1. In your journal, react to a situation or person that you have seen interpreted in starkly different ways.
2. In your journal, make at least three distinctions between a *rebel* and a *traitor*. List several historical figures who might fit into one of those categories.

Writing for Nonacademic Audiences

1. You are asked to return to your middle school and role-play the part of a British historian, defending the actions of the British during the American Revolutionary War. You choose to focus on the events leading up to the Boston Tea Party. Write up the notes you will use to deliver your twenty-minute presentation.
2. Focus on the trial of one person from the twentieth century who was convicted for spying on the United States for the Soviet Union. Write a feature article on that person's trial, a feature that could appear in a prominent newspaper in the United States. Then write another feature article on the same trial, a feature that could have appeared in a prominent Soviet newspaper.

Writing for Academic Audiences

1. Read Richard Hofstadter's essay "Abraham Lincoln and the Self-Made Myth," found in his *The American Political Tradition* (1948). In this essay, Hofstadter proposes a revisionist history of Abraham Lincoln, especially when he comes to deal with the Emancipation Proclamation. Write a short (250-word) review of the article, evaluating the ways in which Hofstadter deals with his evidence.
2. For a course in views on history, write a 1,500-word paper in which you take a position on whether a historian can ever write about events in time without some kind of bias.
3. Read over Graves's first two paragraphs, which interpret the actions of Judas. After reading a Biblical account of Judas's actions (Matthew 26.1-5, 47-56; 27.1-10), write a 750-word essay for an introductory class in historical studies, in which you are studying ways to interpret historical facts. Does the interpretation that Graves gives seem credible? Evaluate his interpretation.
4. Do some research on people in the twentieth century who betrayed secrets of Western countries to countries of the Eastern Bloc. For a history course in Cold War Politics, write a 1,000-word essay analyzing these people's basic motivations.
5. Do some research on the dropping of the nuclear bombs on Nagasaki and Hiroshima in 1945. After reading through contemporary newspaper accounts of

those incidents (you might want to use *The New York Times* for this), find out what the reaction of the Soviet Union was to these bombs. Write a 1,000-word essay for a political science course in international relations describing the Soviet reaction and speculating on why they may have reacted in that manner.

6. For a course in modern American history, write a 1,500-word paper in which you evaluate the claim that American politicians, not American soldiers, lost the war in Vietnam. (You may want to begin by consulting Barbara Tuchman's *The March of Folly* [New York, 1984].)

Fernand Braudel

(1902–1985)

Fernand Braudel is widely regarded as one of the great contemporary historians. During his career he held many different academic positions. As a young man he served as a high school history teacher in Algiers, Algeria. At the time of his death he was an honorary professor of modern history at the College de France.

During World War II, Braudel was captured in France by the Nazis and held as a prisoner of war from 1940–1945. During this time, he performed one of the more amazing feats of memory and scholarship of all time. Drawing upon no written sources, relying only upon his memory of the documents he had explored in archives before the war, he wrote his doctoral dissertation, filling one school copybook after the next and mailing them out of the prison camp to safety. After the war he success-fully defended his dissertation, and later he turned it into a classic of historical schol-arship, the two-volume The Mediterranean and the Mediterranean World in the Age of Philip II. *When this work appeared in English (Volume I in 1972, Volume II in 1973), more and more people were able to recognize it for the masterpiece that it is.*

Braudel belongs to a discourse community often called the Annales School of History. The school got this name because many of its most prominent members at one time or another either edited or contributed to the journal Annales d'histoire économique et sociale, *which was founded in 1929 by Lucien Febvre and Marc Bloch to help express a new approach to history. Annales school writers rejected history as the recounting of great events, the story of the actions of a few great men, and the depiction of a steady stream of progress to a state of spiritual or social perfection. The Annales school writers sought what they called a "total history." They examined as many geographic, ecological, economic, political, religious, and technological forces at work in a period of history as they could. They used these forces to try to explain the collective mental structures of a group of people at a particular time. In this effort, they had to adopt methods from many different academic disciplines.*

Anyone who briefly skims Braudel's The Mediterranean and the Mediterranean World in the Age of Philip II *sees that Braudel examines sources of information that other historians would ignore. He examines schedules for shipping, records about crops, and transcripts of judicial proceedings. Repeatedly he shows how the nature of Spain and the Mediterranean region influenced the policies of King Philip II of Spain.*

In anthologizing only a part of a book, we probably do more injustice to one who tries to write a "total history" than to any other kind of historian. Yet a part of The Mediterranean *can give readers a good indication of what the whole is like. What follows is a selection from Volume I. In it Braudel explores the role of the environ-*

ment in shaping the world for civilization around the Mediterranean Sea during the
fifteenth and sixteenth centuries.

THE MEDITERRANEAN AS A PHYSICAL UNIT: CLIMATE AND HISTORY

> . . . the wanderings of Ulysses, ever under the same climate.
> J. de Barros, *Asia*, I. IV, p. 160.

It would be difficult to recognize any unity in this dense, composite, and ill-   1
defined world we have described at such length other than that of being the
meeting place of many peoples, and the melting-pot of many histories.*
Nevertheless it is significant that at the heart of this human unit, occupying
an area smaller than the whole, there should be a source of physical unity, a
climate, which has imposed its uniformity on both landscape and ways of
life. Its significance is demonstrated by contrast with the Atlantic. The ocean
too is a human unit and one of the most vigorous of the present day world; it
too has been a meeting place and a melting-pot of history. But the Atlantic
complex lacks a homogeneous centre comparable to the source of that even
light which shines at the heart of the Mediterranean. The Atlantic, stretching
from pole to pole, reflects the colours of all the earth's climates.

The Mediterranean of the vines and olive trees consists, as we know,   2
only of a few narrow coastal strips, ribbons of land bordering the sea. This
falls very short of the historical Mediterranean, but it is of great importance
that the Mediterranean complex should have taken its rhythm from the uniform band of climate and culture at its centre, so distinctive that it is to this
that the adjective "Mediterranean" is usually applied. Such a force operating
at the centre could not fail to have far-reaching repercussions, since it affects
all movements into and out of the Mediterranean. Nor is this climate merely
confined to the coastal strips, for since they surround the whole sea, it is also
the climate of the waters in between. That identical or near-identical worlds
should be found on the borders of countries as far apart and in general terms
as different as Greece, Spain, Italy, North Africa; that these worlds should
live at the same rhythm; that men and goods should be able to move from

---

*Paul Valéry, "Réflexions sur l'acier," in: *Acier*, 1938, no. 1. [This and all the following notes
  are Braudel's. Some of them refer to other pages in *The Mediterranean*].

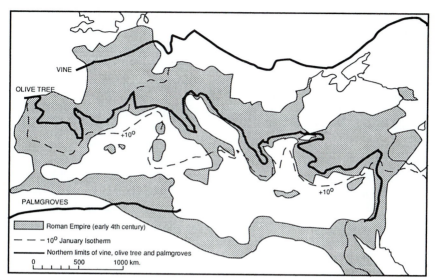

Fig. 1. The *"true"* Mediterranean, from the olive tree to the great palm groves. The limit of the palm groves refers only to *large*, compact groves. The limit for the date-palm growing isolated or in small clumps is much further north.

one to another without any need for acclimatization: such living identity implies the living unity of the sea. It is a great deal more than a beautiful setting.

THE UNITY OF THE CLIMATE

Above the Mediterranean of land and water stretches the Mediterranean of the sky, having little or no connection with the landscapes below and, in fact, independent of local physical conditions. It is created by the breath of two external forces: the Atlantic Ocean, its neighbour to the west, and the Sahara, its neighbour to the south. The Mediterranean itself is not responsible for the sky that looks down on it.*

The Atlantic and the Sahara. Within this open-ended area, two forces are at work, turn by turn: the Sahara brings dry air, clear light, the vast blue sky; the Atlantic, when it is not spreading clouds and rain, sends in abundance that grey mist and moist air which is more widespread than one would think in the Mediterranean atmosphere during the "winter semester." The early Orientalist painters created an enduring false impression with their glowing palettes. In October, 1869, Fromentin, leaving Messina by boat, noted, "grey skies, cold wind, a few drops of rain on the awning. It is sad, it could be the

---

* Emmanuel de Martonne, *Géographie Universelle*, vol. VI, I, 1942, p. 317, ". . . it is not the breath of the Mediterranean which gives Provence its skies."

Baltic."* Earlier, in February, 1848, he had fled towards the Sahara from the persistent grey mists of the Mediterranean winter: "there was no interval that year," he wrote, "between the November rains and the heavy winter rains, which had lasted for three and a half months with hardly a day's respite."† All natives of Algiers must at one time or another have had occasion to see newcomers aghast at the torrential downpours over the city.

The rains have always been a fact of life throughout the region. In Florence, notes a diarist for the entry 24th January, 1651,‡ the inclement weather has lasted five months, "per avere durato a piovere quasi cinque mesi" [Editors' translation: "to have a duration of rain of five months"]. The previous year,§ Capua had been swamped by torrential rains. In fact there was hardly a winter when the rivers did not burst their banks and the towns were not subjected to the terrors and destruction of flooding. Venice suffered more than most, of course. In November, 1443,‖ her losses were enormous, "quasi mezo million di ducati" [Editors' translation: "almost a half million ducats"]; on 18th December, 1600, there was an identical disaster, the *lidi*, the canals, the houses, the private stores at street level, the public stores of salt, grain, and spices all suffering great damage, "con dano di un million d'oro" [Editors' translation: "with damage of a million in gold"], which is also evidence that prices had risen in the meantime.¶

In winter, or more precisely between the September equinox and the March equinox, the Atlantic influence is predominant. The anticyclone over the Azores lets in the Atlantic depressions that move one after another into the warm waters of the Mediterranean; they come in either from the Bay of Biscay, moving quickly over Aquitaine; or, like ships, they enter the Mediterranean by the Straits of Gibraltar and the Spanish coasts. Wherever they enter they cross the Mediterranean from west to east, travelling quickly. They make the winter weather most unsettled, bringing rain, causing sudden winds to spring up, and constantly agitating the sea, which when whipped by the *mistral*, the *noroît* or the *bora*, is often so white with foam, that it looks like a plain covered with snow, or "strewn with ashes" as a sixteenth-century traveller described it.** Above Toledo, the Atlantic humidity contributes in winter to bring those turbulent and dramatic skies of storm and light painted by El Greco.

So every year, and often violently, the Atlantic banishes the desert far away to the south and east. In winter rain falls over the Algerian provinces and sometimes in the heart of the Sahara. Rain falls even on the mountains

---

* *Voyage d'Égypte*, 1935, p. 43.
† *Un été dans le Sahara*, 1908, p. 3.
‡ Baldinucci, *Giornale di ricordi*, 24th January, 1651, Marciana, Ital., **VI, XCIV**.
§ *Recueil des Gazettes*, year 1650, p. 1557, Naples, 2nd November, 1650.
‖ A.d.S. Venice, Cronaca veneta, Brera 51, 10th November, 1443.
¶ Marciana, Cronaca savina, f° 372, 18th December, 1600; there was similar constant rain ("per tre mesi continui") at Christmas 1598, *ibid.*, f° 371 and 371 v°.
** Peter Martyr, *op. cit.*, p. 53 note.

of western Arabia. The anti-desert is not the Mediterranean, as Paul Morand once wrote, but the Atlantic Ocean.

Around the spring equinox, everything changes again, rather suddenly, 8 at about the time when, as the calendar of the Maghreb says, the season for grafting trees arrives, and the first notes of the nightingale are heard.* Of real springtime there is little or none; perhaps a short week that suddenly brings out leaves and flowers. As soon as the winter rains are over, the desert begins to move back and invade the sea, including the surrounding mountains, right up to their peaks. It moves westwards, and above all northwards, passing beyond the furthest limits of the Mediterranean world. In France, the burning air from the south every summer warms the southern Alps, invades most of the Rhône valley, crosses the basin of Aquitaine as a warm current, and often carries the searing drought through the Garonne region to the distant coasts of southern Brittany.†

Torrid summer then reigns uncontested in the centre of the Mediterra- 9 nean zone. The sea is astonishingly calm: in July and August it is like a millpond; little boats sail far out and low-lying galleys could venture without fear from port to port.‡ The summer semester was the best time for shipping, piracy, and war.

The physical causes of this dry, torrid summer are clear. As the sun 10 moves further north, the anticyclone of the Azores increases in size again. When their passage is blocked, the long chain of Atlantic depressions is halted. The obstacle is removed only when autumn approaches; then the Atlantic invasion begins again.

A homogeneous climate. The extreme limits of such a climate could be said 11 to lie far from the shores of the Mediterranean, if they are extended on one side, over Europe, to the regions touched by the Saharan drought in summer, and in the other direction to the regions in Asia and Africa, even in the middle of the vast steppes, which are affected by the rain of the Atlantic depressions. But to set such wide limits is clearly misleading. The Mediterranean climate is neither one nor the other of the forces we have described; it is precisely the zone where they overlap, a combination of the two. To overemphasize either of its components would deform the Mediterranean climate. To extend it too far to the east or south would turn it into a steppe or desert climate, to take it too far north would bring it into the zone where the west winds predominate. The true Mediterranean climate occupies only a fairly narrow zone.

Indeed, it is not easy to define its limits. To do so would require taking 12 note of the smallest details, not necessarily physical, for climates are not mea-

---

Annuaire de monde musulman, 1925, p. 8.
† E. de Martonne, *op. cit.*, p. 296.
‡ Ernest Lavisse, "Sur les galères du Roi," in *Revue de Paris*, November, 1897.

sured only by the usual gauges of temperature, pressure, wind, and rainfall, but can be traced in thousands of signs at ground level, as has been suggested by André Siegfried of the Ardèche,* by Léo Larguier of the border between Languedoc and Lozère,† and J. L. Vaudoyer of the transitional zones between the different parts of Provence.‡ But these are points of detail. In general, the geographer's well-known observation must be accepted without question: the Mediterranean climate lies between the northern limit of the olive tree and the northern limit of the palm grove. Between these frontiers we may count the Italian (or rather Apennine) peninsula, Greece, Cyrenaica, Tunisia, and, elsewhere, a few narrow coastal strips rarely more than 200 kilometres wide. For the mountain barriers soon loom up. The Mediterranean climate is often the climate only of a coastal fringe, the riviera, bordering the sea, a ribbon as narrow as the coastal strip in the Crimea where figs, olives, oranges, and pomegranates all grow freely,§ though only in the southern part of the peninsula.

But this narrow framework, by reason of its very narrowness, provides 13 undeniable homogeneity, both from north to south and from east to west.

From north to south the entire coastal riviera forms only a thin length- 14 wise band on the globe. Its widest point from north to south is the distance of 1100 kilometres from the northern end of the Adriatic to the coast of Tripolitania, and that is an exception. In fact the greatest widths vary on an average between 600 and 800 kilometres for the eastern basin and 740 kilometres between Algiers and Marseilles. The entire area, both land and sea, forms a long belt straddling the 37th and 38th parallels. The differences in latitude are not great. They are sufficient to explain the contrasts between the northern shores and the southern, the latter being the warmer. The mean difference in temperature between Marseilles and Algiers is 4°C. The 10°C. January isotherm on the whole follows the general shape of the sea, cutting off southern Spain and southern Italy, regions that have more in common with Africa than with Europe. In general, all parts of the Mediterranean experience what is perceptibly the same "geometrical" climate.

From east to west there is some variation owing to the fact that moisture 15 from the Atlantic is less pronounced and also later in arrival the further east one travels.

These variations are all worthy of note. At a time when climatologists 16 are attentive to detail, the Mediterranean is rightly regarded by them as a complex of different climates that are to be distinguished one from another.

---

* *Vue générale de la Méditerranée*, 1943, p. 64–65. English translation by D. Hemming, *The Mediterranean*, London, 1948, p. 87.

† Léo Larguier, "Le Gard et les Basses Cévennes," in *Maisons et villages de France, op. cit.*, I, 1943.

‡ *Op. cit.*, p. 183. For the Volterra region, see Paul Bourget, *Sensations d'Italie*, 1902, p. 5.

§ Comte de Rochechouart, *Souvenirs sur la Révolution, L'Empire et la Restauration*, 1889, p. 110; vines from Madeira and Spain had taken to the soil of the Crimea.

But that does not disprove their fundamental, close relationship and undeniable unity. It is a matter of some importance to the historian to find almost everywhere within his field of study the same climate, the same seasonal rhythm, the same vegetation, the same colours and, when the geological architecture recurs, the same landscapes, identical to the point of obsession; in short, the same ways of life. To Michelet, the "stony" Languedoc interior recalled Palestine. For hundreds of writers, Provence has been more Greek than Greece, unless, that is, the true Greece is not to be found on some Sicilian shore. The Iles d'Hyères would not be out of place among the Cyclades, except that they are greener.* The lagoon of Tunis recalls the Lagoon of Chioggia. Morocco is another, more sun-baked Italy.†

Everywhere can be found the same eternal trinity: wheat, olives, and 17 vines, born of the climate and history; in other words an identical agricultural civilization, identical ways of dominating the environment. The different regions of the sea are not, therefore, complementary.‡ They have the same granaries, wine-cellars and oil presses, the same tools, flocks, and often the same agrarian traditions and daily preoccupations. What prospers in one region will do equally well in the next. In the sixteenth century all the coastal regions produced wax, wool, and skins, *montonini* or *vacchini;* they all grew (or could have grown) mulberry trees and raised silkworms. They are all without exception lands of wine and vineyards, even the Moslem countries. Who has praised wine more highly than the poet of Islam? At Tor on the Red Sea there were vines,§ and they even grew in far-off Persia, where the wine of Shīrāz was highly prized.

With such identity of production, it follows that similar goods can be 18 found in any country bordering the sea. In the sixteenth century there was grain from Sicily and grain from Thrace; there was wine from Naples, *greco* or *latino*, the latter more plentiful than the former,‖ but there were also the many casks of wine shipped from Frontignan; there was the Lombardy rice, but also rice from Valencia, Turkey and Egypt. And to compare goods of modest quality, there was wool from North Africa and wool from the Balkans.

The Mediterranean countries, then, were in competition with each 19 other; at least they should have been. They had more goods for exchange outside their climatic environment than within it. But the sixteenth century was a time when the total volume of exchange was small, the prices modest and the distances travelled short. Arrangements had somehow to be reached

---

*Jules Sion, *La France Méditerranéenne*, 1929, p. 77.
†J. and J. Tharaud, *Marrakech ou les seigneurs de l'Atlas*, 1929, p. 135.
‡A. Siegfried, *op. cit.*, p. 148, 326.
§Belon, *op. cit.*, p. 131.
‖A.d.S. Naples, Sommaria Consultationum, 2 f° 223, 2nd October, 1567. In the preceding years, good or bad, the kingdom of Naples had produced: *vini latini 23,667 busti; vini grechi, dulci et Mangiaguera, Manglaguera, 2319 busti.*

between neighbours, between regions that were rich or poor in manpower, and the chief problem was the supply of food for the towns, constantly on the lookout for all kinds of foodstuffs and in particular those that could be transported without too much spoilage: sacks of almonds from the Provençal coast, barrels of salted tunny or meat, sacks of beans from Egypt, not to mention casks of oil and grain, for which, of course, demand was greatest. So identical production did not restrict exchanges within the Mediterranean as much as one might expect, at least during the sixteenth century.

In human terms the unity of the climate* has had many other conse- 20 quences. At a very early stage it prepared the ground for the establishment of identical rural economies. From the first millennium before Christ the civilization of the vine and the olive tree spread westwards from the eastern part of the sea. This basic uniformity was established far back in time, nature and man working to the same end.

As a result, in the sixteenth century, a native of the Mediterranean, 21 wherever he might come from, would never feel out of place in any part of the sea. In former times, it is true, in the heroic age of the first Phoenician and Greek voyages of antiquity, colonization was a dramatic upheaval, but not in later years. To later colonial settlers their journey simply meant finding in a new place the same trees and plants, the same food on the table that they had known in their homeland; it meant living under the same sky, watching the same familiar seasons.

On the other hand when a native of the Mediterranean had to leave the 22 shores of the sea, he was uneasy and homesick; like the soldiers of Alexander the Great when he left Syria and advanced towards the Euphrates;† or the sixteenth-century Spaniards in the Low Countries, miserable among the "fogs of the North." For Alonso Vázquez and the Spaniards of his time (and probably of all time) Flanders was "the land where there grows neither thyme, nor lavender, figs, olives, melons, or almonds; where parsley, onions, and lettuces have neither juice nor taste; where dishes are prepared, strange to relate, with butter from cows instead of oil. . . ."‡ The Cardinal of Aragon, who reached the Netherlands in 1517 with his cook and his own supplies, shared this opinion. "Because of the butter and dairy produce which is so widely used in Flanders and Germany," he concluded, "these countries are

---

*Similarity of climate . . . encourages penetration into regions similar to those left behind, in order that life may continue in accustomed ways," P. Vidal de la Blache, *op. cit.*, p. 179.
†A. Radet, *Alexandre le Grand*, 1931, p. 139.
‡Alonso Vázquez, *Los sucesos de Flandes* . . . extracts published in L. P. Gachard, *Les Biblio-thèques de Madrid* . . ., Brussels, 1875, p. 459, ff., quoted by L. Pfandl, *Jeanne la Folle*, Fr. trans. by R. de Liedekerke, 1938, p. 48, Cf. the following from Maximilien Sorre, *Les Fondements biologiques de la géographie humaine*, 1943, p. 268: "one of the peculiarities of the peoples who lived on the periphery of the Mediterranean world, which most astonished the Ancients, was the use of cows' butter: those accustomed to olive oil viewed this with shocked surprise. Even an Italian, like Pliny, had the same reaction, forgetting that after all the use of olive oil had not been established in Italy for so very long."

overrun with lepers."* A strange land indeed! An Italian cleric stranded at Bayeux in Normandy in the summer of 1529 thought himself "for del mondo"† [Editors' translation: "out of the world"].

This explains the facility with which the Mediterranean dweller trav- 23 elled from port to port; these were not true transplantations, merely removals, and the new occupant would feel quite at home in his new habitat. In striking contrast was the exhausting process of colonizing the New World carried out by the Iberians. Traditional history has preserved, with more or less accuracy, the names of those men and women who were the first to grow wheat, vines, and olives in Peru or in New Spain. Not without courage, battling against the hostile nature of the climate and soil, these Mediterranean expatriates tried to build a new Mediterranean culture in the tropics. The attempt failed. Although there were occasional successes the rural and alimentary civilization of their native lands could not be transplanted to the soil of Spanish and Portuguese America, a zone of maize, manioc, pulque, and before long of rum. One of the great trans-Atlantic supply operations from Spain and Portugal was devoted to maintaining artificially in the New World the alimentary civilization of the Mediterranean: ships laden with flour, wine, and oil left Seville and Lisbon for the other side of the ocean.‡

Yet it was Mediterranean man who almost alone of Europeans survived 24 the transplantation to a new land. Perhaps it was because he was already accustomed to the harsh conditions of one climate, that of the Mediterranean, which is not always kind to the human organism, and was hardened by his struggle against endemic malaria and the regular scourge of plague. Perhaps too it was because he had always been schooled in sobriety and frugality in his native land. The deceptively welcoming climate of the Mediterranean can sometimes be cruel and murderous. It is the filter that has prevented men from distant lands from settling on the shores of the warm sea. They may arrive as conquerors, yesterday's barbarians, today's men of property: but how long can they resist the "scorching heat of summer and . . . the malaria"?§ "The masters come and go," wrote Walter Bauer of Sicily, "the others remain, and it is a romance without words,"‖ always the same.

Drought: The scourge of the Mediterranean. The disadvantage of this cli- 25 mate for human life lies in the annual distribution of rainfall. It rains a good

* Antonio de Beatis, *Itinerario di Monsignor il cardinale de Aragona . . . incominciato nel anno 1517 . . .* ed. L. Pastor, Freiburg-im-Breisgau, 1905, p. 121. Food at the very least "corrompedora dos estômagos" says a Portuguese observer, L. Mendes de Vasconcellos, *Do sitio de Lisboa*, Lisbon, 1608, p. 113. This referred to the "nações do Norte e em parte de França e Lombardia."
† The dean of Bayeux to the Marquis of Mantua, A.d.S., Mantua, Gonzaga, Francia, series E, f° 637, 1st June, 1529.
‡ François Chevalier, "Les cargaisons des flottes de la Nouvelle Espagne vers 1600," in *Revista de Indias*, 1943.
§ P. Vidal de la Blache, *op. cit.*, p. 182; Bonjean, in *Cahiers du Sud*, May, 1943, p. 329–330.
‖ In O. Benndorf, *op. cit.*, p. 62, Colette, *La naissance du Jour*, 1941, p. 8–9.

deal: in some places there is exceedingly high precipitation.* But the rains fall in autumn, winter, and spring, chiefly in autumn and spring. It is broadly the opposite of a monsoon climate. The monsoon climate fruitfully combines warmth and water. The Mediterranean climate separates these two important factors of life, with predictable consequences. The "glorious skies" of the summer semester have their costly drawbacks. Everywhere drought leads to the disappearance or reduction of running waters and natural irrigation: the Mediterranean countries are the zone of the *oueds* and the *fiumari*. It arrests the growth of herbaceous vegetation: so crops and plants must adapt to drought† and learn to use as quickly and profitably as possible the precious sources of water. Wheat, "a winter plant,"‡ hastens to ripen and complete its active cycle by May or June—in Egypt and Andalusia by April.§ The olives of Tunisia are ripened by the autumn rains. From earliest times dry-farming seems to have been practised everywhere, empirically‖ and not only on the initiative of the Phoenicians. From earliest times irrigation in all its diverse forms seems to have penetrated the Mediterranean regions from the East. Today (cf. K. Sapper's map),¶ the limit of the *Kunstbewässerung* is appreciably the same as that of the Mediterranean climate. Many plants, both herbaceous and shrub, which had adapted in the course of evolution to a dry climate, came to the Mediterranean along the same paths as the hydraulic techniques. As we have noted, during the first thousand years before Christ, the culture of the vine and olive spread from the eastern regions of the sea to the West.** The Mediterranean, by its climate was predestined for shrub culture. It is not only a garden, but, providentially, a land of fruit-bearing trees.

On the other hand the climate does not favour the growth of ordinary 26 trees and forest coverings. At any rate it has not protected them. Very early the primeval forests of the Mediterranean were attacked by man and much, too much, reduced. They were either restored incompletely or not at all; hence the large area covered by scrub and underbrush, the debased forms of the forest. Compared to northern Europe, the Mediterranean soon became a deforested region. When Chateaubriand passed through Morea, it was "almost entirely bereft of trees."†† The traveller crossing from the bare stones of Herzegovina to the wooded slopes of Bosnia enters a different world, as

---

* 4 metres a year in the Gulf of Cattaro.
† See the article by Schmidthüser, "Vegetationskunde Süd-Frankreichs und Ost-Spaniens" in *Geogr. Zeitschr.*, 1934, p. 409–422. On deforestation, see H. von Trotha Treyden, "Die Entwaldung der Mittelmeerländer" in *Pet. Mitt.*, 1916, and the bibliography.
‡ According to Woiekof, quoted in Jean Brunhes, *Géographie humaine*, 4th ed., p. 133.
§ G. Botero, *op. cit.*, I, p. 10.
‖ André Siegfried, *op. cit.*, p. 84–85; Jean Brunhes, *op. cit.*, p. 261.
¶ "Die Verbreitung der künstlichen Feldbewässerung," in *Pet. Mitt.*, 1932.
** M. Sorre, *Les foundements biologiques . . . op. cit.*, p. 146.
†† *Itinéraire de Paris a Jerusalem*, 1811, p. 120.

Jean Brunhes has noted.* Almost everywhere, wood was expensive,† often very expensive indeed. At Medina del Campo "richer in fairs than in *montes* [i.e., wooded mountains]," the humanist Antonio de Guevara, reflecting on his budget, concluded, "all told, the wood cost us as much as what was cooking in the pot."‡

Another consequence is the scarcity in the Mediterranean zone of true 27 pastures. As a result there are few of the cattle so useful to the rich farming, necessarily based on the use of manure, practised in the northern countries where the soil is so washed by the rain that it loses its fertile elements—of which the Mediterranean drought is, it is true, a better guardian. Cattle are only found in really large numbers in Egypt and in the rainy Balkans, on the northern margins of the Mediterranean, or on high lands where more rain falls than elsewhere. Sheep and goats (the former raised for their wool more than for their flesh) could not compensate for the deficiency in meat rations. Rabelais' monk of Amiens, "quite angry, scandalized, and out of all patience," who with his travelling companions is contemplating the beauties of Florence has the following to say, "Now at Amiens," he explains, "in four, nay five times less ground than we have trod in our contemplations, I could have shown you above fourteen streets of roasting cooks, most ancient, savoury and aromatic. I cannot imagine what kind of pleasure you have taken in gazing on the lions and Africans (so methinks you call their tigers) near the belfry, or in ogling the porcupines and estridges [ostriches] in the Lord Philip Strozzi's palace. Faith and truth, I had rather see a good fat goose at the spit."§ Apropos of the Mediterranean a geographer once wrote jokingly to me, "Not enough meat and too many bones."‖

To the northerner, even in the sixteenth century, the livestock of the 28 Mediterranean seemed deficient, the cattle often skinny and the sheep weighing little. "In 1577, Montmorency and his army ate 8000 sheep brought from all over lower Languedoc. Their average weight "l'ung portant l'autre" [Editors' translation: "the one carrying the other"] was 30 *livres* per beast, or about 12 modern kilos. This was next to nothing and the animal was almost worthless: 4 *livres* each or a little over an *écu* for a sheep . . . ."¶ At Valladolid, for 11,312 sheep slaughtered between 23rd June and 5th December, 1586, an average yield of 11.960 kilogrammes of meat per beast has been calculated (26 Castilian pounds). Similarly for 2302 cattle slaughtered during the same period, the meat per beast was 148.12 kilogrammes (322 Castilian

---

* *Géographie humaine*, 4th ed., p. 51, note 1.
† Even at Constantinople, Robert Mantran, *Istanbul dans la seconde moitié du XVIIe siècle, Essai d'histoire institutionelle économique et sociale*, 1962, p. 29.
‡ *Biblioteca de Autores Españoles* (B.A.E.), **XIII**, p. 93.
§ *Le Quart livre du noble Pantagruel*, Urquhart & Motteux trans., 1904, ed., p. 49.
‖ Letter from Pierre Gourou, 27th June, 1949.
¶ E. Le Roy Ladurie, *op. cit.*, p. 118–119.

pounds).* So the weight of the stock was low; the same was true of horses. There were some very fine horses in the Mediterranean, Turks, jennets from Naples, Andalusian chargers, and Barbary horses from North Africa, but they were all saddle horses, fast and nimble, and went out of fashion during the following century which was to see the popularity of the heavy horses, asses, and mules of the North. Increasingly, for the mails, for the carriages then coming into fashion, for the artillery's gun-carriages and limbers, the strength of the horses was becoming a decisive factor. Dantiscus, who landed on 4th December, 1522 at Codalia on the Cantabrian coast, set off towards León with six pack horses "non tamen tam bonis," he wrote, "ut sunt apud nos qui plumbum ferunt ex Cracovia in Hungariam . . . ."† [Editors' translation: "Not as good as those that carry lead from Cracow to Hungary."] The comparison with the horses which transported lead from Cracow to Hungary is too spontaneous to be mistaken. Besides what fodder was there for horses in the south? Oats had only just made their appearance in certain regions, such as Languedoc‡ and human mouths competed with the horses for barley. Pity the French horses, who once over the Spanish border began to whinny with dismay, according to Barthélémy Joly, for now they would be on a diet of "short and unappetizing straw."§

Without suggesting that it explains everything, we might note that if   29 the swing-plough, which did little more than scratch the surface of the earth, survived in the Mediterranean countryside, it was not only because of the fragility of the thin layer of loose topsoil, but also because the teams of oxen or mules were not strong enough. Shallow ploughing, the *raies*, were done as often as seven or eight times a year.‖ It would have been better, as time was to prove, to plough more deeply, as in the North, where the wheeled plough with swivelling fore-carriage was a great instrument of progress. In Languedoc, the *mousse* or pseudo-plough imitated from the North, could not fulfil this role and was little used.¶ The poor *aratores* of Languedoc "untiringly scratched the surface of the fallow fields in vain: they bear no comparison" with the hefty *charrueurs* of the Ile-de-France or Picardy.**

The truth is that the Mediterranean has struggled against a fundamen-   30 tal poverty, aggravated but not entirely accounted for by circumstances. It affords a precarious living, in spite of its apparent or real advantages. It is easy to be deceived by its famous charm and beauty. Even as experienced a geographer as Philippson was dazzled, like all visitors from the North, by the

---

* B. Bennassar, "L'alimentation d'une ville espagnole au XVIe siècle. Quelques données sur les approvisionnements et la consommation de Valladolid," in *Annales E.S.C.*, 1961, p. 733.
† Dantiscus to the King of Poland, Valladolid, 4th January, 1523, Czartoryski Library, no. 36, f° 55.
‡ E. Le Roy Ladurie, *op. cit.*, p. 181.
§ Barthélémy Joly, *Voyage en Espagne*, p. 9.
‖ E. Le Roy Ladurie, *op. cit.*, p. 78.
¶ *Ibid.*, p. 80.
** *Ibid.*, p. 79.

sun, the colours, the warmth, the winter roses, the early fruits. Goethe at Vicenza was captivated by the popular street life with its open stalls and dreamed of taking back home with him a little of the magic air of the South. Even when one is aware of the reality it is difficult to associate these scenes of brilliance and gaiety with images of misery and physical hardship. In fact, Mediterranean man gains his daily bread by painful effort. Great tracts of land remain uncultivated and of little use. The land that does yield food is almost everywhere subject to biennial crop rotation that rules out any great productivity. Michelet again was the historian who best understood the basic harshness of all these lands, starting with his own Provence.

There is one visible sign of this poverty: the frugality that has never 31 failed to impress the northerner. The Fleming Busbecq, when in Anatolia, wrote in 1555, "I dare say that a man of our country spends more on food in one day than a Turk in twelve. . . . The Turks are so frugal and think so little of the pleasures of eating that if they have bread, salt, and some garlic or an onion and a kind of sour milk which they call *yoghoort*, they ask nothing more. They dilute this milk with very cold water and crumble bread into it and take it when they are hot and thirsty . . . it is not only palatable and digestible, but also possesses an extraordinary power of quenching the thirst."* This sobriety has often been noted as one of the great strengths of the Turkish soldier on campaign. He would be content with a little rice, ground meat dried in the sun, and bread coarsely cooked in the ashes of the camp fire.† The western soldier was more particular, perhaps because of the example of the many Germans and Swiss.‡

The peasants and even the city-dwellers of Greece, Italy, and Spain 32 were hardly more demanding than these Turks, whose frugal habits were noted only a century ago by Théophile Gautier, who was amazed that the sturdy *caïdjis*, with bulging muscles from their heavy work as oarsmen, could spend the whole day on board their *caïques*, eating almost nothing but raw cucumbers.§ "In Murcia," wrote Alexandre de Laborde in his *Itinéraire descriptif de l'Espagne* (1828), "one cannot find a servant girl during the summer, and many of those who have a position leave it when the fine weather comes. They can then easily find salad, some fruit, melons and especially red peppers, and these provisions are sufficient to keep them."‖ "I invited everyone to supper," writes Montaigne, adding (the incident took place at the

* *The Turkish Letters*, p. 52–53.
† G. Botero, *op. cit.*, **II**, p. 124.
‡ When he was required by Philip II to supply food for the Spanish and German soldiers crossing from Italy to Spain, the Grand Duke of Tuscany preferred to keep the salt meat, of which there was not enough to go round, for the Germans. The Spaniards had arrived first, but would not raise an uproar if they had to be content with rice and biscuit. Felipe Ruiz Martin, Introduction to *Lettres marchandes échangées entre Florence et Medina del Campo*, Paris, 1965.
§ *Voyage a Constantinople*, 1853, p. 97.
‖ P. 112.

Baths of Lucca), "because in Italy a banquet is the equivalent of a light meal in France."*

Commines on the other hand went into raptures over the abundant fare 33 of Venice. He had the excuse of being a foreigner. And Venice was Venice, a town privileged for food. Bandello himself was dazzled by the markets of the town, by the "abbondanza grandissima d'ogni sorte di cose da mangiare"† [Editors' translation: "greatest abundance of every sort of thing to eat"], and he is a reliable witness. But this luxurious market in a rich and well-situated town created, as we know, great problems of supply, and cost the Signoria much anxiety and vigilance.

Has the very small part played in Mediterranean literature by feasts and 34 banquets ever been remarked? Descriptions of meals—except of course princely tables—never suggest plenty.‡ In Bandello's novels, a good meal means a few vegetables, a little Bologna sausage, some tripe, and a cup of wine. In the Spanish literature of the Golden Age an empty stomach is a familiar character. Witness the ultra-classical Lazarillo de Tormes or his brother in *picardia*, Guzmán de Alfarache, eating a crust of hard bread without leaving a crumb for the ants.§ "May God save you from the plague coming down from Castille," the same Guzmán is told, "and from the famine coming up from Andalusia."‖ And we may remember Don Quixote's bills of fare, or the proverb: "If the lark flies over Castille, she must take her grain of corn with her."¶

Although the gardens, orchards, and seafoods may provide varied ad- 35 ditions, they supply what is essentially a frugal diet even today, "bordering on malnutrition in many cases."** This frugality results not from virtue or indifference to food as Busbecq would have called it, but from necessity.

The Mediterranean soil too is responsible for the poverty it inflicts on its 36 peoples, with its infertile limestone, the great stretches blighted with salt, the lands covered with *nitre*, as Pierre Belon called it,†† its rare deposits of loose soil, and the precariousness of its arable land. The thin layers of topsoil, which only the modest wooden swing-plough can scratch, are at the mercy of the wind or the flood waters. They are enabled to survive only by man's constant effort. Given these conditions, if the peasants' vigilance should be distracted during long periods of unrest, not only the peasantry but also the productive soil will be destroyed. During the disturbances of the Thirty Years' War, the German peasantry was decimated, but the land remained and with it the

---

* Journal de voyage en Italie, Collection "Hier" 1932, vol. **III**, p. 242.
† *Op. cit.*, **III**, p. 409.
‡ *Ibid.*, **IV**, p. 233, p. 340, **VI**, p. 400–401. Except in northern Italy.
§ Mateo Aleman, *Vida del picaro Guzmán de Alfarache*, **I**, part **I**, 3, p. 45.
‖ *Ibid.*, part **II**, 2, p. 163.
¶ Bory de Saint-Vincent, *Guide du voyageur en Espagne*, p. 281, quoted by Ch. Weiss, *L'Espagne depuis Philippe* **II**, 1844, vol. **II**, p. 74.
** M. Sorre, *op. cit.*, p. 267.
†† *Op. cit.*, p. 137 v°.

possibility of renewal. Here lay the superiority of the North. In the Mediterranean the soil dies if it is not protected by crops: the desert lies in wait for arable land and never lets go. It is a miracle if it is preserved or reconstituted by the labour of the peasants. Even modern figures prove this. Apart from forests, pastures, and specifically nonproductive land, cultivated land in about 1900 represented 46 per cent of the whole in Italy, 39.1 per cent in Spain, 34.1 per cent in Portugal, and only 18.6 per cent in Greece. On Rhodes, out of a total of 144,000 hectares, 84,000 are still uncultivated today.* On the southern shores of the sea the figures are even more disastrous.

But how much do even the cultivated lands yield? Very little, unless 37 there are exceptional conditions (of irrigation for instance) and for this the climate is responsible.

Harvests, in the Mediterranean, more than elsewhere, are at the mercy 38 of unstable elements. If a south wind blows just before harvest time, the wheat dries before it has completely ripened and reached its normal size; or if already ripe, it drops from the ear. To avoid this disaster in Spain, the peasants would often reap in the cool of the night, for the dry grain would fall to the ground during the day.† If floods lay waste the lowlands in winter, the sowing is endangered. If there are clear skies too early in spring, the crop that has already ripened is attacked by frost, sometimes irremediably. One can never be certain of the harvest until the last moment. At the end of January, 1574, it looked as if there would be a good harvest on Crete; there had been plenty of rain and more seed than usual had been sown. But, adds our source, may not these fine hopes be dashed in countries like this, subject to "pestilential fogs which blight the grain?"‡ The violent winds from the south that are dreaded in the Archipelago often ruined ripe harvests on Corfu§ and are still feared today throughout the cereal growing area of North Africa; this is the *sirocco*, against which there is no remedy and which in three days can destroy a whole year's work. One other item can be added to the list of dangers to the fields of the Mediterranean: the plague of locusts, a greater threat in the past than it is today.‖

In the sixteenth century it was rare for a harvest to escape in turn all 39 the dangers that threatened it. Yields were small, and in view of the limited space devoted to cereal growing, the Mediterranean was always on the verge of famine. A few changes in temperature and a shortage of rainfall were

---

* Charles Parain, *La Méditerranée, les hommes et leurs travaux*, 1936, p. 130.
† Alonso de Herrera, *op. cit.*, 1645, ed., p. 10 v° (particularly true of barley).
‡ A.d.S. Venice, 22nd January, 1574, Capi del C° dei X, Lettere Bª 286, fᵒˢ 8 and 9.
§ G. Botero, *Dell'isole*, p. 72.
‖ G. Vivoli, *Annali di Livorno*, 1842–1846, **III**, p. 18, an invasion of Tuscany by locusts (1541); at Verona, August, 1542 and June, 1553, Ludovico Moscardo, *Historia di Verona*, Verona, 1668, p. 412 and 417; in Hungary, Tebaldo Tebaldi to the Duke of Modena, Venice, 21st August, 1543, A.d.S. Modena; in Egypt, 1544 and 1572, Museo Correr, D. delle Rose, 46, f° 181; on Cyprus, 13th September, 1550, A.d.S. Venice, Senato Mar; 31, f° 42 v° to 43 v°; in the Camargue, 1614, J. F. Noble de la Lauzière, *op. cit.*, p. 446.

enough to endanger human life. Everything was affected accordingly, even politics. If there was no likelihood of a good barley crop on the borders of Hungary (for, in the Mediterranean, barley was the equivalent of oats in the North), it could be assumed that the Grand Turk would not go to war there that year; for how would the horses of the *spahis* be fed? If wheat was also short—as sometimes happened—in the three or four main sources of supply for the sea, whatever the plans of war drawn up during winter or spring, there would be no major war at harvest time, which was also the season of calm seas and great naval campaigns. So immediately brigandage on land and piracy on sea would redouble in vigour. Is it any wonder then, that the only detail of daily life that regularly finds its way into diplomatic correspondence concerns the harvests? It has rained, it has not rained, the wheat has not sprouted; Sicily promises well, but the Turkish harvest was poor, the Grand Turk will certainly not let any wheat out. Will this year be a year of scarcity, of *carestia*, of dearth?

The letters written by the majordomo Francisco Osorio to Philip II in 40 1558 informed the king at great length, in his northern exile, of the weather over the Peninsula. This citizen of Valladolid pays great attention to the colour of the sky, the state of the harvest and the price of bread. On 13th March, 1558, ". . . for two days now," he writes, "the weather here has been clear with plenty of sun and wind. It has not rained since the middle of January. The price of bread has risen somewhat and a 'pragmatic' has been instituted to fix the price in future. Since it was published the other day, the sky has become cloudy. This surely brings hope of rain in April. In Andalusia and Extremadura, as in the kingdom of Toledo it has rained and the weather is very favourable: the price of bread there has fallen greatly."* On 30th October, 1558, he writes: "The wheat harvest was abundant; there is a moderate amount of wine throughout the kingdom, sowing is well advanced everywhere. On the 26th it snowed all morning, with big flakes. Afterwards it rained heavily, which will be of great advantage to the sowing. From the weather here I am sure that it cannot be very warm in Brussels. The price of bread throughout the kingdom has fallen."†

That Philip II should be kept minutely informed of the variations in the 41 weather from seedtime onwards; that the price of bread should rise and fall depending on the rainfall; that these details should be found in a series of letters where one searches in vain for any other precise details of economic history: all this is very revealing of the state of the Mediterranean food supply in the sixteenth century. It was no mere "economic" problem, but a matter of life and death.

For famine, real famine when people died in the streets, was a reality. 42 In 1521, relates the Venetian Navagero, "there was such famine in Andalusia

* *CO DOIN*, **XXVII**, p. 191–192.
† *Ibid.*, p. 194–195.

that countless animals died and the countryside was deserted; many people died also. There was such drought that the wheat was lost and not a blade of grass could any longer be found in the fields; that year the breeds of Andalusian horses for the most part died out and they have not been restored to this day [1525]."* This was an extreme case. But we constantly find *carestia* recorded as the years go past; every government went in search of grain and had to organize public distributions to prevent people from dying of hunger, in which it was not always successful. During the second half of the century a particularly serious crisis affected the whole Mediterranean between 1586 and 1591, and this crisis opened up the Mediterranean to the northern ships. Even in a normal year life was never very comfortable or luxurious. Think of the Tuscans who at the end of the sixteenth century, with all their ploughed lands, vineyards, and mulberry trees, "con tutto ciò non raccolgono vettevaglie per un terzo dell'anno"!† [Editors' translation: "with all those provisions not collected for a third of the year!"]. Or think of the sentence in Guzmán's story, "it was a lean year because of the drought. Seville suffered greatly from it, for the city is sorely strained even in prosperous years. . . ."

A double constraint has always been at the heart of Mediterranean history: poverty and uncertainty of the morrow. This is perhaps the cause of the carefulness, frugality, and industry of the people, the motives that have been behind certain, almost instinctive, forms of imperialism, which are sometimes nothing more than the search for daily bread. To compensate for its weaknesses, the Mediterranean has had to act, to look further afield and take tribute from distant lands, associating itself with their economies: in so doing it has considerably enriched its own history. 43

QUESTIONS ABOUT BRAUDEL'S DISCOURSE COMMUNITY AND HIS CONCERNS IN THIS SELECTION

1. What would you say is Braudel's overall subject in this selection? Is this a legitimate subject for a historian to have, even if it is only one of several other subjects in his two-volume work?
2. Braudel argues that climate imposes uniformity on the way of life in the Mediterranean world. How does climate do this? Does his evidence seem believable to you? Is there enough evidence?
3. Summarize what you take to be Braudel's view of the psychology of the Mediterranean peoples in the sixteenth century.
4. What sense of time seems to inform this selection? Speculate about how writers of the Annales school might view time.
5. Where in this selection do you find evidence of an interdisciplinary approach to history? What different disciplines are represented?

* Andrea Navagero, *Il viaggio fatto in Spagna* . . ., Venice, 1563, p. 27–28.
† G. Botero, *op. cit.*, I, I, p. 40; Marco Foscari, *Relazioni di Firenze*, 1527; E. Albèri, *op. cit.*, II, I, p. 25.

6. In places Braudel includes touches that are nearly poetic. He writes, for instance, about "the season for grafting trees" and "the first notes of the nightingale" (paragraph 8). What are the effects of such passages? Are such passages justified in scholarly history?

7. It is easy to imagine much of what Braudel focuses on. Why is that? What does he do that allows readers to form images of what he describes?

8. Braudel does not translate quotes from other languages. What does this suggest about his view of his readers?

QUESTIONS ABOUT BRAUDEL'S RHETORICAL STRATEGIES

1. What, in order of importance, are the major topics Braudel treats in this selection? Why do you think he uses the order of topics that he does?

2. At several points in this selection, Braudel uses extended contrasts. Describe some of these. Why does he use them? How effective are they?

3. Should a historian be allowed to speculate as much as Braudel does in paragraph twenty-four? Why or why not? Or is he not really speculating?

4. Braudel frequently quotes people who lived in earlier centuries. Why does he do this? What are the advantages and disadvantages of his strategy?

5. When giving evidence for a point, Braudel often cites several other writers who have addressed that point. Is this a wise strategy, or do these citations just get in the reader's way?

6. Where does Braudel use specific details? For what purposes does he use them?

7. Occasionally Braudel tells readers how important certain things are. He writes, for example, that "It is a matter of some importance . . ." (paragraph 16). Is he justified in writing such things, or should they be regarded as unwarranted intrusions?

8. Braudel uses some metaphors in this selection. For example, in paragraph three he talks of "the breath of two external forces . . . ." Find other metaphors. How effective are they? Should a serious historian be allowed to use metaphors? What advantages and disadvantages might metaphors have in writing about history?

WRITING FROM WITHIN AND ABOUT HISTORY AND ITS STUDY

Writing for Yourself

1. In your journal, write about a time when weather or climate noticeably affected your mood and views of the world.

2. In your journal, reflect on someone you know who is very frugal and consider why that person is frugal.

Writing for Nonacademic Audiences

1. For your school's newspaper, write a 500-word description of a country you have visited that has misery and hardship bubbling beneath a surface of wealth and glitter.

2. The editor of your local newspaper has asked you to interview someone who lived through the Great Depression and to work up your reactions to this interview in a 500-word piece for the Variety section of the paper.

Writing for Academic Audiences

1. For your classmates, write a 500-word report on the state of agriculture in the Mediterranean world today.
2. For a local history course, write a 750-word paper in which you try to explain how geography and climate have affected aspects of life in your hometown.
3. Imagine that you are writing an essay question for an examination in a course in the history of the Mediterranean world. The question asks you to evaluate Braudel's claim that in many ways imperialism in the Mediterranean in the fifteenth and sixteenth centuries was linked to the search for daily bread. Write the best answer that you can in the time that you have—fifteen minutes.
4. For a senior seminar in theories of history, write a 1,000-word opinion piece on whether selections such as this one by Braudel can justifiably be considered works of history.
5. For a class in historiography, write a 2,000-word essay in which you try to write as a member of the Annales school. Choose one of the following locales and speculate on how its geography and climate have contributed to the suggested struggle or stance:

the Philippines and the attempt to foster political unity
Haiti and its struggle to overcome massive poverty
Ethiopia and the founding of its communist government
the Antarctic and its status as a noncountry
Switzerland and its traditional stance of neutrality
Nantucket and Martha's Vineyard and their attempts to sever their ties with Massachusetts
Poland and its struggle to exist as a country in its own right free from outside entanglements
Israel in its attempts to fend off Arab pressures

Robert G. L. Waite

(b. 1919)

Robert G. L. Waite, who is Brown Professor of History at Williams College, has spent most of his scholarly career studying modern German history. He has concentrated on the conditions that led to Adolf Hitler's rise to power and on the nature of Nazi Germany. Here we reprint part of his The Psychopathic God, Adolf Hitler, *a work for which Waite found the title in one of W. H. Auden's poems, "September 1, 1939."*

In The Psychopathic God, *Waite pursues what he calls "one of the most intriguing questions of all history: how it is possible for this strange little man [Adolf Hitler], at once so banal and so terrible, to hold a great nation enthralled in cruel yet popular tyranny and to conquer a continent" (Preface to* The Psychopathic God, *p. xi). Waite calls the approach he uses to reach an answer to this question "psychohistory." He calls upon the resources of formal psychology in order to analyze Hitler's personality. Waite's premise is "that Hitler was a pathological personality whose career cannot be understood without a careful examination of his personal life" (Preface to* The Psychopathic God, *p. xv).*

But Waite sets his analysis of Hitler's life in a wider historical context. He examines Hitler's personality traits, but he also relates these traits to Hitler's actions and the constraints of the situations Hitler faced. Waite does not wish to supplant more traditional kinds of historical investigation; rather, he wishes to supplement them with methods and insights derived from psychology.

The picture that Waite leaves us with shows Hitler as a borderline personality, a man with a divided ego. Hitler, Waite writes, was "both a mentally deranged human being and a consummately skillful political leader of high intelligence" (Preface to The Psychopathic God, *p. xvi). To stress one of those sides to the exclusion of the other, Waite argues, produces an incomplete interpretation.*

The section we reproduce is from chapter 3 of The Psychopathic God, *"The Child as Father to the Man."*

HITLER'S "PRIMAL SCENE TRAUMA"*

Alois Hitler [Adolf Hitler's father] was away from home for extended periods 1
during the first three years of Adolf's life. In his absence, the little boy was
drawn very close to his mother, who sometimes took him to bed with her "for
company."† We may speculate that the closer little Adolf felt toward his
mother, the more anxiety he felt about his father; the more he feared his
father, the more he clung to his mother—and the circular anxiety of the
Oedipal conflict was intensified. Fantasied incestuous relations would have
sharpened his hatred of his father as a rival, as well as his fear of paternal
vengeance.

Then one night, when he was about three years old, Adolf saw—or 2
imagined he saw—a scene of horror: his inebriated father attacked his mother
and did something terrible and strange to her. And, most awful of all, she
seemed to enjoy it.

Once again the biographer is confronted with the question of whether 3
his subject "actually experienced" an event or "merely imagined" it. And
once again it must be emphasized that psychologically *it does not make much
difference.* One of Freud's greatest contributions to a biographer's understanding is the insight that neurotic symptoms may not be related to any
actual event at all. They are derived from what is often dismissed as "pure
fantasy." But psychic reality is often more important than objective reality,
and what a subject *imagines* to have happened must therefore be taken seriously. His fantasies, the words and turns of phrase he uses to describe them,
the intensity of his imagery, the number of times he recounts them—none of
this should be written off as accidental or arbitrary. These things are "unconsciously determined" and are very important indeed to the person involved.
From a thousand other events in his life he has chosen these particular incidents; he has described them with these specific words, and not with the
many alternative figures of speech available to him.

We shall never know with finality whether the infant Adolf actually 4
saw the scene of sexual assault. But in his fantasy he did, and it was for him
a "primal scene trauma." Parenthetically, it may be said that, in this instance, fantasy probably coincided with reality.

The best historical source for the incident is Hitler himself. For quite 5
unintentionally in his memoirs he has given us an eyewitness account of his

---

*Primal scene trauma is trauma resulting from a child's actual or imagined first observation of
   his parents engaged in sexual intercourse.
†Hitler told Hanfstaengl that one of his earliest and most pleasant memories was when he was
   permitted to sleep alone with his mother "in the big bed" [Waite's note].

own harrowing experience. Dr. Walter Langer and his psychoanalytical colleagues were the first to notice, in an OSS report of 1943, that a peculiar passage in *Mein Kampf* which ostensibly describes what happened to the little son of a "worker" is, in all probability, a thinly disguised autobiographical memoir. (For purposes of later discussion, some key phrases in the passage have been italicized and numbered.)

> Let us imagine the following: In a basement apartment of two stuffy rooms 6
> lives a worker's family. . . . Among the (1) *five children there is a boy, let us*
> *say, of three.* This is the age at which a child becomes conscious of his first
> impressions. (2) *In gifted people [bei Begabten],* traces of these early memories
> are found even in old age. The (3) *smallness and overcrowding of the rooms* do
> not create favorable conditions. Quarreling and nagging often arise because of
> this. In such circumstances people do not live with one another, but (4) *push*
> *down on top of one another [drücken aufeinander].* Every argument. . . . leads
> to a never-ending, disgusting quarrel. . . . But when the parents fight almost
> daily, their brutality leaves nothing to the imagination; then the results of such
> (5) *visual education* must slowly but inevitably become apparent in the little
> ones . . . especially when the mutual differences express themselves (6) *in the*
> *form of brutal attacks on the part of the father towards the mother or to assaults*
> *due to drunkenness.* The poor little boy (7) *at the age of six,* senses things which
> would (8) *make even a grown-up shudder.* (9) *Morally infected . . .* the young
> "citizen" wanders off to elementary school. . . . The three year old has now
> become a (10) *youth of fifteen* who [has been dismissed from school and] de-
> spises all authority. . . . Now he loiters about and God only knows when he
> comes home. . . . *

The scene at the age of three does not seem at all improbable when one 7 considers how little concerned Alois Hitler was about anybody's knowledge of his sexual life. He was unlikely to be embarrassed by the presence of a little child in the crowded living quarters, particularly if he thought the child was asleep.

The description as given by Hitler contains numerous phrases which 8 reinforce the conclusion that the passage is autobiographical:

(1) *Five children.* For several years as a young boy, Adolf was one of five children, 9
along with Paula and Edmund and his stepbrother and stepsister, Alois Jr. and
Angela.

(2) *in gifted people.* He often referred to himself this way. 10

(3) *smallness and overcrowding of the rooms.* Not an inaccurate description of the 11
close quarters in the inns and mill where the Hitlers lived during Adolf's early
childhood.

(4) *push down on top of one another.* Description of the sex act? 12

(5) *visual education.* Once again, the importance to Hitler of the eyes. 13

(6) *brutal attacks . . . due to drunkenness.* These phrases and images are repeated 14
several times in the chapter.

(7) *at the age of six.* Particularly important to Adolf because when he was six his 15
rival, Edmund, was conceived.

---

*Hitler, *Mein Kampf,* English ed. 42–44; German ed., 32–34. Langer, *Mind of Adolf Hitler,*
142–145 [Waite's note].

(8) *make even a grown-up shudder.* Why should adults *shudder* at sexual inter- 16
course? What kind of attacks was he imagining? Were they particularly sadis-
tic? Would they possibly have been the kind of sadomasochistic sexual deviation
which Hitler himself may later have indulged in? (See below, pp. 237–243.)

(9) *Morally infected.* Note that Hitler associates sexual intercourse with something 17
morally infectious and repulsive.

(10) *Youth of fifteen.* The school dropout who despises authority, loiters about, and 18
stays out until all hours is, as we shall see, an accurate description of Adolf's
own life-style after the death of his father.

Of course, it is not always traumatic for a child to see parents engaged 19
in sex. If it were, thousands upon thousands of Eskimos and Bedouins would,
presumably, be a great deal more neurotic than they seem to be. The experience is traumatic only, as in little Adolf's case, if it reinforces other deeply
disturbing childhood experiences.

In the midst of describing other dreadful incidents involving drunken 20
husbands who are attacking their passive wives, Hitler stops to make a very
important statement: *"I witnessed all this personally in hundreds of scenes
. . . with both disgust and indignation."** We must ask *where* young Adolf
had ever personally witnessed such intimate and, to him, disgusting scenes.
Certainly he had never seen them outside his own home. And he never showed
any interest whatever in observing the workings of a three-year-old mind as
it developed to the age of six and on to fifteen—that is, no such mind except
his own. Then how could he have viewed these things himself "hundreds" of
times?

It is possible that he may never actually have seen them at all, that it 21
was "only a fantasy." But it seems more likely—given the specific details and
turns of phrase in his description—that he did witness such a scene, and that
he had relived the terrifying event hundreds of times in his imagination. Every
psychoanalyst knows from clinical experience that when a patient constantly
repeats an image or an association or has the same dream again and again, it
is an "indication of the depth an impression has made and the intensity of
what he wishes to communicate."†

The professional literature on primal scene trauma is extensive, but a 22
few recurring symptoms may be summarized here. None of these by itself is
decisive, but a combination of them does bespeak serious emotional problems
in many patients as it did, we are suggesting, in Adolf Hitler. All patients
show severe castration anxieties. Indeed, it is an established principle of analysis that severe castration anxiety is a common sequel to the observation of a
primal scene under circumstances that are traumatic to the child. One of
Hitler's most striking illustrations of this symptom was his lifelong preoccupation with decapitation in general and the Medusa's head in particular (see

---

*Hitler, *Mein Kampf*, English ed., 38; German ed., 28; italics are mine [Waite's note].
†Peter Loewenberg, review article, *Central European History* (September 1974): 265 [Waite's
note].

Chapter 1, p. 21f). To decapitate is to castrate as well as to kill; the terror which the Medusa's head evokes is the terror not only of death but also of castration.* The castration fears which so frequently follow a primal scene trauma would have been particularly intense in young Adolf because of his monorchism, for monorchism represents the climax *in reality* of frightening Oedipal fantasies about paternal revenge. Thus, Hitler's anxiety would have been twofold: the actual body damage intensified castration fears, which were further stimulated by the primal scene experience.

Primal scene exposure also awakens in many patients, as it seems to 23 have done in Adolf, incestuous fantasies and fears. The child is both repelled and attracted by the thought of incest, of replacing his father as his mother's sexual partner. Hitler expressed such horror—and infatuation—in many ways. First, as was his habit, he denied vehemently that he himself had any such desires by projecting them onto others. He insisted, for example, that it was not he but the Jews who were guilty of incest.† Or he would say that Vienna was "the personification of incest [*die Verkörperung der Blut-schande*]."‡ The fact that his sexual affairs in later life were with mother substitutes is also strong evidence of incestuous feelings for his mother.

There is other indirect evidence that Adolf had incestuous fantasies 24 about his mother, hated his father as a rival, feared him, and harbored a death wish toward the old man. This is hinted at in his adolescent drama about the Holy Mountain, in which a priest cuts off the head of a sacrificial bull. It seems likely that the bull, a traditional symbol of aggressive sensuality, was to young Hitler a father symbol in this context. Since Adolf was beginning to see himself as a Messiah, he may, unconsciously, have cast himself as the priest sacrificing his father to his own ambition and Oedipal fears.

We have seen that Hitler was also deathly afraid of strangulation. He 25 had written about Dame Poverty as a snake that sought to throttle him. During one of his last "Table Conversations" he said, in an interesting turn of phrase, that the Jews sought to "asphixiate" him. He had nightmares about strangulation, drowning, and shortness of breath. In a classic study of nightmares, Ernest Jones has shown that there is a direct connection between horror dreams of this kind and incestuous desires:

> *The malady known as Nightmare is always an expression of intense mental* 26
> *conflict centering about some form of "repressed" sexual desire.* . . . There is
> no doubt that this concerns the incest trends of sexual life, so that we may
> extend the formula just given and say: *An attack of the Nightmare is an expres-*
> *sion of a mental conflict over an incestuous desire.*§

* Sigmund Freud, "Medusa's Head," in *Works*, Standard ed., 18: 273–274 [Waite's note].
† See letter to Gemlich, 17 September 1919, quoted in Joachim C. Fest, *The Face of the Third Reich: Portraits of the Nazi Leadership*, trans. Michael Bullock (New York, 1970), 16 [Waite's note].
‡ *Mein Kampf*, German Ed., 135 [Waite's note].
§ Conference of 13 February 1945, *Testament*, 51; *OSS Source Book*; Ernest Jones, *On the Nightmare* (New York, 1951), 44; italics in original [Waite's note].

The peculiar biographical fact that both as a young man and as an adult 27 Hitler prided himself on being a "wolf" may be tied-in with his infantile trauma. There are many examples of his identification with wolves, but most significantly, the tune he whistled often and absentmindedly was "Who's Afraid of the Big Bad Wolf?" To those who are acquainted with Freud's celebrated case of the "Wolf-man" or the later publication of the Wolf-man's own memoirs, Hitler's infatuation with the wolf strikes a familiar note. Freud's patient, it will be recalled, had also as an infant watched his parents have intercourse; he subsequently developed a wolf phobia. While we do not know with certainty whether Hitler had a wolf or dog phobia as a child, the defiant tone of the Disney movie song suggests that he may have, and that he learned to defend against this anxiety by associating himself with the object of his fear, by deliberately cultivating it and surrounding himself with it. Familiarity, in this case, bred not contempt but a lessening of anxiety. In identifying himself as the wolf, he was reassuring himself by saying, in effect: "See, I don't need to be afraid of wolves, I myself am the Wolf."*

It is possible that the infant Adolf associated his father with the wolf, 28 since it is known that Alois owned a large dog, possibly an Alsatian (in German, *Wolfshund*). As we have noted, Alois whipped the dog, and in calling for both his dog and his son he gave the same whistle.

There is no doubt that Hitler saw his father as an aggressor against him, 29 as is shown both in the *Mein Kampf* passage and in his many references to the whippings he received as a boy. There is further evidence that Adolf identified with the aggressor-father. He sometimes treated his own *Wolfshund* in the brutal way that he had seen his father whip his own dog. One of the women with whom Hitler had intimate relations during 1926, Maria (or Mimi) Reiter, recalls that she saw him turn savagely on his own dog:

> He whipped his dog like a madman [*Irrsinniger*] with his riding whip as he 30 held him tight on the leash. He became tremendously excited. . . . I could not have believed that this man would ·beat an animal so ruthlessly—an animal about which he had said a moment previously that he could not live without. But now he whipped his most faithful companion!

When Mimi asked him how he could possibly be so brutal, Hitler replied 31 grimly, "That was necessary."† In beating the dog, was Hitler punishing himself for his own guilt feelings, which he had transferred to the animal? He said that he knew his dog had "guilty feelings."

As in the case of Freud's Wolf-man, the horse seems to have replaced 32 the dog or wolf as a phobic object. Hitler, it will be remembered, feared horses. But, as if simultaneously denying that fear and protecting himself

---

*Conversation with Norbert Bromberg, M. D., July 1973 [Waite's note].
†Günter Peis, "Die unbekannte Geliebte," *Stern* Nov. 24 (1959):59 [Waite's note].

from it, he habitually carried a riding whip and surrounded himself with pictures and statues of stallions.*

Among the long-range consequences of Hitler's infantile experience was 33 the belief that coitus is brutal, infectious, and dangerous—so dangerous that the adult Hitler would liken it to going into battle on the Western Front (see Chapter I, p. 52). The sex act also illustrates, as Hitler saw it, women's masochistic need to be overpowered by the audacious man; this reinforced his image of women as weak and deceitful creatures who were not to be trusted. His avoidance of genital intercourse with women may also have been a consequence of his unconscious association of all women with the one woman— his mother—who yielded deceitfully to his father-rival, produced deficient children (who died early in life or were mentally or physically defective), and then nursed them at breasts that later became diseased.†

His infantile experience seems to have had another long-range conse- 34 quence. Phyllis Greenacre has shown that children to whom observation of parental sex was traumatic tend to become prejudiced toward minority groups. Such children emphasize the contrast between themselves and others, stare carefully at strangers, make special note of their physical appearance, and become radically antagonistic toward those whose appearance is different and repugnant to them.‡

It is noteworthy that Hitler's most revealing expression of prejudice in 35 his memoirs emphasizes visual scrutiny and physical appearance. He says that he suffered a profound shock when he first looked at an East European Jew:

> . . . One day when I was walking through the Inner City, I suddenly came 36
> upon a being clad in a long caftan, with black curls.
> "Is this also a Jew?" was my first thought. 37
> At Linz they certainly did not *look* like that. Secretly and cautiously *I* 38
> *watched* the man but the longer *I stared* at this strange face and *scrutinized*
> one feature after the other, the more my mind reshaped the first question into
> another form:
> "Is this also a German?"§ 39

There is another reason why we have dwelt on this infantile experience: 40 the way the mature Hitler remembered his parents' sexual relations reveals modes of thought that had historic consequences when he established his dictatorship. The words, images, and phrases he used in describing the event— or the fantasy—show a clear development of the mistrust and hatred that would determine all his interpersonal relations. His mental picture of the

---

*Freud, "From the History of an Infantile Neurosis," in *Works*, Standard ed., 17:78–79, 82 ff. [Waite's note].

† Conversations with Bromberg [Waite's note].

‡ See Phyllis Greenacre, *Trauma Growth and Personality* (New York, 1952), 132–148, 204–223, 224–238, 293–302; see also Greenacre, "Infantile Trauma," 108–153 [Waite's note].

§ Hitler, *Mein Kampf*, 73; italics are mine [Waite's note].

incident reveals that to his mind sexuality, power, aggression, and cruelty were all fused together in a dangerous, pathologic union: terror, brutalization, and ruthless power were to him the primary features of sex and life.

In short, attitudes revealed here characterized both his own personality 41 and the political system he imposed on his country and much of Europe. *

QUESTIONS ABOUT WAITE'S DISCOURSE COMMUNITY AND HIS CONCERNS IN THIS SELECTION

1. Describe as precisely and concisely as you can the elements of the Oedipal complex or conflict.
2. For the young Adolf Hitler, why would it have been "awful" that his mother "seemed to enjoy" what his father did to her?
3. Do you agree that it makes little difference whether subjects of studies like this "actually experienced" or "merely imagined" an event? Why might the young Hitler have imagined the event involving his mother and father?
4. Does it seem realistic that people might deny a fear by projecting it onto others, as Waite suggests Hitler did with his fear of incest?
5. At one point Waite makes a point about how children who have a traumatic experience observing parental sex "tend to become prejudiced toward minority groups." His evidence for this is a statement to the effect that Phyllis Greenacre has shown this to be true. How adequate is this as a kind of evidence?
6. Does the connection that Waite makes between Hitler's primal scene trauma and later prejudice, aggression, and cruelty seem reasonable to you? Why or why not?
7. This selection is full of speculation and surmise. When is the selection least persuasive? When most?
8. Evaluate the means by which this discourse community chronicles history. What processes does it use to reconstruct historical situations? Do these seem to be reasonable and legitimate processes for a historian to employ?

QUESTIONS ON WAITE'S RHETORICAL STRATEGIES

1. What would you say is the tone of this piece? What elements contribute in a major way to the creation of that tone?
2. Waite frequently uses the word *we*. What is its effect on you as a reader? Is his use of this word defensible?
3. Waite writes that the words "smallness and overcrowding of the rooms" provide "Not an inaccurate description" of where the Hitlers lived during Adolf's early childhood. Why would Waite write "Not an inaccurate description" rather than "An accurate description"?
4. At one point (paragraph 31) Waite asks a question: "In beating the dog, was Hitler punishing himself for his own guilt feelings, which he had transferred to the animal?" Is it a fair practice for a historian to pose such questions? Is it a wise practice?

*Loewenberg, in *Central European History*, 267–268 [Waite's note].

5. Which details that Waite gives about Hitler's life do you find most memorable? Why do you think you find them so?
6. How convincing do you find Waite's analysis of the longer passage from Hitler's *Mein Kampf*? Why do you think that Waite notes that others first pointed out that this passage was probably a "thinly disguised autobiographical memoir"?
7. How compelling do you find the evidence Waite uses in his discussion of the effects on Hitler of his primal scene trauma? Consider the evidence about Hitler's fears of castration, fears of incest, views on sexual intercourse, and prejudice toward minority groups. Some of this evidence is indirect. Is Waite wise to use it?

WRITING FROM WITHIN AND ABOUT HISTORY AND ITS STUDY

Writing for Yourself

1. In your journal, describe someone you know who seems to be trying to overcome a fear by cultivating it and looking for ways to be surrounded by it.
2. In your journal, evaluate Waite's statement that "for a child to see parents engaged in sex" is "traumatic only . . . if it reinforces other deeply disturbing childhood experiences."

Writing for Nonacademic Audiences

1. You have a friend who tends to give a Freudian explanation for almost all examples of human behavior. Write this friend a letter in which you comment on that tendency.

Writing for Academic Audiences

1. You have been asked to give a twenty-minute talk to a high school psychology class (open only to seniors) on Freud's contributions to Western culture. Write that speech.
2. For a college class in psychological disorders, write a 500-word report on borderline personalities.
3. For a class in modern German history, write a 1,000-word essay in which you analyze Theodor Fritsch's effects on Hitler's anti-Semitism.
4. For a class in the history of Nazism, write a 1,000-word essay describing the kind of women the adult Hitler was attracted to.
5. For a class in the history of Nazism, write a 1,500-word essay in which you analyze the appeal that Wagner had for Hitler.
6. Read some reviews of *The Psychopathic God* (the book is reviewed in the following journals: November, 1977, *Choice*; June 15, 1977, *Library Journal*; July 9, 1977, *The Economist*; August 29, 1977, *New Yorker*; July 9–16, 1977, *The New Republic*; August 12, 1977, *New Statesman*; and August 29, 1977, *New York Review of Books*). Then write a 1,000-word essay for a seminar in methods in history describing how Waite's peers judged his practice of psychohistory.

Gerda Lerner

(b. 1920)

One of the more lively current discourse communities is made up of feminist research- ers and writers. These writers, not all of whom are female, have pursued questions in many different academic fields. Thus on a more specific level one can speak of smaller discourse communities made up of feminist literary critics, feminist psychol- ogists, and feminist anthropologists, to name just a few.

The following selection originates in the discourse community of feminist his- torians. It is taken from Gerda Lerner's The Creation of Patriarchy *(1986). Lerner, the Wisconsin Alumni Research Foundation Senior Distinguished Research Professor at the University of Wisconsin, Madison, has focused much of her scholarly attention on the history of American women. In* The Creation of Patriarchy, *however, she focuses more widely, seeking to answer the question of how women in Western cul- ture became trapped in a patriarchal world, a world in which males dominate fe- males in the family and in society. To answer this question, she studies ancient Meso- potamian, Hebrew, and Greek cultures, concentrating on the years between 3100 and 600* B.C. *She is particularly interested in tracing the development of symbol sys- tems that support a patriarchal system of gender in the history of Western civiliza- tion. On the basis of her study, she concludes that "patriarchy as a system is historical; it has a beginning in history" (*The Creation of Patriarchy, *p. 6). She does not believe that male dominance is natural and inevitable. Since the system of patriarchy has a beginning, it can also have an end.*

*On the way to this conclusion, Lerner makes several other claims, many of which are certain to stimulate debate. For example, she argues that the "symbolic devaluing of women in relation to the divine becomes one of the founding metaphors of Western civilization" (*The Creation of Patriarchy, *p. 10). The other founding metaphor comes from Aristotelian philosophy, which stresses that women are incom- plete and damaged human beings. Lerner closes her book by urging upon the reader a feminist worldview, one that "will enable women and men to free their minds from patriarchal thought and practice and at last to build a world free of dominance and hierarchy, a world that is truly human" (*The Creation of Patriarchy, *p. 229).*

The following selection, "The Creation of Patriarchy," is the final chapter of Lerner's book with the same title.

THE CREATION OF PATRIARCHY

Patriarchy is a historic creation formed by men and women in a process which 1
took nearly 2500 years to its completion. In its earliest form patriarchy appeared as the archaic state. The basic unit of its organization was the patriarchal family, which both expressed and constantly generated its rules and values. We have seen how integrally definitions of gender affected the formation
of the state. Let us briefly review the way in which gender became created,
defined, and established.

The roles and behavior deemed appropriate to the sexes were expressed 2
in values, customs, laws, and social roles. They also, and very importantly,
were expressed in leading metaphors, which became part of the cultural construct and explanatory system.

The sexuality of women, consisting of their sexual and their reproduc- 3
tive capacities and services, was commodified even prior to the creation of
Western civilization. The development of agriculture in the Neolithic period*
fostered the inter-tribal "exchange of women," not only as a means of avoid-
ing incessant warfare by the cementing of marriage alliances but also because
societies with more women could produce more children. In contrast to the
economic needs of hunting/gathering societies, agriculturists could use the
labor of children to increase production and accumulate surpluses. Men-as-
a-group had rights in women which women-as-a-group did not have in men.
Women themselves became a resource, acquired by men much as the land
was acquired by men. Women were exchanged or bought in marriages for
the benefit of their families; later, they were conquered or bought in slavery,
where their sexual services were part of their labor and where their children
were the property of their masters. In every known society it was women of
conquered tribes who were first enslaved, whereas men were killed. It was
only after men had learned how to enslave the women of groups who could
be defined as strangers, that they learned how to enslave men of those groups
and, later, subordinates from within their own societies.

Thus, the enslavement of women, combining both racism and sexism, 4
preceded the formation of classes and class oppression. Class differences were,
at their very beginnings, expressed and constituted in terms of patriarchal
relations. Class is not a separate construct from gender; rather, class is expressed in generic terms.

By the second millennium B.C. in Mesopotamian societies, the daugh- 5
ters of the poor were sold into marriage or prostitution in order to advance
the economic interests of their families. The daughters of men of property
could command a bride price, paid by the family of the groom to the family

---

* The last period of the Stone Age, from around 6000 B.C. to 2000 B.C.

of the bride, which frequently enabled the bride's family to secure more financially advantageous marriages for their sons, thus improving the family's economic position. If a husband or father could not pay his debt, his wife and children could be used as pawns, becoming debt slaves to the creditor. These conditions were so firmly established by 1750 B.C. that Hammurabic law made a decisive improvement in the lot of debt pawns by limiting their terms of service to three years, where earlier it had been for life.

The product of this commodification of women—bride price, sale price, 6 and children—was appropriated by men. It may very well represent the first accumulation of private property. The enslavement of women of conquered tribes became not only a status symbol for nobles and warriors, but it actually enabled the conquerors to acquire tangible wealth through selling or trading the product of the slaves' labor and their reproductive product, slave children.

Claude Lévi-Strauss,* to whom we owe the concept of "the exchange 7 of women," speaks of the reification of women, which occurred as its consequence. But it is not women who are reified and commodified, it is women's sexuality and reproductive capacity which is so treated. The distinction is important. Women never became "things," nor were they so perceived. Women, no matter how exploited and abused, retained their power to act and to choose to the same, often very limited extent, as men of their group. But women *always and to this day* lived in a relatively greater state of unfreedom than did men. Since their sexuality, an aspect of their body, was controlled by others, women were not only actually disadvantaged but psychologically restrained in a very special way. For women, as for men of subordinate and oppressed groups, history consisted of their struggle for emancipation and freedom from necessity. But women struggled against different forms of oppression and dominance than did men, and their struggle, up to this time, has lagged behind that of men.

The first gender-defined social role for women was to be those who were 8 exchanged in marriage transactions. The obverse gender role for men was to be those who did the exchanging or who defined the terms of the exchanges.

Another gender-defined role for women was that of the "stand-in" wife, 9 which became established and institutionalized for women of elite groups. This role gave such women considerable power and privileges, but it depended on their attachment to elite men and was based, minimally, on their satisfactory performance in rendering these men sexual and reproductive services. If a woman failed to meet these demands, she was quickly replaced and thereby lost all her privileges and standing.

The gender-defined role of warrior led men to acquire power over men 10 and women of conquered tribes. Such war-induced conquest usually occurred over people already differentiated from the victors by race, ethnicity,

---

* Claude Levi-Strauss (b. 1908) is a famous French social anthropologist.

or simple tribal difference. In its ultimate origin, "difference" as a distinguishing mark between the conquered and the conquerors was based on the first clearly observable difference, that between the sexes. Men had learned how to assert and exercise power over people slightly different from themselves in the primary exchange of women. In so doing, men acquired the knowledge necessary to elevate "difference" of whatever kind into a criterion for dominance.

From its inception in slavery, class dominance took different forms for 11 enslaved men and women: men were primarily exploited as workers; women were always exploited as workers, as providers of sexual services, and as reproducers. The historical record of every slave society offers evidence for this generalization. The sexual exploitation of lower-class women by upper-class men can be shown in antiquity, under feudalism, in the bourgeois households of nineteenth- and twentieth-century Europe, in the complex sex/race relations between women of the colonized countries and their male colonizers—it is ubiquitous and pervasive. For women, sexual exploitation is the very mark of class exploitation.

At any given moment in history, each "class" is constituted of two dis- 12 tinct classes—men and women.

The class position of women became consolidated and actualized 13 through their sexual relationships. It always was expressed within degrees of unfreedom on a spectrum ranging from the slave woman, whose sexual and reproductive capacity was commodified as she herself was; to the slave-concubine, whose sexual performance might elevate her own status or that of her children; then to the "free" wife, whose sexual and reproductive services to one man of the upper classes entitled her to property and legal rights. While each of these groups had vastly different obligations and privileges in regard to property, law, and economic resources, they shared the unfreedom of being sexually and reproductively controlled by men. We can best express the complexity of women's various levels of dependency and freedom by comparing each woman with her brother and considering how the sister's and brother's lives and opportunities would differ.

Class for men was and is based on their relationship to the means of 14 production: those who owned the means of production could dominate those who did not. The owners of the means of production also acquired the commodity of female sexual services, both from women of their own class and from women of the subordinate classes. In Ancient Mesopotamia, in classical antiquity, and in slave societies, dominant males also acquired, as property, the product of the reproductive capacity of subordinate women—children, to be worked, traded, married off, or sold as slaves, as the case might be. For women, class is mediated through their sexual ties to a man. It is through the man that women have access to or are denied access to the means of production and to resources. It is through their sexual behavior that they gain access to class. "Respectable women" gain access to class through their fathers and husbands, but breaking the sexual rules can at once declass them. The gender definition of sexual "deviance" marks a woman as "not respectable," which in fact consigns her to the lowest class status possible. Women who withhold heterosexual services (such as single women, nuns, lesbians) are connected to the dominant man in their family of origin and through him gain access to resources. Or, alternatively, they are declassed. In some historical periods, convents and other enclaves for single women created some sheltered space, in which such women could function and retain their respectability. But the vast majority of single women are, by definition, marginal and dependent on the protection of male kin. This is true throughout historical time up to the middle of the twentieth century in the Western world and still is true in most of the underdeveloped countries today. The group of independent, self-supporting women which exists in every society is small and usually highly vulnerable to economic disaster.

Economic oppression and exploitation are based as much on the com- 15 modification of female sexuality and the appropriation by men of women's labor power and her reproductive power as on the direct economic acquisition of resources and persons.

The archaic state in the Ancient Near East emerged in the second mil- 16 lennium B.C. from the twin roots of men's sexual dominance over women and the exploitation by some men of others. From its inception, the archaic state was organized in such a way that the dependence of male family heads on the king or the state bureaucracy was compensated for by their dominance over their families. Male family heads allocated the resources of society to their families the way the state allocated the resources of society to them. The control of male family heads over their female kin and minor sons was as important to the existence of the state as was the control of the king over his soldiers. This is reflected in the various compilations of Mesopotamian laws, especially in the large number of laws dealing with the regulation of female sexuality.

From the second millennium B.C. forward control over the sexual be- 17 havior of citizens has been a major means of social control in every state society. Conversely, class hierarchy is constantly reconstituted in the family through sexual dominance. Regardless of the political or economic system, the kind of personality which can function in a hierarchical system is created and nurtured within the patriarchal family.

The patriarchal family has been amazingly resilient and varied in dif- 18 ferent times and places. Oriental patriarchy encompassed polygamy and female enclosure in harems. Patriarchy in classical antiquity and in its European development was based upon monogamy, but in all its forms a double sexual standard, which disadvantages women, was part of the system. In modern industrial states, such as in the United States, property relations within the family develop along more egalitarian lines than those in which the father holds absolute power, yet the economic and sexual power relations within the family do not necessarily change. In some cases, sexual relations are more egalitarian, while economic relations remain patriarchal; in other cases the pattern is reversed. In all cases, however, such changes within the family do not alter the basic male dominance in the public realm, in institutions and in government.

The family not merely mirrors the order in the state and educates its 19 children to follow it, it also creates and constantly reinforces that order.

It should be noted that when we speak of relative improvements in the 20 status of women in a given society, this frequently means only that we are seeing improvements in the degree in which their situation affords them opportunities to exert some leverage within the system of patriarchy. Where women have relatively more economic power, they are able to have somewhat more control over their lives than in societies where they have no economic power. Similarly, the existence of women's groups, associations, or economic networks serves to increase the ability of women to counteract the dictates of their particular patriarchal system. Some anthropologists and historians have called this relative improvement women's "freedom." Such a designation is illusory and unwarranted. Reforms and legal changes, while ameliorating the condition of women and an essential part of the process of emancipating them, will not basically change patriarchy. Such reforms need to be integrated within a vast cultural revolution in order to transform patriarchy and thus abolish it.

The system of patriarchy can function only with the cooperation of 21 women. This cooperation is secured by a variety of means: gender indoctrination; educational deprivation; the denial to women of knowledge of their history; the dividing of women, one from the other, by defining "respectability" and "deviance" according to women's sexual activities; by restraints and outright coercion; by discrimination in access to economic resources and political power; and by awarding class privileges to conforming women.

For nearly four thousand years women have shaped their lives and acted 22 under the umbrella of patriarchy, specifically a form of patriarchy best described as paternalistic dominance. The term describes the relationship of a dominant group, considered superior, to a subordinate group, considered inferior, in which the dominance is mitigated by mutual obligations and reciprocal rights. The dominated exchange submission for protection, unpaid labor for maintenance. In the patriarchal family, responsibilities and obligations are not equally distributed among those to be protected: the male children's subordination to the father's dominance is temporary; it lasts until they themselves become heads of households. The subordination of female children and of wives is lifelong. Daughters can escape it only if they place themselves as wives under the dominance/protection of another man. The basis of paternalism is an unwritten contract for exchange: economic support and protection given by the male for subordination in all matters, sexual service, and unpaid domestic service given by the female. Yet the relationship frequently continues in fact and in law, even when the male partner has defaulted on his obligation.

It was a rational choice for women, under conditions of public power- 23
lessness and economic dependency, to choose strong protectors for themselves and their children. Women always shared the class privileges of men of their class *as long as they were under "the protection" of a man.* For women, other than those of the lower classes, the "reciprocal agreement" went like this: in exchange for your sexual, economic, political, and intellectual subordination to men you may share the power of men of your class to exploit men and women of the lower class. In class society it is difficult for people who themselves have some power, however limited and circumscribed, to see themselves also as deprived and subordinated. Class and racial privileges serve to undercut the ability of women to see themselves as part of a coherent group, which, in fact, they are not, since women uniquely of all oppressed groups occur in all strata of the society. The formation of a group consciousness of women must proceed along different lines. That is the reason why theoretical formulations, which have been appropriate to other oppressed groups, are so inadequate in explaining and conceptualizing the subordination of women.

Women have for millennia participated in the process of their own sub- 24
ordination because they have been psychologically shaped so as to internalize the idea of their own inferiority. The unawareness of their own history of struggle and achievement has been one of the major means of keeping women subordinate.

The connectedness of women to familial structures made any develop- 25
ment of female solidarity and group cohesiveness extremely problematic. Each individual woman was linked to her male kin in her family of origin through ties which implied specific obligations. Her indoctrination, from early childhood on, emphasized her obligation not only to make an economic contribution to the kin and household but also to accept a marriage partner in line with family interests. Another way of saying this is to say that sexual control of women was linked to paternalistic protection and that, in the various stages of her life, she exchanged male protectors, but she never outgrew the childlike state of being subordinate and under protection.

Other oppressed classes and groups were impelled toward group con- 26
sciousness by the very conditions of their subordinate status. The slave could clearly mark a line between the interests and bonds to his/her own family and the ties of subservience/protection linking him/her with the master. In fact, protection by slave parents of their own family against the master was one of the most important causes of slave resistance. "Free" women, on the other hand, learned early that their kin would cast them out, should they ever rebel against their dominance. In traditional and peasant societies there are many recorded instances of female family members tolerating and even

participating in the chastisement, torture, even death of a girl who had transgressed against the family "honor." In Biblical times, the entire community gathered to stone the adulteress to death. Similar practices prevailed in Sicily, Greece, and Albania into the twentieth century. Bangladesh fathers and husbands cast out their daughters and wives who had been raped by invading soldiers, consigning them to prostitution. Thus, women were often forced to flee from one "protector" to the other, their "freedom" frequently defined only by their ability to manipulate between these protectors.

Most significant of all the impediments toward developing group con- 27
sciousness for women was the absence of a tradition which would reaffirm the independence and autonomy of women at any period in the past. There had never been any woman or group of women who had lived without male protection, as far as most women knew. There had never been any group of persons like them who had done anything significant for themselves. Women had no history—so they were told; so they believed. Thus, ultimately, it was men's hegemony over the symbol system which most decisively disadvantaged women.

Male hegemony over the symbol system took two forms: educational depri- 28
vation of women and male monopoly on definition. The former happened inadvertently, more the consequence of class dominance and the accession of military elites to power. Throughout historical times, there have always been large loopholes for women of the elite classes, whose access to education was one of the major aspects of their class privilege. But male dominance over definition has been deliberate and pervasive, and the existence of individual highly educated and creative women has, for nearly four thousand years, left barely an imprint on it.

We have seen how men appropriated and then transformed the major 29
symbols of female power: the power of the Mother-Goddess and the fertility-goddesses. We have seen how men constructed theologies based on the counterfactual metaphor of male procreativity and redefined female existence in a narrow and sexually dependent way. We have seen, finally, how the very metaphors for gender have expressed the male as norm and the female as deviant; the male as whole and powerful, the female as unfinished, mutilated, and lacking in autonomy. On the basis of such symbolic constructs, embedded in Greek philosophy, the Judeo-Christian theologies, and the legal tradition on which Western civilization is built, men have explained the world in their own terms and defined the important questions so as to make themselves the center of discourse.

By making the term "man" subsume "woman" and arrogate to itself the 30
representation of all of humanity, men have built a conceptual error of vast proportion into all of their thought. By taking the half for the whole, they have not only missed the essence of whatever they are describing, but they have distorted it in such a fashion that they cannot see it correctly. As long as

men believed the earth to be flat, they could not understand its reality, its function, and its actual relationship to other bodies in the universe. As long as men believe their experiences, their viewpoint, and their ideas represent all of human experience and all of human thought, they are not only unable to define correctly in the abstract, but they are unable to describe reality accurately.

The androcentric fallacy, which is built into all the mental constructs 31 of Western civilization, cannot be rectified simply by "adding women." What it demands for rectification is a radical restructuring of thought and analysis which once and for all accepts the fact that humanity consists in equal parts of men and women and that the experiences, thoughts, and insights of both sexes must be represented in every generalization that is made about human beings.

Today, historical development has for the first time created the necessary 32 conditions by which large groups of women—finally, all women—can emancipate themselves from subordination. Since women's thought has been imprisoned in a confining and erroneous patriarchal framework, the transforming of the consciousness of women about ourselves and our thought is a precondition for change.

We have opened this book with a discussion of the significance of history 33 for human consciousness and psychic well-being. History gives meaning to human life and connects each life to immortality, but history has yet another function. In preserving the collective past and reinterpreting it to the present, human beings define their potential and explore the limits of their possibilities. We learn from the past not only what people before us did and thought and intended, but we also learn how they failed and erred. From the days of the Babylonian king-lists forward, the record of the past has been written and interpreted by men and has primarily focused on the deeds, actions, and intentions of males. With the advent of writing, human knowledge moved forward by tremendous leaps and at a much faster rate than ever before. While, as we have seen, women had participated in maintaining the oral tradition and religious and cultic functions in the preliterate period and for almost a millennium thereafter, their educational disadvantaging and their symbolic dethroning had a profound impact on their future development. The gap between the experience of those who could or might (in the case of lower-class males) participate in the creating of the symbol system and those who merely acted but did not interpret became increasingly greater.

In her brilliant work *The Second Sex*, Simone de Beauvoir focused on 34 the historical end product of this development. She described man as autonomous and transcendent, woman as immanent. But her analysis ignored history. Explaining "why women lack concrete means for organizing themselves into a unit" in defense of their own interests, she stated flatly: "They [women] have no past, no history, no religion of their own."* De Beauvoir is right in her observation that woman has not "transcended," if by transcendence one means the definition and interpretation of human knowledge. But she was wrong in thinking that therefore woman has had no history. Two decades of Women's History scholarship have disproven this fallacy by unearthing an unending list of sources and uncovering and interpreting the hidden history of women. This process of creating a history of women is still ongoing and will need to continue for a long time. We are only beginning to understand its implications.

The myth that women are marginal to the creation of history and civi- 35 lization has profoundly affected the psychology of women and men. It has given men a skewed and essentially erroneous view of their place in human society and in the universe. For women, as shown in the case of Simone de Beauvoir, who surely is one of the best-educated women of her generation, history seemed for millennia to offer only negative lessons and no precedent for significant action, heroism, or liberating example. Most difficult of all was the seeming absence of a tradition which would reaffirm the independence and autonomy of women. It seemed that there had never been any woman or group of women who had lived without male protection. It is significant that all the important examples to the contrary were expressed in myth and fable: amazons, dragon-slayers, women with magic powers. But in real life, women had no history—so they were told and so they believed. And because they had no history they had no future alternatives.

In one sense, class struggle can be described as a struggle for the control 36 of the symbol systems of a given society. The oppressed group, while it shares in and partakes of the leading symbols controlled by the dominant, also develops its own symbols. These become in time of revolutionary change, important forces in the creation of alternatives. Another way of saying this is that revolutionary ideas can be generated only when the oppressed have an alternative to the symbol and meaning system of those who dominate them. Thus, slaves living in an environment controlled by their masters and physically subject to the masters' total control, could maintain their humanity and at times set limits to the masters' power by holding on to their own "culture." Such a culture consisted of collective memories, carefully kept alive, of a prior state of freedom and of alternatives to the masters' ritual, symbols, and beliefs. What was decisive for the individual was the ability to identify him/herself with a state different from that of enslavement or subordination. Thus, all males, whether enslaved or economically or racially oppressed, could still identify with those like them—other males—who showed transcendent qualities in the symbol systems of the master. No matter how degraded, each male slave or peasant was like to the master in his relationship to God. This was

---

* Simone de Beauvoir, *The Second Sex* (New York, 1953), introduction, xxii, both quotes. De Beauvoir based this erroneous generalization on the androcentric historical scholarship available to her at the time of the writing of her book but has to date not corrected it[Lerner's note].

not the case for women. Quite the contrary—in Western civilization up to the time of the Protestant Reformation no woman, no matter how elevated or privileged, could feel her humanity reinforced and confirmed by imagining persons like her—female persons—in positions of intellectual authority and in direct relationship to God.

Where there is no precedent, one cannot imagine alternatives to existing 37 conditions. It is this feature of male hegemony which has been most damaging to women and has ensured their subordinate status for millennia. The denial to women of their history has reinforced their acceptance of the ideology of patriarchy and has undermined the individual woman's sense of self-worth. Men's version of history, legitimized as the "universal truth," has presented women as marginal to civilization and as the victim of historical process. To be so presented and to believe it is almost worse then being entirely forgotten. The picture is false, on both counts, as we now know, but women's progress through history has been marked by their struggle against this disabling distortion.

Moreover, for more than 2500 years women have been educationally 38 disadvantaged and deprived of the conditions under which to develop abstract thought. Obviously thought is not based on sex; the capacity for thought is inherent in humanity; it can be fostered or discouraged, but it cannot ultimately be restrained. This is certainly true for thought generated by and concerned with daily living, the level of thought on which most men and women operate all their lives. But the generating of abstract thought and of new conceptual models—theory formation—is another matter. This activity depends on the individual thinker's education in the best of existing traditions and on the thinker's acceptance by a group of educated persons who, by criticism and interaction, provide "cultural prodding." It depends on having private time. Finally, it depends on the individual thinker being capable of absorbing such knowledge and then making a creative leap into a new ordering. Women, historically, have been unable to avail themselves of all of these necessary preconditions. Educational discrimination has disadvantaged them in access to knowledge; "cultural prodding," which is institutionalized in the upper reaches of the religious and academic establishments, has been unavailable to them. Universally, women of all classes had less leisure time than men, and, due to their child-rearing and family service function, what free time they had was generally not their own. The time of thinking men, their work and study time, has since the inception of Greek philosophy been respected as private. Like Aristotle's slaves, women "who with their bodies minister to the needs of life" have for more than 2500 years suffered the disadvantages of fragmented, constantly interrupted time. Finally, the kind of character development which makes for a mind capable of seeing new connections and fashioning a new order of abstractions has been exactly the opposite of that required of women, trained to accept their subordinate and service-oriented position in society.

Yet there have always existed a tiny minority of privileged women, usu- 39 ally from the ruling elite, who had some access to the same kind of education as did their brothers. From the ranks of such women have come the intellectuals, the thinkers, the writers, the artists. It is such women, throughout history, who have been able to give us a female perspective, an alternative to androcentric thought. They have done so at a tremendous cost and with great difficulty.

Those women, who have been admitted to the center of intellectual 40 activity of their day and especially in the past hundred years, academically trained women, have first had to learn "how to think like a man." In the process, many of them have so internalized that learning that they have lost the ability to conceive of alternatives. The way to think abstractly is to define precisely, to create models in the mind and generalize from them. Such thought, men have taught us, must be based on the exclusion of feelings. Women, like the poor, the subordinate, the marginals, have close knowledge of ambiguity, of feelings mixed with thought, of value judgments coloring abstractions. Women have always experienced the reality of self and community, known it, and shared it with each other. Yet, living in a world in which they are devalued, their experience bears the stigma of insignificance. Thus they have learned to mistrust their own experience and devalue it. What wisdom can there be in menses? What source of knowledge in the milk-filled breast? What food for abstraction in the daily routine of feeding and cleaning? Patriarchal thought has relegated such gender-defined experiences to the realm of the "natural," the non-transcendent. Women's knowledge becomes mere "intuition," women's talk becomes "gossip." Women deal with the irredeemably particular: they experience reality daily, hourly, in their service function (taking care of food and dirt); in their constantly interruptable time; their splintered attention. Can one generalize while the particular tugs at one's sleeve? He who makes symbols and explains the world and she who takes care of his bodily and psychic needs and of his children—the gulf between them is enormous.

Historically, thinking women have had to choose between living a 41 woman's life, with its joys, dailiness, and immediacy, and living a man's life in order to think. The choice for generations of educated women has been cruel and costly. Others have deliberately chosen an existence outside of the sex-gender system, by living alone or with other women. Some of the most significant advances in women's thought were given us by such women, whose personal struggle for an alternative mode of living infused their thinking. But such women, for most of historical time, have been forced to live on the margins of society; they were considered "deviant" and as such found it difficult to generalize from their experience to others and to win influence and approval. Why no female system-builders? Because one cannot think universals when one's self is excluded from the generic.

The social cost of having excluded women from the human enterprise 42 of constructing abstract thought has never been reckoned. We can begin to understand the cost of it to thinking women when we accurately name what was done to us and describe, no matter how painful it may be, the ways in which we have participated in the enterprise. We have long known that rape has been a way of terrorizing us and keeping us in subjection. Now we also know that we have participated, although unwittingly, in the rape of our minds.

Creative women, writers and artists, have similarly struggled against a 43 distorting reality. A literary canon, which defined itself by the Bible, the Greek classics, and Milton, would necessarily bury the significance and the meaning of women's literary work, as historians buried the activities of women. The effort to resurrect this meaning and to re-evaluate women's literary and artistic work is recent. Feminist literary criticism and poetics have introduced us to a reading of women's literature, which finds a hidden, deliberately "slant," yet powerful world-view. Through the reinterpretations of feminist literary critics we are uncovering among women writers of the eighteenth and nineteenth centuries a female language of metaphors, symbols, and myths. Their themes often are profoundly subversive of the male tradition. They feature criticism of the Biblical interpretation of Adam's fall; rejection of the goddess/witch dichotomy; projection or fear of the split self. The powerful aspect of woman's creativity becomes symbolized in heroines endowed with magical powers of goodness or in strong women who are banished to cellars or to live as "the madwoman in the attic." Others write in metaphors upgrading the confined domestic space, making it serve symbolically as the world.*

For centuries, we find in the works of literary women a pathetic, almost 44 desperate search for Women's History, long before historical studies as such exist. Nineteenth-century female writers avidly read the work of eighteenth-century female novelists; over and over again they read the "lives" of queens, abbesses, poets, learned women. Early "compilers" searched the Bible and all historical sources to which they had access to create weighty tomes with female heroines.

Women's literary voices, successfully marginalized and trivialized by 45 the dominant male establishment, nevertheless survived. The voices of anonymous women were present as a steady undercurrent in the oral tradition, in folksong and nursery rhymes, tales of powerful witches and good fairies. In stitchery, embroidery, and quilting women's artistic creativity expressed an alternate vision. In letters, diaries, prayers, and song the symbol-making force of women's creativity pulsed and persisted.

All of this work will be the subject of our inquiry in the next volume. 46 How did women manage to survive under male cultural hegemony; what was their influence and impact on the patriarchal symbol system; how and

---

*Sandra M. Gilbert and Susan Gubar, *The Madwoman in the Attic: The Woman Writer and the Nineteenth Century Imagination* (New Haven, 1984) [Lerner's note].

under what conditions did they come to create an alternate, feminist world-view? These are the questions we will examine in order to chart the rise of feminist consciousness as a historical phenomenon.

Women and men have entered historical process under different condi- 47
tions and have passed through it at different rates of speed. If recording, defining, and interpreting the past marks man's entry into history, this occurred for males in the third millennium B.C. It occurred for women (and only some of them) with a few notable exceptions in the nineteenth century. Until then, all History was for women pre-History.

Women's lack of knowledge of our own history of struggle and achieve- 48
ment has been one of the major means of keeping us subordinate. But even those of us already defining ourselves as feminist thinkers and engaged in the process of critiquing traditional systems of ideas are still held back by unacknowledged restraints embedded deeply within our psyches. Emergent woman faces a challenge to her very definition of self. How can her daring thought—naming the hitherto unnamed, asking the questions defined by all authorities as "non-existent"—how can such thought coexist with her life as woman? In stepping out of the constructs of patriarchal thought, she faces, as Mary Daly put it, "existential nothingness." And more immediately, she fears the threat of loss of communication with, approval by, and love from the man (or the men) in her life. Withdrawal of love and the designation of thinking women as "deviant" have historically been the means of discouraging women's intellectual work. In the past, and now, many emergent women have turned to other women as love objects and reinforcers of self. Heterosexual feminists, too, have throughout the ages drawn strength from their friendships with women, from chosen celibacy, or from the separation of sex from love. No thinking man has ever been threatened in his self-definition and his love life as the price for his thinking. We should not underestimate the significance of that aspect of gender control as a force restraining women from full participation in the process of creating thought systems. Fortunately, for this generation of educated women, liberation has meant the breaking of this emotional hold and the conscious reinforcement of our selves through the support of other women.

Nor is this the end of our difficulties. In line with our historic gender- 49
conditioning, women have aimed to please and have sought to avoid disapproval. This is poor preparation for making the leap into the unknown required of those who fashion new systems. Moreover, each emergent woman has been schooled in patriarchal thought. We each hold at least one great man in our heads. The lack of knowledge of the female past has deprived us of female heroines, a fact which is only recently being corrected through the development of Women's History. So, for a long time, thinking women have refurbished the idea systems created by men, engaging in a dialogue with the great male minds in their heads. Elizabeth Cady Stanton took on the Bible, the Church fathers, the founders of the American republic. Kate Millet ar-

gued with Freud, Norman Mailer, and the liberal literary establishment; Simone de Beauvoir with Sartre, Marx, and Camus; all Marxist-Feminists are in a dialogue with Marx and Engels and some also with Freud. In this dialogue woman intends merely to accept whatever she finds useful to her in the great man's system. But in these systems woman—as a concept, a collective entity, an individual—is marginal or subsumed.

In accepting such dialogue, thinking woman stays far longer than is useful within the boundaries or the question-setting defined by the "great men." And just as long as she does, the source of new insight is closed to her. 50

Revolutionary thought has always been based on upgrading the experi- 51
ence of the oppressed. The peasant had to learn to trust in the significance of his life experience before he could dare to challenge the feudal lords. The industrial worker had to become "class-conscious," the Black "race-conscious" before liberating thought could develop into revolutionary theory. The oppressed have acted and learned simultaneously—the process of becoming the newly conscious person or group is in itself liberating. So with women.

The shift in consciousness we must make occurs in two steps: we must, 52
at least for a time, be woman-centered. We must, as far as possible, leave patriarchal thought behind.

To be woman-centered means: 53
Asking if women were central to this argument, how would it be defined? It means ignoring all evidence of women's marginality, because, even where women appear to be marginal, this is the result of patriarchal intervention; frequently also it is merely an appearance. The basic assumption should be that it is inconceivable for anything ever to have taken place in the world in which women were not involved, except if they were prevented from participation through coercion and repression.

When using methods and concepts from traditional systems of thought, 54
it means using them from the vantage point of the centrality of women. Women cannot be put into the empty spaces of patriarchal thought and systems—in moving to the center, they transform the system.

To step outside of patriarchal thought means: 55
Being skeptical toward every known system of thought; being critical of all assumptions, ordering values and definitions.

Testing one's statement by trusting our own, the female experience. 56
Since such experience has usually been trivialized or ignored, it means overcoming the deep-seated resistance within ourselves toward accepting ourselves and our knowledge as valid. It means getting rid of the great men in our heads and substituting for them ourselves, our sisters, our anonymous foremothers.

Being critical toward our own thought, which is, after all, thought 57
trained in the patriarchal tradition. Finally, it means developing intellectual

courage, the courage to stand alone, the courage to reach farther than our grasp, the courage to risk failure. Perhaps the greatest challenge to thinking women is the challenge to move from the desire for safety and approval to the most "unfeminine" quality of all—that of intellectual arrogance, the supreme hubris which asserts to itself the right to reorder the world. The hubris of the godmakers, the hubris of the male system-builders.

The system of patriarchy is a historic construct; it has a beginning; it 58 will have an end. Its time seems to have nearly run its course—it no longer serves the needs of men or women and in its inextricable linkage to militarism, hierarchy, and racism it threatens the very existence of life on earth.

What will come after, what kind of structure will be the foundation for 59 alternate forms of social organization we cannot yet know. We are living in an age of unprecedented transformation. We are in the process of becoming. But we already know that woman's mind, at last unfettered after so many millennia, will have its share in providing vision, ordering, solutions. Women at long last are demanding, as men did in the Renaissance, the right to explain, the right to define. Women, in thinking themselves out of patriarchy add transforming insights to the process of redefinition.

As long as both men and women regard the subordination of half the 60 human race to the other as "natural," it is impossible to envision a society in which differences do not connote either dominance or subordination. The feminist critique of the patriarchal edifice of knowledge is laying the groundwork for a correct analysis of reality, one which at the very least can distinguish the whole from a part. Women's History, the essential tool in creating feminist consciousness in women, is providing the body of experience against which new theory can be tested and the ground on which women of vision can stand.

A feminist world-view will enable women and men to free their minds 61 from patriarchal thought and practice and at last to build a world free of dominance and hierarchy, a world that is truly human.

QUESTIONS ABOUT LERNER'S DISCOURSE COMMUNITY AND HER CONCERNS IN THIS SELECTION

1. What about women does Lerner argue was reified as a consequence of exchanging them? Do you think all feminists would agree with her?
2. What does Lerner say class for men is based on? What does she say class for women is based on?
3. In Lerner's view, what is it in the system of patriarchy that females receive for "subordination in all matters, sexual service, and unpaid domestic service . . ." (paragraph 22)?
4. According to Lerner, how have men exerted "dominance over definition"? Do

you see signs of such dominance yet today? If so, what examples might you point out?

5. Do you agree with Lerner's analysis of the basic motivation for rape?

6. Why does Lerner claim that using the word *freedom* for past "relative improvements in the status of women" is "illusory and unwarranted"? Do you agree with her?

7. Lerner writes that now, for the first time, historical development has led to conditions that allow all women to emancipate themselves. What do you think those conditions are?

8. What, according to Lerner, are the preconditions for abstract thought? Can you add to her list?

9. Why does Lerner claim that patriarchy is connected to militarism, hierarchy, and racism? Do you agree with her? Do such views themselves show a kind of sexism?

10. Why does Lerner claim history is important for human beings? Do her claims seem reasonable to you?

11. What do you think a feminist worldview would be like? What do you think Lerner would say a feminist worldview would be like?

QUESTIONS ON LERNER'S RHETORICAL STRATEGIES

1. How do you react to Lerner's use of *we*, as in "We have opened this book with a discussion of the significance of history for human consciousness and psychic well-being" (paragraph 33)? Are all her uses of *we* similar? To whom do the various *we*'s refer?

2. In paragraph six, Lerner notes that the product of the "commodification of women . . . may very well represent the first accumulation of private property." How do you react to her words "may very well"? Do they make her seem unsure of herself?

3. Lerner consistently writes about female "sexual services," not so often about love. Why does she do this?

4. In paragraph forty Lerner asks several questions, such as the following: "What source of knowledge in the milk-filled breast?" How do these questions function here? Who is the assumed questioner?

5. What metaphors does Lerner use to characterize the patriarchal system? How effective are they?

6. In this selection, Lerner makes some sweeping generalizations. For example, in paragraph thirty-one she writes that the "androcentric fallacy . . . is built into all the mental constructs of Western civilization. . . ." Does she offer enough evidence for such generalizations?

7. Several of Lerner's paragraphs are only one sentence long. Should any of them be revised?

8. Why does Lerner review the steps in the creation of patriarchy before exploring male control over cultural symbol systems?

9. Consider the conclusion of this selection, where Lerner is addressing the ques-

tion of what it means to be woman-centered. To whom is she addressing the conclusion? Why would she change her stance so dramatically at this point?

WRITING FROM WITHIN AND ABOUT HISTORY AND ITS STUDY

Writing for Yourself

1. In your journal, explore how Lerner's views affect your ideas on dating, courtship, and marriage.
2. In your journal, explore how you think men react to the "thinking woman" today.

Writing for Nonacademic Audiences

1. Since moving away to college, one of your friends has become a rather radical feminist. Write this friend a letter in which you react to radical feminism.
2. Write a 500-word opinion piece for your college newspaper on the metaphors that men use for women on your campus. Are women called foxes, chicks, or what?
3. Write a 500-word opinion piece for your college newspaper on the metaphors that women use for men on your campus. Are men called hunks, studs, or what?

Writing for Academic Audiences

1. Select several derogatory terms, such as *slut* and *harlot*, that have been used to describe a certain type of women. Using the *Oxford English Dictionary*, explore how these words have changed in meaning over time. Write a 750-word essay for a class in semantics; in this paper explain what happened to the meanings of these words and why.
2. Interview some women who you think are successful. Ask them who their heroes and role models were as they were growing up. Then, for a class in modern American history, write a 1,000-word essay in which you analyze what roles heroes play in the lives of successful modern American women.
3. For a class in the history of feminism in America, select a person who contributed to the rise of the movement and write a 1,000-word essay describing aspects of his or her life and contributions to feminism.
4. For a class in modern American history, write a 1,500-word paper in which you defend your answer to the following question: Is the system of patriarchy in America beginning to crumble?
5. For a seminar in the meaning and purposes of history, write a 1,500-word essay in which you evaluate Lerner's claims about the uses of history in people's lives.

Eugene D. Genovese

(b. 1930)

Eugene D. Genovese, who has taught at several North American universities and is now a professor of history at the University of Rochester, is usually associated with the discourse community of Marxist historians. Genovese generally sees history as the result of class struggle and feels the most sympathy for the oppressed masses, but throughout his career his expressions of Marxism have varied in substance and tone.

At times these expressions have been doctrinaire and aggressive. While teaching at Rutgers University from 1963–1967, for instance, he declared that he "welcomed a victory" by the Vietcong in the Vietnam War. Such statements caused such an intense reaction that his appointment at Rutgers became an issue in the 1965 New Jersey gubernatorial campaign. During this campaign, in fact, Richard Nixon called for Genovese's removal from his post on three different occasions.

Genovese's doctrinaire and aggressive expressions of Marxism also appear in some of his writings. In works such as From Rebellion to Revolution: Afro-American Slave Revolts in the Making of the Modern World *(1979) and "Academic Freedom Today" (1980), Genovese applauds Zimbabwe rebels for fanning their countrymen into revolt, expresses some support for Castro's Cuba, and makes some positive judgments on the Soviet Union under Stalin.*

In other works, however, Genovese's expressions of Marxism are more subtle and moderate. In the work for which he is probably best known, Roll, Jordan, Roll: The World the Slaves Made *(1974), his Marxism is sufficiently subtle that some readers miss it altogether. And to a degree, this is understandable, since* Roll, Jordan, Roll *is a masterpiece of quotation, anecdote, and detail relating to nearly every aspect of the slaves' lives prior to the Civil War. But as Michael Bordelon points out in* Twentieth Century American Historians, *Genovese's Marxism is not absent. It shows itself in his focus on slavery as a problem not of race but of class, and in his analysis of how modes of production in the old South led to other aspects of Southern culture without totally determining their development.*

The following selection, "Time and Work Rhythms," is taken from Book Two of Roll, Jordan, Roll.

TIME AND WORK RHYTHMS

It goes without saying that "niggers are lazy": the planters always said so, as 1
did the "poor white trash," whose own famous commitment to hard and
steady work doubtless assured their entrance into John Calvin's Kingdom of
Heaven. Some of the refrain may be dismissed as obvious ideological ratio-
nalization and self-serving cant or a distorted interpretation of the effects of
a lack of adequate incentives. Yet much more needs to be said, for the slaves
themselves sang at their work:

> Nigger mighty happy when he layin' by the corn.   2
> Nigger mighty happy when he hear dat dinner horn;
> But he more happy when de night come on,
> Dat sun's a slantin', as sho's you born!
> Dat old cow's a shakin' dat great big bell,
> And de frogs tunin' up, 'cause de dew's done fell. *

"The white men," Johann David Schoepf observed on his travels during the 3
1780s, "are all the time complaining that the blacks will not work, and they
themselves do nothing." Virginia's great humorist, George W. Bagby, once
reflected on the complacency and self-satisfaction of antebellum life: "Time
was abundant in those days. It was made for slaves, and we had the slaves."†

The slaveholders presided over a plantation system that constituted a 4
halfway house between peasant and factory cultures. The tobacco and cotton
plantations, which dominated the slave economy in the United States, ranged
closer to the peasant than the factory model, in contradistinction to the great
sugar plantations of the Caribbean, which in some respects resembled factories in the field; but even the small holders pushed their laborers toward
modern work discipline. The planters' problem came to this: How could they
themselves preserve as much as possible of that older way of life to which
they aspired and yet convince their slaves to repudiate it? How could they
instill factorylike discipline into a working population engaged in a rural
system that, for all its tendencies toward modern discipline, remained bound
to the rhythms of nature and to traditional ideas of work, time, and leisure?

They succeeded in overcoming this contradiction only to the extent that 5
they got enough work out of their slaves to make the system pay at a level
necessary to their survival as a slaveholding class in a capitalist world market.
But they failed in deeper ways that cast a shadow over the long-range pros-
pects for that very survival and over the future of both blacks and whites in

---

*Rawick, Ed., *Texas Narr.*, V (4) 54. [All of the following, except where noted, are Genovese's
    notes].
†Johann David Schoepf, *Travels in the Confederation, 1783–1784* (2 vols.; trans. A. J. Morri-
    son; Philadelphia, 1911), **II**, 118. The Bagby quotation is from Bancroft, *Slave Trading*,
    p. 88.

American society. Too often they fell back on the whip and thereby taught and learned little. When they went to other incentives, as fortunately most tried to do, they did get satisfactory economic results, but at the same time they reinforced traditional attitudes and values instead of replacing them with more advanced ones.

The black work ethic grew up within a wider Protestant Euro-Ameri- 6 can community with a work ethic of its own. The black ethic represented at once a defense against an enforced system of economic exploitation and an autonomous assertion of values generally associated with preindustrial peoples. As such, it formed part of a more general southern work ethic, which developed in antagonism to that of the wider American society. A Euro-American, basically Anglo-Saxon work ethic helped shape that of southerners in general and slaves in particular and yet, simultaneously, generated a profound antithesis.

In the medieval Catholic formulation the necessity to work both de- 7 rived from the Fall of Man and served as an expression of humility and submission. In the words of Ernst Troeltsch, "Labor is thus both a penalty and a means of salvation."* The Lutheran doctrine of the calling emphasized the means to salvation rather than the penalty, and thereby strengthened the Christian insistence on being satisfied with one's station in life. Calvinism, which so profoundly altered Anglo-American culture, raised the idea of the calling to a religious duty in itself. Whereas in the Lutheran formulation work, with its rigor and anxiety, continued to contradict fundamental features of man's nature, in the Calvinist formulation it became an expression of Grace and therefore an end in itself as a worthy and agreeable means to salvation. Troeltsch writes:

> To people who have been educated on Calvinistic principles the lazy habit 8 of living on an inherited income seems a downright sin; to follow a calling which has no definite end and which yields no material profit seems a foolish waste of time and energy, and failure to make full use of chances of gaining material profit seems like indifference towards God. From the Calvinistic point of view laziness is the most dangerous vice. . . .
>
> The principles and ideals of Ascetic Protestantism may therefore be sum- 9 marized thus: the inner severance of feeling and enjoyment from all the objects of labour; the unceasing harnessing of labour to an aim which lies in the other world, and therefore must occupy us till death; the depreciation of possessions, of all things earthly, to the level of expediency; the habit of industry in order to suppress all distracting and idle impulses; and the willing use of profit for the religious community and for public welfare. . . .†

---

* Troeltsch, *Social Teaching of the Christian Churches*, I, 321.
† *Ibid.*, **II**, 611, 808–809; also **II**, 554, 609. James L. Peacock suggests that Calvinism in the South has substituted fundamentalist attacks on certain social taboos for a worldly asceticism translatable into a bourgeois work ethic. This line of criticism deserves further investigation. See "The Southern Protestant Ethic Disease," in Morland, ed., *The Not So Solid South*, p. 109.

To this stern doctrine of work as duty the slave opposed a religion of joy in 10
life that echoed traditional Africa and, surprising as it may seem, even more
firmly echoed the spirit of the plantation community itself. To speak of a
"calling" or vocation for slaves would be absurd; but more to the point,
worldly asceticism neither corresponded to the sensibilities shaped by the historic development from Africa to the New World nor could take root among
a people who had no material stake in its flowering.

For bourgeois society in sixteenth- and seventeenth-century England a 11
regular rhythm of labor had to be established. From a steady work week
punctuated by one day of Sabbath rest to such household details as regular
mealtimes, the middle classes vigorously campaigned for a philosophy of saving time and doing things on schedule. Work increasingly passed from being
one part of an organically integrated life into being a discrete central fact of
existence. This ideological process, accompanying the transformation of la-
bor-power into a commodity, required and conditioned new personalities for
whom rest and leisure had lower value; for whom life had to be economically
rationalized; and for whom the rising concern with individualism prepared
the way, however ironically, for the subordination of man to the means of
production. *

"World-rejecting asceticism," as Weber called it, led not to a flight from 12
the world but to a continuous battle against it—to the demand to rationalize
everything and to subject all spheres of life to systematic conduct. Such a
world-view, to be transformed into a social power, had to rest on the assent
of free men; it became inseparable from the right of private judgment and its
attendant concern for individual liberty.† A great deal more than the fervor
of white Baptist and Methodist preachers would be required to make the
message meaningful to enslaved Afro-Americans. The Baptist Christianity of
the slaves had neither the capacity nor the aim to do to the slaves what Methodism did to the English working class.

The heart of black slave culture rested in a religion that, however inti- 13
mate its connections with white religion, emerged as a product of the black
experience. For the slaves and for black people generally, religion did not
constitute one feature of life or merely one element in an ideological complex;
rather, it constituted the fundamental spiritual expression of their entire
world-view, as manifested in attitudes toward time and work. An ex-slave
described his conversion experience: "He spoke to me once after I had prayed
and prayed trying to hurry him and get religion. He said, 'I am a time-God.

---

* This discussion has drawn on the perceptive analyses of Christopher Hill, *Century of Revolu-
    tion*, pp. 84–85; Rawick, *Sundown to Sunup*, pp. 128–129; and Michel Foucault, *Mad-
    ness and Civilization: A History of Insanity in the Age of Reason* (trans. R. Howard; New
    York, 1965).

† See esp. Weber, *Sociology of Religion*, pp. 169, 177. Alternatives to this Western tradition do
    exist; see, e.g., Robert N. Bellah, *Tokugawa Religion: The Values of Pre-industrial Japan*
    (Glencoe, Ill., 1957), for the Japanese case.

Behold, I work after the counsel of my own will and in due time I will visit whomsoever I will.' "* The Reverend Henry H. Mitchell has addressed himself to current criticisms that black church services are too long and undisciplined:

> Yet Black tradition holds that the Holy Spirit does not follow white clocks. The   14
> Spirit must have its way, and whatever God does is right on time. It is believed
> that the true Presence is intellectually as well as emotionally enlightening, and
> that it takes *time* for the Spirit to involve a congregation which must first be
> emptied of private concern for mundane interests.

Dr. Mitchell also hints at a special sense of historical time when he notes that   15
blacks see the Bible, not as white fundamentalists do, as the repository of unchanging truths, but as a source of historical experience and a moral context for discussion of their own world.†

The slaves' attitude toward time and work arose primarily from their   16
own experience on the plantations of the South. Comparisons with Africa suggest some important cultural continuities. Traditional African time-reckoning focuses on present and past, not future. Time, being two-dimensional, moves, as it were, backward into a long past; the future, not having been experienced, appears senseless. This idea of time, which inhibited the appearance of an indigenous millennialism prior to Islamic and Christian penetration, encouraged economic attitudes not readily assimilable to early bourgeois demands for saving, thrift, and accumulation.‡ But, however strong the specifically African influence, even more important are those tendencies which characterize preindustrial agricultural peoples in general, for whom the Africans provided a variant or, rather, a series of variants.

G. J. O. Ojo, in *Yoruba Culture*, offers a reference point when he notes   17
that "within the tropics and particularly close to the equator, within about 10°, the almost uniform length of day and night lends itself as the standard reference of time."§ The Yoruba‖ gave no thought to scientific explanations of the day; they began the day at sunrise and measured the month by the phases of the moon. They had the great advantage of a climate in which the sun rarely disappeared behind clouds, but when it did, they estimated time by the amount of work completed and by the behavior of birds and animals. Measurement of a year was not precise, nor need it have been, for the important marks lay in the intersection of work and season.

The Yoruba experience provided one variant of the West African, and   18
the West African provided one complex of variants of a more general traditional, rural preindustrial experience. Traditional society measured its time

---

* Fisk University, *God Struck Me Dead*, p. 7.
† H. H. Mitchell, *Black Preaching*, pp. 107, 113; also p. 130.
‡ Mbiti, *African Religions and Philosophy*, pp. 5, 17, 19; *New Testament Eschatology in an African Background*, Ch. 2.
§ Ojo, *Yoruba Culture*, p. 201.
‖ People of Southwest Nigeria [Editors' note].

by calendars based on agricultural and seasonal patterns, which themselves formed part of an integrated religious world-view. The year proceeded according to a certain rhythm, not according to equal units of time; appropriate festivals and rites broke its continuity and marked the points at which the human spirit celebrated the rhythm of the natural order. Not pure quantities of time obtained, but such flexible units as the beginning of planting and of the harvest. Time became subordinated to the natural order of work and leisure, as their servant rather than their master. *

Whereas in peasant farming the work tasks and such natural conditions 19 as the amount of daylight determine the length of the workday, the acceptable number and duration of breaks, and the amount and type of leisure, in factory work "the arbitrarily fixed time schedule determines the beginning and the end of work periods."† In peasant societies work tasks such as planting and harvesting, which appear to conform to the demands of nature, have oriented the notation of time. E. P. Thompson argues convincingly that this "task orientation" has rendered work more humanly comprehensible: "The peasant or labourer appears to attend upon what is an observed necessity."‡ For the preindustrial English community as a whole the distinction between "work" and "life" was much less clear than it was to become; the working day itself lengthened and contracted according to necessary tasks, and no great conflict appeared between the demands of work and those of leisure. One need not idealize the undoubtedly harsh physical conditions of preindustrial rural life to appreciate the force of Thompson's argument, especially since those who passed under industrial work discipline probably were themselves the ones who came most to idealize their previous existence and thereby to heighten either their resistance or their despair. Eric Hobsbawm writes:

> Industrial labour—and especially mechanized factory labour—imposes a reg- 20
> ularity, routine and monotony quite unlike pre-industrial rhythms of work,
> which depend on the variation of the seasons or the weather, the multiplicity
> of tasks in occupations unaffected by the rational division of labour, the vagar-
> ies of other human beings or animals, or even a man's own desire to play instead
> of working. This was so even in skilled pre-industrial wage-work, such as that

* See esp. Henri Mendras, *The Vanishing Peasant: Innovation and Change in French Agricul-ture* (trans. J. Lerner; Cambridge, Mass., 1970), pp. 55–56.

† *Ibid.*, p. 62. The interesting discussion in Mullin, *Flight and Rebellion*, pp. 42–45, suffers from a failure to relate African time-reckoning to preindustrial European. As Eileen Power notes, Charlemagne named the months of the year precisely according to seasonal work rhythms; in her rendering from the Frankish: Winter, Mud, Spring, Easter, Joy, Plow, Hay, Harvest, Wind, Vintage, Autumn, and Holy Month (*Medieval People*, p. 27). See also Homans, *English Villagers*, esp. Ch. 23. The months as named by Charlemagne strikingly parallel the months designated by Africans; see Eva L. R. Meyerowitz, *The Sacred State of the Akan* (London, 1951), pp. 142–143; Mbiti, *African Religions and Philosophy*, p. 21. Even today, clock sensitivity varies enormously according to class and ethnicity in the United States; see Gay Gaer Luce, *Body Time: Physiological Rhythms and Social Stress* (New York, 1972), p. 13.

‡ E. P. Thompson, "Time, Work Discipline and Industrial Capitalism," *Past and Present*, No. 38 (Dec., 1967), p. 60.

of journeymen craftsmen, whose ineradicable taste for not starting the week's work until the Tuesday ("Saint Monday") was the despair of their masters. Industry brings the tyranny of the clock, the pacesetting machine, and the complex and carefully-timed interaction of processes: the measurement of life, not in seasons ("Michaelmas term" or "Lent term") or even in weeks and days, but in minutes, and above all a mechanized *regularity* of work which conflicts not only with tradition, but with all the inclinations of a humanity as yet unconditioned into it. *

The advent of clock time represented more than a marking of regular 21
work units—of minutes and hours—and of arbitrary schedules, for it supported the increasing division of labor and transformed that division of labor into a division of time itself. Capitalist production had to be measured in units of labor-time, and those units themselves took on the mysterious and apparently self-determining properties of commodities. When Benjamin Franklin said that time is money, he said much more than is generally understood. E. P. Thompson comments: "In a mature capitalist society all time must be consumed, marketed, put to *use*; it is offensive for the labour force merely to pass the time."† Natural rhythms of work and leisure gave place to arbitrary schedules, which were, however, arbitrary only from the point of view of the laborers. The capitalists and those ideologues who were developing a new idea of rationality based on the demands of a rapidly developing economy saw the matter differently. The process of cultural transformation had to rest on economic and extra-economic compulsion and ultimately on violence. It served as the industrial equivalent of that which the West Indian slaveholders, with fewer inhibitions, called "seasoning."

The transformation in the labor force was complete. Thompson writes: 22
"The first generation of factory workers were taught by their masters the importance of time; the second generation formed their short-time committees in the ten-hour movement; the third generation struck for overtime or time-and-a-half. They had accepted the categories of their employers and learned their lesson, that time is money, only too well."‡

The slaves could not reckon time either according to preindustrial peas- 23
ant models or according to industrial factory models. The plantations, especially the sugar plantations that dominated most of the slaveholding regions of the New World, although not of the United States, did resemble factories in the field, but even if we take them as our norm we cannot escape the implications of their preindustrial side. However much their economic organization required and tried to compel quasi-industrial discipline, they also threw up countervailing pressures and embodied inescapable internal contradictions.

* Hobsbawm, *Industry and Empire*, p. 67.
† E. P. Thompson, "Time, Work Discipline and Industrial Capitalism," pp. 90–91.
‡ *Ibid.*, p. 86; Elwin H. Powell, *Design of Discord, Studies of Anomie: Suicide, Urban Society, War* (New York, 1970), p. 8; Karl Marx, *The Grundrisse* (ed. and trans. David McLellan; New York, 1971), p. 148.

The setting remained rural, and the rhythm of work followed seasonal 24
fluctuations. Nature remained the temporal reference point for the slaves.
However much the slaveholders might have wished to transform their slaves
into clock-punchers, they could not, for in a variety of senses both literal and
metaphoric, there were no clocks to punch.* The planters, especially the resident planters of the United States and Brazil but even the typical West Indian agents of absentee owners, hardly lived in a factory world themselves
and at best could only preach what the most docile or stupid slave knew very
well they did not and could not practice. Since the plantation economy required extraordinary exertion at critical points of the year, notably the harvest, it required measures to capitalize on the slaves' willingness to work in
spurts rather than steadily. The slaveholders turned the inclinations of the
slaves to their own advantage, but simultaneously they made far greater
concessions to the value system and collective sensibility of the quarters than
they intended.

The slaveholders, as usual, had their way but paid a price. The slaves, 25
as usual, fell victim to the demands of their exploiters but had some success
in pressing their own advantage. Thus, the plantation system served as a
halfway house for Africans between their agricultural past and their imposed
industrial future. But, it froze them into a position that allowed for their
exploitation on the margins of industrial society. The advantage of this compromise, from the black point of view, lay in the protection it provided for
their rich community life and its cultural consolidation. The disadvantage
lay in its encouragement of a way of life that, however admirable intrinsically, ill prepared black people to compete in the economic world into which
they would be catapulted by emancipation.

John Horton observes, in a stimulating essay entitled "Time and Cool 26
People": "Time in industrial society is clock time. It seems to be an external,
objective regulator of human activities. But for the sociologist . . . time is
diverse; it is always social and subjective. A man's sense of time derives from
his place in the social structure and his lived experience." Horton concludes
that "street people," as he calls them, plan their time quite deliberately and
rationally but in accordance with their own priorities. The same dude who
can never be counted on to show up for work on time will arrive at his girl-
friend's schoolyard precisely at noon to pick her up on her lunch hour. Leith-
man Spinks, an ex-slave from Louisiana, recalled that his master fed the slaves
communally. "Dat de one time," he chuckled, "massa could allus 'pend on
de niggers. When de bell say, 'Come and git it,' all us am there."† And no

---

* "We didn't own no clocks in dem days. We just told de time by de sun in de day and de stars
    at night. If it was clouded we didn't know what time it was" (Jane Simpson, ex-slave, in
    Yetman, ed., *Life Under the "Peculiar Institution,"* p. 279); also Fisk University, *Un-
    written History of Slavery*, p. 146.
† John Horton, "Time and Cool People," in Lee Rainwater, ed., *Soul* (Chicago, 1970), pp. 31–
    50; Rawick, ed., *Texas Narr.*, IV (4), 57. See also the exasperated remarks of Harrod C.
    Anderson, a planter, Diary, Nov. 16, 1855.

one ever accused the slaves of lacking a sense of "time" in their singing. The attitude Horton discusses developed out of the plantation experience, rather than out of the preindustrial agricultural experience in general. It combined the ostensibly natural sense of time found among traditional agriculturalists with an attitude of disguised disobedience—of apparent shiftlessness—which marks a slave class as at once sullen, "stupid," and uncooperative and yet enormously resourceful at doing what it wants to do.

The contradiction between the slave's nature as a human being and his 27
status as a thing with irritating human complications repeatedly drove the slaveholders into responses that, if economically and even socially rational in a direct sense, invariably proved self-defeating with respect to larger ends. Consider Frederick Douglass's bitter indictment:

> I never met with a slave in that part of the country [eastern Maryland] who 28
> could tell me with any certainty how old he was. Few at the time knew any-
> thing of the months of the year or the days of the month. They measured the
> ages of their children by spring-time, winter-time, harvest-time, planting-time,
> and the like. Masters allowed no questions concerning their ages to be put to
> them by slaves. Such questions were regarded by the masters as evidence of an
> impudent curiosity. *

Douglass may have exaggerated the determination of the slaveholders as a 29
class to suppress information and may have underestimated their carelessness and indifference, but most slaves in the South probably did not know their exact age. † On some plantations masters and overseers took care to record birth dates, whether or not they imparted the information to the slaves them-selves; the more paternalistic masters would even record the data in the fam-ily Bible. Many plantation journals, however, contain entries such as these: "List of Negroes of the Estate of William Robertson, with their supposed ages"; "bought a boy . . . about fourteen years old;" or simply a list of slaves with their ages recorded as "about . . ."‡

The slaveholders' objections to having slaves know their age, or their 30
sheer indifference to this feature of the slaves' humanity, proved most ob-viously self-defeating in the element of irrationality it introduced into slave sales. Without adequate records unscrupulous slave dealers could disguise the age of their human commodities with impunity. Even experienced planters could never be certain of what they were buying. George S. Barnsley of Geor-gia wrote in 1860: "Took Dick to Maj. Wooley's to see how old he was. The maj. considers him 40 years old and his present value to be $1100. I don't think that he is much over 33 years old."§

---

* *Life and Times of Frederick Douglass*, p. 27. For other black complaints see WPA, *Negro in Virginia*, pp. 29 ff., and Lester, *To Be a Slave*, p. 30.

† See, e.g., the careful account kept by the overseer on a sugar estate in Louisiana: Seale Diary, 1857.

‡ Printed slave list for 1856 in the Haywood Papers; Bruce Papers, box II, folder 1855; Macrery Papers, 1847; Negro Collection of Duke University (certificates of freedom for New York, from 1799).

§ Barnsley Diary, Jan. 9, 1860.

The planters had to sacrifice more than commercial inconvenience. As 31 Douglass saw, the slave children's imprecise notions about their age reinforced a much more general education in the meaning of time. Carelessness about ages and indifference to or ignorance of exact temporal information reinforced the already strong tendency toward preindustrial and natural patterns of thought. Since children acquire a sense of time from their particular environment, since from an early age they "sense the cycles of change in their environment,"* and since slave children did not normally break into field work until the age of twelve, their masters had an uphill battle to make them time-conscious in the industrial sense of the word. The young slaves began with half-time labor and were eased toward full-time labor over a period of years. Masters and overseers tried to bring them on slowly and safely, but the battle to make them into workers with good Calvinist attitudes had been unwittingly surrendered before it began.

The black view of time, conditioned by the plantation slave experience, 32 has provided a great source of strength for a people at bay, as one of Bishop A. G. Dunston's sermons makes clear:

> You know, that's the way God does it. Same as you can't hurry God—so why 33 don't you wait, just wait. Everybody's ripping and racing and rushing. And God is taking his time. Because he knows that it isn't hurtin' nearly so bad as you and I think it's hurtin'—and that is the way he wants us to go. But by and by he brings relief. . . .†

Black people, in short, learned to take the blow and to parry it as best they 34 could. They found themselves shut out by white racism from part of the dominant culture's value system, and they simultaneously resisted that system both by historically developed sensibility and by necessity. Accordingly, they developed their own values as a force for community cohesion and survival, but in so doing they widened the cultural gap and exposed themselves to even harder blows from a white nation that could neither understand their behavior nor respect its moral foundations.

QUESTIONS ABOUT GENOVESE'S DISCOURSE COMMUNITY AND HIS CONCERNS IN THIS SELECTION

1. How does Genovese describe what he calls the "rural preindustrial experience"? How does this experience relate to the challenge Genovese says the slaveholders faced?
2. What is the connection between the "advent of clock time" and the "division of labor" (paragraph 21)?
3. Genovese writes that the black view of time was a "source of strength for a people at bay" (paragraph 32). Did it also help keep them at bay?

---

* Luce, *Body Time*, p. 114.
† Quoted in H. H. Mitchell, *Black Preaching*, p. 131.

4. From this selection, can you see why some scholars see Calvinism as powerful enough to move people to settle and cultivate continents?

5. How does Genovese characterize the religion of the slaves? How accurate does his characterization seem to you? Does the generalization about "a religion of joy in life" seem too broad?

6. How common do you think it is for a historian to claim, as Genovese does, that the slaves "had some success in pressing their own advantage" (paragraph 25)?

7. In what ways were the emancipated slaves poorly prepared for an industrial world?

8. What specifically Marxist positions do you find in this selection?

9. What do you think Genovese would say is the prime mover in human affairs? What is the primary force behind historical change?

QUESTIONS ABOUT GENOVESE'S RHETORICAL STRATEGIES

1. How would you characterize the tone of the first sentence of this selection? What words and phrases are especially important to the creation of that tone? Is the tone appropriate to Genovese's purpose?

2. Why does Genovese label the Kingdom of Heaven "John Calvin's Kingdom of Heaven"?

3. What connotations does "a halfway house" (paragraph two) carry? Are they appropriate in context?

4. At one point (paragraph 19), Genovese writes that "those who passed under industrial work discipline probably were themselves the ones who came most to idealize their previous existence. . . ." Later (paragraph 29) he writes that "Douglass may have exaggerated the determination of the slaveholders as a class to suppress information. . . ." What is the effect of words like *probably* and *may have*? Should a historian try to avoid such words?

5. What kinds of passages does Genovese quote? For what purposes does he use direct quotes?

6. Summarize the most important points in Genovese's argument. Does he make these as clear as they can possibly be?

7. How successful is Genovese in connecting his generalizations about slaves' sense of time with modern people and their lives?

WRITING FROM WITHIN AND ABOUT HISTORY AND ITS STUDY

Writing for Yourself

1. In your journal, explore how you view work. What place does work have in your life?

2. In your journal, explore how you view time in general. How do you think you would react to "clock time" as Genovese describes it?

Writing for Nonacademic Audiences

1. Focus on a friend or relative who you think does not have a good balance between work and play in his or her life. Write that person a letter in which you try to persuade him or her of the correctness of your view.
2. Some recent research suggests that some young African Americans have difficulty in school because they are unaccustomed to the time frame and orientation of the schools. Read through some of this research and write a brief summary and evaluation of it to be used in a "Focus on Education" supplement that will be included with your local newspaper.

Writing for Academic Audiences

1. For a class in the history of Great Britain, write a 500-word report describing what "Methodism did to the English working class" (Genovese, paragraph 12).
2. For a class on modern American history, write a 750-word essay analyzing how Calvinism affects American culture today.
3. At one point Genovese mentions that some slaveholders used incentives other than whipping to motivate their slaves. For a class in the history of the American South, write a 1,000-word essay describing what the more important of these incentives were.
4. In this selection, Genovese quotes Eric Hobsbawm at some length. And he dedicates one of his other books to Hobsbawm. For a senior-level seminar on approaches to history, write a 500-word report defining Hobsbawm's approach to history.

Robert Hughes

(b. 1936)

In The Fatal Shore: The Epic of Australia's Founding *(1987), Robert Hughes explores the history and effects of Great Britain's policy of transporting thousands of convicts to Australia during the seventeenth and eighteenth centuries. The policy was based on the belief that a specific criminal class existed in British society. If that class could be removed from Britain, then crime in that nation would virtually cease to exist. The fact that England's poor lived under insufferable conditions and were forced, in many instances, to resort to crime to survive was not considered. Nor was the fact that few of Britain's poor knew how to survive in Australia taken into account.*

Born and raised in Sydney, Australia, Hughes has shown himself to be deeply interested in and sympathetic to Australian culture. The author of a standard history of Australian art and since 1970 an art critic for Time *magazine, in* The Fatal Shore *Hughes turns to social history as a way of exploring his own background. In this selection, taken from Hughes's second chapter, "A Horse Foaled by an Acorn," he examines the sweatshops, the child labor, the tenement housing, the diseases of this period in English history. He places these against the world of beauty, grace, and art that the eighteenth century is generally conceived to be. Instead of the stately steps of the minuet, he describes the frenzied hands of children slaving at machines. Instead of the proud porticoes of the country villa, he presents the rat-infested cellars of the London tenements.*

Like Robert Graves, Hughes forces the reader to reevaluate preconceived notions. Here, however, the historian does not deal with a single subject and with several years, but with an entire society and an entire way of life. To challenge our conceptions, the historian evokes the underside of the ordered world of eighteenth-century England.

In evoking this world, Hughes takes on a task similar to that of Gibbon as he evokes the world of the upper classes in ancient Rome. But Hughes's technique is quite different. While Gibbon selects from his material and then crafts it so that we get an anonymous, almost generic picture of the late-Roman leisured class, Hughes has Britain's poorer class speak for itself. Child laborers, nearly blind tailors, arrogant manufacturers all speak to the reader from out of the past. Hughes makes these voices cohere, so that the reader comes away with a new image of a troubled century.

A HORSE FOALED BY AN ACORN

Most educated people have felt twinges of nostalgia for Georgian England.   1

We are tied to the Georgian past through artifacts that we would still   2 like to use, given the chance. The town houses, squares, villas, gardens, paintings, silver and side tables seem to represent an "essence" of the eighteenth century, transcending "mere" politics. Since they present an uncommonly coherent image of elegance, common sense and clarity, we are apt to suppose that English society did too. But argument from design to society, like the syllogism that ascends from the particular to the general, usually goes awry. "We shall learn," wrote one typical English exponent of this approach, "from the architecture and furniture and all other things . . . that nearly everybody in the eighteenth century looked forward to a continuation and an agreeable expansion of gracious fashions."*

"Nearly everybody"—that, until quite recently, was the conventional   3 picture. A passing reference to violence, dirt and gin; a nod in the direction of the scaffold; a highwayman or two, a drunken judge, and some whores for local color; but the rest is all curricles and fanlights. Modern squalor is squalid but Georgian squalor is "Hogarthian," an art form in itself.

Yet most Englishmen and Englishwomen did not live under such roofs,   4 sit on such chairs or eat with such forks. They did not read Johnson† or Pope,‡ for most of them could not read. Antiques say little about the English poor, that vast and as yet unorganized social mass—Samuel Johnson's "rabble," Edmund Burke's§ "swinish multitude"—from whose discontents in the nineteenth century the English working class would shape itself. The Georgian London a modern visitor imagines was not their city. There were two such Londons, their separation symbolized by the cleavage that took place as the rich moved their residences westward from Covent Garden between 1700 and 1750, as the speculators ran up their noble squares and crescents—an absolute gulf between the new West End and the old, rotting East End of the city.

West London had grown rationally. Its streets and squares were   5 planned; property was secured by long leases and enforced standards of building. East London had not. It was a warren of shacks, decaying tene-

---

*John Gloag, *Georgian Grace*, p. 54. This attitude is still very much with us; its recent monument (1985–86) was a vast and theatrical loan exhibition in Washington, D.C., called *Treasure Houses of England*, in which the English country house was presented as the primary "vessel of civilization" and taken as epitomizing the "age" in which it flourished. Modern Americans, in particular, like to fantasize about being Georgian gentlemen.

†Samuel Johnson (1709–1784) was an English author, writer of *A Dictionary of the English Language* [Editors' note].

‡Alexander Pope (1688–1744) was an English poet, well known for his scathing wit [Editors' note].

§Edmund Burke (1729–1797) was a British statesman and political theorist [Editors' note].

ments, and brand-new hovels run up on short leases by jerry-builders restrained by no local ordinances. Georgian residential solidity stopped at the
lower fringe of the middle class. The "rookeries" of the poor formed a laby-
rinth speckled with picturesque names: Turnmill Street, Cow Cross, Chick
Lane, Black Boy Alley, Saffron Hill, the Spittle. West of the old City of London, the worst slum areas in the mid-eighteenth century lay around Covent
Garden, St. Giles, Holborn and the older parts of Westminster. To the east,
they spread through Blackfriars and beyond the Tower, by the Lower Pool
and Limehouse Reach: Wapping, Shadwell, Limehouse, Ratcliffe Highway,
the Jewish ghettos of Stepney and Whitechapel on the north side of the
Thames, the brick canyons of Southwark with its seven prisons on the south
bank. Their courts and alleys were dark, tangled, narrow and choked with
offal. Because men had to live near their work, tenements stood cheek by
jowl with slaughterhouses and tanneries. London was judged the greatest city
in the world, but also the worst smelling. Sewers still ran into open drains;
the largest of these, until it was finally covered in 1765, was the Fleet Ditch.
Armies of rats rose from the tenement cellars to go foraging in daylight.

The living were so crowded that there was scarcely room to bury the 6
dead. Around St. Martin's, St. James's and St. Giles-in-the-Fields, there were
large open pits filled with the rotting cadavers of paupers whose friends could
get them no better burial; they were called "Poor's Holes" and remained a
London commonplace until the 1790s.

Within the rookeries, distinctions of class were seen. Their cellars were 7
rented at 9d. or 1s. a week* to the most miserable tenants—ragpickers, bone-
gatherers or the swelling crowd of Irish casual laborers driven across St.
George's Channel by famine, rural collapse and the lure of the Big City.
Thirty people might be found in a cellar. Before 1800 an artisan might expect
to find a "cheap" furnished room in London for 2s. 6d. a week, and most
London workers lived in such places with no rights of tenancy.

To speak of an eighteenth-century "working class" as though it were a 8
homogeneous entity, united by class-consciousness and solidarity, is both an-
achronistic and abstract. It is a projection of the twentieth century onto the
eighteenth.

Loyalties ran between workers in the same trade but rarely between 9
workers as such. The variety of trades and work underwrote the complexity
of this other London. It contained a huge range of occupations, and a passion
for close divisions of social standing held for workers as well as for gentry.
They too had their pecking orders and were bound by them. At the upper
end of income and comfort, just below the independent shopkeepers, were
the skilled artisans in luxury trades, regularly employed: upholsterers and

---

* In English currency, d. stands for pence (one penny used to be equivalent to $\frac{1}{240}$ of a pound; it
  is now $\frac{1}{100}$ of a pound); s. stands for shilling (one shilling is equivalent to $\frac{1}{20}$ pound, or 12
  pence).

joiners, watch-finishers, coach-painters or lens-grinders. At the lower end were occupations now not only lost but barely recorded: that of the "Pure-finders," for instance, old women who collected dog-turds which they sold to tanneries for a few pence a bucket (the excrement was used as a siccative in dressing fine bookbinding leather). In between lay hundreds of occupations, seasonal or regular. None of them enjoyed any protection, since trade unions and "combinations" were instantly suppressed. There were no wage guarantees, and sweated labor was usual.

Occupational diseases ran rampant. Sawyers went blind young, their conjunctival membranes destroyed by showers of sawdust—hence the difference of status between the "top-notcher," or man on top of the log in the sawpit, and his partner pulling down the saw below. Metalfounders who cast the slugs for Baskerville's elegant type died paralyzed with lead poisoning, and glassblowers' lungs collapsed from silicosis. Hairdressers were prone to lung disease through inhaling the mineral powder used to whiten wigs. The fate of tailors, unchanged until the invention of electric light, was described by one to Henry Mayhew:

> It is not the black clothes that are trying to the sight—black is the steadiest of all colours to work at; white and all bright colours makes the eyes water after looking at 'em for any long time; but of all colours scarlet, such as is used for regimentals, is the most blinding, it seems to burn the eyeballs, and makes them ache dreadful . . . everything seems all of a twitter, and to keep changing its tint. There's more military tailors blind than any others. *

Children went to work after their sixth birthday. The Industrial Revolution did not invent child labor, but it did expand and systematize the exploitation of the very young. The reign of George III saw a rising trade in orphans and pauper children, collected from the parish workhouses of London and Birmingham, who were shipped off in thousands to the new industrial centers of Derbyshire, Nottinghamshire and Lancashire. One London child-slave, Robert Blincoe, who was placed in the St. Pancras Workhouse in 1796 at the age of four and sent off with eighty other abandoned children to the Lambert cotton mill outside Nottingham, gave testimony to a Parliamentary committee on child labor some forty years later:

> Q. Do you have any children?—Three.
> Q. Do you send them to factories?—No; I would rather have them transported. . . . I have seen the time when two hand-vices of a pound weight each, more or less, have been screwed to my ears, at Lytton mill in Derbyshire. These are the scars still remaining behind my ears. Then three or four of us have been hung at once on a cross-beam above the machinery, hanging by our hands, without shirts or stockings. Then we used to stand up, in a skip, without our shirts, and be beaten with straps or sticks; the skip was to prevent us from running away from the straps. . . . Then they used to tie up a 28-pounds'

*Henry Mayhew, *London Labour and the London Poor*, vol. I, pp. 342–43.

weight, one or two at once, according to our size, to hang down our backs, with no shirt on.*

Doctors tended to side with their class allies, the factory-owners, and 15 went on record again and again with their considered opinions that cotton lint, coal dust and phosphorus were harmless to the human lung, that fifteen hours at a machine in a room temperature of 85 degrees did not cause fatigue, that ten-year-olds could work a full night shift without risk of harm. Employers, naturally, resisted the very thought of reform. Some of them were cultivated men like Josiah Wedgwood, uncle to Charles Darwin and heir to his father's great pottery in Staffordshire, who employed 387 people—13 under ten years old, 103 between ten and eighteen—in such work as dipping ware in a glaze partly composed of lead oxide, a deadly poison which, as he admitted, made them "very subject to disease," though no more so than plumbers or painters. Yet "I have a strong opinion," Wedgwood told the Peel Committee in 1816, "that, from all I know at present of manufactories in general, and certainly from all I know of my own, we had better be left alone."†

Of all the testimony offered to the Royal Commissions on factory labor, 16 there is perhaps none more chilling than the evidence of Joseph Badder, a children's overseer in a Leicester mill, to the Factory Commission of 1833. It has a prophetic ring: Here, the factory-induced dystopic visions of man as automation that would run from Mary Shelley's *Frankenstein, or The Modern Prometheus* (1818) to Fritz Lang's *Metropolis* (1926) are made pitiably concrete:

> I used to beat them. . . . I told them I was very sorry after I had done it, but I 17 was forced to it. The masters expected me to do my work, and I could not do mine unless the children did theirs. Then I used to joke with them to keep up their spirits.
> I have seen them fall asleep, and they have been performing their work 18 with their hands until they were asleep, after the billy had stopped, when their work was over. I have stopped and looked at them for two minutes, going through the motions of piecening fast asleep, when there was really no work to do, and when they were really doing nothing.‡

Such flat and distant voices confirm the rhetoric of William Blake: "Grace" 19 is underwritten by constant, speechless suffering, and "culture" begins in the calloused hands of exhausted children, weaving robotically in sleep, "going through the motions . . . when they were really doing nothing." For the first time in human history, the machine dictates the term of organic existence to its servants; the body becomes an inferior machine. If respectability was to be judged by people's endurance of such work, there is no surprise in the

---

* Robert Blincoe to Central Board on Employment of Children in Manufactories, in Parliamentary Papers, Great Britain 1833, xxi. D3:17–18.
† Josiah Wedgwood to Peel Committee, in PP 1816, iii:64.
‡ Joseph Badder to the Factory Commission of 1833, in PP 1833, xx. Cl:191.

growth of crime. In a sense, the children of the mills were inoculated against the dread of punishment; "they appeared as complete prisoners as they would be in gaol," remarked one observer to the Peel Committee.*

But mill labor, at least, was regular and gave fairly steady employment. 20 Not all workers in London had such a prospect. Home industries like weaving were prostrated by industrial competition. To be whip-sawed between long work-hours and patches of unemployment was deeply demoralizing. As Francis Place found, it bred the familiar torpor of the laid-off:

> I know not how to describe the sickening aversion which at times steals over 21
> the working man, and utterly disables him for a longer or shorter time from
> following his usual occupation, and compels him to *idleness*. I have felt it. I
> have been obliged to submit and run away from my work. This is the case with
> every workman I have known; and in such proportion as a man's case is hope-
> less will such fits occur and be of longer duration.†

A common solace was gin. After 1720 this white grain spirit flavored 22 with crushed juniper berries became England's national stupefacient, the heroin of the eighteenth century (but worse, because its use was far wider). Brandy, port, claret and Madeira, the rich man's four tipples, were taxed on import and no workingman could afford them. But gin was made in England and cost next to nothing: "Drunk for a penny, dead drunk for twopence" meant what it said. Its consumption was eagerly promoted by the landed gentry, because England nearly always had a surplus of corn, which gin-distilling used up. Consequently there were no restrictions of any kind on making or selling the liquor until the Gin Act of 1751, by which time London was said to have one gin-shop for every 120 citizens. By 1743 the laboring poor of England were consuming 8 million gallons of gin a year, and they presented a most squalid appearance: "Lazy, sotted and brutish by nature," a French visitor called them in 1777.‡ The contrast between the new, de-graded "mob," sodden with gin, and the honest peasantry, merry with ale, was by now a commonplace with every moralist up to and including William Hogarth, who gave it memorable form in his engravings *Gin Lane* and *Beer Street.*

The "mob," as the urban proletariat was called, had become an object 23 of terror and contempt, but little was known about it. It was seen as a malign fluid, a sort of magma that would burst through any crack in law and cus-tom, quick to riot and easily inflamed to crime by rabble-rousers. This moral prejudice affected most efforts to find out about English crime and English poverty.

Thus Patrick Colquhoun, in his *Treatise on the Police of the Metropolis* 24 (1797), made one of the first attempts to gauge the number of criminals in

---

* Theodore Price to the Peel Committee, in PP 1816, iii:125.
† Francis Place, cit. in Graham Wallas, *Life of Francis Place,* p. 163.
‡ L. Lacombe, *Observations sur Londres. . . .* p. 180.

George III's London. He claimed that there were 115,000 people living off crime in the city—about one Londoner in eight, which constituted a "criminal class" in itself. But who were they, and what did they do? Colquhoun lumped thieves, muggers and forgers, who clearly were criminals, together with scavengers, bear-baiters and gypsies, who were not, or at least not clearly so. He estimated that there were 50,000 "harlots" in London—about 6 percent of its population—but, as Edward P. Thompson pointed out. "[Colquhoun's] prostitutes turn out, on closer inspection, to be 'lewd and immoral women,' including 'the prodigious number among the lower classes who cohabit together without marriage' (and this at a time when divorce for women was an absolute impossibility)."* If the same criteria of whoredom were applied to London today, how many "harlots" would a modern Colquhoun find?

The fact that their superiors *thought* that such people were prostitutes 25 is no guide: In social matters, Georgian Englishmen far preferred generalization to reportage, and there was no eighteenth-century Mayhew. A Spitalfields weaver, an Irish casual laborer and a Scottish ditchdigger might not even understand one another's speech, let alone share any aspirations; but seen from above they all belonged to the "mobbish class of persons." The "mob" was Georgian society's id—the sump of forbidden thoughts and proscribed actions, the locus of the raging will to survive. Amid the general fear of Jacobinism that swept England after the French Revolution, it would seem an even greater menace. Then, the issues of crime and of revolution became conflated, and so the rising crime-rate—or rather, the belief that it was rising—became a potent issue. Accordingly, the Georgian legislators fought back against a threat which they believed came from a whole class. The criminal became the dreaded *sans-culotte*'s cousin. Georgian fear of the "mob" led to Victorian belief in a "criminal class." Against both, the approved weapon was a form of legal terrorism.

QUESTIONS ABOUT HUGHES'S DISCOURSE
COMMUNITY AND HIS CONCERNS
IN THIS SELECTION

1. When we think of eighteenth-century England, we generally think of the highly ordered music of Handel and Haydn, the clean lines of Georgian furniture, classically balanced architecture and poetry, elaborately decorated salons, paintings of languid Greek gods. All the arts reflected the order of the time. How, then, do you account for the side of Georgian life that Hughes depicts in this passage? Is the emphasis on the arts simply a hypocritical lie? Or self-delusion?

*Edward P. Thompson. *The Making of the English Working Class*. pp. 59–60. This casual identification of any woman living out of wedlock as a "whore" would cause grave confusions about the actual morality of transported women convicts in Australia. The results of such assumptions are discussed in Chapter 8.

2. Hughes paints a picture of a society with clearly distinguished classes. Even in so-called classless societies, one can begin to discern distinctions between classes. Do you think there is something inherent in human beings that demands distinctions such as those between classes? Why or why not? Do you think that for some to enjoy elegance and luxuries, others must suffer and sacrifice?

3. What reasons does Hughes suggest for the increasing crime rate of this period? Are the reasons valid? Do these reasons lead the reader to excuse crime because of its social context?

4. Though Hughes is concentrating on what the twentieth century might call the proletariat, he makes occasional references to the upper classes. In what contexts do they appear? How does Hughes go about condemning those classes without actually dealing with them?

5. Would you say that today we have anything comparable to the mob and rabble of Georgian England? If so, is it dangerous?

6. Who is William Hogarth? How does Hughes use Hogarth to make a point about the eighteenth century?

QUESTIONS ABOUT HUGHES'S RHETORICAL STRATEGIES

1. How does Hughes use contemporary reports in this selection? In what contexts do they appear? Are these appropriate evidence for Hughes's argument, or do they necessarily reflect biased views? After reading over the contemporary quotes, describe their effect on you.

2. As Hughes describes the occupations of the lower classes and the diseases those occupations fostered, he is clearly morally outraged. Yet is his tone that of an outraged writer? If not, then how does he suggest his anger? How does he condemn the upper classes as he describes these occupations? Is this a fair way for a historian to depict the upper classes, or is Hughes biased in his argument?

3. How does Hughes depict the conditions of child labor? What rhetorical means does he use to bring the reader to his own point of view?

4. How does Hughes use syntax to imitate the lack of rationality, the random spreading characteristic of the slums of East London in the eighteenth century?

5. How is the image of rookeries especially apt to describe life in the slums of Georgian England?

6. Hughes uses some vivid specific details to move our emotions on behalf of the poor workers of Georgian England. In so doing, is he being fair to those who employed these people?

7. Near the end of this selection, Hughes writes that "If the same criteria of whoredom were applied to London today, how many 'harlots' would a modern Colquhoun find?" Since Hughes is ostensibly trying to show how bad conditions were in Georgian England, why would he use this sentence, which might make us feel conditions were not so bad then? Or is that not the effect Hughes is striving for?

8. Hughes suggests in this selection that usually a writer cannot validly argue from the particular to the general. However, might he be accused of doing just that? How would he answer this charge?

WRITING FROM WITHIN AND ABOUT HISTORY AND ITS STUDY

Writing for Yourself

1. In your journal, react to the account of child labor that you have just read.
2. In your journal, examine your reactions to the times when you did something like assembly-line labor.

Writing for Nonacademic Audiences

1. Take on the persona of a convict on one of the first prison ships to Australia. Write in your diary about your feelings about being transported to a world few had seen.
2. Interview at least five people who are regularly employed. Learn what their attitudes toward their jobs are. Then write a 500-word essay on the modern American social scene, commenting on some attitudes toward work that are prevalent today. This paper will be included as an appendix to an elite college version of Studs Terkel's *Working.*
3. In a debate in an economics club, you have been asked to assume the stance of an eighteenth-century employer and defend the practice of child labor. What arguments will you advance? What arguments will you expect to be raised against you? Write up the notes that you will use in making a fifteen-minute presentation to your peers in this class.

Writing for Academic Audiences

1. As Hughes shows, at one time Australia served as a penal colony for Great Britain. But Australia had penal colonies or outposts of its own, such as the one on Norfolk Island. For a class in Australian history, write a 1,000-word report on what the conditions in such penal outposts were like.
2. For a class in British history, research the introduction of child labor laws and their effects on the economy. Write a paper of 1,250 words based on this research.
3. In a 500-word essay, argue whether or not there is a criminal class, a group almost destined by circumstances or genetics to be criminal in nature. Would the elimination of that group mean the elimination of crime?
4. Research the history of Wedgwood Pottery. In a 1,000-word essay, for a class in art history, discuss the significance of this pottery in the history of English pottery.
5. Hughes claims that eighteenth-century England had a sharply divided class structure. Examine one of the following sharply divided societies and write a 2,000-word essay for a class in economic history that discusses the ultimate effects of that division:

Tsarist Russia of the early twentieth century
France of the late eighteenth century
The Philippines in the early 1980s
Haiti in the mid-1980s.

Fig. 2. William Hogarth, "Gin Lane." 1751.

6. Examine the illustration by William Hogarth (see figure 2). For an interdisciplinary course in culture and society, discuss what this print might suggest about the upper class's vision of "the mob."

INTERCONNECTIONS: QUESTIONS FOR WRITING

Writing for Yourself

1. To someone outside discourse communities in the study of history, it might seem that historical fact is simply that: fact. But a historian would argue that no event is neutral, that every event is subject to the historian's interpretive eye. This suggests that any given narration of historical events is to be understood as one historian's interpretation of those events and their meaning. This raises the possibility that there is no such thing as a truly objective history, that history is constantly being rewritten not only from century to century, but also from

culture to culture, and even from historian to historian. Whether this is a proper state of affairs for discourse communities in the historical sciences is a point of debate. Perhaps pure, objective history is not only impossible, but perhaps it is not even desirable.

In your journal, examine this question as it applies to Bradford, Graves, and Lerner.

Writing for Nonacademic Audiences

1. Should the historian's discourse be true to events in the world or is some invention acceptable? At times, historians, whether through lack of direct evidence or records or through a need to create powerful images, may use conjecture based upon the knowledge that is available. This may lead to surmises about the way something must have been, guesses about a character's attitudes, or speculations about whether actual events ever took place. To advance such speculations and surmises, the historian may turn to reconstructed dialogues and imagined scenes to press a point. Though these are based on conjectures that arise from research, they are still only conjectures.

   Is such conjecture acceptable in historical contexts? Examine this question in relation to Gibbon and Waite, for a short pamphlet designed by history majors of your university. The pamphlet will be used to attract freshmen into that department.

2. To support their interpretations, historians generally amass evidence that illustrates or corroborates their statements. One question that discourse communities in the study of history debate is the nature of that evidence. While some would agree that evidence such as concrete relics or written records are essential, others would argue that those are in a way limiting, that other kinds of evidence are acceptable. These other kinds range from the evidence of first-person accounts to a psychological interpretation of a figure's motivations. One distinction between discourse communities is their acceptance—or lack of acceptance—of another community's evidence.

   What kinds of evidence are acceptable in conducting historical research? Write a 500-word response to that question, considering the perspectives of Bede, Braudel, and Waite. The question appears on your application form for admission to an archeological dig expedition in South America.

3. When a historian deals with a period, he or she must make a choice about what kinds of things should command the reader's attention. What should be the focus of the history? What is the subject? Should the history focus on political controversies, social changes, military upheavals, religious reformations, artistic achievements, scientific advances? Different discourse communities in the historical sciences focus on different kinds of subjects, in addition to handling those subjects in different ways. And each historian must establish his or her own principles for selecting a focus.

   What kinds of foci are legitimate for the historian to choose? What does the choice of a particular focus suggest about a historian's discourse community and his or her approach to the subject? Examine these questions in relation to Braudel or Hughes in a review, to be published in a college newspaper, of either

The Mediterranean and the Mediterranean World in the Age of Philip II or
The Fatal Shore.

4. What is it that pushes history, that causes history to move along? Some historians might assert that history is pushed by time alone and that the historian's
role is to chart historical events by placing them in their chronological contexts.
But it is also legitimate to look for other ways of understanding what it is that
causes historical events to occur. For some, the forces that propel history might
be very personal, perhaps even specific individuals. For others, the forces
might be impersonal, perhaps geographical settings. And for others the forces
might be supernatural, outside human experience.

Examine this question as it relates to Thucydides, Bede, Durant, and
Braudel. Write up your notes for a fifteen-minute presentation to an association
of the American Legion. Write up notes for the same questions to be presented
to an ecumenical gathering of religious leaders. In your journal, explore how
and why your notes for these two presentations differ.

5. One cliché of historical studies is that those who fail to learn the lessons of
history are condemned to repeat it. What does it mean to learn the lessons of
the past? How is one to go about appropriating history and applying it to contemporary circumstances? And if such appropriation is possible, then does it
follow that one of the main roles of the historian is instruction in how to avoid
the failures of the past?

Examine these questions as they relate to Waite and Lerner by writing a
dialogue between those two historians. This will be read dramatically by a local
chapter of a historians' association.

6. What kind of training is essential to obtain work in the discipline of history? Is
academic training essential, and if so, why? Would there be any benefits to not
acquiring academic training?

Examine this question as it applies to Bradford and Graves for a bulletin
to be issued by your college's graduate studies program.

Writing for Academic Audiences

1. William Manchester's recent biography of Winston Churchill, *The Last Lion*
(1983), implies that history is the story of great figures. According to this perspective, if one wishes to understand the history of a particular period, one
must understand how great figures who are responsible for large numbers of
people—kings and queens, popes, prime ministers, military leaders, statesmen—affected events and, in turn, how events affected them. To study Roman
history, then, is to focus on the emperors; to study Canadian history is to focus
on the prime ministers. Recently, however, some historians have challenged
this assumption, arguing that history is the matter of masses of people, not just
their leaders. To study the fall of tsarist Russia, according to this view, is not
just to focus on the failings of Nicholas II, but to concentrate on those forces
working among the Russian people that led to a revolution.

All historians must decide how to approach history. Is it the story of great
figures? Or the study of another group? Or the study of phenomena? Or are
there other choices? For an introductory class in the study of history, examine

this question in a 750-word essay, considering the perspectives of Braudel and Genovese.

2. Historians who assert their own worldviews and perspectives and use them to comment on historical events might be accused of intruding into the history they wish to recount. Another form of intrusion might be the structure that the historian uses to present the material. All historians make decisions about which events or characters they include and which they ignore—or relegate to a minor position. All historians make decisions about how they will order their material and how they will use that ordering to give meaning to the material. But as the historian goes about making and practicing this art, he or she might be accused of too much art and not enough matter.

How much art should a historian use in presenting his or her subject? For a class in historiography, in a 1,000-word essay examine this question as it relates to Gibbon and Hughes.

3. For the historian, one of the most frequently used principles of organizing material is that of chronology. For most western historians, time is a linear phenomenon, and the implication here is that one event leads to another or occurs before another; therefore, that first event should be the one that is recorded or narrated first. But this practice suggests that time is merely a linear progression of events, and not all historians accept that vision of time, particularly as it relates to the organization of their material.

What different approaches to time do historians take, and how do these approaches affect the ways in which a historian presents his or her material? In a 1,000-word essay for a class in ancient history, examine this question in relation to Thucydides, Bede, and Gibbon.

4. How does the field of history make progress? Or, to put it another way, do historians deal with questions that can be fully answered? Or to put it in yet another way, is there such a thing as a definitive historical work? In his essay "Rewriting American History" (1979), Frances Fitzgerald argues that contemporary American historians are rewriting American history to such an extent that those who studied the same period in history in the 1930s would not recognize the kind of history being studied in the 1960s. But perhaps it is the case that each generation rewrites its own history in its own image, in an attempt to understand itself.

Examine these questions as they relate to Graves and Lerner in a 1,500-word essay for a class in contemporary history, using the mode of example to develop your piece.

DISCOURSE
COMMUNITIES
IN THE ARTS

INTRODUCTION

One of our colleagues once visited Boston's Museum of Fine Arts to see its collection of Impressionist paintings. One room held a collection of Monets, and our colleague sat on the cushioned seat in the center of the room to look at them. In the subdued light of the room, the bright colors, the diffused lines, the blurred shapes of the paintings seemed to merge. Soon an elderly woman sat next to him, and, silently, they looked together at a painting of the Riviera. After a time the woman touched him lightly on the shoulder, and when he looked, he saw tears in her eyes. "It looks so much like it," she said softly.

He had never been to the Riviera, but he knew that this painting couldn't possibly look "so much like it." In no place in the real world did shapes blur into each other, did the landscape seem so unreal, did the lines seem so intangible as they did in this painting. So what did the woman mean? And why was she crying?

She might have meant that the Riviera truly did look like that, at a certain time, in a certain light. In that case, the painting was simply an accurate reflection of reality. Or she might have brought certain associations and feelings with her about that place which she found reflected in the tone of the painting. Or she might have found that Monet's feelings about the Riviera as reflected in the painting were exactly those which she felt—at least, insofar as she understood correctly what Monet's feelings might have been. Or she might have felt that what Monet was saying about the Riviera—and perhaps about the world—was significant and meaningful and very moving.

If one were to paraphrase a definition by Northrop Frye regarding literature, one might say that the arts are humanity's messages to itself. According to this view, what Monet was doing in his painting was to send a message to a certain woman—and presumably to anyone else who would look—about his impressions of that particular place at that particular moment. But not all people interpret such a message in the same way. The same image that so moved this woman was to our colleague merely interesting as a historical work of art. To another viewer, the painting might produce a very different reaction. Does this mean that Monet failed to convey his message accurately?

Or that there might be more than one message? Or that whatever we bring with us to any encounter with the arts influences our understanding and reception of the work? Or does it mean that looking for messages in works of art is not a legitimate pursuit? Perhaps art exists simply as and for itself.

In the eighteenth century, John Dryden suggested that "From hence the rudiments of art began, / A coal or chalk first imitated man." This suggestion has two interesting elements. First, in Dryden's view, art is meant to be an imitation; that is, art somehow represents an event in the real world through the medium of the artist's eye. An artist can help us to see the world more clearly by channeling our perceptions through his or her own. Second, Dryden implies that art deals with those things that lie around us, that can be found in the world. Even works of fantasy, such as the paintings of Salvadore Dali or the writings of J.R.R. Tolkien, are composed of elements, however distorted or placed into new contexts, that are still part of the common experience.

But not everyone will agree with Dryden, and in the arts various discourse communities have defined themselves in relation to how they answer questions about the meaning and purpose of the arts. Such communities ask basic questions about art: How do we define something as art? What is the responsibility of art? What do the arts do? How do they do it? What fruitful questions might critics ask about the arts? What are the limits of interpretation? Such questions are important to ask in understanding how any form—dance, film, literature, painting, music—functions as art.

In general, art criticism has focused on an artist's meanings, the contexts in which they are set, and the ways in which they are understood. In the field of music, this may call for an understanding of how a work is structured, and how that structure gives meaning to the overall work and the smaller units within that work. In dance, this may call for an examination of the relationship of movement to music, as well as the cultural meanings of certain movements. In literature, it may call for an understanding of specific uses of imagery in a given work. In film, it may call for an examination of the director's use of editing to create certain effects for his or her audience. In each case, the art critic is asking what the meaning might be and how it is achieved.

In the following selections, critics representing several different discourse communities answer some of these questions in very different ways. Some are concerned with the nature of art itself. The Luttmanns, for example, suggest that the arts are an expression of the communal life of a culture; the arts are meant to pass down a culture's history and traditions to a succeeding generation. To others, such as Sidney, the arts are a production of humanity's creative impulses, springing from the imagination. For Bettelheim, the arts are a working out of our psychological needs within a safe, imaginative context.

Other discourse communities represented here define themselves by the ways in which they approach the meaning of art. Todorov, for example, is principally concerned with the structures of art, whereas Modleski is concerned with approaching art as a feminist. Mao Zedong is interested in the ways in which art functions ideologically, whereas Lamb is interested in the relationship between the morality of art and culture.

The writers collected here focus on many different art forms and disciplines, and these distinctions affect the ways in which they deal with the arts. These essayists deal with literature, music, painting, film, and dance, and while these areas cause some significant differences in approaches, those very distinctions demonstrate some commonalities as well. These common concerns each center on questions such as the following:

> How is it that one distinguishes good art from bad art?
> What purpose does art serve both for the individual and for the group?
> How is an individual work of art affected by the culture out of which it came?
> How does art convey meaning?
> Should artistic production be controlled by forces outside the artist?
> Is there such a thing as a correct interpretation of art?

The different answers given by the following writers are demonstrative of the distinctions in their discourse communities; the fact that they are all asking similar questions, however, unites them in terms of their ultimate goal: to understand what art is and how it conveys meaning.

This may be the most significant question asked by writers in this section: How does art mean? For the woman at the Monet exhibit, art had an extremely personal meaning. What she saw became for her at that moment an expression of reality, or truth. For her, it was irrelevant that our colleague did not share in the truth. It was enough that it was true for her.

Aristotle

(384–323 B.C.)

One could hardly overestimate the influence of Aristotle and his Poetics on the study of literature in western culture. Many people know his views about plot and have memorized his definition of tragedy. Words such as catharsis, which he used to describe the effects of tragedy, come up even in informal conversations. His pronouncements on literature have been regarded as beyond challenge by critics in many ages. And some of his judgments are at the heart of critical discussions even today, particularly discussions of the nature of imitation and representation.

In some ways it is surprising that Aristotle should have exerted such a powerful influence on the study of literature. He was well read and enjoyed watching dramatic productions, but he has never been noted for having a great sensitivity for the music of words or for the metaphysical dimension possible in literature. He has been influential largely because of the analytical powers of his mind. In recognizing the parts of a whole and describing the causes of effects or the effects of causes, few could be more skilled than Aristotle.

His Poetics is essentially a set of notes for lectures that he gave to students at his Lyceum, or school, probably sometime after 335 B.C. The text is therefore more abrupt and elliptical than other works of his. It is also only a remnant; most scholars believe that only one of two parts of the Poetics has survived to modernity.

In the Poetics, Aristotle is working within a discourse community of classical Greek philosophers. And he is addressing thinkers who remembered Plato's having banished the poets from his ideal state. Plato did so partly because poets cater to our emotions, which interfere with the search for truth, and partly because poets only imitated reality and were therefore removed from his ideal forms. In the Poetics, Aristotle sets out to correct what he regards as flaws in Plato's vision; it is no wonder, therefore, that he concentrates on imitation and the emotional effects of tragedy as much as he does.

It is true that there are aspects of literary art that Aristotle does not examine. But those he does examine he treats with impressive analytical abilities. The following selection includes the first nine sections of the Poetics.

ARISTOTLE'S POETICS

Let us here deal with Poetry, its essence and its several species, with the   1
characteristic function of each species and the way in which plots must be
constructed if the poem is to be a success; and also with the number and
character of the constituent parts of a poem, and similarly with all other
matters proper to this same inquiry; and let us, as nature directs, begin first
with first principles.

Epic poetry, then, and the poetry of tragic drama, and, moreover, com-   2
edy and dithyrambic poetry,* and most flute-playing and harp-playing, these,
speaking generally, may all be said to be "representations of life." But they
differ one from another in three ways: either in using means generically dif-
ferent† or in representing different objects or in representing objects not in
the same way but in a different manner. For just as by the use both of colour
and form people represent many objects, making likenesses of them—some
having a knowledge of art and some working empirically—and just as others
use the human voice; so it is also in the arts which we have mentioned, they
all make their representations in rhythm and language and tune, using these
means either separately or in combination. For tune and rhythm alone are
employed in flute-playing and harp-playing and in any other arts which have
a similar function, as, for example, pipe-playing. Rhythm alone without tune
is employed by dancers in their representations, for by means of rhythmical
gestures they represent both character and experiences and actions.

But the art which employs words either in bare prose or in metres,   3
either in one kind of metre or combining several, happens up to the present
day to have no name. For we can find no common term to apply to the mimes
of Sophron and Xenarchus‡ and to the Socratic dialogues: nor again supposing a poet were to make his representation in iambics or elegiacs or any other
such metre—except that people clap the word poet (maker) on to the name
of the metre and speak of elegiac poets and of others as epic poets. Thus they
do not call them poets in virtue of their representation but apply the name
indiscriminately in virtue of the metre. For if people publish medical or scientific treatises in metre the custom is to call them poets. But Homer and
Empedocles§ have nothing in common except the metre, so that it would be
proper to call the one a poet and the other not a poet but a scientist. Similarly
if a man makes his representation by combining all the metres, as Chaeremon
did when he wrote his rhapsody *The Centaur*, a medley of all the metres, he

* Dithyrambic poetry is characterized by enthusiastic and passionate language.
† In other words, the means fall into different categories.
‡ Sophron and Xenarchus, who lived in Syracuse, wrote "mimes," simple and usually farcical
    sketches in prose of everyday events.
§ Homer was a great Greek epic poet, author of *The Iliad* and *The Odyssey*; Empedocles was a
    Greek philosopher and statesman.

too should be given the name of poet. On this point the distinctions thus made may suffice.

There are certain arts which employ all the means which I have men- 4 tioned, such as rhythm and tune and metre—dithyrambic and "nomic" poetry,* for example, and tragedy too and comedy. The difference here is that some use all these at once, others use now one now another. These differences then in the various arts I call the *means* of representation.

Since living persons are objects of representation, these must necessarily 5 be either heroic or inferior—for characters are normally thus distinguished, since ethical differences depend upon vice and virtue—that is to say either better than ourselves or worse or much what we are. It is the same with painters. Polygnotus depicted men as better than they are and Pauson worse, while Dionysius made likenesses.† Clearly each of the above mentioned arts will admit of these distinctions, and they will differ in representing different objects in the way here described. In painting too, and flute-playing and harp-playing, these diversities may certainly be found, and it is the same in prose and in unaccompanied verse. For instance Homer's people are "better," Cleophon's are "like," while in Hegemon of Thasos, the first writer of parodies, and in Nicochares, the author of the *Poltrooniad*, they are "worse." It is the same in dithyrambic and nomic poetry, for instance *** a writer might draw characters like the Cyclops as drawn by Timotheus and Philoxenus.‡ It is just in this respect that tragedy differs from comedy. The latter sets out to represent people as worse than they are to-day, the former as better.

A third difference in these arts is the manner in which one may repre- 6 sent each of these objects. For in representing the same objects by the same means it is possible to proceed either partly by narrative and partly by assuming a character other than your own—this is Homer's method—or by remaining yourself without any such change, or else to represent the characters as carrying out the whole action themselves.

These, as we said above, are the three differences which form the sev- 7 eral species of the art of representation, the means, the objects, and the manner.

It follows that in one respect Sophocles would be the same kind of artist 8 as Homer, for both represent good men, and in another respect he would resemble Aristophanes, for they both represent men in action and doing things. And that is why some people speak of "dramas," because they present people as doing things. And for this reason the Dorians claim as their own both tragedy and comedy—comedy is claimed both by the Megarians in Greece, who say that it originated in the days of the democracy, and by the Megarians in Sicily, for it was from there the poet Epicharmus came, who

---

* The Nome was a vocal solo, accompanied by a harp, to honor Apollo.
† Polygnotus's portraits were in the grand style; Pauson was once called a "perfectly wicked caricaturist"; Dionysius of Colophon had the reputation for producing good likenesses.
‡ Both Timotheus and Philoxenus were famous dithyrambic poets.

was much earlier than Chionides and Magnes; and tragedy some of the Peloponnesians claim. Their evidence is the two names. Their name, they say, for suburb villages is κῶμαι—the Athenians call them "Demes"—and comedians are so called not from κωμάζειν, "to revel," but because they were turned out of the towns and went strolling round the villages (κῶμαι). Their word for action, they add, is δρᾶν, whereas the Athenian word is πράττειν. So much then for the differences, their number, and their nature.

Speaking generally, poetry seems to owe its origin to two particular 9
causes, both natural. From childhood men have an instinct for representation, and in this respect man differs from the other animals that he is far more imitative and learns his first lessons by representing things. And then there is the enjoyment people always get from representations. What happens in actual experience proves this, for we enjoy looking at accurate likenesses of things which are themselves painful to see, obscene beasts, for instance, and corpses. The reason is this. Learning things gives great pleasure not only to philosophers but also in the same way to all other men, though they share this pleasure only to a small degree. The reason why we enjoy seeing likenesses is that, as we look, we learn and infer what each is, for instance, "that is so and so"; for if we have never happened to see the original, our pleasure is not due to the representation as such but to the technique or the colour or some other such cause.

We have, then, a natural instinct for representation and for tune and 10
rhythm—for the metres are obviously sections of rhythms—and starting with these instincts men very gradually developed them until they produced poetry out of their improvisations. Poetry then split into two kinds according to the poet's nature. For the more serious poets represented fine doings and the doings of fine men, while those of a less exalted nature represented the actions of inferior men, at first writing satire just as the others at first wrote hymns and eulogies. Before Homer we cannot indeed name any such poem, though there were probably many satirical poets, but starting from Homer, there is, for instance, his *Margites** and other similar poems. For these the iambic metre was fittingly introduced and that is why it is still called iambic, because it was the metre in which they assailed each other. Of the ancients some wrote heroic verse and some iambic. And just as Homer was a supreme poet in the heroic style, since he alone made his representations not only good but also dramatic, so, too, he was the first to mark out the main lines of comedy, since he made his drama not out of personal satire but out of the laughable as such. His *Margites* indeed provides an analogy: as are the *Iliad* and *Odyssey* to our tragedies, so is the *Margites* to our comedies.

When tragedy and comedy came to light, poets were drawn by their 11
natural bent towards one or the other. Some became writers of comedies

---

* A famous burlesque, or comedy marked by ridiculous exaggeration.

instead of lampoons, the others produced tragedies instead of epics; the reason being that the former is in each case a higher kind of art and has greater value.

To consider whether tragedy proves to have been fully developed by 12 now in all its various species or not, and to criticize it both in itself and in relation to the stage, that is another question. At any rate it originated in improvisation—both tragedy itself and comedy. The one came from the prelude to the dithyramb and the other from the prelude to the phallic songs which still survive as institutions in many cities. Tragedy then gradually evolved as men developed each element that came to light and after going through many changes, it stopped when it had found its natural form. Thus it was Aeschylus who first raised the number of the actors from one to two. He also curtailed the chorus and gave the dialogue the leading part. Three actors and scene-painting Sophocles introduced. Then as to length. Being a development of the Satyr play,* it was quite late before tragedy rose from short plots and comic diction to its full dignity, and that the iambic metre was used instead of the trochaic tetrameter. At first they used the tetrameter because its poetry suited the Satyrs and was better for dancing, but when dialogue was introduced, Nature herself discovered the proper metre. The iambic is indeed the most conversational of metres, and the proof is that in talking to each other we most often use iambic lines but very rarely hexameters and only when we rise above the ordinary pitch of conversation. Then there is the number of acts. The further embellishments,† and the story of their introduction one by one we may take as told, for it would probably be a long task to go through them in detail.

Comedy, as we have said, is a representation of inferior people, not 13 indeed in the full sense of the word bad, but the laughable is a species of the base or ugly. It consists in some blunder or ugliness that does not cause pain or disaster, an obvious example being the comic mask which is ugly and distorted but not painful.

The various stages of tragedy and the originators of each are well 14 known, but comedy remains obscure because it was not at first treated seriously. Indeed it is only quite late in its history that the archon‡ granted a chorus for a comic poet; before that they were volunteers. Comedy had already taken certain forms before there is any mention of those who are called its poets. Who introduced masks or prologues, the number of actors, and so on, is not known. Plot making [Epicharmus and Phormis]§ originally came

---

* The fourth and final play in a cycle of four Greek tragedies. The satyr play, which was intended to bring comic relief to the audience, had the structure of a tragedy but was comic in manner.
† Such as masks and costumes.
‡ A chief magistrate in ancient Athens.
§ Epicharmus and Phormis were early Sicilian comedians. The text is imperfect here.

from Sicily, and of the Athenian poets Crates* was the first to give up the
lampooning form and to generalize his dialogue and plots.

Epic poetry agreed with tragedy only in so far as it was a metrical 15
representation of heroic action, but inasmuch as it has a single metre and is
narrative in that respect they are different. And then as regards length, tragedy tends to fall within a single revolution of the sun or slightly to exceed
that, whereas epic is unlimited in point of time; and that is another difference, although originally the practice was the same in tragedy as in epic
poetry.

The constituent parts are some of them the same and some peculiar to 16
tragedy. Consequently any one who knows about tragedy, good and bad,
knows all about epics too, since tragedy has all the elements of epic poetry,
though the elements of tragedy are not all present in the epic.

With the representation of life in hexameter verse and with comedy we 17
will deal later. We must now treat of tragedy after first gathering up the
definition of its nature which results from what we have said already. Tragedy is, then, a representation of an action that is heroic and complete and of
a certain magnitude—by means of language enriched with all kinds of ornament, each used separately in the different parts of the play: it represents
men in action and does not use narrative, and through pity and fear it effects
relief to these and similar emotions. By "language enriched" I mean that
which has rhythm and tune, *i.e.* song, and by "the kinds separately" I mean
that some effects are produced by verse alone and some again by song.

Since the representation is performed by living persons, it follows at 18
once that one essential part of a tragedy is the spectacular effect, and, besides
that, song-making and diction. For these are the means of the representation.
By "diction" I mean here the metrical arrangement of the words; and "song-
making" I use in the full, obvious sense of the word. And since tragedy represents action and is acted by living agents, who must of necessity have certain qualities of character and thought—for it is these which determine the
quality of an action; indeed thought and character are the natural causes of
any action and it is in virtue of these that all men succeed or fail—it follows
then that it is the plot which represents the action. By "plot" I mean here the
arrangement of the incidents: "character" is that which determines the quality of the agents, and "thought" appears wherever in the dialogue they put
forward an argument or deliver an opinion.

Necessarily then every tragedy has six constituent parts, and on these its 19
quality depends. These are plot, character, diction, thought, spectacle, and
song. Two of these are the means of representation: one is the manner: three
are the objects represented. This list is exhaustive, and practically all the
poets employ these elements, for every drama includes spectacle and character and plot and diction and song and thought.

---

* Fragments of his comedies, dating from the middle of the fifth century B.C., survive.

The most important of these is the arrangement of the incidents,* for 20 tragedy is not a representation of men but of a piece of action, of life, of happiness and unhappiness, which come under the head of action, and the end aimed at is the representation not of qualities of character but of some action; and while character makes men what they are, it is the scenes they act in that make them happy or the opposite. They do not therefore act to represent character, but character-study is included for the sake of the action. It follows that the incidents and the plot are the end at which tragedy aims, and in everything the end aimed at is of prime importance. Moreover, you cannot have a tragedy without action, but you can have one without character-study. Indeed most of the tragedies of our younger men are without this, and, speaking generally, there are many such writers, whose case is like that of Zeuxis compared with Polygnotus.† The latter was good at depicting character, but there is nothing of this in Zeuxis's painting. A further argument is that if a man writes speeches full of character and excellent in point of diction and intelligence, he will not achieve the proper function of tragedy nearly so well as a tragedy which, while inferior in these qualities, has a plot or arrangement of incidents. And furthermore, two of the most important elements in the emotional effect of tragedy, "reversals" and "discoveries," are parts of the plot. And here is further proof: those who try to write tragedy are much sooner successful in language and character-study than in arranging the incidents; for example, almost all the earliest poets.

The plot then is the first principle and as it were the soul of tragedy: 21 character comes second. It is much the same also in painting; if a man smeared a canvas with the loveliest colours at random, it would not give as much pleasure as an outline in black and white. And it is mainly because a play is a representation of action that it also for that reason represents people.

Third comes "thought." This means the ability to say what is possible 22 and appropriate. It comes in the dialogue and is the function of the statesman's or the rhetorician's art. The old writers made their characters talk like statesmen, the moderns like rhetoricians.

Character is that which reveals choice, shows what sort of thing a man 23 chooses or avoids in circumstances where the choice is not obvious, so those speeches convey no character in which there is nothing whatever which the speaker chooses or avoids.

"Thought" you find in speeches which contain an argument that some- 24 thing is or is not, or a general expression of opinion.

The fourth of the literary elements is the language. By this I mean, as 25 we said above, the expression of meaning in words, and this is essentially the same in verse and in prose.

Of the other elements which "enrich" tragedy the most important is 26

---

* That is, the plot.
† These are two Greek painters.

song-making. Scenic display, while highly effective, is yet quite foreign to the art and has nothing to do with poetry. Indeed the effect of tragedy does not depend on its performance by actors, and, moreover, for achieving the scenic effects the art of the stage-carpenter is more authoritative than that of the poet.

After these definitions we must next discuss the proper arrangement of 27 the incidents, since this is the first and most important thing in tragedy. We have laid it down that tragedy is a representation of an action that is whole and complete and of a certain magnitude, since a thing may be a whole and yet have no magnitude. A whole is what has a beginning and middle and end. A beginning is that which is not a necessary consequent of anything else but after which something else exists or happens as a natural result. An end on the contrary is that which is inevitably or, as a rule, the natural result of something else but from which nothing else follows; a middle follows something else and something follows from it. Well constructed plots must not therefore begin and end at random, but must embody the formulae we have stated.

Moreover, in everything that is beautiful, whether it be a living crea- 28 ture or any organism composed of parts, these parts must not only be well arranged but must also have a certain magnitude of their own; for beauty consists in magnitude and arrangement. From which it follows that neither would a very small creature be beautiful—for our view of it is almost instantaneous and therefore confused—nor a very large one, since being unable to view it all at once, we lose the effect of a single whole; for instance, suppose a creature a thousand miles long. As then creatures and other organic structures must have a certain magnitude and yet be easily taken in by the eye, so too with plots: they must have length but must be easily taken in by the memory.

The limit of length considered in relation to competitions and produc- 29 tion before an audience does not concern this treatise. Had it been the rule to produce a hundred tragedies, they would have been regulated by the water clock, as it is said they did once in other days. But as for the natural limit of the action, the longer the better as far as magnitude goes, provided it can all be grasped at once. To give a simple definition: the magnitude which admits of a change from bad fortune to good or from good fortune to bad, in a sequence of events which follow one another either inevitably or according to probability, that is the proper limit.

A plot does not have unity, as some people think, simply because it deals 30 with a single hero. Many and indeed innumerable things happen to an individual, some of which do not go to make up any unity, and similarly an individual is concerned in many actions which do not combine into a single piece of action. It seems therefore that all those poets are wrong who have written a *Heracleid* or *Theseid* or other such poems. They think that because Heracles was a single individual the plot for that reason has unity. But Homer, supreme also in all other respects, was apparently well aware of this truth either by instinct or from knowledge of his art. For in writing an *Odyssey* he did not put in all that ever happened to Odysseus, his being wounded on Parnassus, for instance, or his feigned madness when the host was gathered (these being events neither of which necessarily or probably led to the other), but he constructed his *Odyssey* round a single action in our sense of the phrase. And the *Iliad* the same. As then in the other arts of representation a single representation means a representation of a single object, so too the plot being a representation of a piece of action must represent a single piece of action and the whole of it; and the component incidents must be so arranged that if one of them be altered or removed, the unity of the whole is disturbed and destroyed. For if the presence or absence of a thing makes no visible difference, then it is not an integral part of the whole.

What we have said already makes it further clear that a poet's object is 31 not to tell what actually happened but what could and would happen either probably or inevitably. The difference between a historian and a poet is not that one writes in prose and the other in verse—indeed the writings of Herodotus could be put into verse and yet would still be a kind of history, whether written in metre or not. The real difference is this, that one tells what happened and the other what might happen. For this reason poetry is something more scientific and serious than history, because poetry tends to give general truths while history gives particular facts.

By a "general truth" I mean the sort of thing that a certain type of man 32 will do or say either probably or necessarily. That is what poetry aims at in giving names to the characters. A "particular fact" is what Alcibiades did or what was done to him. In the case of comedy this has now become obvious, for comedians construct their plots out of probable incidents and then put in any names that occur to them. They do not, like the iambic satirists, write about individuals. In tragedy, on the other hand, they keep to real names. The reason is that what is possible carries conviction. If a thing has not happened, we do not yet believe in its possibility, but what has happened is obviously possible. Had it been impossible, it would not have happened. It is true that in some tragedies one or two of the names are familiar and the rest invented; indeed in some they are all invented, as for instance in Agathon's *Antheus*, where both the incidents and the names are invented and yet it is none the less a favourite. One need not therefore endeavour invariably to keep to the traditional stories with which our tragedies deal. Indeed it would be absurd to do that, seeing that the familiar themes are familiar only to a few and yet please all.

It is clear, then, from what we have said that the poet must be a "maker" 33 not of verses but of stories, since he is a poet in virtue of his "representation," and what he represents is action. Even supposing he represents what has actually happened, he is none the less a poet, for there is nothing to prevent some actual occurrences being the sort of thing that would probably or inevitably happen, and it is in virtue of *that* that he is their "maker."

Of "simple" plots and actions the worst are those which are "episodic." 34

By this I mean a plot in which the episodes do not follow each other probably or inevitably. Bad poets write such plays because they cannot help it, and good poets write them to please the actors. Writing as they do for competition, they often strain the plot beyond its capacity and are thus obliged to sacrifice continuity. But this is bad work, since tragedy represents not only a complete action but also incidents that cause fear and pity, and this happens most of all when the incidents are unexpected and yet one is a consequence of the other. For in that way the incidents will cause more amazement than if they happened mechanically and accidentally, since the most amazing accidental occurrences are those which seem to have been providential, for instance when the statue of Mitys at Argos killed the man who caused Mitys's death by falling on him at a festival. Such events do not seem to be mere accidents. So such plots as these must necessarily be the best.

QUESTIONS ON ARISTOTLE'S DISCOURSE COMMUNITY AND HIS CONCERNS IN THIS SELECTION

1. How does Aristotle use the word *poetry*? Is it a more or less general term for him than it is for us?
2. How much of Aristotle's definition of tragedy do you remember?
3. What parts of Aristotle's definition of tragedy (beginning in paragraph 17) would you say still apply to tragedies today? What parts would you say no longer apply to tragedies?
4. How does Aristotle judge whether or not an incident should be a part of a tragic plot? Do you think his criterion is a good one?
5. Do you agree with Aristotle that tragedy represents people as better than they are and that comedy represents people as worse than they are?
6. Aristotle implies that the nature of the poet will determine what kind of poetry he or she will write. Do you agree?
7. Aristotle writes that some arts have more value than others. On what basis does he make this claim?
8. How does Aristotle distinguish the work of the historian from that of the poet? Do you agree with him?

QUESTIONS ON ARISTOTLE'S RHETORICAL STRATEGIES

1. Aristotle is often very careful to make clear how he uses certain words. Do you find these clarifications necessary, or do they get in the way?
2. Aristotle makes some sweeping generalizations. Describe two or three of these. Is he always on safe ground in making these generalizations?
3. How does Aristotle use specific examples? Is his strategy effective?
4. Describe one or two portions of the *Poetics* in which you see especially clearly Aristotle analyzing—that is, breaking things down into parts.
5. How often does Aristotle consider objections to his positions? Do you think that he should do so more often than he does?

6. How would you describe Aristotle's tone in this piece? What elements of the piece contribute most directly to that tone?

WRITING FROM WITHIN AND ABOUT THE ARTS: LITERARY CRITICISM

Writing for Yourself

1. Think back to the time when you were most intensely moved by a piece of literature or a dramatic production. Reflect in your journal about what it was that affected you the most at that time.
2. Reflect in your journal about the criteria you use to judge movies that you see.

Writing for Nonacademic Audiences

1. You have a friend who analyzes every story he or she reads and every movie he or she sees. After not seeing this friend for a while, write him or her a letter in which you comment on this tendency toward analysis.
2. One of your high school friends has always mocked your decision to take a literature course at college. Write him or her a letter in which you defend your choice.

Writing for Academic Audiences

1. For an introductory course in literature, write a 500-word paper in which you define what the essence of the comic is.
2. For a course in modern drama, write a 750-word paper in which you define what the essence of the tragic is and in which you take a position on whether the truly tragic is still possible today.
3. For a class in aesthetics, select a work of literary, dramatic, or cinematic art and write a 750-word paper arguing that it contains a part that is not integral to the whole.
4. One of your literature professors insists that the pleasures of literature center on appreciating well-made aesthetic objects, not on learning general truths about life and humankind. He or she invites you to respond to this claim in a persuasive paper of at least 1,000 words.

Sir Philip Sidney

(1554–1586)

Despite his short life, Sir Philip Sidney represented to many of his countrymen the ideal Elizabethan courtier. Descendent of a royal family, a statesman, a literary craftsman, a soldier, a humanist, a swordsman, he displayed what the Renaissance referred to as "sprezzatura," grace and skill concealing purpose and artistry. Even his death was idealized: Wounded, he gave his bottle of water to a dying soldier, noting that "Thy necessity is greater than mine."

Sidney was well connected on both sides of his family. His father, Sir Henry Sidney, was the lord deputy of Ireland; his mother was the sister of the Earl of Leicester. He attended Christ Church, Oxford, but left without taking a degree when the plague came to that city in 1571. The next year he traveled to France with the entourage of the Earl of Lincoln. While he was there, France underwent the St. Bartholomew's Day massacre, in which hundreds of Protestants were killed; this may have inspired Sidney's own militant Protestantism. From there he traveled to Vienna and Poland, after which he was summoned by Elizabeth I to become a diplomat. In this position he worked to form the Great Protestant League, an alliance of England, the Netherlands, and parts of the Holy Roman Empire against France and Spain.

During his travels, Sidney had become acquainted with European modes of literature, and upon returning to England and taking up a life at court, he continued this interest, associating with such poets as Edmund Spenser. This way of life ended when he incurred the queen's disfavor in 1580 by opposing her proposed match to the Catholic Duke of Anjou. He retired to the home of his sister, the Countess of Pembroke, where he began to write the Arcadia *(which some have seen as the language's first novel) and* An Apologie for Poetrie, *which was in part a response to Stephen Gasson's* The Schoole of Abuse *(1579), an attack on poetry and the theater dedicated to Maistre Philip Sidney.*

In 1583, having regained the queen's favor, Sidney was knighted. Longing to see the New World, he prepared to sail with Sir Francis Drake, but at the last moment he was sent by the queen to the Netherlands, where he was to fight for Protestantism. While attacking a convoy, Sidney was wounded and, after composing a song about his wound, he died twenty-six days later.

The Apology *draws upon many critical texts fashionable in Sidney's discourse community: Plato's* Symposium *and* Phaedrus, *Aristotle's* Poetics *and* Rhetoric, *Horace's* Ars Poetica, *Julius Caesar Scaliger's criticism (from which Sidney frequently uses unattributed quotations). He organized the essay to match Cicero's orations, celebrating a structure that his discourse community of Christian humanists frequently employed. His work stressed an acceptance of classical rules and approaches, while at the same time suggesting an infusion of "energia," an Aristotelian term meaning the employment of vigor and verisimilitude in imaginative work.*

Sidney wrote in a time that saw itself looking backward to the classical world for forms, but also saw itself as looking ahead for its subject matter. Like others writing during the sixteenth century, Sidney held tremendous pride in the vernacular language, and felt that it, adorned with art, could produce literature as great as any that the classical world had seen. For Sidney, this ability to control language was a mark of the civilized man, a true Renaissance man.

The following selection is taken from Sidney's An Apologie for Poetry.

AN APOLOGIE FOR POETRY

But now, let us see how the Greeks named it, and how they deemed of it. 1
The Greeks called him "a poet," which name hath, as the most excellent, gone through other languages. It cometh of this word *Poiein*, which is "to make": wherein, I know not whether by luck or wisdom, we Englishmen have met with the Greeks in calling him "a maker": which name, how high and incomparable a title it is, I had rather were known by marking the scope of other sciences than by my partial allegation.

There is no art delivered to mankind that hath not the works of nature 2
for his principal object, without which they could not consist, and on which they so depend, as they become actors and players, as it were, of what nature will have set forth. So doth the astronomer look upon the stars, and, by that he seeth, setteth down what order nature hath taken therein. So do the geometrician and arithmetician in their diverse sorts of quantities. So doth the musician in times tell you which by nature agree, which not. The natural philosopher thereon hath his name, and the moral philosopher standeth upon the natural virtues, vices, and passions of man; and "follow nature" (saith he) "therein, and thou shalt not err." The lawyer saith what men have determined; the historian what men have done. The grammarian speaketh only of the rules of speech; and the rhetorician and logician, considering what in nature will soonest prove and persuade, thereon give artificial rules, which still are compassed within the circle of a question according to the proposed matter. The physician weigheth the nature of a man's body, and the nature of things helpful or hurtful unto it. And the metaphysic, though it be in the second and abstract notions, and therefore be counted supernatural, yet doth he indeed build upon the depth of nature. Only the poet, disdaining to be tied to any such subjection, lifted up with the vigor of his own invention, doth grow in effect another nature, in making things either better than nature bringeth forth, or, quite anew, forms such as never were in nature, as

the Heroes, Demigods, Cyclops, Chimeras, Furies, and such like:* so as he goeth hand in hand with nature, not enclosed within the narrow warrant of her gifts, but freely ranging only within the zodiac of his own wit.

Nature never set forth the earth in so rich tapestry as divers poets have 3 done—neither with pleasant rivers, fruitful trees, sweet-smelling flowers, nor whatsoever else may make the too much loved earth more lovely. Her world is brazen, the poets only deliver a golden. But let those things alone, and go to man—for whom as the other things are, so it seemeth in him her uttermost cunning is employed—and know whether she have brought forth so true a lover as Theagenes,† so constant a friend as Pylades,‡ so valiant a man as Orlando,§ so right a prince as Xenophon's Cyrus,‖ so excellent a man every way as Virgil's Aeneas.¶ Neither let this be jestingly conceived, because the works of the one be essential, the other in imitation or fiction; for any understanding knoweth the skill of the artificer standeth in that idea or foreconceit of the work, and not in the work itself. And that the poet hath that idea is manifest, by delivering them forth in such excellency as he hath imagined them. Which delivering forth also is not wholly imaginative, as we are wont to say by them that build castles in the air: but so far substantially it worketh, not only to make a Cyrus, which had been but a particular excellency, as nature might have done, but to bestow a Cyrus upon the world, to make many Cyruses, if they will learn aright why and how that maker made him.

Neither let it be deemed too saucy a comparison to balance the highest 4 point of man's wit with the efficacy of nature; but rather give right honor to the heavenly Maker of that maker, who, having made man to his own likeness, set him beyond and over all the works of that second nature: which in nothing he showeth so much as in poetry, when with the force of a divine breath he bringeth things forth far surpassing her doings, with no small argument to the incredulous of that first accursed fall of Adam, since our erected wit maketh us know what perfection is, and yet our infected will keepeth us from reaching unto it. But these arguments will by few be understood, and by fewer granted. Thus much (I hope) will be given me, that the Greeks with some probability of reason gave him the name above all names of learning. Now let us go to a more ordinary opening of him, that the truth may be more palpable: and so I hope, though we get not so unmatched a praise as the

---

* All creatures of Greek mythology. The Cyclops was a one-eyed giant. The chimera had the head of a lion, the body of a goat, and the tail of a serpent; it was judged to be unconquerable. The Furies were creatures who had serpent hair and who wept blood; their task was to pursue sinners.

† Theagenes was the protagonist of *Aethiopica*, which influenced Sidney's *Arcadia*.

‡ Pylades was the steadfast friend of Orestes, who never left him despite Orestes's horrible fate as the descendent of Agamemnon.

§ Orlando is the protagonist of the *Orlando Furioso*, and the Roland figure of the Charlemagne tales, who dies while defending his country's army.

‖ Cyrus the Younger, who enlisted an army of Greeks to fight the Persians.

¶ The hero of the Aeneid, the founder of Rome.

etymology of his names will grant, yet his very description, which no man will deny, shall not justly be barred from a principal commendation.

Poesy therefore is an art of imitation, for so Aristotle termeth* it in his 5 word *Mimesis*, that is to say, a representing, counterfeiting, or figuring forth—to speak metaphorically, a speaking picture; with this end, to teach and delight. Of this have been three several kinds.

The chief, both in antiquity and excellency, were they that did imitate 6 the inconceivable excellencies of God. Such were David in his Psalms; Solomon in his Song of Songs, in his Ecclesiastes, and Proverbs; Moses and Deborah in their Hymns; and the writer of Job which beside other, the learned Emanuel Tremellius and Franciscus Junius† do entitle the poetical part of the Scripture. Against these none will speak that hath the Holy Ghost in due holy reverence. In this kind, though in a full wrong divinity, were Orpheus, Amphion,‡ Homer in his Hymns, and many others, both Greeks and Romans, and this poesy must be used by whosoever will follow St. James's counsel in singing psalms when they are merry, and I know is used with the fruit of comfort by some, when, in sorrowful pangs of their death-bringing sins, they find the consolation of the never-leaving goodness.

The second kind is of them that deal with matters philosophical: either 7 moral, as Tyrtaeus, Phocylides, and Cato;§ or natural, as Lucretius and Virgil's *Georgics*,‖ or astronomical, as Manilius and Pontanus;¶ or historical, as Lucan;** which who mislike, the fault is in their judgments quite out of taste, and not in the sweet food of sweetly uttered knowledge.

But because this second sort is wrapped within the fold of the proposed 8 subject, and takes not the course of his own invention, whether they properly be poets or no let grammarians dispute; and go to the third, indeed right poets, of whom chiefly this question ariseth, betwixt whom and these second is such a kind of difference as betwixt the meaner sort of painters, who counterfeit only such faces as are set before them, and the more excellent, who, having no law but wit, bestow that in colors upon you which is fittest for the eye to see, as the constant though lamenting look of Lucretia,†† when she punished in herself another's fault (wherein he painteth not Lucretia whom

---

*Sidney quotes here from Aristotle's *Poetics*, 1, 2.

†Emanuel Tremellius and Franciscus Junius were two Protestant scholars who in the sixteenth century published a very popular Latin translation of the Bible.

‡A son of Zeus, Amphion's musical powers were so strong that the notes from his lyre moved the stones to build the walls of Thebes.

§Tyrtaeus was a seventh-century-B.C. elegiac Greek poet. Phocylides was a sixth-century B.C. Greek poet. Dionysius Cato was the author of a collection of moral precepts used as a textbook in Elizabethan schoolrooms.

‖Lucretius was a first-century-B.C. Roman poet. Virgil's *Georgics*, finished in 30 B.C., deals with the poet's attempt to find "real life" by living on a farm.

¶Manilius was a first-century-A.D. Roman poet who wrote the *Astronomica*. Jovianus Pontanus was also a Roman poet and astronomer.

**Lucan was a first-century-A.D. Latin poet, forced by Nero to commit suicide.

††Lucretia was raped by Sextus, the son of Tarquinius Superbus.

he never saw, but painteth the outward beauty of such a virtue). For these third be they which most properly do imitate to teach and delight, and to imitate borrow nothing of what is, hath been, or shall be; but range, only reined with learned discretion, into the divine consideration of what may be, and should be. These be they that, as the first and most noble sort may justly be termed *Vates*, so these are waited on in the excellentest languages and best understandings, with the foredescribed name of poets; for these indeed do merely make to imitate, and imitate both to delight and teach, and delight to move men to take that goodness in hand, which without delight they would fly as from a stranger, and teach, to make them know that goodness whereunto they are moved: which being the noblest scope to which ever any learning was directed, yet want there not idle tongues to bark at them.

These be subdivided into sundry more special denominations. The most 9 notable be the heroic, lyric, tragic, comic, satiric, iambic, elegiac, pastoral, and certain others, some of these being termed according to the matter they deal with, some by the sorts of verses they liked best to write in; for indeed the greatest part of poets have appareled their poetical inventions in that numbrous kind of writing which is called verse—indeed but appareled, verse being but an ornament and no cause to poetry, since there have been many most excellent poets that never versified, and now swarm many versifiers that need never answer to the name of poets. For Xenophon,* who did imitate so excellently as to give us *effigiem iusti imperii*, "the portraiture of a just Empire," under name of Cyrus (as Cicero saith of him), made therein an absolute heroical poem. So did Heliodorus in his sugared invention of that picture of love in Theagenes and Chariclea;† and yet both these writ in prose: which I speak to show that it is not rhyming and versing that maketh a poet—no more than a long gown maketh an advocate, who though he pleaded in armor should be an advocate and no soldier. But it is that feigning notable images of virtues, vices, or what else, with that delightful teaching, which must be the right describing note to know a poet by, although indeed the Senate of Poets hath chosen verse as their fittest raiment, meaning, as in matter they passed all in all, so in manner to go beyond them—not speaking (table-talk fashion or like men in a dream) words as they chanceably fall from the mouth, but peizing each syllable of each word by just proportion according to the dignity of the subject.

Now therefore it shall not be amiss first to weigh this latter sort of poetry 10 by his works, and then by his parts, and, if in neither of these anatomies he be condemnable, I hope we shall obtain a more favorable sentence. This purifying of wit, this enriching of memory, enabling of judgment, and enlarging of conceit, which commonly we call learning, under what name soever it come forth, or to what immediate end soever it be directed, the final

*Xenophon was a fourth-century-B.C. Greek historian.
†Heliodorus was the author of *Aethiopica*, in which these two characters figure.

end is to lead and draw us to as high a perfection as our degenerate souls, made worse by their clayey lodgings, can be capable of. This, according to the inclination of the man, bred many formed impressions. For some that thought this felicity principally to be gotten by knowledge and no knowledge to be so high and heavenly as acquaintance with the stars, gave themselves to astronomy; others, persuading themselves to be demigods if they knew the causes of things, became natural and supernatural philosophers; some an admirable delight drew to music; and some the certainty of demonstration to the mathematics. But all, one and other, having this scope—to know, and by knowledge to lift up the mind from the dungeon of the body to the enjoying his own divine essence. But when by the balance of experience it was found that the astronomer looking to the stars might fall into a ditch, that the inquiring philosopher might be blind in himself, and the mathematician might draw forth a straight line with a crooked heart, then, lo, did proof, the overruler of opinions, make manifest that all these are but serving sciences, which, as they have each a private end in themselves, so yet are they all directed to the highest end of the mistress-knowledge, by the Greeks called *Architectonike*, which stands (as I think) in the knowledge of a man's self, in the ethic and politic consideration, with the end of well doing and not of well knowing only:—even as the saddler's next end is to make a good saddle, but his farther end to serve a nobler faculty, which is horsemanship; so the horseman's to soldiery, and the soldier not only to have the skill, but to perform the practice of a soldier. So that, the ending end of all earthly learning being virtuous action, those skills, that most serve to bring forth that, have a most just title to be princes over all the rest. Wherein we can show the poet's nobleness, by setting him before his other competitors, among whom as principal challengers step forth the moral philosophers, whom, methinketh, I see coming towards me with a sullen gravity, as though they could not abide vice by daylight, rudely clothed for to witness outwardly their contempt of outward things, with books in their hands against glory, whereto they set their names, sophistically speaking against subtlety, and angry with any man in whom they see the foul fault of anger. These men casting largesse as they go of definitions, divisions, and distinctions, with a scornful interrogative do soberly ask whether it be possible to find any path so ready to lead a man to virtue as that which teacheth what virtue is—and teacheth it not only by delivering forth his very being, his causes, and effects, but also by making known his enemy, vice (which must be destroyed), and his cumbersome servant, passion (which must be mastered), by showing the generalities that containeth it, and the specialties that are derived from it; lastly, by plain setting down, how it extendeth itself out of the limits of a man's own little world to the government of families, and maintaining of public societies.

The historian scarcely giveth leisure to the moralist to say so much, but 11 that he, laden with old mouse-eaten records, authorizing himself (for the most part) upon other histories, whose greatest authorities are built upon the notable foundation of hearsay; having much ado to accord differing writers and to pick truth out of partiality; better acquainted with a thousand years ago than with the present age, and yet better knowing how this world goeth than how his own wit runneth; curious for antiquities and inquisitive of novelties; a wonder to young folks and a tyrant in table talk, denieth, in a great chafe, that any man for teaching of virtue, and virtuous actions, is comparable to him. "I am *Lux vitae, Temporum magistra, Vita memoriae, Nuncia vetustatis,*"* etc. The philosopher (saith he) "teacheth a disputative virtue, but I do an active. His virtue is excellent in the dangerless Academy of Plato, but mine showeth forth her honorable face in the battles of Marathon, Pharsalia, Poitiers, and Agincourt. He teacheth virtue by certain abstract considerations, but I only bid you follow the footing of them that have gone before you. Old-aged experience goeth beyond the fine-witted philosopher, but I give the experience of many ages. Lastly, if he make the song book, I put the learner's hand to the lute; and if he be the guide, I am the light."

Then would he allege you innumerable examples, conferring story by 12 story, how much the wisest senators and princes have been directed by the credit of history, as Brutus, Alphonsus of Aragon,† and who not, if need be? At length the long line of their disputation maketh a point in this, that the one giveth the precept, and the other the example.

Now, whom shall we find (since the question standeth for the highest 13 form in the school of learning) to be moderator? Truly, as meseemeth, the poet; and if not a moderator, even the man that ought to carry the title from them both, and much more from all other serving sciences. Therefore compare we the poet with the historian, and with the moral philosopher; and, if he go beyond them both, no other human skill can match him. For as for the Divine, with all reverence it is ever to be excepted, not only for having his scope as far beyond any of these as eternity exceedeth a moment, but even for passing each of these in themselves. And for the lawyer, though Jus be the daughter of justice, and justice the chief of virtues, yet because he seeketh to make men good rather *formidine poenae* than *virtutis amore,*‡ or, to say righter, doth not endeavor to make men good, but that their evil hurt not others, having no care, so he be a good citizen, how bad a man he be: therefore, as our wickedness maketh him necessary, and necessity maketh him honorable, so is he not in the deepest truth to stand in rank with these who all endeavor to take naughtiness away, and plant goodness even in the secretest cabinet of our souls. And these four are all that any way deal in that consideration of men's manners, which being the supreme knowledge, they that best breed it deserve the best commendation.

---

* This paraphrase from Cicero's *De oratore* suggests that history is a witness of the times, the light of truth, the life of memory, the mistress of life, the messenger of ancient times.
† Lucius Junius Brutus was the founder of the Roman republic in 510 B.C. Alphonsus was the thirteenth-century coregent of France while Louis IX was on crusade.
‡ This is a quote from Horace's *Epistles:* "rather for fear of punishment than love of virtue."

The philosopher therefore and the historian are they which would win 14
the goal, the one by precept, the other by example. But both, not having
both, do both halt. For the philosopher, setting down with thorny argument
the bare rule, is so hard of utterance, and so misty to be conceived, that one
that hath no other guide but him shall wade in him till he be old before he
shall find sufficient cause to be honest. For his knowledge standeth so upon
the abstract and general, that happy is that man who may understand him,
and more happy that can apply what he doth understand. On the other side,
the historian, wanting the precept, is so tied, not to what should be but to
what is, to the particular truth of things and not to the general reason of
things, that his example draweth no necessary consequence, and therefore a
less fruitful doctrine.

Now doth the peerless poet perform both: for whatsoever the philoso- 15
pher saith should be done, he giveth a perfect picture of it in someone by
whom he presupposeth it was done; so as he coupleth the general notion with
the particular example. A perfect picture I say, for he yieldeth to the powers
of the mind an image of that whereof the philosopher bestoweth but a word-
ish description: which doth neither strike, pierce, nor possess the sight of the
soul so much as that other doth.

For as in outward things, to a man that had never seen an elephant or 16
a rhinoceros, who should tell him most exquisitely all their shapes, color,
bigness, and particular marks, or of a gorgeous palace the architecture, with
declaring the full beauties might well make the hearer able to repeat, as it
were by rote, all he had heard, yet should never satisfy his inward conceits
with being witness to itself of a true lively knowledge: but the same man, as
soon as he might see those beasts well painted, or the house well in model,
should straightways grow, without need of any description, to a judicial comprehending of them: so no doubt the philosopher with his learned definition—be it of virtue, vices, matters of public policy or private government—
replenisheth the memory with many infallible grounds of wisdom, which,
notwithstanding, lie dark before the imaginative and judging power, if they
be not illuminated or figured forth by the speaking picture of poesy.

Tully taketh much pains, and many times not without poetical helps, 17
to make us know the force love of our country hath in us. Let us but hear old
Anchises speaking in the middest of Troy's flames, or see Ulysses in the fullness of all Calypso's delights bewail his absence from barren and beggarly
Ithaca. Anger, the Stoics say, was a short madness: let but Sophocles bring
you Ajax on a stage, killing and whipping sheep and oxen, thinking them the
army of Greeks, with their chieftains Agamemnon and Menelaus, and tell me
if you have not a more familiar insight into anger than finding in the School-
men his genus and difference. See whether wisdom and temperance in Ulysses
and Diomedes, valor in Achilles, friendship in Nisus and Euryalus,* even to

---

*Characters in the *Aeneid*. Nisus died as he sought vengeance for his friend.

an ignorant man carry not an apparent shining, and, contrarily, the remorse of conscience in Oedipus, the soon repenting pride of Agamemnon, the self-devouring cruelty in his father Atreus, the violence of ambition in the two Theban brothers, the sour-sweetness of revenge in Medea, and, to fall lower, the Terentian Gnatho* and our Chaucer's Pandar† so expressed that we now use their names to signify their trades; and finally, all virtues, vices, and passions so in their own natural seats laid to the view, that we seem not to hear of them, but clearly to see through them. But even in the most excellent determination of goodness, what philosopher's counsel can so readily direct a prince, as the feigned Cyrus in Xenophon; or a virtuous man in all fortunes, as Aeneas in Virgil; or a whole Commonwealth, as the way of Sir Thomas More's *Utopia?* I say the way, because where Sir Thomas More erred, it was the fault of the man and not of the poet, for that way of patterning a Commonwealth was most absolute, though he perchance hath not so absolutely performed it. For the question is, whether the feigned image of poesy or the regular instruction of philosophy hath the more force in teaching: wherein if the philosophers have more rightly showed themselves philosophers than the poets have attained to the high top of their profession, as in truth,

Mediocribus esse poetis,   18
Non Di, non homines, non concessere Columnae;‡

it is, I say again, not the fault of the art, but that by few men that art can be   19
accomplished. Certainly, even our Savior Christ could as well have given the moral commonplaces of uncharitableness and humbleness as the divine narration of Dives and Lazarus; or of disobedience and mercy, as that heavenly discourse of the lost child and the gracious father; but that his through-searching wisdom knew the estate of Dives burning in hell, and of Lazarus being in Abraham's bosom, would more constantly (as it were) inhabit both the memory and judgment. Truly, for myself, meseems I see before my eyes the lost child's disdainful prodigality, turned to envy a swine's dinner: which by the learned divines are thought not historical acts, but instructing parables. For conclusion, I say the Philosopher teacheth, but he teacheth obscurely, so as the learned only can understand him; that is to say, he teacheth them that are already taught. But the poet is the food for the tenderest stomachs, the poet is indeed the right popular philosopher, whereof Aesop's tales give good proof: whose pretty allegories, stealing under the formal tales of beasts, make many, more beastly than beasts, begin to hear the sound of virtue from these dumb speakers.

But now may it be alleged that, if this imagining of matters be so fit for   20
the imagination, then must the historian needs surpass, who bringeth you

* Gnatho is a character in Terence's *Eunuchus*.
† Pandar is a character in Chaucer's *Troilus and Criseyde*.
‡ A quote from Horace's *Ars poetica:* "Mediocrity in poets has not been accepted by gods, men, or bookstalls."

images of true matters, such as indeed were done, and not such as fantastically or falsely may be suggested to have been done. Truly, Aristotle himself, in his discourse of poesy, plainly determineth this question, saying that poetry is *Philosophoteron* and *Spoudaioteron*, that is to say, it is more philosophical and more studiously serious than history. His reason is, because poesy dealeth with *Katholou*, that is to say, with the universal consideration, and the history with *Kathekaston*, the particular: "now," saith he, "the universal weighs what is fit to be said or done, either in likelihood or necessity (which the poesy considereth in his imposed names), and the particular only marks whether Alcibiades did, or suffered, this or that." Thus far Aristotle: which reason of his (as all his) is most full of reason. For indeed, if the question were whether it were better to have a particular act truly or falsely set down, there is no doubt which is to be chosen, no more than whether you had rather have Vespasian's picture right as he was, or at the painter's pleasure nothing resembling. But if the question be for your own use and learning, whether it be better to have it set down as it should be, or as it was, then certainly is more doctrinable the feigned Cyrus in Xenophon than the true Cyrus in Justin, and the feigned Aeneas in Virgil than the right Aeneas in Dares Phrygius:* as to a lady that desired to fashion her countenance to the best grace, a painter should more benefit her to portrait a most sweet face, writing Canidia upon it, than to paint Canidia as she was, who, Horace sweareth, was foul and ill favored.

If the poet do his part aright, he will show you in Tantalus, Atreus, and 21 such like, nothing that is not to be shunned; in Cyrus, Aeneas, Ulysses, each thing to be followed; where the historian, bound to tell things as things were, cannot be liberal (without he will be poetical) of a perfect pattern, but, as in Alexander or Scipio himself, show doings, some to be liked, some to be misliked. And then how will you discern what to follow but by your own discretion, which you had without reading Quintus Curtius?† And whereas a man may say, though in universal consideration of doctrine the poet prevaileth, yet that the history, in his saying such a thing was done, doth warrant a man more in that he shall follow; the answer is manifest: that if he stand upon that *was*—as if he should argue, because it rained yesterday, therefore it should rain today—then indeed it hath some advantage to a gross conceit; but if he know an example only informs a conjectured likelihood, and so go by reason, the poet doth so far exceed him, as he is to frame his example to that which is most reasonable, be it in warlike, politic, or private matters; where the historian in his bare *was* hath many times that which we call fortune to overrule the best wisdom. Many times he must tell events whereof he can yield no cause: or, if he do, it must be poetical.

---

* Dares Phrygius was believed by medieval and Renaissance authors to have been an eyewitness to the fall of Troy.
† Quintus Curtius was a Latin author of a history of Alexander the Great.

For that a feigned example hath as much force to teach as a true ex- 22
ample (for as for to move, it is clear, since the feigned may be tuned to the
highest key of passion), let us take one example wherein a poet and a historian
do concur. Herodotus and Justin do both testify that Zopyrus, King Darius's
faithful servant, seeing his master long resisted by the rebellious Babylonians,
feigned himself in extreme disgrace of his king: for verifying of which, he
caused his own nose and ears to be cut off, and so flying to the Babylonians,
was received, and for his known valor so far credited, that he did find means
to deliver them over to Darius. Much like matter doth Livy record of Tarquinius and his son. Xenophon excellently feigneth such another stratagem
performed by Abradates in Cyrus's behalf. Now would I fain know, if occasion be presented unto you to serve your prince by such an honest dissimula-
tion, why you do not as well learn it of Xenophon's fiction as of the other's
verity—and truly so much the better, as you shall save your nose by the bar-
gain; for Abradates did not counterfeit so far. So then the best of the historian
is subject to the poet; for whatsoever action, or faction, whatsoever counsel,
policy, or war stratagem the historian is bound to recite, that may the poet
(if he list) with his imitation make his own, beautifying it both for further
teaching, and more delighting, as it pleaseth him, having all from Dante's
heaven to his hell, under the authority of his pen. Which if I be asked what
poets have done so, as I might well name some, yet say I, and say again, I
speak of the art, and not of the artificer.

QUESTIONS ABOUT SIDNEY'S DISCOURSE COMMUNITY AND HIS CONCERNS IN THIS SELECTION

1. What, according to Sidney, is the etymology of the word *poet?*
2. Sidney suggests that all of the art that humankind engages in—by which he means vocations as well as aesthetic endeavors—has at its root a consideration of nature. This suggestion comes out of the belief within his discourse community that the entire universe was intricately tied together in hierarchical relationships. Do contemporary artists hold to the same beliefs? If not, what factors have contributed to a different point of view?
3. What, according to Sidney, distinguishes the poet from those in all other professions (paragraph 2)? Would a modern poet or writer of fiction make the same kinds of claims?
4. Sidney suggests that poets can create a world even more beautiful than that which nature can produce. "Her [Nature's] world is brazen, the poets only deliver a golden" (paragraph 3). What does this claim suggest about Sidney's perspective on the value and role of poetry?
5. Sidney, following the conventions of his discourse community, suggests that poetry is meant to teach and to delight (paragraph 5). Is this still seen as the function of poetry in the twentieth century?
6. In describing the third category of poetry (paragraph 8), Sidney suggests that poetry serves to hold up models of virtue and therefore inclines one to goodness.

Would proponents of any art form in the twentieth century make a similar claim?

7. What, according to Sidney, is the purpose of learning (paragraph 10)?
8. According to Sidney, why is it legitimate for a poet to portray things not exactly as they are?

QUESTIONS ABOUT SIDNEY'S RHETORICAL STRATEGIES

1. Sidney begins this selection with the words "But now," a technique he uses throughout the *Apologie* whenever he wishes to mark a transition to a new point. Given Sidney's prose style, do you think such transitions are useful?
2. Read over the second paragraph. What rhetorical strategy does Sidney use to illustrate the point he is making? Where else does he use this strategy?
3. Sidney often piles clause upon clause in his sentences. What is the effect on the reader of such a structure? Why is this structure suited to the way Sidney illustrates his points?
4. At times, Sidney uses the rhetorical mode of classification to advance his points. What are the weaknesses and strengths of this mode? In general, does it seem to you that Sidney uses this mode to advantage?
5. Consider the first sentence of paragraph 10. How is Sidney using the pronoun *his* here? What factors might have contributed to that particular usage being dropped soon after the Renaissance?
6. When he comes to describe moral philosophers, Sidney shifts his stance to the dramatic present: "the moral philosophers, whom, me thinketh, I see coming towards me with a sullen gravity, as though they could not abide vice by daylight" (paragraph 10). What is the effect on the reader of this shift in stance?
7. To attack the moral philosophers, Sidney paints a striking image of them. Why does he not simply list their beliefs and approaches? Does it seem to you that this is an appropriate or fair way to attack this group?
8. What examples does Sidney use to suggest that the poet is the moderator of the historian and the moral philosopher? The juxtaposition of several of those examples sounds odd to the modern ear. What does Sidney's willingness to yoke all of these examples together suggest about his discourse community?

WRITING FROM WITHIN AND ABOUT THE ARTS: LITERARY CRITICISM

Writing for Yourself

1. In your journal, reflect on a time in your life when something you have read contributed to a growth in moral awareness.
2. In your journal, reflect on what you take the goal of all learning to be.

Writing for Nonacademic Audiences

1. You have been asked to participate in a debate between students in the departments of history and English literature and language. The question before both sides is which discipline speaks with a stronger voice to the needs of contempo-

rary humanity. You are to deliver the five-minute opening statement for your team. Choose which side you would be on and prepare that statement.

2. The chair of your English department has asked you as a potential English major to write a brief statement expressing whether you believe that the study of literature contributes to moral growth in the individual. The 250-word essay will be part of your permanent file at your university and will be sent on to potential graduate schools or employers along with faculty recommendations.

Writing for Academic Audiences

1. For an introduction to literature class, write a 100-word definition of *poetry*.
2. Research the meaning of the Old English word *scop*, paying close attention to its etymology. For a history of language class, compare the meanings of the Old English *scop* to the term *poet*. Your comparison will be made in a ten-minute oral presentation.
3. Choose a work of fiction you have recently read and evaluate it by using Sidney's criteria of its ability to teach and to delight. Write up your results in a 500-word book review to be printed in a local newspaper.
4. Consider the following passage from Sidney's *Arcadia:*

> There were hills which garnished their proud heights with stately trees; humble valleys whose base estate seemed comforted with refreshing of silver rivers; meadows enamelled with all sorts of eye-pleasing flowers; thickets, which, being lined with most pleasant shade, were witnessed so to by the cheerful deposition of many well-tuned birds; each pasture stored with sheep feeding with sober security, while the pretty lambs with bleating oratory craved the dams' comfort; here a shepherd's boy piping as though he should never be old; there a young shepherdess knitting and withal singing, and it seemed that her voice comforted her hands to work and her hands kept time to her voice's music. As for the houses of the country—for many houses came under their eye—they were all scattered, no two being one by the other, and yet not so far off as that it barred mutual succour: a show, as it were, of an accompanable solitariness and of a civil wildness.

For a class in Renaissance literature, evaluate this passage according to Sidney's claim that nature can create a brazen world while the poet can create a golden one. Write your evaluation in the form of a 750-word essay.

Charles Lamb

(1775–1834)

Charles Lamb is known as one of the finest essayists and critics of the Romantic era in England. He was born in the Inner Temple of the Inns of Court. His father was a lawyer's clerk; we know little about his mother. When Lamb was seven and a half years old, he was sent to Christ's Hospital, a London charity school, where he met Samuel Taylor Coleridge. After he left Christ's Hospital at the age of fifteen, Lamb took a clerkship in the India House, where he worked for thirty years.

Probably the most influential incident in Lamb's life occurred when he was twenty-two. A strain of insanity had been passed down through his mother's side of the family, and Lamb himself suffered from it for a period of time. But his older sister, Mary Ann, suffered from it more often, and when Lamb was twenty-two, he saw Mary Ann in a fit fatally stab their mother. Mary Ann was released into Lamb's custody, and he committed himself to caring for her, which he did until his death.

When Lamb was in his forties, he began to write quite regularly, often under the pen name Elia. In some ways his essays—often sentimental, whimsical, and quaint—would seem to have little appeal for modern readers. But because of his sensitive voice, his humane spirit, and his perceptive arguments, his essays remain popular. And his subjects are often those that we still regard as important. In the following essay, for instance, Lamb focuses on the comedy of manners, the comedy concerned with the manners and morals of the elegant but superficial higher levels of society in the later seventeenth century and the eighteenth century. In his individualism and his looking to the past for subjects to write about, Lamb is typical of essayists of the Romantic period. But he also displays a keen awareness of the moral concerns that we associate with the Victorians. And in his exploration of the comedy of manners and of the relationship between morality and art, Lamb opens up questions that are hotly debated yet today.

ON THE ARTIFICIAL COMEDY
OF THE LAST CENTURY *

The artificial Comedy, or Comedy of Manners, is quite extinct on our stage. 1
Congreve and Farquhar† show their heads once in seven years only, to be
exploded and put down instantly. The times cannot bear them. Is it for a few
wild speeches, an occasional licence of dialogue? I think not altogether. The
business of their dramatic characters will not stand the moral test. We screw
every thing up to that. Idle gallantry in a fiction, a dream, the passing pageant of an evening, startles us in the same way as the alarming indications of
profligacy in a son or ward in real life should startle a parent or guardian.
We have no such middle emotions as dramatic interests left. We see a stage
libertine playing his loose pranks of two hours' duration, and of no after
consequence, with the severe eyes which inspect real vices with their bearings
upon two worlds. We are spectators to a plot or intrigue (not reducible in life
to the point of strict morality) and take it all for truth. We substitute a real
for a dramatic person, and judge him accordingly. We try him in our courts,
from which there is no appeal to the *dramatis personæ*, his peers. We have
been spoiled with—not sentimental comedy—but a tyrant far more pernicious to our pleasures which has succeeded to it, the exclusive and all devouring drama of common life; where the moral point is every thing; where,
instead of the fictitious half-believed personages of the stage (the phantoms
of old comedy) we recognise ourselves, our brothers, aunts, kinsfolk, allies,
patrons, enemies,—the same as in life,—with an interest in what is going on
so hearty and substantial, that we cannot afford our moral judgment, in its
deepest and most vital results, to compromise or slumber for a moment. What
is *there* transacting, by no modification is made to affect us in any other
manner than the same events or characters would do in our relationships of
life. We carry our fire-side concerns to the theatre with us. We do not go
thither, like our ancestors, to escape from the pressure of reality, so much as
to confirm our experience of it; to make assurance double, and take a bond
of fate. We must live our toilsome lives twice over, as it was the mournful
privilege of Ulysses‡ to descend twice to the shades. All that neutral ground
of character, which stood between vice and virtue; or which in fact was
indifferent to neither, where neither properly was called in question; that

---

* Lamb is referring to the eighteenth century.
† William Congreve (1670–1729) and George Farquhar (1678–1707) both wrote comedies of
    manners, although some of Farquhar's later plays helped destroy the artificial style of
    comedy.
‡ Otherwise known as Odysseus.

happy breathing-place from the burthen of a perpetual moral questioning—
the sanctuary and quiet Alsatia* of hunted casuistry—is broken up and dis-
franchised, as injurious to the interests of society. The privileges of the place
are taken away by law. We dare not dally with images, or names, of wrong.
We bark like foolish dogs at shadows. We dread infection from the scenic
representation of disorder; and fear a painted pustule.† In our anxiety that
our morality should not take cold, we wrap it up in a great blanket surtout
of precaution against the breeze and sunshine.

    I confess for myself that (with no great delinquencies to answer for) I 2
am glad for a season to take an airing beyond the diocese of the strict conscience,—not to live always in the precincts of the law-courts—but now and
then, for a dream-while or so, to imagine a world with no meddling restrictions—to get into recesses, whither the hunter cannot follow me—

    —————Secret shades 3
    Of woody Ida's inmost grove,
    While yet there was no fear of Jove—

I come back to my cage and my restraint the fresher and more healthy for it. 4
I wear my shackles more contentedly for having respired the breath of an
imaginary freedom. I do not know how it is with others, but I feel the better
always for the perusal of one of Congreve's—nay, why should I not add even
of Wycherley's‡—comedies. I am the gayer at least for it; and I could never
connect those sports of a witty fancy in any shape with any result to be drawn
from them to imitation in real life. They are a world of themselves almost as
much as fairy-land. Take one of their characters, male or female (with few
exceptions they are alike), and place it in a modern play, and my virtuous
indignation shall rise against the profligate wretch as warmly as the Catos§
of the pit could desire; because in a modern play I am to judge of the right
and the wrong. The standard of *police* is the measure of *political justice*. The
atmosphere will blight it, it cannot live here. It has got into a moral world,
where it has no business, from which it must needs fall headlong; as dizzy,
and incapable of making a stand, as a Swedenborgian‖ bad spirit that has
wandered unawares into the sphere of one of his Good Men or Angels. But in
its own world do we feel the creature is so very bad?—The Fainalls and the
Mirabels, the Dorimants and the Lady Touchwoods,¶ in their own sphere,

---

*Alsatia, or Alsace, is a region between France and Germany. Throughout its history, both
    France and Germany have disputed who should govern it. Before the Reformation, Al-
    sace was also a hotbed of theological debate.
†Resembling a blister or pimple.
‡William Wycherly (1640–1716) was a dramatist known for savage satire and coarse wit.
§Marcus Porcius Cato (234–149 B.C.) was a Roman statesman who fought moral laxity within
    the Roman state.
‖Emanuel Swedenborg (1688–1772) was a Swedish religious teacher and mystic.
¶These are all characters from the drama of the prior century.

do not offend my moral sense; in fact they do not appeal to it at all. They seem engaged in their proper element. They break through no laws, or conscientious restraints. They know of none. They have got out of Christendom into the land—what shall I call it?—of cuckoldry—the Utopia of gallantry, where pleasure is duty, and the manners perfect freedom. It is altogether a speculative scene of things, which has no reference whatever to the world that is. No good person can be justly offended as a spectator, because no good person suffers on the stage. Judged morally, every character in these plays— the few exceptions only are *mistakes*—is alike essentially vain and worthless. The great art of Congreve is especially shown in this, that he has entirely excluded from his scenes,—some little generosities on the part of Angelica perhaps excepted,—not only any thing like a faultless character, but any pretensions to goodness or good feelings whatsoever. Whether he did this designedly, or instinctively, the effect is as happy, as the design (if design) was bold. I used to wonder at the strange power which his *Way of the World* in particular possesses of interesting you all along in the pursuits of characters, for whom you absolutely care nothing—for you neither hate nor love his personages—and I think it is owing to this very indifference for any, that you endure the whole. He has spread a privation of moral light, I will call it, rather than by the ugly name of palpable darkness, over his creations; and his shadows flit before you without distinction or preference. Had he introduced a good character, a single gush of moral feeling, a revulsion of the judgment to actual life and actual duties, the impertinent Goshen would have only lighted to the discovery of deformities, which now are none, because we think them none.

Translated into real life, the characters of his, and his friend Wycher- 5 ley's dramas, are profligates and strumpets,—the business of their brief existence, the undivided pursuit of lawless gallantry. No other spring of action, or possible motive of conduct, is recognised; principles which, universally acted upon, must reduce this frame of things to a chaos. But we do them wrong in so translating them. No such effects are produced in *their* world. When we are among them, we are amongst a chaotic people. We are not to judge them by our usages. No reverend institutions are insulted by their proceedings,—for they have none among them. No peace of families is violated,—for no family ties exist among them. No purity of the marriage bed is stained,—for none is supposed to have a being. No deep affections are disquieted,—no holy wedlock bands are snapped asunder,—for affection's depth and wedded faith are not of the growth of that soil. There is neither right nor wrong,—gratitude or its opposite,—claim or duty,—paternity or sonship. Of what consequence is it to virtue, or how is she at all concerned about it, whether Sir Simon, or Dapperwit, steal away Miss Martha; or who is the father of Lord Froth's, or Sir Paul Pliant's children.

The whole is a passing pageant, where we should sit as unconcerned at 6 the issues, for life or death, as at a battle of the frogs and mice. But, like Don

Quixote,* we take part against the puppets, and quite as impertinently. We dare not contemplate an Atlantis,† a scheme, out of which our coxcombical moral sense is for a little transitory ease excluded. We have not the courage to imagine a state of things for which there is neither reward nor punishment. We cling to the painful necessities of shame and blame. We would indict our very dreams.

Amidst the mortifying circumstances attendant upon growing old, it is 7 something to have seen the *School for Scandal*‡ in its glory. This comedy grew out of Congreve and Wycherley, but gathered some allays of the sentimental comedy§ which followed theirs. It is impossible that it should be now *acted*, though it continues, at long intervals, to be announced in the bills. Its hero, when Palmer played it at least, was Joseph Surface. When I remember the gay boldness, the graceful solemn plausibility, the measured step, the insinuating voice—to express it in a word—the downright *acted* villany of the part, so different from the pressure of conscious actual wickedness,—the hypocritical assumption of hypocrisy,—which made Jack so deservedly a favourite in that character, I must needs conclude the present generation of play-goers more virtuous than myself, or more dense. I freely confess that he divided the palm with me with his better brother; that, in fact, I liked him quite as well. Not but there are passages,—like that, for instance, where Joseph is made to refuse a pittance to a poor relation,—incongruities which Sheridan was forced upon by the attempt to join the artificial with the sentimental comedy, either of which must destroy the other—but over these obstructions Jack's manner floated him so lightly, that a refusal from him no more shocked you, than the easy compliance of Charles gave you in reality any pleasure; you got over the paltry question as quickly as you could, to get back into the regions of pure comedy, where no cold moral reigns. The highly artificial manner of Palmer in this character counteracted every disagreeable impression which you might have received from the contrast, supposing them real, between the two brothers. You did not believe in Joseph with the same faith with which you believed in Charles. The latter was a pleasant reality, the former a no less pleasant poetical foil to it. The comedy, I have said, is incongruous; a mixture of Congreve with sentimental incompatibilities: the gaiety upon the whole is buoyant; but it required the consummate art of Palmer to reconcile the discordant elements.

A player with Jack's talents, if we had one now, would not dare to do 8 the part in the same manner. He would instinctively avoid every turn which might tend to unrealise, and so to make the character fascinating. He must

---

*Don Quixote is the main character in Miguel de Cervantes's *Don Quixote*. He became crazed by reading romances of chivalry.

†A mythical island; the name is sometimes associated with a utopian society.

‡A comedy written by Richard Brinsley Sheridan in 1777.

§Sentimental or "reformed" comedy sprang up early in the eighteenth century as a reaction against the artificial comedy of manners.

take his cue from his spectators, who would expect a bad man and a good man as rigidly opposed to each other as the death-beds of those geniuses are contrasted in the prints, which I am sorry to say have disappeared from the windows of my old friend Carrington Bowles, of St. Paul's Church-yard memory—(an exhibition as venerable as the adjacent cathedral, and almost coeval) of the bad and good man at the hour of death; where the ghastly apprehensions of the former,—and truly the grim phantom with his reality of a toasting fork is not to be despised,—so finely contrast with the meek complacent kissing of the rod,—taking it in like honey and butter,—with which the latter submits to the scythe of the gentle bleeder, Time, who wields his lancet with the apprehensive finger of a popular young ladies' surgeon. What flesh, like loving grass, would not covet to meet half-way the stroke of such a delicate mower?—John Palmer was twice an actor in this exquisite part. He was playing to you all the while that he was playing upon Sir Peter and his lady. You had the first intimation of a sentiment before it was on his lips. His altered voice was meant to you, and you were to suppose that his fictitious co-flutterers on the stage perceived nothing at all of it. What was it to you if that half-reality, the husband, was over-reached by the puppetry— or the thin thing (Lady Teazle's reputation) was persuaded it was dying of a plethory? The fortunes of Othello and Desdemona* were not concerned in it. Poor Jack has passed from the stage in good time, that he did not live to this our age of seriousness. The pleasant old Teazle *King,*† too, is gone in good time. His manner would scarce have passed current in our day. We must love or hate—acquit or condemn—censure or pity—exert our detestable cox-combry of moral judgment upon everything. Joseph Surface, to go down now, must be a downright revolting villain—no compromise—his first appearance must shock and give horror—his specious plausibilities, which the pleasurable faculties of our fathers welcomed with such hearty greetings, knowing that no harm (dramatic harm even) could come, or was meant to come of them, must inspire a cold and killing aversion. Charles‡ (the real canting person of the scene—for the hypocrisy of Joseph has its ulterior legit-imate ends, but his brother's professions of a good heart, centre in downright self-satisfaction) must be *loved*, and Joseph *hated*. To balance one disagree-able reality with another, Sir Peter Teazle must be no longer the comic idea of a fretful old bachelor bridegroom, whose teasings (while King acted it) were evidently as much played off at you, as they were meant to concern any body on the stage,—he must be a real person, capable in law of sustaining an injury—a person towards whom duties are to be acknowledged—the gen-uine crim-con antagonist of the villanous seducer Joseph. To realise him more, his sufferings under his unfortunate match must have the downright pun-

---

* Major characters in Shakespeare's *Othello*.
† An actor who played Sir Peter Teazle in *The School for Scandal*.
‡ Charles is Joseph Surface's brother in *The School for Scandal*.

gency of life—must (or should) make you not mirthful but uncomfortable, just as the same predicament would move you in a neighbour or old friend. The delicious scenes which give the play its name and zest, must affect you in the same serious manner as if you heard the reputation of a dear female friend attacked in your real presence. Crabtree, and Sir Benjamin—those poor snakes that live but in the sunshine of your mirth—must be ripened by this hotbed process of realisation into asps or amphisbænas;* and Mrs. Candour—O! frightful! become a hooded serpent. Oh who that remembers Parsons and Dodd—the wasp and butterfly of the *School for Scandal*—in those two characters; and charming natural Miss Pope, the perfect gentlewoman as distinguished from the fine lady of comedy, in this latter part—would forego the true scenic delight—the escape from life—the oblivion of consequences—the holiday barring out of the pedant Reflection—those Saturnalia† of two or three brief hours, well won from the world—to sit instead at one of our modern plays—to have his coward conscience (that forsooth must not be left for a moment) stimulated with perpetual appeals—dulled rather, and blunted, as a faculty without repose must be—and his moral vanity pampered with images of notional justice, notional beneficences, lives saved without the spectators' risk, and fortunes given away that cost the author nothing?

No piece was, perhaps, ever so completely cast in all its parts as this 9 *manager's comedy*. Miss Farren had succeeded to Mrs. Abingdon in Lady Teazle; and Smith, the original Charles, had retired when I first saw it. The rest of the characters, with very slight exceptions, remained. I remember it was then the fashion to cry down John Kemble, who took the part of Charles after Smith; but, I thought, very unjustly. Smith, I fancy, was more airy, and took the eye with a certain gaiety of person. He brought with him no sombre recollections of tragedy. He had not to expiate the fault of having pleased beforehand in lofty declamation. He had no sins of Hamlet or of Richard to atone for. His failure in these parts was a passport to success in one of so opposite a tendency. But, as far as I could judge, the weighty sense of Kemble made up for more personal incapacity than he had to answer for. His harshest tones in this part came steeped and dulcified in good humour. He made his defects a grace. His exact declamatory manner, as he managed it, only served to convey the points of his dialogue with more precision. It seemed to head the shafts to carry them deeper. Not one of his sparkling sentences was lost. I remember minutely how he delivered each in succession, and cannot by any effort imagine how any of them could be altered for the better. No man could deliver brilliant dialogue—the dialogue of Congreve or of Wycherley—because none understood it—half so well as John Kemble.

* In classical mythology, a serpent with a head on both ends, capable of moving in either direction.
† The festival of Saturn in ancient Rome, which began on December 17. The festival often involved unrestrained, orgiastic celebrations.

His Valentine, in Love for Love,* was, to my recollection, faultless. He flagged sometimes in the intervals of tragic passion. He would slumber over the level parts of an heroic character. His Macbeth has been known to nod. But he always seemed to me to be particularly alive to pointed and witty dialogue. The relaxing levities of tragedy have not been touched by any since him—the playful court-bred spirit in which he condescended to the players in Hamlet—the sportive relief which he threw into the darker shades of Richard—disappeared with him. He had his sluggish moods, his torpors—but they were the halting-stones and resting-places of his tragedy—politic savings, and fetches of the breath—husbandry of the lungs, where nature pointed him to be an economist—rather, I think, than errors of the judgment. They were, at worst, less painful than the eternal tormenting unappeasable vigilance, the "lidless dragon eyes," of present fashionable tragedy.

QUESTIONS ABOUT LAMB'S DISCOURSE
COMMUNITY AND HIS CONCERNS IN THIS ESSAY

1. Why does Lamb say the Comedy of Manners was extinct on the stage at the time of his writing?
2. What does Lamb mean when he writes that "we would indict our very dreams" (paragraph 6)?
3. How convincing is Lamb when he argues that the characters in Comedies of Manners live in the Utopia of gallantry and should not be judged by standards of the world?
4. Lamb claims that we can be interested in characters that we hardly care about. Do you agree? Is this true for you?
5. How does Lamb imply that dramatic art and life ought to be related? Do you agree with him?
6. What does Lamb say are the dangers of keeping one's moral sense operating all the time?

QUESTIONS ABOUT LAMB'S RHETORICAL
STRATEGIES

1. Lamb makes many personal revelations in this essay. How do these strike you?
2. Are Lamb's paragraphs longer or shorter than you prefer? Are his paragraphs unified?
3. Is Lamb foolish to devote so much space to how the actor John Palmer played Joseph Surface in *School for Scandal*? In discussing Palmer, does Lamb stray too far from his main purpose?
4. What metaphors does Lamb use for the world of morality? Are they similar to the ones you would choose for the world of morality?
5. How does Lamb use the pronoun *we*? Does he use it to refer to himself? How effective is this practice?

---

* A comedy (1695) by William Congreve.

6. How does Lamb use the pronoun *you*? Is his strategy effective?
7. Which elements of this essay are hardest for you to understand? Why?

WRITING FROM WITHIN AND ABOUT THE ARTS: LITERARY CRITICISM

Writing for Yourself

1. In your journal, reflect on the funniest dramatic production you have ever seen. Why was it funny?
2. In your journal, reflect on an incident in which you saw someone inappropriately bring a high moral sense to bear on a work of art.

Writing for Nonacademic Audiences

1. On a trip home from school, you let your parents discover that in one of your classes you have just finished reading a story about what many would label sexual immorality. Your parents are shocked, and your stay at home is miserable. When you get back to campus, you write them a letter in which you defend your decision to read the story.
2. Find a review of a work of art in which the critic passes moral judgments on the work. React to the critic's judgments in a letter to the editor of the newspaper or magazine in which the review appeared.
3. *Reader's Digest* is sponsoring a contest for college students. To enter, you must write a 500-word essay on what makes current college students laugh. You decide to enter the contest.
4. The editor of your school newspaper has asked you to write a 500-word reflective piece on whether using art as an escape from the real world is justifiable.

Writing for Academic Audiences

1. For a course that surveys the history of English literature, you are to describe the comedy of manners in a ten-minute talk. Write up your script for that talk.
2. For a course introducing students to literature, write a 1,000-word essay in which you compare and contrast the major effects on viewers of comedy and tragedy.
3. For a course in aesthetics, write a 1,000-word paper in which you argue how the world of a work of art and the real world should be related by readers or viewers.

Roger Fry
(1866–1934)

Roger Fry was born into a Quaker family in Great Britain. He graduated from Cambridge with a degree preparing him for a career in science, but his interest in the graphic arts grew, and he decided to study painting in Italy. Shortly after that he began to lecture and publish on the graphic arts. His first book, on the Venetian Renaissance painter Giovanni Bellini, appeared in 1899, and in 1905 Fry produced an edition of Joshua Reynolds' Discourses.

In 1906 Fry encountered the work of Paul Cézanne, and this experience changed Fry's life. He began to study the works of the French Impressionists and Post-Impressionists. In 1910 he organized a show at the Grafton Galleries which he called "Monet and the Post-Impressionists." He produced a second exhibition of such paintings in 1912. These exhibitions changed aesthetic tastes and standards in England and moved Fry to the cutting edge of art criticism in England.

When Fry began to write art criticism, the dominant critics in Great Britain were those who advocated "art for art's sake." That is, they claimed that graphic artists need not represent anything in the real world and that art has no ethical function in the lives of those who view it. Fry turned away from this movement and helped to found the community of formalist art critics. Fry tended to favor paintings that did indeed represent aspects of the natural world. But as a formalist, he found the primary justification for a painting in its formal structure, in the spatial relations between the objects represented, in its interweaving of surface textures, in the coherence of its tones and colors. To see and understand all the relationships in a work's formal structure, Fry would say, is to have an aesthetic experience. And, he would add, an aesthetic experience has an ethical dimension in that to experience a wonderfully arranged group of forms is an uplifting experience for a human being.

The following essay comes from a point fairly early in Fry's publishing career. In this essay he tries to distinguish real life from the imaginative life and to account for the emotions he asserts people feel in response to various formal properties of works of art.

AN ESSAY IN ÆSTHETICS

A certain painter, not without some reputation at the present day, once wrote 1
a little book on the art he practises, in which he gave a definition of that art
so succinct that I take it as a point of departure for this essay.

"The art of painting," says that eminent authority, "is the art of imitat- 2
ing solid objects upon a flat surface by means of pigments." It is delightfully
simple, but prompts the question—Is that all? And, if so, what a deal of
unnecessary fuss has been made about it. Now, it is useless to deny that our
modern writer has some very respectable authorities behind him. Plato, indeed, gave a very similar account of the affair, and himself put the question—is it then worth while? And, being scrupulously and relentlessly logical, he decided that it was not worth while, and proceeded to turn the artists
out of his ideal republic. For all that, the world has continued obstinately to
consider that painting was worth while, and though, indeed, it has never
quite made up its mind as to what, exactly, the graphic arts did for it, it has
persisted in honouring and admiring its painters.

Can we arrive at any conclusions as to the nature of the graphic arts, 3
which will at all explain our feelings about them, which will at least put them
into some kind of relation with the other arts, and not leave us in the extreme
perplexity, engendered by any theory of mere imitation? For, I suppose, it
must be admitted that if imitation is the sole purpose of the graphic arts, it is
surprising that the works of such arts are ever looked upon as more than
curiosities, or ingenious toys, are ever taken seriously by grown-up people.
Moreover, it will be surprising that they have no recognisable affinity with
other arts, such as music or architecture, in which the imitation of actual
objects is a negligible quantity.

To form such conclusions is the aim I have put before myself in this 4
essay. Even if the results are not decisive, the inquiry may lead us to a view
of the graphic arts that will not be altogether unfruitful.

I must begin with some elementary psychology, with a consideration of 5
the nature of instincts. A great many objects in the world, when presented to
our senses, put in motion a complex nervous machinery, which ends in some
instinctive appropriate action. We see a wild bull in a field; quite without
our conscious interference a nervous process goes on, which, unless we interfere forcibly, ends in the appropriate reaction of flight. The nervous mechanism which results in flight causes a certain state of consciousness, which we
call the emotion of fear. The whole of animal life, and a great part of human
life, is made up of these instinctive reactions to sensible objects, and their
accompanying emotions. But man has the peculiar faculty of calling up again
in his mind the echo of past experiences of this kind, of going over it again,
"in imagination" as we say. He has, therefore, the possibility of a double life;

one the actual life, the other the imaginative life. Between these two lives there is this great distinction, that in the actual life the processes of natural selection have brought it about that the instinctive reaction, such, for instance, as flight from danger, shall be the important part of the whole process, and it is towards this that the man bends his whole conscious endeavour. But in the imaginative life no such action is necessary, and, therefore, the whole consciousness may be focussed upon the perceptive and the emotional aspects of the experience. In this way we get, in the imaginative life, a different set of values, and a different kind of perception.

We can get a curious side glimpse of the nature of this imaginative life 6 from the cinematograph. This resembles actual life in almost every respect, except that what the psychologists call the conative part of our reaction to sensations, that is to say, the appropriate resultant action is cut off. If, in a cinematograph, we see a runaway horse and cart, we do not have to think either of getting out of the way or heroically interposing ourselves. The result is that in the first place we *see* the event much more clearly; see a number of quite interesting but irrelevant things, which in real life could not struggle into our consciousness, bent, as it would be, entirely upon the problem of our appropriate reaction. I remember seeing in a cinematograph the arrival of a train at a foreign station and the people descending from the carriages; there was no platform, and to my intense surprise I saw several people turn right round after reaching the ground, as though to orientate themselves; an almost ridiculous performance, which I had never noticed in all the many hundred occasions on which such a scene had passed before my eyes in real life. The fact being that at a station one is never really a spectator of events, but an actor engaged in the drama of luggage or prospective seats, and one actually sees only so much as may help to the appropriate action.

In the second place, with regard to the visions of the cinematograph, 7 one notices that whatever emotions are aroused by them, though they are likely to be weaker than those of ordinary life, are presented more clearly to the consciousness. If the scene presented be one of an accident, our pity and horror, though weak, since we know that no one is really hurt, are felt quite purely, since they cannot, as they would in life, pass at once into actions of assistance.

A somewhat similar effect to that of the cinematograph can be obtained 8 by watching a mirror in which a street scene is reflected. If we look at the street itself we are almost sure to adjust ourselves in some way to its actual existence. We recognise an acquaintance, and wonder why he looks so dejected this morning, or become interested in a new fashion in hats—the moment we do that the spell is broken, we are reacting to life itself in however slight a degree, but, in the mirror, it is easier to abstract ourselves completely, and look upon the changing scene as a whole. It then, at once, takes on the visionary quality, and we become true spectators, not selecting what we will see, but seeing everything equally, and thereby we come to notice a number of appearances and relations of appearances, which would have escaped our vision before, owing to that perpetual economising by selection of what impressions we will assimilate, which in life we perform by unconscious processes. The frame of the mirror then, does, to some extent, turn the reflected scene from one that belongs to our actual life into one that belongs rather to the imaginative life. The frame of the mirror makes its surface into a very rudimentary work of art, since it helps us to attain to the artistic vision. For that is what, as you will already have guessed, I have been coming to all this time, namely that the work of art is intimately connected with the secondary imaginative life, which all men live to a greater or lesser extent.

That the graphic arts are the expression of the imaginative life rather 9 than a copy of actual life might be guessed from observing children. Children, if left to themselves, never, I believe, copy what they see, never, as we say, "draw from nature," but express, with a delightful freedom and sincerity, the mental images which make up their own imaginative lives.

Art, then, is an expression and a stimulus of this imaginative life, which 10 is separated from actual life by the absence of responsive action. Now this responsive action implies in actual life moral responsibility. In art we have no such moral responsibility—it presents a life freed from the binding necessities of our actual existence.

What then is the justification for this life of the imagination which all 11 human beings live more or less fully? To the pure moralist, who accepts nothing but ethical values, in order to be justified, it must be shown not only *not* to hinder but actually to forward right action, otherwise it is not only useless but, since it absorbs our energies, positively harmful. To such a one two views are possible, one the Puritanical view at its narrowest, which regards the life of the imagination as no better or worse than a life of sensual pleasure, and therefore entirely reprehensible. The other view is to argue that the imaginative life does subserve morality. And this is inevitably the view taken by moralists like Ruskin,* to whom the imaginative life is yet an absolute necessity. It is a view which leads to some very hard special pleading, even to a self-deception which is in itself morally undesirable.

But here comes in the question of religion, for religion is also an affair 12 of the imaginative life, and, though it claims to have a direct effect upon conduct, I do not suppose that the religious person if he were wise would justify religion entirely by its effect on morality, since that, historically speaking, has not been by any means uniformly advantageous. He would probably say that the religious experience was one which corresponded to certain spiritual capacities of human nature, the exercise of which is in itself good and desirable apart from their effect upon actual life. And so, too, I think the artist might if he chose take a mystical attitude, and declare that the fullness

---

*John Ruskin (1819–1900) was an English critic and social theorist whose views set the standard for English judgments on the graphic arts in the mid-nineteenth century.

and completeness of the imaginative life he leads may correspond to an existence more real and more important than any that we know of in mortal life.

And in saying that, his appeal would find a sympathetic echo in most 13 minds, for most people would, I think, say that the pleasures derived from art were of an altogether different character and more fundamental than merely sensual pleasures, that they did exercise some faculties which are felt to belong to whatever part of us there may be which is not entirely ephemeral and material.

It might even be that from this point of view we should rather justify 14 actual life by its relation to the imaginative, justify nature by its likeness to art. I mean this, that since the imaginative life comes in the course of time to represent more or less what mankind feels to be the completest expression of its own nature, the freest use of its innate capacities, the actual life may be explained and justified in its approximation here and there, however partially and inadequately, to that freer and fuller life.

Before leaving this question of the justification of art, let me put it in 15 another way. The imaginative life of a people has very different levels at different times, and these levels do not always correspond with the general level of the morality of actual life. Thus in the thirteenth century we read of barbarity and cruelty which would shock even us; we may I think admit that our moral level, our general humanity is decidedly higher to-day, but the level of our imaginative life is incomparably lower; we are satisfied there with a grossness, a sheer barbarity and squalor which would have shocked the thirteenth century profoundly. Let us admit the moral gain gladly, but do we not also feel a loss; do we not feel that the average business man would be in every way a more admirable, more respectable being if his imaginative life were not so squalid and incoherent? And, if we admit any loss then, there is some function in human nature other than a purely ethical one, which is worthy of exercise.

Now the imaginative life has its own history both in the race and in the 16 individual. In the individual life one of the first effects of freeing experience from the necessities of appropriate responsive action is to indulge recklessly the emotion of self-aggrandisement. The day-dreams of a child are filled with extravagant romances in which he is always the invincible hero. Music— which of all the arts supplies the strongest stimulus to the imaginative life, and at the same time has the least power of controlling its direction—music, at certain stages of people's lives, has the effect merely of arousing in an almost absurd degree this egoistic elation, and Tolstoy* appears to believe that this is its only possible effect. But with the teaching of experience and the growth of character the imaginative life comes to respond to other instincts and to satisfy other desires, until, indeed, it reflects the highest aspirations and the deepest aversions of which human nature is capable.

---

* Count Leo Tolstoy (1828–1910) was a Russian novelist and philosopher.

In dreams and when under the influence of drugs the imaginative life 17 passes out of our own control, and in such cases its experiences may be highly undesirable, but whenever it remains under our own control it must always be on the whole a desirable life. That is not to say that it is always pleasant, for it is pretty clear that mankind is so constituted as to desire much besides pleasure, and we shall meet among the great artists, the great exponents, that is, of the imaginative life, many to whom the merely pleasant is very rarely a part of what is desirable. But this desirability of the imaginative life does distinguish it very sharply from actual life, and is the direct result of that first fundamental difference, its freedom from necessary external conditions. Art, then, is, if I am right, the chief organ of the imaginative life, it is by art that it is stimulated and controlled within us, and, as we have seen, the imaginative life is distinguished by the greater clearness of its perception, and the greater purity and freedom of its emotion.

First with regard to the greater clearness of perception. The needs of 18 our actual life are so imperative, that the sense of vision becomes highly specialised in their service. With an admirable economy we learn to see only so much as is needed for our purposes; but this is in fact very little, just enough to recognise and identify each object or person; that done, they go into an entry in our mental catalogue and are no more really seen. In actual life the normal person really only reads the labels as it were on the objects around him and troubles no further. Almost all the things which are useful in any way put on more or less this cap of invisibility. It is only when an object exists in our lives for no other purpose than to be seen that we really look at it, as for instance at a China ornament or a precious stone, and towards such even the most normal person adopts to some extent the artistic attitude of pure vision abstracted from necessity.

Now this specialisation of vision goes so far that ordinary people have 19 almost no idea of what things really look like, so that oddly enough the one standard that popular criticism applies to painting, namely, whether it is like nature or not, is one which most people are, by the whole tenour of their lives, prevented from applying properly. The only things they have ever really *looked* at being other pictures; the moment an artist who has looked at nature brings to them a clear report of something definitely seen by him, they are wildly indignant at its untruth to nature. This has happened so constantly in our own time that there is no need to prove it. One instance will suffice. Monet* is an artist whose chief claim to recognition lies in the fact of his astonishing power of faithfully reproducing certain aspects of nature, but his really naive innocence and sincerity was taken by the public to be the most audacious humbug, and it required the teaching of men like Bastien-Lepage, who cleverly compromised between the truth and an accepted convention of

---

*Claude Monet (1840–1926) was a famous landscape painter; many critics consider him the founder of Impressionism.

what things looked like, to bring the world gradually round to admitting truths which a single walk in the country with purely unbiased vision would have established beyond doubt.

But though this clarified sense perception which we discover in the   20 imaginative life is of great interest, and although it plays a larger part in the graphic arts than in any other, it might perhaps be doubted whether, interesting, curious, fascinating as it is, this aspect of the imaginative life would ever by itself make art of profound importance to mankind. But it is different, I think, with the emotional aspect. We have admitted that the emotions of the imaginative are generally weaker than those of actual life. The picture of a saint being slowly flayed alive, revolting as it is, will not produce the actual physical sensations of sickening disgust that a modern man would feel if he could assist at the actual event; but they have a compensating clearness of presentment to the consciousness. The more poignant emotions of actual life have, I think, a kind of numbing effect analogous to the paralysing influence of fear in some animals; but even if this experience be not generally admitted, all will admit that the need for responsive action hurries us along and prevents us from ever realising fully what the emotion is that we feel, from co-ordinating it perfectly with other states. In short, the motives we actually experience are too close to us to enable us to feel them clearly. They are in a sense unintelligible. In the imaginative life, on the contrary, we can both feel the emotion and watch it. When we are really moved at the theatre we are always both on the stage and in the auditorium.

Yet another point about the emotions of the imaginative life—since they   21 require no responsive action we can give them a new valuation. In real life we must to some extent cultivate those emotions which lead to useful action, and we are bound to appraise emotions according to the resultant action. So that, for instance, the feelings of rivalry and emulation do get an encouragement which perhaps they scarcely deserve, whereas certain feelings which appear to have a high intrinsic value get almost no stimulus in actual life. For instance, those feelings to which the name of the cosmic emotion has been somewhat unhappily given find almost no place in life, but, since they seem to belong to certain very deep springs of our nature, do become of great importance in the arts.

Morality, then, appreciates emotion by the standard of resultant action.   22 Art appreciates emotion in and for itself.

This view of the essential importance in art of the expression of the   23 emotions is the basis of Tolstoy's marvelously original and yet perverse and even exasperating book, "What is Art," and I willingly confess, while disagreeing with almost all his results, how much I owe to him.

He gives an example of what he means by calling art the means of com-   24 municating emotions. He says, let us suppose a boy to have been pursued in the forest by a bear. If he returns to the village and merely states that he was pursued by a bear and escaped, that is ordinary language, the means of communicating facts or ideas; but if he describes his state first of heedlessness, then of sudden alarm and terror as the bear appears, and finally of relief when he gets away, and describes this so that his hearers share his emotions, then his description is a work of art.

Now in so far as the boy does this in order to urge the villagers to go out 25 and kill the bear, though he may be using artistic methods, his speech is not a pure work of art; but if of a winter evening the boy relates his experience for the sake of the enjoyment of his adventure in retrospect, or better still, if he makes up the whole story for the sake of the imagined emotions, then his speech becomes a pure work of art. But Tolstoy takes the other view, and values the emotions aroused by art entirely for their reaction upon actual life, a view which he courageously maintains even when it leads him to condemn the whole of Michelangelo, Raphael and Titian, and most of Beethoven, not to mention nearly everything he himself has written, as bad or false art.

Such a view would, I think, give pause to any less heroic spirit. He 26 would wonder whether mankind could have always been so radically wrong about a function that, whatever its value be, is almost universal. And in point of fact he will have to find some other word to denote what we now call art. Nor does Tolstoy's theory even carry him safely through his own book, since, in his examples of morally desirable and therefore good art, he has to admit that these are to be found, for the most part, among works of inferior quality. Here, then, is at once the tacit admission that another standard than morality is applicable. We must therefore give up the attempt to judge the work of art by its reaction on life, and consider it as an expression of emotions regarded as ends in themselves. And this brings us back to the idea we had already arrived at, of art as the expression of the imaginative life.

If, then, an object of any kind is created by man not for use, for its 27 fitness to actual life, but as an object of art, an object subserving the imaginative life, what will its qualities be? It must in the first place be adapted to that disinterested intensity of contemplation, which we have found to be the result of cutting off the responsive action. It must be suited to that heightened power of perception which we found to result therefrom.

And the first quality that we demand in our sensations will be order, 28 without which our sensations will be troubled and perplexed, and the other quality will be variety, without which they will not be fully stimulated.

It may be objected that many things in nature, such as flowers, possess 29 these two qualities of order and variety in a high degree, and these objects do undoubtedly stimulate and satisfy that clear disinterested contemplation which is characteristic of the æsthetic attitude. But in our reaction to a work of art there is something more—there is the consciousness of purpose, the consciousness of a peculiar relation of sympathy with the man who made this thing in order to arouse precisely the sensations we experience. And when we come to the higher works of art, where sensations are so arranged that they arouse in us deep emotions, this feeling of a special tie with the man who expressed them becomes very strong. We feel that he has expressed something which was latent in us all the time, but which we never realised, that he has revealed us to ourselves in revealing himself. And this recognition of purpose is, I believe, an essential part of the æsthetic judgment proper.

The perception of purposeful order and variety in an object gives us the 30 feeling which we express by saying that it is beautiful, but when by means of sensations our emotions are aroused we demand purposeful order and variety in them also, and if this can only be brought about by the sacrifice of sensual beauty we willingly overlook its absence.

Thus, there is no excuse for a china pot being ugly, there is every reason 31 why Rembrandt's* and Degas'† pictures should be, from the purely sensual point of view, supremely and magnificently ugly.

This, I think, will explain the apparent contradiction between two dis- 32 tinct uses of the word beauty, one for that which has sensuous charm, and one for the æsthetic approval of works of imaginative art where the objects presented to us are often of extreme ugliness. Beauty in the former sense belongs to works of art where only the perceptual aspect of the imaginative life is exercised, beauty in the second sense becomes as it were supersensual, and is concerned with the appropriateness and intensity of the emotions aroused. When these emotions are aroused in a way that satisfies fully the needs of the imaginative life we approve and delight in the sensations through which we enjoy that heightened experience, because they possess purposeful order and variety in relation to those emotions.

One chief aspect of order in a work of art is unity; unity of some kind is 33 necessary for our restful contemplation of the work of art as a whole, since if it lacks unity we cannot contemplate it in its entirety, but we shall pass outside it to other things necessary to complete its unity.

In a picture this unity is due to a balancing of the attractions to the eye 34 about the central line of the picture. The result of this balance of attractions is that the eye rests willingly within the bounds of the picture. Dr. Denman Ross of Harvard University has made a most valuable study of the elementary considerations upon which this balance is based in his "Theory of Pure Design." He sums up his results in the formula that a composition is of value in proportion to the number of orderly connections which it displays.

Dr. Ross wisely restricts himself to the study of abstract and meaning- 35 less forms. The moment representation is introduced forms have an entirely new set of values. Thus a line which indicated the sudden bend of a head in a certain direction would have far more than its mere value as line in the composition because of the attraction which a marked gesture has for the eye. In almost all paintings this disturbance of the purely decorative values by reason of the representative effect takes place, and the problem becomes too complex for geometrical proof.

---

*Rembrandt van Rijn (1606–1669) was a Dutch painter and etcher.
†Edgar Degas (1834–1917) was a French painter and sculptor.

This merely decorative unity is, moreover, of very different degrees of 36 intensity in different artists and in different periods. The necessity for a closely woven geometrical texture in the composition is much greater in heroic and monumental design than in genre pieces on a small scale.

It seems also probable that our appreciation of unity in pictorial design 37 is of two kinds. We are so accustomed to consider only the unity which results from the balance of a number of attractions presented to the eye simultaneously in a framed picture that we forget the possibility of other pictorial forms.

In certain Chinese paintings the length is so great that we cannot take 38 in the whole picture at once, nor are we intended to do so. Sometimes a landscape is painted upon a roll of silk so long that we can only look at it in successive segments. As we unroll it at one end and roll it up at the other we traverse wide stretches of country, tracing, perhaps, all the vicissitudes of a river from its source to the sea, and yet, when this is well done, we have received a very keen impression of pictorial unity.

Such a successive unity is of course familiar to us in literature and music, 39 and it plays its part in the graphic arts. It depends upon the forms being presented to us in such a sequence that each successive element is felt to have a fundamental and harmonious relation with that which preceded it. I suggest that in looking at drawings our sense of pictorial unity is largely of this nature; we feel, if the drawing be a good one, that each modulation of the line as our eye passes along it gives order and variety to our sensations. Such a drawing may be almost entirely lacking in the geometrical balance which we are accustomed to demand in paintings, and yet have, in a remarkable degree, unity.

Let us now see how the artist passes from the stage of merely gratifying 40 our demand for sensuous order and variety to that where he arouses our emotions. I will call the various methods by which this is effected, the emotional elements of design.

The first element is that of the rhythm of the line with which the forms 41 are delineated.

The drawn line is the record of a gesture, and that gesture is modified 42 by the artist's feeling which is thus communicated to us directly.

The second element is mass. When an object is so represented that we 43 recognise it as having inertia we feel its power of resisting movement, or communicating its own movement to other bodies, and our imaginative reaction to such an image is governed by our experience of mass in actual life.

The third element is space. The same sized square on two pieces of 44 paper can be made by very simple means to appear to represent either a cube two or three inches high, or a cube of hundreds of feet, and our reaction to it is proportionately changed.

The fourth element is that of light and shade. Our feelings towards the 45 same object become totally different according as we see it strongly illuminated against a black background or dark against light.

A fifth element is that of colour. That this has a direct emotional effect 46
is evident from such words as gay, dull, melancholy in relation to colour.

I would suggest the possibility of another element, though perhaps it is 47
only a compound of mass and space: it is that of the inclination to the eye of
a plane, whether it is impending over or leaning away from us.

Now it will be noticed that nearly all these emotional elements of design 48
are connected with essential conditions of our physical existence: rhythm appeals to all the sensations which accompany muscular activity; mass to all
the infinite adaptations to the force of gravity which we are forced to make;
the spatial judgment is equally profound and universal in its application to
life; our feeling about inclined planes is connected with our necessary judgments about the conformation of the earth itself; light, again, is so necessary
a condition of our existence that we become intensely sensitive to changes in
its intensity. Colour is the only one of our elements which is not of critical or
universal importance to life, and its emotional effect is neither so deep nor so
clearly determined as the others. It will be seen, then, that the graphic arts
arouse emotions in us by playing upon what one may call the overtones of
some of our primary physical needs. They have, indeed, this great advantage
over poetry, that they can appeal more directly and immediately to the emotional accompaniments of our bare physical existence.

If we represent these various elements in simple diagrammatic terms, 49
this effect upon the emotions is, it must be confessed, very weak. Rhythm of
line, for instance, is incomparably weaker in its stimulus of the muscular
sense than is rhythm addressed to the ear in music, and such diagrams can at
best arouse only faint ghost-like echoes of emotions of differing qualities; but
when these emotional elements are combined with the presentation of natural appearances, above all with the appearance of the human body, we find
that this effect is indefinitely heightened.

When, for instance, we look at Michelangelo's "Jeremiah," and realise 50
the irresistible momentum his movements would have, we experience powerful sentiments of reverence and awe. Or when we look at Michelangelo's
"Tondo" in the Uffizi, and find a group of figures so arranged that the planes
have a sequence comparable in breadth and dignity to the mouldings of the
earth mounting by clearly-felt gradations to an overtopping summit, innumerable instinctive reactions are brought into play.*

At this point the adversary (as Leonardi da Vinci calls him) is likely 51
enough to retort, "You have abstracted from natural forms a number of so-
called emotional elements which you yourself admit are very weak when
stated with diagrammatic purity; you then put them back, with the help of

---

* Rodin is reported to have said, "A woman, a mountain, a horse—they are all the same thing;
   they are made on the same principles." That is to say, their forms, when viewed with the
   disinterested vision of the imaginative life, have similar emotional elements [Fry's note].

Michelangelo, into the natural forms whence they were derived, and at once they have value, so that after all it appears that the natural forms contain these emotional elements ready made up for us, and all that art need do is to imitate Nature."

But, alas! Nature is heartlessly indifferent to the needs of the imagina- 52 tive life; God causes His rain to fall upon the just and upon the unjust. The sun neglects to provide the appropriate limelight effect even upon a trium-phant Napoleon or a dying Cæsar.* Assuredly we have no guarantee that in nature the emotional elements will be combined appropriately with the de-mands of the imaginative life, and it is, I think, the great occupation of the graphic arts to give us first of all order and variety in the sensuous plane, and then so to arrange the sensuous presentment of objects that the emotional elements are elicited with an order and appropriateness altogether beyond what Nature herself provides.

Let me sum up for a moment what I have said about the relation of art 53 to Nature, which is, perhaps, the greatest stumbling-block to the understand-ing of the graphic arts.

I have admitted that there is beauty in Nature, that is to say, that cer- 54 tain objects constantly do, and perhaps any object may, compel us to regard it with that intense disinterested contemplation that belongs to the imagina-tive life, and which is impossible to the actual life of necessity and action; but that in objects created to arouse the æsthetic feeling we have an added con-sciousness of purpose on the part of the creator, that he made it on purpose not to be used but to be regarded and enjoyed; and that this feeling is char-acteristic of the æsthetic judgment proper.

When the artist passes from pure sensations to emotions aroused by 55 means of sensations, he uses natural forms which, in themselves, are calcu-lated to move our emotions, and he presents these in such a manner that the forms themselves generate in us emotional states, based upon the fundamen-tal necessities of our physical and physiological nature. The artist's attitude to natural form is, therefore, infinitely various according to the emotions he wishes to arouse. He may require for his purpose the most complete represen-tation of a figure, he may be intensely realistic, provided that his present-ment, in spite of its closeness to natural appearance, disengages clearly for us the appropriate emotional elements. Or he may give us the merest suggestion of natural forms, and rely almost entirely upon the force and intensity of the emotional elements involved in his presentment.

We may, then, dispense once for all with the idea of likeness to Nature, 56 of correctness or incorrectness as a test, and consider only whether the emo-

---

*I do not forget that at the death of Tennyson the writer in the *Daily Telegraph* averred that "level beams of the setting moon streamed in upon the face of the dying bard"; but then, after all, in its way the *Daily Telegraph* is a work of art [Fry's note].

tional elements inherent in natural form are adequately discovered, unless, indeed, the emotional idea depends at any point upon likeness, or completeness of representation.

QUESTIONS ABOUT FRY'S DISCOURSE COMMUNITY AND HIS CONCERNS IN THIS ESSAY

1. What is Fry's view on human beings' instinctive reactions to sensible objects? Do you agree with him?
2. How does Fry distinguish actual life from the imaginative life?
3. What does Fry say is the justification for art? Do you agree with him?
4. How does Fry say that the graphic arts arouse emotions in us?
5. What does Fry say are the advantages of the emotions in our imaginative lives over against those in our real lives?
6. How does Fry use the word *beauty* in connection with a work of imaginative art?
7. Where would you say formalist assumptions or concerns show themselves most clearly in this essay?

QUESTIONS ABOUT FRY'S RHETORICAL STRATEGIES

1. Early in this essay, Fry reveals what his aim is. How do you react to this strategy? Does he give away too much information too early?
2. Does Fry seem like an expert in his field? Give reasons for your response.
3. Fry often uses the pronouns *we* and *us*. What effect does he seem to be striving for with these pronouns? Do you think his strategy is effective?
4. When Fry needs evidence for a general point, what kinds does he use? Is his evidence effective?
5. How often does Fry consider possible opposing points of view? Is he wise to bring these up? Would he be smarter simply to ignore objections and points of view other than his own?
6. At the end of this essay, Fry sums up what he has written. Does this strike you as effective? Or does he insult you by telling you what you know already?

WRITING FROM WITHIN AND ABOUT THE ARTS: ART CRITICISM

Writing for Yourself

1. In your journal, write about a time when you saw something and were amazed by it.
2. In your journal, write about a time when you both felt an emotion and were able to watch yourself experiencing it.

Writing for Nonacademic Audiences

1. A controversy has erupted on your campus over a proposed art gallery. Some students claim that no part of their tuition money should be used to finance an art gallery. Others say that it would be fine if their tuition were raised (by 12

percent), with some of the increase going to fund an art gallery. Write a letter to the editor of your school newspaper in which you state and support your position.

2. One of your better friends has gone to a liberal arts college, where, this friend says, the level of the imaginative life is very high. Write this friend a letter in which you comment on the level of the imaginative life on your campus.

3. While you are home from school on a break, you learn that the town council has refused to let an artist show certain paintings at the local art museum. The paintings, you learn, depict some nudes. Write the town council a letter in which you give your reaction to their decision.

Writing for Academic Audiences

1. For a class in recent Western culture, write a 500-word report on the "art-for-art's sake" movement in Great Britain.

2. For a class in art history, write a 500-word analogy paper in which you reveal what the emotions stimulated by a work of art are like.

3. For a class in social psychology, write a 1,000-word paper in which you argue your position on the effectiveness of censoring works of art.

4. For a class in æsthetics, write a 1,500-word paper in which you defend your position on how people should judge the moral nature of a work of art.

Paul Rosenfeld

(1890–1946)

When Paul Rosenfeld published Musical Portraits (1920), his first book, two things happened. First, he was noticed. Though he had published essays in well-known journals, they had been published during World War I, when Americans were preoccupied with European events and America's role in them. Second, he was attacked. His criticism was labeled as excessive, as based upon poor scholarship, and as displaying a lack of musical knowledge. His answer to these charges was to argue for a kind of music criticism different from that of most of his discourse community of music critics, who focused on form and technique. Instead, he focused on content, and tried to match his style of writing to the rhapsodic feelings he encountered as he listened to music.

When he was accused of being subjective, Rosenfeld argued that music was meant to be expressive, to speak to the soul. The critic balances the subjective with the objective, understanding how music speaks out of a historical context to an individual listener. To explain this, Rosenfeld resorted to lyrical prose, metaphoric language, and evocative images to suggest how a musician's piece worked, how it affected a listener. In promoting this vision of musical criticism, Rosenfeld earned the enmity of those in his discourse community who focused on technical matters such as changes in key.

Rosenfeld's interest in music was keenly awakened during a trip to Europe after graduating from Yale and attending the Columbia School of Journalism. Here he saw the many expatriate Americans who journeyed to Europe to find meaning; Rosenfeld rejected this approach and returned to America determined to help develop truly American forms of art. In New York, in 1916, he joined a community of like-minded cultural reformers, the most famous of whom was Van Wyck Brooks. The principle that he worked out in the context of this community was that the artist must give himself or herself totally to art in order for the art to be true; this involved a kind of spiritual growth which, Rosenfeld felt, was just beginning among American artists.

Many of his essays, including the following one, focus on the growth of American music. His voice was heard loudest in his many essays published in his role as musical critic in such journals as The New Republic, Seven Arts, The Dial, and The Nation. This essay on Charles Ives is from Rosenfeld's final collection of essays, Discoveries of a Critic.

CHARLES IVES

The earliest of his compositions Charles E. Ives has chosen to preserve for us 1
are a couple of quicksteps, one of them an arrangement for "kazoo" orchestra
of "The Son of a Gambolier." Dating from his undergraduate days at Yale,
juvenile, and pretty thoroughly in the conventions of the brass band and
college glee club music of the period, they nonetheless stand prophetic of the
composer's highly individual, mature, important works.

They are the expressions of the experiences of a callow American youth 2
of the period through forms scarcely distinguishable from the simple, limited
ones habitual in the composer's native Danbury and New England of the
seventies and the eighties, with its little church choirs, town bands, dance
and theater orchestras. And the later works by Ives, the glorious *Concord
Sonata*, the *Three Places in New England*, the *Suite for Theatre Orchestra*,
and the happy rest, are expressions of an almost national experience, the
relations between the essences affinitive to the American people past and
present through forms in some instances partially, and in others almost
wholly, evolved from those of the American tradition.

Nearly all Ives's characteristic work abounds in minor forms derived 3
directly from this store. In the second number of the orchestral suite *Three
Places in New England*, we hear "The British Grenadiers"—actually one of
the marching songs of the American revolutionary army, which sang it in
superb indifference to its text. In the first movement of the Fourth Symphony, "Old Hundred" sounds; and favorite Virginia reels and other old fid-
dler tunes in the second number of the theater suite, "In the Inn," and in
"Barn Dance"; and "Are You Wash'd in the Blood of the Lamb" in the little
cantata *General Booth Enters Heaven*, to Vachel Lindsay's words; and "Good
Night, Ladies" in *Washington's Birthday;* and various patriotic tunes in the
song "In Flanders Fields," etc. Their function is always a thematic one, sometimes a symbolical and an ironical one, too. But in many of these compositions—curiously abrupt in their contrasts, full of lines finely drawn, and despite their frequent brevity large in their scales of values and deeply expressive
of essences and ideas clearly, boldly felt—the grand forms themselves are
plainly developments and enrichments of the rudimentary musical forms favored by American society. *Putnam's Camp* is first a waltz, then a fox trot,
and last—horridly polytonically and polyrhythmically enough—a military
march. "In the Inn" and "Barn Dance" partake of both the jig and the reel—
indeed may be said to be jigs and reels; in these instances wonderfully shrill,
jagged, and rich of substance. The song "Charlie Rutlage" is an expanded
frontier ballad; the adagio of the Fourth Symphony a hymn tune developed

in fugal form. The Hawthorne movement of the *Concord Sonata* has nicely been called "proto-jazz" by John Kirkpatrick.*

It is even possible that Ives's complex harmonies and rhythms are the development of germs latent in those rudimentary forms. We refer to the clashing harmonies and polyrhythm of his entirely characteristic pieces. . . . Ives in fact is not only one of the most advanced but one of the earliest poly-tonalists and polyrhythmicalists. Aesthetic radicalism was in the air of his home. His father, his first teacher, experimented continuously with acoustics in the conviction that only a fraction of the means of musical expression was being used by musical art; and even invented a quarter-tone instrument; and during his own undergraduate days Ives, it seems, was already experimenting with new chord structures. Ten years in advance of the publication of the score of *Salomé*, he began a composition for the organ with a chord in D minor superimposed on one in C major. These experiments, not only with chord structures but with exotic scales and harmonic rhythms, too, met with the disfavor of his professor in music, Horatio Parker; still, Ives persisted in them, and is said to have tried out his innovations with the help of the orchestra of the old Hyperion Theatre in New Haven. And in 1903, the year of the inception of the sketches for certain of his very personal orchestral pieces, he was already writing completely atonally, thus anticipating similar European innovations; for the atonal passages in Mahler's symphonies are of later date, and the famous *Three Pieces for Pianoforte*, Opus 11, by Schoenberg, the first European pieces completely beyond the tonal system, were published only in 1911. And he has persisted upon his course. The close of *Putnam's Camp*, for example, combines contrapuntally two march tempi in different keys: the one 25 per cent, too, faster than the other. The third and wonderfully fresh section of *Three Places in New England* entitled "The Housatonic at Stockbridge"—a sonorous cataract, easily the jewel of the suite and one of the thrilling American orchestral compositions—includes a rhythm for a solo violin quite independent of that of the rest of the orchestra, and atonal and polytonal figures that clash with the tonic harmonies of the brass and the woodwind. The third of the three pieces comprised in the *Suite for Theatre Orchestra*, the magical, sensuous "In the Night," exhibits another instance of Ives's extreme polyrhythmicality in its combination of a definite rhythm played by horn, bells, and celesta with an extremely indefinite, almost unnumbered one carried by strings and other instruments, and seems to call for the installation in the conductor's stand of a mechanical robot able simultaneously to beat the two extremely distinct and varied measures. Well, these revolutionary forms of Ives's were actually adumbrated by the practice if not by the theory of traditional music. The American composer very early began observing that the melodic, harmonic, and rhythmic distortions of traditional

---

*John Kirkpatrick was a twentieth-century pianist who, in the course of promoting American music, gave the *Concord Sonata* its premier performance, in New York, 1939.

music—frequently of English origin—produced under the stress of excitement by church organists, village bands, country fiddlers, frequently initiated forms truer to their feelings and to the essences and ideas they apprehend than the more regular performances. The untuned organ, the choir soulfully soaring "off key," an organist excitedly striking "false" notes in his musical *élan*, the members of a rural orchestra embroidering individually on the rhythms and wildly playing simultaneously in different tonalities, the clashing bands at Fourth of July celebrations, were actually initiating living forms certainly possessive of a freedom the cut and dried originals did not have, and of a truth of their own. And they actually were, in spite of the fact that the descriptive terms had not as yet been coined, polytonic and polyrhythmical. And in many of Ives's complexly tonic and rhythmical pieces, notably *Putnam's Camp*, "In the Inn," and "Barn Dance," we seem to find not only realizations of these types of forms quite unconsciously suggested by the excited musicians, but of certain of those they shrilly initiated.

This peculiar form of Ives's, and its idiosyncrasies, would appear to be   5
the direct consequence of the nationalistic bent of his mind. We have defined the nationalist as the emergent individual who, in becoming conscious of his own essence, simultaneously becomes conscious of the essences of his nation and its soil, and, put in touch with national ideas by his experience, invests them with worth and realizes them with love. In most instances the musical nationalist apprehends these forces in part through the traditional musical forms of his nation, often the folk music; and often spontaneously expresses his idea with a form inclusive in warp and woof of these traditional bits for the reason that he has long since absorbed them, and that the idea to which they are related calls them forth again. Now Ives is nothing if not a nationalistic American composer. The forces conveyed by his music are deeply, typically American. They are the essences of a practical people, abrupt and nervous and ecstatic in their movements and manifestations—brought into play with a certain reluctance and difficulty, but when finally loosed, jaggedly, abruptly, almost painfully released, with something of an hysteric urgency; manifested sometimes in a bucolic irony and burlesque and sometimes in a religious and mystical elevation, but almost invariably in patterns that have a paroxysmal suddenness and abruptness and violence. We recognize their kin in American humor, in political and revival meetings, whenever and wherever a wholeness has existed in Americans. We have seen their likes through much American literature; one frequently thinks of Twain and Anderson in connection with Ives, as well as of the New England writers whose ideas his music has interpreted. They are curiously like the forces of the abrupt, fierce American Nature herself, who is vernal overnight and summery two weeks after winter has passed away; like the moods of her spring freshets and the floods that pour from the porous soil; and the moods of the vaguely, confusedly, voluptuously sonorous, suddenly swelling night over the towns. Ives has indeed felt the spiritual and moral forces of America past and present

not only through American folk music, but through literary and other artistic expressions, too. Perhaps the richest, most inclusive, most beautifully formed and drawn of all his pieces, the sonata, *Concord, Mass.: 1840–60,* apparently flows from an experience including a discovery of the spirit of transcendentalism as it was contained in the prophetic Emerson, the fantastic Hawthorne, the sturdily sentimental Alcotts, the deeply earth-conscious and lovingly submissive Thoreau. Another piece, the scherzo of the Fourth Symphony, flows from an experience inclusive of another sense of Hawthorne, derived in particular from *The Celestial Railroad;* while the cantata *Lincoln,* on Edwin Markham's words, indicates a creative comprehension quite as much of the figure of the great commoner as of the spirit of the Swan of Staten Island; and the many songs on the words of American poets from Whitman down to Louis Untermeyer and Fenimore Cooper, Jr., and prose men including President Hadley and even obscure newspapermen, the connection of experiences with their verse and prose. And further works demonstrate a stimulation through still other media than musical or literary ones. There is the first of the *Three Places in New England;* called "The Shaw Monument in Boston Common," it conveys a feeling partially crystallized by the Saint-Gaudens. And there is the third of them, "The Housatonic at Stockbridge"; and it refers to a crystallizing object neither artistic nor human: the sweep of the vernal river.

Thus, musically gifted, Ives has been put in the way of the sonorous   6 expression of American life, paralleling—possibly because of the circumstance that he was used, from boyhood up, to expressing himself in terms of the traditional forms—the Russian music of Moussorgsky, the Magyar of Bartók, the Spanish of De Falla.* His characteristically American, jaggedly ecstatic, variously electric and rapturous, almost invariably spasmodic sonorous forms are criticisms, like theirs, of the folk music and the folk itself. Humorous to the paroxysmal point in the cast of "Barn Dance," "In the Inn," and the scherzo of the Fourth Symphony; traversed by an acute sensuousness and voluptuousness in the case of "In the Night"; cataclysmically passionate as in "The Housatonic at Stockbridge"; or rapturous with the quality of slowly groping, reaching intellectual processes ("The Shaw Monument") or with those of religious, prophetic, mystically intuitive moments and their ingredients of insight, faith in the human impulse to perfection, knowledge of the breath of earth ("General Booth Enters Heaven," "Emerson," "The Alcotts," "Thoreau")—his whole so very American expression puts us in touch and harmony, like prose by Twain and Anderson, Cummings or Thoreau and all who have conveyed American essences with fullness and love and beauty, with forces constant in our fellows, selves, soil, and thus with the whole

---

*Modest Petrovich Moussorgsky was a nineteenth-century Russian composer, Bela Bartók a Hungarian composer and collector of folk music, and Manuel de Falla a twentieth-century Spanish composer.

American idea. We feel its parts and their connections, and the breath of the whole.

And the fates have been very generous. They have not even preconfined 7 Ives to a single medium of expression. He has been able to represent his feelings of American life in a prose that, manly as it is racily American, conveys them if not as broadly, nonetheless as truly as the musical medium does. *Essays before a Sonata*, reading-matter intended primarily as a preface or apology for his second piano sonata, the *Concord*, but isolated in a small companion volume for the reason that inclusion with the notes would have made the musical volume as cumbersome as baroque, contributes, together with the composer's very interesting assertion of and generalization about sound's much-questioned ability to convey material, moral, intellectual, or spiritual values, four most poetically penetrating criticisms for the "subjects" of the four movements of the work. Another juicy essay of Ives's is suffixed to the volume in which he has collected a hundred and fourteen of his two hundred-odd songs. Like *Essays before a Sonata*, it also is a sort of smaller twin to the work it is intended to illuminate. This particular one, privately printed too, and now, also, the lucky windfall of secondhand music shops, is one of *the* American books: not only for the reason that it contains most of Ives's first-rate lyrics, among them "Evening" (Milton), "The New River," "Charlie Rutlage," "Like a Sick Eagle" (Keats), "Walt Whitman," and others, but equally for the reason that its very form expresses a distinctly American mode of feeling. That form is extremely miscellaneous. It juxtaposes within a narrow compass—indeed, the volume is a sort of record of Ives's entire development—one hundred and fourteen songs very heterogeneous in point of size, since some are but a few measures long and others cover pages; very heterogeneous in point of idiom and style, for some are based on borrowed and others on original material, and some are diatonic and others impressionistic and others atonal; very heterogeneous too in point of spirit, since certain are homely, certain racy, certain humorous, and others delicate, or intimate, or spiritual; and in point of value, too, since certain are crudely or lightly drawn, and others finely, poignantly, and powerfully. But out of that miscellaneousness, extreme for all the visibility of the personal thread in the intensely disparate fabrics, an idea greets us: the idea that all things possessing breath of their own, no matter how dissimilarly and to what differing degrees, are ultimately consonant. That is good Americanism, and the postscript but re-expresses that feeling and that idea in the maxim, "Everything from a mule to an oak, which nature has given life, has a right to that life; whether they [its values] be approved by a human mind or seen with a human eye, is no concern of that right." And when the prose runs: "I have not written a book for money, for fame, for love, for kindlings. I have merely cleaned house. All that is left is on the clotheslines," we merely recognize anew the American speaking with the spirit of the Artist.

That is Ives: the American as an artist, as a composer, and the foremost 8 of the Americans who have expressed their feeling of life in musical forms; for even Parker's substance is not as mature as some of Ives's, itself unexcelled as yet in point of maturity of substance and richness of feeling by that of any of the younger men. The *Concord Sonata* indeed remains the solidest piece of piano music composed by an American. Its beauty and its significance still surprise us; they still are one of the wonders of the last years, which have revealed them. For Ives had been forced to create in a complete solitude, without external support or recognition. Though individuals able to appreciate the works of literary and pictorial artists as fresh and as significant as his musical ones were not lacking during the first quarter of this century, the musically highly cultured individual was still extremely rare in the American ranks. Lucky for the composer that he was the manager of an insurance company! What porridge he would have had had he been a professional musician can be discerned from the fact that only yesterday one of the white-headed boys of American music, a voice of the official musicality and its conventional criteria, publicly affirmed that those composers who wrote atonically or polytonically did so merely because they were too untalented to compose in the old tonal schemes. But with the multiple appearance of the musically highly cultured individual—composer, performer, or amateur—in the United States a phenomenon one of the most happy of all of those of the last decades, the raising of the curtain on Ives's long-obscured works became almost inevitable. Some intelligence seems to lead the individual almost somnambulistically toward the food he requires for his existence and to bring it toward him, and what comes into the world as an idea does not go lost. In any case, up the curtain went on this good "business man's" music. Henry Bellamann* wrote about it and called it to the attention of the Pro-Musica. The Pro-Musica and later Nicholas Slonimsky, the Pan-Americans, and Copland had some of his pieces performed at their concerts. Henry Cowell began publishing and recording others. The discovery is still an esoteric one. No conductor of a major orchestra has still either seen fit or been able to perform Ives's orchestral pieces. The Second Sonata has never yet been heard in its entirety. And only a few of the songs have as yet figured in song recitals. Still, the curtain *is* up. The music is beginning to be accessible not only in printed but in record form, to the benefit of a world larger than the narrowly musical one.

For artists such as Ives can help enormously to create a democratic so- 9 ciety in America. In investing American essences with worth and presenting them with beauty, they help to convey the national idea as it actually relates these warring and still cognate forces: thus providing a matchlessly practical basis for mutual adjustment.

QUESTIONS ABOUT ROSENFELD'S DISCOURSE COMMUNITY AND HIS CONCERNS IN THIS ESSAY

1. In what ways might music be nationalistic?

---

*Henry Bellamann is a twentieth-century American author and pianist who in 1933 wrote the first critical study of Charles Ives.

2. According to Rosenfeld, what is the function of the well-known American songs that Ives incorporates into his work? Does Rosenfeld's analysis suggest that part of music criticism is a kind of source criticism? How would such an examination of sources be helpful in understanding music?

3. Often Rosenfeld identifies the nature of a piece of music by identifying its genre or similar genres. What does this suggest about the discourse community of music criticism?

4. What differences does Rosenfeld discern between classical music and folk music? What causes those differences? What other differences might you discern?

5. Rosenfeld suggests that much of Ives's work has been shaped by New England. What kinds of evidence does he give for this proposal?

6. Rosenfeld writes that Ives's "very American expression puts us in touch and in harmony . . . with forces constant in our fellows, selves, soil, and thus with the whole American idea" (paragraph 6). What does Rosenfeld mean by this? Is this something that is possible for music to do?

7. What does Rosenfeld mean when he refers to a piece of piano music as "solid" (paragraph 8)?

8. How is it possible for music "to create a democratic society in America" (paragraph 9)?

QUESTIONS ABOUT ROSENFELD'S RHETORICAL STRATEGIES

1. In this essay, Rosenfeld does not take the time to define some of his terms, such as "polytonically" and "polyrhythmically" (paragraph 3). Can you define these terms from the context? If not, why does Rosenfeld not define such terms?

2. At times Rosenfeld startles his readers by bringing together two words that are rarely seen yoked, such as "wonderfully shrill" (paragraph 3) and "voluptuously sonorous" (paragraph 5). Where else does he use this technique? How does it affect the reader?

3. Read through paragraph 4. What does the language of this paragraph suggest about the nature of Rosenfeld's discourse community?

4. In the middle of a paragraph 4, after discussing several of Ives's pieces, Rosenfeld seems to pause, and he indicates this by beginning his sentence, "Well. . . ." Why has Rosenfeld been so desirous of pointing out this pause?

5. In general, what kinds of language does Rosenfeld use when he comes to describe specific pieces by Ives?

6. Consider the following sentence: "They [forces conveyed by Ives's music] are the essences of a practical people, abrupt and nervous and ecstatic in their movements and manifestations—brought into play with a certain reluctance and difficulty, but when finally loosed, jaggedly, abruptly, almost painfully released, with something of a hysteric urgency; manifested sometimes in a bucolic irony and burlesque and sometimes in a religious and mystical elevation, but almost invariably in patterns that have a paroxysmal suddenness and abruptness and violence" (paragraph 5). Where might you divide this into two or even three sentences? Why does Rosenfeld choose not to divide it?

7. In general, are Rosenfeld's paragraphs unified? Why do you think he has chosen to make them so lengthy?

8. Rosenfeld compares Ives's music to the forces of American nature. Is this a logical comparison? If not, why has Rosenfeld chosen to use it?

WRITING FROM WITHIN AND ABOUT THE ARTS: MUSIC CRITICISM

Writing for Yourself

1. In your journal, explore why people's taste in music seems to change as they get older.
2. Explore in your journal your reactions to music that is purposely nationalistic.

Writing for Nonacademic Audiences

1. Choose a song that has had meaning for you for many years. Perhaps the song is memorable because of its religious associations (a hymn, for example), or because of its ethnicity, or because of the context in which you heard it. Research the background of that song and write a 750-word essay to be used as a feature article on music in your university newspaper.
2. Attend a local concert. Write a 750-word review to be printed in your local town newspaper, concentrating on such things as the unity of the pieces, the performance, and how the music affected you.

Writing for Academic Audiences

1. Listen to Ives's piece "Concord, Mass.: 1840–1860." You plan to use this piece as part of a presentation for a course in American literature of the nineteenth century. Your goal is to show how artists other than writers responded to the transcendentalism of Emerson and Thoreau. Write up your notes for the fifteen-minute presentation.
2. For a set of "Concert Notes" to be handed out at a concert featuring new and experimental works, you are to write a short, introductory essay on why it is important for innovation to be occurring continually in all the arts. You are limited to 250 words.
3. For a class in music history, write a 1,250-word essay describing how Ives was influenced by New England.
4. For a class in music criticism, choose one form of music—a fugue, a sonata, a cantata, a symphony, a song—and write a 1,500-word essay that shows how that form either freed or confined a composer of your choice.

Mao Zedong
(1893–1976)

Mao Zedong, who became one of the most powerful political leaders of the twentieth century, was born into a peasant family in China. After graduating from Teacher's College at Changsha in 1918, he held several different jobs. He taught school, worked as a political organizer, and served as a library assistant. In 1921 he helped to found the Communist party in China. What followed was a period of strife and turmoil, during which Mao rose to the top of the Communist party. He helped in struggles against provincial rulers in China, Japanese invaders of mainland China, and the Kuomintang, the nationalist party of China led by Chiang Kai-shek. By 1949 Mao and the Communist party had claimed control over mainland China.

The following selection includes parts II, III, and IV of the concluding talk that Mao gave at Yenan, his headquarters, in 1942, in the face of conflict with the invading Japanese. In it you will find evidence that Mao is working within a Marxist discourse community in the emphases that literary texts are determined by historical conditions and that history changes because of social and economic forces. You will also notice Mao working within a discourse community that he thought needed to be unified and brought more into line with Marxist ideology.

"TALKS AT THE YENAN FORUM ON ART AND LITERATURE"

II

The question of "whom to serve" having been solved, the question of "how 1 to serve" comes up. To put it in the words of our comrades: Should we devote ourselves to elevation or to popularisation?

In the past some comrades rather or even very much despised and ne- 2 glected popularisation and unduly stressed elevation. Elevation should be stressed, but it is wrong to stress it lopsidedly and solely and excessively. The afore-mentioned lack of clarity and thoroughness in the solution of the problem of "for whom," also manifests itself in this connection. As they are not clear about the question, naturally they fail to find any proper criterion for what they mean by "elevation" and "popularisation," let alone the proper relation between the two. Since our art and literature are basically intended for the workers, peasants and soldiers, popularisation means extending art and literature among these people while elevation means raising their level of artistic and literary appreciation. What should we popularise among them? The stuff that is needed and can be readily accepted by the feudal landlord class? Or that which is needed and can be readily accepted by the bourgeoisie?* Or that which is needed and can be readily accepted by the petty-bourgeois intelligentsia?† No, none of these will do. We must popularise what is needed and can be readily accepted by the workers, peasants and soldiers themselves. Consequently the duty of learning from the workers, peasants and soldiers precedes the task of educating them. This is even more true of elevation. There must be a basis to elevate from. When we lift up a bucket of water, for instance, aren't we lifting up something that lies on the ground and does not float in mid-air? What then is the basis from which the standard of our art and literature is to be raised? From the feudal basis? The bourgeois basis? The basis of the petty-bourgeois intelligentsia? No. It can only be raised from the basis of the masses of the workers, peasants and soldiers. This means not that we raise the workers, peasants and soldiers to the level of the feudal class, the bourgeoisie or the petty-bourgeois intelligentsia, but that we raise them up along their own line of advance, along the line of advance of the proletariat.‡ Here again the task of learning from the workers, peasants and soldiers comes in. Only by starting from the workers, peasants and soldiers can we have a correct understanding of elevation and popularisation and find the proper relation between the two.

What after all is the source of any kind of art and literature? An artistic 3 or literary work is ideologically the product of the human brain reflecting the life of a given society. Revolutionary art and literature are the products of the brains of revolutionary artists and writers reflecting the life of the people. In the life of the people itself lies a mine of raw material for art and literature, namely, things in their natural state, things crude, but also most lively, rich and fundamental; in this sense, they throw all art and literature into the shade and provide for them a unique and inexhaustible source. This is the only source, for there can be no other source. Some may ask: Is there not another source in the books, in the artistic and literary works of ancient times and foreign countries? As a matter of fact, artistic and literary works of the past are not the source but the flow; they are the products which the ancients and the foreigners created out of the artistic and literary raw material they

* Often used to refer to the middle class and to those influenced by interest in private property.
† The intelligentsia associated with the petty bourgeoisie, or those among the bourgeoisie with the least wealth and social class.
‡ The lowest social or economic class of a community, the workers.

lit upon in the people's life of their own times and places. We must take over all the fine artistic and literary legacy, critically assimilate from it whatever is beneficial to us and hold it up as an example when we try to work over the artistic and literary raw material derived from the people's life of our own time and place. It makes an enormous difference whether or not one has such examples to look up to, a difference which explains why some works are refined and others crude, some polished and others coarse, some superior and others inferior, some smoothly done and others laboriously executed. Therefore we must not refuse to take over the legacy from the ancients and the foreigners and learn from such examples, whether feudal or bourgeois. But succession to a legacy and learning from examples should never take the place of the creation of our own work, for nothing can take its place. In art and literature, the uncritical appropriation and imitation of the ancients and foreigners represent the most sterile and harmful artistic and literary doctrinairism. All revolutionary artists and writers of China, all artists and writers of high promise, must, for long periods of time, unreservedly and whole-heartedly go into the midst of the masses, the masses of workers, peasants and soldiers; they must go into fiery struggles, go to the only, the broadest, the richest source to observe, learn, study and analyse all men, all classes, all kinds of people, all the vivid patterns of life and struggle and all raw material of art and literature, before they can proceed to creation. Otherwise, for all your labour, you will have nothing to work on and will become the kind of "empty-headed artists or writers" against whom Lu Hsun, in his testament, so earnestly cautioned his son.*

Though man's social life constitutes the only source for art and literature, and is incomparably more vivid and richer than art and literature as such, the people are not satisfied with the former alone and demand the latter. Why? Because, although both are beautiful, life as reflected in artistic and literary works can and ought to be on a higher level and of a greater power and better focused, more typical, nearer the ideal, and therefore more universal than actual everyday life. Revolutionary art and literature should create all kinds of characters on the basis of actual life and help the masses to push history forward. For example, on the one hand there are people suffering from hunger, cold and oppression and on the other hand there are men exploiting and oppressing men—a contrast that exists everywhere and seems quite commonplace to people; artists and writers, however, can create art and literature out of such daily occurrences by organising them, bringing them to a focal point and making the contradictions and struggles in them typical—create art and literature that can awaken and arouse the masses and impel them to unite and struggle to change their environment. If there were no such art and literature, this task could not be fulfilled or at least not effectively and speedily fulfilled.

4

---

*See "Death," *Complete Works of Lu Hsun*, Chinese edition, Vol. VI [Mao's note].

What are popularisation and elevation in art and literature? What is 5 the relation between the two? Works of popularisation are simpler and plainer and therefore more readily accepted by the broad masses of the people of today. Works of a higher level are more polished and therefore more difficult to produce and less likely to win the ready acceptance of the broad masses of people of today. The problem facing the workers, peasants and soldiers today is this: engaged in a ruthless and sanguinary struggle against the enemy, they remain illiterate and uncultured as a result of the prolonged rule of the feudal and bourgeois classes and consequently they badly need a widespread campaign of enlightenment, and they eagerly wish to have culture, knowledge, art and literature which meet their immediate need and are readily acceptable to them so as to heighten their passion for struggle and their confidence in victory, to strengthen their solidarity, and thus to enable them to fight the enemy with one heart and one mind. In meeting their primary need, we are not to "add flowers to a piece of brocade" but "offer fuel to a person in snowy weather." Under the present conditions, therefore, popularisation is the more pressing task. It is wrong to despise and neglect this task.

But popularisation and elevation cannot be sharply separated. Not only 6 is it possible to popularise even now a number of works to a higher level, but the cultural level of the broad masses is also steadily rising. If popularisation remains always on the same level—for one, two or three months, for one, two or three years, dealing out always the same stuff like "Little Cowherd,"* or the characters of "man, hand, mouth, knife, cow, goat,"† then will not the educator and the educated remain much of a muchness? What is such popularisation good for? The people need popularisation, but along with it they need elevation too, elevation month by month and year by year. Popularisation is popularisation for the people, and elevation is elevation of the people. Such elevation does not take place in mid-air, nor behind closed doors, but on the basis of popularisation. It is at once determined by popularisation and gives direction to it. In China, the revolution and revolutionary culture are uneven in their development and they broaden out only gradually; thus in one place the work of popularisation may have been carried out, and also elevation on the basis of popularisation, while in other places the work of popularisation may not yet have begun. Therefore the helpful experiences of elevation on the basis of popularisation in one place may be applied in another, so as to serve as guidance to the work of popularisation and elevation there and save a good deal of labour. Internationally, the helpful experiences of foreign countries, especially the experiences of the Soviet Union, can serve

---

* A popular Chinese operetta with a cast of only two characters, a cowherd and a village girl, carrying on a dialogue in songs. With its songs reworded for the purpose of anti-Japanese propaganda, it enjoyed much popularity in the early days of the War of Resistance [Mao's note].

† In Chinese, these are characters of a few strokes, usually given in the first lessons of old primers [Mao's note].

as our guide. Thus our elevation is on the basis of popularisation while our popularisation is under the guidance of elevation. This being the case, the work of popularisation in our sense not only constitutes no obstacle to elevation but affords a basis for our work of elevation on a limited scale at present, as well as preparing the necessary conditions for our far more extensive work of elevation in the future.

Besides the elevation that directly meets the need of the masses there is 7 the elevation that meets their need indirectly, namely, the elevation needed by the cadres. Being advanced members of the masses, the cadres are generally better educated than the masses, and art and literature of a higher level are entirely necessary to them; and it would be a mistake to ignore this. Anything done for the cadres is also entirely done for the masses, because it is only through the cadres that we can give education and guidance to the masses. If we depart from this objective, if what we give to the cadres cannot help them to educate and guide the masses, then our work of elevation will be like aimless shooting, *i.e.* deviating from our fundamental principle of serving the broad masses of the people.

To sum up: through the creative labour of revolutionary artists and 8 writers the raw material of art and literature in the life of the people becomes art and literature in an ideological form in service of the masses of the people. Hence there are, on the one hand, the more advanced art and literature which are developed upon the basis of elementary art and literature and needed by the elevated section of the masses, or primarily by the cadres; and on the other hand, elementary art and literature which are produced under the guidance of the more advanced art and literature and often meet the urgent need of the broadest masses of today. Whether advanced or elementary, our art and literature are intended for the masses of the people, primarily for the workers, peasants and soldiers, created for them and to be used by them.

Since we have solved the problem of the relation between popularisa- 9 tion and elevation, the problem of the relation between experts and popularisers can also be settled. Our experts should serve not only the cadres but chiefly the masses. Our experts in literature should pay attention to the wall newspapers of the masses and the reportage literature in the army and the villages. Our experts in drama should pay attention to the small troupes in the army and the villages. Our experts in music should pay attention to the songs of the masses. Our experts in the fine arts should pay attention to the fine arts of the masses. All these comrades should keep in close touch with the popularisers of art and literature among the masses, help and guide the popularisers as well as learn from them, and through them draw nourishment from the masses to develop and enrich themselves and to prevent their specialities from becoming empty, lifeless castles in the air detached from the masses and from reality. Experts should be respected; they are very valuable to our cause. But we should also remind them that no revolutionary artist or writer can produce any work of significance unless he has contact with the masses, gives expression to their thoughts and feelings, and becomes their loyal spokesman. Only by speaking for the masses can he educate them and only by becoming their pupil can he become their teacher. If he regards himself as the master of the masses or as an aristocrat who lords it over the "low people", then no matter how great his talent, he will not be needed by the people and his work will have no future.

Is this attitude of ours one of utilitarianism? Materialists are not op-   10 posed to utilitarianism in general, but to the utilitarianism of the feudal, bourgeois and petty-bourgeois classes, to those hypocrites who attack utilitarianism in words but embrace the most selfish and shortsighted utilitarianism in deeds. There is no transcendental utilitarianism in this world, and in a class society utilitarianism is either of this or of that particular class. Being proletarian, revolutionary utilitarians, we take as our point of departure the uniting of the present and future interests of the broadest masses who constitute over 90 per cent of the population; therefore we are revolutionary utilitarians who envisage the interests of the broadest scope and the longest range, not narrow utilitarians who look after only what is partial and immediate. If, for instance, you reproach the masses for their utilitarianism, and yet for the benefit of an individual or a clique you insist upon placing on the market and advertising among the masses a certain work which wins the favour of only a few but proves useless or even harmful to most people, then you are not only insulting the masses but revealing your own lack of self-knowledge. A thing is good only when it brings real benefit to the masses of the people. Granted that your work is as good as "The Spring Snow"; but for the time being it caters only for a few, and the masses are still enjoying the "Pa Emigrants in the Poor Quarters";* if you simply denounce the masses instead of elevating them, you will get nowhere for all your denunciations. The problem now is how to unite "The Spring Snow" with the "Pa Emigrants in the Poor Quarters," to unite elevation with popularisation. If the two are not united, then any artistic work of the highest quality produced by an expert will only have the smallest use and, if one calls that "lofty and pure," one is simply flattering oneself and the masses will not endorse one's opinion.

Having solved the problem concerning the fundamental principle of   11 serving the workers, peasants and soldiers and of the way to serve them, we have also solved such problems as whether to depict the bright or the dark side of life and how to achieve unity among our artists and writers. If this is the fundamental principle we all agree upon, then it must be adhered to by our artists and writers, our schools of art and literature, our artistic and lit-

* This and "The Spring Snow" were songs of the third century B.C. sung by people of Ch'u, one of the largest states in ancient China. They represented respectively music of a lower and a higher order. Sung Yu's "Answer to the King of Ch'u" relates that, in the capital of the state, when a singer sang "The Spring Snow," only a few dozen would join in the chorus, but when he sang the "Pa Emigrants in the Poor Quarters," thousands of people joined in [Mao's note].

erary publications and organisations, and all our artistic and literary activities. It is wrong to deviate from this principle, and anything at variance with it must be duly corrected.

III

Since our art and literature are intended for the broad masses of the people, 12 we can proceed to discuss a problem of inner-Party relations, *i.e.* the relation between the Party's artistic and literary activity and the Party's activity as a whole, and a problem of the Party's external relations, *i.e.* the relation between Party artistic and literary activity and non-Party artistic and literary activity—the problem of the united front in art and literature.

Let us take up the first problem. In the world today all culture, all art 13 and literature belong to definite classes and follow definite political lines. There is in reality no such thing as art for art's sake, art which stands above classes or art which runs parallel to or remains independent of politics. Proletarian art and literature are part of the entire cause of the proletarian revolution, in the words of Lenin, "cogs and screws in the whole machine."* Therefore the Party's artistic and literary activity occupies a definite and assigned position in the Party's total revolutionary work and is subordinated to the prescribed revolutionary task of the Party in a given revolutionary period. Any opposition to this assignment will certainly lead to dualism or pluralism, and in essence amounts to Trotsky's formula: "politics—Marxist; art—bourgeois." We are not in favour of erroneously over-emphasising the importance of art and literature, but neither are we in favour of underestimating it. Art and literature are subordinate to politics, but they in turn also exert a great influence on politics. Revolutionary art and literature are part of the entire cause of the revolution, they are its cogs and screws; though in comparison with certain other parts they may be less important and less urgent and occupy only a secondary position, yet they are, as cogs and screws, indispensable to the whole machine, and form an indispensable part of the entire cause of the revolution. If we had no art and literature even in the broadest and most general sense, then the revolutionary movement could not be carried on to victory. It would be wrong not to realise this. Furthermore, in saying that art and literature are subordinate to politics, we mean here class politics and mass politics, not the politics of a few so-called statesmen. Politics, whether revolutionary or counter-revolutionary, represents the struggle of one class against another, not the activity of a few individuals. Revolutionary struggles on the ideological and artistic fronts must be subordinate to the political struggle because only through politics can the needs of the class and the masses

---

*See V. I. Lenin, *The Party's Organisation and the Party's Literature*, in which he says: "The cause of literature should form a part of the entire cause of the proletariat and become one of the 'cogs and screws' in the great united, social-democratic machine operated by the whole awakened vanguard of the working class" [Mao's note].

be expressed in concentrated form. The revolutionary statesmen or political experts who have mastered the science or art of revolutionary politics are merely leaders of millions of statesmen, namely, the masses, with the task of collecting the ideas of these mass-statesmen, submitting these ideas to a refining process and then passing the refined products back to the masses for them to accept and put into practice; they are therefore not the kind of aristocratic "statesmen" who draw up plans all by themselves with the conceit that they have a monopoly of wisdom—herein lies the difference in principle between the statesmen of the proletariat and those of the decadent bourgeoisie. It is precisely for this reason that the political character of our art and literature becomes entirely at one with its truthfulness. It would be wrong to fail to recognise this point and vulgarise the politics and statesmanship of the proletariat.

Let us take up next the question of the united front in art and literature. 14 Since art and literature are subordinate to politics and since China's first and foremost political problem today is resistance to Japan, Party artists and writers must first of all unite on this issue with all non-Party artists and writers (from Party sympathisers, petty-bourgeois artists and writers to all bourgeois and landlord-class artists and writers who are in favour of resisting Japan). We should also unite with them on the issue of democracy; on this issue, however, not all the anti-Japanese artists and writers agree, so the range of unity will be more limited. Then again, we must unite with them on the special issue in artistic and literary circles—that of method and style in art and literature, but as we are for socialist realism and a section of artists and writers is against it, the range of unity may be further limited. Unity can be achieved on one issue while struggle and criticism take place on another. All the issues are at once separate and connected; thus on the issues which call for unity, such as resistance to Japan, there are at the same time struggle and criticism. In a united front, all unity and no struggle on the one hand, and all struggle and no unity on the other—to put into practice, as some of our comrades did in the past, Right capitulationism, tailism, or "Left" exclusivism and sectarianism—are both wrong policies. This applies to politics as well as to art.

Petty-bourgeois artists and writers in China constitute an important 15 force in the united front of art and literature. Although there are many shortcomings in their ideology and in their works, they are comparatively inclined towards the revolution and comparatively close to the working people. Therefore it is an especially important task to help them to overcome their shortcomings and win them over to the front of serving the working people.

IV

One of the principal methods of struggle in the artistic and literary sphere is 16 art and literary criticism. It should be developed and, as many comrades have rightly pointed out, our work in this respect was quite inadequate in the past. Art and literary criticism presents a complex problem which requires much study of a special kind. Here I shall stress only the basic problem of criteria in criticism. I shall also comment briefly on certain other problems and incorrect views brought up by some comrades.

There are two criteria in art and literary criticism: political and artistic. 17 According to the political criterion, all works are good that facilitate unity and resistance to Japan, that encourage the masses to be of one heart and one mind and that oppose retrogression and promote progress; on the other hand, all works are bad that undermine unity and resistance to Japan, that sow dissension and discord among the masses and that oppose progress and drag the people back. And how can we tell the good from the bad here—by the motive (subjective intention) or by the effect (social practice)? Idealists stress motive and ignore effect, while mechanical materialists stress effect and ignore motive; in contradistinction from either, we dialectical materialists* insist on the unity of motive and effect. The motive of serving the masses is inseparable from the effect of winning their approval, and we must unite the two. The motive of serving the individual or a small clique is not good, nor is the motive of serving the masses good if it does not lead to a result that is welcomed by the masses and confers benefit on them. In examining the subjective intention of an artist, *i.e.* whether his motive is correct and good, we do not look at his declaration but at the effect his activities (mainly his works) produce on society and the masses. Social practice and its effect are the criteria for examining the subjective intention or the motive. We reject sectarianism in our art and literary criticism and, under the general principle of unity and resistance to Japan, we must tolerate all artistic and literary works expressing every kind of political attitude. But at the same time we must firmly uphold our principles in our criticism, and adhere to our standpoint and severely criticise and repudiate all artistic and literary works containing views against the nation, the sciences, the people and communism, because such works, in motive as well as in effect, are detrimental to unity and the resistance to Japan. According to the artistic criterion, all works are good or comparatively good that are relatively high in artistic quality; and bad or comparatively bad that are relatively low in artistic quality. Of course, this distinction also depends on social effect. As there is hardly an artist who does not consider his own work excellent, our criticism ought to permit the free competition of all varieties of artistic works; but it is entirely necessary for us to pass correct judgments on them according to the criteria of the science of art, so that we can gradually raise the art of a lower level to a higher level, and to change the art which does not meet the requirements of the struggle of the broad masses into art that does meet them.

---

* Dialectical materialism is the Marxist theory that reality has a material base and continually changes in a dialectical process.

There is thus the political criterion as well as the artistic criterion. How 18 are the two related? Politics is not the equivalent of art, nor is a general world outlook equivalent to the method of artistic creation and criticism. We believe there is neither an abstract and absolutely unchangeable political criterion, nor an abstract and absolutely unchangeable artistic criterion, for every class in a class society has its own political and artistic criteria. But all classes in all class societies place the political criterion first and the artistic criterion second. The bourgeoisie always rejects proletarian artistic and literary works, no matter how great their artistic achievement. As for the proletariat, they must treat the art and literature of the past according to their attitude towards the people and whether they are progressive in the light of history. Some things which are basically reactionary from the political point of view may yet be artistically good. But the more artistic such a work may be, the greater harm will it do to the people, and the more reason for us to reject it. The contradiction between reactionary political content and artistic form is a common characteristic of the art and literature of all exploiting classes in their decline. What we demand is unity of politics and art, of content and form, and of the revolutionary political content and the highest possible degree of perfection in artistic form. Works of art, however politically progressive, are powerless if they lack artistic quality. Therefore we are equally opposed to works with wrong political approaches and to the tendency towards so-called "poster and slogan style" which is correct only in political approach but lacks artistic power. We must carry on a two-front struggle in art and literature.

Both tendencies can be found in the ideologies of many of our com- 19 rades. Those comrades who tend to neglect artistic quality should pay attention to its improvement. But as I see it, the political side is more of a problem at present. Some comrades lack elementary political knowledge and consequently all kinds of muddled ideas arise. Let me give a few instances found in Yenan.

"The theory of human nature." Is there such a thing as human nature? 20 Of course there is. But there is only human nature in the concrete, no human nature in the abstract. In a class society there is only human nature that bears the stamp of a class, but no human nature transcending classes. We uphold the human nature of the proletariat and of the great masses of the people, while the landlord and bourgeois classes uphold the nature of their own classes as if—though they do not say so outright—it were the only kind of human nature. The human nature boosted by certain petty-bourgeois intellectuals is also divorced from or opposed to that of the great masses of the people; what they call human nature is in substance nothing but bourgeois individualism, and consequently in their eyes proletarian human nature is contrary to their human nature. This is the "theory of human nature" advocated by some people in Yenan as the so-called basis of their theory of art and literature, which is utterly mistaken.

"The fundamental point of departure for art and literature is love, the 21 love of mankind." Now love may serve as a point of departure, but there is still a more basic one. Love is a concept, a product of objective practice. Fundamentally, we do not start from a concept but from objective practice. Our artists and writers who come from the intelligentsia love the proletariat because social life has made them feel that they share the same fate with the proletariat. We hate Japanese imperialism because the Japanese imperialists oppress us. There is no love or hatred in the world that has not its cause. As to the so-called "love of mankind," there has been no such all-embracing love since humanity was divided into classes. All the ruling classes in the past liked to advocate it, and many so-called sages and wise men also did the same, but nobody has ever really practised it, for it is impracticable in a class society. Genuine love of mankind will be born only when class distinctions have been eliminated throughout the world. The classes have caused the division of society into many opposites and as soon as they are eliminated there will be love of all mankind, but not now. We cannot love our enemies, we cannot love social evils, and our aim is to exterminate them. How can our artists and writers fail to understand such a common sense matter?

"Art and literature have always described the bright as well as the dark 22 side of things impartially, on a fifty-fifty basis." This statement contains a number of muddled ideas. Art and literature have not always done so. Many petty-bourgeois writers have never found the bright side and their works are devoted to exposing the dark side, the so-called "literature of exposure"; there are even works which specialise in propagating pessimism and misanthropy. On the other hand, Soviet literature during the period of socialist reconstruction portrays mainly the bright side. It also describes shortcomings in work and villainous characters, but such descriptions serve only to bring out the brightness of the whole picture, and not on a "compensating basis." Bourgeois writers of reactionary periods portray the revolutionary masses as ruffians and describe the bourgeois as saints, thus reversing the so-called bright and dark sides. Only truly revolutionary artists and writers can correctly solve the problem whether to praise or to expose. All dark forces which endanger the masses of the people must be exposed while all revolutionary struggles of the masses must be praised—this is the basic task of all revolutionary artists and writers.

"The task of art and literature has always been to expose." This sort of 23 argument, like the one mentioned above, arises from the lack of knowledge of the science of history. We have already shown that the task of art and literature does not consist solely in exposure. For the revolutionary artists and writers the objects to be exposed can never be the masses of the people, but only the aggressors, exploiters and oppressors and their evil aftermath brought to the people. The people have their shortcomings too, but these are to be overcome by means of criticism and self-criticism within the ranks of the people themselves, and to carry on such criticism and self-criticism is also one of the most important tasks of art and literature. However, we should not call that "exposing the people." As for the people, our problem is basically one of how to educate them and raise their level. Only counter-revolutionary artists and writers describe the people as "born fools" and the revolutionary masses as "tyrannical mobs."

"This is still a period of the essay, and the style should still be that of 24 Lu Hsun." Living under the rule of the dark forces, deprived of freedom of speech, Lu Hsun had to fight by means of burning satire and freezing irony cast in essay form, and in this he was entirely correct. We too must hold up to sharp ridicule the fascists, the Chinese reactionaries and everything endangering the people; but in our border region of Shensi-Kansu-Ningsia and the anti-Japanese base areas in the enemy's rear, where revolutionary artists and writers are given full freedom and democracy and only counter-revolutionaries are deprived of them, essays must not be written simply in the same style as Lu Hsun's. Here we can shout at the top of our voice, and need not resort to obscure and veiled expressions which would tax the understanding of the broad masses of the people. In dealing with the people themselves and not the enemies of the people, Lu Hsun even in his "essay period" did not mock or attack the revolutionary masses and the revolutionary parties, and his style was also entirely different from that employed in his essays on the enemy. We have already said that we must criticise the shortcomings of the people, but be sure that we criticise from the standpoint of the people and out of a whole-hearted eagerness to defend and educate them. If we treat our comrades like enemies, then we are taking the standpoint of the enemy. Are we then to give up satire altogether? No. Satire is always necessary. But there are all kinds of satire; the kind for our enemies, the kind for our allies and the kind for our own ranks—each of them assumes a different attitude. We are not opposed to satire as a whole, but we must not abuse it.

"I am not given to praise and eulogy; works which extol the bright side 25 of things are not necessarily great, nor are works which depict the dark side necessarily poor." If you are a bourgeois artist or writer, you will extol not the proletariat but the bourgeoisie, and if you are a proletarian artist or writer, you will extol not the bourgeoisie but the proletariat and the working people: you must do one or the other. Those works which extol the bright side of the bourgeoisie are not necessarily great while those which depict its dark side are not necessarily poor, and those works which extol the bright side of the proletariat are not necessarily poor, while those works which depict the so-called "dark side" of the proletariat are certainly poor—are these not facts recorded in the history of art and literature? Why should we not extol the people, the creator of the history of the human world? Why should we not extol the proletariat, the Communist Party, the New Democracy and socialism? Of course, there are persons who have no enthusiasm for the people's cause and stand aloof, looking with cold indifference on the struggle and the victory of the proletariat and its vanguard; and they only take pleasure in singing endless praises of themselves, plus perhaps a few persons in their own coterie. Such petty-bourgeois individualists are naturally unwilling to praise the meritorious deeds of the revolutionary masses or to heighten their courage in struggle and confidence in victory. Such people are the black sheep in the revolutionary ranks and the revolutionary masses have indeed no use for such "singers."

"It is not a matter of standpoint; the standpoint is correct, the intention 26 good, and the ideas are all right, but the expression is faulty and produces a bad effect." I have already spoken about the dialectical materialist view of motive and effect, and now I want to ask: Is the question of effect not one of standpoint? A person who, in doing a job, minds only the motive and pays no regard to the effect, is very much like a doctor who hands out prescriptions and does not care how many patients may die of them. Suppose, again, a political party keeps on making pronouncements while paying not the least attention to carrying them out. We may well ask, is such a standpoint correct? Are such intentions good? Of course, a person is liable to make mistakes in estimating the result of an action before it is taken; but are his intentions really good if he adheres to the same old rut even when facts prove that it leads to bad results? In judging a party or a doctor, we must look at the practice and the effect, and the same applies in judging an artist or a writer. One who has a truly good intention must take the effect into consideration by summing up experiences and studying methods or, in the case of creative work, the means of expression. One who has a truly good intention must criticise with the utmost candour his own shortcomings and mistakes in work, and make up his mind to correct them. That is why the Communists have adopted the method of self-criticism. Only such a standpoint is the correct one. At the same time it is only through such a process of practice carried out conscientiously and responsibly that we can gradually understand what the correct point of view is and have a firm grasp of it. If we refuse to do this in practice, then we are really ignorant of the correct point of view, despite our conceited assertion to the contrary.

"To call on us to study Marxism may again lead us to take the repetition 27 of dialectical materialist formulas for literary creation, and this will stifle our creative impulse." We study Marxism in order to apply the dialectical materialist and historical materialist* viewpoint in our observation of the world, society and art and literature, and not in order to write philosophical discourses in our works of art and literature. Marxism embraces realism in artistic and literary creation but cannot replace it, just as it embraces atomics and electronics in physics but cannot replace them. Empty, cut-and-dried dog-

---

* Historical materialism is a Marxist theory that ideas and social institutions develop only on a material economic base.

mas and formulas will certainly destroy our creative impulse; moreover, they first of all destroy Marxism. Dogmatic "Marxism" is not Marxist but anti-Marxist. But will Marxism not destroy any creative impulse? It will; it will certainly destroy the creative impulse that is feudal, bourgeois, petty-bourgeois, liberal, individualistic, nihilistic, art-for-art's-sake, aristocratic, decadent or pessimistic, and any creative impulse that is not of the people and of the proletariat. As far as the artists and writers of the proletariat are concerned, ought not these kinds of impulse to be done away with? I think they ought; they should be utterly destroyed, and while they are being destroyed, new things can be built up.

QUESTIONS ABOUT MAO'S DISCOURSE COMMUNITY
AND HIS CONCERNS IN THIS ESSAY

1. What kinds of feelings does Mao seem to have for the masses?
2. Education was obviously very important to Mao. Why do you think that was the case?
3. For whom does Mao say that the art and literature of the Communist party is intended? For whom is this art and literature not intended?
4. What does Mao say is the chief purpose of art and literature? Do you agree with him?
5. Mao says that all art and literature follow definite political lines. Do you agree with him?
6. How do you react to Mao's ideas on the relation between human nature and social class?
7. How much resistance to the goals of the Communist party on the part of artists does Mao seem inclined to allow? What is your evidence for this judgment?

QUESTIONS ABOUT MAO'S RHETORICAL
STRATEGIES

1. What do the members of Mao's audience seem to be like? To whom does he appear to be talking?
2. How would you characterize Mao's tone in this selection? What elements of the selection are particularly instrumental in creating that tone?
3. Mao uses many sweeping generalizations. Do you find them all justified?
4. How does Mao use questions in this piece? Is his practice effective?
5. Mao does a good deal of summing up, of letting his audience know where he has been. Knowing what you do about Mao's original context, would you say that he does too much summing up?
6. Examine Mao's definition of the artistic criterion of evaluation (paragraph two of section IV). How adequate do you find it?
7. Mao calls art a " science." Is his choice of words wise? How might his Marxism have contributed to this choice of words?

WRITING FROM WITHIN AND ABOUT THE ARTS: LITERARY CRITICISM

Writing for Yourself

1. In your journal, reflect on how your view of the value of individuals compares to Mao's view.
2. In your journal, reflect on how an individual in a Marxist regime is probably led to see his or her ultimate purpose.

Writing for Nonacademic Audiences

1. A controversy has been raging in the letters column of your hometown newspaper on the extent to which the government should control what individuals read and view as art. You decide to join the fray. Write a 250-word letter to the editor, giving your views succinctly.
2. On a trip home from school you tell your grandfather that you have been reading Marxist literary criticism. A veteran of the Korean War, he is aghast. After you get back to school, you write him a letter in which you try to explain the value of that reading.
3. Write a 500-word column for your university newspaper on what it is about North American capitalism that does the most to make Marxism appealing to you.
4. How necessary to a democracy is literacy? Respond to this question in an essay that you will submit to the *Reader's Digest*.

Writing for Academic Audiences

1. In an introduction to literature class, your instructor writes the following on the chalkboard: "Art with a political message is bad art." He or she then asks you to write a 500-word paper in which you react to the statement.
2. For a class in aesthetics, write a 1,000-word comparison-contrast paper on how being an artist in a democracy is probably similar to and different from being an artist in a Marxist country.

Bruno Bettelheim

(1903–1990)

Born in Vienna in 1903, Bruno Bettelheim took all of his education in that city through his doctorate, which he received in psychology and philosophy from the University of Vienna in 1938. In that same year, Nazi Germany took over Austria. Bettelheim, a Jewish intellectual, was imprisoned first at Dachau and then at Buchenwald. Released in 1939, Bettelheim emigrated to the United States, where he lived the rest of his life.

In 1939, Bettelheim began his thirty-four-year association with the University of Chicago. He directed the university's Orthogenic School, a residential treatment center for children aged six to fourteen with emotional disturbances. His goal was to relieve the enormous emotional suffering of autistic children, and he argued that this would never come about through mere restraint, that if a child was to be able to function in society, there must be true education and continual contact with others.

In 1943, Bettelheim published an article that brought him wide recognition: "Individual and Mass Behavior in Extreme Situations," based on his observations during his incarceration in the concentration camps. He continued to use his powers of observation as the basis for his writings. Dialogues with Mothers *(1962), based on observations at the Orthogenic School, dealt with the child's need to develop autonomy.* Children of the Dream *(1967) examined the communal upbringing of children in Israeli Kibbutzim and suggested that traditional family structures should be re-examined based on the experiment.*

The Uses of Enchantment *(1975) was similarly based on observation, though this work came out of a need that Bettelheim perceived in children. In his introduction to the text he wrote:*

> *As an educator and therapist of severely disturbed children, my main task was to restore meaning to their lives. This work made it obvious to me that if children were reared so that life was meaningful to them, they would not need special help. I was confronted with the problem of deducing what experiences in a child's life are most suited to promote his ability to find meaning in his life; to endow life in general with more meaning. Regarding this task, nothing is more important than the impact of parents and others who take care of the child; second in importance is our cultural heritage, when transmitted to the child in the right manner. When children are young, it is literature that carries such information best.*

His approach to folklore was to find how tales became meaningful; his answer came through a psychoanalytic, Freudian approach.

Bettelheim argues that fairy tales are important for child development because

they enable children to come to grips with realities of the outside or adult world. He
suggests that these tales deal with inner pressures that children feel as they approach
sexual maturity and are faced with changing relationships to their parents; the tales
help children to deal with these pressures by presenting them in such a way that the
child unconsciously recognizes them and finds in the stories both temporary and per-
manent solutions. In pursuing this approach, Bettelheim places himself in the dis-
course community of Freudian literary criticism, which uses psychoanalytic princi-
ples to explain and understand literary works.

   The following excerpt is from the second part of The Uses of Enchantment,
which examines the meaning of specific tales.

"JACK AND THE BEANSTALK"

Fairy tales deal in literary form with the basic problems of life, particularly 1
those inherent in the struggle to achieve maturity. They caution against the
destructive consequences if one fails to develop higher levels of responsible
selfhood, setting warning examples such as the older brothers in "The Three
Feathers," the stepsisters in "Cinderella," the wolf in "Little Red Cap." To
the child, these tales subtly suggest why he ought to strive for higher integration, and what is involved in it.

   These same stories also intimate to a parent that he ought to be aware 2
of the risks involved in his child's development, so that he may be alert to
them and protect the child when necessary to prevent a catastrophe; and that
he ought to support and encourage his child's personal and sexual development when and where this is appropriate.

   The tales of the Jack cycle are of British origin; from there they became 3
diffused throughout the English-speaking world. By far the best-known and
most interesting story of this cycle is "Jack and the Beanstalk." Important
elements of this fairy tale appear in many stories all over the world: the seemingly stupid exchange which provides something of magic power; the miraculous seed from which a tree grows that reaches into heaven; the cannibalistic ogre that is outwitted and robbed; the hen that lays golden eggs or the
golden goose; the musical instrument that talks. But their combination into
a story which asserts the desirability of social and sexual self-assertion in the
pubertal boy, and the foolishness of a mother who belittles this, is what makes
"Jack and the Beanstalk" such a meaningful fairy tale.

   One of the oldest stories of the Jack cycle is "Jack and His Bargains." In 4
it the original conflict is not between a son and his mother who thinks him a
fool, but a battle for dominance between son and father. This story presents

some problems of the social-sexual development of the male in clearer form than "Jack and the Beanstalk," and the underlying message of the latter can be understood more readily in the light of this earlier tale.

In "Jack and His Bargains" we are told that Jack is a wild boy, of no help to his father. Worse, because of Jack the father has fallen on hard times and must meet all kinds of debts. So he has sent Jack with one of the family's seven cows to the fair, to sell it for as much money as he can get for it. On the way to the fair Jack meets a man who asks him where he is headed. Jack tells him, and the man offers to swap the cow for a wondrous stick: all its owner has to say is "Up stick and at it" and the stick will beat all enemies senseless. Jack makes the exchange. When he comes home, the father, who has expected to receive money for his cow, gets so furious that he fetches a stick to beat Jack with. In self-defense Jack calls on *his* stick, which beats the father until he cries for mercy. This establishes Jack's ascendancy over his father in the home, but does not provide the money they need. So Jack is sent to the next fair to sell another cow. He meets the same man and exchanges the cow for a bee that sings beautiful songs. The need for money increases, and Jack is sent to sell a third cow. Once more he meets the man, and exchanges this cow for a fiddle which plays marvelous tunes.

Now the scene shifts. The king who rules in this part of the world has a daughter who is unable to smile. Her father promises to marry her to the man who can make her merry. Many princes and rich men try in vain to amuse her. Jack, in his ragged clothes, gets the better of all the highborn competitors, because the princess smiles when she hears the bee sing and the fiddle play so beautifully. She laughs outright as the stick beats up all the mighty suitors. So Jack is to marry her.

Before the marriage is to take place, the two are to spend a night in bed together. There Jack lies stock still and makes no move toward the princess. This greatly offends both her and her father; but the king soothes his daughter, and suggests that Jack may be scared of her and the new situation in which he finds himself. So on the following night another try is made, but the night passes as did the first. When on a third try Jack still does not move toward the princess in bed, the angry king has him thrown into a pit full of lions and tigers. Jack's stick beats these wild animals into submission, at which the princess marvels at "what a proper man he was." They get married "and had baskets full of children."

The story is somewhat incomplete. For example, while the number three is emphasized repeatedly—three encounters with the man, three exchanges of a cow for a magic object, three nights with the princess without Jack's "turning to her"—it remains unclear why seven cows are mentioned at the beginning and then we hear no more about the four cows remaining after three have been exchanged for the magic objects. Secondly, while there are many other fairy tales in which a man remains unresponsive to his love for three consecutive days or nights, usually this is explained in some fashion;* Jack's behavior in this regard, however, is left quite unexplained, and so we have to rely on our imagination for its meaning.

The magic formula "Up stick and at it" suggests phallic associations, as 9 does the fact that only this new acquisition permits Jack to hold his own in relation to his father, who up to now has dominated him. It is this stick which gains him victory in the competition with all suitors—a competition which is a sexual contest, since the prize is marrying the princess. It is the stick that finally leads to sexual possession of the princess, after it has beaten the wild animals into submission. While the lovely singing of the bee and the beautiful tunes of the fiddle make the princess smile, it is the stick's beating up the pretentious suitors, and thus making a shambles of what we may assume was their masculine posturing, that makes her laugh.† But if these sexual connotations were all there was to this story, it would not be a fairy tale, or not a very meaningful one. For its deeper significance we have to consider the other magic objects, and the nights during which Jack rests unmovingly beside the princess as if he himself were a stick.

Phallic potency, the story implies, is not enough. In itself it does not 10 lead to better and higher things, nor does it make for sexual maturity. The bee—a symbol of hard work and sweetness, as it gives us honey, hence its delightful songs—stands for work and its enjoyment. Constructive labor as symbolized by the bee is a stark contrast to Jack's original wildness and laziness. After puberty, a boy must find constructive goals and work for them to become a useful member of society. That is why Jack is first provided with the stick, before he is given the bee and fiddle. The fiddle, the last present, symbolizes artistic achievement, and with it the highest human accomplishment. To win the princess, the power of the stick and what it symbolizes sexually is not sufficient. The power of the stick (sexual prowess) must become controlled, as suggested by the three nights in bed during which Jack does

*For example, in the Brothers Grimm's tale "The Raven," a queen's daughter turned into a raven can be freed from her enchantment if the hero awaits her fully awake on the following afternoon. The raven warns him that to remain awake he must not eat or drink of anything an old woman will offer him. He promises, but on three consecutive days permits himself to be induced to take something and in consequence falls asleep at the appointed time when the raven-princess comes to meet him. Here it is an old woman's jealousy and a young man's selfish cupidity which explain his falling asleep when he should be wide awake for his beloved.

†There are many fairy tales in which an all-too-serious princess is won by the man who can make her laugh—that is, free her emotionally. This is frequently achieved by the hero's making persons who normally command respect look ridiculous. For example, in the Brothers Grimm's story "The Golden Goose," Simpleton, the youngest of three sons, because of his kindness to an old dwarf is given a goose with golden feathers. Cupidity induces various people to try to pull a feather off, but for this they get stuck to the goose, and to each other. Finally a parson and a sexton get stuck, too, and have to run after Simpleton and his goose. They look so ridiculous that on seeing this procession, the princess laughs.

not move. By such behavior he demonstrates his self-control; with it he no longer rests his case on the display of phallic masculinity; he does not wish to win the princess by overpowering her. Through his subjugation of the wild animals Jack shows that he uses his strength to control those lower tendencies—the ferocity of lion and tiger, his wildness and irresponsibility which had piled up debts for his father—and with it becomes worthy of princess and kingdom. The princess recognizes this. Jack at first has made her only laugh, but at the end when he has demonstrated not only (sexual) power but also (sexual) self-control, he is recognized by her as a proper man with whom she can be happy and have many children.*

"Jack and His Bargains" begins with adolescent phallic self-assertion 11 ("Up stick and at it") and ends with personal and social maturity as self-control and valuation of the higher things in life are achieved. The much-better-known "Jack and the Beanstalk" story starts and ends considerably earlier in a male's sexual development. While loss of infantile pleasure is barely hinted at in the first story with the need to sell the cows, this is a central issue in "Jack and the Beanstalk." We are told that the good cow Milky White, which until then had supported child and mother, has suddenly stopped giving milk. Thus the expulsion from an infantile paradise begins; it continues with the mother's deriding Jack's belief in the magic power of his seeds. The phallic beanstalk permits Jack to engage in oedipal conflict with the ogre, which he survives and finally wins, thanks only to the oedipal mother's taking his side against her own husband. Jack relinquishes his reliance on the belief in the magic power of phallic self-assertion as he cuts down the beanstalk; and this opens the way toward a development of mature masculinity. Thus, both versions of the Jack story together cover the entire male development.

Infancy ends when the belief in an unending supply of love and nutri- 12 ment proves to be an irrealistic fantasy. Childhood begins with an equally irrealistic belief in what the child's own body in general, and specifically one aspect of it—his newly discovered sexual equipment—can achieve for him. As in infancy the mother's breast was symbol of all the child wanted of life and seemed to receive from her, so now his body, including his genitals, will do all that for the child, or so he wishes to believe. This is equally true for boys and girls; that is why "Jack and the Beanstalk" is enjoyed by children of both sexes. The end of childhood, as suggested before, is reached when such

---

*The Brothers Grimm's story "The Raven" may serve as a comparison to support the idea that three-times-repeated self-control over instinctual tendencies demonstrates sexual maturity, while its absence indicates an immaturity that prevents the gaining of one's true love. Unlike Jack, the hero in "The Raven," instead of controlling his desire for food and drink and for falling asleep, succumbs three times to the temptation by accepting the old woman's saying "One time is no time"—that is, it doesn't count—which shows his moral immaturity. He thus loses the princess. He finally gains her only after many errands through which he grows.

childish dreams of glory are given up and self-assertion, even against a parent, becomes the order of the day.

Every child can easily grasp the unconscious meaning of the tragedy 13 when the good cow Milky White, who provided all that was needed, suddenly stops giving milk. It arouses dim memories of that tragic time when the flow of milk ceased for the child, when he was weaned. That is the time when the mother demands that the child must learn to make do with what the outside world can offer. This is symbolized by Jack's mother sending him out into the world to arrange for something (the money he is expected to get for the cow) that will provide sustenance. But Jack's belief in magic supplies has not prepared him for meeting the world realistically.

If up until now Mother (the cow, in fairy-tale metaphor) has supplied 14 all that was needed and she now no longer does so, the child will naturally turn to his father—represented in the story by the man encountered on the way—expecting Father to supply magically to the child all he needs. Deprived of the "magic" supplies which up to then have been assured, and which he has felt were his unquestionable "rights," Jack is more than ready to exchange the cow for any promise of a magic solution to the impasse in living in which he finds himself.

It is not just Mother who tells Jack to sell the cow because it no longer 15 gives milk; Jack also wants to get rid of this no-good cow that disappoints him. If Mother, in the form of Milky White, deprives and makes it imperative to change things, then Jack is going to exchange the cow not for what Mother wants, but for what seems more desirable to him.

To be sent out to encounter the world means the end of infancy. The 16 child then has to begin the long and difficult process of turning himself into an adult. The first step on this road is relinquishing reliance on oral solutions to all of life's problems. Oral dependency has to be replaced by what the child can do for himself, on his own initiative. In "Jack and His Bargains" the hero is handed all three magic objects and only by means of them gains his independence; these objects do everything for him. His only contribution, while it shows self-control, is a rather passive one: he does nothing while in bed with the princess. When he is thrown into a pit with the wild animals, he is rescued not by his courage or intelligence, but only by the magic power of his stick.

Things are very different in "Jack and the Beanstalk." This story tells 17 that while belief in magic can help in daring to meet the world on our own, in the last analysis we must take the initiative and be willing to run the risks involved in mastering life. When Jack is given the magic seeds, he climbs the beanstalk on his own initiative, not because somebody else suggested it. Jack uses his body's strength skillfully in climbing the beanstalk, and risks his life three times to gain the magic objects. At the end of the story he cuts down the beanstalk and in this way makes secure his possession of the magic objects which he has gained through his own cunning.

Giving up oral dependency is acceptable only if the child can find se- 18
curity in a realistic—or, more likely, a fantastically exaggerated—belief in
what his body and its organs will do for him. But a child sees in sexuality not
something based on a relation between a man and a woman, but something
that he can achieve all by himself. Disappointed in his mother, a little boy is
not likely to accept the idea that to achieve his masculinity he requires a
woman. Without such (unrealistic) belief in himself, the child is not able to
meet the world. The story tells that Jack looked for work, but didn't succeed
in finding it; he is not yet able to manage realistically; this the man who gives
him the magic seeds understands, although his mother does not. Only trust
in what his own body—or, more specifically, his budding sexuality—can
achieve for him permits the child to give up reliance on oral satisfaction; this
is another reason why Jack is ready to exchange cow for seeds.

If his mother would accept Jack's wish to believe that his seeds and what 19
they eventually may grow into are as valuable now as cow milk was in the
past, then Jack would have less need to take recourse to fantasy satisfactions,
such as the belief in magic phallic powers as symbolized by the huge beanstalk. Instead of approving of Jack's first act of independence and initiative—
exchanging the cow for seeds—his mother ridicules what he has done, is angry with him for it, beats him, and, worst of all, falls back on the exercise of
her depriving oral power: as punishment for having shown initiative, Jack is
sent to bed without being given any food.

There, while he is in bed, reality having proven so disappointing, fan- 20
tasy satisfaction takes over. The psychological subtlety of fairy stories which
gives what they tell the ring of truth is shown once more in the fact that it is
during the night that the seeds grow into the huge beanstalk. No normal boy
could during the day exaggerate so fantastically the hopes which his newly
discovered masculinity evokes in him. But during the night, in his dreams, it
appears to him in extravagant images, such as the beanstalk on which he will
climb to the gates of heaven. The story tells that when Jack awakes, his room
is partly dark, the beanstalk shutting off the light. This is another hint that
all that takes place—Jack's climbing into the sky on the beanstalk, his encounters with the ogre, etc.—is but dreams, dreams which give a boy hope
for the great things he will one day accomplish.

The fantastic growth of the humble but magic seeds during the night is 21
understood by children as a symbol of the miraculous power and of the satisfactions Jack's sexual development can bring about: the phallic phase is replacing the oral one; the beanstalk has replaced Milky White. On this beanstalk the child will climb into the sky to achieve a higher existence.

But, the story warns, this is not without its great dangers. Getting stuck 22
in the phallic phase is little progress over fixation on the oral phase. Only
when the relative independence acquired due to the new social and sexual
development is used to solve the old oedipal problems will it lead to true
human progress. Hence Jack's dangerous encounters with the ogre, as the
oedipal father. But Jack also receives help from the ogre's wife, without which

he would be destroyed by the ogre. How insecure Jack in "Jack and the Bean-stalk" is about his newly discovered masculine strength is illustrated by his "regression" to orality whenever he feels threatened: he hides twice in the oven, and finally in a "copper," a large cooking vessel. His immaturity is further suggested by his stealing the magic objects which are the ogre's pos-sessions, which he gets away with only because the ogre is asleep.* Jack's essential unreadiness to trust his newly found masculinity is indicated by his asking the ogre's wife for food because he is so hungry.

In fairy-tale fashion, this story depicts the stages of development a boy 23
has to go through to become an independent human being, and shows how this is possible, even enjoyable, despite all dangers, and most advantageous. Giving up relying on oral satisfactions—or rather having been forced out of it by circumstances—and replacing them with phallic satisfaction as solution to all of life's problems are not enough: one has also to add, step by step, higher values to the ones already achieved. Before this can happen, one needs to work through the oedipal situation, which begins with deep disappoint-ment in the mother and involves intense competition with and jealousy of the father. The boy does not yet trust Father enough to relate openly to him. To master the difficulties of this period, the boy needs a mother's understanding help: only because the ogre's wife protects and hides Jack can he acquire the ogre-father's powers.

On his first trip Jack steals a bag filled with gold. This gives him and his 24
mother the resources to buy what they need, but eventually they run out of money. So Jack repeats his excursion, although he now knows that in doing so he risks his life.†

On his second trip Jack gains the hen that lays the golden eggs: he has 25

---

* How different is the behavior of Jack in "Jack and His Bargains," who trusts his newly gained strength. He does not hide or get things on the sly; on the contrary, when in a dangerous situation, whether with his father, his competitors for the princess, or the wild beasts, he openly uses the power of his stick to gain his goals.

† On some level, climbing up the beanstalk symbolizes not only the "magic" power of the phallus to rise, but also a boy's feelings connected with masturbation. The child who masturbates fears that if he is found out, he will suffer terrible punishment, as symbolized by the ogre's doing away with him if he should discover what Jack is up to. But the child also feels as if he is, in masturbating, "stealing" some of his parent's powers. The child who, on an unconscious level, understands this meaning of the story derives reassurance that his mas-turbation anxieties are invalid. His "phallic" excursion into the world of the grown-up giant-ogres, far from leading to his destruction, gains him advantages he is able to enjoy permanently.

Here is another example of how the fairy tale permits the child to understand and be helped on an unconscious level without his having to become aware on a conscious level of what the story is dealing with. The fairy tale represents in images what goes on in the unconscious or preconscious of the child: how his awakening sexuality seems like a miracle that happens in the darkness of the night, or in his dream. Climbing up the beanstalk, and what it symbolizes, creates the anxiety that at the end of this experience he will be destroyed for his daring. The child fears that his desire to become sexually active amounts to stealing parental powers and prerogatives, and that therefore this can be done only on the sly, when the adults are unable to see what goes on. After the story has given body to these anxieties, it assures the child that the ending will be a good one.

learned that one runs out of things if one cannot produce them or have them produced. With the hen Jack could be content, since now all physical needs are permanently satisfied. So it is not necessity which motivates Jack's last trip, but the desire for daring and adventure—the wish to find something better than mere material goods. Thus, Jack next attains the golden harp, which symbolizes beauty, art, the higher things in life. This is followed by the last growth experience, in which Jack learns that it will not do to rely on magic for solving life's problems.

As Jack gains full humanity by striving for and gaining what the harp 26 represents, he is also forcefully made aware—through the ogre's nearly catching him—that if he continues to rely on magic solutions, he will end up destroyed. As the ogre pursues him down the beanstalk, Jack calls out to his mother to get the ax and cut the beanstalk. The mother brings the ax as told, but on seeing the giant's huge legs coming down the beanstalk, she freezes into immobility; she is unable to deal with phallic objects. On a different level, the mother's freezing signifies that while a mother may protect her boy against the dangers involved in striving for manhood—as the ogre's wife did in hiding Jack—she cannot gain it for him; only he himself can do that. Jack grabs the ax and cuts off the beanstalk, and with it brings down the ogre, who perishes from his fall. In doing so, Jack rids himself of the father who is experienced on the oral level: as a jealous ogre who wants to devour.

But in cutting down the beanstalk Jack not only frees himself from a 27 view of the father as a destructive and devouring ogre; he also thus relinquishes his belief in the magic power of the phallus as the means for gaining him all the good things in life. In putting the ax to the beanstalk, Jack forswears magic solutions; he becomes "his own man." He no longer will take from others, but neither will he live in mortal fear of ogres, nor rely on Mother's hiding him in an oven (regressing to orality).

As the story of "Jack and the Beanstalk" ends, Jack is ready to give up 28 phallic and oedipal fantasies and instead try to live in reality, as much as a boy his age can do so. The next development may see him no longer trying to trick a sleeping father out of his possessions, nor fantasizing that a mother figure will for his sake betray her husband, but ready to strive openly for his social and sexual ascendency. This is where "Jack and His Bargains" begins, which sees its hero attain such maturity.

This fairy tale, like many others, could teach parents much as it helps 29 children grow up. It tells mothers what little boys need to solve their oedipal problems: Mother must side with the boy's masculine daring, surreptitious though it may still be, and protect him against the dangers which might be inherent in masculine assertion, particularly when directed against the father.

The mother in "Jack and the Beanstalk" fails her son because, instead 30 of supporting his developing masculinity, she denies its validity. The parent of the other sex ought to encourage a child's pubertal sexual development, particularly as he seeks goals and achievements in the wider world. Jack's mother, who thought her son utterly foolish for the trading he had done, stands revealed as the foolish one because she failed to recognize the development from child to adolescent which was taking place in her son. If she had had her way, Jack would have remained an immature child, and neither he nor his mother would have escaped their misery. Jack, motivated by his budding manhood, undeterred by his mother's low opinion of him, gains great fortune through his courageous actions. This story teaches—as do many other fairy tales, such as "The Three Languages"—that the parents' error is basically the lack of an appropriate and sensitive response to the various problems involved in a child's maturing personally, socially, and sexually.

The oedipal conflict within the boy in this fairy tale is conveniently 31 externalized onto two very distant figures who exist somewhere in a castle in the sky: the ogre and his wife. It is many a child's experience that most of the time, when Father—like the ogre in the tale—is out of the home, the child and his mother have a good time together, as do Jack and the ogre's wife. Then suddenly Father comes home, asking for his meal, which spoils everything for the child, who is not made welcome by his father. If a child is not given the feeling that his father is happy to find him home, he will be afraid of what he fantasized while Father was away, because it didn't include Father. Since the child wants to rob Father of his most prized possessions, how natural that he should fear being destroyed in retaliation.

Given all the dangers of regressing to orality, here is another implied 32 message of the Jack story: it was not at all bad that Milky White stopped giving milk. Had this not happened, Jack would not have gotten the seeds out of which the beanstalk grew. Orality thus not only sustains—when hung on to too long, it prevents further development; it even destroys, as does the orally fixated ogre. Orality can be left safely behind for masculinity if Mother approves and continues to offer protection. The ogre's wife hides Jack in a safe, confined place, as Mother's womb had provided safety against all dangers. Such a short regression to a previous stage of development provides the security and strength needed for the next step in independence and self-assertion. It permits the little boy to enjoy fully the advantages of the phallic development he is now entering. And if the bag of gold and, even more, the hen that lays the golden eggs stand for anal ideas of possession, the story assures that the child will not get stuck in the anal stage of development: he will soon realize that he must sublimate such primitive views and become dissatisfied with them. He will then settle for nothing less than the golden harp and what it symbolizes.*

---

* Unfortunately, "Jack and the Beanstalk" is often reprinted in a form that contains many changes and additions, mostly the result of efforts to provide moral justification for Jack's robbing the giant. These changes, however, destroy the story's poetic impact and rob it of its deeper psychological meaning. In this bowdlerized version, a fairy tells Jack that the giant's castle and the magic objects were once the possessions of Jack's father, which the giant took after killing him; and that Jack is therefore to slay the giant and gain rightful possession of the magic objects. This makes all that happens to Jack a moral tale of retribution rather than a story of manhood achieved.

QUESTIONS ABOUT BETTELHEIM'S DISCOURSE COMMUNITY AND HIS CONCERNS IN THIS ESSAY

1. What is a fairy tale?
2. Does it seem credible to you that fairy tales deal with such things as the struggle to achieve maturity? Is Bettelheim asserting more than he can possibly prove by such a claim? Does it seem to be the case that children would actually internalize, consciously or unconsciously, the concerns that Bettelheim attributes to fairy tales?
3. Fairy tales and most folklore were originally meant for an adult audience; only since the seventeenth century have these tales become the property of children as well. Does this awareness of the tales' primary audience affect a reader's response to Bettelheim's proposals at all?
4. How does Bettelheim interpret the symbolic meaning of the three gifts Jack receives in "Jack and His Bargains"? What specific details in the rest of the story support these interpretations?
5. How does Bettelheim interpret the phrase "a proper man" from the end of "Jack and His Bargains"? How else might this phrase be interpreted?
6. In paragraph 13, Bettelheim suggests that the loss of milk at the beginning of "Jack and the Beanstalk" arouses a child's memory of being weaned. Is this a credible claim? How would Bettelheim go about supporting such a claim? What evidence would he use?
7. According to Bettelheim, what encourages Jack's entrance into fantasy and the climb up the beanstalk?
8. In paragraph 21, what kind of higher existence is Bettelheim imagining?

QUESTIONS ABOUT BETTELHEIM'S RHETORICAL STRATEGIES

1. In structuring this selection, Bettelheim chose to deal with "Jack and His Bargains" before "Jack and the Beanstalk," even though the latter story deals with an earlier stage of the child's maturity, according to Bettelheim. Why did he choose this order?
2. Bettelheim uses male pronouns throughout this selection, even when he is refer-

---

The original "Jack and the Beanstalk" is the odyssey of a boy striving to gain independence from a mother who thinks little of him, and on his own achieving greatness. In the bowdlerized version, Jack does only what another powerful older female, the fairy, orders him to do.

One last example of how those who think they are improving on a traditional fairy tale actually do the opposite. In both versions, when Jack seizes the magic harp, it cries out "Master, Master," awakening the ogre, who then pursues Jack with the intention of killing him. That a talking harp arouses its rightful master when being stolen makes good fairy-tale sense. But what is the child to think of a magic harp which was not only stolen from its rightful master, but stolen by the man who vilely killed him, and which in the process of being regained by his rightful master's son nevertheless arouses the thief and murderer? Changing such details robs the story of its magic impact, as it deprives the magic objects—and everything else that happens in the story—of their symbolic meaning as external representations of inner processes.

ring to a parent. Do you find this to be problematic, or is there a specific and justifiable rhetorical strategy behind this language?

3. Consider the long sentence in paragraph three. Why does Bettelheim choose this construction? What expectations about his readers do you think he has?

4. In paragraph three, Bettelheim asserts that the Jack stories are tales about "the desirability of social and sexual self-assertion." Is it problematic that Bettelheim does not qualify this claim? For example, why does he not write, "One of the ways in which the Jack stories may be interpreted . . ."?

5. Read over Bettelheim's summary of "Jack and His Bargains" (paragraph 5–7). How does Bettelheim's style here differ from that of the rest of the selection? Why would he make these stylistic changes for his summary?

6. Bettelheim makes many asides that he puts into the form of footnotes. In general, what kind of information is included in these notes? Is his practice justified?

7. What does Bettelheim use as evidence for the claims he makes? Which discourse communities might not accept the kind of evidence he uses?

8. The last four paragraphs of this essay seem in some ways to provide a summary of the argument. How else do they serve to conclude the piece?

WRITING FROM WITHIN AND ABOUT THE ARTS: THE STUDY OF FOLKLORE

Writing for Yourself

1. In your journal, reflect on whether or not you believe people can be helped on their conscious levels by what they experience on their unconscious levels.

2. In your journal, reflect on a fairy tale that you remember from your childhood. What is it about that tale that makes you still remember it?

Writing for Nonacademic Audiences

1. Write a 250-word response essay to Bettelheim, either supporting or attacking his approach to the Jack tales.

Writing for Academic Audiences

1. For a course in folk literature, read several different versions of "Snow White." Then prepare three retellings that you will read to your peers in class. One should emphasize Freudian elements. A second should emphasize feminist elements. A third should be a bowdlerized version. Prepare a brief concluding statement in which you tell which version you find to be most effective for a child audience.

2. For a course in folk literature, write a 750-word essay on the origins of the Jack tales, considering especially their audience.

3. For an introductory course in literary criticism, write a 750-word essay in which you interpret "Jack and the Beanstalk" as a Marxist critic might approach the tale.

4. Bettelheim's approach to the folktale suggests that literature can embed psycho-

logical truth in its images and plot situations. Examine the following tale collected by the Grimm brothers and then write a 1,000-word essay examining the ways in which the story conveys psychological truth.

THE ELF

There was once upon a time a rich King who had three daughters, who daily 1
went to walk in the palace garden. The King was a great lover of all kinds of
fine trees, but there was one for which he had such an affection that if anyone
gathered an apple from it he wished him a hundred fathoms under ground.
And when harvest time came, the apples on this tree were all as red as blood.
The three daughters went every day beneath the tree, and looked to see if the
wind had not blown down an apple, but they never by any chance found
one, and the tree was so loaded with them that it was almost breaking, and
the branches hung down to the ground.

    The King's youngest child had a great desire for an apple, and said to 2
her sisters, "Our father loves us far too much to wish us underground; it is
my belief that he would only do that to people who were strangers." And
while she was speaking, the child plucked off quite a large apple, and ran to
her sisters, saying, "Just taste, my dear little sisters, for never in my life have
I tasted anything so delightful." Then the two other sisters also ate some of
the apple, whereupon all three sank deep down into the earth, where they
could hear no cock crow.

    When mid-day came, the King wished to call them to come to dinner, 3
but they were nowhere to be found. He sought them everywhere in the palace and garden, but could not find them. Then he was much troubled, and
made known to the whole land that whosoever brought his daughters back
again should have one of them to wife. Hereupon so many young men went
about the country in search, that there was no counting them, for every one
loved the three children because they were so kind to all, and so fair of face.
Three young huntsmen also went out, and when they had traveled about for
eight days, they arrived at a great castle, in which were beautiful apartments, and in one room a table was laid on which were delicate dishes which
were still so warm that they were smoking, but in the whole of the castle no
human being was either to be seen or heard.

    They waited there for half a day, and the food still remained warm and 4
smoking, and at length they were so hungry that they sat down and ate, and
agreed with each other that they would stay and live in that castle, and that
one of them, who should be chosen by casting lots, should remain in the
house, and the two others seek the King's daughters. They cast lots, and the

lot fell on the eldest; so next day the two younger went out to seek, and the eldest had to stay at home.

At mid-day came a small, small mannikin and begged for a piece of bread; then the huntsman took the bread which he had found there, and cut a round off the loaf and was about to give it to him, but while he was giving it to the mannikin, the latter let it fall, and asked the huntsman to be so good as to give him that piece again. The huntsman was about to do so and stooped, on which the mannikin took a stick, seized him by the hair, and gave him a good beating.

Next day, the second stayed at home, and he fared no better. When the two others returned in the evening, the eldest said, "Well, how have you got on?" "Oh, very badly," said he, and then they lamented their misfortune together, but they said nothing about it to the youngest, for they did not like him at all, and always called him Stupid Hans, because he did not exactly belong to the forest.

On the third day, the youngest stayed at home, and again the little mannikin came and begged for a piece of bread. When the youth gave it to him, the elf let it fall as before, and asked him to be so good as to give him that piece again. Then said Hans to the little mannikin, "What! canst thou not pick up that piece thyself? If thou wilt not take as much trouble as that for thy daily bread, thou dost not deserve to have it." Then the mannikin grew very angry and said he was to do it, but the huntsman would not, and took my dear mannikin, and gave him a thorough beating. Then the mannikin screamed terribly, and cried, "Stop, stop, and let me go, and I will tell thee where the King's daughters are."

When Hans heard that, he left off beating him and the mannikin told him that he was an earth-mannikin, and that there were more than a thousand like him, and that if he would go with him he would show him where the King's daughters were. Then he showed him a deep well, but there was no water in it. And the elf said that he knew well that the companions Hans had with him did not intend to deal honorably with him; therefore if he wished to deliver the King's children, he must do it alone. The two other brothers would also be very glad to recover the King's daughters, but they did not want to have any trouble or danger. Hans was therefore to take a large basket, and he must seat himself in it with his hanger and a bell, and be let down. Below were three rooms, and in each of them was a Princess, with a many-headed dragon, whose heads she was to comb and trim, but he must cut them off. And having said all this, the elf vanished.

When it was evening the two brothers came and asked how he had got on, and he said, "pretty well so far," and that he had seen no one except at mid-day when a little mannikin had come who had begged for a piece of bread, that he had given some to him, but that the mannikin had let it fall and had asked him to pick it up again; but as he did not choose to do that, the elf had begun to lose his temper, and that he had done what he ought not, and had given the elf a beating, on which he had told him where the King's daughters were. Then the two were so angry at this that they grew green and yellow.

Next morning they went to the well together, and drew lots who should 10 first seat himself in the basket, and again the lot fell on the eldest, and he was to seat himself in it, and take the bell with him. Then he said, "If I ring, you must draw me up again immediately." When he had gone down for a short distance, he rang, and they at once drew him up again. Then the second seated himself in the basket, but he did just the same as the first, and then it was the turn of the youngest, but he let himself be lowered quite to the bottom. When he had got out of the basket, he took his hanger, and went and stood outside the first door and listened, and heard the dragon snoring quite loudly. He opened the door slowly, and one of the Princesses was sitting there, and had nine dragon's heads lying upon her lap, and was combing them. Then he took his hanger and hewed at them, and the nine fell off. The Princess sprang up, threw her arms round his neck, embraced and kissed him repeatedly, and took her stomacher, which was made of red gold, and hung it round his neck. Then he went to the second Princess, who had a dragon with five heads to comb, and delivered her also, and to the youngest, who had a dragon with four heads, he went likewise. And they all rejoiced, and embraced him and kissed him without stopping.

Then he rang very loud, so that those above heard him, and he placed 11 the Princesses one after the other in the basket, and had them all drawn up, but when it came to his own turn he remembered the words of the elf, who had told him that his comrades did not mean well by him. So he took a great stone which was lying there, and placed it in the basket, and when it was about half way up, his false brothers above cut the rope, so that the basket with the stone fell to the ground, and they thought that he was dead, and ran away with the three Princesses, making them promise to tell their father that it was they who had delivered them, and then they went to the King, and each demanded a Princess in marriage.

In the meantime the youngest huntsman was wandering about the three 12 chambers in great trouble, fully expecting to have to end his days there, when he saw, hanging on the wall, a flute; then said he, "Why do you hang there, no one can be merry here?" He looked at the dragon's head likewise and said, "You cannot help me now." He walked backwards and forwards for such a long time that he made the surface of the ground quite smooth. At last other thoughts came to his mind, and he took the flute from the wall, and played a few notes on it, and suddenly a number of elves appeared, and with every note that he sounded one more came.

He played until the room was entirely filled. They all asked what he 13 desired, so he said he wished to get above ground back to daylight, on which they seized him by every hair that grew on his head, and thus they flew with him on to the earth again. When he was above ground, he at once went to

the King's palace just as the wedding of one Princess was about to be celebrated, and he went to the room where the King and his three daughters
were. When the Princesses saw him they fainted. Hereupon the King was
angry, and ordered him to be put in prison at once, because he thought he
must have done some injury to the children. When the Princesses came to
themselves, however, they entreated the King to set him free again. The King
asked why, and they said that they were not allowed to tell that, but their
father said that they were to tell it to the stove. And he went out, listened at
the door, and heard everything. Then he caused the two brothers to be hanged
on the gallows, and to the third he gave his youngest daughter, and on that
occasion I wore a pair of glass shoes, and I struck them against a stone, and
they said, "Klink," and were broken.

Tzvetan Todorov

(b. 1939)

Tzvetan Todorov was born in Sofia, Bulgaria, where he spent most of his early life, eventually taking an M.A. at the University of Sofia. Later Todorov moved to Paris, where he earned two doctorates from the University of Paris. He stayed in Paris, becoming recognized as a literary theorist and an authority on Slavic literature. Since 1968 he has worked at the Centre Nationale de la Recherche Scientifique in Paris.

Among literary theorists, Todorov has worked mainly within the discourse community of structuralists. In fact, he played a major role in forming this community with his translations into French of the work of the Russian Formalists. Taking their lead from scholars such as Charles Sanders Peirce and Ferdinand de Saussure, structuralists see nearly all cultural phenomena, and especially language, as manifesting underlying systems of signification.

Such systems have elemental units of meaning, and one of the structuralists' goals is to try to discover the elemental units of meaning of whatever phenomenon they are investigating, be it a popular spectator sport, an advertising campaign, or a work of literature. Such systems also have rules for how the basic units of meaning can be combined. Structuralists often speak and write of the "grammar" or "grammars" of various phenomena, meaning by grammar *the set of rules that govern how elemental units of meaning can be combined. Once such grammars are constructed, it is natural for structuralists to work at comparisons and classifications, trying to show how the resources for and organizations of meaning for one cultural phenomenon compare to those for another. Underlying all this activity are assumptions that most human beings organize experience in similar ways.*

The following selection comes from Todorov's The Poetics of Prose. *In it, Todorov examines different kinds of detective fiction.*

THE TYPOLOGY OF DETECTIVE FICTION

Detective fiction cannot be subdivided into kinds. It merely offers historically different forms.

Boileau and Narcejac
Le Roman policier, 1964

If I use this observation as the epigraph to an article dealing precisely with 1 "kinds" of "detective fiction," it is not to emphasize my disagreement with the authors in question, but because their attitude is very widespread; hence it is the first thing we must confront. Detective fiction has nothing to do with this question: for nearly two centuries, there has been a powerful reaction in literary studies against the very notion of genre.* We write either about literature in general or about a single work, and it is a tacit convention that to classify several works in a genre is to devalue them. There is a good historical explanation for this attitude: literary reflection of the classical period, which concerned genres more than works, also manifested a penalizing tendency— a work was judged poor if it did not sufficiently obey the rules of its genre. Hence such criticism sought not only to describe genres but also to prescribe them; the grid of genre preceded literary creation instead of following it.

The reaction was radical: the romantics and their present-day descen- 2 dants have refused not only to conform to the rules of the genres (which was indeed their privilege) but also to recognize the very existence of such a notion. Hence the theory of genres has remained singularly undeveloped until very recently. Yet now there is a tendency to seek an intermediary between the too-general notion of literature and those individual objects which are works. The delay doubtless comes from the fact that typology implies and is implied by the description of these individual works; yet this task of description is still far from having received satisfactory solutions. So long as we cannot describe the structure of works, we must be content to compare certain measurable elements, such as meter. Despite the immediate interest in an investigation of genres (as Albert Thibaudet remarked, such an investigation concerns the problem of universals), we cannot undertake it without first elaborating structural description: only the criticism of the classical period could permit itself to deduce genres from abstract logical schemas.

An additional difficulty besets the study of genres, one which has to do 3 with the specific character of every esthetic norm. The major work creates, in a sense, a new genre and at the same time transgresses the previously valid

---

* *Genre* refers to a category, such as epic poetry, that literary works have traditionally been assigned to.

rules of the genre. The genre of *The Charterhouse of Parma*,* that is, the norm to which this novel refers, is not the French novel of the early nineteenth century; it is the genre "Stendhalian novel" which is created by precisely this work and a few others. One might say that every great book establishes the existence of two genres, the reality of two norms: that of the genre it transgresses, which dominated the preceding literature, and that of the genre it creates.

Yet there is a happy realm where this dialectical contradiction between   4 the work and its genre does not exist: that of popular literature. As a rule, the literary masterpiece does not enter any genre save perhaps its own; but the masterpiece of popular literature is precisely the book which best fits its genre. Detective fiction has its norms; to "develop" them is also to disappoint them: to "improve upon" detective fiction is to write "literature," not detective fiction. The whodunit par excellence is not the one which transgresses the rules of the genre, but the one which conforms to them: *No Orchids for Miss Blandish* is an incarnation of its genre, not a transcendence. If we had properly described the genres of popular literature, there would no longer be an occasion to speak of its masterpieces. They are one and the same thing; the best novel will be the one about which there is nothing to say. This is a generally unnoticed phenomenon, whose consequences affect every esthetic category. We are today in the presence of a discrepancy between two essential manifestations; no longer is there one single esthetic norm in our society, but two; the same measurements do not apply to "high" art and "popular" art.

The articulation of genres within detective fiction therefore promises to   5 be relatively easy. But we must begin with the description of "kinds," which also means with their delimitation. We shall take as our point of departure the classic detective fiction which reached its peak between the two world wars and is often called the whodunit. Several attempts have already been made to specify the rules of this genre (we shall return below to S. S. Van Dine's twenty rules); but the best general characterization I know is the one Butor† gives in his own novel *Passing Time (L'Emploi du temps)*. George Burton, the author of many murder mysteries, explains to the narrator that "all detective fiction is based on two murders of which the first, committed by the murderer, is merely the occasion for the second, in which he is the victim of the pure and unpunishable murderer, the detective," and that "the narrative . . . superimposes two temporal series: the days of the investigation which begin with the crime, and the days of the drama which lead up to it."

At the base of the whodunit we find a duality, and it is this duality   6 which will guide our description. This novel contains not one but two stories:

---

* *The Charterhouse of Parma* (1839) is a historical novel by Stendhal (pen name of Marie Henri Beyle, 1783–1842).
† Michel Butor (b. 1926) is a French novelist and essayist.

the story of the crime and the story of the investigation. In their purest form, these two stories have no point in common. Here are the first lines of a "pure" whodunit:

> a small green index-card on which is typed: 7
>   Odel, Margaret.
> 184 W. Seventy-first Street. Murder: Strangled about
> 11 P.M. Apartment robbed. Jewels stolen. Body found by
> Amy Gibson, maid
>   [S. S. Van Dine, *The "Canary" Murder Case*]

The first story, that of the crime, ends before the second begins. But 8 what happens in the second? Not much. The characters of this second story, the story of the investigation, do not act, they learn. Nothing can happen to them: a rule of the genre postulates the detective's immunity. We cannot imagine Hercule Poirot* or Philo Vance† threatened by some danger, attacked, wounded, even killed. The hundred and fifty pages which separate the discovery of the crime from the revelation of the killer are devoted to a slow apprenticeship: we examine clue after clue, lead after lead. The whodunit thus tends toward a purely geometric architecture: Agatha Christie's *Murder on the Orient Express*, for example, offers twelve suspects; the book consists of twelve chapters, and again twelve interrogations, a prologue, and an epilogue (that is, the discovery of the crime and the discovery of the killer).

This second story, the story of the investigation, thereby enjoys a partic- 9 ular status. It is no accident that it is often told by a friend of the detective, who explicitly acknowledges that he is writing a book; the second story consists, in fact, in explaining how this very book came to be written. The first story ignores the book completely, that is, it never confesses its literary nature (no author of detective fiction can permit himself to indicate directly the imaginary character of the story, as it happens in "literature"). On the other hand, the second story is not only supposed to take the reality of the book into account, but it is precisely the story of that very book.

We might further characterize these two stories by saying that the first— 10 the story of the crime—tells "what really happened," whereas the second— the story of the investigation—explains "how the reader (or the narrator) has come to know about it." But these definitions concern not only the two stories in detective fiction, but also two aspects of every literary work which the Russian Formalists‡ isolated forty years ago. They distinguished, in fact, the *fable* (story) from the *subject* (plot) of a narrative: the story is what has happened in life, the plot is the way the author presents it to us. The first notion corresponds to the reality evoked, to events similar to those which take place in our lives; the second, to the book itself, to the narrative, to the literary

---

* The famous Belgian detective created by Agatha Christie.
† The New York City detective created by S. S. Van Dine.
‡ Russian literary theorists during the 1920s; they were interested more in the aesthetic and formal nature of art than in its social aspects.

devices the author employs. In the story, there is no inversion in time, actions follow their natural order; in the plot, the author can present results before their causes, the end before the beginning. These two notions do not characterize two parts of the story or two different works, but two aspects of one and the same work; they are two points of view about the same thing. How does it happen then that detective fiction manages to make both of them present, to put them side by side?

To explain this paradox, we must first recall the special status of the two stories. The first, that of the crime, is in fact the story of an absence: its most accurate characteristic is that it cannot be immediately present in the book. In other words, the narrator cannot transmit directly the conversations of the characters who are implicated, nor describe their actions: to do so, he must necessarily employ the intermediary of another (or the same) character who will report, in the second story, the words heard or the actions observed. The status of the second story is, as we have seen, just as excessive; it is a story which has no importance in itself, which serves only as a mediator between the reader and the story of the crime. Theoreticians of detective fiction have always agreed that style, in this type of literature, must be perfectly transparent, imperceptible; the only requirement it obeys is to be simple, clear, direct. It has even been attempted—significantly—to suppress this second story altogether. One publisher put out real dossiers, consisting of police reports, interrogations, photographs, fingerprints, even locks of hair; these "authentic" documents were to lead the reader to the discovery of the criminal (in case of failure, a sealed envelope, pasted on the last page, gave the answer to the puzzle: for example, the judge's verdict).

We are concerned then in the whodunit with two stories of which one is absent but real, the other present but insignificant. This presence and this absence explain the existence of the two in the continuity of the narrative. The first involves so many conventions and literary devices (which are in fact the "plot" aspects of the narrative) that the author cannot leave them unexplained. These devices are, we may note, of essentially two types, temporal inversions and individual "points of view": the tenor of each piece of information is determined by the person who transmits it, no observation exists without an observer; the author cannot, by definition, be omniscient as he was in the classical novel. The second story then appears as a place where all these devices are justified and "naturalized": to give them a "natural" quality, the author must explain that he is writing a book! And to keep this second story from becoming opaque, from casting a useless shadow on the first, the style is to be kept neutral and plain, to the point where it is rendered imperceptible.

Now let us examine another genre within detective fiction, the genre created in the United States just before and particularly after World War II, and which is published in France under the rubric "*série noire*" (the thriller); this kind of detective fiction fuses the two stories or, in other words, suppresses the first and vitalizes the second. We are no longer told about a crime anterior to the moment of the narrative; the narrative coincides with the action. No thriller is presented in the form of memoirs: there is no point reached where the narrator comprehends all past events, we do not even know if he will reach the end of the story alive. Prospection takes the place of retrospection.

There is no story to be guessed; and there is no mystery, in the sense 14 that it was present in the whodunit. But the reader's interest is not thereby diminished; we realize here that two entirely different forms of interest exist. The first can be called *curiosity*; it proceeds from effect to cause: starting from a certain effect (a corpse and certain clues) we must find its cause (the culprit and his motive). The second form is *suspense*, and here the movement is from cause to effect: we are first shown the causes, the initial *données* (gangsters preparing a heist), and our interest is sustained by the expectation of what will happen, that is, certain effects (corpses, crimes, fights). This type of interest was inconceivable in the whodunit, for its chief characters (the detective and his friend the narrator) were, by definition, immunized: nothing could happen to them. The situation is reversed in the thriller: everything is possible, and the detective risks his health, if not his life.

I have presented the opposition between the whodunit and the thriller 15 as an opposition between two stories and a single one; but this is a logical, not a historical classification. The thriller did not need to perform this specific transformation in order to appear on the scene. Unfortunately for logic, genres are not constituted in conformity with structural descriptions; a new genre is created around an element which was not obligatory in the old one: the two encode different elements. For this reason the poetics of classicism was wasting its time seeking a logical classification of genres. The contemporary thriller has been constituted not around a method of presentation but around the milieu represented, around specific characters and behavior; in other words, its constitutive character is in its themes. This is how it was described, in 1945, by Marcel Duhamel, its promoter in France: in it we find "violence—in all its forms, and especially the most shameful—beatings, killings. . . . Immorality is as much at home here as noble feelings. . . . There is also love—preferably vile—violent passion, implacable hatred." Indeed it is around these few constants that the thriller is constituted: violence, generally sordid crime, the amorality of the characters. Necessarily, too, the "second story," the one taking place in the present, occupies a central place. But the suppression of the first story is not an obligatory feature: the early authors of the thriller, Dashiell Hammett and Raymond Chandler, preserve the element of mystery; the important thing is that it now has a secondary function, subordinate and no longer central as in the whodunit.

This restriction in the milieu described also distinguishes the thriller 16 from the adventure story, though this limit is not very distinct. We can see that the properties listed up to now—danger, pursuit, combat—are also to be found in an adventure story; yet the thriller keeps its autonomy. We must distinguish several reasons for this: the relative effacement of the adventure story and its replacement by the spy novel; then the thriller's tendency toward the marvelous and the exotic, which brings it closer on the one hand to the travel narrative, and on the other to contemporary science fiction; last, a tendency to description which remains entirely alien to the detective novel. The difference in the milieu and behavior described must be added to these other distinctions, and precisely this difference has permitted the thriller to be constituted as a genre.

One particularly dogmatic author of detective fiction, S. S. Van Dine, 17 laid down, in 1928, twenty rules to which any self-respecting author of detective fiction must conform. These rules have been frequently reproduced since then (see for instance the book, already quoted from, by Boileau and Narcejac*) and frequently contested. Since we are not concerned with prescribing procedures for the writer but with describing the genres of detective fiction, we may profitably consider these rules a moment. In their original form, they are quite prolix and may be readily summarized by the eight following points:

1. The novel must have at most one detective and one criminal, and at least one 18 victim (a corpse).
2. The culprit must not be a professional criminal, must not be the detective, must 19 kill for personal reasons.
3. Love has no place in detective fiction.   20
4. The culprit must have a certain importance: 21
   (a) in life: not be a butler or a chambermaid.
   (b) in the book: must be one of the main characters.
5. Everything must be explained rationally; the fantastic is not admitted.   22
6. There is no place for descriptions nor for psychological analyses.   23
7. With regard to information about the story, the following homology must be 24 observed: "author: reader = criminal: detective."
8. Banal situations and solutions must be avoided (Van Dine lists ten).   25

If we compare this list with the description of the thriller, we will dis- 26 cover an interesting phenomenon. A portion of Van Dine's rules apparently refers to all detective fiction, another portion to the whodunit. This distribution coincides, curiously, with the field of application of the rules: those which concern the themes, the life represented (the "first story"), are limited to the whodunit (rules 1–4a); those which refer to discourse, to the book (to the "second story"), are equally valid for the thriller (rules 4b–7; rule 8 is of a much broader generality). Indeed in the thriller there is often more than one detective (Chester Himes's *For Love of Imabelle*) and more than one criminal (James Hadley Chase's *The Fast Buck*). The criminal is almost obliged to be a professional and does not kill for personal reasons ("the hired killer"); further, he is often a policeman. Love—"preferably vile"—also has

* In the epigraph to this essay.

its place here. On the other hand, fantastic explanations, descriptions, and psychological analyses remain banished; the criminal must still be one of the main characters. As for rule 7, it has lost its pertinence with the disappearance of the double story. This proves that the development has chiefly affected the thematic part, and not the structure of the discourse itself (Van Dine does not note the necessity of mystery and consequently of the double story, doubtless considering this self-evident).

Certain apparently insignificant features can be codified in either type 27 of detective fiction: a genre unites particularities located on different levels of generality. Hence the thriller, to which any accent on literary devices is alien, does not reserve its surprises for the last lines of the chapter; whereas the whodunit, which legalizes the literary convention by making it explicit in its "second story," will often terminate the chapter by a particular revelation ("You are the murderer," Poirot says to the narrator of *The Murder of Roger Ackroyd*). Further, certain stylistic features in the thriller belong to it specifically. Descriptions are made without rhetoric, coldly, even if dreadful things are being described; one might say "cynically" ("Joe was bleeding like a pig. Incredible that an old man could bleed so much," Horace McCoy, *Kiss Tomorrow Goodbye*). The comparisons suggest a certain brutality (description of hands: "I felt that if ever his hands got around my throat, they would make the blood gush out of my ears," Chase, *You Never Know with Women*). It is enough to read such a passage to be sure one has a thriller in hand.

It is not surprising that between two such different forms there has de- 28 veloped a third, which combines their properties: the suspense novel. It keeps the mystery of the whodunit and also the two stories, that of the past and that of the present; but it refuses to reduce the second to a simple detection of the truth. As in the thriller, it is this second story which here occupies the central place. The reader is interested not only by what has happened but also by what will happen next; he wonders as much about the future as about the past. The two types of interest are thus united here—there is the curiosity to learn how past events are to be explained; and there is also the suspense: what will happen to the main characters? These characters enjoyed an immunity, it will be recalled, in the whodunit; here they constantly risk their lives. Mystery has a function different from the one it had in the whodunit: it is actually a point of departure, the main interest deriving from the second story, the one taking place in the present.

Historically, this form of detective fiction appeared at two moments: it 29 served as transition between the whodunit and the thriller and it existed at the same time as the latter. To these two periods correspond two subtypes of the suspense novel. The first, which might be called "the story of the vulnerable detective" is mainly illustrated by the novels of Hammett and Chandler. Its chief feature is that the detective loses his immunity, gets beaten up, badly hurt, constantly risks his life, in short, he is integrated into the universe of the other characters, instead of being an independent observer as the reader is (we recall Van Dine's detective-as-reader analogy). These novels are habitually classified as thrillers because of the milieu they describe, but we see that their composition brings them closer to suspense novels.

The second type of suspense novel has in fact sought to get rid of the 30 conventional milieu of professional crime and to return to the personal crime on the whodunit, though conforming to the new structure. From it has resulted a novel we might call "the story of the suspect-as-detective." In this case, a crime is committed in the first pages and all the evidence in the hands of the police points to a certain person (who is the main character). In order to prove his innocence, this person must himself find the real culprit, even if he risks his life in doing so. We might say that, in this case, this character is at the same time the detective, the culprit (in the eyes of the police), and the victim (potential victim of the real murderers). Many novels by William Irish, Patrick Quentin, and Charles Williams are constructed on this model.

It is quite difficult to say whether the forms we have just described 31 correspond to the stages of an evolution or else can exist simultaneously. The fact that we can encounter several types by the same author, such as Arthur Conan Doyle or Maurice Leblanc, preceding the great flowering of detective fiction, would make us tend to the second solution, particularly since these three forms coexist today. But it is remarkable that the evolution of detective fiction in its broad outlines has followed precisely the succession of these forms. We might say that at a certain point detective fiction experiences as an unjustified burden the constraints of this or that genre and gets rid of them in order to constitute a new code. The rule of the genre is perceived as a constraint once it becomes pure form and is no longer justified by the structure of the whole. Hence in novels by Hammett and Chandler, mystery had become a pure pretext, and the thriller which succeeded the whodunit got rid of it, in order to elaborate a new form of interest, suspense, and to concentrate on the description of a milieu. The suspense novel, which appeared after the great years of the thriller, experienced this milieu as a useless attribute, and retained only the suspense itself. But it has been necessary at the same time to reinforce the plot and to re-establish the former mystery. Novels which have tried to do without both mystery and the milieu proper to the thriller—for example, Francis Iles's *Premeditations* and Patricia Highsmith's *The Talented Mr Ripley*—are too few to be considered a separate genre.

Here we reach a final question: what is to be done with the novels which 32 do not fit our classification? It is no accident, it seems to me, that the reader habitually considers novels such as those I have just mentioned marginal to the genre, an intermediary form between detective fiction and the novel itself. Yet if this form (or some other) becomes the germ of a new genre of detective fiction, this will not in itself constitute an argument against the classification proposed; as I have already said, the new genre is not necessarily constituted by the negation of the main feature of the old, but from a different complex of properties, not by necessity logically harmonious with the first form.

QUESTIONS ABOUT TODOROV'S DISCOURSE COMMUNITY AND HIS CONCERNS IN THIS ESSAY

1. How does Todorov say that great literature differs from popular literature in the matter of genre? Do you agree with him?
2. What two stories does Todorov say the typical detective novel contains?
3. Why can detective novels not have omniscient narrators?
4. Why does Todorov say that the second story in a detective novel must be written in a neutral and plain style?
5. Explain the distinctions Todorov draws between the whodunit kind of detective fiction and the thriller kind of detective fiction.
6. How does Todorov say a new genre of detective fiction grows out of an established one?
7. How easy would it be to do the kind of critical work that Todorov does here? What, above all else, would be necessary to do this kind of work?
8. Where do you see structuralist methods most clearly in this essay?

QUESTIONS ABOUT TODOROV'S RHETORICAL STRATEGIES

1. How does the epigraph function in this essay? Is it necessary?
2. In general, what kinds of evidence does Todorov use in this essay? How would you evaluate it?
3. How does Todorov use Van Dine's rules for authors of detective fiction? Do you have any objections to his use of these rules?
4. Todorov seems very confident in this essay. What specific elements contribute to the tone of this piece?
5. In making one of his points, Todorov uses the words "We might further characterize . . ." (paragraph 10). What effect does the word *might* have on the tone of this piece?
6. Many commentators call Todorov's style clear and economical. Would you agree? Why or why not?
7. Would a summary of Todorov's main points and distinctions have helped you at the end of this essay? Why do you think he does not include one?

WRITING FROM WITHIN AND ABOUT THE ARTS: LITERARY AND FILM CRITICISM

Writing for Yourself

1. In your journal, reflect on what you read purely for pleasure and on why that material gives you pleasure.
2. In your journal, reflect on the assumptions that writers of detective fiction make about order in the world.

Writing for Nonacademic Audiences

1. On a trip home from college, you get into a debate with your older brother, who never went to college, on why one should read great literature, not just popular fiction. Your brother does not see this distinction, so when you get back

to school, you write him a letter in which you try to make clear to him how great literature differs from popular fiction.

2. A reviewer for your college newspaper recently wrote a scathingly negative review of the worth of detective fiction. You like detective fiction, so you decide to write a letter of rebuttal to the newspaper.

Writing for Academic Audiences

1. You have been asked to talk to a high school modern media class about recent movies that seem intended to terrify audiences. You decide to show how all these movies use the same plot formula. Prepare the text for this talk; the talk may last no longer than twenty minutes.

2. For a college class in world literature, read a detective novel and write a 500-word classification of it according to Todorov's categories. If the categories do not fit perfectly, explain how they should be changed.

3. For a college class introducing students to literature, you have been assigned to write a 750-word paper defining a literary genre.

4. For a college class introducing students to literature, write a 1,000-word essay in which you state and defend your position on what great literature is supposed to do for those who read it.

5. Choose one of the following novels and, for a course in popular literature, write a 1,000-word essay showing how that novel pushes the conventions of the detective genre without breaking those conventions.

P. D. James, *A Taste of Death*
Agatha Christie, *The Final Curtain*
Dorothy Sayers, *Strong Poison*
G. K. Chesterton, *The Man Who Was Thursday*
Umberto Eco, *The Name of the Rose*

Tania Modleski

(b. 1949)

In Rear Window, *a recently rereleased film directed by Alfred Hitchcock, the main characters, Jeff and Lisa, struggle to find the parameters of their relationship. Outside the rear window of Jeff's apartment, similar struggles are being enacted: One woman yearns for male companionship, another fights off that companionship, a married couple encounters extremes of emotion, and an older couple's emotion leads to murder. The method of the murder and the identity of the murderer are all given in the film; a spectator is not unraveling a mystery. What is most interesting about the film is the set of connections that are established among the various characters.*

In The Women Who Knew Too Much, *Tania Modleski examines these relationships from the viewpoint of the feminist film critic. A professor of film and literature in the English Department of the University of Southern California, Modleski asserts that Hitchcock as a director is deeply ambivalent about his women characters. Though he has been depicted as both a misogynist and one who is sympathetic to women's roles in a male-dominated society, Modleski finds neither extreme helpful. She asserts that Hitchcock's complicated attitude towards femininity, which she explores in the following examination of* Rear Window, *has severe implications for an audience viewing Hitchcock's films.*

Modleski asks some of the central questions that feminist film criticism has been dealing with in the last decade. Is film narrative generally male dominated in terms of its point of view and structure? Is the spectator of Hollywood films generally assumed to be male, and what implications might that have for the interpretation of films? Is the female spectator participating in a passive role, both as viewer and as one who is being viewed? How should women respond to what Modleski calls patriarchal cinema? In this first full-length feminist study of Hitchcock's films, and particularly in her discussion of Rear Window, *Modleski deals with each of these questions.*

The following selection is chapter 5, "The Master's Dollhouse: Rear Window," *of Tania Modleski's* The Women Who Knew Too Much: Hitchcock and Feminist Theory.

THE MASTER'S DOLLHOUSE:
REAR WINDOW

In "Visual Pleasure and Narrative Cinema." Laura Mulvey uses two Hitch- 1
cock films to exemplify her theory. According to Mulvey, both *Rear Window*
(1954) and *Vertigo* (1958) are films "cut to the measure of male desire"—
tailored, that is, to the fears and fantasies of the male spectator, who, because
of the threat of castration posed by the woman's image, needs to see her
fetishized and controlled in the course of the narrative.* Certainly, these two
films appear perfectly to support Mulvey's thesis that classic narrative film
negates woman's view, since each of them seems to confine us to the hero's
vision of events and to insist on that vision by literally stressing the man's
point of view throughout. The film spectator apparently has no choice *but* to
identify with the male protagonist, who exerts an active, controlling gaze
over a passive female object. In *Rear Window*. Mulvey writes, "Lisa's exhi-
bitionism [is] established by her obsessive interest in dress and style, in being
a passive image of visual perfection: Jeffries's voyeurism and activity [are]
established through his work as a photojournalist, a maker of stories and
captor of images. However, his enforced inactivity, binding him to his seat
as a spectator, puts him squarely in the phantasy position of the cinema audience."†

This last observation connects Mulvey to a tradition of criticism of the 2
film that begins with the work of the French critic Jean Douchet and that
sees the film as a metacinematic commentary: spectators identifying with the
chair-bound, voyeuristic protagonist find themselves in complicity with his
guilty desires.‡ Because of Hitchcock's relentless insistence on the male gaze,
even critics like Robin Wood, who are anxious to save the film for feminism,
restrict themselves to discussing the film's critique of the position of the hero
and, by extension, of the *male* spectator whose "phantasy position the hero
occupies."§ But what happens, in the words of a recent relevant article by
Linda Williams, "when the woman looks"?‖ I shall argue, against the grain

---

* Laura Mulvey, "Visual Pleasure and Narrative Cinema," *Screen* 16, no. 3 (1975): 17. [Modle-
ski's note.]

† Mulvey, "Visual Pleasure," p. 16. [Modleski's note.]

‡ Jean Douchet, "Hitch et son Public," *Cahiers du Cinéma*, no. 113 (November 1960): 10. For
the most recent discussion of the film in relation to questions of spectatorship, see R.
Barton Palmer. "The Metafictional Hitchcock: The Experience of Viewing and the Viewing of Experience in *Rear Window* and *Psycho*." *Cinema Journal* 26, no. 2 (Winter 1986):
4–29. [Modleski's note.]

§ Robin Wood, "Fear of Spying," *American Film* (November 1982): 31–32. [Modleski's note.]

‖ Linda Williams, "When the Woman Looks," in *Revision: Essays in Feminist Film Criticism*,
ed . Mary Ann Doane, Patricia Mellencamp, and Williams. The American Film Institute
Monograph Series, Vol. 3 (Frederick, MD: University Publications of America, 1984).
[Modleski's note.]

of critical consensus, that the film actually has something to say about this question.*

Rear Window is the story of photojournalist, L. B. Jeffries (James Stew- 3 art), who, as a result of an accident on the job, is confined to a wheel chair in his apartment, where he whiles away the time spying on his neighbors. These include a middle-aged, alcoholic musician with composer's block; a newlywed couple who spend all their time in bed behind closed shades; a childless couple who sleep on the balcony at night and own a little dog; a voluptuous dancer, "Miss Torso," who practices her suggestive dance routines as she goes about her daily chores; "Miss Lonelyhearts," who fantasizes about gentlemen callers; and Lars Thorwald, a costume jewelry salesman with a nagging, invalid wife.

The film opens with the camera panning the courtyard of a lower east 4 side housing development and then moving back through a window where we see L. B. Jeffries asleep, his chair turned away from the window, beads of sweat on his face. There is a cut to a thermometer, which registers over ninety degrees, and then the camera tilts down Jeffries's body to reveal that his leg is in a cast. The camera proceeds to explore the apartment, calling our attention to some smashed camera equipment, a photograph of a car acci-dent, some other photographs Jeff has taken in his travels, and, finally, a negative of a blonde woman's face followed by a "positive" photograph of her on the cover of *Life* magazine. When Jeff wakes up, he begins to observe his neighbors and then complains on the phone to his editor that if he doesn't get back to the job soon, he's going to do "something drastic like get mar-ried." While he speaks of the horrors of marriage, we watch from his point of view as Thorwald (Raymond Burr) returns home to be greeted by a nag-ging wife.

Soon after, Stella (Thelma Ritter), the insurance company nurse, comes 5 in to give Jeff a massage. She immediately begins to scold him for being a Peeping Tom, and tries to persuade him to marry Lisa Freemont, claiming that his lukewarm attitude to the woman he claims is "too perfect" is abnor-mal. Later that evening, Lisa (Grace Kelly) comes to visit, dressed in an $1100 gown and accompanied by a waiter from the Twenty One Club, who is delivering their dinner. Lisa and Jeff have an argument as he tells her that marriage to him, given his grueling life style and her pampered one, is out of the question. When she goes home, Jeff begins to watch the neighbors again and observes some strange movements on the part of Lars Thorwald. Even-tually Jeff falls asleep, and we see Thorwald and a woman leaving Thor-wald's apartment. The next day Jeff notices that Mrs. Thorwald has gone,

---

*Robert Stam and Roberta Pearson do, however, devote one brief paragraph to this issue in their article, "Hitchcock's *Rear Window*: Reflexivity and the Critique of Voyeurism," *Enclitic* 7, no. 1 (Spring 1983): 143. [Modleski's note.]

and he becomes convinced that Thorwald has murdered his wife—a conviction that becomes more and more obsessive as the film progresses—to the point where he uses first binoculars and then a huge telephoto lens to see more closely. He attempts to persuade Lisa, Stella, and his friend, policeman Tom Doyle (Wendell Corey), of his interpretation of the events across the way. Though Doyle remains skeptical, the women eventually come to accept Jeff's view and actually go looking for clues.

Lisa is caught by Thorwald as she searches his apartment for the wedding ring that will prove Jeff's theory, and Jeff is forced to look helplessly on as Thorwald pushes her around. Jeff warns the police, whom he has just contacted on the phone to alert them that Miss Lonelyhearts is about to take an overdose of pills. The police arrive in time to prevent any harm from befalling Lisa, and they take her to jail. After Jeff sends Stella off with the bail money, he finds himself face to face with the guilty Thorwald, who asks, "What is it you want of me?" and steps forward menacingly. Jeff tries to keep him at bay by popping off flashbulbs in his face, but Thorwald manages to grab him and, during a struggle, Jeff falls to the ground from a window ledge. 6

The film ends with another pan around the courtyard. The various plots featuring the neighbors have been resolved: workmen are repainting the bathroom of Thorwald's apartment, where blood had splattered when Thorwald murdered his wife and cut her up in pieces; Miss Lonelyhearts, whose suicide was prevented when she heard the musician's beautiful song, has formed a relationship with the musician: Miss Torso's little soldier boyfriend Stanley arrives and asks what's in the refrigerator; the childless couple, whose dog was murdered by Thorwald because it was digging in the flower garden where evidence was buried (the dog who "knew too much," as Lisa puts it), have gotten another dog; and the newlywed wife is nagging her husband because he has lost his job. The camera tracks back into the window to show L.B. asleep, as before, only this time both his legs are in casts. The camera movement ends on a medium shot of Lisa lying on Jeff's bed, in pants and shirt, and reading a book entitled *Beyond the High Himalayas*. She steals a glance at Jeff to make sure he is still asleep, puts down the book, and picks up a copy of Harper's *Bazaar*. On the soundtrack is the musician's song, "Lisa," finally completed, like the narrative itself. 7

A number of critics, most of whom center their analyses around the film's critique of voyeurism, have pointed out that the film's protagonist is fixated at an infantile level of sexual development and must in the course of the narrative grow into "mature sexuality": "Jeffries's voyeurism goes hand in hand with an absorbing fear of mature sexuality. Indeed, the film begins by hinting at a serious case of psychosexual pathology. The first image of Jeffries, asleep with hand on thigh is quietly masturbatory, as if he were an 8 invalid who had just abused himself in the dark."* By the end of the film Jeff has supposedly learned his lesson and "has realized the corollary psychic costs of both voyeurism and solitude": he is now ready for the marriage he has all along resisted and for the "mature" sexual relation that this implies. Yet there is a sense in which the image of Lisa in masculine clothes, absorbed in "masculine" interests only places Jeff—and the audience—more squarely than ever in the Imaginary. For as the narrative proceeds, the sexuality of the woman, which is all along presented as threatening, is first combated by the fantasy of female dismemberment and then, finally, by a re-membering of the woman according to the little boy's fantasy that the female is no different from himself.†

Jeff claims that Lisa is "too perfect." On the face of it, of course, this 9 reason for resisting marriage is patently absurd, as Stella does not fail to point out. (This absurdity leads one critic to argue that the project of the film is to stimulate the audience's desire for the couple's union by inducing frustration at "Jeff's indifference to her allure."‡ But, while it may indeed be "unrealistic" that any red-blooded man would reject Grace Kelly, there is a certain psychological plausibility in Jeff's fear of Lisa's "perfection"—a fear that is related to man's fear of women's difference and his suspicion that they may not, after all, be mutilated (imperfect) men, may not be what, as Susan Lurie puts it, *men* would be if they lacked penises—"bereft of sexuality, helpless, incapable."§ Lurie's words certainly describe the situation of Jeff, whose impotence is suggested by the enormous cast on his leg and his consequent inability to move about, so that ultimately he is unable to rescue the woman he loves from danger. By contrast, Lisa Freemont is anything but helpless and incapable, despite Mulvey's characterization of her as a "passive image of visual perfection"—and this is where the "problem" lies.

In our very first view of her, Lisa is experienced as an overwhelmingly 10 powerful presence. Jeff is asleep in his chair, the camera positioned over him, when suddenly an ominous shadow crosses his face. There is a cut to a closeup of Grace Kelly, a vision of loveliness, bending down toward him and us: the princess-to-be waking Sleeping Beauty with a kiss. These two shots—shadow and vibrant image—suggest the underlying threat posed by the desirable woman and recall the negative and positive images of the woman on the

---

*Stam and Pearson, "Hitchcock's *Rear Window*: Reflexivity," p. 140. [Modleski's note.]

†A constant theme in the writings of Stephen Health is the way cinema works to "remember" the (male) spectator: e.g., "the historical reality it encounters [is] a permanent crisis of identity that must be permanently resolved by remembering the history of the individual subject." "Film Performance," *Questions of Cinema* (Bloomington: Indiana University Press, 1981), p. 125. [Modleski's note.]

‡Ruth Perlmutter, "*Rear Window*: A Construction Story," *Journal of Film and Video* 37 (Spring 1985): 59. [Modleski's note.]

§Susan Lurie, "Pornography and the Dread of Women: The Male Sexual Dilemma," *Take Back the Night: Women on Pornography*, ed. Laura Lederer (New York: William Morrow, 1980), p. 166. [Modleski's note.]

cover of *Life*. When Jeff jokingly inquires, "Who are you?" Lisa turns on three lamps, replies, "Reading from top to bottom, Lisa . . . Carol . . . Freemont," and strikes a pose. While the pose confirms the view of her as exhibitionist, her confident nomination of herself reveals her to be extremely self-possessed—in contrast to the man who is known by only one of *his* three names. The two engage in small talk as Lisa sets about preparing the dinner brought in from the Twenty One Club, and Jeff makes continual jibes about married life. Lisa ends the conversation by claiming, "At least you can't say the dinner's not alright," and over a shot of a very appetizing meal, Jeff replies, exasperated, "Lisa, it's perfect, as *always*." In the meantime we have witnessed Thorwald taking dinner in to his wife, who pushes it from her in disgust and flings away the rose he has placed on the tray.

Important parallels are thus set up between Lisa and Thorwald, on the   11 one hand, and Jeff and the wife, on the other. Critics have seldom picked up on this parallelism, preferring instead to stress a symmetry along sexual lines— that is, Jeff's similarity to Thorwald and Lisa's resemblance to the blonde wife. Interestingly, Hitchcock himself was quite explicit about the gender reversal: "The symmetry is the same as in *Shadow of a Doubt*. On one side of the yard you have the Stewart-Kelly couple, with him immobilized by his leg in a cast, while she can move about freely. And on the other side there is a sick woman who's confined to her bed, while the husband comes and goes."* Raymond Bellour has shown how in classic cinema a binary opposition between movement and stasis generally works to establish male superiority in classical narrative cinema.† In *Rear Window*, however, the *woman* is continually shown to be physically superior to the hero, not only in her physical movements but also in her dominance within the frame: she towers over Jeff in nearly every shot in which they both appear.

Given this emphasis on the woman's mobility, freedom, and power, it   12 seems odd that an astute critic like Mulvey sees in the image of Lisa Freemont only a passive object of the male gaze. Mulvey bases her judgment on the fact that Lisa appears to be "obsessed with dress and style," continually putting herself on visual display for Jeff so that he will notice her and turn his gaze away from the neighbors.‡ (In this respect, the "project" of the film resembles that of *Rebecca*, which also deals with a woman's efforts to get the man she loves to look at her.) It is important, however, not to dismiss out of hand Lisa's professional and personal involvement with fashion but to consider all

---

* François Truffaut, *Hitchcock* (New York: Simon and Schuster, 1983), p. 166. [Modleski's note.]
† This point is developed at great length in Raymond Bellour, "*The Birds*: Analysis of a Sequence." Mimeograph. The British Film Institute Advisory Service. n.d. [Modleski's note.]
‡ That he is so reluctant to do so provides an interesting confirmation of Christian Metz's thesis that in narrative cinema, it is the story, rather than any particular character, that "exhibits itself." "History/discourse: a note on two voyeurisms." *Theories of Authorship*, ed. John Caughie (London: Routledge & Kegan Paul, 1981), p. 231. [Modleski's note.]

the ways this involvement *functions* in the narrative. This is no simple matter. For if, on the one hand, woman's concern with fashion quite obviously serves patriarchal interests, on the other hand, this very concern is often denigrated and ridiculed by men (as it is by Jeff throughout the film)—thus putting women in a familiar double bind by which they are first assigned a restricted place in patriarchy and then condemned for occupying it. For feminist criticism to ignore the full complexity of woman's contradictory situation is to risk acquiescing in masculine contempt for female activities. In *A Room of One's Own*, Virginia Woolf suggested that a necessary, if not sufficient, feminist strategy must be to reclaim and revalue women's actual experience under patriarchy. The example Woolf gives of the double literary standard operating against this experience is telling, and relevant to our discussion here: "Speaking crudely, football and sport are important, the worship of fashion, the buying of clothes trivial, and these values are inevitably transferred from life to fiction."* Certainly these two sets of values are counterpoised in the fiction of *Rear Window* (Jeff has, after all, broken his leg at a *sporting* event, where he stepped in front of an oncoming race car to get a spectacular photograph) and are the source of the couple's quarrels. Jeff dwells on the hardships of his manly life style and belittles Lisa's work when she enthusiastically describes her day to him. In the film, then, "fashion" is far from representing woman's unproblematic assimilation to the patriarchal system, but functions to some extent as a signifier of feminine desire and female sexual difference.

Throughout the film, Lisa's exquisite costumes give her the appearance 13 of an alien presence in Jeff's milieu, more strange and marvelous than the various exotic wonders he has encountered in his travels—a strangeness that is fascinating and threatening at the same time. The threat becomes especially evident in the sequence in which Lisa boldly acts on her desire for Jeff and comes to spend the night with him. Significantly, this is the night when she becomes convinced of the truth of Thorwald's guilt. Jeff has just observed Thorwald talking on the phone and sorting through some jewelry, which includes a wedding ring, in his wife's purse. In Hitchcock's films, women's purses (and their jewelry) take on a vulgar Freudian significance relating to female sexuality and to men's attempts to investigate it. One might think, for example, of the purse in the opening closeup shot of *Marnie* (1964) that contains Marnie's "identity" cards and the booty of her theft from patriarchy. In *Rear Window*, Lisa concludes that Mrs. Thorwald *must* have been murdered rather than, as Tom Doyle believes, sent on a trip because no woman would leave behind her favorite purse (to say nothing of her wedding ring). As she muses, Lisa picks up her own designer purse, which we discover is a kind of "trick" purse; it is really a tiny suitcase, and in one of her many lines that sound like sexual double entendres (this one unwittingly echoing the Freud-

---

* Virginia Woolf. *A Room of One's Own* (New York: Harbinger, 1957), p. 77. [Modleski's note.]

ian notion of male and female sexuality, but reversing their values since it takes the latter as the standard), she says, "I'll bet *yours* isn't this small." When she opens the case, an elaborate and expensive negligee comes tumbling out, along with a pair of lovely slippers. The purse connects Lisa to the victimized woman, as does the negligee, since the invalid Mrs. Thorwald was always seen wearing a nightgown; but it also, importantly, connects her to the criminal, Lars Thorwald, and so is an overdetermined image like the images in the Freudian dreamwork. Thus when Tom Doyle comes to Jeff's apartment later in the evening, he keeps casting meaningful glances at the nightgown as if it were an incriminating object; when Jeff asks why Thorwald didn't tell his landlord where he was going, Doyle looks at the suitcase and asks pointedly, "Do you tell *your* landlord everything?" After Doyle has gone, Lisa picks up the suitcase, offering Jeff a "preview of coming attractions," and as she goes into the bathroom to change, she asks, "Do you think Mr. Doyle thought I stole this case?"

Lisa's aggressive sexuality, which is thus humorously labelled "crimi- 14 nal," would seem to provoke in Jeff and the male spectator a retaliatory aggression that finds an outlet in Thorwald's acts of murder and dismemberment. The interpretation of *Rear Window* which critics like Robin Wood take to be primary—that Lars Thorwald's murder of his wife enacts a wish on the part of Jeff to be rid of Lisa—is persuasive as far as it goes, but this wish may further be analyzed as a response to the male fear of impotence and lack. Jeff's impairment—his helplessness, passivity, and invalidism—impel him to construct a story that, in the words of Kaja Silverman (describing the male's psychic trajectory), attempts to "resituate . . . loss at the level of the female anatomy, thereby restoring to the [male] an imaginary wholeness."* Hence the fantasy of female dismemberment that pervades the film: not only are there many gruesome jokes about Lars Thorwald's cutting up his wife's body, but Jeff also names the women across the way according to body parts: Miss Lonelyhearts and Miss Torso—yet another decapitated woman.†

This response is a psychic consequence of Jeff's placement at the mirror 15 stage of development, a placement that, as critics like to point out, makes him very much like Christian Metz's cinematic spectator, who occupies a transcendent, godlike position in relation to the screen.‡ To some extent,

---

* Kaja Silverman. "Lost Objects and Mistaken Subjects: Film Theory's Structuring Lack." *Wide Angle* 7. nos. 1–2 (1985): 24. In many respects. Silverman's position is close to Lurie's. However, Lurie, in common with many "American" feminists (as opposed to French or French-influenced feminists), seems to share to some extent the little boy's fantasy, which he comes to deny, of woman's "wholeness," whereas for Silverman all subjects are inevitably divided, but in patriarchal culture men are able to project division on to women, thus maintaining the illusion of their own completeness. [Modleski's note.]

† On this point see Perlmutter, "*Rear Window*: A Construction Story," p. 58. [Modleski's note.]

‡ Metz speaks of "that *other* mirror, the cinema screen, in this respect a veritable psychical substitute, a prosthesis for our primally dislocated limbs." Quoted in Stam and Pearson. "Hitchcock's *Rear Window*: Reflexivity," p. 138. [Modleski's note.]

however, this analogy between the windows across the way and the cinema screen is misleading, since it is the very *difference* between the world observed by Jeff and the larger-than-life-world of most films that accounts for the strong effect of transcendence evoked by *Rear Window*. For Jeff's world is a miniature one, like a dollhouse—a world, as Susan Stewart writes, "of inversion [wherein] contamination and crudeness are controlled . . . by an absolute manipulation of space and time."* Resembling other fantasy structures, . . . even sleep," the miniature, according to Stewart, "tends toward tableau rather than narrative" and "is against speech, particularly as speech reveals an inner dialectical, or dialogic, nature. . . . All senses are reduced to the visual, a sense which in its transcendence remains ironically and tragically remote" (pp. 66–67).† It is significant that in *Rear Window* only little snatches of conversation may be heard across the way; generally the events proceed mutely, with diegetic noises and music filling the soundtrack (one song even proclaims the primacy of the visual: Bing Crosby's "To See You is to Love You," playing, ironically, while Miss Lonelyhearts entertains a phantom lover). Moreover, the tableau-like spaces of the microscreens across the way find their temporal equivalent in the device of the fade which punctuates the film, likewise creating a sense of a sealed-off fantasy world impervious to the dialogic, "contaminated" world of lived experience.

Just as the cinema, in its resemblance to the mirror at the mirror stage, 16 offers the viewer an image of wholeness and plenitude, so too does the dollhouse world of the apartment buildings Jeff watches. In fact, one of the reasons the miniature is so appealing is that is suggests completeness and "perfection," as in the description of Tom Thumb quoted by Stewart: "No mis-shapen limbs, no contorted features were there, but all was sweet and beautiful" (p. 46; unlike, say, Gulliver's ugly Brobdingnags, whose every imperfection is magnified a hundredfold). But just as this passage must raise the spectre of physical mutilation in order to banish it, the mirror phase—the phase at which the child first "anticipates . . . the apprehension and mastery of its bodily unity"—evokes retroactively in the child a phantasy of *"the-body-in pieces."*‡ This fantasy, according to Lacan, corresponds to the autoerotic stage preceding the formation of the ego (precisely the stage evoked

---

*Susan Stewart, *On Longing: Narratives of the Miniature, the Gigantic, the Souvenir, the Collection* (Baltimore: Johns Hopkins University Press, 1984), p. 63. It is important to recognize, as John Belton has pointed out, that Jeff does not merely watch, but actively manipulates his neighbors, "writing a blackmail letter ('What have you done with her?') which keeps the suspected killer from leaving town and later luring him out of his apartment with a phone call so that it can be searched." *Cinema Stylists* (Metuchen, N.J.: Scarecrow, 1983), p. 15. Stewart hereafter cited in the text. [Modleski's note.]

†In his meditation on the miniature in *The Poetics of Space*, Gaston Bachelard makes a similar point. However, unlike Stewart, Bachelard celebrates the tendency of the miniature to place us in a position of transcendence. See *The Poetics of Space*, trans. Maria Jolas (Boston: Beacon,. 1964), pp. 148–82. [Modleski's note.]

‡Jean Laplanche and J.-B. Pontalis, *The Language of Psychoanalysis*. Trans. Donald Nicholson Smith (London: Hogarth. 1973), p. 251. [Modleski's note.]

by the "quietly masturbatory" image of the "mutilated" Jeff at the film's opening).* On the one hand, then, there is the anticipation of bodily "perfection" and unity which is, importantly, first promised by the body of the woman; on the other hand, the fantasy of dismemberment, a fantasy that gets disavowed by projecting it onto the body of the woman, who, in an interpretation which reverses the state of affairs the male child most fears, eventually comes to be perceived as castrated, mutilated, "imperfect."

Similarly, Jeff's interpretation of the events he sees across the way—his 17 piecing together the fragments of evidence he observes in the Thorwald apartment into a coherent narrative—is designed to reverse the situation in his own apartment, to invalid-ate the female and assure his own control and dominance. It is not enough, however, for him to construct an interpretation that victimizes woman; for patriarchal interpretations to work, they require her assent: man's conviction must become woman's conviction—in a double sense. Those critics who emphasize the film's restriction of point of view to the male character neglect the fact that it increasingly stresses a *dual* point of view, with the reverse shots finding *both* Jeff and Lisa intently staring out the window at the neighbors across the way. It seems possible, then, to consider Lisa as a representative of the *female* spectator at the cinema. And through her, we can ask if it is true that the female spectator simply acquiesces in the male's view or, if, on the contrary, her relationship to the spectacle and the narrative is different from his?

From the outset, Lisa is less interested than Jeff in spying on the neigh- 18 bors and adopting a transcendent and controlling relation to the texts of their lives; rather, she relates to the "characters" through empathy and identification. Early in the film, Jeff jokingly points out a similarity between her apartment and that of Miss Torso, who at the time is seen entertaining several men. Jeff says, "she's like a queen bee with her pick of the drones," to which Lisa responds, "I'd say she's doing a woman's hardest job—juggling wolves." Miss Torso accompanies one of the men onto the balcony where she kisses him briefly and tries to go back inside while he attempts to restrain her. Jeff says, "she sure picked the most prosperous looking one," and Lisa disparages this notion, claiming, "she's not in love with *him*—or with any of them for that matter." When Jeff asks her how she can be so certain, she replies, "you *said* it resembled my apartment didn't you?" Later the same man forces himself on Miss Torso, who has to fight him off, and still later—at the end of the film— Miss Torso's true love, Stanley, will come to visit her. Thus despite critics' emphasis on the film's limited point of view, Lisa and Jeff have very *different* interpretations about the woman's desire in this scene fraught with erotic and violent potential, and it is *Lisa's* interpretation, arrived at through identification, that is ultimately validated.

---

* Jacques Lacan, *Ecrits: A Selection*. trans. Alan Sheridan (New York: Norton, 1977), pp. 1–7. [Modleski's note.]

Whereas Jeff sees Miss Torso as "queen bee," Lisa significantly changes 19 the metaphor: Miss Torso is prey to "wolves." In fact, Lisa's increasing absorption in Jeff's story, her fascination with his murderous, misogynist tale, is accompanied by a corresponding discovery of women's victimization at the hands of men. At one point in the film, Lisa can be seen staring even more intently than Jeff: that is, when Miss Lonelyhearts picks up a young man at a bar and brings him home, only to be assaulted by him. As Lisa stares and Jeff looks away in some embarrassment, the song "Mona Lisa" is heard, sung by drunken revellers at the musician's party. The title of the song suggests an important link between the two women ("is it only cause you're *lonely*, Mona Lisa"), and between the male fantasies that are projected onto woman ("Mona Lisa, Mona Lisa, men have named you"; and "many dreams have been brought to your doorstep") and the brutal reality of male violence to which women are frequently subjected.

Of course, the most brutal act of all is Thorwald's butchering of his 20 wife's body—an act devoutly desired by Jeff—and later, by Lisa herself. At one level, *Rear Window* may be seen as a parable of the dangers involved for women of becoming invested in male stories and male interpretations. Or perhaps we should say "overinvested"—unable, as Mary Ann Doane maintains, to adopt, as men do, the appropriate, voyeuristic distance from the text.* Rather, women supposedly "enter into" films so thoroughly that they tend to confuse the very boundary between fantasy and reality—like Lisa crossing over and merging into the "screen" opposite Jeff's window. This merger is a logical extension of her ready identification with the victimized woman, an identification that actually leads to the solution of the crime. Lisa is able to provide the missing evidence because she claims a special knowledge of women that men lack: the knowledge, in this case, that no woman would go on a trip and leave behind her purse and her wedding ring. Lisa appeals to the authority of Stella, asking her if she would ever go somewhere without her ring, and Stella replies, "They'd have to cut off my finger."

Embarking on a search for this incriminating ring, Lisa becomes trap- 21 ped in Thorwald's apartment when he returns unobserved by Stella and Jeff, who have been preoccupied by the sight of Miss Lonelyhearts about to kill herself. Jeff alerts the police and then watches in agonized helplessness as Lisa is flung about the room by Thorwald. The police arrive in time to prevent another woman from being cut up, and as Lisa stands with her back to the screen—caught, like so many Hitchcock heroines, between the criminal and the legal authorities—she points to the wedding ring on her finger. François Truffaut has admired this touch:

> One of the things I enjoyed in the film was the dual significance of that wedding 22
> ring. Grace Kelly wants to get married but James Stewart doesn't see it that

---

*I again refer the reader to the opening pages of Mary Ann Doane's *The Desire to Desire: The Woman's Film of the 1940's* (Bloomington: Indiana University Press, 1987). [Modleski's note.]

way. She breaks into the killer's apartment to search for evidence and she finds the wedding ring. She puts it on her finger and waves her hand behind her back so that James Stewart, looking over from the other side of the yard with his spyglasses, can see it. To Grace Kelly, that ring is a double victory; not only is it the evidence she was looking for, but who knows, it may inspire Stewart to propose to her. After all, she's already got the ring.*

Thus speaks the male critic, who has habitually considered the film to be a 23 reflection on marriage from the man's point of view. A female spectator of *Rear Window* may, however, use her special knowledge of women and their position in patriarchy to see another kind of significance in the ring; to the woman identifying, like Lisa herself, with the female protagonist of the story, the episode may be read as pointing up the victimization of women by men. Just as Miss Lonelyhearts, pictured right below Lisa in a kind of "split screen" effect, has gone looking for a little companionship and romance and ended up nearly being raped, so Lisa's ardent desire for marriage leads straight to a symbolic wedding with a wife-murderer. For so many women in Hitchcock—and this is the point of his continual reworking of the "female Gothic"—"wedlock is deadlock" indeed.†

But it is not only the female spectator who is bound to identify with 24 Lisa at this climactic moment in the story—the moment which seems actually to be the point of the film. Jeff himself—and, by extension, the male film viewer—is forced to identify with the woman and to become aware of his *own* passivity and helplessness in relation to the events unfolding before his eyes. Thus, all Jeff's efforts to repudiate the feminine identification the film originally sets up (Jeff and Anna Thorwald as mirror images) end in resounding failure, and he is forced to be, in turn, the victim of *Hitchcock's* cinematic manipulations of space and time. In a discussion with Truffaut about his theory of suspense, Hitchcock uses this scene with Grace Kelly as his chief example of how to create "the public's identification" with an endangered person, even when that person is an unlikable "snooper." "Of course," he explains, "when the character is attractive, as for instance Grace Kelly in *Rear Window*, the public's emotion is greatly intensified" (p. 73). The implication here is that in scenes of suspense, which in Hitchcock films, as in other thrillers, usually take woman as their object as well as their subject, our identification is generally with the imperiled woman. In this respect, we do in fact all become masochists at the cinema—and it is extremely interesting to note that Theodor Reik considered suspense to be a major factor in masochistic fantasies.‡

* Truffaut, *Hitchcock*, p. 223. Hereafter cited in the text. [Modleski's note.]

† The phrase is taken from James B. McLaughlin's excellent discussion of Hitchcock's *Shadow of a Doubt*. "All in the Family: Alfred Hitchcock's *Shadow of a Doubt*." *Wide Angle* 4, no. 1 (1980): 18. [Modleski's note.]

‡ Theodor Reik, *Masochism and Modern Man*. trans. Margaret H. Biegel and Gertrud M. Kurth (New York: Farrar, Straus, 1941), pp. 59–71. On the primacy of masochism in human development, see Jean Laplanche, *Life and Death in Psychoanalysis*, trans. Jeffrey Mehlman (Baltimore: Johns Hopkins University Press, 1976), p. 89. [Modleski's note.]

Suspense, Truffaut has claimed, "is simply the dramatization of a film's 25 narrative material, or, if you will, the most intense presentation possible of dramatic situations"; suspense is not "a minor form of the spectacle," but "*the* spectacle in itself" (p. 15). Granted this equivalence between suspense and "*the* spectacle," *the* narrative, might we not then say that spectatorship and "narrativity" are themselves "feminine" (to the male psyche) in that they place the spectator in a passive position and in a submissive relation to the text? Robert Scholes has observed that "narrativity" —the "process by which a perceiver actively constructs a story from the fictional data provided by any narrative medium.* (the process, that is, which is inscribed in *Rear Window* through the character of Jeff)—is a situation of "licensed and benign paranoia" in that "it assumes a purposefulness in the activities of narration which, if it existed in the world, would be truly destructive of individuality and personality as we know them" (p. 396).† Narrativity involves, in Scholes's words, a "quality of submission and abandon" (we may recall the paranoid Dr. Schreber's attitude of "voluptuousness" toward God's grand narrative which featured a plot to impregnate the feminized doctor). This quality once noted by Scholes leads him to call for stories which reward the "most energetic and rigorous kinds of narrativity" as a means of exercising control over the text that seeks to manipulate and seduce its audience (p. 397). Of course, it is precisely Jeff's suspicion that there is a "purposefulness" to the activities across the way that impels him to adopt an "energetic and rigorous"—i.e., controlling, transcendent, and, above all, "*masculine*"—narrativity.

At this moment in the film the camera traces a triangular trajectory 26 from Jeff's gaze at the ring to Thorwald, who sees the ring and then looks up at Jeff, returning the gaze for the first time. And then Thorwald proceeds to complete the "feminization" process by crossing over to Jeff's apartment and placing Jeff in the role previously played by Mrs. Thorwald and then by Lisa—that of victim to male violence. Jeff's "distancing" techniques, of course, no longer work, and the flashing bulbs only manage to slow Thorwald down a bit. Like Lisa, Jeff finally becomes a participant in his story, though *his* identification with the female character is involuntary, imposed on him by Thorwald, whose visit comes like the return of the repressed.

Although Jeff's interpretation of the Thorwald story has been validated 27 by the end of the film, Jeff himself remains *invalided*, ending up with *two* broken legs, the body less "perfect" than ever, while Lisa, lounging on the bed, has become the mirror image of the man—dressed in masculine clothes

---

* Robert Scholes, "Narration and Narrativity in Film," in *Film Theory and Criticism*, ed. Gerald Mast and Marshall Cohen (New York: Oxford University Press, 1985), p. 393. Hereafter cited in the text. [Modleski's note.]

† Peter Brooks speaks of the same activity in similar terms, terms recalling the way in which "femininity" is perceived and constructed under patriarchy: "The assumption of another's story, the entry into narratives not one's own, runs the risk of an alienation from self that in Balzac's work repeatedly evokes the threat of madness and aphasia." See his *Reading for the Plot: Design and Intention in Narrative* (New York: Vintage, 1985), p. 219. [Modleski's note.]

and reading a book of male adventure. No longer representing sexual difference, nominating herself and speaking her own desire. Lisa is now spoken *by* the male artist—by the musician, whose completed song "Lisa" plays on the soundtrack ("men have named you," indeed), and ultimately by Hitchcock himself, who earlier made his appearance in the musician's apartment. More clearly than most, the film's ending and its "narrative image" of Lisa in masculine drag* reveals the way in which acceptable femininity is a construct of male narcissistic desire, despite Freud's claim that women tend to be more narcissistic than men, who supposedly possess a greater capacity for object love.† The film has consistently shown the opposite state of affairs to be the case, and in particular has revealed Jeff to be unable to care for Lisa except insofar as she affirms and mirrors him: significantly, he becomes erotically attracted to her only when she begins to corroborate his interpretation of the world around him (the first time he looks at her with real desire is not, as Mulvey claims, when she goes into the Thorwald apartment and becomes the object of his voyeurism, but when she begins to supply arguments in favor of his version of events).

One of the most highly reflexive of films, *Rear Window* indicates that what Jean-Louis Baudry has argued to be characteristic of the cinematic apparatus as a whole—and in particular of *projection*—is also true at the level of narrative, which functions as masculine fantasy *projected* onto the body of woman. Baudry maintains that because film projection depends on negation of the individual image as such "we could say that film . . . lives on the denial of difference: the difference is necessary for it to live, but it lives on its negation."‡ Similarly, much narrative cinema negates the *sexual* difference that nevertheless sustains it—negates it in the dual sense of transforming women into Woman and Woman into man's mirror. (Thus Baudry's analogy between cinema and woman is more revealing than he seems to know: speaking of our tendency to "go to movies before deciding which film we want to see," Baudry writes that cinéphiles "seem just as blind in their passion as those lovers who imagine they love a woman because of her qualities or because of her beauty. They need good movies, but most of all, to rationalize

28

---

*Teresa de Lauretis borrows this term, "narrative image," from Stephen Heath: "In cinema . . . woman properly represents the fulfillment of the narrative promise (made, as we know, to the little boy), and that representation works to support the male status of the mythical subject. The female position, produced as the end result of narrativization, is the figure of narrative closure, the narrative image in which the film, as Heath says, 'comes together.'" *Alice Doesn't: Feminism, Semiotics, Cinema* (Bloomington: Indiana University Press, 1984), p. 140. [Modleski's note.]

†Sigmund Freud, "On Narcissism: An Introduction," *The Standard Edition of the Complete Psychological Works of Sigmund Freud*, Vol. 14, trans. James Strachey (London: Hogarth, 1974), pp. 88–89. [Modleski's note.]

‡Jean-Louis Baudry, "Ideological Effects of the Basic Cinematographic Apparatus," trans. Alan Williams, *Apparatus: Cinematographic Apparatus: Selected Writings*, ed. Theresa Hak Kyung Cha (New York: Tanam, 1980), p. 29. [Modleski's note.]

their need for cinema."* Any woman, like any movie, will do to fulfill man's "need." Put a paper bag over their heads and all women are like Miss Torso or the headless "Hunger" sculpture of the female artist in Jeff's courtyard, both of whom function, like the cinematic apparatus itself, to displace male fears of fragmentation. "What might one say," Baudry asks, "of the function of the head in this captivation [of the spectator at the movies]: it suffices to recall that for Bataille materialism makes itself headless—like a wound that bleeds and thus transfuses."†

That "difference is necessary" for cinema to live and therefore can never 29 be destroyed, but only continually negated, is implied by the ending of *Rear Window*. Jeff is once again asleep, in the same position as he was at the film's opening, and Lisa, after assuring herself that he is *not* watching her (in contrast to former times when she had worked so hard to attract his gaze), puts away his book and picks up her own magazine. As important as this gesture is, even more important is the fact that the film gives her the last look. This is, after all, the conclusion of a movie that all critics agree is about the power the man attempts to wield through exercising the gaze. We are left with the suspicion (a preview, perhaps, of coming attractions) that while men sleep and dream their dreams of omnipotence over a safely reduced world, women are not where they appear to be, locked into male "views" of them, imprisoned in their master's dollhouse.

QUESTIONS ABOUT MODLESKI'S DISCOURSE COMMUNITY AND HER CONCERNS IN THIS SELECTION

1. At the beginning of the essay, Modleski seems to claim that films told from a male's point of view make the audience identify with that point of view. Does point of view always lead to such identification?
2. Modleski examines the stereotypical vision of men as active creatures and women as passive creatures. What forces might have given rise to such a stereotype? Does it seem to you to be the case that mobility by film characters implies power? What recent films might support or contradict this notion?
3. In *Rear Window*, the character of Jeff is made into a voyeur, one who surreptitiously looks out his window at the little dramas being played out across the courtyard. Critics have claimed that the director, Hitchcock, is simply putting Jeff in the position of the movie spectator. How does Modleski interpret this connection?
4. In examining *Rear Window*, Modleski assumes that visual images carry many layers of meaning. Jeff's cast, for example, suggests his own impotence and

---

* Jean-Louis Baudry, "Author and Analyzable Subject," in *Apparatus*, p. 68. [Modleski's note.]
† Baudry, "Ideological Effects," p. 32. In light of the "headless woman" motif in Hitchcock, consider the following remark by Joan Copjec, "We know that the dreamer dreams of himself when he dreams of a person whose head he cannot see." "The Anxiety of the Influencing Machine," *October 23 (Winter 1982): 44.* [Modleski's note.]

inability to react. She does not discuss the large negative in Jeff's apartment, which is actually a picture of Lisa herself. What might be the significance of the fact that Jeff keeps a negative, rather than a positive, print?

5. Several times, Modleski refers to "the male fear of impotence and lack" (paragraph 14). Does this emphasis suggest that Modleski is working both as a Freudian and a feminist critic?

6. Modleski suggests that "women supposedly 'enter into' films so thoroughly that they tend to confuse the very boundary between fantasy and reality" (paragraph 20). Do you agree? What kind of evidence would be needed to support this claim?

7. In paragraph 23, Modleski disparages François Truffaut's comments: "Thus speaks the male critic." Is this a fair generalization? How is she here defining her own views of her discourse community?

8. According to Modleski, in what ways is spectatorship feminine? How does the film *Rear Window* support this view?

QUESTIONS ABOUT MODLESKI'S RHETORICAL STRATEGIES

1. Modleski begins this chapter by examining work by Laura Mulvey. What purpose does such a beginning serve? In general, is it a good practice to begin with someone else's work, rather than your own? Which discourse communities might be more inclined to accept that practice?

2. The end of the second paragraph contains an announcement of what Modleski will be doing in the remainder of this examination. Is this giving away too much too early, or is such an announcement helpful?

3. Modleski includes a rather lengthy summary of the film, despite the fact that most readers of this book will already know the film. Indeed, much of the rest of the argument depends on the reader's knowledge of the film. What, then, is the purpose of the summary? Might this simply be an expectation of Modleski's discourse community of film critics?

4. In general, how does Modleski use quotations from the film? How does her use of these differ in purpose from her use of quotes from other film critics? Which are more effective in terms of advancing her argument?

5. In paragraph 13, Modleski refers to *Marnie*, another Hitchcock film. What purpose does that reference serve? What might references of this sort suggest about Modleski's discourse community?

6. Read over paragraph 15. What terms here are technical terms that refer to aspects of cinematography? What does Modleski's use of these terms suggest about her assumptions about her audience?

7. Why does Modleski hyphenate *invalidate* in paragraph 17? Is this a legitimate procedure?

8. In paragraph 22, Modleski quotes Truffaut's interpretation of the meaning of the wedding ring, and then dismisses that interpretation. But she does not state clearly that the interpretation was made in an interview with Alfred Hitchcock himself, and that Hitchcock's reply was "Exactly. That was an ironic touch." Does Hitchcock's affirmation of Truffaut's interpretation negate Modleski's view?

WRITING FROM WITHIN AND ABOUT THE ARTS: FILM CRITICISM

Writing for Yourself

1. In your journal, reflect upon a film you have recently seen that deals in some way with a male-female relationship. How are the two characters depicted? Is mobility of those characters an important factor in your understanding of them?

Writing for Nonacademic Audiences

1. As a member of the film arts committee of your college, respond to a letter in your college newspaper condemning your committee for showing Hitchcock films, films that, the letter states, show only the male point of view. Your letter of response is limited to 500 words.

Writing for Academic Audiences

1. Choose one of the following films by Hitchcock and write a 750-word review for a women's studies interdisciplinary course: *North by Northwest*, *Vertigo*, or *Marnie*.
2. For an introductory humanities course, write a 500-word essay in which you take a position on whether or not modern horror films intended for an audience of teenagers are shot from the masculine point of view.
3. In an introduction to film studies, you are to write a 750-word essay examining the use of editing in one scene from a Hitchcock film. Choose one of the following scenes and write that essay:

   The scene in which Melanie waits outside the Bodega Bay school in *The Birds*
   The gunfight scene in *The Lady Vanishes*
   The death of Schmidt in *Lifeboat*
   The shower scene in *Psycho*
   The scene in *Sabotage* in which the young boy carries the bomb
4. Jimmy Stewart has often been cited as a film icon, a character who in some ways never changes. Examine the validity of this view in a 1,000-word essay for an introductory course in film by comparing his characterization in a drama (*Rear Window* or *Mr. Smith Goes to Washington*), a western (*The Man Who Shot Liberty Valance*), a romance (*It's A Wonderful Life*), and a comedy (*Harvey*).

Gail (Luttmann) Damerow and Rick Luttmann

(b. 1944); (b. 1940)

Gail Damerow and Rick Luttmann both came to the discourse community of dance criticism from the point of view of dancers. Gail Damerow, a folk dancer, combined her interests in folk dancing and anthropology by pursuing graduate studies at Alaska Methodist University, in Anchorage. For four years, from 1967 through 1970, she conducted research on Eskimo culture, concentrating particularly on dance. In 1976 she filmed a documentary on Eskimo dance in Kotzebue.

Rick Luttmann, a professor of mathematics at Sonoma State University in Cotati, California, became interested in dance while at Stanford University pursuing his master's degree in mathematics. Since that time he has founded two university dance groups and, while teaching at Alaska Methodist University, engaged in research on dance in arctic cultures. Much of this research has been conducted through fieldwork. Together they have published "Dance in Eskimo Society—A Historical Perspective," in Dance Heritage *(1977). The following article, also written collaboratively, was published in the* Dance Research Annual *(vol. 15) in 1985.*

In examining movement and meaning in Eskimo dance, the Luttmanns make reference to Eskimo carving and methods of storytelling. Their argument is that patterns in one art form may reproduce themselves in another art form within the same culture. Furthermore, they argue that, although dance by definition is ephemeral, using ancient artifacts might lead to some accurate conjectures about dance in Eskimo culture before it was tainted by contact with Western cultures.

The use of evidence from other art forms to explain the processes of another art form is not a new technique. In 1967, for example, John Leyerle used the patterns of the Lindisfarn Gospels to explain the interlacing structures of the Anglo-Saxon poem Beowulf *(University of Toronto Quarterly, vol. 37). But in making such connections, writers are engaged in combining the concerns of two discourse communities, with all the attendant difficulties of appealing to communities that may perceive forms of evidence and qualities of proof in very different ways.*

As the Luttmanns note, dance criticism is hampered by the fact that dance is a performed art; even videotapes capture only a replication of the actual performance. Their essay is in part an attempt to rectify this difficulty within their discourse community.

AESTHETICS OF ESKIMO DANCE:
A COMPARISON METHODOLOGY

It's wonderful to make up songs,   1
but all too many of them fail . . .
I recognize what I want to put into words,
But it does not come well-arranged,
It does not become worth listening to.
Something that is well-arranged,
something well worth hearing
hastily to put that together
that is often difficult.
An awkward one—maybe so—I have put together
                    Utkuh Eskimo Song
                    (Lowenstein 1973: xvi)

Introduction

In an effort to reach a deeper understanding of the aesthetics of traditional 2
Eskimo dances of northwestern Alaska* we have sought to establish parallels
with another traditional Eskimo aesthetic form, carving. We also examined
the art of storytelling for independent corroboration.

This methodological approach suggested itself because, in contrast with 3
the tangible arts, dance by its very nature is ephemeral and therefore can be
difficult to study. It is done and enjoyed, then it is over and gone. The dancer
and the dancer's audience may feel fulfilled, but the scholar does not. He can
study the dance only in memory or by insisting on unnaturally extended repetition or by making some sort of visual record. The contrast with the student
of the plastic arts is obvious. There is accordingly a great deal more written
and photographic documentation of Eskimo carving than Eskimo dance.

Our hypothesis then is the following: to get at dance through carving 4
we will contemplate carving and think of dance. We will regard statements
made about carving and consider whether, on the basis of our observations
and the available literature, they can be verified or refuted when transferred
to dance. Our motivation in relating here the method as well as the conclusions is our belief that the method might be useful to other researchers in
dance.

Carving and dance among the Eskimo are closely related aesthetic 5
forms. Each served as a medium for the often very lucid expression of the
Eskimos' deepest perceptions about the human experience. In a seminomadic
and nonliterate culture, these two along with storytelling were virtually the
only such media. They were poetry, story, drama, history, theology, philos-

---

* This paper is based on the results of field research in Alaska during 1968–70 and 1976.

ophy, satire, and political debate. They were both used in conjunction with religious ceremonies; both had important connections with hunting and other subsistence activities and had these activities as their principal themes; both were substantial factors in the socialization of the young. The contexts of both carving and dance have metamorphosed dramatically with the Westernization of Eskimo culture over the last century, particularly as opportunities have arisen within the tourist trade to make a living as a "professional" Eskimo.

Some immediately recognizable parallels come to mind which further   6 confirm that the proposed technique is likely to be fruitful: the phenomenal powers of observation for which the Eskimo is legendary, the low-relief treatment of human figures, the decrease in quality and quantity over recent decades, and the dual processes of creation and execution—all of these are evident in both art forms.

There is an added benefit to the study of the correlation of dance and   7 carving besides those named: it may become possible to frame meaningful hypotheses about the nature of dance in prehistoric Eskimo cultures on the basis of the archaeological evidence. Dance is never dug up by archaeologists, but carvings are. If sufficiently compelling connections are established between the two art forms throughout the documentable past, then it would be reasonable to extrapolate backward and make some plausible conjectures. Such inferences would of course be highly tentative, but methods of independent corroboration might suggest themselves after a coherent theory emerged.

For this study we have examined two northwestern Alaskan dance   8 forms: Atuutipiaq and Sayuun (Sevek 1976). Both are performed primarily with arm and upper torso motions, and have little floor pattern (except in special cases). Atuutipiaq or "common dance" is a freestyle absolute dance form consisting of a series of stylized extemporized motions. Since it is open to group participation, Atuutipiaq is sometimes called "invitational dance" or "real dance for all people" (Green 1959). Sayuun or "motion action" dance, on the other hand, is rehearsed and done "solo," although it may be performed by two or more persons who have attained sufficient proficiency to dance in unison. It is a dance of presentation rather than participation, and an important factor is the interaction of performer and spectator. Sayuun involves fixed sequences of expressive movements. These often symbolic and descriptive mime-like sequences have been characterized as "story dances," although "dance poems" may be a more apt term. Like Eskimo tales, these dances have little "plot" in the Western sense. And like the Eskimo languages themselves, a Sayuun tends to be a complex knot of allusions without linearity or direct reference and without a fixed point of view.

Dance motions are similar for men and women, but the men's style is   9 vigorous and angular while the women's is softer and more fluid. Dancers are accompanied by an ensemble of male drummers and singers, backed by a chorus of female singers. The sole instrument is a large narrow-frame drum fashioned from a hoop of hardwood over which is stretched a single membrane of organic origin. The drum is held by an ivory or bone handle and beaten vigorously with a thin wooden stick on the underside of the rim.

Background

Aesthetic talents were once the cultural norm among the Eskimo for, as in 10 certain other non-Western cultures, "art" was not a thing apart. Ornamentation of subsistence equipment, decoration of clothing, and creation of ceremonial objects and dances to please the spirits were traditional (Ray 1977). The aesthetic and utilitarian were thus inseparable. The male activity of carving, for instance, was as significant as the also masculine activity of hunting, and even in recent times the two have been thought of as reciprocal (Ray 1961). A similar relationship existed between dance and subsistence patterns. Through dance an adolescent could demonstrate acquired knowledge and capabilities in the roles to be played in life, a significant outlet in a culture which censured any form of overt bragging or self-congratulation. Young men learned that their imitative ability in dance went hand in hand with their success in hunting and fishing (J. Senungetuk 1971), and was regarded by their elders as a confirmation of their maturity. A young marriageable woman could demonstrate her desirability as a spouse by miming her talents in dance. Aesthetics, so well integrated with the basic subsistence activities, were also inseparable from the ceremonies that provided for the continuing success of those activities by propitiating the spirits.

With the intensification of outside contact toward the end of the nine- 11 teenth century, Western behavior and implements increasingly took the place of their precontact counterparts. Modern implements did not readily lend themselves to precontact aesthetic treatment, and traditional ceremonial objects and activities were discouraged by the missionaries of various Christian sects (Luttmann 1977). At the same time that traditional aesthetics were becoming irrelevant to their own material and spiritual culture, the Eskimo found that these aesthetic activities had a certain marketability among outsiders. The same aesthetics which had formerly brought not only personal pleasure but also success in obtaining necessities through pleasing the spirits, were now providing secondary fulfillment of their needs through pleasing more secular parties. The souvenirs and "native experiences" sought by whalers, miners, trappers, and adventurers are today still much in demand by the tourist trade. The sale of Eskimo carvings and demonstrations of native skills including dance have become an integral part of the packaged Arctic tour.

Since the passage of the Alaska Native Land Claims Settlement Act by 12 Congress in 1971, which provided extensive funds and landholdings collectively to Alaskan natives, there has been a renewed interest in traditional dance and other activities (Johnston 1975). This, together with the current general trend to seek out one's cultural roots as a means of becoming secure in one's own personal identity, has stirred a revival among the younger Eskimo in the more traditional aspects of Eskimo life. Inevitably, however, there is a heavily Western aspect to this interest and, rather than learning through observation and imitation of older relatives, as traditionally they would have done, Eskimo children now often learn their skills in the classroom. Though dancing and carving are still sometimes done strictly for pleasure by "amateurs," carving has essentially become a specialized activity, and dancing is often done by special troupes which design costumes and properties, practice together, and travel throughout the state and sometimes "outside" to perform.

Process

Ethnographic accounts have continually attested to the remarkable ability of   13
the Eskimo to observe and memorize, to imitate and copy, and this is borne out in modern times as well as through archaeological finds (Ray 1961). The Eskimo socialization process has adapted to the demands of Arctic hunting by stressing sensitivity to visual information (Kleinfeld 1971). Undoubtedly the seemingly featureless monochromatic environment of the Arctic has made it imperative to become an acute and shrewd observer in order to avoid being lost, surprised by bad weather, or outwitted by elusive game. Both carving and dancing play a role in teaching attention to detail through their imitative aspect, emphasizing recognition of that which is considered significant or important for survival.

The carver works entirely from memory, yet is expected to create a   14
realistic sensitive rendition of his subject, as must also the originator of a Sayuun. Those who later learn the dance and accompaniment are expected to do so rapidly, and permanently. Just as the skilled Eskimo storyteller must be able to repeat the tale exactly as he heard it, performers of a Sayuun, without watching fellow dancers for cues, must faithfully reproduce the dance as it was created. Even the maker of the dance does not change it once it has been introduced and performed. An incident bearing out this Eskimo facility for rapid learning and excellent retention took place so unobtrusively in our presence that the significance of it escaped us at the time. We were present among a group of dancers when one uttered a few words in Inupiat, the indigenous language, and then sang a song once through. There followed a period of silence. Later we were made aware that a new dance song had been taught and mastered on that fleeting occasion.

Another parallel between carving and dance is the importance of the   15
ability to depict a wide range of subjects. However, in both cases this must never be at the expense of treating each subject carefully and with appropriate competence. The Eskimo carver does not skip around superficially from theme to theme but sticks with one until it is fully developed and polished to his satisfaction. A carver once tellingly commented that if a new theme were

chosen for each carved piece, it would look like the work of a beginner (Ray 1961). Similarly, a good dancer is one who has a large repertoire, although today a dancer may be recognized for the ability to perform proficiently just one dance and appreciated for skill in that dance alone. Though proficiency comes through the repetition of a carved theme or the continued performance of a given Sayuun, repetition must not dull the creativeness of each endeavor. Something of the spirit must be put into the work each time, so that it appears to be spontaneous.

Since in general a storyteller's skill is not in creating an exciting new 16 narrative, but in identically repeating a story as it was first heard, the pleasure must come in the telling—in the activity of storytelling. Similarly, the same Sayuun may be done repeatedly on different occasions for the same audience, so it must likewise be in the skillful and accurate repetition that pleasure is derived for both the dancer and the observer. The audience may know a tale or a dance as well as the performer, and yet anticipate with delight the narrator's or dancer's expressive ability. We observed a dance event in which the audience was already laughing as the next dancer made his way to the floor, evidently anticipating what they knew would be an outstanding rendition of a favorite humorous Sayuun. (The dance, incidentally, was a take-off on various styles of dancing.)

In light of the carver's comment that the continual carving of new 17 themes gives the appearance of a beginner's work, it is interesting that a young Eskimo is expected first to learn Atuutipiaq which, since it is extemporaneous, is a "new" dance with each performance. In contrast, the mark of an experienced dancer is the skillful execution of a Sayuun, a dance that must be repeated each time exactly as it was first learned. It is quite typical of indigenous dancers to regard freestyle dances as easier for beginners to learn than fixed-form dances. It undoubtedly is so for persons raised within their culture. However, extemporizing is extremely challenging to an outsider, who normally would not intuitively sense the limited range of forms to which so-called "free form" movements will necessarily be confined by those within the culture. For the outsiders, it is always safer to learn fixed-form dances first until they become accustomed to the feeling and flavor of the inventiveness permitted in the idiom. On this theory we began our own learning of Eskimo dances with the Sayuun and have never quite mastered the subtleties of the Atuutipiaq. We understand, but cannot help being amused by the awe with which our teachers regard our willingness to attempt Sayuun without having first conquered Atuutipiaq.

Product

Even though heavily influenced by outside forces, the carving and Sayuun 18 motifs used today reflect the traditional Eskimo concern with hunting, fishing, boating, and other subsistence activities. The enduring popularity of

animal themes attests to the continuing close association of the modern Eskimo with traditional subsistence. An interesting comment was made by Etok
(Gallagher 1974), a young Northwest Alaskan Eskimo lobbyist for "Eskimo
Power," that when he finds himself alone in the nation's capital he likes to go
to the Washington Zoo to watch the animals. "All my life I have watched
animals," he says, "how they move, what they eat, how they interact." Thus
the modern sophisticated Eskimo retains the traditional interest of his culture
in animal behavior. Intimate knowledge of a variety of animal behaviors is,
of course, essential to the hunter. It is also essential to the realistic carving of
animals, and to the convincing imitative Sayuun.

Dance and carving are each appropriate themes for the other, and thus   19
the two aesthetic forms come together. The act of carving is occasionally
mimed by the dancer, and traditional festivals and dance activities are commonly portrayed by the graphic artist. Sometimes dance even turns in on
itself. Interestingly, a large number of references to dance are made within
dances, some direct, others oblique, but usually suggesting in one way or
another the enormous enjoyment and pleasure dancing brings. There is even
some evidence that dances purporting to be fragments of traditional ceremonial dances are in fact more recent dances about no-longer-done ceremonial dances that have ceased to be relevant to modern life. Thus the old traditional dance festivals have apparently become subjects for contemporary
Sayuuns.

As convincing and lifelike as carved and danced portrayals can be, out-   20
siders are often struck by their economy and simplicity. Close examination of
the techniques employed in attaining this realism suggests that the secret is in
the ability to focus on the most revealing clues and exclude all irrelevant
information, just as the hunter can determine at a glance that which he needs
to know about his prey or the weather or the terrain. The observation of the
minutest and subtlest details in the environment and the recognition of the
characteristic diagnostic features and postural attitudes so important to the
hunter are equally important to the skillful carver, storyteller, and dancer.
These diagnostic features are often depicted through conventionalizations,
some mimetic, others symbolic. Thus realism is not created through a slav-
ishly exact and mechanically detailed reproduction that would overwhelm
and obscure the essence of the matter.

Rolfe (1969/70) might well have been speaking of Eskimo aesthetic con-   21
cepts instead of mime when she stated that the elimination of trivial gesture
gives meaning to small gesture; the recognition of the essential leads to the
recognition of what is inessential; the emptying of physical space fills imaginative space; and the removal of superficial communication reveals deeper
layers of communication. Descriptive detail in a carving merely functions to
arrest the eye, narrative description suspends the action, and in dance inessential motions interrupt its dynamics.

Detail that is merely descriptive and "chatty" is rarely used to create   22 realism in carving, for only those features which are essential to recognition are included. The Eskimo storyteller similarly focuses on the action, never using description for its own sake. There is thus a dearth of adjectives and adverbs in Eskimo tales (Arron 1957). But it may be noted that the nouns of Inupiat are singularly specific, and thus a remarkable degree of detail is compressed into the structure of the language itself. An Eskimo speaks not of loons, foxes, and winds, but of king loons, red foxes, and the south wind, each with a single substantive. There can be no mistake because there is no generality. Each concept is defined by man's relation to it. The language contains a system of localizers which enables the speaker to specify the form of an object and its spatial location as an integral part of the word for the object. The Eskimo is thus able to code a larger amount of information into fewer words (Kleinfeld 1971).

Motions or song-words may be so sparse in a typical Sayuun that, unless 23 the dancer and audience have firsthand personal knowledge of the action being depicted, the dance may have no meaning for them whatsoever. This is frustrating to outsiders observing a dance event, who may rightly feel that something is going over their heads. Actually, something may easily be going over the Eskimos' heads as well, if they lack the necessary referents to catch the allusions. This is especially true today since there is much less spontaneity and creativity in dance than formerly. In consequence dances today have very long life expectancies and a greater proportion of dancers are learning and repeating dances of others instead of constantly renewing their repertoires by creating their own, as in former times. Owing to the subtlety and allusiveness of many dances, their significance can, like a joke among intimate friends, be lost after a few years or after passing too far from the source.

One of the consequences of the commercialization of both carving and 24 dancing, and the associated changes in their emphasis from process to product, has been what we might call a blurring or loss of subtlety and a concomitant shortening or condensation of the time consumed. Both attest to a waning of interest and real concern by the artists. As the monetary compensation takes the place of the joy of doing as a motivational factor, carvers no longer add the subtleties they were known for in the past. Presumably such time-consuming work would never be compensated adequately in the marketplace. In dance, many of the subtleties of movement that were reported by early observers and still remembered by the older dancers today have vanished from the dance floor, or are disappearing with the cycling of the generations.

Essential to the well carved piece of ivory is a sense of fluidity and grace, 25 a suggestion of movement generated from within. Lack of fluidity in carving is attributed by older carvers to the work of boys (Ray 1961). Stiffness in dance is similarly considered a sign of immaturity. The proficiency that comes with a lifetime of practice results in more expansive gestures and in considerably more integrated use of the head, arms, shoulders, knees, and torso. A seasoned dancer shows more control over subtle movements while at the same time retaining much of the suppleness and liveliness of youth (Eskimo attributes of a good dancer). It is remarkable to see a young dancer spring eagerly to the dance floor, spry, energetic, and enthusiastic, but give a disappointing and awkward performance, while an aging dancer who must be led to the dance floor blind and hobbling is transfigured at the first drumbeat into an angel of grace.

Fluidity and minimal indication work together in defining space, which   26
to the Eskimo is more important than filling space. The carver is not concerned with covering ivory with designs since the medium itself is as important as the object it will become. In fact, the very shape of the piece to be carved determines what will be carved from it. When asked how he decided what to carve, an Eskimo of our acquaintance told us that he drew his ideas from the shape of the raw material.

Dramatic effect in carving is created through judicious use of a few   27
black strokes against the smooth white surface. Similar dramatic effect is found in dance in the contrast of stillness with motion, silence with sound. Fleeting pauses marking the end of each individual motion heighten this effect, and the dance is heavily accented with rhythmic pulsations. Accompaniment provides further contrast: the loud beating of the drum may be alternated with the softer clicking of the stick against the rim, or the drumming and singing may cease, separately or together, to emphasize certain actions in the dance. Yet the motions, song, and drumming are well integrated. The booming drums are conducive to the typical staccato style of northwestern Alaskan Eskimo dance, and to the pulsating of sustained tones in the song.

In developing their themes, Eskimo carvers are fond of the use of mul-   28
tiple perspective. This multiplicity takes two forms: more than one perspective can be given to one object, or the object may take on more than one identity depending on its orientation. In sketches, an Eskimo artist may draw the same activity from different perspectives, or may draw within the same scene activities that would not in actual fact take place in close spatial or temporal proximity to each other. Multiple perspective may show different related activities or the various sequential activities of one person or group. Storytellers also shun single perspective. Carpenter (1973) puts it well (in speaking of the Aivilik Eskimo of Eastern Canada): the narrator verbally moves about, letting the story itself speak, asserting its own form unhampered by fixed perspective. It is the same for the dancer, who may first be the hunter, next the terrain over which the hunter travels, then the prey, and finally the arrow seeking its mark. Or he may be now the boatman, now the boat, now the waves upon which the boat glides. Perspective may jump from that of a person within the boat to that of one watching from the shore. Western observers are often struck by this apparent discontinuity in perspective (or perhaps more accurately, lack of preoccupation with continuity). The interest of storyteller and audience seems to be in vignettes rather than

in the chronological narrative so typical of Western tales. The narrator may end his tale before the denouement, leaving the scene in the perpetual uncertainty of Arctic life. A Sayuun, too, often focuses on a significant activity but without providing a definitive beginning or end. Lacking crisis or resolution, Eskimo tales and Eskimo dances seem to the Westerner to ramble on, and end without point or punch line.

Conclusion

As a methodological approach to understanding the aesthetic aspects of 29 northwestern Alaskan Eskimo dance, parallels with the indigenous aesthetic form of carving were sought. Independent corroboration was made through examination of the art of Eskimo narration.

Through a combination of field research and review of the literature, 30 numerous similarities were found between carving and dancing. Both play reciprocal roles in the traditional hunting subsistence pattern, and both are of economic importance in the expanding industry of tourism. Behavioral elements of both are important to the socialization process and both embody many of the same cultural values.

The end products of carvers and dancers share such elements as realism, 31 contrast, simplicity, fluidity, choice of motifs, and multiple perspective.

This comparative approach has proven useful in attempting to identify aesthetic aspects of northwestern Alaskan Eskimo dance.

REFERENCES

Arron, Walter Jack. 1957. Aspects of the epic in Eskimo folklore. *Anthropological Papers* (University of Alaska) 5(2):119–141.
Carpenter, Edmund. 1973, *Eskimo Realities*. New York: Holt, Rinehart and Winston.
Gallagher, H. C. 1974. *Etok—A Story of Eskimo Power*. New York: G. P. Putnam's Sons.
Green, Paul. 1959. *I Am Eskimo, Aknik My Name*. Juneau: Alaska Northwest Publishing Company.
Johnston, Thomas F. 1975. Alaskan Eskimo dance in cultural context. *Dance Research Journal* VII(2):1–11.
Kleinfeld, Judith. 1971. Visual memory in village Eskimo and urban Caucasian children. *Arctic* 24(2):132–138.
Lowenstein, Tom. 1973. *Eskimo Poems from Canada and Greenland*. Pittsburgh: University of Pittsburgh Press.
Luttmann, Rick and Gail. 1977. Dance in Eskimo society—a historical perspective, in *Dance Heritage*. Focus on Dance VIII. Washington, D.C.: AAHPER.
Ray, Dorothy Jean. 1977. *Eskimo Art: Tradition and Innovation in North Alaska*. Seattle: University of Washington Press.
———. 1961, *Artists of the Tundra and the Sea*. Seattle: University of Washington Press.
Rolfe, Bari. 1969/70. Mime—paradigm of paradox. *Impulse* 37–38.
Senungetuk, Joseph E. 1971. *Give or Take a Century: An Eskimo Chronicle*. San Francisco: The Indian Historian Press.
Sevek, Chester. 1976. "I'm going to tell you something about Eskimo dances." Presentation sponsored by Alaska Tour and Marketing Service, Kotzebue, Alaska.
———. 1974. A preliminary analysis of symbolism in Eskimo art and culture, in *Proceeding of the XL International Congress of Americanists, Rome 1972*. Volume 2. Genova: Tilgher.

Other Sources

Ager, Lynn Price. 1975. Eskimo dance and cultural values in an Alaskan village. *Dance Research Journal* VIII(1):7–12.

Canadian Eskimo Arts Council, 1971, *Sculpture/Inuit*. Toronto: University of Toronto Press.

Carpenter, Edmund. 1971. Life as it was, in *I Breathe a New Song*, Richard Lewis, ed. New York: Simon and Schuster

———. 1955. Eskimo poetry and word magic. *Explorations in Culture* 4:101–111.

Graburn, Nelson H. H. 1976. *Nalunaikutanga*: signs and symbols in Canadian Inuit arts and culture. *Polarforschung* (Muenster, West Germany) 46(1):1–11.

Hall, Edwin S., Jr. 1975. *The Eskimo Storyteller*. Knoxville: The University of Tennessee Press.

Hippler, Arthur E. 1974. The North Alaskan Eskimos: a culture and personality perspective. *American Ethnologist* 1(3):449–469.

Martijn, Charles A. 1967. A retrospective glance at Canadian Eskimo carving. *The Beaver*, Autumn:5–19.

Riesman, Paul. 1966. The Eskimo discovery of man's place in the universe, in *Sign, Image, and Symbol*, Gyorgy Kepes, ed. New York: George Braziller.

Senungetuk, Ronald. 1970. The artist speaks, in *Cross-Cultural Arts in Alaska*, O. W. Frost, ed. Anchorage: Alaska Methodist University Press.

Swinton, George. 1972. *Sculpture of the Eskimo*. Greenwich, CT: New York Graphic Society, Ltd.

QUESTIONS ABOUT DAMEROW AND LUTTMANN'S DISCOURSE COMMUNITY AND THEIR CONCERNS IN THIS ESSAY

1. In general, is it legitimate to make connections between different art forms within a single culture? What might be the strengths of this approach? What might be its dangers? Damerow and Luttmann examine dance, carving, and storytelling. What do these three art forms have in common? Are their differences such that they would preclude any effective comparison?

2. According to Damerow and Luttmann, what difficulties does the scholar face in writing about dance? What other difficulties can you imagine?

3. Damerow and Luttmann state their hypothesis as follows: "to get at dance through carving we will contemplate carving and think of dance" (paragraph 3). Is this actually a hypothesis?

4. In what ways might dance express "deepest perceptions about the human experience" (paragraph 5)?

5. In what ways has westernization affected Eskimo art forms? What kinds of evidence would be necessary to verify these effects? According to Damerow and Luttmann, what roles did dance play in early Eskimo culture? What might those roles suggest about the role of art in general in that culture? Might dance fill any of those same roles in contemporary North American culture?

6. Damerow and Luttmann note that traditional Eskimo dances are now done by specialized troupes; they are no longer part of the culture at large. How might this process affect those traditional dances?

7. What are the differences between Sayuun and Atuutipiaq? How are they viewed differently by different cultures?

8. In paragraph 24, the Luttmanns connect the loss of subtlety in carving with the loss of intricate dance steps. Is this a logical connection?

QUESTIONS ABOUT DAMEROW AND LUTTMANN'S RHETORICAL STRATEGIES

1. Part of the structuring of the Damerow and Luttmann essay comes through the headings they include. Are these headings effective? Could Damerow and Luttmann be accused of using these as transition devices rather than making transitions with text?

2. Why do Damerow and Luttmann use the first person so frequently in the introduction to this essay? Is this an appropriate stance in an introduction?

3. In the context of the introduction to the essay, what is the purpose of paragraph 7? Would this information be equally effective if it were put in the conclusion of the essay?

4. In paragraph 3, the Luttmanns use the following sentence: "It [dance] is done and enjoyed, then it is over and gone." From a technical point of view, the comma in this sentence should be replaced by a semicolon. But what case could the Luttmanns make for retaining the comma?

5. At times, the Luttmanns use language peculiar to the discourse community of dance criticism. For example, they speak of dances that have "little floor pattern" (paragraph 8). How have they used this language in ways that allow a reader to interpret the language accurately?

6. Consider the sentence structures of paragraph 9, which describe the dance and its setting. What is the general pattern of sentence construction in this paragraph? Is that an effective pattern for a descriptive passage?

7. At times the authors record firsthand observations of Eskimo dances. Are these observations strong evidence?

8. Damerow and Luttmann note that "the Eskimo is thus able to code a larger amount of information into fewer words" (paragraph 22). With what are they comparing this language?

WRITING FROM WITHIN AND ABOUT THE ARTS: DANCE CRITICISM

Writing for Yourself

1. In your journal, compare any two contemporary North American art forms with which you are familiar.

2. In your journal, describe in what ways art might be considered "a thing apart" in North American society.

Writing for Nonacademic Audiences

1. Your first assignment in a dance education course—a course you have taken to fulfill a physical education requirement—is to write an honest 250-word essay on why you feel that dance is or is not important to you.

2. For your school newspaper, review a dance performance, focusing on what it might express about its contextual culture. You are limited to 500 words.

3. Write a 750-word letter to the National Endowment for the Humanities explaining why you feel that the NEH should fund dance troupes around the country.

Writing for Academic Audiences

1. The Luttmanns note that the nouns in Inupiat are "singularly specific." Could this fact be related to the primarily oral culture of the Eskimos? Respond in a 300-word essay for an introductory course in language and linguistics.
2. You have been asked to contribute to a collection of 1,250-word essays that deal with ethnic traditions and their survival in North America. Write this essay, using your own experience as your principal resource.
3. For a class in dance history, write a 750-word essay on the contributions of Isadora Duncan to American dance.
4. Using the references provided by the Luttmanns, write an article for a journal like *National Geographic* in which you explore the place of dance in Eskimo society. You have a 1,500-word limit.
5. For a course in art criticism, write a 1,500-word essay showing how the spirit of an age may influence artistic styles. You might look at such "spirits" as Renaissance humanism, social realism, modern abstract art, or medieval Gothic art.

INTERCONNECTIONS: QUESTIONS FOR WRITING

Writing for Yourself

1. What is art? How does a movement or a sound or a drawing or a piece of writing qualify as art? On what do we base our judgments as we define something as a work of art?

   Reflect on these questions in your journal, making reference to how Sidney, Fry, and Mao Zedong would have dealt with these same issues.
2. One of the questions we must deal with in examining the arts is how closely they mirror real life. Are the arts meant to be mirrors, images that reflect our lives so that we may see ourselves more clearly? Or do they have their own reality apart from that function?

   Reflect on these questions in your journal, making reference to the perspectives that Sidney and Lamb might have had on these issues.
3. How important is the moral order of the work of art in one's reaction to it? Or does art never show any kind of moral order?

   In your journal, reflect on these questions as they relate to the claims of Lamb and Fry.

Writing for Nonacademic Audiences

1. The arts are the productions of a creative individual or community. Yet at the same time, they are the outgrowth of a specific culture. How is art affected by culture? Is it possible for people of one culture to ever fully participate in and understand the art of another culture?

   Examine these questions by crafting a conversation between Lamb, Bettelheim, and Damerow and Luttmann, in which they discuss these issues.

2. In what ways does art deal with issues contemporary in a given culture? If art does deal with such issues, does it become dated and irrelevant outside the context of that culture and those issues?

   Deal with these questions in a feature article for a newsletter published by your local historical society, discussing the question of whether the Vietnam War Memorial can be called a work of art. In formulating your response, consider how Aristotle and Modleski might have responded to those questions.

3. Can art be dangerous?

   Examine this question in a letter to the local newspaper, written after *Huckleberry Finn*, *Go Ask Alice*, or *The Chocolate War* has been censored in your community high school. As you formulate your response, consider how Modleski and Mao Zedong might have responded to the question.

Writing for Academic Audiences

1. All of the discourse communities represented in this section have varying approaches to the art with which they deal. One decision they must each make, though, is whether to examine the work of art as a whole or to divide it into its component parts. Does dividing a work of art destroy one's ability to understand it as an integral whole? Does maintaining its unity downplay the role of each individual part in contributing to the whole?

   For a class in the criticism of art, of dance, or of literature, examine these questions in an essay of 1,000 words, relating your discussion to the perspectives of Aristotle, Todorov, and Rosenfeld.

2. What is the purpose of art in society? What roles does it play in the group?

   For a class on the history of music or film, write a 1,250-word essay in which you deal with how Fry, Modleski, and Damerow and Luttmann might respond to these questions.

3. How does one develop criticism to judge good art from bad art? What is the nature of such criticism? Who establishes this criticism? How is it valuable?

   For a class in aesthetics, write a 1,000-word essay examining these questions as they relate to positions taken by Aristotle, Lamb, and Rosenfeld.

DISCOURSE
COMMUNITIES IN
PHILOSOPHY

INTRODUCTION

When in the sixth century B.C. the Greek philosopher Pythagoras defined philosophy as the love of and search for wisdom, he established a discourse community that would wrestle with some of the deepest questions about the nature and purpose of humanity. As philosophy developed, it began to define the search for wisdom more sharply, seeing it as both a kind of speculation into the nature of humanity and as a criticism of moral, political, ethical, and logical structures. Today, philosophy is divided into a number of narrowly defined disciplines, such as ethics, epistemology, metaphysics, aesthetics, logic, social philosophy, philosophy of law, philosophy of physical science, and the philosophy of religion, among others.

Many of these disciplines define philosophy in distinct ways. Philosophers of the physical sciences work to define phenomena such as the nature of time, which the natural sciences in their present stages cannot explain. Logicians examine systems of thought, critically analyzing their consistency. Ethicists examine the nature of morality, while social philosophers deal with humanity's relationship to itself and to the world. And within these disciplines, certain discourse communities define philosophy even more sharply. A Marxist, for example, defines philosophy as an examination of ideology. Pragmatists see the task of philosophy as analyzing and improving society.

At first glance it might seem that such specialization would sharpen the discipline's focus and put it at the forefront of a liberal arts education. Certainly it occupied such a position in the Middle Ages and even into the Renaissance. But since that time philosophy has been dethroned and may no longer be said to be the queen of sciences—at the least, that title would have no meaning today.

In the eighteenth century, David Hume complained in his "Of Essay Writing" that "philosophy went to wreck by [its] moping recluse method of study and became as chimerical in her conclusions, as she was unintelligible in her style and manner of delivery." Today, that same complaint may still be heard in charges that philosophy is too abstract and airy to have any real significance for the contemporary student. While some students see a course in philosophy simply as a hurdle set up in a liberal arts core curriculum, others may dismiss it as "boring," "irrelevant" or "out of touch with the real world." One student's question—"What has this got to do with anything?"—represents a charge that Pythagoras might not even have understood. And certainly Socrates would find it an odd complaint: His famous sentiment that "the unexamined life is not worth living" is, he might claim, no less true today, despite its becoming a cliché.

It is the task of the philosopher to examine life, to ask the kind of foundational questions that pierce through shoddy thinking and ill-formed opinion. If Socrates is to be taken as a model, then the philosopher should challenge us, make us uneasy, shake our presumptions. Such a task might be aimed toward the individual or the community, but its function is to probe beneath assumptions to test their validity.

The following sections from widely different discourse communities within philosophy represent differing definitions of philosophy's task. For some writers, such as Augustine and Julian of Norwich, philosophy relates to the individual, particularly in terms of an individual's spiritual questions. Others, such as Locke, Descartes, and Sartre, work out of a particular movement (e.g., the Enlightenment, Existentialism) in defining an individual's meaning. Whorf and Kuhn work out of particular disciplines and apply their definitions of philosophy to their respective disciplines, while others, such as Thomas Merton, use one philosophy and its cultural background to critique other philosophical positions.

Philosophy is generally conducted in one of two ways: through critical analysis or speculation. Critical philosophy attempts to express beliefs and assumptions in very specific, precise, and explicit language. Among the following selections, one sees this in Descartes's attempt to strip away all but that which can be absolutely proven. Speculative philosophy attempts to establish general categories and concepts to explain the human experience, as in Plato's call for humanity to emerge from the cave. But these two broad ways of conducting philosophy are themselves subject to competing visions of how philosophy as a discipline is to proceed. While Socrates and Pythagoras argued that philosophy is the search for wisdom, others have claimed that philosophy has other roles. Bertrand Russell, for example, has argued that philosophy's methodology should consist of the clear statement of problems; once such problems are stated, they enter the realm of science for specific analysis. The logical positivists have argued that philosophy should be about the business of examining the methods of science. Analytic philosophers assert that philosophy proceeds through the analysis of language. Pragmatists insist that philosophy analyzes society, whereas existentialists see philosophy's role in the larger analysis of the human condition.

Clearly each discourse community within the discipline of philosophy writes according to its own understanding of how philosophy should be practiced. The philosophers in this section represent a number of these approaches as they attempt to deal with questions such as the following:

What is the nature and purpose of humanity?

How do we decide what is good? How do we decide what is evil?

What is the nature of reality, and how can we be sure that we are perceiving it accurately?

What lies beyond the realm of the senses?

In what does an individual find value?

What is the relationship of the individual to the community? To the earth?

Is truth relative, or is truth the same regardless of the time or the culture?

Can we be absolutely sure of anything? Or are the basic principles upon which we base our lives things to be accepted on faith?

Perhaps the large questions could be dismissed as being too abstract and airy if, as the following group of philosophers claims, they did not directly touch upon more immediate questions:

How do I live my life justly?

How do my assumptions about who I am affect the decisions I make about my vocation?

How do I define wealth, and how do I use it wisely?

What questions do I ask in choosing a major?

What responsibilities do I have to my society? What is the source of those responsibilities?

These and other questions follow from the larger questions which the philosophers in the following section examine.

Though philosophy is no longer queen of the sciences, certainly the questions she asks command our attention. Amidst the many competing calls that crowd upon us in the last decade of a century of remarkable change, the calls of Pythagoras and Socrates to search for wisdom and justice and the examined life have not changed.

As western nations deal with Arab nations whose mindset they have never fully understood, as Britain struggles with tensions in Ireland, as South Africa feels the rising power of its black citizens, as China seems to be settling back into repression, each nation must examine its corporate life and search out justice. And as a college freshman chooses a major and a career or decides on how he or she should care for a neighbor, a loved one, a planet; as he or she makes decisions about how to divide time between a job, classes, recreation, community commitments, and other people—here too philosophy's call to examine one's life is pressing.

Plato

(c. 428 B.C.–c. 348 B.C.)

Plato was born into one of the most distinguished families of Athens, in ancient Greece; on his father's side, he traced his lineage back to Poseidon, the god of the sea. For a time he cherished hopes of becoming active in politics, but the violent acts of a conservative faction that supported him, the attempt by some politicians to implicate Socrates, Plato's mentor, in an illegal execution, and the condemning of Socrates to his death all convinced Plato that it was not possible for a man of conscience to be active in the political arena. Plato, together with other students of Socrates, left Athens to travel in Italy, Egypt, and Greece.

Plato returned to Athens sometime around 387 B.C., when he founded his Academy. Dedicated to research in science and philosophy, which he saw as intimately wedded, Plato taught for the rest of his life. Though little survives telling of what life was like at the Academy, it seems that Plato based his own teaching on that of Socrates, lecturing without notes and setting problems that groups would work on together, arriving at joint solutions. Upon his death, Plato was buried at the Academy.

Though Plato himself saw the Academy as his major contribution to the science of philosophy, later centuries have found his Dialogues to be more important, and they have led to his reputation as one of the greatest philosophers of the West. Many of these were written during his time in the Academy, though apparently they were not aimed at his students. Instead, they were aimed at an educated class that had not trained at his Academy, in the hope that they would interest those not at the Academy in his methods and, primarily, in the ideas being examined by Plato and his students. One of those ideas is the doctrine of Ideal Forms—that the physical world points to more substantial realities beyond itself—which would become an important part of Plato's most famous dialogue, The Republic.

The central concern of The Republic *is the nature of justice. This concern leads Plato to speculate on the structures of a society and, passing from the communal to the individual, on the ethics and virtues of the private citizen. For both the individual and the community, Plato suggested four principal virtues: justice, prudence or wisdom, fortitude or courage, and temperance; these would become the four cardinal virtues of the Middle Ages. All of these virtues come only through a period of hard thinking and evaluation, of coming out of the cave into the light.*

The following selection, "The Allegory of the Cave," is taken from Plato's Republic. It consists of Plato's reconstructed dialogue between his mentor Socrates and Glaucon, one of Socrates' students.

THE ALLEGORY OF THE CAVE

Socrates: And now, I said, let me show in a figure* how far our nature is 1
enlightened or unenlightened:—Behold! human beings living in an underground den, which has a mouth open towards the light and reaching all along
the den; here they have been from their childhood, and have their legs and
necks chained so that they cannot move, and can only see before them, being
prevented by the chains from turning round their heads. Above and behind
them a fire is blazing at a distance, and between the fire and the prisoners
there is a raised way; and you will see, if you look, a low wall built along the
way, like the screen which marionette players have in front of them, over
which they show the puppets.

Glaucon: I see. 2

And do you see, I said, men passing along the wall carrying all sorts of 3
vessels, and statues and figures of animals made of wood and stone and various materials, which appear over the wall? Some of them are talking, others
silent.

You have shown me a strange image, and they are strange prisoners. 4

Like ourselves, I replied; and they see only their own shadows, or the 5
shadows of one another, which the fire throws on the opposite wall of the
cave?

True, he said; how could they see anything but the shadows if they were 6
never allowed to move their heads?

And of the objects which are being carried in like manner they would 7
only see the shadows?

Yes, he said. 8

And if they were able to converse with one another, would they not 9
suppose that they were naming what was actually before them?

Very true. 10

And suppose further that the prison had an echo which came from the 11
other side, would they not be sure to fancy when one of the passers-by spoke
that the voice which they heard came from the passing shadow?

No question, he replied. 12

To them, I said, the truth would be literally nothing but the shadows 13
of the images.

That is certain. 14

And now look again, and see what will naturally follow if the prisoners 15
are released and disabused of their error. At first, when any of them is liber-
ated and compelled suddenly to stand up and turn his neck round and walk
and look towards the light, he will suffer sharp pains; the glare will distress

* That is, an allegorical image.

him, and he will be unable to see the realities of which in his former state he had seen the shadows; and then conceive some one saying to him, that what he saw before was an illusion, but that now, when he is approaching nearer to being and his eye is turned towards more real existence, he has a clearer vision,—what will be his reply? And you may further imagine that his instructor is pointing to the objects as they pass and requiring him to name them,—will he not be perplexed? Will he not fancy that the shadows which he formerly saw are truer than the objects which are now shown to him?

Far truer.   16

And if he is compelled to look straight at the light, will he not have a   17 pain in his eyes which will make him turn away to take refuge in the objects of vision which he can see, and which he will conceive to be in reality clearer than the things which are now being shown to him?

True, he said.   18

And suppose once more, that he is reluctantly dragged up a steep and   19 rugged ascent, and held fast until he is forced into the presence of the sun himself, is he not likely to be pained and irritated? When he approaches the light his eyes will be dazzled, and he will not be able to see anything at all of what are now called realities.

Not all in a moment, he said.   20

He will require to grow accustomed to the sight of the upper world.   21 And first he will see the shadows best, next the reflections of men and other objects in the water, and then the objects themselves; then he will gaze upon the light of the moon and the stars and the spangled heaven; and he will see the sky and the stars by night better than the sun or the light of the sun by day?

Certainly.   22

Last of all he will be able to see the sun, and not mere reflections of him   23 in the water, but he will see him in his own proper place, and not in another; and he will contemplate him as he is.

Certainly.   24

He will then proceed to argue that this is he who gives the seasons and   25 the years, and is the guardian of all that is in the visible world, and in a certain way the cause of all things which he and his fellows have been accustomed to behold?

Clearly, he said, he would first see the sun and then reason about him.   26

And when he remembered his old habitation, and the wisdom of the   27 den and his fellow-prisoners, do you not suppose that he would felicitate himself on the change, and pity them?

Certainly, he would.   28

And if they were in the habit of conferring honours among themselves   29 on those who were quickest to observe the passing shadows and to remark which of them went before, and which followed after, and which were together; and who were therefore best able to draw conclusions as to the future, do you think that he would care for such honours and glories, or envy the possessors of them? Would he not say with Homer,

"Better to be the poor servant of a poor master."   30

and to endure anything, rather than think as they do and live after their   31
manner?

Yes, he said, I think that he would rather suffer anything than entertain   32
those false notions and live in this miserable manner.

Imagine once more, I said, such an one coming suddenly out of the sun   33
to be replaced in his old situation; would he not be certain to have his eyes
full of darkness?

To be sure, he said.   34

And if there were a contest, and he had to compete in measuring the   35
shadows with the prisoners who had never moved out of the den, while his
sight was still weak, and before his eyes had become steady (and the time
which would be needed to acquire this new habit of sight might be very
considerable), would he not be ridiculous? Men would say of him that up he
went and down he came without his eyes; and that it was better not even to
think of ascending; and if any one tried to loose another and lead him up to
the light, let them only catch the offender, and they would put him to death.

No question, he said.   36

This entire allegory, I said, you may now append, dear Glaucon, to the   37
previous argument; the prison-house is the world of sight, the light of the fire
is the sun, and you will not misapprehend me if you interpret the journey
upwards to be the ascent of the soul into the intellectual world according to
my poor belief, which, at your desire, I have expressed—whether rightly or
wrongly God knows. But, whether true or false, my opinion is that in the
world of knowledge the idea of good appears last of all, and is seen only with
an effort; and when seen, is also inferred to be the universal author of all
things beautiful and right, parent of light and of the lord of light in this
visible world, and the immediate source of reason and truth in the intellectual; and that this is the power upon which he who would act rationally
either in public or private life must have his eye fixed.

I agree, he said, as far as I am able to understand you.   38

QUESTIONS ABOUT PLATO'S DISCOURSE COMMUNITY AND HIS CONCERNS IN THIS SELECTION

1. Socrates describes men who see only shadows, although they define those shadows as realities. What would cause those men to define a shadow as a reality?
2. When one of the prisoners is released, he turns and is startled by a sharp light.
   What is that light meant to symbolize?
3. How many levels of reality does Socrates point to in this selection? How do you
   as a contemporary reader respond to these levels? Do they seem to be mere

fictions, or is there some way in which they actually function in your own experience?

4. What kinds of forces would Plato see as liberating one from the cave?

5. What does the sun represent for Plato?

6. For Socrates, the world of sight—of the physical reality that lies around us—is less "real" than the intellectual world. How do you react to this? What precisely does Socrates mean by the intellectual world?

7. What is the good, according to Socrates? Why should it be the last thing we apprehend?

8. How do you think Socrates would respond to T. S. Eliot's suggestion in *The Four Quartets*, "Burnt Norton," that "human kind/Cannot bear very much reality"? (11.42–43).

QUESTIONS ABOUT PLATO'S RHETORICAL STRATEGIES

1. Plato organizes this selection as a dialogue between Socrates and Glaucon. Since *The Republic* was written many years after the death of Socrates, a reader is undoubtedly not expected to believe that this is a verbatim account of a conversation. What purpose, then, does the dialogue form serve?

2. Why would the dialogue form be particularly suited for a discourse community within philosophy?

3. What are the advantages and limitations of using an analogy to make a point? In what discourse communities would an analogy be particularly appropriate?

4. Why does Plato include the replies of Glaucon, since they are very short and almost all the same? Do they serve any purpose other than maintaining the fiction of a conversation?

5. Why does Socrates use so many rhetorical questions? How do they serve to lead the listener in the direction that Socrates wants to take?

6. Why does Socrates explain the entire allegory at the end of this selection? Is such an explanation really necessary?

WRITING FROM WITHIN AND ABOUT PHILOSOPHY

Writing for Yourself

1. In your journal, respond to a case of someone you know who wished to persist in living with an illusion.

2. In your journal, respond to Socrates' contention that the intellectual world is more real than the physical world around us.

Writing for Nonacademic Audiences

1. Analogy is often cited as a particularly effective rhetorical device. Choose one of the following and develop an analogy that you will use in a debate on the subject. Sketch out the analogy in about 150 words, which you will use in preparation for the debate:

future relations between the United States and Iran
experiments with chimpanzees and language
how one decides whether to obey the law or one's superior
how one decides whether or not a work of art is beautiful

2. As a student recruiting for your university, you have been asked by a high school student contemplating enrolling at your school why anyone should major in philosophy. Respond to that student in a 300-word letter.

3. You accept an invitation to write a short (500-word) description of the Socratic method, to be used by your institution's Education Department as a handout in classes on methods of teaching high school students.

4. For a college pamphlet expressing some of the questions addressed by philosophy courses at your university, summarize in about 50 words the major questions posed by Plato's "Allegory of the Cave."

5. Read *The Place of the Lion*, by Charles Williams, a difficult novel that has as its central image the Ideal Forms that Plato envisioned. After reading the novel, write a book review to appear in a religious periodical that explores how Williams used Plato.

Writing for Academic Audiences

1. For an introductory course in philosophy, write a 750-word essay dealing with those forces that tend to keep our natures unenlightened.

2. Taking the stance of Socrates, write a 1,000-word dialogue in which you explore one of the following:

the virtues of solitude compared to the virtues of community
the nature of a democratic system
what one can perceive with the senses
how one can know what, if anything, lies beyond the senses
how all actions are supported by philosophical assumptions

Augustine

(354–430)

Augustine was born into a family of minor importance that was divided in its religious loyalties. His father was a pagan, his mother a Christian, though still new to her faith. (His father eventually became a Christian when Augustine was sixteen, and his mother eventually was elevated to sainthood by the Catholic church.) For four years Augustine studied at Madur (now Mdaurouch, in present-day Algiers) and then Carthage. During his years at Carthage, Augustine, by his own account, led a dissolute life, fathering an illegitimate son, Adeodatus, whom he faithfully cared for. He taught rhetoric, which also involved matters of ethics and philosophy, in Carthage and Milan until his conversion to Christianity in 386.

After his conversion Augustine experienced two tragedies: the death of his mother in 387 and of his son in 388. He turned to monastic life, studying, writing, and devoting himself to the church. In 391 he visited the city of Hippo and founded a monastery there, eventually becoming the bishop of Hippo. From this vantage point he wrote Confessions (397), numerous attacks on heretical movements, and City of God (413–426), a response to the sacking of Rome. In 430 Hippo was besieged by vandals, and during the siege Augustine died.

In some ways Confessions is a very personal document, a monologue directed toward God. It is certainly one of the West's great spiritual autobiographies. It is also a statement of faith, an affirmation of the beliefs that Augustine had held for eleven or twelve years. As such, it is similar to the discourse of medieval theologians.

But it is also aimed at a wider audience. By 397, Augustine was already gaining a reputation within Christendom for his personal sanctity. He understood that his reputation would affect the way people read his works, and in Confessions he uses his considerable rhetorical skill to dissuade his admirers, to show that he was not a spiritual superman. This goal did not arise out of false modesty; Augustine had a doctrinal purpose behind Confessions: to show that all goodness comes from God alone, and that God's grace alone had saved him from his sin. The whole of Confessions points to this affirmation.

The following selection is Book II of Confessions.

CONFESSIONS

1

I must now carry my thoughts back to the abominable things I did in those   1
days, the sins of the flesh which defiled my soul. I do this, my God, not
because I love those sins, but so that I may love you. For love of your love I
shall retrace my wicked ways. The memory is bitter, but it will help me to
savour your sweetness, the sweetness that does not deceive but brings real joy
and never fails. For love of your love I shall retrieve myself from the havoc
of disruption which tore me to pieces when I turned away from you, whom
alone I should have sought, and lost myself instead on many a different quest.
For as I grew to manhood I was inflamed with desire for a surfeit of hell's
pleasures. Foolhardy as I was, I ran wild with lust that was manifold and
rank. In your eyes my beauty vanished and I was foul to the core, yet I was
pleased with my own condition and anxious to be pleasing in the eyes of men.

2

I cared for nothing but to love and be loved. But my love went beyond the   2
affection of one mind for another, beyond the arc of the bright beam of
friendship. Bodily desire, like a morass, and adolescent sex welling up within
me exuded mists which clouded over and obscured my heart, so that I could
not distinguish the clear light of true love from the murk of lust. Love and
lust together seethed within me. In my tender youth they swept me away
over the precipice of my body's appetites and plunged me in the whirlpool of
sin. More and more I angered you, unawares. For I had been deafened by
the clank of my chains, the fetters of the death which was my due to punish
the pride in my soul. I strayed still farther from you and you did not restrain
me. I was tossed and spilled, floundering in the broiling sea of my fornication, and you said no word. How long it was before I learned that you were
my true joy! You were silent then, and I went on my way, farther and farther
from you, proud in my distress and restless in fatigue, sowing more and more
seeds whose only crop was grief.

Was there no one to lull my distress, to turn the fleeting beauty of these   3
new-found attractions to good purpose and set up a goal for their charms, so
that the high tide of my youth might have rolled in upon the shore of marriage? The surge might have been calmed and contented by the procreation
of children, which is the purpose of marriage, as your law prescribes, O Lord.
By this means you form the offspring of our fallen nature, and with a gentle
hand you prune back the thorns that have no place in your paradise. For
your almighty power is not far from us, even when we are far from you. Or,
again, I might have listened more attentively to your voice from the clouds,

saying of those who marry that they will *meet with outward distress, but I leave you your freedom; that a man does well to abstain from all commerce with women,* and that *he who is unmarried is concerned with God's claim, asking how he is to please God; whereas the married man is concerned with the world's claim, asking how he is to please his wife.* These were the words to which I should have listened with more care, and if I had made myself a *eunuch for love of the kingdom of heaven,* I should have awaited your embrace with all the greater joy.

But, instead, I was in a ferment of wickedness. I deserted you and al- 4 lowed myself to be carried away by the sweep of the tide. I broke all your lawful bounds and did not escape your lash. For what man can escape it? You were always present, angry and merciful at once, strewing the pangs of bitterness over all my lawless pleasures to lead me on to look for others unallied with pain. You meant me to find them nowhere but in yourself, O Lord, for you teach us by inflicting pain, you smite so that you may heal, and you kill us so that we may not die away from you. Where was I then and how far was I banished from the bliss of your house in that sixteenth year of my life? This was the age at which the frenzy gripped me and I surrendered myself entirely to lust, which your law forbids but human hearts are not ashamed to sanction. My family made no effort to save me from my fall by marriage. Their only concern was that I should learn how to make a good speech and how to persuade others by my words.

3

In the same year my studies were interrupted. I had already begun to go to 5 the near-by town of Madaura to study literature and the art of public speaking, but I was brought back home while my father, a modest citizen of Thagaste whose determination was greater than his means, saved up the money to send me farther afield to Carthage. I need not tell all this to you, my God, but in your presence I tell it to my own kind, to those other men, however few, who may perhaps pick up this book. And I tell it so that I and all who read my words may realize the depths from which we are to cry to you. Your ears will surely listen to the cry of a penitent heart which lives the life of faith.

No one had anything but praise for my father who, despite his slender 6 resources, was ready to provide his son with all that was needed to enable him to travel so far for the purpose of study. Many of our townsmen, far richer than my father, went to no such trouble for their children's sake. Yet this same father of mine took no trouble at all to see how I was growing in your sight or whether I was chaste or not. He cared only that I should have a fertile tongue, leaving my heart to bear none of your fruits, my God, though you are the only Master, true and good, of its husbandry.

In the meanwhile, during my sixteenth year, the narrow means of my 7 family obliged me to leave school and live idly at home with my parents. The brambles of lust grew high above my head and there was no one to root them out, certainly not my father. One day at the public baths he saw the signs of active virility coming to life in me and this was enough to make him relish the thought of having grandchildren. He was happy to tell my mother about it, for his happiness was due to the intoxication which causes the world to forget you, its Creator, and to love the things you have created instead of loving you, because the world is drunk with the invisible wine of its own perverted, earthbound will. But in my mother's heart you had already begun to build your temple and laid the foundations of your holy dwelling, while my father was still a catechumen and a new one at that. So, in her piety, she became alarmed and apprehensive, and although I had not yet been baptized, she began to dread that I might follow in the crooked path of those who do not keep their eyes on you but turn their backs instead.

How presumptuous it was of me to say that you were silent, my God, 8 when I drifted farther and farther away from you! Can it be true that you said nothing to me at that time? Surely the words which rang in my ears, spoken by your faithful servant, my mother, could have come from none but you? Yet none of them sank into my heart to make me do as you said. I well remember what her wishes were and how she most earnestly warned me not to commit fornication and above all not to seduce any man's wife. It all seemed womanish advice to me and I should have blushed to accept it. Yet the words were yours, though I did not know it. I thought that you were silent and that she was speaking, but all the while you were speaking to me through her, and when I disregarded her, your handmaid, I was disregarding you, though I was both her son and your servant. But I did this unawares and continued headlong on my way. I was so blind to the truth that among my companions I was ashamed to be less dissolute than they were. For I heard them bragging of their depravity, and the greater the sin the more they gloried in it, so that I took pleasure in the same vices not only for the enjoyment of what I did, but also for the applause I won.

Nothing deserves to be despised more than vice; yet I gave in more and 9 more to vice simply in order not to be despised. If I had not sinned enough to rival other sinners, I used to pretend that I had done things I had not done at all, because I was afraid that innocence would be taken for cowardice and chastity for weakness. These were the companions with whom I walked the streets of Babylon. I wallowed in its mire as if it were made of spices and precious ointments, and to fix me all the faster in the very depths of sin the unseen enemy trod me underfoot and enticed me to himself, because I was an easy prey for his seductions. For even my mother, who by now had escaped from the centre of Babylon, though she still loitered in its outskirts, did not act upon what she had heard about me from her husband with the same earnestness as she had advised me about chastity. She saw that I was already infected with a disease that would become dangerous later on, but if the growth of my passions could not be cut back to the quick, she did not think it right to restrict them to the bounds of married love. This was because she was afraid that the bonds of marriage might be a hindrance to my hopes for the future—not of course the hope of the life to come, which she reposed in you, but my hopes of success at my studies. Both my parents were unduly eager for me to learn, my father because he gave next to no thought to you and only shallow thought to me, and my mother because she thought that the usual course of study would certainly not hinder me, but would even help me, in my approach to you. To the best of my memory this is how I construe the characters of my parents. Furthermore, I was given a free rein to amuse myself beyond the strict limits of discipline, so that I lost myself in many kinds of evil ways, in all of which a pall of darkness hung between me and the bright light of your truth, my God. What malice proceeded from my pampered heart!

4

It is certain, O Lord, that theft is punished by your law, the law that is 10 written in men's hearts and cannot be erased however sinful they are. For no thief can bear that another thief should steal from him, even if he is rich and the other is driven to it by want. Yet I was willing to steal, and steal I did, although I was not compelled by any lack, unless it were the lack of a sense of justice or a distaste for what was right and a greedy love of doing wrong. For of what I stole I already had plenty, and much better at that, and I had no wish to enjoy the things I coveted by stealing, but only to enjoy the theft itself and the sin. There was a pear-tree near our vineyard, loaded with fruit that was attractive neither to look at nor to taste. Late one night a band of ruffians, myself included, went off to shake down the fruit and carry it away, for we had continued our games out of doors until well after dark, as was our pernicious habit. We took away an enormous quantity of pears, not to eat them ourselves, but simply to throw them to the pigs. Perhaps we ate some of them, but our real pleasure consisted in doing something that was forbidden.

Look into my heart, O God, the same heart on which you took pity 11 when it was in the depths of the abyss. Let my heart now tell you what prompted me to do wrong for no purpose, and why it was only my own love of mischief that made me do it. The evil in me was foul, but I loved it. I loved my own perdition and my own faults, not the things for which I committed wrong, but the wrong itself. My soul was vicious and broke away from your safe keeping to seek its own destruction, looking for no profit in disgrace but only for disgrace itself.

5

The eye is attracted by beautiful objects, by gold and silver and all such 12 things. There is great pleasure, too, in feeling something agreeable to the touch, and material things have various qualities to please each of the other senses. Again, it is gratifying to be held in esteem by other men and to have the power of giving them orders and gaining the mastery over them. This is also the reason why revenge is sweet. But our ambition to obtain all these things must not lead us astray from you, O Lord, nor must we depart from what your law allows. The life we live on earth has its own attractions as well, because it has a certain beauty of its own in harmony with all the rest of this world's beauty. Friendship among men, too, is a delightful bond, uniting many souls in one. All these things and their like can be occasions of sin because, good though they are, they are of the lowest order of good, and if we are too much tempted by them we abandon those higher and better things, your truth, your law, and you yourself, O Lord our God. For these earthly things, too, can give joy, though not such joy as my God, who made them all, can give, because *honest men will rejoice in the Lord; upright hearts will not boast in vain.*

When there is an inquiry to discover why a crime has been committed, 13 normally no one is satisfied until it has been shown that the motive might have been either the desire of gaining, or the fear of losing, one of those good things which I said were of the lowest order. For such things are attractive and have beauty, although they are paltry trifles in comparison with the worth of God's blessed treasures. A man commits murder and we ask the reason. He did it because he wanted his victim's wife or estates for himself, or so that he might live on the proceeds of robbery, or because he was afraid that the other might defraud him of something, or because he had been wronged and was burning for revenge. Surely no one would believe that he would commit murder for no reason but the sheer delight of killing? Sallust tells us that Catiline was a man of insane ferocity, "who chose to be cruel and vicious without apparent reason"; but we are also told that his purpose was "not to allow his men to lose heart or waste their skill through lack of practice." If we ask the reason for this, it is obvious that he meant that once he had made himself master of the government by means of this continual violence, he would obtain honour, power, and wealth and would no longer go in fear of the law because of his crimes or have to face difficulties through lack of funds. So even Catiline did not love crime for crime's sake. He loved something quite different, for the sake of which he committed his crimes.

6

If the crime of theft which I committed that night as a boy of sixteen were a 14 living thing, I could speak to it and ask what it was that, to my shame, I loved in it. It had no beauty because it was a robbery. It is true that the pears which we stole had beauty, because they were created by you, the good God, who are the most beautiful of all beings and the Creator of all things, the supreme Good and my own true Good. But it was not the pears that my unhappy soul desired. I had plenty of my own, better than those, and I only picked them so that I might steal. For no sooner had I picked them than I threw them away, and tasted nothing in them but my own sin, which I relished and enjoyed. If any part of one of those pears passed my lips, it was the sin that gave it flavour.

And now, O Lord my God, now that I ask what pleasure I had in that 15 theft, I find that it had no beauty to attract me. I do not mean beauty of the sort that justice and prudence possess, nor the beauty that is in man's mind and in his memory and in the life that animates him, nor the beauty of the stars in their allotted places or of the earth and sea, teeming with new life born to replace the old as it passes away. It did not even have the shadowy, deceptive beauty which makes vice attractive—pride, for instance, which is a pretence of superiority, imitating yours, for you alone are God, supreme over all; or ambition, which is only a craving for honour and glory, when you alone are to be honoured before all and you alone are glorious for ever. Cruelty is the weapon of the powerful, used to make others fear them: yet no one is to be feared but God alone, from whose power nothing can be snatched away or stolen by any man at any time or place or by any means. The lustful use caresses to win the love they crave for, yet no caress is sweeter than your charity and no love is more rewarding than the love of your truth, which shines in beauty above all else. Inquisitiveness has all the appearance of a thirst for knowledge, yet you have supreme knowledge of all things. Ignorance, too, and stupidity choose to go under the mask of simplicity and innocence, because you are simplicity itself and no innocence is greater than yours. You are innocent even of the harm which overtakes the wicked, for it is the result of their own actions. Sloth poses as the love of peace; yet what certain peace is there besides the Lord? Extravagance masquerades as fullness and abundance: but you are the full, unfailing store of never-dying sweetness. The spendthrift makes a pretence of liberality: but you are the most generous dispenser of all good. The covetous want many possessions for themselves: you possess all. The envious struggle for preferment: but what is to be preferred before you? Anger demands revenge: but what vengeance is as just as yours? Fear shrinks from any sudden, unwonted danger which threatens the things that it loves, for its only care is safety: but to you nothing is strange, nothing unforeseen. No one can part you from the things that you love, and safety is assured nowhere but in you. Grief eats away its heart for the loss of things which it took pleasure in desiring, because it wants to be like you, from whom nothing can be taken away.

So the soul defiles itself with unchaste love when it turns away from you 16 and looks elsewhere for things which it cannot find pure and unsullied except by returning to you. All who desert you and set themselves up against you merely copy you in a perverse way; but by this very act of imitation they only show that you are the Creator of all nature and, consequently, that there is no place whatever where man may hide away from you.

What was it, then, that pleased me in that act of theft? Which of my 17
Lord's powers did I imitate in a perverse and wicked way? Since I had no
real power to break his law, was it that I enjoyed at least the pretence of
doing so, like a prisoner who creates for himself the illusion of liberty by
doing something wrong, when he has no fear of punishment, under a feeble
hallucination of power? Here was the slave who ran away from his master
and chased a shadow instead! What an abomination! What a parody of life!
What abysmal death! Could I enjoy doing wrong for no other reason than
that it was wrong?

7

What return shall I make to the Lord for my ability to recall these things 18
with no fear in my soul? I will love you, Lord, and thank you, and praise
your name, because you have forgiven me such great sins and such wicked
deeds. I acknowledge that it was by your grace and mercy that you melted
away my sins like ice. I acknowledge, too, that by your grace I was preserved
from whatever sins I did not commit, for there was no knowing what I might
have done, since I loved evil even if it served no purpose. I avow that you
have forgiven me all, both the sins which I committed of my own accord and
those which by your guidance I was spared from committing.

What man who reflects upon his own weakness can dare to claim that 19
his own efforts have made him chaste and free from sin, as though this entitled him to love you the less, on the ground that he had less need of the mercy
by which you forgive the sins of the penitent? There are some who have been
called by you and because they have listened to your voice they have avoided
the sins which I here record and confess for them to read. But let them not
deride me for having been cured by the same Doctor who preserved them
from sickness, or at least from such grave sickness as mine. Let them love you
just as much, or even more, than I do, for they can see that the same healing
hand which rid me of the great fever of my sins protects them from falling
sick of the same disease.

8

It brought me no happiness, for *what harvest did I reap from acts which now* 20
make me blush, particularly from that act of theft? I loved nothing in it
except the thieving, though I cannot truly speak of that as a "thing" that I
could love, and I was only the more miserable because of it. And yet, as I
recall my feelings at the time, I am quite sure that I would not have done it
on my own. Was it then that I also enjoyed the company of those with whom
I committed the crime? If this is so, there was something else I loved besides
the act of theft; but I cannot call it "something else," because companionship,
like theft, is not a thing at all.

No one can tell me the truth of it except my God, who enlightens my 21 mind and dispels its shadows. What conclusion am I trying to reach from these questions and this discussion? It is true that if the pears which I stole had been to my taste, and if I had wanted to get them for myself, I might have committed the crime on my own if I had needed to do no more than that to win myself the pleasure. I should have had no need to kindle my glowing desire by rubbing shoulders with a gang of accomplices. But as it was not the fruit that gave me pleasure, I must have got it from the crime itself, from the thrill of having partners in sin.

9

How can I explain my mood? It was certainly a very vile frame of mind and 22 one for which I suffered; but how can I account for it? *Who knows his own frailties?*

We were tickled to laughter by the prank we had played, because no 23 one suspected us of it although the owners were furious. Why was it, then, that I thought it fun not to have been the only culprit? Perhaps it was because we do not easily laugh when we are alone. True enough: but even when a man is all by himself and quite alone, sometimes he cannot help laughing if he thinks or hears or sees something especially funny. All the same, I am quite sure that I would never have done this thing on my own.

My God, I lay all this before you, for it is still alive in my memory. By 24 myself I would not have committed that robbery. It was not the takings that attracted me but the raid itself, and yet to do it by myself would have been no fun and I should not have done it. This was friendship of a most un-friendly sort, bewitching my mind in an inexplicable way. For the sake of a laugh, a little sport, I was glad to do harm and anxious to damage another; and that without thought of profit for myself or retaliation for injuries re-ceived! And all because we are ashamed to hold back when others say "Come on! Let's do it!"

10

Can anyone unravel this twisted tangle of knots? I shudder to look at it or 25 think of such abomination. I long instead for innocence and justice, graceful and splendid in eyes whose sight is undefiled. My longing fills me and yet it cannot cloy. With them is certain peace and life that cannot be disturbed. The man who enters their domain goes to *share the joy of his Lord*. He shall know no fear and shall lack no good. In him that is goodness itself he shall find his own best way of life. But I deserted you, my God. In my youth I wandered away, too far from your sustaining hand, and created of myself a barren waste.

QUESTIONS ABOUT AUGUSTINE'S DISCOURSE COMMUNITY AND HIS CONCERNS IN THIS SELECTION

1. How would you define the intended audience of Augustine's *Confessions*? Would you say that there are multiple audiences?

2. How does Augustine distinguish between human desire and moral law? Is there such a thing as a moral law that applies to all people?
3. Read over those passages that deal with Augustine's father. What are some of his highest values? How does Augustine, at the time of this writing, feel about those values? Does he reject them completely? Does he despise his father, for example, for sending him to study at Carthage?
4. What benefits did Augustine's parents hope would come to him from the process of education?
5. Does it seem to you from this passage that Augustine would agree with those of his contemporaries who advised Christians to reject the world and to retire into communities set apart from the world?
6. Speculate on how Augustine would have answered the question of how God speaks to humanity.
7. In section 8, Augustine speculates on the source of the pleasure he received from the theft of the pears. What is that source? Would you say that it is still a source of pleasure for people?
8. Does it seem to you that Augustine was as dreadful a scoundrel as he seems to indicate in this selection?
9. Augustine writes that as he began to sin in his youth "in your eyes my beauty vanished and I was foul to the core" (section one). What does this suggest about Augustine's vision of the nature of sin?

QUESTIONS ABOUT AUGUSTINE'S RHETORICAL STRATEGIES

1. Frequently in *Confessions* Augustine addresses God directly. What effect do you think this would have had upon Augustine's contemporaries? What effect does this have upon the modern reader?
2. Especially in the early parts of this selection, Augustine uses metaphors to vivify his description of his sinful state. What do most of these metaphors bring to mind? Do they work well to describe a sinful condition?
3. Read over the first paragraph of section 2. What dominant rhetorical strategy is Augustine using here? Is it effective?
4. In section 2, Augustine inserts several Biblical quotations into his prose. Why might he do this? What effect does it have upon the reader's perception of the nature of the writer?
5. Toward the end of section 2, Augustine uses the rhetorical technique of paradox: "[F]or you teach us by inflicting pain, you smite so that you may heal, and you kill us so that we may not die away from you." Do you find this to be an effective technique within this discourse community? Which modern discourse communities might not find this kind of technique useful?
6. How does Augustine use the story of Catiline to advance his argument (section 5)?
7. In section 6, Augustine arranges part of his material by following the order of what the Middle Ages called the seven deadly sins. Why would such a patterning be effective within his discourse community?
8. Section 7 of this selection does not really advance the narrative. What is the rhetorical purpose of this section?

WRITING FROM WITHIN AND ABOUT PHILOSOPHY

Writing for Yourself

1. In your journal, discuss whether it is possible for anyone to know his or her own frailties fully.
2. An old cliché claims that confession is good for the soul. In your journal, reflect on whether there is any truth to this cliché.
3. Augustine writes that "the life we live on earth has its own attractions as well because it has a certain beauty of its own in harmony with all the rest of this world's beauty." In your journal, discuss what the certain beauty of life might be.

Writing for Nonacademic Audiences

1. Your closest friend in high school, who went to a different college than you did, has recently experienced great suffering: His or her father has developed Alzheimer's disease. After learning of this in a letter, you write a letter back in which you comment on your view of the cause and purpose of suffering in life.
2. You have been asked to give a fifteen-minute talk to high school students on the good and bad sides of peer pressure. Prepare the text for that talk.
3. After a recent football game, many students on your campus became unruly to the point of violence. For an underground newspaper distributed on your campus, write a 500-word piece satirizing the reasons for this violent behavior.
4. For a religious periodical, write a 500-word feature article dealing with why it might be valuable for a modern reader to study Augustine, who wrote almost 1,600 years ago. Use the selection included here as the basis for your essay.

Writing for Academic Audiences

1. For a class in philosophy and religion, write a 500-word essay in which you explore the question of whether or not there is such a thing as sin.
2. For a class in aesthetics, write a 750-word essay evaluating Augustine's claim that God is the source of all beauty (section 6).

Julian of Norwich

(1342–c. 1416)

Very little is known about the life of one of England's major mystical writers. Her date of birth has been calculated from her own notation that in 1373, when she was thirty and a half years old, she was gravely ill. The last known date when she was alive was 1416, when she was named the beneficiary of a will. That will refers to her as the "recluse atte Norwyche," a title supported by long tradition. She experienced spiritual revelations on May 8, 1373, when she was probably living in her mother's house during an illness. She writes that she brooded on these for twenty years, afterwards writing her Revelations of Divine Love.

Sometime before 1400, Julian had become an anchoress, or recluse. This kind of solitary life was meant to be devoted to fasting and prayer. If one felt called to it and one could provide for oneself—and could prove these two points to the church leadership—one would be approved for such confinement, where the anchorite or anchoress would essentially live in a cell, virtually alone, for the rest of his or her life. The service of enclosure itself involved the Mass for the Dead, for the anchoress would now be dead to the world but alive to God. During the service, the cell was blessed, the occupant blessed, prayers offered, and then the anchoress invited to enter the "tomb." Afterwards, the bishop would leave the cell and the entrance would be blocked.

For some, this meant a completely solitary life; for others things were not so harsh. Many had a window that was always open to the world, and consequently some rules for anchoresses warned against gossip. Some had servants (Julian had at least two at one time) as well as visitors, particularly if they became known, like Julian, as effective spiritual counselors. Some kept gardens and even cattle. But the core of a solitary's life was meant to be prayer, organized according to a tight schedule of rules.

Julian lived and wrote during the reigns of Edward III and Richard II, a time in England when both church and state were corrupt and barren. She aimed her work at an audience affected by this barrenness, speaking in simple terms of the love of God, which she at times expressed as the Motherhood of God (she sometimes referred to Jesus as our Kind Mother, Gracious Mother, Very Mother). She understood that her writing came out of a need to communicate what God had shown to her. In chapter 6 of Revelations of Divine Love *she wrote, "I know well this that I say—I have it on the showing of him who is a sovereign Teacher—and truly charity urgeth me to tell you of it, for I would that God were known and my fellow-Christian helped (as I would be myself), to the more hating of sin and loving of God."*

As her work was copied and distributed in manuscript form, her fame spread, and it was recognized—although none of her contemporaries would have expressed it this way—that she was writing within the discourse community of the religious mystic. The Christian mystic in the fourteenth and later centuries was perceived to be one who, through prayer, had become united with God and experienced some form of intimacy with God.

The following selection contains chapters 14 through 18 of Revelations of Divine Love.

REVELATIONS OF DIVINE LOVE

CHAPTER 14: *The sixth revelation: the great honour of Christ's gratitude with which he rewards his servants; its three joys*

After this the Lord said, "Thank you for all your suffering, the suffering of 1 your youth."

I saw in my imagination heaven, and our Lord as the head of his own 2 house, who had invited all his dear servants and friends to a great feast. The Lord, I saw, occupied no one place in particular in his house, but presided regally over it all, suffusing it with joy and cheer. Utterly at home, and with perfect courtesy, himself was the eternal happiness and comfort of his beloved friends, the marvelous music of his unending love showing in the beauty of his blessed face. Which glorious countenance of the Godhead fills heaven full of joy and delight.

God showed me the three degrees of bliss enjoyed by every soul who has 3 served him deliberately in any way on earth: (i) The most valuable thanks that God shall give him when he is relieved of his suffering. This gratitude is so supremely worthwhile that a man would think he was filled with it even if there were no more. I thought that *all* the pain and suffering experienced by mankind would not merit the worth of the gratitude that a single soul shall get for having deliberately served God! (ii) All blessed heavenly beings are aware of that most worthwhile gratitude, for God makes a man's service known to all heaven. An example of this was given: If a king thanks his servants, they value it greatly, but if he makes it known throughout his realm, then is its value greatly increased. (iii) The freshness and pleasure with which it is at first received shall last for ever.

This also was disclosed to me, with delightful simplicity, that every 4 man's age is to be made known in heaven, and his reward is governed by the willingness of his service and its duration. In particular those who willingly and freely offer their youth to God are rewarded and thanked, supremely and wonderfully. But I saw that if a man or woman was genuinely turned to God for however long or short a time, even if it were for a single day of service given with an eternal intention, he should experience all three degrees of delight. The more the loving soul sees this courtesy of God, the more gladly will he serve him all the days of his life.

CHAPTER 15: *The seventh revelation: the recurring experience of delight and depression; it is good for man sometimes not to know comfort; it is not necessarily caused by sin*

After this he treated my soul to a supreme and spiritual pleasure. I was filled 5 with an eternal assurance, which was powerfully maintained, without the least sort of grievous fear. This experience was so happy spiritually that I felt completely at peace and relaxed: nothing on earth could have disturbed me.

But this lasted only a short while and I began to react with a sense of 6 loneliness and depression, and the futility of life; I was so tired of myself that I could scarcely bother to live. No comfort or relaxation now, just "faith, hope, and charity." And not much of these in feeling, but only in bare fact. Yet soon after this our blessed Lord gave once again that comfort and rest, so pleasant and sure, so delightful and powerful, that no fear, or sorrow, or physical suffering could have discomposed me. And then I felt the pain again; then the joy and pleasure; now it was one, and now the other, many times— I imagine quite twenty. When I was glad I was ready to say with St. Paul, "Nothing shall separate me from the love of Christ," and when I suffered, I could have said with St. Peter, "Lord, save me; I perish!"

I understood this vision to mean that it was for their own good that 7 some souls should have this sort of experience: sometimes to be consoled; sometimes to be bereft and left to themselves. The will of God is that we should know he keeps us safely, alike "in weal or woe." For his own soul's good a man is sometimes left to himself. This is not invariably due to sin, for certainly I had not sinned when I was left alone—it happened all too suddenly. On the other hand I did not deserve to have this experience of blessedness. But our Lord gives it as and when he pleases, just as he sometimes permits us to know its opposite. Both are equally his love. For it is God's will that we should know the greatest happiness we are capable of, for this bliss is to last for ever. Suffering is transient for those who are to be saved, and will ultimately vanish completely. It is not God's will therefore that we should grieve and sorrow over our present sufferings, but rather that we should leave them at once, and keep ourselves in his everlasting joy.

CHAPTER 16: *The eighth revelation: the pitiful suffering of Christ as he dies, his discoloured face, and dried-up body*

It was after this that Christ showed me something of his passion near the time 8 of his dying. I saw his dear face, dry, bloodless, and pallid with death. It became more pale, deathly and lifeless. Then, dead, it turned a blue colour, gradually changing to a browny blue, as the flesh continued to die. For me his passion was shown primarily through his blessed face, and particularly by his lips. There too I saw these same four colours, though previously they had been, as I had seen, fresh, red, and lovely. It was a sorry business to see him change as he progressively died. His nostrils too shrivelled and dried before my eyes, and his dear body became black and brown as it dried up in death; it was no longer its own fair, living colour.

For at the same time as our blessed Lord and Saviour was dying on the   9 cross there was, in my picture of it, a strong, dry, and piercingly cold wind. Even when the precious blood was all drained from that dear body, there still remained a certain moisture in his flesh, as was shown me. The loss of blood and the pain within, the gale and the cold without, met together in his dear body. Between them the four (two outside, two in) with the passage of time dried up the flesh of Christ. The pain, sharp and bitter, lasted a very long time, and I could see it painfully drying up the natural vitality of his flesh. I saw his dear body gradually dry out, bit by bit, withering with dreadful suffering. And while there remained any natural vitality, so long he suffered pain. And it seemed to me, that with all this drawn-out pain, he had been a week in dying, dying and on the point of passing all that time he endured this final suffering. When I say "it seemed to me that he had been a week in dying" I am only meaning that his dear body was so discoloured and dry, so shrivelled, deathly, and pitiful, that he might well have been seven nights in dying. And I thought to myself that the withering of his flesh was the severest part, as it was the last, of all Christ's passion.

CHAPTER 17: *The dreadful, physical thirst of Christ; the four reasons for this; his pitiful crowning; a lover's greatest pain*

And the words of Christ dying came to mind, "I thirst." I saw that he was   10 thirsty in a twofold sense, physical and spiritual—of this latter I shall be speaking in the thirty-first chapter. The immediate purpose of this particular word was to stress the physical thirst, which I assumed to be caused by drying up of the moisture. For that blessed flesh and frame was drained of all blood and moisture. Because of the pull of the nails and the weight of that blessed body it was a long time suffering. For I could see that the great, hard, hurtful nails in those dear and tender hands and feet caused the wounds to gape wide and the body to sag forward under its own weight, and because of the time it hung there. His head was scarred and torn, and the crown was sticking to it, congealed with blood; his dear hair and his withered flesh was entangled with the thorns, and they with it. At first, when the flesh was still fresh and bleeding the constant pressure of the thorns made the wounds even deeper. Furthermore, I could see that the dear skin and tender flesh, the hair and the blood, were hanging loose from the bone, gouged by the thorns in many places. It seemed about to drop off, heavy and loose, still holding its natural moisture, sagging like a cloth. The sight caused me dreadful and great grief;

I would have died rather than see it fall off. What the cause of it was I could not see, but I assumed that it was due to the sharp thorns, and the rough and cruel way the garland was pressed home heartlessly and pitilessly. All this continued awhile, and then it began to change before my very eyes, and I marvelled. I saw that it was beginning to dry, and therefore to lose weight, and to congeal around the garland. And as it went right round the head, it made another garland under the first. The garland of thorns was dyed the colour of his blood, and this second garland of blood, and his head generally, were the colour of blood that is congealed and dry. What could be seen of the skin of the face was covered with tiny wrinkles, and was tan coloured; it was like a plank when it has been planed and dried out. The face was browner than the body.

The cause of dryness was fourfold: the first was caused by his bloodless- 11 ness; the second by the ensuing pain; the third by his hanging in the air, like some cloth hung out to dry; the fourth was due to his physical need of drink— and there was no comfort to relieve all his suffering and discomfort. Hard and grievous pain! But much harder and more grievous still when the moisture ceased, and all began to dry!

The pains experienced in that blessed head were these: the first was 12 known in the act of dying, while the body was still moist, and the other was that killing, contracting drying which, with the strong wind blowing, shrivelled and hurt him with cold more than I could possibly imagine. And there were other pains beyond power to describe—for I recognize that whatever I might say about them would be quite inadequate.

This showing of Christ's pain filled me with pain myself. For though I 13 was fully aware that he suffered only once, it seemed as if he wanted to show it all to me, and to fill my mind with it as indeed I had asked. All the while he was suffering I personally felt no pain but for him. And I thought to myself, "I know but little of the pain that I asked for," and, wretch that I am, at once repented, thinking that had I known what it would have been I should have hesitated before making such a prayer. For my pains, I thought, passed beyond any physical death. Was there any pain like this? And my reason answered, "Hell is a different pain, for there there is despair as well. But of all the pains that lead to salvation this is the greatest, to see your Love suffer. How could there be greater pain than to see him suffer, who is all my life, my bliss, my joy?" Here it was that I truly felt that I loved Christ so much more than myself, and that there could be no pain comparable to the sorrow caused by seeing him in pain.

CHAPTER 18: *The spiritual martyrdom of our Lady, and others of Christ's lovers; all things suffer with him, good and bad alike*

Because of all this I was able to understand something of the compassion of 14 our Lady St. Mary. She and Christ were so one in their love that the greatness of her love caused the greatness of her suffering. In this I found an example of that instinctive love that creation has to him—and which develops by grace. This sort of love was most fully and supremely shown in his dear Mother. Just because she loved him more than did anyone else, so much the more did her sufferings transcend theirs. The higher, and greater, and sweeter our love, so much deeper will be our sorrow when we see the body of our beloved suffer. All his disciples and real lovers suffered more greatly here than at their own dying. I felt quite certain that the very least of them loved Christ much more than they loved themselves, and quite beyond my power to describe.

Here too I saw a close affinity between Christ and ourselves—at least, 15 so I thought—for when he suffered, we suffered. All creatures capable of suffering pain suffered with him; I mean, all creatures that God has made for our use. Even heaven and earth languished for grief in their own peculiar way when Christ died. It is their nature to know him to be their God, from whom they draw all their powers. When he failed, then needs must that they too most properly should fail to the limit of their ability, grieving for his pains. So too his friends suffered pain because they loved him. Speaking generally we can say that all suffered, for even those who did not know him suffered when the normal conditions of life failed—though the mighty, secret keeping of God did not fail. I am thinking of two kinds of people, exemplified by two quite different types: Pilate, and St. Denis of France, who at that time was a pagan. When he saw the extraordinary and frightening portents of that day he said, "Either the world is now at its end, or its Maker is suffering." So he wrote upon an altar, "This is the Altar of the Unknown God." God in his goodness makes planets and the elements to work according to their nature for good and bad alike, but on that day it was withdrawn from both. So it was that even those who did not know him sorrowed at that time.

Thus was our Lord Jesus set at nought for us, and we too with him 16 stand to suffer in a similar way, until such time as we come to his glory, as I shall explain later.

QUESTIONS ABOUT JULIAN OF NORWICH'S DISCOURSE COMMUNITY AND HER CONCERNS IN THIS SELECTION

1. Define a revelation as Julian would understand it.
2. The modern imagination conceives of medieval visions as lurid scenes of hell, or beatific scenes of heaven, or very visual and sensory scenes of the Passion of Christ. Certainly some of these conceptions apply to the work of Julian, but as this selection shows, not all revelations were primarily visual. How would you define the nature of the three visions included in this selection?
3. In an earlier chapter (2), Julian describes herself as "unlettered," and indeed a scribe recorded all of her revelations. But what in this selection suggests that

Julian is at least not completely "unlettered"? What forces would lead her to make such a disclaimer?

4. Julian clearly assumes here that she is addressing an audience that accepts the validity of the religious experience. But a contemporary audience might not be so accepting. What has changed in Western culture that would lead to a modern audience's rejection of the validity of these visions?

5. In chapter 15, Julian laments that her experience of faith, hope, and charity was not so much in feeling but in bare fact. What does she mean by this? Could Julian be accused of depending on her emotions alone, rather than on emotion and intellect, in her religious experience?

6. In chapter 15, Julian deals with the fact that it seems that God gives both "woe and weal." What is her rationale for this apparent oddity? Does her reasoning here strike you as sound?

7. In chapter 15, Julian suggests that "it is not God's will therefore that we should grieve and sorrow over our present sufferings. But rather that we should leave them at once, and keep ourselves in his everlasting joy." She makes no attempt here to show how one should go about this. Is this a flaw in her work?

8. Many medieval sermon writers, lyricists, and mystics used elements of Christ's passion to focus one's religious experience. The reader or listener was enjoined to imagine dreadful torment not to delight in gore, but, it was claimed, to understand the depth of God's mercy. Where do you see this approach in Julian's work? Is it effective for a modern reader?

QUESTIONS ABOUT JULIAN OF NORWICH'S RHETORICAL STRATEGIES

1. Julian is particularly noted for the simplicity of her diction, even when she is dealing with very complicated theological matters. Where in this passage do you see such simplicity?

2. Julian's style bears some similarity to that of other British mystics of her time. Does her use of a style that was fairly widespread in her culture diminish the power or authenticity of these visions?

3. Read over Julian's description of the heavenly feast in chapter 14. Then consider the scriptural passage in which heaven is imaged as a wedding feast (Matthew 22:1–14). How does she adapt the metaphor to her own purposes?

4. One very typical medieval rhetorical strategy was listing. Where in this passage do you see such a strategy? What benefits does Julian derive from it?

5. Characterize Julian's use of adjectives. How many does she use? Where does she use them? To what purpose does she use them? How do they strike the modern ear?

6. Julian frequently moves from a discussion of delight and peace to a discussion of pain and fear and horror. Sometimes these alternate feelings are paired in the same sentence. What theological point might Julian be heading toward by using this rhetorical strategy?

7. Read over Julian's description of the decaying body at the beginning of chapter 16. How does she go about horrifying her audience? What purpose might such horror have?

8. How does Julian make a transition between her own very personal reactions to the passion to a more universal reaction (chapter 18)?

WRITING FROM WITHIN AND ABOUT PHILOSOPHY

Writing for Yourself

1. In your journal, reflect on what you conceive to be the source of Julian's visions. What beliefs and assumptions do you hold that affect the way you respond to these visions?
2. In your journal, reflect on whether great suffering must precede great joy.

Writing for Nonacademic Audiences

1. If one were to travel through old Quebec, one would come upon many churches that hold what some would see as gory images of Christ's passion. In a 500-word feature article for a touring guide to this region, discuss your reactions to such images.
2. One of the most popular television and movie series of the last two decades has been "Star Trek." Some have speculated that the major characters in the show reflect a conflict within the personality: Spock is pure intellect, McCoy is pure emotion, and Kirk is the fusion of the two. Using the rhetorical mode of example, write a 750-word essay exploring this speculation for a science-fiction journal.

Writing for Academic Audiences

1. For a class in the philosophy of religion, write a 250-word essay in which you define what has been called the problem of pain. How is it that a just God can allow evil in the world? Remember here that you are defining the nature of the problem, not posing solutions.
2. Choose three of the following discourse communities and, in 150 words, explain how each of those communities might respond to a religious vision. Your audience for each of these is an introductory class in these communities.

Science	Anthropology
History	Psychology
Philosophy	Literary criticism

3. Julian's prose is particularly striking because of its simplicity. Another religious work noted for its simple yet powerful diction is the King James Version of the Bible. Choose a passage from that version, perhaps the creation account in Genesis 1, and write a 500-word analysis of its diction for an audience of your peers.
4. Margery Kempe once visited Julian, and her impressions are recorded in *The Book of Margery Kempe*. Read her account of this visit and, for an oral presentation for a course in the history of religious philosophy, prepare a 500-word essay using Kempe's description and this selection from *Revelations of Divine Love* to define Julian's character and principal concerns.

5. For a class in ethics, write a 500-word essay describing how much one's life should be guided by emotion and how much by intellect.
6. For a class in the history of philosophy, write a 1,500-word essay in which you discuss the main tenets of the mysticism of one of the great English medieval mystics: Richard Rolle, Walter Hilton, Julian of Norwich, or Margery Kempe.

René Descartes

(1596–1650)

René Descartes, who saw in his lifetime the condemnation of Galileo, was, like Galileo, a scientist, a mathematician, and a shaper of modern scientific and philosophical thought. He was born in La Haye, a small town in France, and educated at the Jesuit college of La Flèche. He would later claim that of his instruction there, only mathematics, with its sure proof systems, had given him any certain knowledge; the rest of the instruction was little more than a passing on of ancient tradition. Discouraged with this system of learning, he traveled to Holland in 1618, where he served in the army of Maurice of Nassau. While with that army in Germany, he dreamed of some kind of unity between the sciences and mathematics. He interpreted that dream to be a divine sign of his intended career.

Ten years later, Descartes engaged in a debate in Paris where he argued that science, despite current beliefs that it could be based on probabilities, should be based only on certainty. The remainder of his life's work was a working out of a method to achieve that certainty, to eliminate probability, to establish and then build on only what can be known for certain. He first worked on this methodology in Holland, and in 1634 he published Le Monde, *though he had it suppressed when he heard of Galileo's condemnation. Seven years later, though, he published what would become one of his most famous works:* Meditations de Prima Philosophia, *together with sets of objections and replies to his thought. A more formal study, less narrative in tone, was published in 1644:* Principia Philosophiae. *Both works brought him fame—a murderous fame, as it turned out. In 1649 he was invited by Queen Christina of Sweden to come to her court and instruct her in philosophy. Overcoming his own reluctance, he went, and in 1650 died as a result of pneumonia brought on by the Swedish climate and exhaustion from the Queen's demands.*

Descartes established a discourse community of objective philosophy. He argued that all science could be unified under mathematical systems. Such systems established paradigms or models for establishing knowledge with certitude. Extending this notion, Descartes asserted that all knowledge, not just that of the natural sciences, could be tested by criteria based upon mathematical models. This led Descartes to hold that he would accept only beliefs that were "clearly and distinctly true," beliefs that were incapable of being doubted. One of these beliefs was in his own existence, which could not be doubted, because he was thinking: "cogito, ergo sum"— "I think, therefore I am."

The central question that Descartes posed—"How do I know?"—has affected virtually every philosopher since the sixteenth century. Philosophers began to ask not only what the world was like, but how could one know what the world was like. He

also gave to philosophy the premise that one can answer this question only by begin-
ning with one's consciousness and moving out to the external world.

The following selection includes the first and second meditations of Descartes'
Meditations on First Philosophy *(1641).*

MEDITATIONS ON FIRST PHILOSOPHY

in which are demonstrated the existence of God and the distinction between
the human soul and the body

FIRST MEDITATION: *What can be called into doubt*

Some years ago I was struck by the large number of falsehoods that I had 1
accepted as true in my childhood, and by the highly doubtful nature of the
whole edifice that I had subsequently based on them. I realized that it was
necessary, once in the course of my life, to demolish everything completely
and start again right from the foundations if I wanted to establish anything
at all in the sciences that was stable and likely to last. But the task looked an
enormous one, and I began to wait until I should reach a mature enough age
to ensure that no subsequent time of life would be more suitable for tackling
such inquiries. This led me to put the project off for so long that I would now
be to blame if by pondering over it any further I wasted the time still left for
carrying it out. So today I have expressly rid my mind of all worries and
arranged for myself a clear stretch of free time. I am here quite alone, and at
last I will devote myself sincerely and without reservation to the general dem-
olition of my opinions.

But to accomplish this, it will not be necessary for me to show that all 2
my opinions are false, which is something I could perhaps never manage.
Reason now leads me to think that I should hold back my assent from opinions which are not completely certain and indubitable just as carefully as I
do from those which are patently false. So, for the purpose of rejecting all
my opinions, it will be enough if I find in each of them at least some reason
for doubt. And to do this I will not need to run through them all individually,
which would be an endless task. Once the foundations of a building are undermined, anything built on them collapses of its own accord; so I will go
straight for the basic principles on which all my former beliefs rested.

Whatever I have up till now accepted as most true I have acquired 3
either from the senses or through the senses. But from time to time I have

found that the senses deceive, and it is prudent never to trust completely those who have deceived us even once.

Yet although the senses occasionally deceive us with respect to objects 4 which are very small or in the distance, there are many other beliefs about which doubt is quite impossible, even though they are derived from the senses—for example, that I am here, sitting by the fire, wearing a winter dressing-gown, holding this piece of paper in my hands, and so on. Again, how could it be denied that these hands or this whole body are mine? Unless perhaps I were to liken myself to madmen, whose brains are so damaged by the persistent vapours of melancholia that they firmly maintain they are kings when they are paupers, or say they are dressed in purple when they are naked, or that their heads are made of earthenware, or that they are pumpkins, or made of glass. But such people are insane, and I would be thought equally mad if I took anything from them as a model for myself.

A brilliant piece of reasoning! As if I were not a man who sleeps at 5 night, and regularly has all the same experiences while asleep as madmen do when awake—indeed sometimes even more improbable ones. How often, asleep at night, am I convinced of just such familiar events—that I am here in my dressing-gown, sitting by the fire—when in fact I am lying undressed in bed! Yet at the moment my eyes are certainly wide awake when I look at this piece of paper; I shake my head and it is not asleep; as I stretch out and feel my hand I do so deliberately, and I know what I am doing. All this would not happen with such distinctness to someone asleep. Indeed! As if I did not remember other occasions when I have been tricked by exactly similar thoughts while asleep! As I think about this more carefully, I see plainly that there are never any sure signs by means of which being awake can be distinguished from being asleep. The result is that I begin to feel dazed, and this very feeling only reinforces the notion that I may be asleep.

Suppose then that I am dreaming, and that these particulars—that my 6 eyes are open, that I am moving my head and stretching out my hands—are not true. Perhaps, indeed, I do not even have such hands or such a body at all. Nonetheless, it must surely be admitted that the visions which come in sleep are like paintings, which must have been fashioned in the likeness of things that are real, and hence that at least these general kinds of things— eyes, head, hands and the body as a whole—are things which are not imaginary but are real and exist. For even when painters try to create sirens and satyrs with the most extraordinary bodies, they cannot give them natures which are new in all respects; they simply jumble up the limbs of different animals. Or if perhaps they manage to think up something so new that nothing remotely similar has ever been seen before—something which is therefore completely fictitious and unreal—at least the colours used in the composition must be real. By similar reasoning, although these general kinds of things— eyes, head, hands and so on—could be imaginary, it must at least be admitted that certain other even simpler and more universal things are real. These are as it were the real colours from which we form all the images of things, whether true or false, that occur in our thought.

This class appears to include corporeal nature in general, and its exten- 7 sion; the shape of extended things; the quantity, or size and number of these things; the place in which they may exist, the time through which they may endure, and so on.

So a reasonable conclusion from this might be that physics, astronomy, 8 medicine, and all other disciplines which depend on the study of composite things, are doubtful; while arithmetic, geometry and other subjects of this kind, which deal only with the simplest and most general things, regardless of whether they really exist in nature or not, contain something certain and indubitable. For whether I am awake or asleep, two and three added together are five, and a square has no more than four sides. It seems impossible that such transparent truths should incur any suspicion of being false.

And yet firmly rooted in my mind is the long-standing opinion that 9 there is an omnipotent God who made me the kind of creature that I am. How do I know that he has not brought it about that there is no earth, no sky, no extended thing, no shape, no size, no place, while at the same time ensuring that all these things appear to me to exist just as they do now? What is more, since I sometimes believe that others go astray in cases where they think they have the most perfect knowledge, may I not similarly go wrong every time I add two and three or count the sides of a square, or in some even simpler matter, if that is imaginable? But perhaps God would not have allowed me to be deceived in this way, since he is said to be supremely good. But if it were inconsistent with his goodness to have created me such that I am deceived all the time, it would seem equally foreign to his goodness to allow me to be deceived even occasionally; yet this last assertion cannot be made.

Perhaps there may be some who would prefer to deny the existence of 10 so powerful a God rather than believe that everything else is uncertain. Let us not argue with them, but grant them that everything said about God is a fiction. According to their supposition, then, I have arrived at my present state by fate or chance or a continuous chain of events, or by some other means; yet since deception and error seem to be imperfections, the less powerful they make my original cause, the more likely it is that I am so imperfect as to be deceived all the time. I have no answer to these arguments, but am finally compelled to admit that there is not one of my former beliefs about which a doubt may not properly be raised; and this is not a flippant or ill-considered conclusion, but is based on powerful and well thought-out reasons. So in future I must withhold my assent from these former beliefs just as carefully as I would from obvious falsehoods, if I want to discover any certainty.

But it is not enough merely to have noticed this; I must make an effort 11 to remember it. My habitual opinions keep coming back, and, despite my wishes, they capture my belief, which is as it were bound over to them as a result of long occupation and the law of custom. I shall never get out of the habit of confidently assenting to these opinions, so long as I suppose them to be what in fact they are, namely highly probable opinions—opinions which, despite the fact that they are in a sense doubtful, as has just been shown, it is still much more reasonable to believe than to deny. In view of this, I think it will be a good plan to turn my will in completely the opposite direction and deceive myself, by pretending for a time that these former opinions are utterly false and imaginary. I shall do this until the weight of preconceived opinion is counter-balanced and the distorting influence of habit no longer prevents my judgement from perceiving things correctly. In the meantime, I know that no danger or error will result from my plan, and that I cannot possibly go too far in my distrustful attitude. This is because the task now in hand does not involve action but merely the acquisition of knowledge.

I will suppose therefore that not God, who is supremely good and the   12
source of truth, but rather some malicious demon of the utmost power and cunning has employed all his energies in order to deceive me. I shall think that the sky, the air, the earth, colours, shapes, sounds and all external things are merely the delusions of dreams which he has devised to ensnare my judgement. I shall consider myself as not having hands or eyes, or flesh, or blood or senses, but as falsely believing that I have all these things. I shall stubbornly and firmly persist in this meditation; and, even if it is not in my power to know any truth, I shall at least do what is in my power, that is, resolutely guard against assenting to any falsehoods, so that the deceiver, however powerful and cunning he may be, will be unable to impose on me in the slightest degree. But this is an arduous undertaking, and a kind of laziness brings me back to normal life. I am like a prisoner who is enjoying an imaginary freedom while asleep; as he begins to suspect that he is asleep, he dreads being woken up, and goes along with the pleasant illusion as long as he can. In the same way, I happily slide back into my old opinions and dread being shaken out of them, for fear that my peaceful sleep may be followed by hard labour when I wake, and that I shall have to toil not in the light, but amid the inextricable darkness of the problems I have now raised.

SECOND MEDITATION: *The nature of the human mind, and how it is better known than the body*

So serious are the doubts into which I have been thrown as a result of yester-   13
day's meditation that I can neither put them out of my mind nor see any way of resolving them. It feels as if I have fallen unexpectedly into a deep whirlpool which tumbles me around so that I can neither stand on the bottom nor swim up to the top. Nevertheless I will make an effort and once more attempt the same path which I started on yesterday. Anything which admits of the slightest doubt I will set aside just as if I had found it to be wholly false; and

I will proceed in this way until I recognize something certain, or, if nothing else, until I at least recognize for certain that there is no certainty. Archimedes* used to demand just one firm and immovable point in order to shift the entire earth; so I too can hope for great things if I manage to find just one thing, however slight, that is certain and unshakable.

I will suppose then, that everything I see is spurious. I will believe that 14 my memory tells me lies, and that none of the things that it reports ever happened. I have no senses. Body, shape, extension, movement and place are chimeras. So what remains true? Perhaps just the one fact that nothing is certain.

Yet apart from everything I have just listed, how do I know that there 15 is not something else which does not allow even the slightest occasion for doubt? Is there not a God, or whatever I may call him, who puts into me the thoughts I am now having? But why do I think this, since I myself may perhaps be the author of these thoughts? In that case am not I, at least, something? But I have just said that I have no senses and no body. This is the sticking point: what follows from this? Am I not so bound up with a body and with senses that I cannot exist without them? But I have convinced myself that there is absolutely nothing in the world, no sky, no earth, no minds, no bodies. Does it now follow that I too do not exist? No: if I convinced myself of something then I certainly existed. But there is a deceiver of supreme power and cunning who is deliberately and constantly deceiving me. In that case I too undoubtedly exist, if he is deceiving me; and let him deceive me as much as he can, he will never bring it about that I am nothing so long as I think that I am something. So after considering everything very thoroughly, I must finally conclude that this proposition, *I am, I exist*, is necessarily true whenever it is put forward by me or conceived in my mind.

But I do not yet have a sufficient understanding of what this "I" is, that 16 now necessarily exists. So I must be on my guard against carelessly taking something else to be this "I," and so making a mistake in the very item of knowledge that I maintain is the most certain and evident of all. I will therefore go back and meditate on what I originally believed myself to be, before I embarked on this present train of thought. I will then subtract anything capable of being weakened, even minimally, by the arguments now introduced, so that what is left at the end may be exactly and only what is certain and unshakable.

What then did I formerly think I was? A man. But what is a man? Shall 17 I say "a rational animal"? No; for then I should have to inquire what an animal is, what rationality is, and in this way one question would lead me down the slope to other harder ones, and I do not now have the time to waste on subtleties of this kind. Instead I propose to concentrate on what came into my thoughts spontaneously and quite naturally whenever I used to consider

*Archimedes (287–212 B.C.) was a Greek mathematician, physicist, and inventor.

what I was. Well, the first thought to come to mind was that I had a face, hands, arms and the whole mechanical structure of limbs which can be seen in a corpse, and which I called the body. The next thought was that I was nourished, that I moved about, and that I engaged in sense-perception and thinking; and these actions I attributed to the soul. But as to the nature of this soul, either I did not think about this or else I imagined it to be something tenuous, like a wind or fire or ether, which permeated my more solid parts. As to the body, however, I had no doubts about it, but thought I knew its nature distinctly. If I had tried to describe the mental conception I had of it, I would have expressed it as follows: by a body I understand whatever has a determinable shape and a definable location and can occupy a space in such a way as to exclude any other body; it can be perceived by touch, sight, hearing, taste or smell, and can be moved in various ways, not by itself but by whatever else comes into contact with it. For, according to my judgement, the power of self-movement, like the power of sensation or of thought, was quite foreign to the nature of a body; indeed, it was a source of wonder to me that certain bodies were found to contain faculties of this kind.

But what shall I now say that I am, when I am supposing that there is 18
some supremely powerful and, if it is permissible to say so, malicious deceiver, who is deliberately trying to trick me in every way he can? Can I now assert that I possess even the most insignificant of all the attributes which I have just said belong to the nature of a body? I scrutinize them, think about them, go over them again, but nothing suggests itself; it is tiresome and pointless to go through the list once more. But what about the attributes I assigned to the soul? Nutrition or movement? Since now I do not have a body, these are mere fabrications. Sense-perception? This surely does not occur without a body, and besides, when asleep I have appeared to perceive through the senses many things which I afterwards realized I did not perceive through the senses at all. Thinking? At last I have discovered it—thought; this alone is inseparable from me. I am, I exist—that is certain. But for how long? For as long as I am thinking. For it could be that were I totally to cease from thinking, I should totally cease to exist. At present I am not admitting anything except what is necessarily true. I am, then, in the strict sense only a thing that thinks; that is, I am a mind, or intelligence, or intellect, or reason—words whose meaning I have been ignorant of until now. But for all that I am a thing which is real and which truly exists. But what kind of a thing? As I have just said—a thinking thing.

What else am I? I will use my imagination. I am not that structure of 19
limbs which is called a human body. I am not even some thin vapour which permeates the limbs—a wind, fire, air, breath, or whatever I depict in my imagination; for these are things which I have supposed to be nothing. Let this supposition stand; for all that I am still something. And yet may it not perhaps be the case that these very things which I am supposing to be nothing, because they are unknown to me, are in reality identical with the "I" of

which I am aware? I do not know, and for the moment I shall not argue the point, since I can make judgements only about things which are known to me. I know that I exist; the question is, what is this "I" that I know? If the "I" is understood strictly as we have been taking it, then it is quite certain that knowledge of it does not depend on things of whose existence I am as yet unaware; so it cannot depend on any of the things which I invent in my imagination. And this very word "invent" shows me my mistake. It would indeed be a case of fictitious invention if I used my imagination to establish that I was something or other; for imagining is simply contemplating the shape or image of a corporeal thing. Yet now I know for certain both that I exist and at the same time that all such images and, in general, everything relating to the nature of body, could be mere dreams ⟨and chimeras⟩. Once this point has been grasped, to say "I will use my imagination to get to know more distinctly what I am" would seem to be as silly as saying "I am now awake, and see some truth; but since my vision is not yet clear enough, I will deliberately fall asleep so that my dreams may provide a truer and clearer representation." I thus realize that none of the things that the imagination enables me to grasp is at all relevant to this knowledge of myself which I possess, and that the mind must therefore be most carefully diverted from such things if it is to perceive its own nature as distinctly as possible.

But what then am I? A thing that thinks. What is that? A thing that 20 doubts, understands, affirms, denies, is willing, is unwilling, and also imagines and has sensory perceptions.

This is a considerable list, if everything on it belongs to me. But does it? 21 Is it not one and the same "I" who is now doubting almost everything, who nonetheless understands some things, who affirms that this one thing is true, denies everything else, desires to know more, is unwilling to be deceived, imagines many things even involuntarily, and is aware of many things which apparently come from the senses? Are not all these things just as true as the fact that I exist, even if I am asleep all the time, and even if he who created me is doing all he can to deceive me? Which of all these activities is distinct from my thinking? Which of them can be said to be separate from myself? The fact that it is I who am doubting and understanding and willing is so evident that I see no way of making it any clearer. But it is also the case that the "I" who imagines is the same "I." For even if, as I have supposed, none of the objects of imagination are real, the power of imagination is something which really exists and is part of my thinking. Lastly, it is also the same "I" who has sensory perceptions, or is aware of bodily things as it were through the senses. For example, I am now seeing light, hearing a noise, feeling heat. But I am asleep, so all this is false. Yet I certainly *seem* to see, to hear, and to be warmed. This cannot be false; what is called "having a sensory perception" is strictly just this, and in this restricted sense of the term it is simply thinking.

From all this I am beginning to have a rather better understanding of 22 what I am. But it still appears—and I cannot stop thinking this—that the corporeal things of which images are formed in my thought, and which the senses investigate, are known with much more distinctness than this puzzling "I" which cannot be pictured in the imagination. And yet it is surely surprising that I should have a more distinct grasp of things which I realize are doubtful, unknown and foreign to me, than I have of that which is true and known—my own self. But I see what it is: my mind enjoys wandering off and will not yet submit to being restrained within the bounds of truth. Very well then; just this once let us give it a completely free rein, so that after a while, when it is time to tighten the reins, it may more readily submit to being curbed.

Let us consider the things which people commonly think they under-   23
stand most distinctly of all; that is, the bodies which we touch and see. I do not mean bodies in general—for general perceptions are apt to be somewhat more confused—but one particular body. Let us take, for example, this piece of wax. It has just been taken from the honeycomb; it has not yet quite lost the taste of the honey; it retains some of the scent of the flowers from which it was gathered; its colour, shape and size are plain to see; it is hard, cold and can be handled without difficulty; if you rap it with your knuckle it makes a sound. In short, it has everything which appears necessary to enable a body to be known as distinctly as possible. But even as I speak, I put the wax by the fire, and look: the residual taste is eliminated, the smell goes away, the colour changes, the shape is lost, the size increases; it becomes liquid and hot; you can hardly touch it, and if you strike it, it no longer makes a sound. But does the same wax remain? It must be admitted that it does; no one denies it, no one thinks otherwise. So what was it in the wax that I understood with such distinctness? Evidently none of the features which I arrived at by means of the senses; for whatever came under taste, smell, sight, touch or hearing has now altered—yet the wax remains.

Perhaps the answer lies in the thought which now comes to my mind;   24
namely, the wax was not after all the sweetness of the honey, or the fragrance of the flowers, or the whiteness, or the shape, or the sound, but was rather a body which presented itself to me in these various forms a little while ago, but which now exhibits different ones. But what exactly is it that I am now imagining? Let us concentrate, take away everything which does not belong to the wax, and see what is left: merely something extended, flexible and changeable. But what is meant here by "flexible" and "changeable"? Is it what I picture in my imagination: that this piece of wax is capable of changing from a round shape to a square shape, or from a square shape to a triangular shape? Not at all; for I can grasp that the wax is capable of countless changes of this kind, yet I am unable to run through this immeasurable number of changes in my imagination, from which it follows that it is not the faculty of imagination that gives me my grasp of the wax as flexible and changeable. And what is meant by "extended"? Is the extension of the wax

also unknown? For it increases if the wax melts, increases again if it boils, and is greater still if the heat is increased. I would not be making a correct judgement about the nature of wax unless I believed it capable of being extended in many more different ways than I will ever encompass in my imagination. I must therefore admit that the nature of this piece of wax is in no way revealed by my imagination, but is perceived by the mind alone. (I am speaking of this particular piece of wax; the point is even clearer with regard to wax in general.) But what is this wax which is perceived by the mind alone? It is of course the same wax which I see, which I touch, which I picture in my imagination, in short the same wax which I thought it to be from the start. And yet, and here is the point, the perception I have of it is a case not of vision or touch or imagination—nor has it ever been, despite previous appearances—but of purely mental scrutiny; and this can be imperfect and confused, as it was before, or clear and distinct as it is now, depending on how carefully I concentrate on what the wax consists in.

But as I reach this conclusion I am amazed at how ⟨weak and⟩ prone 25 to error my mind is. For although I am thinking about these matters within myself, silently and without speaking, nonetheless the actual words bring me up short, and I am almost tricked by ordinary ways of talking. We say that we see the wax itself, if it is there before us, not that we judge it to be there from its colour or shape; and this might lead me to conclude without more ado that knowledge of the wax comes from what the eye sees, and not from the scrutiny of the mind alone. But then if I look out of the window and see men crossing the square, as I just happen to have done, I normally say that I see the men themselves, just as I say that I see the wax. Yet do I see any more than hats and coats which could conceal automatons? I *judge* that they are men. And so something which I thought I was seeing with my eyes is in fact grasped solely by the faculty of judgement which is in my mind.

However, one who wants to achieve knowledge above the ordinary level 26 should feel ashamed at having taken ordinary ways of talking as a basis for doubt. So let us proceed, and consider on which occasion my perception of the nature of the wax was more perfect and evident. Was it when I first looked at it, and believed I knew it by my external senses, or at least by what they call the "common" sense—that is, the power of imagination? Or is my knowledge more perfect now, after a more careful investigation of the nature of the wax and of the means by which it is known? Any doubt on this issue would clearly be foolish; for what distinctness was there in my earlier perception? Was there anything in it which an animal could not possess? But when I distinguish the wax from its outward forms—take the clothes off, as it were, and consider it naked—then although my judgement may still contain errors, at least my perception now requires a human mind.

But what am I to say about this mind, or about myself? (So far, remem- 27 ber, I am not admitting that there is anything else in me except a mind.) What, I ask, is this "I" which seems to perceive the wax so distinctly? Surely my awareness of my own self is not merely much truer and more certain than my awareness of the wax, but also much more distinct and evident. For if I judge that the wax exists from the fact that I see it, clearly this same fact entails much more evidently that I myself also exist. It is possible that what I see is not really the wax; it is possible that I do not even have eyes with which to see anything. But when I see, or think I see (I am not here distinguishing the two), it is simply not possible that I who am now thinking am not something. By the same token, if I judge that the wax exists from the fact that I touch it, the same result follows, namely that I exist. If I judge that it exists from the fact that I imagine it, or for any other reason, exactly the same thing follows. And the result that I have grasped in the case of the wax may be applied to everything else located outside me. Moreover, if my perception of the wax seemed more distinct after it was established not just by sight or touch but by many other considerations, it must be admitted that I now know myself even more distinctly. This is because every consideration whatsoever which contributes to my perception of the wax, or of any other body, cannot but establish even more effectively the nature of my own mind. But besides this, there is so much else in the mind itself which can serve to make my knowledge of it more distinct, that it scarcely seems worth going through the contributions made by considering bodily things.

I see that without any effort I have now finally got back to where I wanted. I now know that even bodies are not strictly perceived by the senses or the faculty of imagination but by the intellect alone, and that this perception derives not from their being touched or seen but from their being understood; and in view of this I know plainly that I can achieve an easier and more evident perception of my own mind than of anything else. But since the habit of holding on to old opinions cannot be set aside so quickly, I should like to stop here and meditate for some time on this new knowledge I have gained, so as to fix it more deeply in my memory.

QUESTIONS ABOUT DESCARTES' DISCOURSE COMMUNITY AND HIS CONCERNS IN THIS SELECTION

1. Does it seem logical to you that one should demolish all theoretical beliefs in order to devise new, and potentially more accurate, ones?
2. Descartes argues that he should withhold his assent from claims that are obviously false equally as with claims that are not completely certain. Do you agree with this approach?
3. What role(s) do the senses play in what we learn? What kinds of knowledge do we gain apart from the senses? Is it possible for knowledge gained without the use of the senses to be objectively confirmed?
4. Early in the first meditation, Descartes postulates that he might be asleep, that his meditations might be a deception. How would you answer that?
5. For a time Descartes assumes "that certain kinds of simple and universal things must be considered to be real." For example, a square will always have four

sides. But how does he throw doubt upon even that? Do you think those doubts are indeed legitimate and worth consideration? Couldn't it simply be argued that a square is a square by definition? Anything without four equal sides that intersect at right angles is by definition not a square.

6. At the beginning of the second meditation Descartes convinces himself of the fact of his existence because he is able to think: "as long as I think I am something." Does this seem to you to be an adequate proof for one's existence? Or is it too limited?

7. Descartes refuses to define man as a "rational animal." Would you say that his reasons for this refusal are merely pragmatic, or is there a deeper cause for this refusal?

8. Descartes claims that he is "a thing that doubts, understands, affirms, denies, is willing, is unwilling, and also imagines and has sensory perceptions." He then goes on to show that all of these attributes are related to thinking. Do you find this to be a convincing conclusion and argument?

QUESTIONS ABOUT DESCARTES' RHETORICAL STRATEGIES

1. In this selection, Descartes constructs a kind of gentle fiction. In the first meditation it seems that he is sitting by a fireside, wearing a winter dressing gown. In the second meditation he seems to be sitting by a window overlooking a busy city square. Do you think that these are accurate portrayals of where he is during the writing of these meditations? Would the argument be affected if they were not? Why would Descartes want to include this kind of material?

2. Descartes uses several different rhetorical modes here, including narrative, classification, and contrast. Do all of these strategies work together to form a unified piece? If so, how?

3. In some ways these meditations are the rambling thoughts of a philosopher beginning to consider a topic. How does Descartes make the argument progress when it seems to have the appearance of being discursive?

4. When dealing with the question of whether he might be insane or asleep, Descartes seems, at the same time, to both accept and reject the options. Does this seem to you to be a rhetorically sound way to proceed in an argument? Which discourse communities might not accept this methodology?

5. These two meditations are highly personal, using the first-person pronoun quite frequently. Is this rhetorical strategy appropriate for a "meditation"? Does it hinder a universal application of Descartes' ideas?

6. Throughout the meditations, Descartes employs rhetorical questions. In general, how does he use these?

7. Descartes uses a specific example—the piece of wax—to advance his argument on the relationship between thought and sensory experience. Is this an effective strategy to advance this argument?

WRITING FROM WITHIN AND ABOUT PHILOSOPHY

Writing for Yourself

1. In this essay, Descartes searches for one indisputable fact. In your journal, reflect on whether there is such an indisputable fact for you.

Writing for Nonacademic Audiences

1. A potential employer questions your choice of a major in philosophy, using Descartes as an example of esoteric thought that has no connection to the real world. In a 250-word letter to be submitted to that employer before your interview, defend your choice of a major.
2. For a journal like the *Reader's Digest*, write a 500-word narrative describing a time when your senses have deceived you.
3. Philosophers of religion have recently developed some ingenious arguments for the existence of God. As a senior philosophy major, you have been asked to give a fifteen-minute talk describing the more prominent of these arguments to a philosophy club on your campus. Write up that talk.
4. For *Literary Cavalcade*, a journal aimed at a high school audience, write a narrative that deals with philosophical assumptions that you once held but now have rejected. This feature article should be 750 words long.

Writing for Academic Audiences

1. For an interdisciplinary course in philosophy and psychology, write a 500-word evaluation of the adequacy of the definition of human beings as rational animals.
2. One of Descartes' most famous claims is "je pense, donc je suis"—"I think, therefore I am." For an introductory philosophy class, write a 750-word essay on whether thought is proof of existence.
3. For a class in logic, write a 750-word essay in which you attempt to prove that physical entities that we perceive through the senses have a reality independent of ourselves.
4. For an introductory philosophy class, write a 750-word essay dealing with whether or not we can accept knowledge not derived from the senses.
5. For a class in the history of philosophy, write a 1,500-word essay describing the influence of Cartesian philosophy on any one school of philosophy in the twentieth century.

John Locke

(1632–1704)

John Locke is often regarded as the father of the Age of Reason in England, and his ideas are still widely discussed today. He had a standard classical education at Westminster School from 1647 through 1652. In 1652 he began study at Oxford University, where he received his B.A. in 1656 and his M.A. in 1658. Afterwards, he was elected tutor at Oxford, in which capacity he was serving at the time of the restoration of the monarchy in 1660. Locke also earned a medical degree in 1675.

Locke is known now primarily as a thinker and writer, but in his day he often became embroiled in political activities. In 1666 he became personal secretary to Lord Shaftesbury, who became involved in activities regarded as treasonous. Lord Shaftesbury eventually had to flee to the Netherlands, and in 1684 Locke, fearing he might be suspected because of his association with Shaftesbury, also fled to the Netherlands. He was able to return to England once William of Orange became king.

Locke wrote about many subjects—religion, education, politics, medicine, and theories of knowledge. We include him in this book primarily because of his work in forming a discourse community concerned with theories of knowledge or with epistemology. Locke reacted against claims that human beings are endowed with innate ideas and that they can work out through reason the secrets of the universe. In many cases he argues against claims made by medieval scholastics and by Descartes. Locke argues for empiricism. He claims that we know things on the basis of experience and observation and on the basis of reflection upon experience. On a foundation of experience and reflection, we can perform more complicated mental operations.

The selection that follows is the first chapter of book 2 of Locke's An Essay Concerning Human Understanding. *Locke produced two drafts of this work in 1671 and then revised it from time to time over the next eighteen years. It was published in 1689, with all copies dated 1690.*

BOOK II: CHAPTER I

of ideas in general, and their original

1. Idea is the object of thinking.—Every man being conscious to himself, 1
that he thinks, and that which his mind is applied about, whilst thinking,
being the ideas that are there, it is past doubt that men have in their mind
several ideas, such as are those expressed by the words, "whiteness, hardness,
sweetness, thinking, motion, man, elephant, army, drunkenness," and others. It is in the first place then to be inquired, How he comes by them? I know
it is a received doctrine, that men have native ideas and original characters
stamped upon their minds in their very first being. This opinion I have at
large examined already; and, I suppose, what I have said in the foregoing
book will be much more easily admitted, when I have shown whence the
understanding may get all the ideas it has, and by what ways and degrees
they may come into the mind; for which I shall appeal to every one's own
observation and experience.

    2. All ideas come from sensation or reflection.—Let us then suppose 2
the mind to be, as we say, white paper, void of all characters, without any
ideas; how comes it to be furnished? Whence comes it by that vast store,
which the busy and boundless fancy of man has painted on it with an almost
endless variety? Whence has it all the materials of reason and knowledge? To
this I answer, in one word, From experience; in that all our knowledge is
founded, and from that it ultimately derives itself. Our observation, employed either about external sensible objects, or about the internal operations
of our minds, perceived and reflected on by ourselves, is that which supplies
our understandings with all the materials of thinking. These two are the
fountains of knowledge, from whence all the ideas we have, or can naturally
have, do spring.

    3. The object of sensation one source of ideas.—First. Our senses, con- 3
versant about particular sensible objects, do convey into the mind several
distinct perceptions of things, according to those various ways wherein those
objects do affect them; and thus we come by those ideas we have of yellow,
white, heat, cold, soft, hard, bitter, sweet, and all those which we call sensible qualities; which when I say the senses convey into the mind, I mean,
they from external objects convey into the mind what produces there those
perceptions. This great source of most of the ideas we have, depending wholly
upon our senses, and derived by them to the understanding, I call, "sensation."

    4. The operations of our minds the other source of them.—Secondly. 4
The other fountain, from which experience furnisheth the understanding with
ideas, is the perception of the operations of our own minds within us, as it is

employed about the ideas it has got; which operations, when the soul comes to reflect on and consider, do furnish the understanding with another set of ideas which could not be had from things without; and such are perception, thinking, doubting, believing, reasoning, knowing, willing, and all the different actings of our own minds; which we, being conscious of, and observing in ourselves, do from these receive into our understandings as distinct ideas, as we do from bodies affecting our senses. This source of ideas every man has wholly in himself; and though it be not sense as having nothing to do with external objects, yet it is very like it, and might properly enough be called "internal sense." But as I call the other "sensation," so I call this "reflection," the ideas it affords being such only as the mind gets by reflecting on its own operations within itself. By reflection, then, in the following part of this discourse, I would be understood to mean that notice which the mind takes of its own operations, and the manner of them, by reason whereof there come to be ideas of these operations in the understanding. These two, I say, viz., external material things as the objects of sensation, and the operations of our own minds within as the objects of reflection, are, to me, the only originals from whence all our ideas take their beginnings. The term "operations" here, I use in a large sense, as comprehending not barely the actions of the mind about its ideas, but some sort of passions arising sometimes from them, such as is the satisfaction or uneasiness arising from any thought.

5. *All our ideas are of the one or the other of these.*—The understand- 5 ing seems to me not to have the least glimmering of any ideas which it doth not receive from one of these two. External objects furnish the mind with the ideas of sensible qualities, which are all those different perceptions they produce in us; and the mind furnishes the understanding with ideas of its own operations.

These, when we have taken a full survey of them, and their several 6 modes, combinations, and relations, we shall find to contain all our whole stock of ideas; and that we have nothing in our minds which did not come in one of these two ways. Let any one examine his own thoughts, and thoroughly search into his understanding, and then let him tell me, whether all the original ideas he has there, are any other than of the objects of his senses, or of the operations of his mind considered as objects of his reflection; and how great a mass of knowledge soever he imagines to be lodged there, he will, upon taking a strict view see that he has not any idea in his mind but what one of these two have imprinted, though perhaps with infinite variety compounded and enlarged by the understanding, as we shall see hereafter.

6. *Observable in children.*—He that attentively considers the state of a 7 child at his first coming into the world, will have little reason to think him stored with plenty of ideas that are to be the matter of his future knowledge. It is by degrees he comes to be furnished with them; and though the ideas of obvious and familiar qualities imprint themselves before the memory begins to keep a register of time and order, yet it is often so late before some unusual

qualities come in the way, that there are few men that cannot recollect the beginning of their acquaintance with them: and, if it were worth while, no doubt a child might be so ordered as to have but a very few even of the ordinary ideas till he were grown up to a man. But all that are born into the world being surrounded with bodies that perpetually and diversely affect them, variety of ideas whether care be taken about it, or no, are imprinted on the minds of children. Light and colours are busy at hand every where when the eye is but open; sounds and some tangible qualities fail not to solicit their proper senses, and force an entrance to the mind; but yet I think it will be granted easily, that if a child were kept in a place where he never saw any other but black and white till he were a man, he would have no more ideas of scarlet or green, than he that from his childhood never tasted an oyster or a pine-apple has of those particular relishes.

7. *Men are differently furnished with these according to the different* 8 *objects they converse with.*—Men then come to be furnished with fewer or more simple ideas from without, according as the objects they converse with afford greater or less variety; and from the operations of their minds within, according as they more or less reflect on them. For, though he that contemplates the operations of his mind cannot but have plain and clear ideas of them; yet, unless he turn his thoughts that way, and considers them attentively, he will no more have clear and distinct ideas of all the operations of his mind, and all that may be observed therein, than he will have all the particular ideas of any landscape, or of the parts and motions of a clock, who will not turn his eyes to it, and with attention heed all the parts of it. The picture or clock may be so placed, that they may come in his way every day; but yet he will have but a confused idea of all the parts they are made of, till he applies himself with attention to consider them each in particular.

8. *Ideas of reflection later, because they need attention.*—And hence 9 we see the reason why it is pretty late before most children get ideas of the operations of their own minds; and some have not any very clear or perfect ideas of the greatest part of them all their lives:—because, though they pass there continually, yet like floating visions, they make not deep impressions enough to leave in the mind, clear, distinct, lasting ideas, till the understanding turns inwards upon itself, reflects on its own operations, and makes them the object of its own contemplation. Children, when they come first into it, are surrounded with a world of new things, which, by a constant solicitation of their senses, draw the mind constantly to them, forward to take notice of new, and apt to be delighted with the variety of changing objects. Thus the first years are usually employed and diverted in looking abroad. Men's business in them is to acquaint themselves with what is to be found without; and so, growing up in a constant attention to outward sensations, seldom make any considerable reflection on what passes within them till they come to be of riper years; and some scarce ever at all.

9. *The soul begins to have ideas when it begins to perceive.*—To ask, 10

at what time a man has first any ideas, is to ask when he begins to perceive; having ideas, and perception, being the same thing. I know it is an opinion, that the soul always thinks; and that it has the actual perception of ideas within itself constantly, as long as it exists; and that actual thinking is as inseparable from the soul, as actual extension is from the body: which if true, to inquire after the beginning of a man's ideas is the same as to inquire after the beginning of his soul. For, by this account, soul and its ideas, as body and its extension, will begin to exist both at the same time.

10. *The soul thinks not always; for this wants proofs.*—But whether 11 the soul be supposed to exist antecedent to, or coeval with, or some time after, the first rudiments or organization, or the beginnings of life in the body, I leave to be disputed by those who have better thought of that matter. I confess myself to have one of those dull souls that doth not perceive itself always to contemplate ideas; nor can conceive it any more necessary for the soul always to think, than for the body always to move; the perception of ideas being, as I conceive, to the soul, what motion is to the body: not its essence, but one of its operations; and, therefore, though thinking be supposed never so much the proper action of the soul, yet it is not necessary to suppose that it should be always thinking, always in action: that, perhaps, is the privilege of the infinite Author and Preserver of things, "who never slumbers nor sleeps;" but it is not competent to any finite being, at least not to the soul of man. We know certainly by experience, that we sometimes think; and thence draw this infallible consequence,—that there is something in us that has power to think; but whether that substance perpetually thinks, or no, we can be no farther assured than experience informs us. For to say, that actual thinking is essential to the soul and inseparable from it, is to beg what is in question, and not to prove it by reason; which is necessary to be done, if it be not a self-evident proposition. But whether this—that "the soul always thinks," be a self-evident proposition, that every body assents to on first hearing, I appeal to mankind. It is doubted whether I thought all last night, or no; the question being about a matter of fact, it is begging it to bring as a proof for it an hypothesis which is the very thing in dispute; by which way one may prove any thing; and it is but supposing that all watches, whilst the balance beats, think, and it is sufficiently proved, and past doubt, that my watch thought all last night. But he that would not deceive himself ought to build his hypothesis on matter of fact, and make it out by sensible experience, and not presume on matter of fact because of his hypothesis; that is, because he supposes it to be so; which way of proving amounts to this,—that I must necessarily think all last night because another supposes I always think, though I myself cannot perceive that I always do so.

But men in love with their opinions may not only suppose what is in 12 question, but allege wrong matter of fact. How else could any one make it an inference of mine, that a thing is not, because we are not sensible of it in our sleep? I do not say, there is no soul in a man because he is not sensible of it in his sleep; but I do say, he cannot think at any time, waking, or sleeping, without being sensible of it. Our being sensible of it is not necessary to any thing but to our thoughts; and to them it is, and to them it will always be, necessary, till we can think without being conscious of it.

11. *It is not always conscious of it.*—I grant that the soul in a waking 13 man is never without thought, because it is the condition of being awake; but whether sleeping without dreaming be not an affection of the whole man, mind as well as body, may be worth a waking man's consideration; it being hard to conceive that any thing should think and not be conscious of it. If the soul doth think in a sleeping man without being conscious of it, I ask, whether, during such thinking, it has any pleasure or pain, or be capable of happiness or misery? I am sure the man is not, no more than the bed or earth he lies on. For to be happy or miserable without being conscious of it, seems to me utterly inconsistent and impossible. Or if it be possible that the soul can, whilst the body is sleeping, have its thinking, enjoyments, and concerns, its pleasure or pain, apart, which the man is not conscious of, nor partakes in, it is certain that Socrates asleep, and Socrates awake, is not the same person; but his soul when he sleeps, and Socrates the man, consisting of body and soul, when he is waking, are two persons; since waking Socrates has no knowledge of, or concernment for that happiness or misery of his soul which it enjoys alone by itself whilst he sleeps, without perceiving any thing of it, no more than he has for the happiness or misery of a man in the Indies, whom he knows not. For if we take wholly away all consciousness of our actions and sensations, especially of pleasure and pain, and the concernment that accompanies it, it will be hard to know wherein to place personal identity.

12. *If a sleeping man thinks without knowing it, the sleeping and wak-* 14 *ing man are two persons.*—"The soul, during sound sleep, thinks," say these men. Whilst it thinks and perceives, it is capable, certainly, of those of delight or trouble, as well as any other perceptions; and it must necessarily be conscious of its own perceptions. But it has all this apart. The sleeping man, it is plain, is conscious of nothing of all this. Let us suppose, then, the soul of Castor, whilst he is sleeping, retired from his body; which is no impossible supposition for the men I have here to do with, who so liberally allow life without a thinking soul to all other animals. These men cannot, then, judge it impossible, or a contradiction, that the body should live without the soul; nor that the soul should subsist and think, or have perception, even perception of happiness or misery, without the body. Let us, then, as I say, suppose the soul of Castor separated, during his sleep, from his body, to think apart. Let us suppose, too, that it chooses for its scene of thinking the body of another man, v.g. Pollux, who is sleeping without a soul: for if Castor's soul can think whilst Castor is asleep, what Castor is never conscious of, it is no matter what place it chooses to think in. We have here, then, the bodies of two men with only one soul between them, which we will suppose to sleep and wake by turns; and the soul still thinking in the waking man, whereof

the sleeping man is never conscious, has never the least perception. I ask, then, whether Castor and Pollux, thus, with only one soul between them, which thinks and perceives in one what the other is never conscious of, nor is concerned for, are not two as distinct persons as Castor and Hercules, or as Socrates and Plato were ? and whether one of them might not be very happy and the other very miserable? Just by the same reason they make the soul and the man two persons, who make the soul think apart what the man is not conscious of. For, I suppose, nobody will make identity of persons to consist in the soul's being united to the very same numerical particles of matter; for if that be necessary to identity, it will be impossible, in that constant flux of the particles of our bodies, that any man should be the same person two days or two moments together.

13. Impossible to convince those that sleep without dreaming, that they think. —Thus, methinks, every drowsy nod shakes their doctrine who teach that their soul is always thinking. Those, at least, who do at any time sleep without dreaming can never be convinced that their thoughts are sometimes for hours busy without their knowing of it; and if they are taken in the very act, waked in the middle of that sleeping contemplation, can give no manner of account of it.

14. That men dream without remembering it, in vain urged. —It will perhaps be said, that the soul thinks even in the soundest sleep, but the memory retains it not. That the soul in a sleeping man should be this moment busy a-thinking, and the next moment in a waking man not remember, nor be able to recollect one jot of all those thoughts, is very hard to be conceived, and would need some better proof than bare assertion to make it be believed. For who can without any more ado but being barely told so, imagine that the greatest part of men do, during all their lives, for several hours every day think of something which, if they were asked even in the middle of these thoughts, they could remember nothing at all of? Most men, I think, pass a great part of their sleep without dreaming. I once knew a man that was a bred a scholar, and had no bad memory, who told me, he had never dreamed in his life till he had that fever he was then newly recovered of, which was about the five-or-six-and-twentieth year of his age. I suppose the world affords more such instances; at least, every one's acquaintance will furnish him with examples enough of such as pass most of their nights without dreaming.

15. Upon this hypothesis, the thoughts of a sleeping man ought to be most rational. —To think often and never to retain it so much as one moment, is a very useless sort of thinking; and the soul, in such a state of thinking, does very little if at all excel that of a looking-glass, which constantly receives a variety of images, or ideas, but retains none; they disappear and vanish, and there remain no footsteps of them; the looking-glass is never the better for such ideas, nor the soul for such thoughts. Perhaps it will be said, "that in a waking man the materials of the body are employed and made use of in thinking; and that the memory of thoughts is retained by the impressions that are made on the brain, and the traces there left after such thinking; but that in the thinking of the soul which is not perceived in a sleeping man, there the soul thinks apart, and, making no use of the organs of the body, leaves no impressions on it and consequently no memory of such thoughts." Not to mention again the absurdity of two distinct persons, which follows from this supposition, I answer farther, that whatever ideas the mind can receive and contemplate without the help of the body, it is reasonable to conclude it can retain without the help of the body too; or else the soul, or any separate spirit, will have but little advantage by thinking. If it has no memory of its own thoughts if it cannot lay them up for its use, and be able to recall them upon occasion; if it cannot reflect upon what is past, and make use of its former experiences, reasonings, and contemplations; to what purpose does it think? They who make the soul a thinking thing, at this rate will not make it a much more noble being than those do whom they condemn for allowing it to be nothing but the subtilest parts of matter. Characters drawn on dust that the first breath of wind effaces, or impressions made on a heap of atoms or animal spirits, are altogether as useful, and render the subject as noble, as the thoughts of a soul that perish in thinking; that, once out of sight, are gone for ever, and leave no memory of themselves behind them. Nature never makes excellent things for mean or no uses; and it is hardly to be conceived that our infinitely wise Creator should make so admirable a faculty as the power of thinking, that faculty which comes nearest the excellency of his own incomprehensible being, to be so idly and uselessly employed, at least a fourth part of its time here, as to think constantly without remembering any of those thoughts, without doing any good to itself or others, or being any way useful to any other part of the creation. If we will examine it, we shall not find, I suppose, the motion of dull and senseless matter any where in the universe made so little use of, and so wholly thrown away.

16. *On this hypothesis, the soul must have ideas not derived from sen-* 18 *sation or reflection, of which there is no appearance.* —It is true, we have sometimes instances of perception whilst we are asleep, and retain the memory of those thoughts: but how extravagant and incoherent for the most part they are, how little conformable to the perfection and order of a rational being, those who are acquainted with dreams need not be told. This I would willingly be satisfied in: Whether the soul, when it thinks thus apart, and as it were separate from the body, acts less rationally than when conjointly with it, or no? If its separate thoughts be less rational, then these men must say that the soul owes the perfection of rational thinking to the body; if it does not, it is a wonder that our dreams should be for the most part so frivolous and irrational, and that the soul should retain none of its more rational soliloquies and meditations.

17. *If I think when I know it not, nobody else can know it.* —Those 19 who so confidently tell us, that the soul always actually thinks, I would they would also tell us what those ideas are that are in the soul of a child before

or just at the union with the body, before it hath received any by sensation. The dreams of sleeping men are, as I take it, all made up of the waking man's ideas, though for the most part oddly put together. It is strange, if the soul has ideas of its own that it derived not from sensation or reflection (as it must have, if it thought before it received any impression from the body), that it should never in its private thinking (so private, that the man himself perceives it not), retain any of them the very moment it wakes out of them, and then make the man glad with new discoveries. Who can find it reasonable that the soul should in its retirement, during sleep, have so many hours' thoughts, and yet never light on any of those ideas it borrowed not from sensation or reflection, or at least preserve the memory of none but such which, being occasioned from the body, must needs be less natural to a spirit? It is strange the soul should never once in a man's whole life recall over any of its pure, native thoughts, and those ideas it had before it borrowed any thing from the body; never bring into the waking man's view any other ideas but what have a tang of the cask, and manifestly derive their original from that union. If it always thinks, and so had ideas before it was united, or before it received any from the body, it is not to be supposed but that during sleep it recollects its native ideas; and during that retirement from communicating with the body, whilst it thinks by itself, the ideas it is busied about should be, sometimes at least, those more natural and congenial ones which it had in itself, underived from the body, or its own operations about them; which since the waking man never remembers, we must from this hypothesis conclude, either that the soul remembers something that the man does not, or else that memory belongs only to such ideas as are derived from the body, or the mind's operations about them.

18. *How knows any one that the soul always thinks? For if it be not a* 20 *self-evident proposition, it needs proof.*—I would be glad also to learn from these men, who so confidently pronounce that the human soul, or, which is all one, that a man, always thinks, how they come to know it; nay, how they come to know that they themselves think, when they themselves do not perceive it? This, I am afraid, is to be sure without proofs, and to know without perceiving. It is, I suspect, a confused notion taken up to serve an hypothesis; and none of those clear truths that either their own evidence forces us to admit, or common experience makes it impudence to deny. For the most that can be said of it is, that it is possible the soul may always think, but not always retain it in memory; and I say, it is as possible that the soul may not always think, and much more probable that it should sometimes not think, than that it should often think, and that a long while together, and not be conscious to itself, the next moment after, that it had thought.

19. *That a man should be busy in thinking, and yet not retain it the* 21 *next moment, very improbable.*—To suppose the soul to think, and the man not to perceive it, is, as has been said, to make two persons in one man; and if one considers well these men's way of speaking, one should be led into a

suspicion that they do so. For they who tell us that the soul always thinks, do never, that I remember, say, that a man always thinks. Can the soul think, and not the man? or a man think, and not be conscious of it? This perhaps would be suspected of jargon in others. If they say, "The man thinks always, but is not always conscious of it," they may as well say, his body is extended without having parts. For it is altogether as intelligible to say, that a body is extended without parts, as that any thing thinks without being conscious of it, or perceiving that it does so. They who talk thus may, with as much reason, if it be necessary to their hypothesis, say, that a man is always hungry, but that he does not always feel it: whereas hunger consists in that very sensation, as thinking consists in being conscious that one thinks. If they say, that a man is always conscious to himself of thinking, I ask how they know it? Consciousness is the perception of what passes in a man's own mind. Can another man perceive that I am conscious of any thing, when I perceive it not myself? No man's knowledge here can go beyond his experience. Wake a man out of a sound sleep, and ask him what he was that moment thinking on. If he himself be conscious of nothing he then thought on, he must be a notable diviner of thoughts that can assure him that he was thinking: may he not with more reason assure him he was not asleep? This is something beyond philosophy; and it cannot be less than revelation that discovers to another thoughts in my mind when I can find none there myself: and they must needs have a penetrating sight who can certainly see that I think, when I cannot perceive it myself, and when I declare that I do not; and yet can see that dogs or elephants do not think, when they give all the demonstration of it imaginable, except only telling us that they do so. This some may suspect to be a step beyond the Rosicrucians; it seeming easier to make one's self invisible to others than to make another's thoughts visible to me, which are not visible to himself. But it is but defining the soul to be a substance that always thinks, and the business is done. If such definition be of any authority, I know not what it can serve for, but to make many men suspect that they have no souls at all, since they find a good part of their lives pass away without thinking. For no definitions that I know, no suppositions of any sect, are of force enough to destroy constant experience; and perhaps it is the affectation of knowing beyond what we perceive that makes so much useless dispute and noise in the world.

20. *No ideas but from sensation or reflection evident, if we observe* 22
children.—I see no reason therefore to believe that the soul thinks before the senses have furnished it with ideas to think on; and as those are increased and retained, so it comes by exercise to improve its faculty of thinking in the several parts of it; as well as afterwards, by compounding those ideas and reflecting on its own operations, it increases its stock, as well as facility in remembering, imagining, reasoning, and other modes of thinking.

21. He that will suffer himself to be informed by observation and ex- 23

uctory class in epistemology, write a 500-word paper definin
k an idea is.
mental psychology class, do some research in language acquisition
750-word paper comparing and contrasting those findings with
ns.
at Locke has been brought to the present time and becomes ac-
ith recent dream research. For a class in cognitive psychology, write
l paper analyzing how you think he would respond to the findings in
n dreams.
s in ethics, write a 750-word paper on how you define personhood.

perience, and not make his own hypothesis the rule of nature, will find few signs of a soul accustomed to much thinking in a new-born child, and much fewer of any reasoning at all. And yet it is hard to imagine, that the rational soul should think so much and not reason at all. And he that will consider that infants newly come into the world, spend the greatest part of their time in sleep, and are seldom awake, but when either hunger calls for the teat, or some pain (the most importunate of all sensations), or some other violent impression on the body, forces the mind to perceive and attend to it:—he, I say, who considers this will, perhaps, find reason to imagine, that a fœtus in the mother's womb differs not much from the state of a vegetable; but passes the greatest part of its time without perception or thought, doing very little but sleep in a place where it needs not seek for food, and is surrounded with liquor always equally soft, and near of the same temper; where the eyes have no light, and the ears so shut up are not very susceptible of sounds; and where there is little or no variety or change of objects to move the senses.

22. Follow a child from its birth, and observe the alterations that time 24 makes, and you shall find, as the mind by the senses comes more and more to be furnished with ideas, it comes to be more and more awake, thinks more the more it has matter to think on. After some time it begins to know the objects which, being most familiar with it, have made lasting impressions. Thus it comes by degrees to know the persons it daily converses with, and distinguish them from strangers; which are instances and effects of its coming to retain and distinguish the ideas the senses convey to it: and so we may observe how the mind, by degrees, improves in these, and advances to the exercise of those other faculties of enlarging, compounding, and abstracting its ideas, and of reasoning about them, and reflecting upon all these; of which I shall have occasion to speak more hereafter.

23. If it shall be demanded, then, when a man begins to have any ideas? 25 I think, the true answer is, When he first has any sensation. For since there appear not to be any ideas in the mind before the senses have conveyed any in, I conceive that ideas in the understanding are coeval with sensation; which is such an impression or motion made in some part of the body as produces some perception in the understanding. It is about these impressions made on our senses by outward objects that the mind seems first to employ itself in such operations as we call "perception, remembering, consideration, reasoning," &c.

24. *The original of all our knowledge.*—In time the mind comes to 26 reflect on its own operations about the ideas got by sensation, and thereby stores itself with a new set of ideas, which I call "ideas of reflection." These are the impressions that are made on our senses by outward objects, that are extrinsical to the mind; and its own operations, proceeding from powers intrinsical and proper to itself, which, when reflected on by itself, become also objects of its contemplation, are, as I have said, the original of all knowledge.

Thus the first capacity of human intellect is, that the mind is fitted to receive the impressions made on it, either through the senses by outward objects, or by its own operations when it reflects on them. This is the first step a man makes towards the discovery of any thing, and the ground-work whereon to build all those notions which ever he shall have naturally in this world. All those sublime thoughts which tower above the clouds, and reach as high as heaven itself, take their rise and footing here: in all that great extent wherein the mind wanders in those remote speculations it may seem to be elevated with, it stirs not one jot beyond those ideas which sense or reflection have offered for its contemplation.

25. *In the reception of simple ideas, the understanding is for the most part passive.* —In this part the understanding is merely passive; and whether or no it will have these beginnings and, as it were, materials of knowledge, is not in its own power. For the objects of our senses do many of them obtrude their particular ideas upon our minds, whether we will or no; and the operations of our minds will not let us be without at least some obscure notions of them. No man can be wholly ignorant of what he does when he thinks. These simple ideas, when offered to the mind, the understanding can no more refuse to have, nor alter when they are imprinted, nor blot them out and make new ones itself, than a mirror can refuse, alter or obliterate the images or ideas, which the objects set before it do therein produce. As the bodies that surround us do diversely affect our organs, the mind is forced to receive the impressions, and cannot avoid the perception of those ideas that are annexed to them.

QUESTIONS ABOUT LOCKE'S DISCOURSE COMMUNITY AND HIS CONCERNS IN THIS SELECTION

1. How does Locke define an idea? How would you define one?
2. Locke claims that the mind starts out as a "white paper." Do you agree that we have no innate ideas? What community of psychologists seems to have taken its lead from Locke?
3. What does Locke mean by *sensation*? What does he mean by *reflection*?
4. What does Locke mean when he writes that in receiving simple ideas, the mind is primarily passive? Do you agree with him?
5. How does Locke define *consciousness*? How adequate do you think his definition is?
6. How do you think Locke would explain the fact that some people have more and better ideas than others?
7. Would knowledge of hypnosis have changed any of Locke's views? How?
8. How do you react to Locke's claim that it is "the affectation of knowing beyond what we perceive that makes so much useless dispute and noise in the world" (end of section 19)?

QUESTIONS ABOUT L... STRATEGIES

1. Locke divides his chapte... tions for. Do you find this... this practice?
2. Locke writes about *men* inst... *men* to refer to people of both...
3. When does Locke use terms su... them?
4. What figures of speech does Lock... with his literal claims about the m...
5. What are some general characteris... vide clarity and precision, or does it...
6. How persuasive do you find Locke's... do you think his original readers woul...
7. Why does Locke write so much about... guing for?
8. How does Locke use opponents' ideas in... tice effective?
9. Is Locke arguing fairly when he claims tha... advance their own and argue for them on... (section 10)?

WRITING FROM WITHIN AND ABOUT PHIL...

Writing for Yourself

1. In your journal, reflect on your first memories. What... you been able to retain them?
2. In your journal, reflect on what ideas in this selection ap... ideas repulse you most?
3. In an introductory psychology class, the instructor writes... lowing claim: "At our births, our brains are like sheets of w... the world writes." The instructor then asks you to freewri... for five minutes.

Writing for Nonacademic Audiences

1. After some time away at college, you return home and your gra... you what you are studying. "Oh," you say, "in one of my classes... cussing how it is we come to have ideas." Write a sketch of how yo... conversation would proceed from that point.
2. When children are born, what do they know? Write two feature articl... subject for the Sunday edition of your local newspaper. Each may be n... than 750 words.

Writing for A...

1. For an introd... what you thi...
2. For a develop... and write a... Locke's clai...
3. Imagine th... quainted w... a 750-wor... research o...
4. For a clas...

Benjamin Lee Whorf

(1897–1941)

Benjamin Lee Whorf grew up in Winthrop, north of Boston Harbor. In 1914 he enrolled at the Massachusetts Institute of Technology to study chemical engineering. After graduation, he was employed as a fire prevention inspector for the Hartford Fire Insurance Agency, where he worked until his death.

In 1924, largely because he wanted to bridge the apparent gap between modern science and the Biblical account of creation, in his spare time Whorf began to study Hebrew. He soon began to study other languages as well, Aztec in 1926 and Mayan hieroglyphics in 1928.

In 1928 Whorf also met Edward Sapir, a noted linguist and anthropologist. In 1931, Sapir accepted a position at Yale University, and Whorf attended as many classes and discussions with Sapir and his graduate students as his job would allow him. Sapir encouraged Whorf to use his keen linguistic abilities to analyze Hopi and other Native American languages. Whorf began his work with a native speaker of Hopi living in New York City, and as he continued, he took leaves of absence from his insurance work to make field trips to the American West. Whorf never became a full-time, academic linguist, but his work on Native American languages is brilliant.

Today Whorf is best known for his work within a discourse community comprised of scholars called philosophers of language. Under Sapir's intellectual influence, Whorf developed a fascinating hypothesis, which is variously known as the Whorfian hypothesis, the Sapir-Whorf hypothesis, or the theory of linguistic relativity and determinism.

Whorf's hypothesis begins with the claim that all of our higher thought processes depend on language. Based on his work with Hopi, he went on to argue that all languages dissect reality differently from each other. In other words, each language carries with it a view of the world that is different from the views associated with other languages. This idea is known as linguistic relativity. Beyond this, one can take a strong view of linguistic determinism and argue that each language locks its speakers into its own way of viewing the world. Or one can take a weaker view and argue that each language habituates its speakers into seeing the world in a certain way but does not lock them into it.

Note: The manuscript of this article, together with pertinent linguistic notes, was among the papers left by Whorf at his death and turned over to George L. Trager. Dr. Trager and Dr. E. A. Kennard edited the manuscript for publication, making no substantial changes, and the paper is presented here in the form in which it appeared in the *Int. J. Amer. Linguistics*, 16:67–72 (1950). Internal evidence and certain comments found in Whorf's correspondence suggest that the paper was written in about 1936. [This note is by John B. Carroll, who edited *Language, Thought, and Reality*].

It is difficult to tell precisely how strong a view of linguistic determinism Whorf takes. It is clear, however, that his views have stimulated a great deal of discussion on the relationship between thought and language, between language and world-views, and between worldviews and actions. Many tests of his hypothesis have been conducted, but it is debatable whether researchers will ever be able to control all the variables that present themselves in such tests.

The following selection is taken from Language, Thought and Reality, *a collection of Whorf's writings edited after Whorf's untimely death. This selection was probably written about 1936.*

AN AMERICAN INDIAN MODEL OF THE UNIVERSE

I find it gratuitous to assume that a Hopi who knows only the Hopi language 1 and the cultural ideas of his own society has the same notions, often supposed to be intuitions, of time and space that we have, and that are generally assumed to be universal. In particular, he has no general notion or intuition of TIME as a smooth flowing continuum in which everything in the universe proceeds at an equal rate, out of a future, through a present, into a past; or, in which, to reverse the picture, the observer is being carried in the stream of duration continuously away from a past and into a future.

After long and careful study and analysis, the Hopi language is seen to 2 contain no words, grammatical forms, constructions or expressions that refer directly to what we call "time," or to past, present, or future, or to enduring or lasting, or to motion as kinematic rather than dynamic (i.e., as a continuous translation in space and time rather than as an exhibition of dynamic effort in a certain process), or that even refer to space in such a way as to exclude that element of extension or existence that we call "time," and so by implication leave a residue that could be referred to as "time." Hence, the Hopi language contains no reference to "time," either explicit or implicit.

At the same time, the Hopi language is capable of accounting for and 3 describing correctly, in a pragmatic or operational sense, all observable phenomena of the universe. Hence, I find it gratuitous to assume that Hopi thinking contains any such notion as the supposed intuitively felt flowing of "time," or that the intuition of a Hopi gives him this as one of its data. Just as it is possible to have any number of geometries other than the Euclidean* which give an equally perfect account of space configurations, so it is possible

---

*Euclid was a Greek mathematician who lived about 300 B.C. The geometry he developed is the one most commonly studied in North American schools.

to have descriptions of the universe, all equally valid, that do not contain our familiar contrasts of time and space. The relativity viewpoint of modern physics is one such view, conceived in mathematical terms, and the Hopi Weltanschauung is another and quite different one, nonmathematical and linguistic.

Thus, the Hopi language and culture conceals a METAPHYSICS, such as 4 our so-called naïve view of space and time does, or as the relativity theory does; yet it is a different metaphysics from either. In order to describe the structure of the universe according to the Hopi, it is necessary to attempt—insofar as it is possible—to make explicit this metaphysics, properly describable only in the Hopi language, by means of an approximation expressed in our own language, somewhat inadequately it is true, yet by availing ourselves of such concepts as we have worked up into relative consonance with the system underlying the Hopi view of the universe.

In this Hopi view, time disappears and space is altered, so that it is no 5 longer the homogeneous and instantaneous timeless space of our supposed intuition or of classical Newtonian mechanics. At the same time, new concepts and abstractions flow into the picture, taking up the task of describing the universe without reference to such time or space—abstractions for which our language lacks adequate terms. These abstractions, by approximations of which we attempt to reconstruct for ourselves the metaphysics of the Hopi, will undoubtedly appear to us as psychological or even mystical in character. They are ideas which we are accustomed to consider as part and parcel either of so-called animistic or vitalistic beliefs, or of those transcendental unifications of experience and intuitions of things unseen that are felt by the consciousness of the mystic, or which are given out in mystical and (or) so-called occult systems of thought. These abstractions are definitely given either explicitly in words—psychological or metaphysical terms—in the Hopi language, or, even more, are implicit in the very structure and grammar of that language, as well as being observable in Hopi culture and behavior. They are not, so far as I can consciously avoid it, projections of other systems upon the Hopi language and culture made by me in my attempt at an objective analysis. Yet, if MYSTICAL be perchance a term of abuse in the eyes of a modern Western scientist, it must be emphasized that these underlying abstractions and postulates of the Hopian metaphysics are, from a detached viewpoint, equally (or to the Hopi, more) justified pragmatically and experientially, as compared to the flowing time and static space of our own metaphysics, which are *au fond** equally mystical. The Hopi postulates equally account for all phenomena and their interrelations, and lend themselves even better to the integration of Hopi culture in all its phases.

The metaphysics underlying our own language, thinking, and modern 6 culture (I speak not of the recent and quite different relativity metaphysics of

---

* At bottom, fundamentally.

modern science) imposes upon the universe two grand COSMIC FORMS, space and time; static three-dimensional infinite space, and kinetic one-dimensional uniformly and perpetually flowing time—two utterly separate and unconnected aspects of reality (according to this familiar way of thinking). The flowing realm of time is, in turn, the subject of a threefold division: past, present, and future.

The Hopi metaphysics also has its cosmic forms comparable to these in scale and scope. What are they? It imposes upon the universe two grand cosmic forms, which as a first approximation in terminology we may call MANIFESTED and MANIFESTING (or, UNMANIFEST) or, again, OBJECTIVE and SUBJECTIVE. The objective or manifested comprises all that is or has been accessible to the senses, the historical physical universe, in fact, with no attempt to distinguish between present and past, but excluding everything that we call future. The subjective or manifesting comprises all that we call future, BUT NOT MERELY THIS; it includes equally and indistinguishably all that we call mental—everything that appears or exists in the mind, or, as the Hopi would prefer to say, in the HEART, not only the heart of man, but the heart of animals, plants, and things, and behind and within all the forms and appearances of nature in the heart of nature, and by an implication and extension which has been felt by more than one anthropologist, yet would hardly ever be spoken of by a Hopi himself, so charged is the idea with religious and magical awesomeness, in the very heart of the Cosmos, itself.* The subjective realm (subjective from our viewpoint, but intensely real and quivering with life, power, and potency to the Hopi) embraces not only our FUTURE, much of which the Hopi regards as more or less predestined in essence if not in exact form, but also all mentality, intellection, and emotion, the essence and typical form of which is the striving of purposeful desire, intelligent in character, toward manifestation—a manifestation which is much resisted and delayed, but in some form or other is inevitable. It is the realm of expectancy, of desire and purpose, of vitalizing life, of efficient causes, of thought thinking itself out from an inner realm (the Hopian HEART) into manifestation. It is in a dynamic state, yet not a state of motion—it is not advancing toward us out of a future, but ALREADY WITH US in vital and mental form, and its dynamism is at work in the field of eventuating or manifesting, i.e., evolving without motion from the subjective by degrees to a result which is the objective. In translating into English, the Hopi will say that these entities in process of causation "will come" or that they—the Hopi—"will come to" them, but, in their own language, there are no verbs corresponding to our "come" and "go" that mean simple and abstract motion, our purely kinematic concept. The words in this case translated "come" refer to the process of even-

7

---

* This idea is sometimes alluded to as the "spirit of the Breath" (*hikwsu*) and as the "Mighty Something" (*ʔaʔne himu*), although these terms may have lower and less cosmic though always awesome connotations. [Whorf's note].

tuating without calling it motion—they are "eventuates to here" (*pew'i*) or "eventuates from it" (*angqö*) or "arrived" (*pitu*, pl. *öki*) which refers only to the terminal manifestation, the actual arrival at a given point, not to any motion preceding it.

This realm of the subjective or of the process of manifestation, as distin- 8 guished from the objective, the result of this universal process, includes also— on its border but still pertaining to its own realm—an aspect of existence that we include in our present time. It is that which is beginning to emerge into manifestation; that is, something which is beginning to be done, like going to sleep or starting to write, but is not yet in full operation. This can be and usually is referred to by the same verb form (the EXPECTIVE form in my ter- minology of Hopi grammar) that refers to our future, or to wishing, wanting, intending, etc. Thus, this nearer edge of the subjective cuts across and in- cludes a part of our present time, viz. the moment of inception, but most of our present belongs in the Hopi scheme to the objective realm and so is indis- tinguishable from our past. There is also a verb form, the INCEPTIVE which refers to this EDGE of emergent manifestation in the reverse way—as belong- ing to the objective, as the edge at which objectivity is attained; this is used to indicate beginning or starting, and in most cases there is no difference apparent in the translation from the similar use of the expective. But, at certain crucial points, significant and fundamental differences appear. The inceptive, referring to the objective and result side, and not like the expective to the subjective and causal side, implies the ending of the work of causation in the same breath that it states the beginning of manifestation. If the verb has a suffix which answers somewhat to our passive, but really means that causation impinges upon a subject to effect a certain result—i.e. "the food is being eaten," then addition of the INCEPTIVE suffix in such a way as to refer to the basic action produces a meaning of causal cessation. The basic action is in the inceptive state; hence whatever causation is behind it is ceasing; the causation explicitly referred to by the causal suffix is hence such as WE would call past time, and the verb includes this and the incepting and the decausat- ing of the final state (a state of partial or total eatenness) in one statement. The translation is "it stops getting eaten." Without knowing the underlying Hopian metaphysics, it would be impossible to understand how the same suffix may denote starting or stopping.

If we were to approximate our metaphysical terminology more closely 9 to Hopian terms, we should probably speak of the subjective realm as the realm of HOPE or HOPING. Every language contains terms that have come to attain cosmic scope of reference, that crystallize in themselves the basic pos- tulates of an unformulated philosophy, in which is couched the thought of a people, a culture, a civilization, even of an era. Such are our words "reality, substance, matter, cause," and as we have seen "space, time, past, present, future." Such a term in Hopi is the word most often translated "hope"— *tunátya*—"it is in the action of hoping, it hopes, it is hoped for, it thinks or is thought of with hope," etc. Most metaphysical words in Hopi are verbs, not nouns as in European languages. The verb *tunátya* contains in its idea of hope something of our words "thought," "desire," and "cause," which sometimes must be used to translate it. The word is really a term which crystallizes the Hopi philosophy of the universe in respect to its grand dualism of objective and subjective; it is the Hopi term for SUBJECTIVE. It refers to the state of the subjective, unmanifest, vital and causal aspect of the Cosmos, and the fermenting activity toward fruition and manifestation with which it seethes—an action of HOPING; i.e., mental-causal activity, which is forever pressing upon and into the manifested realm. As anyone acquainted with Hopi society knows, the Hopi see this burgeoning activity in the growing of plants, the forming of clouds and their condensation in rain, the careful planning out of the communal activities of agriculture and architecture, and in all human hoping, wishing, striving, and taking thought: and as most especially concentrated in prayer, the constant hopeful praying of the Hopi community, assisted by their exoteric communal ceremonies and their secret, esoteric rituals in the underground kivas—prayer which conducts the pressure of the collective Hopi thought and will out of the subjective into the objective. The inceptive form of *tunátya*, which is *tunátyava*, does not mean "begins to hope," but rather "comes true, being hoped for." Why it must logically have this meaning will be clear from what has already been said. The inceptive denotes the first appearance of the objective, but the basic meaning of *tunátya* is subjective activity or force; the inceptive is then the terminus of such activity. It might then be said that *tunátya* "coming true" is the Hopi term for objective, as contrasted with subjective, the two terms being simply two different inflectional nuances of the same verbal root, as the two cosmic forms are the two aspects of one reality.

As far as space is concerned, the subjective is a mental realm, a realm 10 of no space in the objective sense, but it seems to be symbolically related to the vertical dimension and its poles the zenith and the underground, as well as to the "heart" of things, which corresponds to our word "inner" in the metaphorical sense. Corresponding to each point in the objective world is such a vertical and vitally INNER AXIS which is what we call the wellspring of the future. But to the Hopi there is no temporal future; there is nothing in the subjective state corresponding to the sequences and successions conjoined with distances and changing physical configurations that we find in the objective state. From each subjective axis, which may be thought of as more or less vertical and like the growth-axis of a plant, extends the objective realm in every physical direction, though these directions are typified more especially by the horizontal plane and its four cardinal points. The objective is the great cosmic form of extension; it takes in all the strictly extensional aspects of existence, and it includes all intervals and distances, all seriations and number. Its DISTANCE includes what we call time in the sense of the temporal relation between events which have already happened. The Hopi conceive time and motion in the objective realm in a purely operational sense—a matter of the complexity and magnitude of operations connecting events—so that the element of time is not separated from whatever element of space enters into the operations. Two events in the past occurred a long "time" apart (the Hopi language has no word quite equivalent to our "time") when many periodic physical motions have occurred between them in such a way as to traverse much distance or accumulate magnitude of physical display in other ways. The Hopi metaphysics does not raise the question whether the things in a distant village exist at the same present moment as those in one's own village, for it is frankly pragmatic on this score and says that any "events" in the distant village can be compared to any events in one's own village only by an interval of magnitude that has both time and space forms in it. Events at a distance from the observer can only be known objectively when they are "past" (i.e., posited in the objective) and the more distant, the more "past" (the more worked upon from the subjective side). Hopi, with its preference for verbs, as contrasted to our own liking for nouns, perpetually turns our propositions about things into propositions about events. What happens at a distant village, if actual (objective) and not a conjecture (subjective) can be known "here" only later. If it does not happen "at this place," it does not happen "at this time"; it happens at "that" place and at "that" time. Both the "here" happening and the "there" happening are in the objective, corresponding in general to our past, but the "there" happening is the more objectively distant, meaning, from our standpoint, that it is further away in the past just as it is further away from us in space than the "here" happening.

As the objective realm displaying its characteristic attribute of extension 11
stretches away from the observer toward that unfathomable remoteness which is both far away in space and long past in time, there comes a point where extension in detail ceases to be knowable and is lost in the vast distance, and where the subjective, creeping behind the scenes as it were, merges into the objective, so that at this inconceivable distance from the observer— from all observers—there is an all-encircling end and beginning of things where it might be said that existence, itself, swallows up the objective and the subjective. The borderland of this realm is as much subjective as objective. It is the abysm of antiquity, the time and place told about in the myths, which is known only subjectively or mentally—the Hopi realize and even express in their grammar that the things told in myths or stories do not have the same kind of reality or validity as things of the present day, the things of practical concern. As for the far distances of the sky and stars, what is known and said about them is supposititious, inferential—hence, in a way subjective—reached more through the inner vertical axis and the pole of the zenith than through the objective distances and the objective processes of vision and locomotion. So the dim past of myths is that corresponding distance on earth (rather than in the heavens) which is reached subjectively as myth through

the vertical axis of reality via the pole of the nadir—hence it is placed BELOW the present surface of the earth, though this does not mean that the nadir-land of the origin myths is a hole or cavern as we should understand it. It is *Palátkwapi* "At the Red Mountains," a land like our present earth, but to which our earth bears the relation of a distant sky—and similarly the sky of our earth is penetrated by the heroes of tales, who find another earthlike realm above it.

It may now be seen how the Hopi do not need to use terms that refer to 12 space or time as such. Such terms in our language are recast into expressions of extension, operation, and cyclic process provided they refer to the solid objective realm. They are recast into expressions of subjectivity if they refer to the subjective realm—the future, the psychic-mental, the mythical period, and the invisibly distant and conjectural generally. Thus, the Hopi language gets along perfectly without tenses for its verbs.

QUESTIONS ABOUT WHORF'S DISCOURSE COMMUNITY AND HIS CONCERNS IN THIS ESSAY

1. Is Whorf justified in writing with certainty that a Hopi who knows only the Hopi language has no intuition of time as a continuum? On what basis does he make this claim?
2. What is the basis for Whorf's claim that the Hopi language gets along perfectly without verb tenses? What does it mean for a language to get along perfectly?
3. If Whorf's claims about Hopi are true, do you think non-Hopi speakers could ever see the universe as Hopi speakers do?
4. If Whorf's claims in this essay are correct, how possible is translation from one language into another?
5. How does Whorf characterize Hopi metaphysics? What cosmic forms does it impose on the universe?
6. Where do you see evidence that Whorf assumes that most forms of thinking depend on language?
7. Do you think it is true that most metaphysical words in English are nouns? If so, is this significant? Why?
8. Do you think that an oral culture (one without written texts) would favor verbs (rather than nouns) more than a highly literate culture would?
9. Some people claim that speakers of English would be better off morally if the language forced them to give an expression of validity to all that they say. Do you agree?

QUESTIONS ABOUT WHORF'S RHETORICAL STRATEGIES

1. Consider Whorf's first sentence carefully. Does he seem too combative here? Would this sentence put some readers off?
2. Examine the first sentence of Whorf's second paragraph. Should it be broken down, or is it manageable as it is? Is Whorf trying to imitate something?
3. Describe the readers Whorf is addressing. Whom does the *we* he uses refer to?

4. How clearly does Whorf explain the Hopi conception of space? How could he have done this more clearly?
5. How well does Whorf's analogy between different systems of geometry and different views of the universe work?
6. In paragraph 9, Whorf makes a sweeping generalization about "every language." Is he justified in making such a generalization?
7. Whorf writes that different systems of metaphysics impose different cosmic forms on the universe. What view of knowledge and knowing lies behind the word *impose?*

WRITING FROM WITHIN AND ABOUT PHILOSOPHY

Writing for Yourself

1. In your journal, reflect on some of your experiences that have led you either to believe or disbelieve the claim that languages dissect reality differently from one another.
2. In your journal, reflect on your most embarrassing experience with a speaker of another language.

Writing for Nonacademic Audiences

1. Interview an exchange student on your campus, asking particularly about how many of his or her difficult adjustments have involved language. Use this interview for a 500-word feature article in your campus newspaper.
2. You work at an off-campus center as a tutor in the English language for students whose first language is not English. At one point, one of these students quits learning English, claiming he does not want to start seeing the world as an American. You must file a report on this student with your supervisor. Explain what the student said and evaluate it. This should be no longer than 500 words.
3. As an intern for the United States Department of State, you are asked to prepare a paper on your position on whether one worldview can be more valid than another. The paper must not exceed 1,000 words.

Writing for Academic Audiences

1. What would you say is the dominant worldview in the United States today? Respond in a 500-word analytical paper for a class in the sociology of the modern United States.
2. Research the history of some important international treaty or negotiation. Did different languages affect these negotiations? How? To what extent? Write up your findings in a paper for a class in international relations; the paper should be about 750 words long.
3. For a course in epistemology, write a 500-word paper in which you argue your position on the extent to which thought depends on language.
4. For a course in epistemology, write a 1,000-word paper in which you argue your position on whether most aspects of the world can be seen either as things or as processes. Also give your position on the implications of seeing aspects either as things or as processes.

Jean-Paul Sartre

(1905–1980)

Jean-Paul Sartre, in addition to being one of the West's great exponents of the philosophy of existentialism, was also one of France's more important playwrights and novelists. His novels Nausea *(1928),* The Age of Reason *(1947),* The Reprieve *(1947), and* Troubled Sleep *(1955) were to earn him the Nobel Prize for Literature in 1964, but he declined the award after deciding that novels were not particularly effective ways to communicate philosophical ideas. Instead he turned to plays, such as* No Exit *(1946), set in hell. This iconoclasm would mark his entire life.*

Sartre grew up with his maternal grandfather, Carl Schweitzer, the uncle of Albert Schweitzer. Rejected by his peers because of his slight build and crossed eyes, Sartre retreated with his mother to a sixth-story apartment, where he began to exercise his imagination and form the plan of becoming a writer. He attended the prestigious École Normale Supérieure and the Sorbonne, graduating from each and meeting Simone de Beauvoir (with whom he would maintain a lifelong attachment), Simone Weil, Claude Lévi-Strauss, and others who would become France's great writers of the twentieth century.

During the 1930s and 1940s Sartre wrote strong defenses of human dignity and human freedom in such works as Being and Nothingness *(1943). He argued in this work that consciousness, by definition, escapes all determinism. This assertion led to a greater concern for social responsibilities during the 1950s, and he himself began to act for the poor and disinherited, arguing that freedom carried along with it social responsibility. Towards this end Sartre looked to the Soviet Union, hoping that Communism in that country would bring about greater social responsibility. These hopes were crushed when the Soviet Union invaded Hungary in 1956. Four years later he wrote a critique of Marxism that suggested that the present form of that philosophy had ossified.*

From 1960 to 1971 Sartre worked on a biography of Gustave Flaubert, using Marxist and Freudian approaches, but the four-volume project was abandoned as Sartre began to believe that action was more important than the word. He left his desk more and more often, but towards the end of the 1970s he became blind. His death in 1980 attracted little official recognition, but twenty-five thousand people attended his funeral, a testament to his concern for freedom and dignity for all people.

Sartre's primary discourse community is generally agreed to be that of the existential philosopher. As a member of this tradition, he argued that each person gives meaning and order to the world. People become free as they recognize this role, though that freedom itself brings enormous responsibility. Sartre is somewhat pessimistic, however. The observation at the end of No Exit *that hell is other people sug-*

gests his belief that human relations menace personal integrity and can lead to self-deception.

The following selection is his essay "Existentialism."

EXISTENTIALISM

Man is nothing else but what he makes of himself. Such is the first principle 1 of existentialism. It is also what is called subjectivity, the name we are labeled with when charges are brought against us. But what do we mean by this, if not that man has a greater dignity than a stone or table? For we mean that man first exists, that is, that man first of all is the being who hurls himself toward a future and who is conscious of imagining himself as being in the future. Man is at the start a plan which is aware of itself, rather than a patch of moss, a piece of garbage, or a cauliflower; nothing exists prior to this plan; there is nothing in heaven; man will be what he will have planned to be. Not what he will want to be. Because by the word "will" we generally mean a conscious decision, which is subsequent to what we have already made of ourselves. I may want to belong to a political party, write a book, get married; but all that is only a manifestation of an earlier, more spontaneous choice that is called "will." But if existence really does precede essence, man is responsible for what he is. Thus, existentialism's first move is to make every man aware of what he is and to make the full responsibility of his existence rest on him. And when we say that a man is responsible for himself, we do not only mean that he is responsible for his own individuality, but that he is responsible for all men.

The word "subjectivism" has two meanings, and our opponents play on 2 the two. Subjectivism means, on the one hand, that an individual chooses and makes himself; and, on the other, that it is impossible for man to transcend human subjectivity. The second of these is the essential meaning of existentialism. When we say that man chooses his own self, we mean that every one of us does likewise; but we also mean by that that in making this choice he also chooses all men. In fact, in creating the man that we want to be, there is not a single one of our acts which does not at the same time create an image of man as we think he ought to be. To choose to be this or that is to affirm at the same time the value of what we choose, because we can never choose evil. We always choose the good, and nothing can be good for us without being good for all.

If, on the other hand, existence precedes essence, and if we grant that 3 we exist and fashion our image at one and the same time, the image is valid for everybody and for our whole age. Thus, our responsibility is much greater than we might have supposed, because it involves all mankind. If I am a workingman and choose to join a Christian trade union rather than be a Communist, and if by being a member, I want to show that the best thing for man is resignation, that the kingdom of man is not of this world, I am not only involving my own case—I want to be resigned for everyone. As a result, my action has involved all humanity. To take a more individual matter, if I want to marry, to have children, even if this marriage depends solely on my own circumstances or passion or wish, I am involving all humanity in monogamy and not merely myself. Therefore, I am responsible for myself and for everyone else. I am creating a certain image of man of my own choosing. In choosing myself, I choose man.

This helps us understand what the actual content is of such rather gran- 4 diloquent words as anguish, forlornness, despair. As you will see, it's all quite simple.

First, what is meant by anguish? The existentialists say at once that man 5 is anguish. What that means is this: the man who involves himself and who realizes that he is not only the person he chooses to be, but also a lawmaker who is, at the same time, choosing all mankind as well as himself, cannot help escape the feeling of his total and deep responsibility. Of course, there are many people who are not anxious; but we claim that they are hiding their anxiety, that they are fleeing from it. Certainly, many people believe that when they do something, they themselves are the only ones involved, and when someone says to them, "What if everyone acted that way?" they shrug their shoulders and answer, "Everyone doesn't act that way." But really, one should always ask himself, "What would happen if everybody looked at things that way?" There is no escaping this disturbing thought except by a kind of doubledealing. A man who lies and makes excuses for himself by saying "not everybody does that," is someone with an uneasy conscience, because the act of lying implies that a universal value is conferred upon the lie.

Anguish is evident even when it conceals itself. This is the anguish that 6 Kierkegaard called the anguish of Abraham. You know the story: an angel has ordered Abraham to sacrifice his son; if it really were an angel who has come and said, "You are Abraham, you shall sacrifice your son," everything would be all right. But everyone might first wonder, "Is it really an angel, and am I really Abraham? What proof do I have?"

There was a madwoman who had hallucinations; someone used to speak 7 to her on the telephone and give her orders. Her doctor asked her, "Who is it who talks to you?" She answered, "He says it's God." What proof did she really have that it was God? If an angel comes to me, what proof is there that it's an angel? And if I hear voices, what proof is there that they come from heaven and not from hell, or from the subconscious, or a pathological condition? What proves that they are addressed to me? What proof is there that I have been appointed to impose my choice and my conception of man on humanity? I'll never find any proof or sign to convince me of that. If a voice addresses me, it is always for me to decide that this is the angel's voice; if I consider that such an act is a good one, it is I who will choose to say that it is good rather than bad.

Now, I'm not being singled out as an Abraham, and yet at every mo- 8 ment I'm obliged to perform exemplary acts. For every man, everything happens as if all mankind had its eyes fixed on him and were guiding itself by what he does. And every man ought to say to himself, "Am I really the kind of man who has the right to act in such a way that humanity might guide itself by my actions?" And if he does not say that to himself, he is masking his anguish.

There is no question here of the kind of anguish which would lead to 9 quietism, to inaction. It is a matter of a simple sort of anguish that anybody who has had responsibilities is familiar with. For example, when a military officer takes the responsibility for an attack and sends a certain number of men to death, he chooses to do so, and in the main he alone makes the choice. Doubtless, orders come from above, but they are too broad; he interprets them, and on this interpretation depend the lives of ten or fourteen or twenty men. In making a decision he cannot help having a certain anguish. All leaders know this anguish. That doesn't keep them from acting; on the contrary, it is the very condition of their action. For it implies that they envisage a number of possibilities, and when they choose one, they realize that it has value only because it is chosen. We shall see that this kind of anguish, which is the kind that existentialism describes, is explained, in addition, by a direct responsibility to the other men whom it involves. It is not a curtain separating us from action, but is part of action itself.

When we speak of forlornness, a term Heidegger* was fond of, we mean 10 only that God does not exist and that we have to face all the consequences of this. This existentialist is strongly opposed to a certain kind of secular ethics which would like to abolish God with the least possible expense. About 1880, some French teachers tried to set up a secular ethics which went something like this: God is a useless and costly hypothesis; we are discarding it; but, meanwhile, in order for there to be an ethics, a society, a civilization, it is essential that certain values be taken seriously and that they be considered as having an *a priori* existence. It must be obligatory, *a priori*, to be honest, not to lie, not to beat your wife, to have children, etc., etc. So we're going to try a little device which will make it possible to show that values exist all the same, inscribed in a heaven of ideas, though otherwise God does not exist. In other words—and this, I believe, is the tendency of everything called reformism in France—nothing will be changed if God does not exist. We shall find ourselves with the same norms of honesty, progress, and humanism, and we shall have made of God an outdated hypothesis which will peacefully die off by itself.

The existentialist, on the contrary, thinks it very distressing that God 11

---

*Martin Heidegger was a twentieth-century German philosopher.

does not exist, because all possibility of finding values in a heaven of ideas disappears along with Him; there can no longer be an *a priori* Good, since there is no infinite and perfect consciousness to think it. Nowhere is it written that the Good exists, that we must be honest, that we must not lie; because the fact is we are on a plane where there are only men. Dostoievsky* said, "If God didn't exist, everything would be possible." That is the very starting point of existentialism. Indeed, everything is permissible if God does not exist, and as a result man is forlorn, because neither within him nor without does he find anything to cling to. He can't start making excuses for himself.

If existence really does precede essence, there is no explaining things 12 away by reference to a fixed and given human nature. In other words, there is no determinism, man is free, man is freedom. On the other hand, if God does not exist, we find no values or commands to turn to which legitimize our conduct. So, in the bright realm of values, we have no excuse behind us, nor justification before us. We are alone, with no excuses.

That is the idea I shall try to convey when I say that man is condemned 13 to be free. Condemned, because he did not create himself, yet, in other respects is free; because, once thrown into the world, he is responsible for everything he does. The existentialist does not believe in the power of passion. He will never agree that a sweeping passion is a ravaging torrent which fatally leads a man to certain acts and is therefore an excuse. He thinks that man is responsible for his passion.

The existentialist does not think that man is going to help himself by 14 finding in the world some omen by which to orient himself. Because he thinks that man will interpret the omen to suit himself. Therefore, he thinks that man, with no support and no aid, is condemned every moment to invent man. Ponge,† in a very fine article, has said, "Man is the future of man." That's exactly it. But if it is taken to mean that this future is recorded in heaven, that God sees it, then it is false, because it would really no longer be a future. If it is taken to mean that, whatever a man may be, there is a future to be forged, a virgin future before him, then this remark is sound. But then we are forlorn.

To give you an example which will enable you to understand forlorn- 15 ness better, I shall cite the case of one of my students who came to see me under the following circumstances: his father was on bad terms with his mother, and, moreover, was inclined to be a collaborationist,‡ his older brother had been killed in the German offensive of 1940, and the young man, with somewhat immature but generous feelings, wanted to avenge him. His mother lived alone with him, very much upset by the half-treason of her husband and the death of her older son; the boy was her only consolation.

* Feodor Mikhailovich Dostoyevsky (1821–1881) was a Russian novelist, one of the great figures of world literature.
† Francis Ponge was a twentieth-century French essayist and poet.
‡ One who willingly worked with the occupying German army during World War II.

The boy was faced with the choice of leaving for England and joining 16 the Free French forces—that is, leaving his mother behind—or remaining with his mother and helping her to carry on. He was fully aware that the woman lived only for him and that his going off—and perhaps his death— would plunge her into despair. He was also aware that every act that he did for his mother's sake was a sure thing, in the sense that it was helping her to carry on, whereas every effort he made toward going off and fighting was an uncertain move which might run aground and prove completely useless; for example, on his way to England he might, while passing through Spain, be detained indefinitely in a Spanish camp; he might reach England or Algiers and be stuck in an office at a desk job. As a result, he was faced with two very different kinds of action: one, concrete, immediate, but concerning only one individual; the other concerned an incomparably vaster group, a national collectivity, but for that very reason was dubious, and might be interrupted en route. And, at the same time, he was wavering between two kinds of ethics. On the one hand, an ethics of sympathy, of personal devotion; on the other, a broader ethics, but one whose efficacy was more dubious. He had to choose between the two.

Who could help him choose? Christian doctrine? No. Christian doctrine 17 says, "Be charitable, love your neighbor, take the more rugged path, etc., etc." But which is the more rugged path? Whom should he love as a brother? The fighting man or his mother? Which does the greater good, the vague act of fighting in a group, or the concrete one of helping a particular human being to go on living? Who can decide *a priori*? Nobody. No book of ethics can tell him. The Kantian* ethics says, "Never treat any person as a means, but as an end." Very well, if I stay with my mother, I'll treat her as an end and not as a means; but by virtue of this very fact, I'm running the risk of treating the people around me who are fighting, as means; and, conversely, if I go to join those who are fighting, I'll be treating them as an end, and, by doing that, I run the risk of treating my mother as a means.

If values are vague, and if they are always too broad for the concrete 18 and specific case that we are considering, the only thing left for us is to trust our instincts. That's what this young man tried to do; and when I saw him, he said, "In the end, feeling is what counts. I ought to choose whichever pushes me in one direction. If I feel that I love my mother enough to sacrifice everything else for her—my desire for vengeance, for action, for adventure— then I'll stay with her. If, on the contrary, I feel that my love for my mother isn't enough, I'll leave."

But how is the value of a feeling determined? What gives his feeling for 19 his mother value? Precisely the fact that he remained with her. I may say that I like so-and-so well enough to sacrifice a certain amount of money for him, but I may say so only if I've done it. I may say "I love my mother well

---

*Immanuel Kant (1724–1804) was a German metaphysician.

enough to remain with her" if I have remained with her. The only way to determine the value of this affection is, precisely, to perform an act which confirms and defines it. But, since I require this affection to justify my act, I find myself caught in a vicious circle.

On the other hand, Gide* has well said that a mock feeling and a true 20 feeling are almost indistinguishable; to decide that I love my mother and will remain with her, or to remain with her by putting on an act, amount somewhat to the same thing. In other words, the feeling is formed by the acts one performs; so, I cannot refer to it in order to act upon it. Which means that I can neither seek within myself the true condition which will impel me to act, nor apply to a system of ethics for concepts which will permit me to act. You will say, "At least, he did go to a teacher for advice." But if you seek advice from a priest, for example, you have chosen this priest; you already knew, more or less, just about what advice he was going to give you. In other words, choosing your adviser is involving yourself. The proof of this is that if you are a Christian, you will say, "Consult a priest." But some priests are collaborating, some are just marking time, some are resisting. Which to choose? If the young man chooses a priest who is resisting or collaborating, he has already decided on the kind of advice he's going to get. Therefore, in coming to see me he knew the answer I was going to give him, and I had only one answer to give: "You're free, choose, that is, invent." No general ethics can show you what is to be done; there are no omens in the world. The Catholics will reply, "But there are." Granted—but, in any case, I myself choose the meaning they have.

When I was a prisoner, I knew a rather remarkable young man who 21 was a Jesuit. He had entered the Jesuit order in the following way: he had had a number of very bad breaks; in childhood, his father died, leaving him in poverty, and he was a scholarship student at a religious institution where he was constantly made to feel that he was being kept out of charity; then, he failed to get any of the honors and distinctions that children like; later on, at about eighteen, he bungled a love affair; finally, at twenty-two, he failed in military training, a childish enough matter, but it was the last straw.

This young fellow might well have felt that he had botched everything. 22 It was a sign of something, but of what? He might have taken refuge in bitterness or despair. But he very wisely looked upon all this as a sign that he was not made for secular triumphs, and that only the triumphs of religion, holiness, and faith were open to him. He saw the hand of God in all this, and so he entered the order. Who can help seeing that he alone decided what the sign meant?

Some other interpretation might have been drawn from this series of 23 setbacks; for example, that he might have done better to turn carpenter or

---

* André Gide (1869–1951) was a French writer who achieved fame for his unconventional style of novel writing.

revolutionist. Therefore, he is fully responsible for the interpretation. Forlornness implies that we ourselves choose our being. Forlornness and anguish go together.

As for despair, the term has a very simple meaning. It means that we 24 shall confine ourselves to reckoning only with what depends upon our will, or on the ensemble of probabilities which make our action possible. When we want something, we always have to reckon with probabilities. I may be counting on the arrival of a friend. The friend is coming by rail or streetcar; this supposes that the train will arrive on schedule, or that the streetcar will not jump the track. I am left in the realm of possibility; but possibilities are to be reckoned with only to the point where my action comports with the ensemble of these possibilities, and no further. The moment the possibilities I am considering are not rigorously involved by my action, I ought to disengage myself from them, because no God, no scheme, can adapt the world and its possibilities to my will. When Descartes* said, "Conquer yourself rather than the world," he meant essentially the same thing.

The Marxists to whom I have spoken reply, "You can rely on the sup- 25 port of others in your action, which obviously has certain limits because you're not going to live forever. That means: rely on both what others are doing elsewhere to help you, in China, in Russia, and what they will do later on, after your death, to carry on the action and lead it to its fulfillment, which will be the revolution. You even *have* to rely upon that, otherwise you're immoral." I reply at once that I will always rely on fellow-fighters insofar as these comrades are involved with me in a common struggle, in the unity of a party or a group in which I can more or less make my weight felt; that is, one whose ranks I am in as a fighter and whose movements I am aware of at every moment. In such a situation, relying on the unity and will of the party is exactly like counting on the fact that the train will arrive on time or that the car won't jump the track. But, given that man is free and that there is no human nature for me to depend on, I cannot count on men whom I do not know by relying on human goodness or man's concern for the good of society. I don't know what will become of the Russian revolution; I may make an example of it to the extent that at the present time it is apparent that the proletariat plays a part in Russia that it plays in no other nation. But I can't swear that this will inevitably lead to a triumph of the proletariat. I've got to limit myself to what I see.

Given that men are free and that tomorrow they will freely decide what 26 man will be, I cannot be sure that, after my death, fellow-fighters will carry on my work to bring it to its maximum perfection. Tomorrow, after my death, some men may decide to set up Fascism, and the others may be cowardly and muddled enough to let them do it. Fascism will then be the human reality, so much the worse for us.

* René Descartes (1596–1650) was a French philosopher and scientist.

Actually, things will be as man will have decided they are to be. Does 27
that mean that I should abandon myself to quietism? No. First, I should
involve myself; then, act on the old saw, "Nothing ventured, nothing gained."
Nor does it mean that I shouldn't belong to a party, but rather that I shall
have no illusions and shall do what I can. For example, suppose I ask myself,
"Will socialization, as such, ever come about?" I know nothing about it. All
I know is that I'm going to do everything in my power to bring it about.
Beyond that, I can't count on anything. Quietism is the attitude of people
who say, "Let others do what I can't do." The doctrine I am presenting is the
very opposite of quietism, since it declares, "There is no reality except in
action." Moreover, it goes further, since it adds, "Man is nothing else than
his plan; he exists only to the extent that he fulfills himself; he is therefore
nothing else than the ensemble of his acts, nothing else than his life."

According to this, we can understand why our doctrine horrifies certain 28
people. Because often the only way they can bear their wretchedness is to
think, "Circumstances have been against me. What I've been and done doesn't
show my true worth. To be sure, I've had no great love, no great friendship,
but that's because I haven't met a man or woman who was worthy. The
books I've written haven't been very good because I haven't had the proper
leisure. I haven't had children to devote myself to because I didn't find a man
with whom I could have spent my life. So there remains within me, unused
and quite viable, a host of propensities, inclinations, possibilities, that one
wouldn't guess from the mere series of things I've done."

Now, for the existentialist there is really no love other than one which 29
manifests itself in a person's being in love. There is no genius other than one
which is expressed in works of art; the genius of Proust* is the sum of Proust's
works; the genius of Racine† is his series of tragedies. Outside of that, there
is nothing. Why say that Racine could have written another tragedy, when
he didn't write it? A man is involved in life, leaves his impress on it, and
outside of that there is nothing. To be sure, this may seem a harsh thought to
someone whose life hasn't been a success. But, on the other hand, it prompts
people to understand that reality alone is what counts, that dreams, expectations, and hopes warrant no more than to define a man as a disappointed
dream, as miscarried hopes, as vain expectations. In other words, to define
him negatively and not positively. However, when we say, "You are nothing
else than your life," that does not imply that the artist will be judged solely
on the basis of his works of art; a thousand other things will contribute toward summing him up. What we mean is that a man is nothing else than a
series of undertakings, that he is the sum, the organization, the ensemble of
the relationships which make up these undertakings.

When all is said and done, what we are accused of, at bottom, is not 30

---

* Marcel Proust (1871–1922) was a French novelist.
† Jean Racine (1639–1699) was a French dramatist.

our pessimism, but an optimistic toughness. If people throw up to us our works of fiction in which we write about people who are soft, weak, cowardly, and sometimes even downright bad, it's not because these people are soft, weak, cowardly, or bad; because if we were to say, as Zola* did, that they are that way because of heredity, the workings of environment, society, because of biological or psychological determinism, people would be reassured. They would say, "Well, that's what we're like, no one can do anything about it." But when the existentialist writes about a coward, he says that this coward is responsible for his cowardice. He's not like that because he has a cowardly heart or lung or brain; he's not like that on account of his physiological make-up; but he's like that because he has made himself a coward by his acts. There's no such thing as a cowardly constitution; there are nervous constitutions; there is poor blood, as the common people say, or strong constitutions. But the man whose blood is poor is not a coward on that account, for what makes cowardice is the act of renouncing or yielding. A constitution is not an act; the coward is defined on the basis of the acts he performs. People feel, in a vague sort of way, that this coward we're talking about is guilty of being a coward, and the thought frightens them. What people would like is that a coward or a hero be born that way. . . .

From these few reflections it is evident that nothing is more unjust than 31 the objections that have been raised against us. Existentialism is nothing else than an attempt to draw all the consequences of a coherent atheistic position. It isn't trying to plunge man into despair at all. But if one calls every attitude of unbelief despair, like the Christians, then the word is not being used in its original sense. Existentialism isn't so atheistic that it wears itself out showing that God doesn't exist. Rather, it declares that even if God did exist, that would change nothing. There you've got our point of view. Not that we believe that God exists, but we think that the problem of His existence is not the issue. In this sense existentialism is optimistic, a doctrine of action, and it is plain dishonesty for Christians to make no distinction between their own despair and ours and then to call us despairing.

QUESTIONS ABOUT SARTRE'S DISCOURSE
COMMUNITY AND HIS CONCERNS IN THIS ESSAY

1. What does Sartre mean when he claims that "man is nothing else but what he makes of himself" (paragraph 1)? How does this claim lead to a charge of "subjectivity"?
2. According to Sartre, for what reason is each person responsible for himself or herself? In what sense is each person responsible "for all men"? What is the source of this responsibility?
3. According to Sartre, upon what basis do people make ethical and moral decisions?

---

* Émile Zola (1840–1902) was a French novelist.

4. Is it the case that a person "can never choose evil" (paragraph 2)? How do you think Sartre accounts for the presence of evil in the world?
5. Define *anguish* in Sartre's sense of the word. According to Sartre, what is the basis for this anguish? Do you agree that those people who are not experiencing this anguish are merely hiding their anxiety (paragraph 5)?
6. Sartre rejects the notion of faith, insisting that decisions must be based upon personal choice. Is it necessarily the case that a choice to have faith in something is the opposite of remaining free to make personal choices?
7. According to Sartre, what does it mean to be forlorn? Why should this be a desirable condition?
8. Is it the case that "there is no reality except in action" (paragraph 27)?

QUESTIONS ABOUT SARTRE'S RHETORICAL STRATEGIES

1. How would you characterize the tone of this essay? Which of its elements are particularly significant in the creation of that tone?
2. In the first two paragraphs, Sartre seems to be responding to opponents who make certain charges against existentialists. Why does he begin this way? Why does he not identify his opponents at this time? Does it seem to you that the opponents he has in mind at the beginning of the essay are the same as those mentioned in the conclusion?
3. In general, how does Sartre use examples in this essay? Characterize those examples. Which discourse communities might not accept this kind of example? Why?
4. Why does Sartre assure the reader that "it's all quite simple" when he comes to define certain terms (paragraph 4)?
5. How does Sartre's use of the story of Abraham help to advance his argument?
6. Sartre frequently defines existentialism by opposing it to other schools of thought. Is this an effective rhetorical strategy?
7. Read over paragraph seventeen. The stance of the writer here seems very personal, almost as though the writer is carrying on a dialogue with the reader. Is this an effective stance? Where else does Sartre use it in this essay?
8. At times Sartre will use phrases that sound like slogans: "There is no reality except in action" (paragraph 27); "Man is nothing else than his plan" (paragraph 27). Does Sartre mean for these to work upon the reader as a slogan might? If so, why?

WRITING FROM WITHIN AND ABOUT PHILOSOPHY

Writing for Yourself

1. In your journal, reflect on whether we fashion and shape ourselves only by acts of our own will or whether we are influenced by other forces.
2. In your journal, reflect on what the foundations of your deepest values are.

Writing for Nonacademic Audiences

1. For a high school class beginning to study the works of the French existential-ists, prepare a ten-minute talk in which you define the terms *anguish, forlorn-ness,* and *despair.*
2. In a recent movie review printed in your institution's newspaper, a student critic calls a character in a movie an existentialist because for that character life has absolutely no meaning. In a letter to the editor, you react to the critic's conception of existentialism.

Writing for Academic Audiences

1. Write a 50-word abstract for this essay, to be used as a header for the essay in a volume of Sartre's work.
2. For a class in ethics, write a 250-word essay in which you suggest a resolution to the conflict Sartre describes in paragraphs fifteen and sixteen. Should the boy go to the front or stay with his mother?
3. Sartre refuses to accept the validity of the claim that existentialism is a philos-ophy of despair. For an introduction to philosophy course, write a 500-word essay that is based upon this selection and that evaluates the validity of the charge.

Thomas Merton

(1915–1968)

Born into a family of artists in France, Thomas Merton would later comment that he was born into a world at war. While he was being born, rotting bodies were being buried along the Marne, the detritus of one of the grimmest battles of World War I. In his autobiography, The Seven Story Mountain, *Merton would continually use the metaphor of war and conflict as he discusses his youth and eventual entrance into a Trappist monastery.*

Merton studied at Cambridge University and Columbia University, where he was converted to Roman Catholicism. He became a Trappist monk at the age of 26, entering the Abbey of Our Lady of Gethsemani, in Kentucky, where he was to live for much of the remainder of his life. A poet and a literary critic, Merton is best known for his theological writing, his autobiography, and his history of the Trappists, The Waters of Siloe.

Merton held a lifelong interest in Eastern religions, and in 1968 he traveled to an ecumenical council of Catholic and Buddhist monks, held in Bangkok, Thailand, to discuss the future of monastic life in Asia. While there, he died in an electrical accident. He left behind him about twelve essays that dealt with Zen Buddhism, each of which works not only at explaining the main tenets of Zen and its influence on and importance for the Western world, but also at reconciling two discourse communities—Roman Catholicism and Zen Buddhism—which had historically been at odds.

*The following essay, "Zen Buddhist Monasticism," is an example of his attempt at reconciling these communities. It was first published in his collection of essays on mysticism—*Mystics and Zen Masters *(1967), and later reprinted in a posthumous collection entitled* Thomas Merton on Zen *(1976). The editor of that volume, Irmgard Schloegl, suggested the root of Merton's interest in Zen:*

> *Thomas Merton went down the Christian branch of religion to the root. Nourished by that, he saw the other branches. Is it so surprising that his writings in Zen come from a depth of understanding rather than from a surface comparison? When the dogmatists meet, there is great argument. When the practicians meet, there is a nodding agreement (vii–viii).*

ZEN BUDDHIST MONASTICISM

A description of the observances of Japanese Zen monasteries might prove 1
entertaining and indeed instructive. But such a description would be worse
than useless without some understanding of the nature of Zen. Since Zen is
one of the most mysterious of all spiritualities—being so full of impudent
paradox that it is at first a real scandal to the rational spirit of the West—it
is not at all easy to make it accessible to the modern Western reader.

This article will therefore be divided into two parts. In the first we will 2
consider the meaning of Zen to discover the motivation that brings the postulant to a Zen monastery. The second part will be shorter and will give a
description of life in the monastery. Those who would be confused or repelled
by the mystery of Zen teaching might read the second part first.

The approach will be one of sympathetic objectivity. Neither the space 3
at our disposal nor the climate of dialogue permit, in such an essay, any
destructive criticism of an Asian religious mentality which is in any case very
difficult to understand precisely in our Western terms.

I

Writers with a superficial knowledge of monasticism in Christianity and in 4
Buddhism sometimes compare the Zen Buddhist monks with the Cistercians.
There are, indeed, obvious analogies. The Zen monks are noted for the simplicity and austerity of their lives, their uncompromising poverty, their manual work, the extreme strictness and plainness of the common life. We frequently encounter in Zen those deliberate and sometimes violent tactics of
punishment and humiliation which can remind one of the methods of Abbot
de Rancé and the spirituality of La Trappe. Later in this article we shall take
note of many monastic practices in Zen which recall to mind some of the
most basic monastic traditions of the West. But it must be said right at the
beginning that from a certain point of view Zen monasticism has a quite
different purpose from ours, and if, in describing the life of the *Zendo*, we
unconsciously project our own monastic ideals, aims, and problems into the
context of Japanese Buddhism, we will certainly fail to understand what Zen
is all about, and we will fail to grasp any possible meaning that Zen might
have for ourselves.*

Our own view of monasticism, as Cistercians, is of course first of all 5

---

*Dom Aelred Graham, O.S.B., in his *Zen Catholicism* (New York, 1963) has given us a useful
demonstration of the value, even for Christians and Christian monks, of a certain Zen
way of looking at life. Not that we should necessarily imitate the rather drastic methods
of Zen, but there is a directness and a simplicity in the Zen attitude toward life that is
spiritually and psychologically healthy, provided of course that it is properly understood.
Dom Graham advances the merits of this simplicity as against rigidly artificial and self-
conscious programs in the spiritual life. [Merton's note.]

focused on a lifetime consecration to God in a monastery in which, further-more, we have a vow of stability. The Zen monk is doubtless no less deter-mined than we are to devote his life to the purpose of attaining salvation. But for him, the monastery is not what it is for St. Benedict: a permanent "work-shop in which all the instruments of perfection are to be employed . . . a school in which one perseveres until death in patience, and in participation in the sufferings of Christ."*

The Zen monastery with its common meditation hall, or *Zendo*, is in a 6 sense more like a seminary than a monastic family. It is a place of formation and training. Hence the intensity and pressure of the discipline of the *Zendo* is easier to understand when we realize that it is intended to be lived only for a few years and not for a whole lifetime.

In fact, far from a lifetime commitment to remain in one community, 7 the Zen monk is bound only for a relatively short period, analogous to a scholastic "term." At the end of this he is free to leave for another monastery (as one might change to a different school or university). He is also subject to examinations, and if he fails to meet the standards he is not allowed to return to the monastery and he will even be refused in other monasteries.

The purpose of this formation, as we shall see in a moment, is to give 8 the monk, as quickly and as effectively as possible, a degree of spiritual ma-turity and liberty which will enable him to stand on his own feet and pursue, on his own, the path to enlightenment by the traditional practice of the Bud-dhist precepts (*sila*), meditation (*dhyana*), and wisdom (*prajna*). Once he attains this mature formation, he may leave the monastery to dwell as a priest in some city, or perhaps as a hermit in a lonely mountain temple. He may go to another monastery, he may go on pilgrimage, or he may return to business or professional life as a layman. Or he may remain in the monastery to teach and guide others. But, in any case, we see immediately that, in Zen at least, the Buddhist monk is not incorporated for life in one monastic family. In fact, as in primitive Christian eremitism, the Zen monk seeks out a particular monastery more because of a *Roshi*, or "venerable teacher," who is found there, than for the sake of the community or the rule. His aim is to attain to direct spiritual insight that will qualify him to live on his own.

In order to understand something of the spirit of Zen, we might quote 9 a frankly anti-monastic statement attributed to Buddha in one of his last discourses.†

Knowing that the Master was about to die, his favorite disciple, Ananda, 10 asked him to leave final instructions, perhaps in the form of a rule, for his disciples. But the Buddha refused to do so. He explicitly refrained from be-coming the "founder of an order" which would follow special methods to

---

*See *Rule of St. Benedict*, C. 4 end, Prol. end, etc.

† From the *Digha Nikaya*, which is a Pali text belonging to the Theravada (Hinayana) tradition. Zen is of course in the Mahayana tradition. But the text nevertheless throws light on the Zen spirit. The translation used here is taken from *Sources of Indian Tradition*, by De Bary, Hay, Weiler, and Yarrow (New York, 1958), p. 113. [Merton's note.]

attain perfection or would deliver an esoteric teaching inaccessible to ordinary people. It will be remembered that in his own life Sakyamuni (Buddha) had been disillusioned with extreme asceticism as well as with the worldly life of hedonism, and followed the "middle path" between them. Now, in reply to Ananda, he said:

> If anyone thinks "It is I who will lead the Order" or "The Order depends on 11
> me," he is the one who should lay down instructions concerning the Order. But
> the Tathagatha [Buddha] has no such thought, so why should he leave instructions?

And the Buddha goes on: 12

> So, Ananda, you must be your own lamps, be your own refuges. Take refuge 13
> in nothing outside yourselves. Hold firm to the truth as a lamp and a refuge,
> and do not look for a refuge in anything besides yourselves. A monk becomes
> his own lamp and refuge by continually looking on his body, feelings, percep-
> tions, moods and ideas in such a manner that he conquers the cravings and
> depressions of ordinary men and is always strenuous, self-possessed and col-
> lected in mind. Whoever among my monks does this, either now or when I am
> dead, if he is anxious to learn, will reach the summit. *

The tone of this passage is altogether that of the individualist asceticism 14
of southern (Theravada or Hinayana) Buddhism. We see, of course, how far
the Buddhist ascetic ideal is from the Christian dependence on grace, which
demands a total self surrender and a complete dependence on Christ. However, we must be on our guard against interpreting an Asian text in the context of our own Pelagian and semi-Pelagian controversies. The Buddha is
warning his disciples against reliance on external means, ritual forms, and
ascetic systems. He is by no means telling them to rely on themselves "instead
of" on "grace" (a concept which does not enter into consideration at this
point). They are to rely on nothing but "the truth" as they experience it directly. Hence, they must not even prefer an authoritative statement by the
Buddha to the direct insight into truth in their own lives.

The purpose of the text just quoted seems therefore to be an express 15
prohibition, on the part of Buddha, forbidding his disciples to treat him as a
god or as a source of grace, or as a semi-deified monastic patriarch. In Mahayana Buddhism we later find a complete reliance on Buddha as Savior (in
Amidism). The spirit of Zen, on the other hand, takes the same view of Buddha that we have seen in this Theravada text.† Zen places no reliance upon

---

* Ibid. This translation is also a condensation of the original text and it avoids the technical
   Buddhist emphasis of the original, conveying instead a genuine idea of ascetic impassibil-
   ity. This gives it a more "Pelagian" tone. [Merton's note.]
† In fact Chao Chou (Japanese, Joshu, ninth century) once slapped a disciple whom he found
   bowing down before an image of Buddha. The disciple complained: "Is it not a laudable
   thing to pay respect to Buddha?" Joshu replied: "Yes, but it is better even to renounce a
   laudable thing!" Suzuki comments (*Introduction to Zen Buddhism*, London, 1960,
   p. 53): "Does this attitude savour of anything nihilistic and iconoclastic? Superficially,
   yes, but let us dive deep into the spirit of Joshu out of the depths of which this utterance
   comes, and we will find ourselves confronting an absolute affirmation quite beyond the
   ken of our discursive understanding." [Merton's note.]

the authority of scriptures (sutras) as do other Buddhist sects, and it does not place any confidence in special rules or methods, since its main aim is to bring the monk to a state of enlightenment and spiritual liberty in which he has no need of methods because he is in direct and immediate contact with light and reality in their existential source. Zen is, in fact, an Asian form of religious existentialism. It aims at breaking through the conventional structures of thought and ritual in order that the subject may attain to an authentic personal experience of the inner meaning of life.*

A famous four-line stanza attributed to the semi-legendary founder of   16
Chinese Zen, Bodhidharma (sixth century A.D.), sums up the Zen program:

> *A special tradition outside the scriptures*   17
> *No dependence upon words and letters;*
> *Direct pointing at the soul of man;*
> *Seeing into one's own nature and the attainment of Buddhahood.* †

Zen discards the elaborate metaphysical speculations that came to China   18
with Indian Buddhism. It can indeed be said to have no doctrine at all.‡ For this reason, the Zen monks have often been accused, as have the Cistercians and for much the same reasons, of being anti-intellectual. Certainly there is some basis to the accusation, if it is understood in the light of the following typical Zen story. A disciple once asked a Zen master: "I wish to read the sutras, and what would you advise me to do about it?" The master replied: "Do you think a merchant who deals in millions would bother about making a few pennies?"§

---

* Martin Heidegger, the German existentialist, in a conversation with the Japanese writer on Zen, Daisetz Suzuki, remarked on the basic similarity of their purposes. A succinct statement of Heidegger's philosophical aim may be quoted here, as it throws light on Zen. "Heidegger uses Being as the 'inner light,' that illumination through which we become conscious of our meaning or of our existence and of existence itself. The light allows us to know that we are beings. It illumines the ground which makes this knowledge possible . . . The Heideggerian approach forces us to return, and this path of return leads us to a correspondence with the source and primordial structure of all being, the Being of being. Man must seek himself in the ground of life, the *Urgrund*, the Being of beings . . . Man is neither explained economically, rationally nor politically, his meaning lies in the ontological structure of his reality." From the Introduction to Heidegger's *What is Philosophy?* by W. Klubach and Jean Wild (1958), p. 9. [Merton's note.]

† See Heinrich Dumoulin, S.J.: *A History of Zen Buddhism* (New York, 1963), p. 67. [Merton's note.]

‡ "There are in Zen no sacred books or dogmatic tenets, nor are there any symbolic formulae through which an access might be gained into the signification of Zen. If I am asked, then, what Zen teaches, I would answer Zen teaches nothing. Whatever teachings there are in Zen, they come out of one's own mind. We teach ourselves; Zen merely points the way. Unless this pointing is teaching, there is certainly nothing in Zen purposely set up as its cardinal doctrines or as its fundamental philosophy." D. T. Suzuki: *Introduction to Zen Buddhism*. This statement must of course be balanced with others made by the same author. We shall see that, in fact, the Buddhist scriptures are normally read and recited as part of the daily life of the Zen monastery. [Merton's note.]

§ See Suzuki: *The Training of the Zen Buddhist Monk* (New York, 1959), p. 113. The insistence on direct insight rather than speculative knowledge can be compared to the aims and methods of Socrates, except that Zen is never dialectical. "Knowledge of values, in fact, is a matter of direct insight like seeing that the sky is blue, the grass green. It does not

The Zen monks traditionally preferred direct experience to abstract and 19 theoretical knowledge gained by reading and study. But of course they never denied that reading and study could, in their proper place, contribute to the validity of their spiritual training. The harm comes from placing one's whole trust in books and in learning, and neglecting the direct grasp of life which is had only by living it in all its existential reality.

Another Zen master, when asked if a monk should read the sutras, re- 20 plied in characteristic Zen style: "There are no byroads and no crossroads here; the mountains are all the year round fresh and green; east or west, in whichever direction, you may have a fine walk." The monk asked for more explicit instructions. The master replied: "It is not the sun's fault if the blind cannot see their way."*

Since attachment even to the teaching of Buddha himself could produce 21 spiritual blindness, the Zen masters were very careful to prevent any disciple from becoming attached to their teaching. That is why so many of the sayings of the Zen masters seem to us to be pure nonsense. They were often, in fact, deliberately meaningless from a logical viewpoint. The Zen masters did not want disciples simply to memorize something they had said. Yet, paradoxically, Zen literature consists of almost nothing but quotations of the Zen masters!

One of the Zen masters was asked by a postulant to accept him as a 22 disciple in his monastery and teach him the truth of Buddhism. The master replied:

Why do you seek such a thing here? Why do you wander about neglecting your 23 own precious treasure at home? I have nothing to give you, and what truth of Buddhism do you desire to find in my monastery? There is nothing, absolutely nothing!†

We know that the Desert Fathers of Egypt, particularly those in the 24 Evagrian tradition, whose doctrine was transmitted to the West by Cassian,

---

consist of pieces of information that can be handed from one mind to another. In the last resort every individual must see and judge for himself what is good for him to do. The individual, if he is to be a complete man, must become morally autonomous, and take his own life into his own control. This is a responsibility that no individual can escape. He can indeed, once for all, accept some external authority and thenceforward treat this authority as responsible for what it tells him to do. But he remains responsible for his original choice of an authority to be obeyed. Socrates held that the judge within each of us cannot depute his functions to another." F. M. Cornford: *Before and After Socrates* (Cambridge, 1960), pp. 46–7. [Merton's note.]

*Suzuki: *Training*, p. 113. Once again we can profitably compare this intention with that of Socrates, though the means used are very different. "As with the bodily eye, the soul's vision may be clouded and dim, and it may be deceived with false appearances. Pleasure, for instance, is constantly mistaken for good, when it is not really good. But when the eye of the soul does see straight and clearly, then there is no appeal from its decision. In the field of conduct, education (after the necessary tutelage of childhood) is not teaching; it is opening the eye of the soul and clearing its vision from the distorting mists of prejudice and from the conceit of knowledge which is really no more than secondhand opinion." Cornford: op. cit., p. 47. [Merton's note.]

†Quoted in Suzuki: *Introduction to Zen Buddhism*, p. 49. [Merton's note.]

sought a perfect purity of heart, and for this reason they avoided making learning or conceptual knowledge too much of an end in itself. We find in Zen an analogous striving for non-attachment, and an apophatic contemplation which is summed up in the term "no-mind" or *wu nien*. But the "emptiness" and "objectlessness" of the Zen way of "no-mind" must be well understood, for in such a delicate matter the slightest error is disastrous. To become attached to emptiness itself and to an imaginary "purity of heart" that is conceived as an object which one can attain is to miss the target altogether, even though it may seem to be the highest point of the mystical life. Hence, the Zen masters refuse to countenance any deliberate cultivation of a state of negative inner silence, still less of unconsciousness. A Chinese Zen master, Hui Neng, said: "If you cherish the notion of purity and cling to it, you turn purity into falsehood . . . Purity has neither form nor shape, and when you claim an achievement by establishing a form to be known as purity . . . you are purity-bound [i.e., imprisoned by your limited and illusory concept of purity]."*

Shen Hui, a disciple of Hui Neng, said: "If disciples cultivate [a state   25 of] unreality and stay put in unreality, then they are chained to unreality. If they cultivate contemplation and stay put in it, the very contemplation enchains them; when they cultivate the silence of the beyond and stay put in it, the very silence of the beyond enchains them."†

In other words, Zen, as properly understood, refuses to countenance   26 the deliberate cultivation of a state of inner emptiness from which one might systematically exclude all external images and all concepts in order to experience oneself resting in a well-defined condition of silence, tranquillity, and peace. It is not, as so many Westerners imagine, a mere quietistic cult of inner silence, to be achieved by complete withdrawal from ordinary life. On the contrary, the true Zen enlightenment, according to the Zen masters, is found in action (though not necessarily in activity, still less in *activism*). Zen is a full awareness of the dynamism and spontaneity of life, and hence it cannot be grasped by mere introspection, still less by dreaming. Suzuki says, "Zen must be seized with bare hands, with no gloves on."‡ It requires a real alertness and effort, and one's entire, undivided attention: however, the attention is given not to a theory or to an abstract truth, but to life in its concrete, existential reality, here and now. The Zen masters would doubtless like the maxim *age quod agis*.§ They seek Zen in the ordinary conduct of everyday life, since "one's ordinary mind is the *Tao*." If one must not vainly seek a special enlightenment in the sutras, one must also avoid the delusion that enlightenment is to be found by sitting for hours in quiet meditation. In truth,

---

*Suzuki: *The Zen Doctrine of No-Mind* (London, 1958), p. 27. The quotation is from the Platform Scripture (*T'an Ching*) of Hui Neng. [Merton's note.]

†Quoted in Fung Yu Lan: *The Spirit of Chinese Philosophy* (Boston, 1962), p. 164. [Merton's note.]

‡Suzuki: *Introduction*, p. 51. [Merton's note.]

§ Lit. "Do what you are doing."

one must be free from all bondage to any system whatever. "The whole system of Zen," says Suzuki, "may thus be said to be nothing but a series of attempts to set us free from all forms of bondage . . . [The advocates of inner purity] still have traces of clinging [attachment], setting up a certain state of mind and taking it for ultimate emancipation. So long as the seeing is something to see, it is not the real one; only when the seeing is no-seeing—that is, when the seeing is not a specific act of seeing into a definite circumscribed state of consciousness—is it the 'seeing into one's self-nature.' Paradoxically stated, when seeing is no-seeing, this is real seeing; when hearing is no-hearing, there is real hearing."*

A Chinese Zen master, Shu Chou, spoke of two great diseases of the 27 mind which afflict contemplatives. He described these diseases in simple images as "looking for the ass on which you are actually riding" and "having realized that you are riding on the ass, being unwilling to get off." From the Zen point of view, looking for the ass is looking for some special secret of spiritual perfection, some hidden infallible method, some esoteric state of mind which is the property of initiates, making them superior to everyone else. We are already riding on the ass; that is to say, the ordinary experience of everyday life is the "place" where enlightenment is to be sought. "I tell you," says Shu Chou, "do not search for the ass." On the other hand: "Having found the ass, but being unwilling to dismount: this disease is the hardest to heal." Here he means that one becomes attached to the special awareness that one's everyday mind contains the secret one has been looking for. One is now secure that one possesses "the answer," and therefore one clings to it, one puts one's security in the fact of "having an answer." But one must get off the ass, one must forget even that one has the answer. "What I say to you is: do not ride. You yourself are the ass, and everything is the ass. Why do you go on riding? If you do, you cannot dispel your disease."† If the whole purpose of Zen training is, then, simply to show the monk that he does not need to look for the ass upon which he is already riding and that he ought to have enough sense to get off the ass when there is no longer any need to ride, one may wonder why the discipline of the Zen monastery is so terribly strict, and why such costly sacrifices are demanded of the monks. Are all these things really necessary, in order merely to bring one to a simple recognition that one can find the answer to life's problems by oneself, since they are right in front of one's nose?

It is at this point that Western understanding of Zen usually breaks 28

---

* *Zen Doctrine of No-Mind*, pp. 27-8. [Merton's note.]
† Fung Yu Lan: op. cit., p. 169. Another Zen master (Yengo) said: "People of the world seek the truth outside themselves. What a pity that the thing they are so earnestly looking for is being trodden under their own feet . . . We see the thing and yet it is not seen; we hear it and yet it is not heard; we talk about it and yet it is not talked about; we know it and it is not known. Let me ask, how does it so happen?" Quoted in Suzuki: *Introduction*, p. 55. [Merton's note.]

down completely and, in some cases, disastrously. The trouble arises from the fact that Western thought is, in one way or another, much more individualistic than Asian thought. Even where Western thought is given a collective and social orientation, and even when its individualism is no longer an enforcement of the "I" but its renunciation, the "I" nevertheless remains the starting point of everything. It is the subject endowed with freedom and with the capacity to know and to love. For a Christian, of course, the "I" needs to be transformed and elevated by grace. But from the moment one speaks of spontaneity, freedom, etc., the Western mind thinks at once of the empirical ego-subject. Hence, recognizing "the ass" and situating oneself in one's everyday existence is simply recognizing and indeed affirming the empirical self, the "I." This being the case, one would scarcely need the grueling discipline of Zen in order to discover oneself on this level.

But for Zen (backed as it is by a Buddhist ontology), things are just the 29 opposite. The empirical ego is in fact the source and center of every illusion. The "ass" to be recognized in meditation is not the empirical "I," but the ground of Being which the "I" prevents us from recognizing. (Getting off the ass is then a matter of even renouncing one's "experience" and "idea" of the ground of Being conceived as an object.)

Therefore, instead of simply affirming the "I," with its spontaneous de- 30 sires and joys, the Zen man seeks to accomplish the long and difficult labor of divesting himself completely of this "I" and all its works, in order to discover the deeper spontaneity that comes out of the ground of Being—in Buddhist terms, from the "original self," the "Buddha mind," or *prajna*; in Chinese terms, from *Tao*. This corresponds roughly to the kind of life the New Testament writers and the Fathers describe as "Life in the Spirit," always allowing for the differences involved by a new and supernatural perspective.

Since the work of getting rid of the "I" is in fact so difficult and so subtle 31 as to be completely impossible without the help of others, the disciple must submit unconditionally to the most rigorous obedience and discipline. He must take without question and without murmur every possible difficulty and hardship. He must bear insult, weariness, labor, opprobrium. The attitude he takes toward these things is, however, somewhat different from the Christian attitude, because of his different concept of the self. Where the Christian has Christ and the Cross, the Zen Buddhist has not Buddha as a person but *sunyata*, the Void. This implies very special difficulties and, indeed, unusual dispositions of mind and heart.

Hence, the Zen monk must be persuaded first of all that if he merely 32 relies on his own ability to meditate and to discipline himself, to seek perfection by himself, he is on the way to ruin and perhaps to insanity. Thus, the saying of Buddha—"be lamps for yourselves"—becomes dangerously paradoxical if one takes the "self" to mean simply the empirical "I." In order to become a "lamp for oneself," one must first completely die to one's empirical "I," and to do this, one must submit completely to another who is himself enlightened and who knows exactly how to bring one through the perilous ways of transformation and enlightenment. But in no case must one become attached to the methods, the teaching, the "system" (if any) even of this master.

Western monks who get a taste of Zen by superficial reading and who 33 imagine that it represents a wonderful new world of liberty to do as one pleases without restraint, and indeed to act a little madly at times, if they underestimate the severity and ruthlessness of Zen discipline, are completely misled, and they would do well to recognize that dabbling in Zen will be, for them, a very serious danger.

II

Having become acquainted with the general principles behind Zen monasti- 34 cism, we must now consider, in broad outline, the nature of the monastic life and monastic formation in Zen. We shall come across numerous analogies with our own monastic tradition.

The Buddhist monastic life is essentially a life of pilgrimage *(angya)*. It 35 is as a pilgrim that the newcomer presents himself at the monastery door, whether he be a monk already experienced and trained in another monastery, or a postulant newly arrived from secular life with a letter from his spiritual father. He comes on foot as a "homeless one," a wanderer, wearing the traditional bamboo hat and straw sandals, carrying all his belongings in a small papier-mâché box slung round his neck. All he has are his clothes, his razor, his begging bowl, and a couple of books perhaps. There is a small sum of money in his box, enough to pay for his burial if he is found dead by the roadside. On his way to his chosen monastery, the pilgrim will spend the nights sleeping in temples or in roadside shrines, if not in the open fields.

The purpose of *angya*, or pilgrimage, is to convince the monk of the 36 fact that his whole life is a search, in exile, for his true home. And he must seek earnestly, not be diverted by the trivial incidents he meets along his way. The "Song of Pilgrimage," composed by a Chinese Zen monk, describes the mentality of the pilgrim monk:

> *His conduct is to be transparent as ice or crystal*   37
> *He is not to seek fame or wealth*
> *He is to rid himself of defilements of all sorts.*
> *He has no other way open to him but to go about and inquire;*
> *Let him be trained in mind and body by walking over the mountains and ford-*
> *ing the rivers;*
> *Let him befriend wise men in the Dharma (Law) and pay them respect wher-*
> *ever he may accost them;*
> *Let him brave the snow, tread on the frosty roads, not minding the severity of*
> *the weather;*
> *Let him cross the waves and penetrate the clouds, chasing away dragons and*
> *evil spirits. **

* Suzuki: *Training*, p. 5. [Merton's note.]

This pilgrimage, let us repeat it, does not end at the monastery gate. 38
When his period of training has ended, the monk will once again take to the
road and continue his search, though now, we hope, it will have a totally
new dimension. His whole monastic life is a pilgrimage, and his stay in the
monastery is only one of the incidents in his journey. Not even the monastery
and the training, the discipline, the teaching and the observance, are permitted to become ends in themselves. However, in practice, it is no longer possible or usual for Zen monks to live the true pilgrimage life that was led by
their fathers. Yet, if they return to the world, they must live in it with the
mentality of pilgrims.

On arriving at the monastery, the pilgrim, even if he is an experienced 39
monk, receives the same kind of treatment as prescribed by St. Benedict for
the reception of postulants. Even though he presents a letter of introduction,
the newcomer is politely but firmly told to go elsewhere. There is no room
for him here! The aspirant knows well enough that this refusal is not to be
taken seriously, so he remains in an attitude of supplication at the gate. When
evening comes, he will probably be invited inside the gate for the night. He
will pray or sleep on the ground and thus he will undergo a period of proba-
tion in the outer court. After about five days he may enter the monastery
itself. When he is allowed to come to the *Zendo* or meditation hall, he begins
to take part in the life of the community.

The *Zendo* is the place where, for several hours a day, the monk must 40
sit in the lotus posture meditating. Each monk has a small space about three
by six feet allotted to him, and when night comes, he unrolls his quilt and
sleeps there on the floor. When meditation is in progress, he is not allowed to
leave the *Zendo* except to see the spiritual master (*Roshi*). To break the mo-
notony and to relax their limbs, the monks at regular intervals get up together
and walk briskly around the hall a few times, then resume their meditation,
which, in times of special retreat, can go on for eight or ten hours of the day.

On what does the Zen monk meditate? Here we come face to face with 41
the famous *koan* which is so often bafflingly described in Zen literature. But
we must remember that the *koan* meditation is favored only by one school of
Zen, that of Rinzai. Hence, we need not devote too much space to it here.
But it must be mentioned, since it is an original creation of Zen. The *koan* is
an enigmatic saying which the *Roshi* may assign to the disciple as a topic for
meditation. The disciple may spend hours and days trying to analyze the
saying, or interpreting it symbolically, but each time he returns to the master
he is sent away to continue seeking the "answer." Gradually he begins to
realize that the nature of his *koan* is such that it cannot be analyzed or interpreted intellectually. Yet it does in some sense have a "solution," though the
solution is not "an answer." It is in fact a solution that can be known only by
being lived. The true *koan* meditation is one in which the disciple comes to
be so identified with the *koan* that he experiences his whole self as a riddle
without an answer. This may be for him an utterly hopeless experience, but

if he continues to struggle he may one day suddenly accept himself precisely as he is, as a riddle *without an answer that is communicable to others in an objective manner.** If he is capable of "illumination," he will at that moment taste the delight of recognizing that his own incommunicable experience of the ground of his being, his own total acceptance of his own nothingness, far from constituting a problem, is in fact the source and center of inexpressible joy: in Christian terms, one can hardly help feeling that the illumination of the genuine Zen experience seems to open out into an unconscious demand for grace—a demand that is perhaps answered without being understood. Is it perhaps already grace?

There is also a certain amount of liturgical prayer in the *Zendo*, but it 42 remains very simple. In spite of the fact that the Zen tradition seems to reject the reading of sutras and to despise ritualism, we find that the sutras are nevertheless read. The practice of reading sutras corresponds to our psalmody. There are also other rites, the offering of incense before a statue of Buddha and so on. But the ritual is never very elaborate and there is nothing that would correspond to our conventual Mass.

A daily sermon or conference may be given by the *Roshi*. From the 43 literature on the subject, one gets the impression that this has now become a very formal and perhaps artificial exercise lacking the vitality and spontaneity of the exchanges which, in the ancient texts, took place between the *Roshi* and his disciples. Nevertheless, a collection of Zen conferences given in recent years on the Japanese radio can be read in English translation, and they have a very definite spiritual interest.†

Undoubtedly, one of the most essential elements of the Zen training is 44 encountered in interviews with the *Roshi*. These are deliberately humiliating and frustrating, for the spiritual master is determined to waste no time tolerating the illusions and spiritual self-gratifications that may be cherished by his disciples. If necessary, he will still resort (as did famous Zen masters in the past) to slapping, kicking, and other forms of physical violence. It may also be mentioned that in the *Zendo* there is always one monk on guard with a stick, with which he does not hesitate to strike the shoulders of anyone who is not manifestly awake. Far from fearing to create tension, the Zen masters deliberately make severe demands upon their disciples, and it is understood that one cannot really attain to enlightenment unless one is pressed to the limit. One might almost say that one of the purposes of the Zen training is to push the monk by force into a kind of dark night, and to bring him as quickly and efficaciously as possible into a quandary where, forced to face and to reject his most cherished illusions, driven almost to despair, he abandons all

---

* This experience is not, however, regarded as pure solipsism, for it is in enlightenment that the Zen monk also experiences himself as one with other men and with all beings; not in metaphysical immersion or confusion, but also in love above all. [Merton's note.]

† See Abbot Amakuki's lectures on Hakuin's "Song of Meditation," published in *A First Zen Reader*, compiled by Trevor Leggett (Tokyo, 1960). [Merton's note.]

false hopes and makes a breakthrough into a complete humility, detachment, and spiritual poverty. Unfortunately, however, experience in the monastic life everywhere teaches that this severe training may, in fact, simply make the monk tough, callous, stubborn, perhaps even incurably proud, rather than purifying his heart. This would of course be especially true in a case where the spiritual master, instead of being a genuinely spiritual and holy man, is only a self-opinionated bully with a taste for pushing people around. All methods have their risks!

We must not, however, simply imagine the Zen monk sitting cross-   45
legged and straining his mind almost to the breaking point, with no hope of any relaxation all day long. On the contrary, they have a daily tea ceremony and occasional recreation in the form of judo wrestling bouts among themselves! Also, on the more serious side, the monks go out to beg, and they also work in the garden or around the monastery. Both begging and manual work are important in Zen monasticism, since they inculcate the spirit of poverty and humility. But, in addition to this, the monk enters into contact with "the world" by his begging and by his work, which is the same as that of the farmers among whom he lives. This reminds him of the realities of life, and he shares in the hardships of the poor, of whom he is one. His meditation and his inner purity are what he offers to the world in return, and he feels that he cannot be entitled to share the bread (or the rice) of the poor if he is not completely serious in his efforts to become enlightened, and open his spiritual "eye of wisdom" (the *prajna* eye). Suzuki quotes a text which brings home to the monk his responsibility to be truly what his fellow Buddhists in the world expect him to be, for in traditional Buddhism the monk has a very important part to play. He indeed is one to whom the rest of the Buddhist world looks for help and for salvation. The Triple refuge of the Buddhist is the *Buddha*, the *Dharma* (law), and the *Samgha*, or the monastic order.

> O monks, you are all sons of the Buddha; every thread of the dress you wear   46
> comes from the loom of the hard-working weaver, and every grain you con-
> sume is indicative of the sweat of the farmer's brow. If your prajna eye is not
> yet opened, what claim can you ever have on those precious gifts from your
> fellow beings? Do you wish to know what animals they are that are covered
> with fur and carry a pair of horns on their heads? They are no other than those
> monks who accept shamelessly all the pious offerings from their devotees. Monks
> are not to eat while not hungry, they are not to wear anything more than they
> actually need. Instead of accepting from their pious-minded devotees fine rai-
> ment, a bowl of rice or a hut, let monks wear a dress of red hot steel, make a
> meal of molten metal, and live in a blazing kiln, if their hearts have not yet
> burned with the desire to save themselves as well as all beings from the despot-
> ism of birth and death, and if they are not straining all their spiritual energy
> toward the attaining of this end.*

Zen monasticism is currently in crisis, as is monasticism everywhere,   47
and doubtless the question of poverty and living on alms as well as work will

---

* A traditional text, quoted in Suzuki: *Training*, pp. 97, 98. [Merton's note.]

be a matter of urgent concern with them as well as among us. But the Zen monk has always had a definite sense of being "in the world though not of it," and the mature monk is one who does not shrink from the needs of those who come to him for spiritual help. Another page of a traditional text, moving in its simplicity, tells us this:

> Monks ought to behave like a grinding stone: Chang-san comes to sharpen his 48
> knife, Li-szu comes to grind his axe, everybody and anybody who wants to have his metal improved in any way comes and makes use of the stone. Each time the stone is rubbed, it wears out, but it makes no complaint, nor does it boast of its usefulness. And those who come, go home fully benefitted; some of them may not be quite appreciative of the stone; but the stone itself remains ever contented . . .*

This readiness to be completely "available" to others is more character- 49 istic of the Zen monk's life as priest in the world or as *Roshi* in the monastery. It represents the active side of the Zen life, and does not normally interfere with the *Zendo* training and contemplation.

Zen monasticism, as we have briefly described it here, still exists and 50 flourishes in Japan. It has ceased to exist in China, where it was already in decline before the Communist takeover. In spite of the fact that there has been considerable interest in Zen on the part of Americans and Europeans, the Zen masters themselves feel that the future is not all bright for Zen monasticism. The kind of life we have described is a life bound up with medieval Japanese culture and it is understandable that modern men who are looking for the answer to the confusing spiritual problems of our time may no longer be able, in large numbers, to take on the severe discipline of the *Zendo*, meditate on the *koan*, or submit to the rough tactics of the *Roshi*. Zen, too, may go through a period of adaptation. It is certain that non-Buddhist students who have been allowed to participate in the life of Zen monasteries do not receive all the traditional harsh treatment. Among such guests of Zen monasteries there has been a Jesuit father, Enomiye Lassalle, who has written an interesting account of his experience.†

There have been attempts on a small scale to transplant Zen monasti- 51 cism to America and Europe. But these remain study and training centers rather than monasteries where the Zen life is lived in all its fullness. Yet Zen remains the object of great popular interest in the West. There are many books and articles published on the subject, far more, perhaps, than about Yoga and other Asian spiritualities. These books are generally of excellent quality and are read in intellectual and artistic circles. Why? Probably because of the widespread dissatisfaction with the spiritual sterility of mass society dominated by technology and propaganda, in which there is no room

---

*Ibid., p. 98. [Merton's note.]
† H. M. Enomiye Lassalle, S.J.: *Zen, Weg zur Erleuchtung* (Wien, 1960). See *Collectanea*, Jan.–Mar. 1965. [Merton's note.]

left for personal spontaneity. Perhaps also because of modern man's disgust with all that claims to offer him yet another final and complete answer to all questions. The frank, thoroughgoing existentialism and dynamism of Zen continue to appeal to the kind of men who, suspicious at once of Marx and of organized religion, live in the existentialist climate which we owe not so much to Sartre and to the literary existentialists as to Husserl and to Heidegger.* Though perhaps not Christian, this climate does seem to have a certain spiritual seriousness, as is shown by the fact that Edith Stein, for instance, began as a disciple of Husserl but became a follower of St. John of the Cross and eventually gave up her life at Auschwitz.

Is it enough to say that Zen is a philosophic and existentialist type of   52 spirituality, capable of bringing man into an authentic confrontation with himself, with reality, and with his fellow man, or shall we see in it a deeper religious quality? Without discussing this question in detail, we might at least consider that without this religious dimension it would be hard to see how Zen monasticism could have survived for so many centuries and played such a role in the history of Asian religious culture. But perhaps the most reasonable conclusion would be to reprint here a Zen text of unusual interest, and leave it to speak for itself. The words are those of a Chinese master, Shih Shuang (Japanese: Sekiso), quoted by Suzuki.† Another Zen master, Yuan-Wu, comments:

"Stop all your hankerings; let the mildew grow on your lips; make your-   53 self like a perfect piece of immaculate silk; let your one thought be eternity; let yourself be like dead ashes, cold and lifeless; again let yourself be like an old censer in a deserted village shrine.

"Putting your simple faith in this, discipline yourself accordingly; let   54 your body and your mind be turned into an inanimate object of nature like a piece of stone or wood; when a state of perfect motionlessness and unawareness is obtained, all the signs of life will depart and also every trace of limitation will vanish. Not a single idea will disturb your consciousness when lo! all of a sudden you will come to realize a light abounding in full gladness. It is like coming across a light in thick darkness; it is like receiving treasure in poverty. The four elements and the five aggregates are no more felt as burdens; so light, so easy, so free you are. Your very existence has been delivered from all limitations: you have become open, light and transparent. You gain an illuminating insight into the very nature of things, which now appear to you as so many fairy-like flowers having no graspable realities. Here is manifested the unsophisticated self which is the original face of your being; here is shown bare the most beautiful landscape of your birthplace. There is but one straight passage open and unobstructed through and through. This is so

---

* Edmund Husserl (1859–1938) was a German philosopher who explored the ways in which the consciousness perceived its experience. Martin Heidegger was influenced by Husserl; his major concern was with what he defined as the problem of being. [Merton's note.]

† *Introduction*, pp. 46–7. [Merton's note.]

when you surrender all—your body, your life, and all that belongs to your inmost self. This is where you gain peace, ease, nondoing and inexpressible delight. All the sutras and sastras are no more than communications of this fact; all the sages, ancient as well as modern, have exhausted their ingenuity and imagination to no other purpose than to point the way to this. It is like unlocking the door to a treasure; when the entrance is once gained, every object coming into your view is yours, every opportunity that presents itself is available for your use; for are they not, however multitudinous, all possessions obtainable within the original being of yourself? Every treasure there is but waiting your pleasure and utilization. This is what is meant by 'once gained, eternally gained, even to the end of time.' Yet really there is nothing gained; what you have gained is no gain, and yet there is truly something gained in this!"

QUESTIONS ABOUT THOMAS MERTON'S DISCOURSE COMMUNITY AND HIS CONCERNS IN THIS ESSAY

1. In this essay, Merton is bringing together two radically different discourse communities—Zen Buddhism and Roman Catholicism—as subjects of investigation. What evidence is there in the essay that Merton was attempting to effect a kind of reconciliation between these two different communities, or at least to foster a new understanding between them? Do you think that Merton would agree that these are two distinct discourse communities?

2. In the beginning of this essay, Merton refers to Zen as "mysterious" and "full of impudent paradox." Does it seem to you, after reading this essay, that this early characterization is true? Why or why not?

3. Merton quotes the Buddha (paragraph 13) as saying, "Take refuge in nothing outside yourselves. Hold firm to the truth as a lamp and a refuge, and do not look for a refuge in anything besides yourselves." How does Merton react to this advice?

4. Merton often speaks of searching for "the truth." What do you think he means by "the truth"?

5. Merton insists that Zen enlightenment is found in action, everyday action, not in mere contemplation. What role, then, might contemplation have?

6. Merton suggests that the student of Zen studies "in order to discover the deeper spontaneity that comes out of the ground of Being" (paragraph 30). Here he is using Eastern terms that apparently have no exact equivalent Western terms. What might Merton mean by "the ground of Being"?

7. Merton suggests that the student of Zen may eventually come to understand himself "as a riddle without an answer that is communicable to others in an objective manner" (paragraph 41). What precisely does he mean by this?

8. Where does Merton, in the second part of this essay, find direct links between Christianity and Zen Buddhism?

9. Merton notes that monasticism is "in crisis" around the world (paragraph 47). He wrote this in the early 1960s, but it is still the case in the early 1990s. Why might monasticism be "in crisis"?

QUESTIONS ABOUT THOMAS MERTON'S RHETORICAL STRATEGIES

1. Merton's primary audience for this essay is his fellow Cistercian monks. Where in this essay is it evident that he is addressing that audience directly? Are there any clues here that Merton was also aware that this essay would address a wider community as well?

2. One basic rhetorical strategy used in this selection is that of contrast, used to distinguish between Zen monasticism and Christian monasticism. Which side does Merton deal with more fully? Why? What does this suggest about the writer's relationship to his or her audience?

3. Read over the third paragraph. Why does Merton name his tone "sympathetic objectivity"? What does he mean by this? Is it consistent throughout the essay? Does Merton's reference to "destructive criticism" imply that he could, if he wished, attack Zen?

4. In paragraph four, Merton uses the rhetorical technique of establishing common ground and then establishing distinctions. Is this an effective technique in this context? Where else does Merton use this technique?

5. Though Merton uses the term *Zen monastery*, it is clear that *monastery* does not really describe the kind of institution (if even that word fits) within which one learns Zen. Could Merton be accused here of foisting a Western conception onto an Eastern institution? If so, what does that suggest about the limitations of language within a discourse community?

6. At times Merton records a *koan*, a short, cryptic story about a Zen master and his disciple. What rhetorical purposes do these stories serve?

7. How does Merton use the rhetorical strategy of analogy in paragraph 27? Why might this be an effective rhetorical technique, given Merton's audience?

8. At the end of paragraph 41, Merton asks a speculative question: "Is it perhaps already grace?" How do you think he expects his audience to respond to this question?

WRITING FROM WITHIN AND ABOUT PHILOSOPHY

Writing for Yourself

1. Most Westerners are not particularly familiar with Zen; many are hostile to it, seeing it as a rather alien philosophy of mysticism. In your journal, reflect upon your own reactions to Zen philosophy. Why do you react the way you do?

2. In your journal, reflect on your own ideas about the validity of a cloistered life.

Writing for Nonacademic Audiences

1. Your friends are amazed to find that you have been studying Zen Buddhism, which they have dismissed as mere mystical hocus-pocus. Write a 500-word letter to one of these friends explaining why the study of Zen Buddhism might be helpful in a Westerner's life.

2. Choose one of the koans recounted by Merton and prepare a ten-minute oral presentation for your peers in an introductory philosophy class, showing how that koan defies any kind of simple, intellectual interpretation.

3. You will be traveling with a group of your peers to spend one semester at a Japanese university. In preparation for that trip, you have each been assigned topic areas about which you are to prepare discussion questions. You have been assigned to write five discussion questions on Zen Buddhism. Prepare these questions.

4. While you are home over Christmas break, your uncle learns that you have been reading about Zen Buddhism. He wonders what it is. You agree to write him a letter, in which you will provide a short explanation of Zen. Once back at school, you write that letter.

5. Interview a member of a cloistered religious order, focusing on the question of whether monasticism is in crisis. Use this interview as the basis for an editorial on monasticism to appear in the *Boston Globe* (recognizing that Boston has a large Catholic population).

6. After conducting the interview in question 5, write up your results for a feature article in your university's newspaper.

Writing for Academic Audiences

1. Your philosophy department has begun a study of how aware modern North Americans are of the philosophical assumptions that undergird and guide their actions. Choose any organized group on your campus and interview three of the students who have joined, focusing on why they have decided to take that action. Write up your findings as a report to the department.

2. For a class in the philosophy of eastern religions, write a 500-word essay defining the Zen understanding of "enlightenment."

3. Choose one of the following books by Thomas Merton and write a book review of it, to be included in a quarterly departmental newsletter put out by your university's philosophy department and distributed to philosophy majors: *The Wisdom of the Desert, The Asian Journal, The Silent Life, The Seven Story Mountain.*

4. Merton notes that Zen is sometimes accused of being anti-intellectualist; it certainly is not the only religious community that has been charged with this. One North American community that has often been labeled as anti-intellectual is the Amish community. For a class in the philosophy of religion, discuss why the Amish community is perceived to be anti-intellectual, whether in fact it is anti-intellectual, and what philosophical positions it holds that touch on the life of the mind. Limit yourself to 1,250 words.

Thomas S. Kuhn

(b. 1922)

Thomas S. Kuhn works with the history and philosophy of science. He studied at Harvard University, where he earned a B.S. in 1943, an M.A. in 1946, and a Ph.D. in physics in 1949. Since earning his Ph.D., Kuhn has held positions at Howard University, the University of California at Berkeley, and Princeton University. Since 1978 he has served as a professor of philosophy and the history of science at the Massachusetts Institute of Technology. During his career, Kuhn has received several awards and honorary degrees.

Kuhn is best known for his work in the community of philosophers of science. His most influential book, The Structure of Scientific Revolutions, *examines how science has progressed over the ages. The popular view is that science has progressed bit by bit primarily in the same line and with similar methods. Kuhn holds that this popular conception is wrong. Science, he maintains, progresses by undergoing revolutions.*

Central to his view is his idea about a scientific paradigm. A paradigm, Kuhn says, is a model that scientists at a given time accept and work with. It indicates what problems they should try to solve, and it sets the standards for methods of investigation and kinds of evidence. As scientists work within a paradigm, they usually encounter problems that the paradigm seems poorly suited to address. These problems can help scientists extend and refine a paradigm, but if the problems accumulate in great numbers and persist for long periods of time, they can lead scientists to abandon the paradigm they had worked with and develop a new one. When this happens, Kuhn says, science undergoes a revolution.

Kuhn's views have been controversial, probably because they imply that scientific revolutions are motivated by no independent and objective body of evidence but by scientists coming to see their work in a new way. Those who accept Kuhn's ideas often investigate the psychological and social causes for a scientific revolution rather than the nature of a world that exists independent of scientists' interaction with it.

The following selection is the second chapter of The Structure of Scientific Revolutions.

THE ROUTE TO NORMAL SCIENCE

In this essay, "normal science" means research firmly based upon one or more 1 past scientific achievements, achievements that some particular scientific community acknowledges for a time as supplying the foundation for its further practice. Today such achievements are recounted, though seldom in their original form, by science textbooks, elementary and advanced. These textbooks expound the body of accepted theory, illustrate many or all of its successful applications, and compare these applications with exemplary observations and experiments. Before such books became popular early in the nineteenth century (and until even more recently in the newly matured sciences), many of the famous classics of science fulfilled a similar function. Aristotle's *Physica*, Ptolemy's *Almagest*, Newton's *Principia* and *Opticks*, Franklin's *Electricity*, Lavoisier's *Chemistry*, and Lyell's *Geology*—these and many other works served for a time implicitly to define the legitimate problems and methods of a research field for succeeding generations of practitioners. They were able to do so because they shared two essential characteristics. Their achievement was sufficiently unprecedented to attract an enduring group of adherents away from competing modes of scientific activity. Simultaneously, it was sufficiently open-ended to leave all sorts of problems for the redefined group of practitioners to resolve.

Achievements that share these two characteristics I shall henceforth re- 2 fer to as "paradigms," a term that relates closely to "normal science." By choosing it, I mean to suggest that some accepted examples of actual scientific practice—examples which include law, theory, application, and instrumentation together—provide models from which spring particular coherent traditions of scientific research. These are the traditions which the historian describes under such rubrics as "Ptolemaic astronomy" (or "Copernican"), "Aristotelian dynamics" (or "Newtonian"), "corpuscular optics" (or "wave optics"), and so on. The study of paradigms, including many that are far more specialized than those named illustratively above, is what mainly prepares the student for membership in the particular scientific community with which he will later practice. Because he there joins men who learned the bases of their field from the same concrete models, his subsequent practice will seldom evoke overt disagreement over fundamentals. Men whose research is based on shared paradigms are committed to the same rules and standards for scientific practice. That commitment and the apparent consensus it produces are prerequisites for normal science, i.e., for the genesis and continuation of a particular research tradition.

Because in this essay the concept of a paradigm will often substitute for 3 a variety of familiar notions, more will need to be said about the reasons for its introduction. Why is the concrete scientific achievement, as a locus of professional commitment, prior to the various concepts, laws, theories, and points of view that may be abstracted from it? In what sense is the shared paradigm a fundamental unit for the student of scientific development, a unit that cannot be fully reduced to logically atomic components which might function in its stead? When we encounter them in Section V, answers to these questions and to others like them will prove basic to an understanding both of normal science and of the associated concept of paradigms. That more abstract discussion will depend, however, upon a previous exposure to examples of normal science or of paradigms in operation. In particular, both these related concepts will be clarified by noting that there can be a sort of scientific research without paradigms, or at least without any so unequivocal and so binding as the ones named above. Acquisition of a paradigm and of the more esoteric type of research it permits is a sign of maturity in the development of any given scientific field.

If the historian traces the scientific knowledge of any selected group of 4 related phenomena backward in time, he is likely to encounter some minor variant of a pattern here illustrated from the history of physical optics. Today's physics textbooks tell the student that light is photons, i.e., quantum-mechanical entities that exhibit some characteristics of waves and some of particles. Research proceeds accordingly, or rather according to the more elaborate and mathematical characterization from which this usual verbalization is derived. That characterization of light is, however, scarcely half a century old. Before it was developed by Planck, Einstein, and others early in this century, physics texts taught that light was transverse wave motion, a conception rooted in a paradigm that derived ultimately from the optical writings of Young and Fresnel in the early nineteenth century. Nor was the wave theory the first to be embraced by almost all practitioners of optical science. During the eighteenth century the paradigm for this field was provided by Newton's *Opticks*, which taught that light was material corpuscles. At that time physicists sought evidence, as the early wave theorists had not, of the pressure exerted by light particles impinging on solid bodies. *

These transformations of the paradigms of physical optics are scientific 5 revolutions, and the successive transition from one paradigm to another via revolution is the usual developmental pattern of mature science. It is not, however, the pattern characteristic of the period before Newton's work, and that is the contrast that concerns us here. No period between remote antiquity and the end of the seventeenth century exhibited a single generally accepted view about the nature of light. Instead there were a number of competing schools and subschools, most of them espousing one variant or another of Epicurean, Aristotelian, or Platonic theory. One group took light to be particles emanating from material bodies; for another it was a modification

---

* Joseph Priestley, *The History and Present State of Discoveries Relating to Vision, Light, and Colours* (London, 1772), pp. 385–90. [Kuhn's note].

of the medium that intervened between the body and the eye; still another explained light in terms of an interaction of the medium with an emanation from the eye; and there were other combinations and modifications besides. Each of the corresponding schools derived strength from its relation to some particular metaphysic, and each emphasized, as paradigmatic observations, the particular cluster of optical phenomena that its own theory could do most to explain. Other observations were dealt with by *ad hoc* elaborations, or they remained as outstanding problems for further research. *

At various times all these schools made significant contributions to the 6 body of concepts, phenomena, and techniques from which Newton drew the first nearly uniformly accepted paradigm for physical optics. Any definition of the scientist that excludes at least the more creative members of these various schools will exclude their modern successors as well. Those men were scientists. Yet anyone examining a survey of physical optics before Newton may well conclude that, though the field's practitioners were scientists, the net result of their activity was something less than science. Being able to take no common body of belief for granted, each writer on physical optics felt forced to build his field anew from its foundations. In doing so, his choice of supporting observation and experiment was relatively free, for there was no standard set of methods or of phenomena that every optical writer felt forced to employ and explain. Under these circumstances, the dialogue of the resulting books was often directed as much to the members of other schools as it was to nature. That pattern is not unfamiliar in a number of creative fields today, nor is it incompatible with significant discovery and invention. It is not, however, the pattern of development that physical optics acquired after Newton and that other natural sciences make familiar today.

The history of electrical research in the first half of the eighteenth cen- 7 tury provides a more concrete and better known example of the way a science develops before it acquires its first universally received paradigm. During that period there were almost as many views about the nature of electricity as there were important electrical experimenters, men like Hauksbee, Gray, Desaguliers, Du Fay, Nollett, Watson, Franklin, and others. All their numerous concepts of electricity had something in common—they were partially derived from one or another version of the mechanico-corpuscular philosophy that guided all scientific research of the day. In addition, all were components of real scientific theories, of theories that had been drawn in part from experiment and observation and that partially determined the choice and interpretation of additional problems undertaken in research. Yet though all the experiments were electrical and though most of the experimenters read each other's works, their theories had no more than a family resemblance.†

---

* Vasco Ronchi, *Histoire de la lumière*, trans. Jean Taton (Paris, 1956), chaps. i–iv [Kuhn's note].
† Duane Roller and Duane H. D. Roller, *The Development of the Concept of Electric Charge: Electricity from the Greeks to Coulomb* ("Harvard Case Histories in Experimental Sci-

One early group of theories, following seventeenth-century practice, 8 regarded attraction and frictional generation as the fundamental electrical phenomena. This group tended to treat repulsion as a secondary effect due to some sort of mechanical rebounding and also to postpone for as long as possible both discussion and systematic research on Gray's newly discovered effect, electrical conduction. Other "electricians" (the term is their own) took attraction and repulsion to be equally elementary manifestations of electricity and modified their theories and research accordingly. (Actually, this group is remarkably small—even Franklin's theory never quite accounted for the mutual repulsion of two negatively charged bodies.) But they had as much difficulty as the first group in accounting simultaneously for any but the simplest conduction effects. Those effects, however, provided the starting point for still a third group, one which tended to speak of electricity as a "fluid" that could run through conductors rather than as an "effluvium" that emanated from non-conductors. This group, in its turn, had difficulty reconciling its theory with a number of attractive and repulsive effects. Only through the work of Franklin and his immediate successors did a theory arise that could account with something like equal facility for very nearly all these effects and that therefore could and did provide a subsequent generation of "electricians" with a common paradigm for its research.

Excluding those fields, like mathematics and astronomy, in which the 9 first firm paradigms date from prehistory and also those, like biochemistry, that arose by division and recombination of specialties already matured, the situations outlined above are historically typical. Though it involves my continuing to employ the unfortunate simplification that tags an extended historical episode with a single and somewhat arbitrarily chosen name (e.g., Newton or Franklin), I suggest that similar fundamental disagreements characterized, for example, the study of motion before Aristotle and of statics before Archimedes, the study of heat before Black, of chemistry before Boyle and Boerhaave, and of historical geology before Hutton. In parts of biology—the study of heredity, for example—the first universally received paradigms are still more recent; and it remains an open question what parts of social science have yet acquired such paradigms at all. History suggests that the road to a firm research consensus is extraordinarily arduous.

History also suggests, however, some reasons for the difficulties encoun- 10 tered on that road. In the absence of a paradigm or some candidate for par-

---

ence," Case 8; Cambridge, Mass., 1954); and I. B. Cohen, *Franklin and Newton: An Inquiry into Speculative Newtonian Experimental Science and Franklin's Work in Electricity as an Example Thereof* (Philadelphia, 1956), chaps. vii–xii. For some of the analytic detail in the paragraph that follows in the text, I am indebted to a still unpublished paper by my student John L. Heilbron. Pending its publication, a somewhat more extended and more precise account of the emergence of Franklin's paradigm is included in T. S. Kuhn, "The Function of Dogma in Scientific Research," in A. C. Crombie (ed.), "Symposium on the History of Science, University of Oxford, July 9–15, 1961," to be published by Heinemann Educational Books, Ltd. [Kuhn's note].

adigm, all of the facts that could possibly pertain to the development of a given science are likely to seem equally relevant. As a result, early fact-gathering is a far more nearly random activity than the one that subsequent scientific development makes familiar. Furthermore, in the absence of a reason for seeking some particular form of more recondite information, early fact-gathering is usually restricted to the wealth of data that lie ready to hand. The resulting pool of facts contains those accessible to casual observation and experiment together with some of the more esoteric data retrievable from established crafts like medicine, calendar making, and metallurgy. Because the crafts are one readily accessible source of facts that could not have been casually discovered, technology has often played a vital role in the emergence of new sciences.

But though this sort of fact-collecting has been essential to the origin of 11 many significant sciences, anyone who examines, for example, Pliny's encyclopedic writings or the Baconian natural histories of the seventeenth century will discover that it produces a morass. One somehow hesitates to call the literature that results scientific. The Baconian "histories" of heat, color, wind, mining, and so on, are filled with information, some of it recondite. But they juxtapose facts that will later prove revealing (e.g., heating by mixture) with others (e.g., the warmth of dung heaps) that will for some time remain too complex to be integrated with theory at all.* In addition, since any description must be partial, the typical natural history often omits from its immensely circumstantial accounts just those details that later scientists will find sources of important illumination. Almost none of the early "histories" of electricity, for example, mention that chaff, attracted to a rubbed glass rod, bounces off again. That effect seemed mechanical, not electrical.† Moreover, since the casual fact-gatherer seldom possesses the time or the tools to be critical, the natural histories often juxtapose descriptions like the above with others, say, heating by antiperistasis (or by cooling), that we are now quite unable to confirm.‡ Only very occasionally, as in the cases of ancient statics, dynamics, and geometrical optics, do facts collected with so little guidance from pre-established theory speak with sufficient clarity to permit the emergence of a first paradigm.

This is the situation that creates the schools characteristic of the early 12 stages of a science's development. No natural history can be interpreted in

---

* Compare the sketch for a natural history of heat in Bacon's *Novum Organum*, Vol. VIII of *The Works of Francis Bacon*, ed. J. Spedding, R. L. Ellis, and D. D. Heath (New York, 1869), pp. 179–203. [Kuhn's note].

† Roller and Roller, *op. cit.*, pp. 14, 22, 28, 43. Only after the work recorded in the last of these citations do repulsive effects gain general recognition as unequivocally electrical. [Kuhn's note].

‡ Bacon, *op. cit.*, pp. 235, 337, says, "Water slightly warm is more easily frozen than quite cold." For a partial account of the earlier history of this strange observation, see Marshall Clagett, *Giovanni Marliani and Late Medieval Physics* (New York, 1941), chap. iv. [Kuhn's note].

the absence of at least some implicit body of intertwined theoretical and methodological belief that permits selection, evaluation, and criticism. If that body of belief is not already implicit in the collection of facts—in which case more than "mere facts" are at hand—it must be externally supplied, perhaps by a current metaphysic, by another science, or by personal and historical accident. No wonder, then, that in the early stages of the development of any science different men confronting the same range of phenomena, but not usually all the same particular phenomena, describe and interpret them in different ways. What is surprising, and perhaps also unique in its degree to the fields we call science, is that such initial divergences should ever largely disappear.

For they do disappear to a very considerable extent and then apparently 13 once and for all. Furthermore, their disappearance is usually caused by the triumph of one of the pre-paradigm schools, which, because of its own characteristic beliefs and preconceptions, emphasized only some special part of the too sizable and inchoate pool of information. Those electricians who thought electricity a fluid and therefore gave particular emphasis to conduction provide an excellent case in point. Led by this belief, which could scarcely cope with the known multiplicity of attractive and repulsive effects, several of them conceived the idea of bottling the electrical fluid. The immediate fruit of their efforts was the Leyden jar, a device which might never have been discovered by a man exploring nature casually or at random, but which was in fact independently developed by at least two investigators in the early 1740's.* Almost from the start of his electrical researches, Franklin was particularly concerned to explain that strange and, in the event, particularly revealing piece of special apparatus. His success in doing so provided the most effective of the arguments that made his theory a paradigm, though one that was still unable to account for quite all the known cases of electrical repulsion.† To be accepted as a paradigm, a theory must seem better than its competitors, but it need not, and in fact never does, explain all the facts with which it can be confronted.

What the fluid theory of electricity did for the subgroup that held it, 14 the Franklinian paradigm later did for the entire group of electricians. It suggested which experiments would be worth performing and which, because directed to secondary or to overly complex manifestations of electricity, would not. Only the paradigm did the job far more effectively, partly because the end of interschool debate ended the constant reiteration of fundamentals and partly because the confidence that they were on the right track encouraged scientists to undertake more precise, esoteric, and consuming sorts

---

* Roller and Roller, *op. cit.*, pp. 51–54. [Kuhn's note].
† The troublesome case was the mutual repulsion of negatively charged bodies, for which see Cohen, *op. cit.*, pp. 491–94, 531–43. [Kuhn's note].

of work.* Freed from the concern with any and all electrical phenomena, the united group of electricians could pursue selected phenomena in far more detail, designing much special equipment for the task and employing it more stubbornly and systematically than electricians had ever done before. Both fact collection and theory articulation became highly directed activities. The effectiveness and efficiency of electrical research increased accordingly, providing evidence for a societal version of Francis Bacon's acute methodological dictum: "Truth emerges more readily from error than from confusion."†

We shall be examining the nature of this highly directed or paradigm-based research in the next section, but must first note briefly how the emergence of a paradigm affects the structure of the group that practices the field. When, in the development of a natural science, an individual or group first produces a synthesis able to attract most of the next generation's practitioners, the older schools gradually disappear. In part their disappearance is caused by their members' conversion to the new paradigm. But there are always some men who cling to one or another of the older views, and they are simply read out of the profession, which thereafter ignores their work. The new paradigm implies a new and more rigid definition of the field. Those unwilling or unable to accommodate their work to it must proceed in isolation or attach themselves to some other group.‡ Historically, they have often simply stayed in the departments of philosophy from which so many of the special sciences have been spawned. As these indications hint, it is sometimes just its reception of a paradigm that transforms a group previously interested merely in the study of nature into a profession or, at least, a discipline. In the

*It should be noted that the acceptance of Franklin's theory did not end quite all debate. In 1759 Robert Symmer proposed a two-fluid version of that theory, and for many years thereafter electricians were divided about whether electricity was a single fluid or two. But the debates on this subject only confirm what has been said above about the manner in which a universally recognized achievement unites the profession. Electricians, though they continued divided on this point, rapidly concluded that no experimental tests could distinguish the two versions of the theory and that they were therefore equivalent. After that, both schools could and did exploit all the benefits that the Franklinian theory provided (*ibid.*, pp. 543–46, 548–54). [Kuhn's note].

† Bacon, *op. cit.*, p. 210. [Kuhn's note].

‡ The history of electricity provides an excellent example which could be duplicated from the careers of Priestley, Kelvin, and others. Franklin reports that Nollet, who at mid-century was the most influential of the Continental electricians, "lived to see himself the last of his Sect, except Mr. B.—his Eleve and immediate Disciple" (Max Farrand [ed.], *Benjamin Franklin's Memoirs* [Berkeley, Calif., 1949], pp. 384–86). More interesting, however, is the endurance of whole schools in increasing isolation from professional science. Consider, for example, the case of astrology, which was once an integral part of astronomy. Or consider the continuation in the late eighteenth and early nineteenth centuries of a previously respected tradition of "romantic" chemistry. This is the tradition discussed by Charles C. Gillispie in "The *Encyclopédie* and the Jacobin Philosophy of Science: A Study in Ideas and Consequences," *Critical Problems in the History of Science*, ed. Marshall Clagett (Madison, Wis., 1959), pp. 255–89; and "The Formation of Lamarck's Evolutionary Theory," *Archives internationales d'histoire des sciences*, XXXVII (1956), 323–38. [Kuhn's note].

sciences (though not in fields like medicine, technology, and law, of which the principal *raison d'être* is an external social need), the formation of specialized journals, the foundation of specialists' societies, and the claim for a special place in the curriculum have usually been associated with a group's first reception of a single paradigm. At least this was the case between the time, a century and a half ago, when the institutional pattern of scientific specialization first developed and the very recent time when the paraphernalia of specialization acquired a prestige of their own.

The more rigid definition of the scientific group has other consequences. 16 When the individual scientist can take a paradigm for granted, he need no longer, in his major works, attempt to build his field anew, starting from first principles and justifying the use of each concept introduced. That can be left to the writer of textbooks. Given a textbook, however, the creative scientist can begin his research where it leaves off and thus concentrate exclusively upon the subtlest and most esoteric aspects of the natural phenomena that concern his group. And as he does this, his research communiqués will begin to change in ways whose evolution has been too little studied but whose modern end products are obvious to all and oppressive to many. No longer will his researches usually be embodied in books addressed, like Franklin's *Experiments . . . on Electricity* or Darwin's *Origin of Species*, to anyone who might be interested in the subject matter of the field. Instead they will usually appear as brief articles addressed only to professional colleagues, the men whose knowledge of a shared paradigm can be assumed and who prove to be the only ones able to read the papers addressed to them.

Today in the sciences, books are usually either texts or retrospective 17 reflections upon one aspect or another of the scientific life. The scientist who writes one is more likely to find his professional reputation impaired than enhanced. Only in the earlier, pre-paradigm, stages of the development of the various sciences did the book ordinarily possess the same relation to professional achievement that it still retains in other creative fields. And only in those fields that still retain the book, with or without the article, as a vehicle for research communication are the lines of professionalization still so loosely drawn that the layman may hope to follow progress by reading the practitioners' original reports. Both in mathematics and astronomy, research reports had ceased already in antiquity to be intelligible to a generally educated audience. In dynamics, research became similarly esoteric in the later Middle Ages, and it recaptured general intelligibility only briefly during the early seventeenth century when a new paradigm replaced the one that had guided medieval research. Electrical research began to require translation for the layman before the end of the eighteenth century, and most other fields of physical science ceased to be generally accessible in the nineteenth. During the same two centuries similar transitions can be isolated in the various parts of the biological sciences. In parts of the social sciences they may well be occurring today. Although it has become customary, and is surely proper, to deplore the widening gulf that separates the professional scientist from his colleagues in other fields, too little attention is paid to the essential relationship between that gulf and the mechanisms intrinsic to scientific advance.

Ever since prehistoric antiquity one field of study after another has [18] crossed the divide between what the historian might call its prehistory as a science and its history proper. These transitions to maturity have seldom been so sudden or so unequivocal as my necessarily schematic discussion may have implied. But neither have they been historically gradual, coextensive, that is to say, with the entire development of the fields within which they occurred. Writers on electricity during the first four decades of the eighteenth century possessed far more information about electrical phenomena than had their sixteenth-century predecessors. During the half-century after 1740, few new sorts of electrical phenomena were added to their lists. Nevertheless, in important respects, the electrical writings of Cavendish, Coulomb, and Volta in the last third of the eighteenth century seem further removed from those of Gray, Du Fay, and even Franklin than are the writings of these early eighteenth-century electrical discoverers from those of the sixteenth century.* Sometime between 1740 and 1780, electricians were for the first time enabled to take the foundations of their field for granted. From that point they pushed on to more concrete and recondite problems, and increasingly they then reported their results in articles addressed to other electricians rather than in books addressed to the learned world at large. As a group they achieved what had been gained by astronomers in antiquity and by students of motion in the Middle Ages, of physical optics in the late seventeenth century, and of historical geology in the early nineteenth. They had, that is, achieved a paradigm that proved able to guide the whole group's research. Except with the advantage of hindsight, it is hard to find another criterion that so clearly proclaims a field a science.

QUESTIONS ABOUT KUHN'S DISCOURSE
COMMUNITY AND HIS CONCERNS IN THIS ESSAY

1. Kuhn says that publications that have defined problems and methods for scientists share two characteristics. What are they?
2. What does Kuhn mean by *normal science*?
3. What does Kuhn say is necessary for a paradigm to be accepted?
4. Is it good or bad for science that a paradigm never explains all the facts that it confronts?

---

* The post-Franklinian developments include an immense increase in the sensitivity of charge detectors, the first reliable and generally diffused techniques for measuring charge, the evolution of the concept of capacity and its relation to a newly refined notion of electric tension, and the quantification of electrostatic force. On all of these see Roller and Roller, *op. cit.*, pp. 66–81; W. C. Walker, "The Detection and Estimation of Electric Charges in the Eighteenth Century," *Annals of Science*, I (1936), 66–100; and Edmund Hoppe, *Geschichte der Elektrizität* (Leipzig, 1884), Part I, chaps. iii–iv. [Kuhn's note].

5. List some of the consequences that the acceptance of a paradigm in a scientific field usually has.
6. Why is it important for scientists not to have to build their field "anew from its foundations" (paragraph 6)?
7. Is there any danger in that today scientists generally write only to professional colleagues working in very specialized areas? Are there advantages to this?
8. We usually think of science as leading to new technologies. Why does Kuhn say that technology often leads to new sciences?

QUESTIONS ABOUT KUHN'S RHETORICAL STRATEGIES

1. Kuhn begins by defining "normal science." Is this a fair tactic? Are there any advantages in authors' defining terms for their readers? What else does he define? Are there any dangers?
2. How does Kuhn define true science as distinct from other activities?
3. Kuhn refers to scientists with masculine terms. Do you think this is merely a convention?
4. In a couple of places, Kuhn addresses the reader directly, indicating what he will focus on in later chapters. How do you react to such addresses?
5. What does Kuhn depend on for the bulk of his evidence? What kind of evidence does he use? How do you evaluate it?
6. Why do you think Kuhn first chooses to illustrate the process of revolutions in science with the case of physical optics? Would other cases work just as well? Is it necessary for him to use such illustrations at all?
7. In paragraph 6, Kuhn writes about scientists and bodies of "belief." Why does he use the word *belief*? Do you think it is wise for him to use *belief* here?

WRITING FROM WITHIN AND ABOUT PHILOSOPHY

Writing for Yourself

1. In your journal, reflect on the advantages and disadvantages of a system of scientific research that becomes more and more specialized.
2. In your journal, reflect on a time when you found some "truth from error."

Writing for Nonacademic Audiences

1. For your campus newspaper, write a 500-word persuasive piece on the biggest threat that specialization in science poses to modern society.
2. A debate has erupted on the pages of your campus newspaper in response to a letter from a physics major who has claimed that only in science will anyone ever be able to discover the nature of reality. You decide to respond in a letter to the editor in which you satirize the physics major's claim.

Writing for Academic Audiences

1. For a class in the history of science, write a 500-word description of one of the scientific revolutions that Kuhn mentions.

2. You have been asked to explain Kuhn's concept of a scientific paradigm to a group of high school National Merit finalists who intend to major in a science in college. You have approximately twenty minutes. Write a draft of this speech.
3. The chairman of the department of your major has asked you to write up a 500-word explanation of what work in your major is like. What kind of questions do you ask? How do you do research? What is valid evidence? How do you report results? Your piece will become part of a handbook for students wishing to major in your field.
4. Interview several specialists in a scientific field about how they would characterize the paradigm that they work with. Generalize about their positions in a 750-word explanatory paper for a philosophy of science class.

Virginia Essene

(b. 1928)

The following selection comes from Virginia Essene's Secret Truths, *a book aimed at people in their teens and twenties. This book follows Essene's earlier work,* New Techniques for an Awakening Humanity. *The title of the earlier work, in addition to the fact that Essene says she did not write* Secret Truths *by herself but channeled it from higher energy forms, shows that Essene works within the discourse community of New Age thinkers. This community has received a great deal of publicity in recent years, largely because of the writings of Shirley MacLaine.*

New Age thinkers may differ from one another in some details of their philosophies, but most of them would agree with the following statements, some of which have connections to traditional philosophies:

(1) *A new age of spirituality that will lead to peace and harmony is coming to earth.*

(2) *We must work to transform our consciousness, using whatever means are necessary to combat the distractions of the world and to seek the higher truths.*

(3) *All aspects of reality are interrelated and flow throughout our consciousness.*

(4) *God is everything, and everything is God.*

(5) *Therefore, each of us is a part of God. We should learn to recognize and celebrate our deity.*

Many of these ideas are present in the following selection, which is the first chapter of Secret Truths.

WHY YOU CAME TO PLANET EARTH

And so it is time for you to know the truth about who you are and why you ¹ are living on the planet earth during this period of time called the 20th Century, A.D.

You chose to come and help rescue the planet. There are only a few ² adults on your planet who have learned the great secret teachings and can tell you these things. Perhaps you are a fortunate person who lives among adults of great knowing. All the better if you are. But if you are not, it is very important that you be told immediately about these coming years. This is because there likely will be great earth changes to be experienced in order that you might have a peaceful planet.

The purpose of these changes will be explained to you in this book, so that you will not be confused or unprepared for the things which will surely come if your peoples and your nations do not seek peace! The monstrous attitudes of war, violence and negative thinking, which are so prevalent on your planet at this time, must be reversed. These attitudes threaten to snuff out a majority of the life you now take for granted—not only the life of human beings but also the life of animals, birds, plants, trees, flowers, and every other living organism that creates the great web of interrelated life where you are. These attitudes must change if life is to continue peacefully on planet earth! 3

You are one of millions of young adults on the planet, one of 30–40 million just in the United States alone—and time is short! This book is for you and those like you who are ready to remember your true origins and your life's purpose as a Caretaker of planet earth. 4

Then let us begin at the beginning, before life as you know it existed on this planet earth, and share what the truth of your soul is. 5

Over eight million years ago, you were a light body similar to that of beings you call angels. Your body weight and structure were very different then, and you had only a few of the physical characteristics that you know as "normal" today. Let us say you were glowing with a beautiful light, that you had an outline similar in design to what you have now. Remember, you are not just the physical body which you see reflected in mirrors and which appears to be the great certainty of your existence. No, you are still that light, that glowing brilliance encased or temporarily residing in your physical body. Yes, now you have taken on the physicalness of earth, to be able to stay in what is called a third-dimensional world, for learning and service. You are learning to love and care for God and for all of life in its various forms. 6

Actually, your source of this light and energy—something like electricity, if you can imagine that—has a homeland far from this one, which you are capable of visiting sometimes during sleep. And you and all life energy were created by what you call God. 7

Who or what are you? YOU ARE LIGHT AND ENERGY! When something happens to your body or "earth suit," your higher and more knowledgeable self returns to its higher life, or dimensions, or activities, to that world your holy books have called "heaven." 8

Heaven is merely a general word that lumps together the places where life continues after that experience called "death." And, in a way, you died when you left your magnificent eternal homeland, heaven, and entered this phase of learning experience or school called earth. Here it is nearly impossible to remember what we are speaking of, but be assured, your life will 9 continue when you exit from this "Earth School," even as you lived before visiting this planet.

Can you grasp a little bit of what we are saying? When that great ONE   10
called God, Source, or Force created you of Itself, your nature was light and energy. When this life giving energy burst forth into its two aspects—the gold and silver rays—trillions and trillions of energy particles were later created by them, which eventually expanded into twelve holy light Universes. These worlds beyond counting cradled multiple lifeforms and planets, stars, star clusters, galaxies, novas, and glowing suns and much more than is spoken of in your field of astronomy. The reality of all this is far greater than we can briefly describe or than you can see when you look up at the night sky. But by watching the night sky some of the sparkling proof of what we have mentioned may arouse your soul's recollection about your origin and purpose on earth.

More, even, than the flowers that bloom, than the sand on the beaches,   11
or the drops of water in the oceans—more than all this is the magnificent, ever-growing family of God, scattered far beyond your ability to count or measure. It is too vast for you to experience presently and yet it is all related by the common heritage of energy and light that created it.

Know, then, that a spark of the Divine or unlimited Creator resides in   12
you, even though you left your higher life to visit the planet earth for additional schooling and service.

Now, you may be wondering, "Why would I leave my homeland to   13
come to earth?" This is a logical question. Let it be answered this way. Whenever a new planet is made ready for life of any kind, including that which you call human, those of the spiritual eternal flame quality are asked if they would like to have an adventure in growth and learning. And those who volunteer, who are appraised to be suitable and who pledge to complete their mission, are given the opportunity to join others on the new planet which needs Caretakers to oversee the unfolding of life in all its expressions. You came to earth as one of the Caretakers of its life eight million years ago. Then you did not have a dense physical body as you have now.

Like a great armada, those spiritualized energies came to earth, to-   14
gether constituting the spiritual family of Caretakers to complete the task they had chosen. All was in readiness for a great adventure. Those millions of glowing, non-physical souls were excited and challenged by their new environment and, above the planet's surface they discovered, learned, and cared for the life they found. They were wonderfully happy and lived in their light bodies for many thousands of years.

In fact, for nearly a million years life was truly enjoyable. And then a   15
great change occurred.

In their original agreement to come to earth, the light beings had prom-   16
ised that, no matter what happened, they would always remember their Creator with love and reverence, and would always stay true to the purpose of preservation of all life on the planet.

The planet was created as an experiment in free will, so you live on a 17
FREE WILL planet. (Free will means each soul can choose whatever it
wishes to do.) Since only positive energy had been present for a million years,
there was nothing of negativity to unbalance this beautiful free will creation.
But then negativity was allowed to enter the planetary area, so a true free
will situation would exist. And that, Children of the Light, is where the trouble began.

Ever since they had left their homelands behind, these spiritual pioneers 18
still maintained communication with their former existence by means of what
you might call mental telepathy. It was a lifeline to those former homelands
and enabled them to receive guidance about problems, difficulties, or concerns they were having. It was similar to a two-way radio, walkie-talkie set
or mental TV. You can understand that this communication link was vital
for those on this spiritual outpost in a far corner of the Universe.

Since the purpose of coming to earth as a Caretaker was to learn to love 19
God through every difficulty and not to abandon belief in the Parent which
had created it, each soul was now put to a crucial test as part of its learning
experience—something like an examination in a school course.

Up until this moment on the planet, the beings of light were all peace 20
and harmony. They cared for all lifeforms who needed assistance, aided one
another if help was necessary, and lived a glorious life of beauty and serenity.
Their minds were connected both to one another and to God. And because
of this communication, life proceeded naturally as had been planned.

Then the challenge came.   21

Only a few of your earth books speak of that time of darkness or sepa- 22
ration in true perspective which is why you are being given this information
now. Many of your teachings do say there came a deep sleep, a separation,
or a falling away from the God who had created them. But most teachings
fail to explain that you had volunteered to come to the planet to learn self-
mastery as love-beings. They do not tell you that the time in which you live
today is the final time, the end of that great eight million year period you
began so long ago. It is the closure of many cycles; it is the time of graduation.

When the power of negative thinking began on earth, many of the light 23
beings began to get involved with and in the lifeforms which they were supposedly caring for, and there was an intermingling of their light with the
grossness of the lesser, material world. This has been called temptation by
some holy books. The temptation to go off and do whatever the individual
soul chose to do prevailed, and the messages of support and warning that still
could be heard within the mind as if by radio or TV were ignored. Thus the
lowering of sound and light vibrations continued for eons, until many were
no longer capable of hearing the God voice within.

Much of this happened after a negative, unloving power came to en- 24
courage the light people to ignore what they had agreed to do. This dark
influence over the formerly loving Caretakers continued for millions of years,

with only a minority of the people able to remember God, to hear constructive guidance on that inner home telephone. And, although there were many
"rescue teams" sent to remind the light beings, now fallen, of their need to
return to their original agreements, if they were to have self-mastery and
receive what you might call a promotion into higher cosmic activities, none
had much real effect.

Now you are here—eight million years later—with one last opportunity 25
in that asked-for self-mastery course you undertook. While there is still time
to re-establish peace on earth, you are challenged to preserve all life and to
revere and remember God, that great ONE from which all life sprang.

So that is the setting in which your own personal life now exists. And 26
the questions we ask you to consider are: Do you wish to remember why you
came to earth long ago? Will you join your efforts with millions of others like
yourself who are just now awakening?—just now ready to pick up the torch
of certainty and commitment and move into a graduation of your soul's planetary initiation? You live on the earth, but this is not your primary heritage.
It is a step, a stage, part of a vast learning process from which you may be
promoted to even greater opportunities. Or you can be the foundation of a
great new civilization of heaven on earth, if you wish. The world needs peace!
Will you bring that message and be its model?

There will be those who insist, "Prove what you say" or "How can I 27
know this is the truth?" Our reply to this doubt would be that you listen with
your heart. That is the one infallible tool humanity has possessed since its fall
from that former ability to communicate with God. For your heart feels and
remembers God. It is your soul connection to the Cosmos.

Today your only true guide is that spark of God within you that will 28
direct your path and make your journey as easy as possible. This is the present
plight of your fellow beings on the planet: they are asleep; they have forgotten; they are unconscious. But that unconsciousness must be ended if peace is
to return to the planet and if you are to escape the ravages of a self-created
nuclear war, the effects of underground explosions, Star Wars weaponry, or
worse.

Your proof of any new information is the way you feel inside. For in- 29
stance, if this message rings within you an inner bell of some kind, it is your
truth. If not, you may find other helpful information or you may continue to
sleep until one day, in some faraway place, you will again be given the chance
to learn this commitment of caring through thick and thin, of loving God
without ceasing.

Time means nothing to God. Only in these physical worlds does it exist, 30
and time has a way of being interminable and exhausting. Let your heart
remember your mission, then, and please use these remaining years to good
benefit. Your task can still be completed, whether you are an angel that forgot itself, a child of angels that forgot, a rescuer of angels that became en-

trapped here, or a soul which still prefers to do as it pleases regardless of the original earth agreement.

If you dare to remember your true inheritance, God's love corps welcomes you home again and seeks to bring about the completion of that adventure which you undertook so long ago. Jesus the Christ was one being who, along with others down through time, remembered fully and completely his true God-identity while living in a body. Christ means light! You are light remembering itself—its true self. And you have many great opportunities now to achieve the goal, set eight million years ago, before the earth was physically populated. 31

The present difficult circumstances on earth involve karmic law (or the principle of cause and effect), and it is consequently a time of intense challenge for the planet and all of humanity because of those returning negative effects that must now be faced. 32

During this time the call is going out to many like yourself; it is the call to work together in order to save planet earth from disaster. You will not be alone. You are needed! Can we count on you? 33

Humanity and the planet must be healed! All of you can help with this regardless of your age, size, color, or religion. Yes, this is the Time of Awakening. Will you receive God's love and energy and awaken to your true spiritual identity? 34

If, as a young person, you have not read of these things in your history books or if you have not gleaned them from the books you call the holy scriptures or from the teachings of a religion, do not be surprised. You are still one of the Caretakers of the earth, even if nearly everyone on this planet has forgotten what this means. 35

If you awaken now, perhaps you can help persuade your sleeping fellow humans to give up war, attack, and killing, and to model peace as an example to others. Humanity must learn to care for all of life with great intensity, whether it be the minerals, the animals, the plants and trees, or the birds and mammals of land and sea. 36

Being, then, a responsible person—whatever your age—you will recognize in your heart that the future of planet earth is partially in your hands. There are many who have totally forgotten their mission, who have forgotten who they are in the spiritual realms, who have aligned themselves with pursuits and interests which do not acknowledge the need for peace and the preservation of all life. Yet they can still awaken to their souls' and God's calling. 37

Then share the truth of who and what you are: *energy* (something like electricity or electromagnetic energy). Share that you have a common identity springing from that great ONE who is often called God. Share that in this relationship between you and God, or you and your creative source, the Parent-of-all, you have a purpose far beyond the little planet you live upon 38 now. You have relationships in vast corners of this Universe and you have power and responsibilities at many other levels. You have the type of power that is creative in nature, if accompanied by a nurturing and caring attitude. Nothing here on earth has been created that is not cared about by the spiritual ones who assist you!

The very act of creating anything—whether a tree house, a toy, a picture, a song, a home or airplane of some kind—begins with a thought, a picture, a blueprint, or an idea seeking fulfillment. Even God's energy, in the creation of your planet, had an idea or concept to follow or you would not be here. For the idea contained the visualization of what would happen after it was finished. The expectation was that, over eons of time, the individual cellular, molecular, microbiological lifeforms would grow and expand and, one day, would create the basis of a simple pattern out of which much else would follow. 39

And in all of this planning there was peace and harmony, excitement and joy, and the interest to see how it would all work out eventually, so that each lifeform would be honored. For God is not limited by time. Time is only a measurement for you on earth to segregate and separate things and people, one from another. Since God knows no separation, there is, in truth, no time. 40

The most important thing for you as a young person to understand is that each little piece of life or creation is vital. All are part of a gigantic undertaking of wholeness and relationship called symbiosis. Symbiosis, or harmony in and through relationships, has its cycles and nothing remains static or changeless for long, except God and God's first creations. 41

This planet is not a duplicate of any other planet. It is unique. The thing that is unique or most unusual about it is that God's creative force wanted this planet to be one of *caring and peace*, although free will in nature. For not all planets are of this type. Since earth was set in motion to be both free will and a loving peaceful planet, you who live here cannot change that pattern—you can only demonstrate it. Its purpose is already defined, just as the purposes of the other planets in your solar system have been defined. 42

Then ponder what has been said. Close your eyes, shut the book and hold it in your lap a few minutes. 43

Be quiet for a while and listen within. 44

. . . . 45

Only if you really feel drawn to continue reading this book should you do so. For some people are ready to remember and some are not. 46

Follow your inner knowing only, not the senseless monkey-mind chatter of the limited human personality which is an illusionary substitute for God's truth and peace. 47

Ask the God-spark within you what your course of action should be, for 48 in spite of this long spiritual sleep, that spark can glow again and bring you back to God. It is an infallible map to buried treasures of spiritual gold and silver. It is your return ticket to Cosmic truth.

QUESTIONS ABOUT ESSENE'S DISCOURSE COMMUNITY AND HER CONCERNS IN THIS SELECTION

1. What does Essene claim is the most important thing for young people to understand?
2. Essene writes that each of us once existed in what state?
3. Why does she say we chose to come to this planet?
4. How is free will dependent on negativity? Does Essene adequately show where the power of negativity came from?
5. Does Essene exaggerate the seriousness of the threats to life on earth?
6. In what ways does Essene seem to have drawn from other religions and philosophies?
7. Which of Essene's points do you think would be most attractive to people in their teens or twenties? Why?

QUESTIONS ABOUT ESSENE'S RHETORICAL STRATEGIES

1. How do you read Essene's first sentence? What is its tone? Is there anything combative about it?
2. In paragraph 6, Essene uses the words "Let us say." Why would she use the word *us* and not *me*? Who is the narrator of this piece?
3. In general, how would you characterize Essene's attitude toward her readers? Are you attracted to her writing voice? Why or why not?
4. What kind of strategy is Essene using when she writes that each of her readers is "a responsible person"?
5. How does Essene use italicized and capitalized words? Is her strategy effective?
6. Examine the metaphors Essene uses. What is she trying to do with them? How effective are they?
7. What kind of evidence does Essene use? How do you evaluate it?
8. For Essene, what constitutes proof? Do you agree with her?
9. How does Essene try to get you to want to read more of this book? Does she succeed? Why or why not?

WRITING FROM WITHIN AND ABOUT PHILOSOPHY

Writing for Yourself

1. In your journal explore your reactions to the claim that everything is God.
2. In your journal explore your reactions to claims commonly made about reincarnation.

Writing for Nonacademic Audiences

1. Interview several students on your campus about what threats to the planet they see, if any. Then write a 500-word summary article on this subject for a column in your school newspaper entitled "What They're Thinking on Campus."
2. What elements of current popular movies seem to be derived from New Age thinking? Respond in a 750-word analytical essay for your school's monthly anthology of student writing.

Writing for Academic Audiences

1. For a philosophy of religion course, write a 750-word analysis of why you think so many religions adopt the metaphor of light to describe God and gods.
2. For a sociology of religion course, write a 1,000-word cause-and-effect paper on what moves young people to be attracted to New Age thinking.
3. For a philosophy of religion course, write a 1,250-word analysis of the main philosophical connections between New Age thinkers and other religious leaders.

INTERCONNECTIONS: QUESTIONS FOR WRITING

Writing for Yourself

1. Speculative philosophy often deals with what lies beyond the realm of the senses and whether we can ever approach that realm. Some philosophers have suggested that that realm is indeed accessible. Others, such as the logical positivists, have argued that we can talk only about what is patently before us in the physical world. Still others suggest that we cannot trust our senses, that even the apparent reality of the physical world may not be actual reality.

    Examine this question in your journal, reflecting on how Julian of Norwich, Descartes, and Essene might have responded.
2. What is it that gives meaning to one's life? How can one be sure that one's life has meaning?

    In your journal, examine this question as it relates to Plato, Augustine, and Sartre.

Writing for Nonacademic Audiences

1. Many philosophers have attempted to define the nature of humankind. What is it about humanity that sets it apart from the rest of the natural world?

    Examine this question as it relates to Augustine, Kuhn, and Essene. Prepare your response in the form of notes for a thirty-minute lecture to be delivered to a study group of a local religious community. Prepare a similar set of notes to be delivered to your university's biology club.
2. How important is one's culture in shaping one's philosophical positions? By using the word *shaping*, this question includes positions that agree with and are opposed to the culture's positions. Is it possible for an individual to arrive at

philosophical positions unencumbered by traditions from his or her own culture?

Examine this question as it relates to Descartes and Whorf. Your response will appear in a collection of essays by college-age writers. Half of these writers will be of Native American descent; half will be of European descent.

3. What kinds of evidence can a philosopher appeal to? Is a philosophical argument capable of being proven, or are proofs irrelevant to philosophical arguments?

Examine these questions by writing an informal dialogue between Plato, Descartes, and Sartre. This will be used as a script for a twenty-minute radio presentation to be broadcast by your university's radio station.

4. Should the philosopher be present in his or her own writing? That is, should the stance be one that reflects the philosopher's own self? Or should the writer be utterly detached?

Examine these questions as they relate to Augustine, Descartes, Whorf, or Essene by choosing one of their pieces and rewriting a 750-word section of that piece, omitting as much as possible the presence of the philosopher. Then, in a 250-word letter to that philosopher, explain how your version improves upon or detracts from the original.

Writing for Academic Audiences

1. Is it possible for philosophy as a discourse community to make progress? And if so, what does that progress look like and how might it be measured?

Examine this question as it relates to Merton and Kuhn in a 500-word essay for an introductory philosophy course.

2. In twentieth-century North America, mysticism is often viewed warily. A society built upon empirical science is hardly likely to embrace mystical precepts. But some philosophers have argued that mysticism is a valid way of understanding ourselves in relation to the rest of the world.

Examine this problem as it relates to Julian of Norwich, Locke, and Merton in a 750-word opinion essay for a course in world religions.

3. Are there any empirical tests that can be used to judge the rightness or wrongness of philosophical positions? Or would such tests be completely irrelevant to philosophical thought?

Examine this question as it relates to Augustine, Descartes, and Essene in a 1,000-word essay for a sophomore-level course in the philosophy department of your university.

4. Philosophical writing has often been characterized as dense and obtuse by those outside the discourse community. One question that a philosopher—and really any writer—must answer is whether he or she wishes to appeal to those outside the discourse community. If the answer to this question is yes, then the philosopher must deal with elements within a text that would put off an outside reader. Many of these elements are part of the content, but some are part of style as well. Is there a general style that characterizes philosophical writing? If so, what elements of that style would need to be adapted?

Examine these questions as they relate to Locke, Sartre, and Merton. Your response should come in the form of a 500-word essay for your university's freshman writing course.

DISCOURSE
COMMUNITIES IN
THE SOCIAL SCIENCES

INTRODUCTION

Those who conduct research within the social sciences work with the behavior of individuals or groups within specific contexts. The angle from which researchers approach such study depends upon the kind of behavior that they are most interested in exploring: the inner life of an individual's dreams, the mythic underpinnings of a society, the structure of societal order that a people has established for itself, the force of societal patterns upon individual behavior. All are areas which social scientists examine.

The following essays are written by avowed capitalists and fervid communists, Freudians and behaviorists, Darwinists and moral theorists, functionalists and social constructionists and feminists. Each uses the assets and assumptions and understandings of his or her discourse community to probe into questions of human behavior, dealing with a subject that is by its very nature nebulous and changing and difficult to define.

The essayists represented here ask questions such as the following:

How does an individual define a place for himself or herself in the context of a group?
What role does the past play in determining future behavior?
How do traditional roles change? Are such changes amoral?
How do societies and individuals govern themselves?
How does a society make progress? How is such progress to be defined? Is such progress amoral in nature?

Whether questions such as these can ever be resolved is open to debate. Certainly these writers point towards some answers.

Because social scientists are dealing with behaviors, theirs might be judged to be a somewhat inexact science. Evidence might have to be collected from very subjective sources and its accuracy judged. (Recently, for example, some of the subjects who provided so much information to anthropologist Margaret Mead for her book *Coming of Age in Samoa* [1928] have suggested that some of their information was purposefully misleading; such suggestions have cast doubt upon Mead's work.) Conclusions about a group may not necessarily be applicable to each individual within that group. Nor can conclusions about one group or individual necessarily be used to understand another group or individual, especially ones separated by culture, time, and experience. In the face of these obstacles, the work of the social scientist is to come to limited conclusions about a certain people at a certain time, based upon observations of that people.

Yet here, too, the research of the social scientist becomes thorny. How strongly does the very presence of the researcher affect the research? Can the Trobriand Islanders be completely themselves if Malinowski is there beside them (see 484)? Can Katharina be completely uninhibited in her talks with Freud, a relative stranger (see 458)? Can Ouchi observe a corporation while remaining unobserved himself—and at the same time holding in check his own subjective judgments (see 549)?

The last point is yet another issue for the social scientist: How does one battle one's own preconceptions to present an objective picture of another? Like the historian, the social scientist must recognize his or her own cultural biases and perceptions and overcome them if that scientist is to report accurately and fairly on life on a remote island, on the nature of democracy or capitalism, on the relationship between the sexes, on the deep sources of behavior. Among the ten writers in the following section, some may not be said to have accomplished this very successfully. Some do not try.

The nature of the evidence that social scientists collect and the methods by which they gather it vary considerably among discourse communities within the social sciences. The cultural anthropologist, collecting information on a culture other than his or her own, uses fieldwork to observe and interview those within that culture. He or she may need to turn to other discourse communities to supplement these observations: to archeology, perhaps, to examine past evidence, or to biology to examine skeletal remains and conjecture upon such things as diet. Each observation in the course of such research represents another stroke in putting together a picture of a culture.

Economists and political scientists also examine large groups, and they too may use field work. However, they focus on a single aspect of the group's behavior, rather than its overall culture. These social scientists look for patterns of behavior in the economic and political spheres: How does the group produce and use its wealth? How is wealth distributed among members of the group? How does the society create order within itself? How does a government function efficiently and with justice? The evidence that will lead to answers for these questions may be expressed statistically, rather than as a narrative or a description.

For the psychologist, field research may be only a small part of a larger understanding that he or she is trying to develop about an individual. As the psychologist deals with an individual's behavior, he or she pieces together a series of observations, trying to discern inner motivations from outer actions. Those actions are themselves only bits of evidence that point to hidden causes.

But each writer, as he or she comes to the task of writing within the social sciences, must gather evidence—much of it anecdotal and subjective—

and come to conclusions based upon that evidence. Encapsulated in the essay must be a statement of the evidence, an evaluation of its usefulness, and a rationale for the conclusions drawn from it. Such conclusions become less and less tentative as the writer amasses evidence which on some level is verifiable.

The following selections represent five different areas of study within the social sciences. Marx, Engels, and Lasswell represent the political sciences, examining the structures that humanity establishes to govern itself. Adam Smith and Ouchi are economists, studying how economic systems function. Malinowski is an anthropologist, researching cultural patterns. Durkheim is a sociologist, examining the behavior of groups. Freud, Skinner, Gilligan, and Kessler and McKenna are psychologists, focusing on the inner, sometimes unconscious, life of the individual and how it develops.

Other discourse communities cut across the boundaries of the five social sciences just mentioned. These influence the ways in which the represented writers come to their subject matters. These discourse communities are affected by time—Adam Smith writing in eighteenth-century Britain, William Ouchi working within the context of strained trade relationships between Japan and the United States in the late twentieth century. They are affected by gender concerns. They are affected by theoretical choices made about the way evidence ought to be collected and the manner in which it is to be interpreted. And they are affected by their place within the larger discipline of the social sciences.

Adam Smith

(1723–1790)

Certainly before 1776, the notion of political economy had been examined; in universities it was considered to be part of the discipline of moral philosophy. But until Adam Smith's An Inquiry into the Nature and Causes of the Wealth of Nations, *economics had never been envisioned as a separate discourse community. After that work, it would never again be seen as a discourse community subject to the constructs of another community. Like other writers of this section, Smith founded a discipline by organizing and articulating principles, and by using those principles to interpret the world around him.*

That Adam Smith would be the one to articulate this community is perhaps remarkable. He was known to be absent-minded; he once walked into a pit while conversing with a friend, and another time he walked fifteen miles in only a dressing gown. His lectures were reputed to be hardly vigorous, yet he searched out fundamental ideas that would give unity to a universe that was apparently chaotic—a philosophical bent that would not seem at first to tend toward economics. Smith looked around him and envisioned a uniform set of laws that determined the economy of a nation and, inevitably, its wealth. Whether, as he observed the factory system that was sprawling across England and on up into Scotland and Glasgow, where Smith taught, he failed to see the seven-year-old children who worked fourteen hours a day in a mine shaft or at a loom and failed to account for this moral horror is a valid question.

The Wealth of Nations *began in a fit of boredom. Smith was tutoring Charles Townshend's son as that scion was making a grand tour of Europe. (Townshend is best remembered as the one responsible for imposing the tea tax on the American colonies that would lead to the Boston Tea Party). Smith began the book while traveling through the provinces of France. When he returned to England, he was determined to show that agriculture was not the only source of a nation's wealth, as many argued. Instead, wealth lay also in the hands of the mercantile classes. Twelve years later, he would publish the book.*

The book drew from a number of prominent eighteenth-century writers, particularly John Locke and David Hume; it cites over one hundred authors by name. Its greatness lies in the fact that for the first time, a large work had dealt with exclusively economic issues, bringing together many bits and pieces of economic theory. It is not a book known for conciseness, and often the details and sidelights are so labored and meticulously handled that they cloud the arguments. But it has one central thesis to which everything else is subordinate: that wealth is that which is produced and consumed by an entire nation. Wealth is not that which is held in a king's treasury, but that which is held in the hands of a country's populace. This new, radical under-

standing of wealth would define a discourse community and influence economists for the next two centuries.

The following selection is the opening chapter of Wealth of Nations, *dealing with the division of labor, a development Smith saw as responsible for increasing productivity and, hence, a nation's wealth.*

OF THE DIVISION OF LABOUR

The greatest improvement in the productive powers of labour, and the greater 1 part of the skill, dexterity, and judgment with which it is any where directed, or applied, seem to have been the effects of the division of labour.

The effects of the division of labour, in the general business of society, 2 will be more easily understood, by considering in what manner it operates in some particular manufactures. It is commonly supposed to be carried furthest in some very trifling ones; not perhaps that it really is carried further in them than in others of more importance: but in those trifling manufactures which are destined to supply the small wants of but a small number of people, the whole number of workmen must necessarily be small; and those employed in every different branch of the work can often be collected into the same work-house, and placed at once under the view of the spectator.

In those great manufactures, on the contrary, which are destined to 3 supply the great wants of the great body of the people, every different branch of the work employs so great a number of workmen, that it is impossible to collect them all into the same workhouse. We can seldom see more, at one time, than those employed in one single branch. Though in such manufactures, therefore, the work may really be divided into a much greater number of parts, than in those of a more trifling nature, the division is not near so obvious, and has accordingly been much less observed.

To take an example, therefore, from a very trifling manufacture; but 4 one in which the division of labour has been very often taken notice of, the trade of the pin-maker; a workman not educated to this business (which the division of labour has rendered a distinct trade), nor acquainted with the use of the machinery employed in it (to the invention of which the same division of labour has probably given occasion), could scarce, perhaps, with his utmost industry, make one pin in a day, and certainly could not make twenty. But in the way in which this business is now carried on, not only the whole work is a peculiar trade, but it is divided into a number of branches, of which the greater part are likewise peculiar trades. One man draws out the wire, another straights it, a third cuts it, a fourth points it, a fifth grinds it at the top for receiving the head; to make the head requires two or three distinct operations; to put it on, is a peculiar business, to whiten the pins is another; it is even a trade by itself to put them into the paper; and the important business of making a pin is, in this manner, divided into about eighteen distinct operations, which, in some manufactories, are all performed by distinct hands, though in others the same man will sometimes perform two or three of them. I have seen a small manufactory of this kind where ten men only were employed, and where some of them consequently performed two or three distinct operations. But though they were very poor, and therefore but indifferently accommodated with the necessary machinery, they could, when they exerted themselves, make among them about twelve pounds of pins in a day. There are in a pound upwards of four thousand pins of a middling size. Those ten persons, therefore, could make among them upwards of forty-eight thousand pins in a day. Each person, therefore, making a tenth part of forty-eight thousand pins, might be considered as making four thousand eight hundred pins in a day. But if they had all wrought separately and independently, and without any of them having been educated to this peculiar business, they certainly could not each of them have made twenty, perhaps not one pin in a day; that is, certainly, not the two hundred and fortieth, perhaps not the four thousand eight hundredth part of what they are at present capable of performing, in consequence of a proper division and combination of their different operations.

In every other art and manufacture, the effects of the division of labour 5 are similar to what they are in this very trifling one; though, in many of them, the labour can neither be so much subdivided, nor reduced to so great a simplicity of operation. The division of labour, however, so far as it can be introduced, occasions, in every art, a proportionate increase of the productive powers of labour. The separation of different trades and employments from one another, seems to have taken place, in consequence of this advantage. This separation too is generally carried furthest in those countries which enjoy the highest degree of industry and improvement; what is the work of one man in a rude state of society, being generally that of several in an improved one. In every improved society, the farmer is generally nothing but a farmer; the manufacturer, nothing but a manufacturer. The labour too which is necessary to produce any one complete manufacture, is almost always divided among a great number of hands. How many different trades are employed in each branch of the linen and woollen manufacturers, from the growers of the flax and the wool, to the bleachers and smoothers of the linen, or to the dyers and dressers of the cloth! The nature of agriculture, indeed, does not admit of so many subdivisions of labour, nor of so complete a separation of one business from another, as manufactures. It is impossible to separate so entirely, the business of the grazier from that of the corn-farmer, as the trade of carpenter is commonly separated from that of the smith. The spinner is almost always a distinct person from the weaver; but the ploughman, the harrower, the sower of the seed, and the reaper of the corn, are often the same. The occasions for those different sorts of labour returning with the different seasons of the year, it is impossible that one man should be constantly employed in any one of them. This impossibility of making so complete and entire a separation of all the different branches of labour employed in agriculture, is perhaps the reason why the improvement of the productive powers of labour in this art, does not always keep pace with their improvement in manufactures. The most opulent nations, indeed, generally excel all their neighbours in agriculture as well as in manufactures; but they are commonly more distinguished by their superiority in the latter than in the former. Their lands are in general better cultivated, and having more labour and expence bestowed upon them, produce more in proportion to the extent and natural fertility of the ground. But this superiority of produce is seldom much more than in proportion to the superiority of labour and expence. In agriculture, the labour of the rich country is not always much more productive than that of the poor; or, at least, it is never so much more productive, as it commonly is in manufactures. The corn of the rich country, therefore, will not always, in the same degree of goodness, come cheaper to market than that of the poor. The corn of Poland, in the same degree of goodness, is as cheap as that of France, notwithstanding the superior opulence and improvement of the latter country. The corn of France is, in the corn provinces, fully as good, and in most years nearly about the same price with the corn of England, though, in opulence and improvement, France is perhaps inferior to England. The corn-lands of England, however, are better cultivated than those of France, and the corn-lands of France are said to be much better cultivated than those of Poland. But though the poor country, notwithstanding the inferiority of its cultivation, can, in some measure, rival the rich in the cheapness and goodness of its corn, it can pretend to no such competition in its manufactures; at least if those manufactures suit the soil, climate, and situation of the rich country. The silks of France are better and cheaper than those of England, because the silk manufacture, at least under the present high duties upon the importation of raw silk, does not so well suit the climate of England as that of France. But the hard-ware and the coarse woollens of England are beyond all comparison superior to those of France, and much cheaper too in the same degree of goodness. In Poland there are said to be scarce any manufactures of any kind, a few of those coarser household manufactures excepted, without which no country can well subsist.

This great increase of the quantity of work, which, in consequence of 6 the division of labour, the same number of people are capable of performing, is owing to three different circumstances; first, to the increase of dexterity in every particular workman; secondly, to the saving of the time which is commonly lost in passing from one species of work to another; and lastly, to the invention of a great number of machines which facilitate and abridge labour, and enable one man to do the work of many.

First, the improvement of the dexterity of the workman necessarily in- 7 creases the quantity of the work he can perform; and the division of labour, by reducing every man's business to some one simple operation, and by making this operation the sole employment of his life, necessarily increases very much the dexterity of the workman. A common smith, who, though accustomed to handle the hammer, has never been used to make nails, if upon some particular occasion he is obliged to attempt it, will scarce, I am assured, be able to make above two or three hundred nails in a day, and those too very bad ones. A smith who has been accustomed to make nails, but whose sole or principal business has not been that of a nailer, can seldom with his utmost diligence make more than eight hundred or a thousand nails in a day. I have seen several boys under twenty years of age who had never exercised any other trade but that of making nails, and who, when they exerted themselves, could make, each of them, upwards of two thousand three hundred nails in a day. The making of a nail, however, is by no means one of the simplest operations. The same person blows the bellows, stirs or mends the fire as there is occasion, heats the iron, and forges every part of the nail: In forging the head too he is obliged to change his tools. The different operations into which the making of a pin, or of a metal button, is subdivided, are all of them much more simple, and the dexterity of the person, of whose life it has been the sole business to perform them, is usually much greater. The rapidity with which some of the operations of those manufactures are performed, exceeds what the human hand could, by those who had never seen them, be supposed capable of acquiring.

Secondly, the advantage which is gained by saving the time commonly 8 lost in passing from one sort of work to another, is much greater than we should at first view be apt to imagine it. It is impossible to pass very quickly from one kind of work to another, that is carried on in a different place, and with quite different tools. A country weaver, who cultivates a small farm, must lose a good deal of time in passing from his loom to the field, and from the field to his loom. When the two trades can be carried on in the same workhouse, the loss of time is no doubt much less. It is even in this case, however, very considerable. A man commonly saunters a little in turning his hand from one sort of employment to another. When he first begins the new work he is seldom very keen and hearty; his mind, as they say, does not go to it, and for some time he rather trifles than applies to good purpose. The habit of sauntering and of indolent careless application, which is naturally, or rather necessarily acquired by every country workman who is obliged to change his work and his tools every half hour, and to apply his hand in twenty different ways almost every day of his life; renders him almost always slothful and lazy, and incapable of any vigorous application even on the most pressing occasions. Independent, therefore, of his deficiency in point of dexterity, this cause alone must always reduce considerably the quantity of work which he is capable of performing.

Thirdly, and lastly, every body must be sensible how much labour is 9 facilitated and abridged by the application of proper machinery. It is unnecessary to give any example. I shall only observe, therefore, that the invention of all those machines by which labour is so much facilitated and abridged, seems to have been originally owing to the division of labour. Men are much more likely to discover easier and readier methods of attaining any object, when the whole attention of their minds is directed towards that single object, than when it is dissipated among a great variety of things. But in consequence of the division of labour, the whole of every man's attention comes naturally to be directed towards some one very simple object. It is naturally to be expected, therefore, that some one or other of those who are employed in each particular branch of labour should soon find out easier and readier methods of performing their own particular work, wherever the nature of it admits of such improvement. A great part of the machines made use of in those manufactures in which labour is most subdivided, were originally the inventions of common workmen, who, being each of them employed in some very simple operation, naturally turned their thoughts towards finding out easier and readier methods of performing it. Whoever has been much accustomed to visit such manufactures, must frequently have been shewn very pretty machines, which were the inventions of such workmen, in order to facilitate and quicken their own particular part of the work. In the first fire-engines, a boy was constantly employed to open and shut alternately the communication between the boiler and the cylinder, according as the piston either ascended or descended. One of those boys, who loved to play with his companions, observed that, by tying a string from the handle of the valve which opened this communication to another part of the machine, the valve would open and shut without his assistance, and leave him at liberty to divert himself with his play-fellows. One of the greatest improvements that has been made upon this machine, since it was first invented, was in this manner the discovery of a boy who wanted to save his own labour.

All the improvements in machinery, however, have by no means been 10 the inventions of those who had occasion to use the machines. Many improvements have been made by the ingenuity of the makers of the machines, when to make them became the business of a peculiar trade; and some by that of those who are called philosophers or men of speculation, whose trade it is not to do any thing, but to observe every thing; and who, upon that account, are often capable of combining together the powers of the most distant and dissimilar objects. In the progress of society, philosophy or speculation becomes, like every other employment, the principal or sole trade and occupation of a particular class of citizens. Like every other employment too, it is subdivided into a great number of different branches, each of which affords occupation to a peculiar tribe or class of philosophers; and this subdivision of employment in philosophy, as well as in every other business, improves dexterity, and saves time. Each individual becomes more expert in his own peculiar branch, more work is done upon the whole, and the quantity of science is considerably increased by it.

It is the great multiplication of the productions of all the different arts, 11 in consequence of the division of labour, which occasions, in a well-governed society, that universal opulence which extends itself to the lowest ranks of the people. Every workman has a great quantity of his own work to dispose of beyond what he himself has occasion for; and every other workman being exactly in the same situation, he is enabled to exchange a great quantity of his own goods for a great quantity, or, what comes to the same thing, for the price of a great quantity of theirs. He supplies them abundantly with what they have occasion for, and they accommodate him as amply with what he has occasion for, and a general plenty diffuses itself through all the different ranks of the society.

Observe the accommodation of the most common artificer or day- 12 labourer in a civilized and thriving country, and you will perceive that the number of people of whose industry a part, though but a small part, has been employed in procuring him this accommodation, exceeds all computation. The woollen coat, for example, which covers the day-labourer, as coarse and rough as it may appear, is the produce of the joint labour of a great multitude of workmen. The shepherd, the sorter of the wool, the wool-comber or carder, the dyer, the scribbler, the spinner, the weaver, the fuller, the dresser, with many others, must all join their different arts in order to complete even this homely production. How many merchants and carriers, besides, must have been employed in transporting the materials from some of those work-men to others who often live in a very distant part of the country! How much commerce and navigation in particular, how many ship-builders, sailors, sail-makers, rope-makers, must have been employed in order to bring together the different drugs made use of by the dyer, which often come from the re-motest corners of the world! What a variety of labour too is necessary in order to produce the tools of the meanest of those workmen! To say nothing of such complicated machines as the ship of the sailor, the mill of the fuller, or even the loom of the weaver, let us consider only what a variety of labour is req-uisite in order to form that very simple machine, the shears with which the shepherd clips the wool. The miner, the builder of the furnace for smelting the ore, the feller of the timber, the burner of the charcoal to be made use of in the smelting-house, the brick-maker, the brick-layer, the workmen who attend the furnace, the mill-wright, the forger, the smith, must all of them join their different arts in order to produce them. Were we to examine, in the same manner, all the different parts of his dress and household furniture, the coarse linen shirt which he wears next his skin, the shoes which cover his feet, the bed which he lies on, and all the different parts which compose it, the kitchen-grate at which he prepares his victuals, the coals which he makes use of for that purpose, dug from the bowels of the earth, and brought to him perhaps by a long sea and a long land carriage, all the other utensils of his kitchen, all the furniture of his table, the knives and forks, the earthen or pewter plates upon which he serves up and divides his victuals, the different hands employed in preparing his bread and his beer, the glass window which lets in the heat and the light, and keeps out the wind and the rain, with all the knowledge and art requisite for preparing that beautiful and happy invention, without which these northern parts of the world could scarce have afforded a very comfortable habitation, together with the tools of all the different workmen employed in producing those different conveniences; if we examine, I say, all these things, and consider what a variety of labour is employed about each of them, we shall be sensible that without the assistance and co-operation of many thousands, the very meanest person in a civilized country could not be provided, even according to, what we very falsely imagine, the easy and simple manner in which he is commonly accommodated. Compared, indeed, with the more extravagant luxury of the great, his accommodation must no doubt appear extremely simple and easy; and yet it may be true, perhaps, that the accommodation of an European prince does not always so much exceed that of an industrious and frugal peasant, as the accommodation of the latter exceeds that of many an African king, the absolute master of the lives and liberties of ten thousand naked savages.

QUESTIONS ABOUT ADAM SMITH'S DISCOURSE COMMUNITY AND HIS CONCERNS IN THIS SELECTION

1. What does Smith understand to be labor? Would his definition of this term be the same as that of a contemporary economist? What does Smith mean by the division of labor?
2. The division of labor has sometimes been attacked because of its stultifying effects on workers and on the quality of the product. Smith never addresses the effects of this specialization upon the individual worker, except for a brief and perhaps overly optimistic and naive comment at the essay's conclusion. Why do you think he did not address this issue? Does that omission hurt his credibility?
3. Based on the fourth paragraph, what, according to Smith, is the chief value of the division of labor? Do you agree that this is a praiseworthy value?
4. Smith asserts that "the division of labour . . . so far as it can be introduced, occasions, in every art, a proportionate increase of the productive powers of labor" (paragraph 5). Do you agree with this generalization? What industries, does it seem to you, might not be aided by the specialization of labor?
5. How do you respond to Smith's comments about the individual country laborer (paragraph eight)? What do his comments suggest about his own position in society? Does it seem to you that Smith is qualified to make these kinds of generalizations?
6. In this chapter, Smith frequently refers to simplicity. What role does simplicity play in industry, according to Smith? Do you think that simplicity is necessarily a virtue in this context?
7. In paragraph ten, Smith argues that society itself is divided according to specialties, and the division leads to an increase in the amount of work done. A Marxist economist might argue that such a view perpetuates the unfair division of classes. Which side would you lean toward? Why?

8. Smith observes that, in a land that uses the division of labor, "a general plenty diffuses itself through all the different ranks of the society" (paragraph 11). Yet surely Smith must have known of the abject poverty throughout England in the eighteenth century. Is he merely ignoring this poverty? Rationalizing it away? Being purposefully ignorant? Or is there some other reason for this optimistic observation?

QUESTIONS ABOUT SMITH'S RHETORICAL STRATEGIES

1. What functions does the first sentence of this chapter serve? When Smith uses the word *seem*, does it sound as though he is unsure of his ideas?
2. At times throughout this chapter, Smith uses the rhetorical mode of development by example. Read over paragraph four. Do you think that this mode of development is effective at this point in the selection? Why or why not? Does it seem to you that this mode of development would be particularly effective in the discourse community of economics?
3. In the *Wealth of Nations*, Smith is essentially founding a discourse community. Is there any evidence in the rhetorical strategies of this piece that Smith was aware of his role?
4. In paragraph five, Smith cites cases in England, France, and Poland in order to advance his argument. Much of what he writes is subjective, however. Does it seem to you that his examples need greater solidity, more accuracy, than they have? Could a contemporary economist use such examples?
5. Toward the end of paragraph five Smith writes that "In Poland there are said to be scarce any manufactures of any kind. . . ." Could a contemporary economist ever write such a sentence for publication? Why or why not?
6. Beginning with the sixth paragraph, Smith moves very clearly over three different "circumstances." Evaluate the structure of this part of the chapter. Does the nature of the material demand such a clear structure?
7. Does the example of the boy and the valve in paragraph nine seem credible? Why, does it seem to you, does Smith not give any source for this example?
8. How effective is the conclusion of the essay? How would you describe Smith's stance towards his audience in this essay?

WRITING FROM WITHIN AND ABOUT THE SOCIAL SCIENCES: ECONOMICS

Writing for Yourself

1. In your journal, reflect on the effects of Smith's division of labor on the individual worker. What effect might such a division have upon an individual's creative life?
2. In your journal, make a list of those values which you feel an industry should uphold. After the list, reflect on whether or not those virtues are commonly upheld.

Writing for Nonacademic Audiences

1. In 1989, an oil tanker ran aground on the Alaskan coast, spilling millions of gallons of oil into the water, an enormous environmental disaster. Smith would probably have seen this as a glitch in the division of labor, an error by one area of specialization. For a popular journal like *Reader's Digest*, write a 250-word essay in which you speculate how Smith might have advised handling this oil spill.
2. Interview a local union leader and a local owner of an industrial plant. Are the goals of these two with regard to the company's workers significantly different? Write a feature article of 750 words for an issue of your university's newspaper that will be devoted to jobs and job searches.
3. Since the "back to nature" movement of the late 1960s, some people have rejected the notion of the division of labor and have begun baking their own bread, tending vegetable gardens, riding bicycles rather than cars, sewing their own clothes. For a journal like *National Geographic*, speculate in a 500-word essay on whether this kind of lifestyle threatens industrial society.
4. Your local newspaper is soliciting articles for a series on modern working conditions. You decide to submit a piece, which can be no longer than 500 words, on assembly-line conditions. Interview several assembly-line workers and then write up the feature article.
5. Harvard Business School is noted for its use of the case study method in its courses. The dean of the business school of your university has been interested in promoting this method, and he is soliciting student responses to the case study method. You are one of the students asked to study the method, evaluate its strengths and weaknesses, and then write a 750-word report for the dean of the business school.

Writing for Academic Audiences

1. Today, it is commonly agreed that the family farm, which has dominated the midwestern states for more than a century, is in trouble. Many of those family farms have been taken over by large corporations, whose owners may never set foot on the land they have acquired. According to Smith, what forces might have led to this change? Write a 1,000-word essay for a class in economic theory exploring those forces and speculating on how those forces might be countered.
2. The division of labor has sometimes been attacked for its effects upon workers. Research those effects in the automobile industry and evaluate the ways in which that industry is trying to combat those effects. Based upon this research, write a 1,250-word essay for an introductory class in economics.

Karl Marx   and   Friedrich Engels
(1818–1883)   (1820–1895)

Together, Karl Marx and Friedrich Engels are known as the founders of Marxist Socialism. Marx was born in Germany, and his studious nature led him to earn a doctorate in philosophy at the University of Jena. His radical ideas, however, led to a denial of a university position, and he began to make his livelihood through journalism. But he became a political nomad, forced from Prussia to Paris, and from Paris to Brussels; eventually, after additional moves around the continent, he settled in London in 1849. He was to live there until his death, founding the International Workingmen's Association (1864) and writing his most famous work, Das Kapital *(1867).*

Engels was also German, and he also knew England well. His first work was The Condition of the Working Class in England in 1844 *(1845). He collaborated with Marx on several important socialist works, most notably* The Communist Manifesto *(1848) and the second and third volumes of* Das Kapital *(1885–1894), which he edited from Marx's notes. He also helped to support Marx and his family while they were living in London.*

Though the ideas that Marx and Engels presented in the Communist Manifesto *were not widely discussed upon their publication (this would wait until the prominence of one of their disciples, Vladimir Lenin) they have since exerted an enormous influence upon the modern world. Marx and Engels argued that history was teleological, that it moved inevitably and perhaps even consciously toward a certain specific end. For Marx and Engels this end was the revolution to dialectical materialism, a notion derived from Georg Hegel, who asserted that historical events are produced by tensions and conflicts between two economic groups. In the* Communist Manifesto, *Marx and Engels defined these two groups as the bourgeoisie (the ruling class) and the proletariat (the working class), giving new meanings and connotations to those two old terms.*

Though Marx and Engels would have seen themselves as working within already defined discourse communities—political science and economic theory—they also founded a new discourse community commonly known today as Marxism. This community would establish other similarly oriented communities in the social sciences, history, literature, and the sciences.

The following selection is the opening section of The Communist Manifesto, *translated by Samuel Moore.*

THE COMMUNIST MANIFESTO

A specter is haunting Europe—the specter of Communism. All the Powers of 1
old Europe have entered into a holy alliance to exorcise this specter; Pope
and Czar, Metternich* and Guizot,† French Radicals‡ and German police-
spies.

    Where is the party in opposition that has not been decried as commu- 2
nistic by its opponents in power? Where the Opposition that has not hurled
back the branding reproach of Communism against the more advanced opposition parties, as well as against its reactionary adversaries?

    Two things result from this fact. 3

    I. Communism is already acknowledged by all European Powers to be 4
itself a Power.

    II. It is high time that Communists should openly, in the face of the 5
whole world, publish their views, their aims, their tendencies, and meet this
nursery tale of the specter of Communism with a Manifesto of the party itself.

    To this end, Communists of various nationalities have assembled in 6
London and sketched the following Manifesto, to be published in the English, French, German, Italian, Flemish and Danish languages.

BOURGEOIS AND PROLETARIANS

The history of all hitherto existing society is the history of class struggles. 7

    Freeman and slave, patrician and plebeian, lord and serf, guild-master 8
and journeyman, in a word, oppressor and oppressed, stood in constant opposition to one another, carried on uninterrupted, now hidden, now open
fight, a fight that each time ended, either in a revolutionary re-constitution
of society at large, or in the common ruin of the contending classes.

    In the earlier epochs of history we find almost everywhere a compli- 9
cated arrangement of society into various orders, a manifold gradation of
social rank. In ancient Rome we have patricians, knights, plebeians, slaves;
in the Middle Ages, feudal lords, vassals, guild-masters, journeymen, appren-
tices, serfs; in almost all of these classes, again, subordinate gradations.

    The modern bourgeois society that has sprouted from the ruins of feudal 10
society, has not done away with class antagonisms. It has but established new
classes, new conditions of oppression, new forms of struggle in place of the
old ones.

    Our epoch, the epoch of the bourgeoisie, possesses, however, this dis- 11
tinctive feature; it has simplified the class antagonisms. Society as a whole is

---

*Klemens von Metternich (1773–1859) was an influential Austrian political leader who helped
    to establish peace in Europe after the defeat of Napoleon.

†Francois Pierre Guizot (1787–1874) was a French statesman who opposed communism.

‡The French Radicals were a political group urging a return to a republic.

more and more splitting up into two great hostile camps, into two great classes directly facing each other: Bourgeoisie and Proletariat.

From the serfs of the Middle Ages sprang the chartered burghers of the 12 earliest towns. From these burgesses the first elements of the bourgeoisie were developed.

The discovery of America, the rounding of the Cape,* opened up fresh 13 ground for the rising bourgeoisie. The East Indian and Chinese markets, the colonization of America, trade with the colonies, the increase in the means of exchange and in commodities generally, gave to commerce, to navigation, to industry, an impulse never before known, and thereby, to the revolutionary element in the tottering feudal society, a rapid development.

The feudal system of industry, under which industrial production was 14 monopolized by closed guilds, now no longer sufficed for the growing wants of the new market. The manufacturing system took its place. The guild-masters were pushed on one side by the manufacturing middle-class: division of labor between the different corporate guilds vanished in the face of division of labor in each single workshop.

Meantime the markets kept ever growing, the demand ever rising. Even 15 manufacture no longer sufficed. Thereupon, steam and machinery revolutionized industrial production. The place of manufacture was taken by the giant, Modern Industry, the place of the industrial middle-class, by industrial millionaires, the leaders of whole industrial armies, the modern bourgeois.

Modern industry has established the world market, for which the dis- 16 covery of America paved the way. This market has given an immense development to commerce, to navigation, to communication by land. This development has, in its turn, reacted on the extension of industry; and in proportion as industry, commerce, navigation, railways extended, in the same proportion the bourgeoisie developed, increased its capital, and pushed into the background every class handed down from the Middle Ages.

We see, therefore, how the modern bourgeoisie is itself the product of a 17 long course of development, of a series of revolutions in the modes of production and of exchange.

Each step in the development of the bourgeoisie was accompanied by a 18 corresponding political advance of that class. An oppressed class under the sway of the feudal nobility, an armed and self-governing association in the medieval commune, here independent urban republic (as in Italy and Germany), there taxable "third estate" of the monarchy (as in France), afterwards, in the period of manufacture proper, serving either the semi-feudal or the absolute monarchy as a counterpoise against nobility, and, in fact, corner stone of the great monarchies in general, the bourgeoisie has at last, since the establishment of Modern Industry and of the world-market, conquered for itself, in the modern representative State, exclusive political sway.

* The Cape of Good Hope is the southernmost tip of Africa.

The executive of the modern State is but a committee for managing the common affairs of the whole bourgeoisie.

The bourgeoisie, historically, has played a most revolutionary part.   19

The bourgeoisie, wherever it has got the upper hand, has put an end to   20 all feudal, patriarchal, idyllic relations. It has pitilessly torn asunder the motley feudal ties that bound man to his "natural superiors," and has left no other nexus between man and man than naked self-interest, than callous "cash payment." It has drowned the most heavenly ecstasies of religious fervor, of chivalrous enthusiasm, of Philistine sentimentalism, in the icy water of egotistical calculation. It has resolved personal worth into exchange value, and in place of the numberless indefeasible chartered freedoms, has set up that single, unconscionable freedom—Free Trade. In one word, for exploitation, veiled by religious and political illusions, it has substituted naked, shameless, direct, brutal exploitation.

The bourgeoisie has stripped of its halo every occupation hitherto   21 honored and looked up to with reverent awe. It has converted the physician, the lawyer, the priest, the poet, the man of science, into its paid wage laborers.

The bourgeoisie has torn away from the family its sentimental veil, and   22 has reduced the family relation to a mere money relation.

The bourgeoisie has disclosed how it came to pass that the brutal display   23 of vigor in the Middle Ages, which reactionists so much admire, found its fitting complement in the most slothful indolence. It has been the first to show what man's activity can bring about. It has accomplished wonders far surpassing Egyptian pyramids, Roman aqueducts and Gothic cathedrals; it has conducted expeditions that put in the shade all former Exoduses of nations and crusades.

The bourgeoisie cannot exist without constantly revolutionizing the in-   24 struments of production, and thereby the relations of production, and with them the whole relations of society. Conservation of the old modes of production in unaltered form was, on the contrary, the first condition of existence for all earlier industrial classes. Constant revolutionizing of production, uninterrupted disturbance of all social conditions, everlasting uncertainty and agitation distinguish the bourgeois epoch from all earlier ones. All fixed, fast frozen relations, with their train of ancient and venerable prejudices and opinions, are swept away, all new formed ones become antiquated before they can ossify. All that is solid melts into the air, all that is holy is profaned, and man is at last compelled to face with sober senses, his real conditions of life, and his relations with his kind.

The need of a constantly expanding market for its products chases the   25 bourgeoisie over the whole surface of the globe. It must nestle everywhere, settle everywhere, establish connections everywhere.

The bourgeoisie has through its exploitation of the world-market given   26 a cosmopolitan character to production and consumption in every country.

To the great chagrin of reactionists, it has drawn from under the feet of industry the national ground on which it stood. All old-established national industries have been destroyed or are daily being destroyed. They are dislodged by new industries, whose introduction becomes a life and death question for all civilized nations, by industries that no longer work up indigenous raw material, but raw material drawn from the remotest zones; industries whose products are consumed, not only at home, but in every quarter of the globe. In place of the old wants, satisfied by the productions of the country, we find new wants, requiring for their satisfaction the products of distant lands and climes. In place of the old local and national seclusion and self-sufficiency, we have intercourse in every direction, universal interdependence of nations. And as in material, so also in intellectual production. The intellectual creations of individual nations become common property. National onesidedness and narrowmindedness become more and more impossible, and from the numerous national and local literatures there arises a world-literature.

The bourgeoisie, by the rapid improvement of all instruments of pro- 27 duction, by the immensely facilitated means of communication, draws all, even the most barbarian nations into civilization. The cheap prices of its commodities are the heavy artillery with which it batters down all Chinese walls, with which it forces the barbarians' intensely obstinate hatred of foreigners to capitulate. It compels all nations, on pain of extinction, to adopt the bourgeois mode of production; it compels them to introduce what it calls civilization into their midst, i.e., to become bourgeois themselves. In a word, it creates a world after its own image.

The bourgeoisie has subjected the country to the rule of the towns. It 28 has created enormous cities, has greatly increased the urban population as compared with the rural and has thus rescued a considerable part of the population from the idiocy of rural life. Just as it has made the country dependent on the towns, so it has made barbarian and semi-barbarian countries dependent on civilized ones, nations of peasants on nations of bourgeois, the East on the West.

The bourgeoisie keeps more and more doing away with the scattered 29 state of the population, of the means of production, and of property. It has agglomerated population, centralized means of production, and has concentrated property in a few hands. The necessary consequence of this was political centralization. Independent, or but loosely connected provinces, with separate interests, laws, governments, and systems of taxation, became lumped together in one nation, with one government, one code of laws, one national class interest, one frontier and one customs tariff.

The bourgeoisie, during its rule of scarce one hundred years, has cre- 30 ated more massive and more colossal productive forces than have all preceding generations together. Subjection of Nature's forces to man, machinery, application of chemistry to industry and agriculture, steam-navigation, railways, electric telegraphs, clearing of whole continents for cultivation, canalization of rivers, whole populations conjured out of the ground—what earlier century had even a presentiment that such productive forces slumbered in the lap of social labor?

We see then: the means of production and of exchange on whose foundation the bourgeoisie built itself up, were generated in feudal society. At a certain stage in the development of these means of production and of exchange, the conditions under which feudal society produced and exchanged, the feudal organization of agriculture and manufacturing industry, in one word, the feudal relations of property became no longer compatible with the already developed productive forces; they became so many fetters. They had to burst asunder; they were burst asunder. 31

Into their place stepped free competition, accompanied by a social and political constitution adapted to it, and by the economical and political sway of the bourgeois class. 32

A similar movement is going on before our own eyes. Modern bourgeois society with its relations of production, of exchange and of property, a society that has conjured up such gigantic means of production and of exchange, is like the sorcerer, who is no longer able to control the powers of the nether world whom he has called up by his spells. For many a decade past, the history of industry and commerce is but the history of the revolt of modern productive forces against modern conditions of production, against the property relations that are the conditions for the existence of the bourgeoisie and of its rule. It is enough to mention the commercial crises that by their periodical return put on its trial, each time more threateningly, the existence of the entire bourgeois society. In these crises a great part not only of the existing products, but also of the previously created productive forces, are periodically destroyed. In these crises there breaks out an epidemic that, in all earlier epochs, would have seemed an absurdity—the epidemic of overproduction. Society suddenly finds itself put back into a state of momentary barbarism; it appears as if a famine, a universal war of devastation, had cut off the supply of every means of subsistence; industry and commerce seem to be destroyed; and why? Because there is too much civilization, too much means of subsistence, too much industry, too much commerce. The productive forces at the disposal of society no longer tend to further the development of the conditions of the bourgeois property; on the contrary, they have become too powerful for these conditions by which they are fettered, and as soon as they overcome these fetters they bring disorder into the whole of bourgeois society, endanger the existence of bourgeois property. The conditions of bourgeois society are too narrow to comprise the wealth created by them. And how does the bourgeoisie get over these crises? On the one hand by enforced destruction of a mass of productive forces; on the other, by the conquest of new markets, 33 and by the more thorough exploitation of the old ones. That is to say, by paving the way for more extensive and more destructive crises, and by diminishing the means whereby crises are prevented.

The weapons with which the bourgeoisie felled feudalism to the ground 34 are now turned against the bourgeoisie itself.

But not only has the bourgeoisie forged the weapons that bring death to 35 itself; it has also called into existence the men who are to wield those weapons—the modern working class—the proletarians.

In proportion as the bourgeoisie, i.e., capital, is developed, in the same 36 proportion is the proletariat, the modern working class, developed, a class of laborers who live only so long as they find work, and who find work only so long as their labor increases capital. These laborers, who must sell themselves piecemeal, are a commodity, like every other article of commerce, and are consequently exposed to all the vicissitudes of competition, to all the fluctuations of the market.

Owing to the extensive use of machinery and to division of labor, the 37 work of the proletarians has lost all individual character, and, consequently, all charm for the workman. He becomes an appendage of the machine, and it is only the most simple, most monotonous and most easily acquired knack that is required of him. Hence, the cost of production of a workman is restricted almost entirely to the means of subsistence that he requires for his maintenance, and for the propagation of his race. But the price of a commodity, and also of labor, is equal to its cost of production. In proportion, therefore, as the repulsiveness of the work increases the wage decreases. Nay more, in proportion as the use of machinery and division of labor increases, in the same proportion the burden of toil increases, whether by prolongation of the working hours, by increase of the work enacted in a given time, or by increased speed of the machinery, etc.

Modern industry has converted the little workshop of the patriarchal 38 master into the great factory of the industrial capitalist. Masses of laborers, crowded into factories, are organized like soldiers. As privates of the industrial army they are placed under the command of a perfect hierarchy of officers and sergeants. Not only are they the slaves of the bourgeois class and of the bourgeois state, they are daily and hourly enslaved by the machine, by the overlooker, and, above all, by the individual bourgeois manufacturer himself. The more openly this despotism proclaims gain to be its end and aim, the more petty, the more hateful and the more embittering it is.

The less the skill and exertion or strength implied in manual labor, in 39 other words, the more modern industry becomes developed, the more is the labor of men superseded by that of women. Differences of age and sex have no longer any distinctive social validity for the working class. All are instruments of labor, more or less expensive to use, according to their age and sex.

No sooner is the exploitation of the laborer by the manufacturer, so far 40 at an end, that he receives his wages in cash, than he is set upon by the other portions of the bourgeoisie, the landlord, the shopkeeper, the pawnbroker, etc.

The lower strata of the middle class—the small trades-people, shop- 41 keepers and retired tradesmen generally, the handicraftsmen and peasants— all these sink gradually into the proletariat, partly because their diminutive capital does not suffice for the scale on which Modern Industry is carried on, and is swamped in the competition with the large capitalists, partly because their specialized skill is rendered worthless by new methods of production. Thus the proletariat is recruited from all classes of the population.

The proletariat goes through various stages of development. With its 42 birth begins its struggle with the bourgeoisie. At first the contest is carried on by individual laborers, then by the workpeople of a factory, then by the operatives of one trade, in one locality, against the individual bourgeois who directly exploits them. They direct their attacks not against the bourgeois conditions of production, but against the instruments of production themselves; they destroy imported wares that compete with their labor, they smash to pieces machinery, they set factories ablaze, they seek to restore by force the vanished status of the workman of the Middle Ages.

At this stage the laborers still form an incoherent mass scattered over 43 the whole country, and broken up by their mutual competition. If anywhere they unite to form more compact bodies, this is not yet the consequence of their own active union, but of the union of the bourgeoisie, which class, in order to attain its own political ends, is compelled to set the whole proletariat in motion, and is moreover yet, for a time, able to do so. At this stage, therefore, the proletarians do not fight their enemies, but the enemies of their enemies, the remnants of absolute monarchy, the landowners, the non-industrial bourgeois, the petty bourgeoisie. Thus the whole historical movement is concentrated in the hands of the bourgeoisie, every victory so obtained is a victory for the bourgeoisie.

But with the development of industry the proletariat not only increases 44 in number; it becomes concentrated in greater masses, its strength grows and it feels that strength more. The various interests and conditions of life within the ranks of the proletariat are more and more equalized, in proportion as machinery obliterates all distinctions of labor, and nearly everywhere reduces wages to the same low level. The growing competition among the bourgeois, and the resulting commercial crisis, make the wages of the workers even more fluctuating. The unceasing improvement of machinery, ever more rapidly developing, makes their livelihood more and more precarious; the collisions between individual workmen and individual bourgeois take more and more the character of collisions between two classes. Thereupon the workers begin to form combinations (Trades' Unions) against the bourgeois; they club together in order to keep up the rate of wages; they found permanent associations in order to make provision beforehand for these occasional revolts. Here and there the contest breaks out into riots.

Now and then the workers are victorious, but only for a time. The real 45
fruit of their battle lies not in the immediate result but in the ever-expanding
union of workers. This union is helped on by the improved means of communication that are created by modern industry, and that places the workers
of different localities in contact with one another. It was just this contact that
was needed to centralize the numerous local struggles, all of the same character, into one national struggle between classes. But every class struggle is a
political struggle. And that union, to attain which the burghers of the Middle
Ages with their miserable highways, required centuries, the modern proletarians, thanks to railways, achieve in a few years.

This organization of the proletarians into a class, and consequently into 46
a political party, is continually being upset again by the competition between
the workers themselves. But it ever rises up again, stronger, firmer, mightier.
It compels legislative recognition of particular interests of the workers by
taking advantage of the divisions among the bourgeoisie itself. Thus the ten
hours' bill in England* was carried.

Altogether collisions between the classes of the old society further, in 47
many ways, the course of development of the proletariat. The bourgeoisie
finds itself involved in a constant battle. At first with the aristocracy; later
on, with those portions of the bourgeoisie itself whose interests have become
antagonistic to the progress of industry; at all times, with the bourgeoisie of
foreign countries. In all these battles it sees itself compelled to appeal to the
proletariat, to ask for its help, and thus, to drag it into the political arena.
The bourgeoisie itself, therefore, supplies the proletariat with its own elements of political and general education; in other words, it furnishes the
proletariat with weapons for fighting the bourgeoisie.

Further, as we have already seen, entire sections of the ruling classes 48
are, by the advance of industry, precipitated into the proletariat, or are at
least threatened in their conditions of existence. These also supply the proletariat with fresh elements of enlightenment and progress.

Finally, in times when the class-struggle nears the decisive hour, the 49
process of dissolution going on within the ruling class—in fact, within the
whole range of an old society—assumes such a violent, glaring character that
a small section of the ruling class cuts itself adrift and joins the revolutionary
class, the class that holds the future in its hands. Just as, therefore, at an
earlier period, a section of the nobility went over to the bourgeoisie, so now
a portion of the bourgeoisie goes over to the proletariat, and in particular, a
portion of the bourgeois ideologists, who have raised themselves to the level
of comprehending theoretically the historical movements as a whole.

Of all the classes that stand face to face with the bourgeoisie today the 50
proletariat alone is a really revolutionary class. The other classes decay and
finally disappear in the face of modern industry; the proletariat is its special
and essential product.

* This bill, passed in 1847, limited the working day to ten hours.

The lower middle class, the small manufacturer, the shopkeeper, the 51 artisan, the peasant, all these fight against the bourgeoisie, to save from extinction their existence as fractions of the middle class. They are therefore not revolutionary, but conservative. Nay, more; they are reactionary, for they try to roll back the wheel of history. If by chance they are revolutionary, they are so only in view of their impending transfer into the proletariat; they thus defend not their present, but their future interests; they desert their own standpoint to place themselves at that of the proletariat.

The "dangerous class," the social scum, that passively rotting mass 52 thrown off by the lowest layers of old society, may, here and there, be swept into the movement by a proletarian revolution; its conditions of life, however, prepare it far more for the part of a bribed tool of reactionary intrigue.

In the conditions of the proletariat, those of the old society at large are 53 already virtually swamped. The proletarian is without property; his relation to his wife and children has no longer anything in common with the bourgeois family relations; modern industrial labor, modern subjection to capital, the same in England as in France, in America as in Germany, has stripped him of every trace of national character. Law, morality, religion, are to him so many bourgeois prejudices, behind which lurk in ambush just as many bourgeois interests.

All the preceding classes that got the upper hand sought to fortify their 54 already acquired status by subjecting society at large to their conditions of appropriation. The proletarians cannot become masters of the productive forces of society, except by abolishing their own previous mode of appropriation, and thereby also every other previous mode of appropriation. They have nothing of their own to secure and to fortify; their mission is to destroy all previous securities for and insurances of individual property.

All previous historical movements were movements of minorities, or in 55 the interest of minorities. The proletarian movement is the selfconscious, independent movement of the immense majority. The proletariat, the lowest stratum of our present society, cannot stir, cannot raise itself up without the whole superincumbent strata of official society being sprung into the air.

Though not in substance, yet in form, the struggle of the proletariat 56 with the bourgeoisie is at first a national struggle. The proletariat of each country must, of course, first of all settle matters with its own bourgeoisie.

In depicting the most general phases of the development of the prole- 57 tariat, we traced the more or less veiled civil war, raging within existing society, up to the point where that war breaks out into open revolution, and where the violent overthrow of the bourgeoisie, lays the foundations for the sway of the proletariat.

Hitherto every form of society has been based, as we have already seen, 58 on the antagonism of oppressing and oppressed classes. But in order to oppress a class, certain conditions must be assured to it under which it can, at least, continue its slavish existence. The serf, in the period of serfdom, raised himself to membership in the commune, just as the petty bourgeois, under the yoke of feudal absolutism, managed to develop into a bourgeois. The modern laborer, on the contrary, instead of rising with the progress of industry, sinks deeper and deeper below the conditions of existence of his own class. He becomes a pauper, and pauperism develops more rapidly than population and wealth. And here it becomes evident that the bourgeoisie is unfit any longer to be the ruling class in society, and to impose its conditions of existence upon society as an over-riding law. It is unfit to rule, because it is incompetent to assure an existence to its slave within his slavery, because it cannot help letting him sink into such a state that it has to feed him, instead of being fed by him. Society can no longer live under this bourgeoisie; in other words, its existence is no longer compatible with society.

The essential condition for the existence, and for the sway of the bour- 59 geois class, is the formation and augmentation of capital; the condition for capital is wage labor. Wage labor rests exclusively on competition between the laborers. The advance of industry, whose involuntary promoter is the bourgeoisie, replaces the isolation of the laborers, due to competition, by their involuntary combination, due to association. The development of Modern Industry, therefore, cuts from under its feet the very foundation on which the bourgeoisie produces and appropriates products. What the bourgeoisie therefore produces, above all, are its own grave diggers. Its fall and the victory of the proletariat are equally inevitable.

QUESTIONS ABOUT THE DISCOURSE COMMUNITY OF MARX AND ENGELS AND THEIR CONCERNS IN THIS SELECTION

1. Does it seem to you to be the case that "the history of all hitherto existing society is the history of class struggles" (paragraph 7)?
2. What do Marx and Engels mean when they speak of the bourgeoisie? Is the group they are describing uniform enough to be described with one term?
3. How do Marx and Engels evaluate the division of labor (paragraph 14)? What reasons do they advance for their evaluation?
4. Read over paragraph 15, in which Marx and Engels propose a specific chain of events. Does this seem to you to be a likely chain? Are there other influences and trends that Marx and Engels do not mention that might have contributed to the growth of modern industry?
5. In paragraph 20, Marx and Engels claim that the bourgeoisie, "for exploitation, veiled by religious and political illusions . . . has substituted naked, shameless, direct, brutal exploitation." What specifically might Marx and Engels be thinking of when they refer to "religious and political illusions"?
6. What are some of the potential abuses of free competition? What might be some effective responses to those abuses?
7. Marx and Engels speak of the class struggle as moving towards a "decisive hour" (paragraph 49). What might they mean by that decisive hour?
8. Marx and Engels speak of the proletariat as a "revolutionary class" (paragraph 50). What might they mean by revolutionary?

QUESTIONS ABOUT THE RHETORICAL STRATEGIES OF MARX AND ENGELS

1. What is the purpose of the ghost or specter analogy in the first paragraph? What kinds of connotations does it carry? Do you find this to be an effective opening?
2. One thing that a reader sees at a glance is that the writers employ very short paragraphs. What might be the purpose of these? In an era dominated by prose writers who used rather lengthy paragraphs, why might Marx and Engels have chosen an opposing strategy?
3. Paragraph 7 is one of the more famous definitions in political science. Why might it have been imperative to give this short sentence its own paragraph? Where else are short sentences made into single paragraphs? Why?
4. Although *The Communist Manifesto* is a political document, it is an economic one as well. Where do Marx and Engels bring together the concerns of these two discourse communities? For what purpose?
5. What in the diction suggests the nature of the audience that Marx and Engels are trying to reach?
6. How do Marx and Engels use diction and sentence structure in paragraphs 19 to 23 to castigate the bourgeoisie? Is there a reason for their not even trying to seem objective in this passage?
7. Why, from paragraphs 19 through 30, do Marx and Engels begin almost every paragraph with the words *The bourgeoisie*? What effect does this have on the reader?
8. When Marx and Engels describe the growth of the proletariat (paragraphs 42 to 44), they use much longer paragraphs than they had used earlier in the essay. What might be the reason for this?

WRITING FROM WITHIN AND ABOUT THE SOCIAL SCIENCES: POLITICAL SCIENCE AND ECONOMICS

Writing for Yourself

1. In your journal, reflect on whether you believe that "the history of all hitherto existing society is the history of class struggles" (paragraph 7).
2. In your journal, reflect on whether, in contemporary North America, the family relation has been reduced "to a mere money relation" (paragraph 22).

Writing for Nonacademic Audiences

1. Prepare a ten-minute talk for a high school class in which you distinguish between the bourgeoisie and the proletarians. Also, prepare a list of four or five discussion questions to be used by the class after your talk that center on whether those distinctions apply to contemporary North American society.
2. In paragraphs 36 through 38, Marx and Engels describe the situation of the modern worker. Consider the case of the migrant worker who works in the United States, particularly in the Southwest. For a local journal in a southern California orange tree region, write a 500-word editorial on whether or not such workers should be protected by state regulations.

3. For the journal put out by economics majors on your campus, write a 500-word opinion piece on capitalism at its worst.
4. For a journal put out by the political science majors at your university, dedicated to increasing political awareness on campus, write a 750-word feature article on a local small business or artisan who is feeling the pressure of competition with big business. In your article, address the question of whether the solution to this problem should be political or not.

Writing for Academic Audiences

1. What capitalistic elements are being introduced into communist or formerly communist countries? Why are they being introduced? Write up your findings in a 500-word paper that will be used as a handout in introductory economics classes at your university.
2. For an introductory class in political economy, write a 750-word essay describing the feudal system of industry and how it might have affected and been affected by the political situation of western Europe during the Middle Ages.
3. For a class in political history, research the relationship between the United States and Fidel Castro as Castro was gaining power in the early 1960s. In a 1,000-word essay, discuss what first attracted American officials to Castro, and then describe what led to the break.

Sigmund Freud

(1856–1939)

Born in Freiberg, Moravia, Sigmund Freud was destined to have an enormous influence on a number of discourse communities, particularly those of the social sciences such as anthropology and education. Though his contributions to these social sciences is direct, his work has also contributed to the criticism of art and literature, as well as to an understanding of historical forces. His greatest contribution, however, was essentially the founding of a discourse community, that which we today label as psychoanalysis.

Between 1880 and 1882, Josef Breuer had begun to treat hysteria not as a nervous disease to be treated with drugs but as what a modern analysist would term a psychological disorder. Freud began to work with Breuer when Freud returned to Vienna after 1886. By using hypnosis, Freud and Breuer demonstrated that many of the nervous symptoms of hysteria were traceable not to a physical cause, but to early childhood trauma. This marked the beginning of psychoanalysis. Breuer and Freud would eventually publish Studies in Hysteria *(1895), a carefully worked-out description of their ten years of research.*

The careful language of the reports in Studies in Hysteria, *the balanced tone, the nonaggressive assertions hedged with multiple justifications, the structuring of the sequence of interviews—all suggest that Freud and Breuer recognized that they were developing a new science that would probably meet with some resistance. It did. Toward the end of his career, Freud described the early days in* The History of the Psychoanalytic Movement:

> *. . . I was entirely isolated and in the confusion of problems and the accumulation of difficulties, I often feared lest I should lose my orientation and my confidence. . . . But as my conviction of the general accuracy of my observations and the conclusions grew and grew, and as my faith in my own judgement and my moral courage were by no means small, there could be no doubt about the issue of this situation. I was imbued with the conviction that it fell to my lot to discover particularly imperfect connections, and was prepared to accept the fate which sometimes accompanies such discoveries. [A. A. Ball, ed. and trans. (1938).* The Basic Writings of Sigmund Freud. *New York: The Modern Library. 942–943.]*

But even after Freud's ideas found greater acceptance and carved out their own discourse community, Freud found himself attacked and rejected. Breuer disagreed sharply with Freud over the source of the early trauma, rejecting Freud's belief that the source of most trauma was sexual. Carl Jung and Alfred Adler joined Freud in 1906 but five years later left to found their own schools, protesting Freud's emphasis on infantile sexuality. Others rejected his analysis of dreams, his use of hypnosis, his division of the personality into the ego, superego, and id. But Freud persevered, working in Vienna until he was arrested by the Nazis in 1938; upon his release that same year, he moved to London, where he died in 1939.

Despite disagreements, the discourse community of psychoanalysis is heavily indebted to Freud's careful, painstaking, patient work in establishing the sources of neuroses. Many of his methods and much of his terminology remain in use in the 1990s.

The following selection is the fourth case recounted in Studies in Hysteria.

CASE 4: KATHARINA

In the summer vacation of the year 189- I made an excursion into the Hohe 1
Tauern* so that for a while I might forget medicine and more particularly the neuroses. I had almost succeeded in this when one day I turned aside from the main road to climb a mountain which lay somewhat apart and which was renowned for its views and for its well-run refuge hut. I reached the top after a strenuous climb and, feeling refreshed and rested, was sitting deep in contemplation of the charm of the distant prospect. I was so lost in thought that at first I did not connect it with myself when these words reached my ears: "Are you a doctor, sir?" But the question was addressed to me, and by the rather sulky-looking girl of perhaps eighteen who had served my meal and had been spoken to by the landlady as "Katharina." To judge by her dress and bearing, she could not be a servant, but must no doubt be a daughter or relative of the landlady's.

Coming to myself I replied: "Yes, I'm a doctor: but how did you know 2
that?"

"You wrote your name in the Visitors' Book, sir. And I thought if you 3
had a few moments to spare . . . The truth is, sir, my nerves are bad. I went to see a doctor in L_____ about them and he gave me something for them; but I'm not well yet."

So there I was with the neuroses once again—for nothing else could very 4
well be the matter with this strong, well-built girl with her unhappy look. I was interested to find that neuroses could flourish in this way at a height of over 6,000 feet; I questioned her further therefore. I report the conversation that followed between us just as it is impressed on my memory and I have not altered the patient's dialect.

"Well, what is it you suffer from?"   5

* A mountain range in the eastern Alps.

"I get so out of breath. Not always. But sometimes it catches me so that 6
I think I shall suffocate."

This did not, at first sight, sound like a nervous symptom. But soon it 7
occurred to me that probably it was only a description that stood for an
anxiety attack: she was choosing shortness of breath out of the complex of
sensations arising from anxiety and laying undue stress on that single factor.

"Sit down here. What is it like when you get 'out of breath'?"   8

"It comes over me all at once. First of all it's like something pressing on 9
my eyes. My head gets so heavy, there's a dreadful buzzing, and I feel so
giddy that I almost fall over. Then there's something crushing my chest so
that I can't get my breath."

"And you don't notice anything in your throat?"   10

"My throat's squeezed together as though I were going to choke."   11

"Does anything else happen in your head?"   12

"Yes, there's a hammering, enough to burst it."   13

"And don't you feel at all frightened while this is going on?"   14

"I always think I'm going to die. I'm brave as a rule and go about 15
everywhere by myself—into the cellar and all over the mountain. But on a
day when that happens I don't dare to go anywhere; I think all the time
someone's standing behind me and going to catch hold of me all at once."

So it was in fact an anxiety attack, and introduced by the signs of a 16
hysterical "aura"*—or, more correctly, it was a hysterical attack the content
of which was anxiety. Might there not probably be some other content as
well?

"When you have an attack do you think of something? and always the 17
same thing? or do you see something in front of you?"

"Yes. I always see an awful face that looks at me in a dreadful way, so 18
that I'm frightened."

Perhaps this might offer a quick means of getting to the heart of the 19
matter.

"Do you recognize the face? I mean, is it a face that you've really seen 20
some time?"

"No."
                                                                        21
"Do you know what your attacks come from?"   22
"No."   23
"When did you first have them?"   24

"Two years ago, while I was still living on the other mountain with my 25
aunt. (She used to run a refuge hut there, and we moved here eighteen months
ago.) But they keep on happening."

Was I to make an attempt at an analysis? I could not venture to trans- 26
plant hypnosis to these altitudes, but perhaps I might succeed with a simple
talk. I should have to try a lucky guess. I had found often enough that in girls'

---

* Sensations immediately preceding a hysterical or epileptic attack.

anxiety was a consequence of the horror by which a virginal mind is overcome when it is faced for the first time with the world of sexuality.*

So I said: "If you don't know, I'll tell you how *I* think you got your 27
attacks. At that time, two years ago, you must have seen or heard something
that very much embarrassed you, and that you'd much rather not have seen."

"Heavens, yes!" she replied, "that was when I caught my uncle with 28
the girl, with Franziska, my cousin."

"What's this story about a girl? Won't you tell me all about it?" 29

"You can say *anything* to a doctor, I suppose. Well, at that time, you 30
know, my uncle—the husband of the aunt you've seen here—kept the inn on
the _____kogel. Now they're divorced, and it's my fault they were divorced,
because it was through me that it came out that he was carrying on with
Franziska."

"And how did you discover it?" 31

"This way. One day two years ago some gentlemen had climbed the 32
mountain and asked for something to eat. My aunt wasn't at home, and
Franziska, who always did the cooking, was nowhere to be found. And my
uncle was not to be found either. We looked everywhere, and at last Alois,
the little boy, my cousin, said: 'Why, Franziska must be in Father's room!'
And we both laughed; but we weren't thinking anything bad. Then we went
to my uncle's room but found it locked. That seemed strange to me. Then
Alois said: 'There's a window in the passage where you can look into the
room.' We went into the passage; but Alois wouldn't go to the window and
said he was afraid. So I said: 'You silly boy! I'll go. I'm not a bit afraid.' And
I had nothing bad in my mind. I looked in. The room was rather dark, but I
saw my uncle and Franziska; he was lying on her."

"Well?" 33

"I came away from the window at once, and leant up against the wall 34
and couldn't get my breath—just what happens to me since. Everything went
blank, my eyelids were forced together and there was a hammering and
buzzing in my head."

"Did you tell your aunt that very same day?" 35

"Oh no, I said nothing." 36

"Then why were you so frightened when you found them together? Did 37
you understand it? Did you know what was going on?"

---

*I will quote here the case in which I first recognized this causal connection. I was treating a
young married woman who was suffering from a complicated neurosis and, once again
[cf. p. 150 n.], was unwilling to admit that her illness arose from her married life. She
objected that while she was still a girl she had had attacks of anxiety, ending in fainting
fits. I remained firm. When we had come to know each other better she suddenly said to
me one day: "I'll tell you now how I came by my attacks of anxiety when I was a girl. At
that time I used to sleep in a room next to my parents'; the door was left open and a night-
light used to burn on the table. So more than once I saw my father get into bed with my
mother and heard sounds that greatly excited me. It was then that my attacks came on."
[Freud's note].

"Oh no. I didn't understand anything at that time. I was only sixteen. 38
I don't know what I was frightened about."

"Fräulein Katharina, if you could remember now what was happening 39
in you at that time, when you had your first attack, what you thought about
it—it would help you."

"Yes, if I could. But I was so frightened that I've forgotten everything." 40

(Translated into the terminology of our "Preliminary Communication" 41
this means: "The affect itself created a hypnoid state, whose products were
then cut off from associative connection with the ego-consciousness.")

"Tell me, Fräulein. Can it be that the head that you always see when 42
you lose your breath is Franziska's head, as you saw it then?"

"Oh no, she didn't look so awful. Besides, it's a man's head." 43

"Or perhaps your uncle's?" 44

"I didn't see his face as clearly as that. It was too dark in the room. And 45
why should he have been making such a dreadful face just then?"

"You're quite right." 46

(The road suddenly seemed blocked. Perhaps something might turn up 47
in the rest of her story.)

"And what happened then?" 48

"Well, those two must have heard a noise, because they came out soon 49
afterwards. I felt very bad the whole time. I always kept thinking about it.
Then two days later it was a Sunday and there was a great deal to do and I
worked all day long. And on the Monday morning I felt giddy again and was
sick, and I stopped in bed and was sick without stopping for three days."

We [Breuer and I] had often compared the symptomatology of hysteria 50
with a pictographic script which has become intelligible after the discovery
of a few bilingual inscriptions. In that alphabet being sick means disgust. So
I said: "If you were sick three days later, I believe that means that when you
looked into the room you felt disgusted."

"Yes, I'm sure I felt disgusted," she said reflectively, "but disgusted at 51
what?"

"Perhaps you saw something naked? What sort of state were they in?" 52

"It was too dark to see anything; besides they both of them had their 53
clothes on. Oh, if only I knew what it was I felt disgusted at!"

I had no idea either. But I told her to go on and tell me whatever oc- 54
curred to her, in the confident expectation that she would think of precisely
what I needed to explain the case.

Well, she went on to describe how at last she reported her discovery to 55
her aunt, who found that she was changed and suspected her of concealing
some secret. There followed some very disagreeable scenes between her uncle
and aunt, in the course of which the children came to hear a number of things
which opened their eyes in many ways and which it would have been better
for them not to have heard. At last her aunt decided to move with her children and niece and take over the present inn, leaving her uncle alone with

Franziska, who had meanwhile become pregnant. After this, however, to my astonishment she dropped these threads and began to tell me two sets of older stories, which went back two or three years earlier than the traumatic moment. The first set related to occasions on which the same uncle had made sexual advances to her herself, when she was only fourteen years old. She described how she had once gone with him on an expedition down into the valley in the winter and had spent the night in the inn there. He sat in the bar drinking and playing cards, but she felt sleepy and went up to bed early in the room they were to share on the upper floor. She was not quite asleep when he came up; then she fell asleep again and woke up suddenly "feeling his body" in the bed. She jumped up and remonstrated with him: "What are you up to, Uncle? Why don't you stay in your own bed?" He tried to pacify her: "Go on, you silly girl, keep still. You don't know how nice it is."—"I don't like your 'nice' things; you don't even let one sleep in peace." She remained standing by the door, ready to take refuge outside in the passage, till at last he gave up and went to sleep himself. Then she went back to her own bed and slept till morning. From the way in which she reported having defended herself it seems to follow that she did not clearly recognize the attack as a sexual one. When I asked her if she knew what he was trying to do to her, she replied: "Not at the time." It had become clear to her much later on, she said; she had resisted because it was unpleasant to be disturbed in one's sleep and "because it wasn't nice."

I have been obliged to relate this in detail, because of its great impor- 56 tance for understanding everything that followed.—She went on to tell me of yet other experiences of somewhat later date: how she had once again had to defend herself against him in an inn when he was completely drunk, and similar stories. In answer to a question as to whether on these occasions she had felt anything resembling her later loss of breath, she answered with decision that she had every time felt the pressure on her eyes and chest, but with nothing like the strength that had characterized the scene of discovery.

Immediately she had finished this set of memories she began to tell me 57 a second set, which dealt with occasions on which she had noticed something between her uncle and Franziska. Once the whole family had spent the night in their clothes in a hay loft and she was woken up suddenly by a noise; she thought she noticed that her uncle, who had been lying between her and Franziska, was turning away, and that Franziska was just lying down. Another time they were stopping the night at an inn at the village of N——; she and her uncle were in one room and Franziska in an adjoining one. She woke up suddenly in the night and saw a tall white figure by the door, on the point of turning the handle: "Goodness, is that you, Uncle? What are you doing at the door?"—"Keep quiet. I was only looking for something."—"But the way out's by the *other* door."—"I'd just made a mistake" . . . and so on.

I asked her if she had been suspicious at that time. "No, I didn't think 58 anything about it; I only just noticed it and thought no more about it." When

I enquired whether she had been frightened on these occasions too, she replied that she thought so, but she was not so sure of it this time.

At the end of these two sets of memories she came to a stop. She was 59 like someone transformed. The sulky, unhappy face had grown lively, her eyes were bright, she was lightened and exalted. Meanwhile the understanding of her case had become clear to me. The later part of what she had told me, in an apparently aimless fashion, provided an admirable explanation of her behavior at the scene of the discovery. At that time she had carried about with her two sets of experiences which she remembered but did not understand, and from which she drew no inferences. When she caught sight of the couple in intercourse, she at once established a connection between the new impression and these two sets of recollections, she began to understand them and at the same time to fend them off. There then followed a short period of working-out, of "incubation," after which the symptoms of conversion set in, the vomiting as a substitute for moral and physical disgust. This solved the riddle. She had not been disgusted by the sight of the two people but by the memory which that sight had stirred up in her. And, taking everything into account, this could only be the memory of the attempt on her at night when she had "felt her uncle's body."

So when she had finished her confession I said to her: "I know now what 60 it was you thought when you looked into the room. You thought: 'Now he's doing with her what he wanted to do with me that night and those other times.' That was what you were disgusted at, because you remembered the feeling when you woke up in the night and felt his body."

"It may well be," she replied, "that that was what I was disgusted at 61 and that that was what I thought."

"Tell me just one thing more. You're a grown-up girl now and know all 62 sorts of things . . ."

"Yes, now I am." 63

"Tell me just one thing. What part of his body was it that you felt that 64 night?"

But she gave me no more definite answer. She smiled in an embarrassed 65 way, as though she had been found out, like someone who is obliged to admit that a fundamental position has been reached where there is not much more to be said. I could imagine what the tactile sensation was which she had later learnt to interpret. Her facial expression seemed to me to be saying that she supposed that I was right in my conjecture. But I could not penetrate further, and in any case I owed her a debt of gratitude for having made it so much easier for me to talk to her than to the prudish ladies of my city practice, who regard whatever is natural as shameful.

Thus the case was cleared up.—But stop a moment! What about the 66 recurrent hallucination of the head, which appeared during her attacks and struck terror into her? Where did it come from? I proceeded to ask her about it, and, as though *her* knowledge, too, had been extended by our conversation, she promptly replied: "Yes, I know now. The head is my uncle's head—I recognize it now—but not from *that* time. Later, when all the disputes had broken out, my uncle gave way to a senseless rage against me. He kept saying that it was all my fault: if I hadn't chattered, it would never have come to a divorce. He kept threatening he would do something to me; and if he caught sight of me at a distance his face would get distorted with rage and he would make for me with his hand raised. I always ran away from him, and always felt terrified that he would catch me some time unawares. The face I always see now is his face when he was in a rage."

This information reminded me that her first hysterical symptom, the 67 vomiting, had passed away; the anxiety attack remained and acquired a fresh content. Accordingly, what we were dealing with was a hysteria which had to a considerable extent been abreacted. And in fact she had reported her discovery to her aunt soon after it happened.

"Did you tell your aunt the other stories—about his making advances 68 to you?"

"Yes. Not at once, but later on, when there was already talk of a di- 69 vorce. My aunt said: 'We'll keep that in reserve. If he causes trouble in the Court, we'll say that too.'"

I can well understand that it should have been precisely this last pe- 70 riod—when there were more and more agitating scenes in the house and when her own state ceased to interest her aunt, who was entirely occupied with the dispute—that it should have been this period of accumulation and retention that left her the legacy of the mnemic symbol [of the hallucinated face].

I hope this girl, whose sexual sensibility had been injured at such an 71 early age, derived some benefit from our conversation. I have not seen her since.

DISCUSSION

If someone were to assert that the present case history is not so much an 72 analyzed case of hysteria as a case solved by guessing, I should have nothing to say against him. It is true that the patient agreed that what I interpolated into her story was probably true; but she was not in a position to recognize it as something she had experienced. I believe it would have required hypnosis to bring that about. Assuming that my guesses were correct, I will now attempt to fit the case into the schematic picture of an "acquired" hysteria on the lines suggested by Case 3. It seems plausible, then, to compare the two sets of erotic experiences with "traumatic" moments and the scene of discovering the couple with an "auxiliary" moment. The similarity lies in the fact that in the former experiences an element of consciousness was created which was excluded from the thought-activity of the ego and remained, as it were, in storage, while in the latter scene a new impression forcibly brought about an associative connection between this separated group and the ego. On the other hand there are dissimilarities which cannot be overlooked. The cause of the isolation was not, as in Case 3, an act of will on the part of the ego but *ignorance* on the part of the ego, which was not yet capable of coping with sexual experiences. In this respect the case of Katharina is typical. In every analysis of a case of hysteria based on sexual traumas we find that impressions from the pre-sexual period which produced no effect on the child attain traumatic power at a later date as memories, when the girl or married woman has acquired an understanding of sexual life. The splitting-off of psychical groups may be said to be a normal process in adolescent development; and it is easy to see that their later reception into the ego affords frequent opportunities for psychical disturbances. Moreover, I should like at this point to express a doubt as to whether a splitting of consciousness due to ignorance is really different from one due to conscious rejection, and whether even adolescents do not possess sexual knowledge far oftener than is supposed or than they themselves believe.

A further distinction in the psychical mechanism of this case lies in the 73 fact that the scene of discovery, which we have described as "auxiliary," deserves equally to be called "traumatic." It was operative on account of its own content and not merely as something that revived previous traumatic experiences. It combined the characteristics of an "auxiliary" and a "traumatic" moment. There seems no reason, however, why this coincidence should lead us to abandon a conceptual separation which in other cases corresponds also to a separation in time. Another peculiarity of Katharina's case, which, incidentally, has long been familiar to us, is seen in the circumstance that the conversion, the production of the hysterical phenomena, did not occur immediately after the trauma but after an interval of incubation. Charcot liked to describe this interval as the "period of psychical working out" [*élaboration*].

The anxiety from which Katharina suffered in her attacks was a hyster- 74 ical one; that is, it was a reproduction of the anxiety which had appeared in connection with each of the sexual traumas. I shall not here comment on the fact which I have found regularly present in a very large number of cases— namely that a mere suspicion of sexual relations calls up the affect of anxiety in virginal individuals.*

QUESTIONS ABOUT FREUD'S DISCOURSE
COMMUNITY AND HIS CONCERNS IN THIS ESSAY

1. Do you believe Freud's account of his trip to the Alps? Does it seem likely to you that someone whom Freud describes as "the rather sulky-looking girl of

---

* (*Footnote added* 1924:) I venture after the lapse of so many years to lift the veil of discretion and reveal the fact that Katharina was not the niece but the daughter of the landlady. The girl fell ill, therefore, as a result of sexual attempts on the part of her own father. Distortions like the one which I introduced in the present instance should be altogether avoided in reporting a case history. From the point of view of understanding the case, a distortion of this kind is not, of course, a matter of such indifference as would be shifting the scene from one mountain to another. [Freud's note]

perhaps eighteen" would reveal to a stranger the things that she reveals? Does Freud make any attempt to explain her lack of reticence?

2. It seems unlikely that Freud could remember this long conversation verbatim, nor is there any indication that he was taking notes. Would it be legitimate to conclude, then, that this is a reconstructed conversation, with quotes that are not quite exact, material that has been left out or reordered? Does this negate the legitimacy of this case? Does it seem to you that this case description would be accepted by a discourse community in psychology in the 1990s?

3. When Katharina first begins to describe her symptoms, Freud comments, "So there I was with the neuroses once again—for nothing else could very well be the matter with this strong, well-built girl with her unhappy look. I was interested to find that neuroses could flourish in this way at a height of over 6,000 feet; I questioned her further therefore" (paragraph 4). What assumptions about neuroses do you find here? What, according to this passage, is Freud's motive for questioning Katharina? Do you think that this is his entire motivation?

4. Much of this case proceeds by assumption and guesswork. How does Freud account for this process? Does it seem as if this is a legitimate way to proceed in this case? Are there any ethical questions to consider here?

5. At first Katharina does not recognize the awful face that she sees during her attacks, but later she does. Are we to assume from this that Freud's analysis helped her to this recognition?

6. Why does Freud hide the fact that the uncle described here is really Katharina's father? Why did Freud wait thirty years before revealing that fact? Would such forms of discretion be accepted in a contemporary report of this type?

7. What evidence do you see in this passage that Freud is trying to legitimize a science? Who is his intended audience?

8. Freud leaves Katharina without being sure that she did indeed derive "some benefit" from their conversation. Was this ethical on his part? Once he agrees to listen, should he commit himself to curing her?

QUESTIONS ABOUT FREUD'S RHETORICAL STRATEGIES

1. Why does Freud frame his description of Katharina's case with an account of his travels into the eastern Alps? Does it seem to you that this is a very nonscientific way to proceed? Might this frame be influenced by Freud's sense that he was trying to justify the validity of this new science—psychoanalysis?

2. Much of the description of this case comes through dialogue between Freud and Katharina. Is this the most effective technique that Freud could have used? Why might he have used this strategy in the retelling?

3. Freud frequently intersperses analytical comments into his account of the dialogue. For example, he notes that "[t]his did not, at first sight, sound like a nervous symptom." What is the rhetorical purpose of these comments? Do you think that Freud includes them because of the needs of his discourse community?

4. Freud is here writing about a topic that many people would find delicate. In

such a situation, writers frequently resort to euphemism. What euphemisms do you find in this selection? Is the use of euphemism appropriate to this discourse community? When are euphemisms acceptable? Not acceptable?

5. Read over paragraph 41. Why does Freud change his stance so dramatically at this point?
6. Speaking of the scene between Katharina's "uncle" and Franziska, Freud asks, "Perhaps you saw something naked?" Why does he use the word *something* instead of *someone?*
7. In paragraph 55, Freud changes his rhetorical strategies, combining his direct quotes with indirect quotations, summaries, and paraphrasing. Why does he do this, especially since this is a critical part of their conversation?
8. Paragraph 59 is, in a way, the climax of the selection. How does Freud signal that this is, in the essay's structure, a climax?

WRITING FROM WITHIN AND ABOUT THE SOCIAL SCIENCES: PSYCHOLOGY

Writing for Yourself

1. In your journal, write an informal definition of a neurosis and give a specific example.
2. In your journal, write a brief statement on your views of hypnosis. Do you believe that hypnosis is a legitimate tool for the psychologist to use?

Writing for Nonacademic Audiences

1. Think about your earliest childhood memory. Write a letter home describing why you have held onto that particular memory.
2. Read over Oliver Sacks's *The Man Who Mistook His Wife For a Hat and Other Clinical Tales* (1986). For a newsletter put out by the psychology department of your university and sent to all psychology majors, write a 250-word review that examines the use of narrative art in this book.

Writing for Academic Audiences

1. Freud remarks on "the prudish ladies of my city practice, who regard whatever is natural as shameful." For an introductory class in psychology, write a 500-word essay that explains, in part, the source of embarrassment or at least reticence, that many people feel when dealing with "whatever is natural."
2. Many of us have certain patterns of behavior that we enter into in certain situations. This might be something like drumming one's fingers before an exam, tapping a pencil on a table while one is concentrating, jingling coins in one's pocket while standing in line, pacing a room when one is worried. Observe someone close to you and keep a record of such behavior patterns. Then, for a class in behavioral psychology, write up a 750-word description of the behavior, its duration, the kind of situation that triggers it, and the subject's awareness of it.

3. After conducting the observational experiment in the previous question, write a 500-word essay dealing with the ethics of conducting research and reporting on that research. Is it legitimate to conduct research on an unaware subject?
4. For a class in child psychology, write a 750-word position paper on what parents should do to best prepare their children for the "world of sexuality."
5. For a class in the history of psychology, write a 2,000-word essay exploring the reception that Freud's ideas found in his own immediate discourse community.

Émile Durkheim

(1858–1917)

Émile Durkheim is widely viewed as the father of the French school of sociology. He was a remarkably disciplined young man, a fact that helped him shoulder the heavy responsibilities imposed on him after the death of his father when the young Durkheim was only twenty. In 1879, Durkheim was accepted into the École Normale Supérieure in Paris, which was the most prestigious teacher-preparation college in France. After graduating in 1882, Durkheim held a series of positions in the secondary schools of France until 1887. Then he received an appointment to the University of Bordeaux, where he taught social philosophy until 1902. At that time Durkheim moved to the University of Paris, becoming a full professor in 1906.

His last years were difficult. Along with other professors at the University of Paris, Durkheim was accused of respecting German scholarship too much. World War I came as an especially severe blow to him. He had worked so hard for social reform that the outbreak of war was almost more than he could endure. Then, in 1916, his only son was killed while fighting in the Balkans. Durkheim appeared more and more gaunt and distressed, and in November of 1917 he died.

In many respects Durkheim's sociology resembles moral philosophy. He saw much in French society that frightened and saddened him. Many people displayed what he called anomie, a feeling of not belonging and of not having much worth. He felt that prosperity had encouraged greed and other passions that threatened the fabric of society. He also believed that advances in technology and mechanization had separated workers from each other and from the feeling of accomplishment that comes with making a whole product by oneself.

Durkheim was a sociologist who wedded empirical research with sociological theorizing. He did groundbreaking work on the role of individuals in a society and on how properties of a society can arise from interactions among individuals, even though none of the individuals alone possesses those properties. But Durkheim did not leave his findings and theories in the scholarly journals; he regarded himself as an educator of society and worked hard for social reform in France. He tried to make French society more closely approximate his vision of a healthy and moral society.

The following selection, on human nature and its social conditions, was published originally in 1914 in the journal Scientia.

THE DUALISM OF HUMAN NATURE AND ITS SOCIAL CONDITIONS

Although sociology is defined as the science of societies, it cannot, in reality, 1
deal with the human groups that are the immediate object of its investigation
without eventually touching on the individual who is the basic element of
which these groups are composed. For society can exist only if it penetrates
the consciousness of individuals and fashions it in "its image and resemblance." We can say, therefore, with assurance and without being excessively
dogmatic, that a great number of our mental states, including some of the
most important ones, are of social origin. In this case, then, it is the whole
that, in a large measure, produces the part; consequently, it is impossible to
attempt to explain the whole without explaining the part—without explaining, at least, the part as a result of the whole. The supreme product of collective activity is that ensemble of intellectual and moral goods that we call
civilization; it is for this reason that Auguste Comte* referred to sociology as
the science of civilization. However, it is civilization that has made man what
he is; it is what distinguishes him from the animal: man is man only because
he is civilized. To look for the causes and conditions upon which civilization
depends is, therefore, to seek out also the causes and conditions of what is
most specifically human in man. And so sociology, which draws on psychology and could not do without it, brings to it, in a just return, a contribution
that equals and surpasses in importance the services that it receives from it.
It is only by historical analysis that we can discover what makes up man,
since it is only in the course of history that he is formed.

The work that we recently published, *The Elementary Forms of the* 2
Religious Life,† offers an example of this general truth. In attempting to
study religious phenomena from the sociological point of view, we came to
envisage a way of explaining scientifically one of the most characteristic peculiarities of our nature. Since the critics who have discussed the book up to
the present have not—to our great surprise—perceived the principle upon
which this explanation rests, it seemed to us that a brief outline of it would
be of some interest to the readers of *Scientia*.

The peculiarity referred to is the constitutional duality of human na- 3
ture. In every age, man has been intensely aware of this duality. He has, in

---

*Auguste Comte (1798–1857) was a French philosopher; he brought the word *sociology* into
    common use.
†*Les formes élémentaires de la vie religieuse* (Paris: Félix Alean, 1912). [Translated as *The
    Elementary Forms of the Religious Life* by Joseph Ward Swain ([1915] Glencoe, Ill.: Free
    Press of Glencoe, Illinois, 1947). Durkheim's note].

fact, everywhere conceived of himself as being formed of two radically heterogeneous beings: the body and the soul. Even when the soul is represented
in a material form, its substance is not thought of as being of the same nature
as the body. It is said that it is more ethereal, more subtle, more plastic, that
it does not affect the senses as do the other objects to which they react, that
it is not subject to the same laws as these objects, and so on. And not only are
these two beings substantially different, they are in a large measure independent of each other, and are often even in conflict. For centuries it was believed that after this life the soul could escape from the body and lead an
autonomous existence far from it. This independence was made manifest at
the time of death when the body dissolved and disappeared and the soul
survived and continued to follow, under new conditions and for varying
lengths of time, the path of its own destiny. It can even be said that although
the body and the soul are closely associated, they do not belong to the same
world. The body is an integral part of the material universe, as it is made
known to us by sensory experience; the abode of the soul is elsewhere, and
the soul tends ceaselessly to return to it. This abode is the world of the sacred.
Therefore, the soul is invested with a dignity that has always been denied the
body, which is considered essentially profane, and it inspires those feelings
that are everywhere reserved for that which is divine. It is made of the same
substance as are the sacred beings: it differs from them only in degree.

A belief that is as universal and permanent as this cannot be purely 4
illusory. There must be something in man that gives rise to this feeling that
his nature is dual, a feeling that men in all known civilizations have experienced. Psychological analysis has, in fact, confirmed the existence of this
duality: it finds it at the very heart of our inner life.

Our intelligence, like our activity, presents two very different forms: on 5
the one hand, are sensations* and sensory tendencies; on the other, conceptual thought and moral activity. Each of these two parts of ourselves represents a separate pole of our being, and these two poles are not only distinct
from one another but are opposed to one another. Our sensory appetites are
necessarily egoistic: they have our individuality and it alone as their object.
When we satisfy our hunger, our thirst, and so on, without bringing any
other tendency into play, it is ourselves, and ourselves alone, that we satisfy.†
[Conceptual thought] and moral activity are, on the contrary, distinguished
by the fact that the rules of conduct to which they conform can be universalized. Therefore, by definition, they pursue impersonal ends. Morality begins

---

* To sensations, one should add images, but since images are only sensations that survive them-
　　selves, it is useless to mention them separately. The same is true for those conglomerations
　　of images and sensations which are called perceptions [Durkheim's note].
† No doubt there are egoistic desires that do not have material things as their objects, but the
　　sensory appetites are the type par excellence of egoistic tendencies. We believe that desires
　　for objects of a different kind imply—although the egoistic motive may play a role in
　　them—a movement out of ourselves which surpasses pure egoism. This is the case, for
　　example, with love of glory, power, and so on [Durkheim's note].

with disinterest, with attachment to something other than ourselves.* A sensation of color or sound is closely dependent on my individual organism, and I cannot detach the sensation from my organism. In addition, it is impossible for me to make my awareness pass over into someone else. I can, of course, invite another person to face the same object and expose himself to its effect, but the perception that he will have of it will be his own work and will be proper to him, as mine is proper to me. Concepts, on the contrary, are always common to a plurality of men. They are constituted by means of words, and neither the vocabulary nor the grammar of a language is the work or product of one particular person. They are rather the result of a collective elaboration, and they express the anonymous collectivity that employs them. The ideas of *man* or *animal* are not personal and are not restricted to me; I share them, to a large degree, with all the men who belong to the same social group that I do. Because they are held in common, concepts are the supreme instrument of all intellectual exchange. By means of them minds communicate. Doubtless, when one thinks through the concepts that he receives from the community, he individualizes them and marks them with his personal imprint, but there is nothing personal that is not susceptible to this type of individualization.†

These two aspects of our psychic life are, therefore, opposed to each 6 other as are the personal and the impersonal. There is in us a being that represents everything in relation to itself and from its own point of view; in everything that it does, this being has no other object but itself. There is another being in us, however, which knows things *sub specie aeternitis*, as if it were participating in some thought other than its own, and which, in its acts, tends to accomplish ends that surpass its own. The old formula *homo duplex* is therefore verified by the facts. Far from being simple, our inner life has something that is like a double center of gravity. On the one hand is our individuality—and, more particularly, our body in which it is based;‡ on the other is everything in us that expresses something other than ourselves.

Not only are these two groups of states of consciousness different in their 7 origins and their properties, but there is a true antagonism between them.

---

* Cf. our communication to the French Philosophical Society, "La détermination du fait moral," *Bulletin de la Société francaise de philosophie*, VI, (1906), 113–39. [Translated as "The Determination of Moral Facts," in Durkheim, *Sociology and Philosophy*, trans. D. F. Pocock, with an Introduction by J. G. Peristiany (Glencoe, Ill.: Free Press of Glencoe, Illinois, 1953), pp. 35–62. Durkheim's note].

† We do not mean to deny the individual the capacity to form concepts. He learns to form representations of this kind from the collectivity, but even the concepts he forms in this way have the same character as the others: They are constructed in such a way that they can be universalized. Even when they are the product of a personality, they are in part impersonal [Durkheim's note].

‡ We say our individuality and not *our personality*. Although the two words are often used synonymously, they must be distinguished with the greatest possible care, for the personality is made up essentially of supraindividual elements. Cf., on this point, *Les formes élémentaires de la vie religieuse*, pp. 386–90 [Durkheim's note].

They mutually contradict and deny each other. We cannot pursue moral ends without causing a split within ourselves, without offending the instincts and the penchants that are the most deeply rooted in our bodies. There is no moral act that does not imply a sacrifice, for, as Kant* has shown, the law of duty cannot be obeyed without humiliating our individual, or, as he calls it, our "empirical" sensitivity. We can accept this sacrifice without resistance and even with enthusiasm, but even when it is accomplished in a surge of joy, the sacrifice is no less real. The pain that the ascetic seeks is pain nonetheless, and this antinomy is so deep and so radical that it can never be completely resolved. How can we belong entirely to ourselves, and entirely to others at one and the same time? The ego cannot be something completely other than itself, for, if it were, it would vanish—this is what happens in ecstasy. In order to think, we must be, we must have an individuality. On the other hand, however, the ego cannot be entirely and exclusively itself, for, if it were, it would be emptied of all content. If we must be in order to think, then we must have something to think about. To what would consciousness be reduced if it expressed nothing but the body and its states? We cannot live without representing to ourselves the world around us and the objects of every sort which fill it. And because we represent it to ourselves, it enters into us and becomes part of us. Consequently, we value the world and are attached to it just as we are to ourselves. Something else in us besides ourselves stimulates us to act. It is an error to believe that it is easy to live as egoists. Absolute egoism, like absolute altruism, is an ideal limit which can never be attained in reality. Both are states that we can approach indefinitely without ever realizing them completely.

It is no different in the sphere of our knowledge. We understand only 8 when we think in concepts. But sensory reality is not made to enter the framework of our concepts spontaneously and by itself. It resists, and, in order to make it conform, we have to do some violence to it, we have to submit it to all sorts of laborious operations that alter it so that the mind can assimilate it. However, we never completely succeed in triumphing over its resistance. Our concepts never succeed in mastering our sensations and in translating them completely into intelligible terms. They take on a conceptual form only by losing that which is most concrete in them, that which causes them to speak to our sensory being and to involve it in action; and, in so doing, they become something fixed and dead. Therefore, we cannot understand things without partially renouncing a feeling for their life, and we cannot feel that life without renouncing the understanding of it. Doubtless, we sometimes dream of a science that would adequately express all of reality; but this is an ideal that we can only approach ceaselessly, not one that is possible for us to attain.

This inner contradiction is one of the characteristics of our nature. 9

---

* Immanuel Kant (1724–1804) was one of the world's great philosophers.

According to Pascal's* formula, man is both "angel and beast" and not exclusively one or the other. The result is that we are never completely in accord with ourselves for we cannot follow one of our two natures without causing the other to suffer. Our joys can never be pure; there is always some pain mixed with them; for we cannot simultaneously satisfy the two beings that are within us. It is this disagreement, this perpetual division against ourselves, that produces both our grandeur and our misery: our misery because we are thus condemned to live in suffering; and our grandeur because it is this division that distinguishes us from all other beings. The animal proceeds to his pleasure in a single and exclusive movement; man alone is normally obliged to make a place for suffering in his life.

Thus the traditional antithesis of the body and soul is not a vain myth- 10 ological concept that is without foundation in reality. It is true that we are double, that we are the realization of an antinomy. In connection with this truth, however, a question arises that philosophy and even positive psychology cannot avoid: Where do this duality and this antinomy come from? How is it that each of us is, to quote another of Pascal's phrases, a "monster of contradictions" that can never completely satisfy itself? And, certainly, if this odd condition is one of the distinctive traits of humanity, the science of man must try to account for it.

The proposed solutions to this problem are neither numerous nor var- 11 ied. Two doctrines that occupy an important place in the history of thought held that the difficulty could be removed by denying it; that is, by calling the duality of man an illusion. These doctrines are empirical monism and idealistic monism.

According to the first of these doctrines, concepts are only more or less 12 elaborate sensations. They consist entirely of groups of similar images, groups that have a kind of individuality because each of the images that comprise the group is identified by the same word; however, outside of these images and sensations of which they are the extension, concepts have no reality at all. In the same way, this doctrine holds, moral activity is only another aspect of self-interested activity: the man who obeys the call of duty is merely pursuing his own self-interest as he understands it. When our nature is seen in this way, the problem of its duality disappears: man is one, and if there are serious strains within him, it is because he is not acting in conformity with his nature. If properly interpreted, a concept cannot be contrary to the sensation to which it owes its existence; and the moral act cannot be in conflict with the egoistic act, because, fundamentally, it derives from utilitarian motives.

Unfortunately, however, the facts that posed the question in the first 13 place still exist. It is still true that at all times man has been disquieted and

---

*Blaise Pascal (1623–1662) was a French scientist and religious philosopher.

malcontent. He has always felt that he is pulled apart, divided against himself; and the beliefs and practices to which, in all societies and all civilizations, he has always attached the greatest value, have as their object not to suppress these inevitable divisions but to attenuate their consequences, to give them meaning and purpose, to make them more bearable, and at the very least, to console man for their existence. We cannot admit that this universal and chronic state of malaise is the product of a simple aberration, that man has been the creator of his own suffering, and that he has stupidly persisted in it, although his nature truly predisposed him to live harmoniously. Experience should have corrected such a deplorable error long ago. At the very least, it should be able to explain the origin of this inconceivable blindness. Moreover, the serious objections to the hypothesis of empirical monism are well known. It has never been able to explain how the inferior can become the superior; or how individual sensation, which is obscure and confused, can become the clear and distinct impersonal concept; or how self-interest can be transformed into disinterest.

It is no different with the absolute idealist. For him, too, reality is one; but for him it is made up entirely of concepts, while for the empiricist it is made up entirely of sensations. According to the idealist, an absolute intelligence seeing things as they are would find that the world is a system of definite ideas connected with each other in relationships that are equally definite. To the idealist, sensations are nothing by themselves; they are only concepts that are not clear and are intermixed. They assume the particular aspect in which they are revealed to us in experience only because we do not know how to distinguish their elements. If we knew how, there would be no fundamental opposition between the world and ourselves or between the different parts of ourselves. The opposition that we think we perceive is due to a simple error in perspective that needs only to be corrected. However, if this were true, we should be able to establish that this error diminishes to the degree that the domain of conceptual thought is extended and we learn to think less by sensation and more in concepts; to the degree, that is, that science develops and becomes a more important factor in our mental life. But, unfortunately, history is far from confirming these optimistic hopes. It seems that, on the contrary, human malaise continues to increase. The great religions of modern man are those which insist the most on the existence of the contradictions in the midst of which we struggle. These continue to depict us as tormented and suffering, while only the crude cults of inferior societies breathe forth and inspire a joyful confidence.* For what religions express is the experience through which humanity has lived, and it would be very surprising if our nature became unified and harmonious when we feel that our discords are increasing. Moreover, even if we assume that these discords are only superficial and apparent, it is still necessary to take this appearance into

---

*Cf. *ibid.*, pp. 320–321, 580 [Durkheim's note].

consideration. If the sensations are nothing outside of concepts, it is still necessary to determine why it is that the latter do not appear to us as they really are, but seem to us mixed and confused. What is it that has imposed on them a lack of distinctness that is contrary to their nature? Idealism faces considerable difficulty in trying to solve these problems, and its failure to do so gives rise to objections that are precisely the opposite of those that have so often and so legitimately been made against empiricism. The latter has never explained how the inferior can become the superior—that is, how a sensation can be raised to the dignity of a concept while remaining unchanged; and the former faces equal difficulty in explaining how the superior can become the inferior, how the concept can wither and degenerate in such a way as to become sensation. This degeneration cannot be spontaneous; it must be determined by some contradictory principle. However, there is no place for a principle of this kind in a doctrine that is essentially monistic.

If we reject the theories which eliminate the problem rather than solve 15 it, the only remaining ones that are valid and merit examination are those which limit themselves to affirming the fact that must be explained, but which do not account for it.

First of all, there is the ontological explanation for which Plato gave the 16 formula. Man is double because two worlds meet in him: that of non-intelligent and amoral matter, on the one hand, and that of ideas, the spirit, and the good, on the other. Because these two worlds are naturally opposed, they struggle within us; and, because we are part of both, we are necessarily in conflict with ourselves. But if this answer—completely metaphysical as it is—has the merit of affirming the fact that must be interpreted without trying to weaken it, it does confine itself, nevertheless, to distinguishing the two aspects of human nature and does not account for them. To say that we are double because there are two contrary forces in us is to repeat the problem in different terms: it does not resolve it. It is still necessary to explain their opposition. Doubtless, one can admit that because of the excellence that is attributed to it the world of ideas and of good contains within itself the reason for its existence: but how does it happen that outside of it there is a principle of evil, of darkness, of non-being? And what is the function of this principle?

We understand even less how these two worlds which are wholly op- 17 posite, and which, consequently, should repulse and exclude each other, tend, nevertheless, to unite and interpenetrate in such a way as to produce the mixed and contradictory being that is man; for it seems that their antagonism should keep them apart and make their union impossible. To borrow the language of Plato, the Idea, which is perfect by definition, possesses the plenitude of being, and is, therefore, sufficient in itself, and needs only itself in order to exist. Why, then, should it lower itself toward matter when contact with it can only alter its nature and make it sink below its former level? But, on the other hand, why should matter aspire to the contrary principle—a principle that it denies—and permit itself to be penetrated by it? And, finally, it is man that is the theatre par excellence of the struggle that we have described, a struggle that is not found in other beings; according to the hypothesis, however, man is not the only place where the two worlds ought to meet.

The theory that is most widely accepted at present offers an even less 18 satisfactory explanation of human dualism: it does not base it on two metaphysical principles that are the basis of all reality, but on the existence of two antithetical faculties within us. We possess both a faculty for thinking as individuals and a faculty for thinking in universal and impersonal terms. The first is called sensitivity, and the second reason. Our activity can, therefore, manifest two completely opposed characters depending on whether it is based on sensory or on rational motives. Kant more than anyone else has insisted on this contrast between reason and sensitivity, between rational activity and sensory activity. But even if this classification is perfectly legitimate, it offers no solution to the problem that occupies us here; for the important thing to determine from our consideration of the fact that we have aptitudes for living both a personal and an impersonal life, is not what name it is proper to give to these contrary aptitudes, but how it is that in spite of their opposition, they exist in a single and identical being. How is it that we can participate concurrently in these two existences? How is it that we are made up of two halves that appear to belong to two different beings? Merely to give a name to each being does nothing toward answering the fundamental question.

If we have too often been satisfied with this purely verbal answer, it is 19 because we have generally thought of man's mental nature as a sort of ultimate given which need not be accounted for. Thus we tend to believe that all has been said and done when we attach such and such a fact, whose causes we are seeking, to a human faculty. But why should the human spirit, which is—to put it briefly—only a system of phenomena that are comparable in all ways to other observable phenomena, be outside and above explanation? We know that our organism is the product of a genesis; why should it be otherwise with our psychic constitution? And if there is anything in us that urgently requires explanation, it is precisely this strange antithesis which is involved in this constitution.

The statement made previously that human dualism has always 20 expressed itself in religious form is sufficient to suggest that the answer to our question must be sought in a quite different direction. As we have said, the soul has everywhere been considered something sacred; it has been viewed as a bit of divinity which lives only a brief terrestrial life and tends, as if by itself, to return to its place of origin. Thus the soul is opposed to the body, which is regarded as profane; and everything in our mental life that is related to the body—the sensations and the sensory appetites—has this same character. For this reason, we think that sensations are inferior forms of our activity, and we attribute a higher dignity to reason and moral activity which are the faculties by which, so we are told, we communicate with God. Even the man who is most free of professed belief makes a distinction of this kind, attributing an unequal value to our varying psychic functions, and giving to each, according to its relative value, a place in a hierarchy, in which those that are most closely related to the body are at the bottom. Furthermore, as we have shown,* there is no morality that is not infused with religiosity. Even to the secular mind, duty, the moral imperative, is something august and sacred; and reason, the indispensable ally of moral activity, naturally inspires similar feelings. The duality of our nature is thus only a particular case of that division of things into the sacred and the profane that is the foundation of all religions, and it must be explained on the basis of the same principles.

It is precisely this explanation that we attempted in the previously cited 21 work, *The Elementary Forms of the Religious Life*, where we tried to show that sacred things are simply collective ideals that have fixed themselves on material objects.† The ideas and sentiments that are elaborated by a collectivity, whatever it may be, are invested by reason of their origin with an ascendancy and an authority that cause the particular individuals who think them and believe in them to represent them in the form of moral forces that dominate and sustain them. When these ideals move our wills, we feel that we are being led, directed, and carried along by singular energies that, manifested, do not come from us but are imposed on us from the outside. Our feelings toward them are respect and reverent fear, as well as gratitude for the comfort that we receive from them: for they cannot communicate themselves to us without increasing our vitality. And the particular virtues that we attribute to these ideals are not due to any mysterious action of an external agency; they are simply the effects of that singularly creative and fertile psychic operation—which is scientifically analyzable—by which a plurality of individual consciousnesses enter into communion and are fused into a common consciousness.

From another point of view, however, collective representations origi- 22 nate only when they are embodied in material objects, things, or beings of every sort—figures, movements, sounds, words, and so on—that symbolize and delineate them in some outward appearance. For it is only by expressing their feelings, by translating them into signs, by symbolizing them externally, that the individual consciousnesses, which are, by nature, closed to each other, can feel that they are communicating and are in unison.‡ The things that embody the collective representations arouse the same feelings as do the mental states that they represent and, in a manner of speaking, materialize. They, too, are respected, feared, and sought after as helping powers. Consequently, they are not placed on the same plane as the vulgar things that

* Cf. "La détermination du fait moral," p. 125 [Durkheim's note].
† Cf. *Les formes élémentaires de la vie religieuse*, pp. 268–342 [Durkheim's note].
‡ *Ibid.*, pp. 329 ff. [Durkheim's note].

interest only our physical individualities, but are set apart from them. There-fore, we assign them a completely different place in the complex of reality and separate them; and it is this radical separation that constitutes the es-sence of their sacred character.* This system of conceptions is not purely imaginary and hallucinatory, for the moral forces that these things awaken in us are quite real—as real as the ideas that words recall to us after they have served to form the ideas. This is the dynamogenic influence that reli-gions have always exercised on men.

However, these ideals, these products of group life, cannot originate— 23 let alone persist—unless they penetrate the individual consciousness where they are organized in a lasting fashion. Once the group has dissolved and the social communion has done its work, the individuals carry away within themselves these great religious, moral, and intellectual conceptions that so-cieties draw from their very hearts during their periods of greatest creativity. Doubtless, once the creativity has ceased and each individual has again taken up his private existence, removing himself from the source of his inspiration, the vitality of these conceptions is not maintained at the same intensity. It is not extinguished, however; for the action of the group does not cease alto-gether: it perpetually gives back to the great ideals a little of the strength that the egoistic passions and daily personal preoccupations tend to take away from them. This replenishment is the function of public festivals, ceremonies, and rites of all kinds.

In mingling with our individual lives in this way, however, these var- 24 ious ideals are themselves individualized. Because they are in a close relation with our other representations, they harmonize with them, and with our temperaments, characters, habits, and so on. Each of us puts his own mark on them; and this accounts for the fact that each person has his own partic-ular way of thinking about the beliefs of his church, the rules of common morality, and the fundamental notions that serve as the framework of con-ceptual thought. But even while they are being individualized—and thus be-coming elements of our personalities—collective ideals preserve their char-acteristic property: the prestige with which they are clothed. Although they are our own, they speak in us with a tone and an accent that are entirely different from those of our other states of consciousness. They command us; they impose respect on us; we do not feel ourselves to be on an even footing with them. We realize that they represent something within us that is supe-rior to us.

It is not without reason, therefore, that man feels himself to be double: 25 he actually is double. There are in him two classes of states of consciousness that differ from each other in origin and nature, and in the ends toward which they aim. One class merely expresses our organisms and the objects to which they are most directly related. Strictly individual, the states of con-

* *Ibid.*, pp. 53 ff. [Durkheim's note].

sciousness of this class connect us only with ourselves, and we can no more detach them from us than we can detach ourselves from our bodies. The states of consciousness of the other class, on the contrary, come to us from society; they transfer society into us and connect us with something that surpasses us. Being collective, they are impersonal; they turn us toward ends that we hold in common with other men; it is through them and them alone that we can communicate with others. It is, therefore, quite true that we are made up of two parts, and are like two beings, which, although they are closely associated, are composed of very different elements and orient us in opposite directions.

In brief, this duality corresponds to the double existence that we lead 26 concurrently: the one purely individual and rooted in our organisms, the other social and nothing but an extension of society. The origin of the antagonism that we have described is evident from the very nature of the elements involved in it. The conflicts of which we have given examples are between the sensations and the sensory appetites, on the one hand, and the intellectual and moral life, on the other; and it is evident that passions and egoistic tendencies derive from our individual constitutions, while our rational activity— whether theoretical or practical—is dependent on social causes. We have often had occasion to prove that the rules of morality are norms that have been elaborated by society;* the obligatory character with which they are marked is nothing but the authority of society, communicating itself to everything that comes from it. In the book that is the occasion of the present study but which we can only mention here, we have tried to demonstrate that concepts, the material of all logical thought, were originally collective representations. The impersonality that characterizes them is proof that they are the product of an anonymous and impersonal action.† We have even found a basis for conjecturing that the fundamental and lofty concepts that we call categories are formed on the model of social phenomena.‡

The painful character of the dualism of human nature is explained by 27 this hypothesis. There is no doubt that if society were only the natural and spontaneous development of the individual, these two parts of ourselves would harmonize and adjust to each other without clashing and without friction: the first part, since it is only the extension and, in a way, the complement of the second, would encounter no resistance from the latter. In fact, however, society has its own nature, and, consequently, its requirements are quite different from those of our nature as individuals: the interests of the whole are not necessarily those of the part. Therefore, society cannot be formed or maintained without our being required to make perpetual and costly sacri-

---

*Cf. *De la division du travail social* ([1893] 3rd ed.; Paris: Félix Alcan, 1907), *passim* and esp. pp. 391 ff. [Translated as *The Division of Labor in Society*, by George Simpson ([1933] Glencoe, Ill.: Free Press of Glencoe, Illinois, 1947). Durkheim's note].

† *Les formes élémentaires de la vie religieuse*, pp. 616 ff. [Durkheim's note].

‡ *Ibid.*, pp. 12–28 ff., 205 ff., 336, 386, 508, 627 [Durkheim's note].

fices. Because society surpasses us, it obliges us to surpass ourselves; and to surpass itself, a being must, to some degree, depart from its nature—a departure that does not take place without causing more or less painful tensions. We know that only the action of society arouses us to give our attention voluntarily. Attention presupposes effort: to be attentive we must suspend the spontaneous course of our representations and prevent our consciousness from pursuing the dispersive movement that is its natural course. We must, in a word, do violence to certain of our strongest inclinations. Therefore, since the role of the social being in our single selves will grow ever more important as history moves ahead, it is wholly improbable that there will ever be an era in which man is required to resist himself to a lesser degree, an era in which he can live a life that is easier and less full of tension. To the contrary, all evidence compels us to expect our effort in the struggle between the two beings within us to increase with the growth of civilization.

QUESTIONS ON DURKHEIM'S DISCOURSE COMMUNITY AND HIS CONCERNS IN THIS ESSAY

1. Is the individual a proper subject for sociology? Why or why not?
2. How does Durkheim distinguish perceptions and conceptions? Do you agree with his treatment?
3. Why does Durkheim claim that if the ego were entirely itself, it "would be emptied of all content"? Do you agree with him?
4. Durkheim writes that "man is man only because he is civilized." Do you agree? How would you define humankind?
5. Durkheim calls some societies inferior. On what basis would he probably have made such a judgment?
6. Do you agree with Durkheim that some of our personal traits derive not from our own individual nature but from our social group?
7. In Durkheim's view, what is the source of the rules of morality? Do you agree with him?
8. Do you agree with Durkheim that we are "condemned to live in suffering"?

QUESTIONS ON DURKHEIM'S RHETORICAL STRATEGIES

1. How well does Durkheim lead the reader through this selection? How is it organized on its most general level?
2. When Durkheim begins to detail the nature of the mind-body dualism, he repeatedly uses the pronoun *our* ("our intelligence," "our being," "our sensory appetites"). What are the advantages of this practice?
3. Often Durkheim attacks a position by asking questions about it. How effective do you think this strategy is?
4. After dismissing several explanations for the duality of our nature, Durkheim asserts that this duality is only one case of how religions divide up the world. How persuasive do you think this assertion is?

5. What kind of evidence does Durkheim offer for the existence of the soul? Does this evidence seem sufficient to you?
6. How well does Durkheim make the case that the nature of society is different from the nature of individuals? In the light of the fact that this selection appeared as a self-contained piece in a journal, do you think he could be expected to provide more evidence?
7. Durkheim writes that he has often proved that morality derives from society. Is *proved* too strong of a word? Do you think it is possible for him to prove this?
8. What is Durkheim attempting to achieve with his conclusion? How effective is it?

WRITING ABOUT AND FROM WITHIN THE SOCIAL SCIENCES: SOCIOLOGY

Writing for Yourself

1. In your journal, reflect on how suffering affects human character.
2. In your journal, reflect on how sensitive you have been at different stages of your life to pressures from your peers.

Writing for Nonacademic Audiences

1. For the opinion column in your school newspaper, write a 250-word piece in which you argue that an individual on your campus can make an important difference to campus life.
2. Can North American society force individuals to surpass themselves, to grow in ways they could not without societal pressure? You have been asked to write a 500-word opinion piece in response to this question. The *Chronicle of Higher Education* is soliciting opinion pieces on this topic from various college students; it will print about a dozen of the more provocative ones.

Writing for Academic Audiences

1. For a class in the sociology of religion, write a 750-word description of liberation theology. Try also to explain its appeal in Central and South America today.
2. For a course in the sociology of religion, write a 1,000-word analysis of the current appeal of evangelical Protestantism in the United States.
3. For a class in the sociology of religion, write a 1,000-word analysis of the difficulties that traditional mainline Protestant churches have had lately in the United States in attracting and holding members.
4. In your opinion, what is the source of morality? Respond in a 1,000-word persuasive piece for a course in the sociology of religion.
5. For a senior seminar in sociology, write a 1,000-word argument on the extent to which sociologists must study the nature of the individual.

Bronislaw Malinowski

(1884–1942)

Bronislaw Malinowski is widely regarded as a leading anthropologist of the twentieth century and as the founder of the field of social anthropology.

Malinowski was born in Kraków, Poland. His father was a professor of Slavic philology at Jagiellonian University in Kraków, and his mother was a skilled linguist. After receiving much of his early education at home, Malinowski entered Jagiellonian University, where he earned a doctorate in philosophy in 1908. Shortly after that, he read Sir James Frazier's The Golden Bough, *a work describing religious and magical practices around the world, and Malinowski became fascinated with such work. As a result, in 1910 he enrolled at the London School of Economics, which included anthropology among its fields of study. After anthropological field research in New Guinea, he earned a doctorate in anthropology. Later Malinowski was to draw extensively on this field research, as well as on that which he conducted in the Trobriand Islands. In 1938, Malinowski visited the United States, and when World War II broke out, he decided to stay in the United States, accepting a professorship at Yale University.*

Malinowski developed a functional theory of anthropology. He believed that every custom, saying, object, practice, and belief of a culture has a distinct function in that culture. One could not fully understand a part of a culture until he or she could see what function it fulfilled in that culture. Malinowski's aim was to investigate a culture in its totality and to pursue the functional interconnection of all its parts. He believed that each culture in its totality is unique; he saw little point in trying to compare one culture with another.

The following selection is taken from the first chapter of the first volume of Malinowski's Coral Gardens and Their Magic. *The two volumes of* Coral Gardens *focus on the methods of tilling the soil and the magical rites governing crop production that Malinowski studied in the Trobriand Islands, flat coral islands off the east coast of New Guinea. In the following selection, one can see how Malinowski investigates both the work of raising crops and the rites of magic used to protect the crops. Repeatedly he attends to the issue of how work and magic fulfill organizing functions in the lives of the Trobriand Islanders.*

CORAL GARDENS AND THEIR MAGIC

THE SEVERAL ASPECTS OF TROBRIAND AGRICULTURE

In the Introduction I have shown in a concrete manner how agriculture per- 1
meates tribal life. Now let us see how other aspects of Trobriand culture enter
into the system of gardening. Any observer who has lived, worked, and con-
versed with the natives, would be impressed by the sheer bulk, complexity,
and abundant detail of their gardening occupations, and the number of ex-
traneous and supererogatory activities which cluster about these.

Gardening is associated with an extremely complicated and important 2
body of magic, which, in turn, has its mythology, traditional charters and
privileges. Magic appears side by side with work, not accidentally or sporad-
ically as occasion arises or as whim dictates, but as an essential part of the
whole scheme and in a way which does not permit any honest observer to
dismiss it as a mere excrescence* (cf. App. I).

Agriculture also has its legal aspect. When we come to the distribution 3
of plots for cultivation, we shall see that a complex system of privileges and
claims and duties is involved, accompanied by semi-ceremonial transactions
which the natives by no means treat as trivial or irrelevant.

Again the sociology of garden-making is intricate. The parts played by 4
the chief or headman of the community, by the official garden magician, by
the owners of the soil, by those who lease garden plots, by those who benefit
from the harvest, dovetail and intertwine into a complex economic and social
network which constitutes the land-tenure of these natives (cf. Chs. VI, XI,
and XII). Another important aspect of culture into which gardening enters
directly is social organisation, notably the kinship system and political power.
The natives usually harvest a large surplus over and above what is necessary
to nourish them; and this surplus figures in tribute and the marriage gift.
When we study the distribution of yams at harvest (Chs. V to VIII) we shall
see that the best produce is always given by the gardener to his sister and her
husband, and, owing to the system of polygamous marriage which is definitely the privilege of rank and chieftainship, a large proportion of such ma-
trimonial gifts finds its way to the storehouses of various chiefs and notables.
The whole institution of chieftainship is founded on the large tribute in staple
crops which the chief receives from the maternal kinsmen of his wives (cf.
Part I, Sec. 10 and Ch. VI, Sec. 2). The enormous quantity of yams thus
placed at his disposal, he in turn has to distribute, partly in the financing of
feasts and tribal enterprises and partly in maintaining a number of industrial

---

* An excrescence is an abnormal and usually useless outgrowth or enlargement [Editors' note].

workers who produce objects of permanent wealth for him (Part I, Secs. 4, 6 and 10). Gardening, and effective gardening at that, with a large surplus produce, lies at the root of all tribal authority as well as of the kinship system and communal organisation of the Islanders.

Finally, among other apparently extrinsic elements, we find a surpris- 5 ing care for the aesthetics of gardening. The gardens of the community are not merely a means to food; they are a source of pride and the main object of collective ambition. Care is lavished upon effects of beauty, pleasing to the eye and the heart of the Trobriander, upon the finish of the work, the perfection of various contrivances and the show of food. We shall also see how other incentives besides mere greed and anxiety are brought into action by joint family farmings and competitive display. A further complexity is added to Trobriand gardening by the diversity of crops, the various kinds of gardens, and the differentiation of plots according to their magical, aesthetic and practical function.

The theoretical synthesis of all these elements—the meaning and func- 6 tion of magic, the part played by elegance and aesthetic finish, the relations between the privileges of kinship and the influence of myth—are subjects which we shall be discussing in the following chapters. At present, so as not to lose our way through the detailed accounts which follow, we must lay down a few general principles.

A WALK THROUGH THE GARDENS

We have gathered something of the work and care lavished upon gardens 7 through our somewhat desultory visit to them in the Introduction. The landscape of the Trobriands is not at first sight beautiful. We are on a flat, even, coral foundation, covered for the most part with fertile black soil, interspersed with patches of swampy ground, and of drier, stonier soil. Round the northern and eastern shores of the main island and of Vakuta* there runs a low, irregular, coral ridge, named by the natives *rayboag*, which is covered with primeval forest. The remainder is almost entirely under intermittent cultivation, so that the bush, cleared away every few years, cannot grow to any height. When you walk across the country, therefore, you either move between two green walls of low, dense jungle of recent growth, or you pass through gardens. Glancing at Plates 18 and 19 we see parties of men and women carrying tubers—a sight typical of the district at harvest-time, when food is constantly being transported from gardens to villages, or, again, when there is a competitive food display between two villages (Ch. V, Secs. 5 and 6). Women carry in bell-shaped baskets on their heads; men in oblong, valise-shaped baskets or, in the case of the very big long yams, they shoulder their

---

* Vakuta Island is the southernmost of the Trobriand Islands [Editors' note].

Plate 18

burden. On Plate 18 we see a party on a road through the low jungle, and on Plate 19 another passing through a harvested garden.

The gardens are certainly the more attractive part of the landscape. We 8 pass over completely cleared ground which leaves an open view into the distance, where the horizon is broken by an occasional clump of trees marking the site of a *boma* (sacred grove) or one of the numerous villages; or else our eye travels towards the jungle on the coral ridge or sweeps across the green lagoon between the islands. The gardens shown on Plate 20, which was taken towards the end of the clearing and after most of the preliminary crops had been planted, illustrates such a view. These crops can be seen already growing, the tall tufts of sugar-cane, the young heart-shaped leaves of the taro, and here and there an early yam vine of the large variety (*kuvi*) climbing round the stems left standing after the cutting and burning (Ch. II, Sec. 5, Ch. III, Sec. 1). In the foreground we see the poles already laid which divide the gardens like a chessboard into squares. In the background the scrub, which in this case was almost at the foot of the coral ridge, rises behind the fence. A group of men are seen at work.

Or again we traverse a yam garden in full development, reminiscent 9 somewhat of a Kentish hop-field and unquestionably more attractive. The exuberant vines climb round tall stout poles, their full shady garlands of foliage rising like fountains of green, or spilling downwards; producing the

Plate 19

effect of abundance and darkness so often referred to in native spells (Pl. 21). Even the gardens already harvested, in which here and there a banana tree is left growing and the old crop of sweet potatoes still continues, have their charm, the charm of an old untidy orchard. In the marshy districts we might pass by a taro garden with its array of scarecrows and wind rattles, a new stout fence encircling the low flat surface of broad green leaves. We would meet a somewhat different picture in the south, where patches of fertile soil are scarce and small gardens are often wedged in between jungle, mangrove swamp, and stony coral outcrops. Plate 22 shows such a taro garden. The new plants are seen growing among large heaps of stones; a small *kamkokola* stands near the well-built fence. On the other side of the fence is the site of an old garden. Walking along the coral ridge we would, from time to time, come across a more or less deep hole in the dead coral filled with black humus, and planted with the large variety of yam which grows specially well in this soil, the vine trained round one or two supports and spreading over the rim.

On a rough computation I estimated that about one-fifth or perhaps one-quarter of the total area is under tillage at any one time. The cultivation of this area is very varied because, in the first place, the natives have two entirely different types of garden—the *tapopu*, exclusively planted with taro, and the gardens in which the yam predominates; and in the second place,

487

Plate 20

these latter are of two kinds, the earlier, *kaymugwa*, and the main gardens, *kaymata*. The *kaymugwa* are made on a smaller scale and planted with very much more mixed crops than the *kaymata*, which are almost all taytu. With the various stages of decaying, flourishing and harvested crops, the occasional plantations of banana and sugar-cane, and the cultivated holes in the coral ridge, the complexity of gardening and its claim on human attention and labour become patent.*

A closer inspection of the gardens reveals other interesting details. For instance, some plots are much more carefully worked than others. These are usually the most advanced, and the surrounding fence, the vine supports and certain large magical structures called *kamkokola*, display a better finish and are of bigger proportions. Usually these plots will be the first we meet on entering the gardens from the village. They have a special name, *leywota*, and we shall designate them throughout as "standard plots." They are generally cultivated by some important persons and play a leading part in magic and in gardening.† They are in a way representative plots as the work on them has to be done with full aesthetic finish and the maximum of perfection;

*On the relation between the early and the main gardens, see Note 2 in Sec. 4 of App. II [Malinowski's note].
† See Note 3 in Sec. 4 of App. II [Malinowski's note].

Plate 21

on them no magical rite may be omitted, and some ceremonies are performed on them only, though meant indirectly to benefit the rest of the gardens. These plots are the pride of the community and the focus of all magical activities.

Thus even an occasional visitor would find the Trobriand gardens not only attractive but intriguing in their detail. The ethnographer finds them, even during his preliminary explorations, full of interest and significance. The obviously non-utilitarian, geometrical erections at the corners of each plot, the *kamkokola*, promise well for what might be called the magical or esoteric dimension in gardening. A careful inspection of the corners on which the biggest *kamkokola* stand, the "magical corners" as we shall call them, would reveal further details: a small construction of sticks, *si bwala baloma*, "the house of spirits" as it is called by the natives; a miniature *kamkokola* made of slender sticks; a group of special plants leaning against the *kamkokola*; some herbs inserted into it; and again, a strand of tough grass wound round the pole. Sooner or later the ethnographer discovers that these are traces of magical activities, and indeed, in any of his walks he might come across the magician leaning over a *kamkokola* and reciting his spells. On Plate 23 which was taken during an actual performance, we see a clump of plants in the magical corner. The large *kamkokola*, as well as the miniature replica, can also be seen, together with a row of large poles, ready to be put

12

489

Plate 22

up as yam supports (cf. Ch. III, Sec. 4). Starting from such visible signs, he is led gradually to discover the world of mythology and magic, the ideas of value and the sentiments of a sociological nature which surround gardening.

When he walks with the natives through a well-tilled fully developed 13 garden in a year of plenty, he realises that to the Trobriander the whole garden oozes prosperity (*malia*). When he watches the natives at their communal work during the preliminary clearing or the planting of the seeds, when he accompanies a family at some other stage of gardening and spends the whole day with them in their open-air work, he comes to understand how much of sociable life centres round the gardens and gardening. Spice is given to routine by competitive efforts—at times on a tribal scale, at times in a much smaller way as between families or individuals.

To possess a good and showy garden is not only a matter of pride, it is 14 also a privilege. Only chiefs, or those who make their gardens for a chief, are allowed to have absolutely first-class gardens. For men of lesser rank to be too successful would entail serious consequences to themselves.

A man who had no gardens would be an outcast, whereas a man who 15 for one reason or another is no good at gardening is an object for contempt. Everybody has to make gardens, and the more garden plots a man is capable of tilling, the greater is his renown. The average number that a strong, grown-up married man can manage with the help of his wife is three to six. A boy

Plate 23

or youth would make one or two; exceptionally strong men eight to ten. But we shall return to the question of work and its division between the men and the women; and to the question of land tenure and the right of each man to cultivate as many plots as he needs (cf. Sec. 8 of this chapter; and Chs. XI and XII).

The age at which boys begin to make their own gardens is exceedingly 16 early. A small boy in Omarakana,* by name Bwoysabwoyse, honoured me with his friendship and often visited me, his favourite place to dispose his person being a five-pound tin of biscuits, whence he watched the proceedings in the tent. Even on such an unmonumental basis he looked diminutive, and he could hardly have been more than six years old. When walking through the gardens once, I was told that we were crossing the plot of Bwoysabwoyse. I looked upon this simply as a joke, and it was only after I had received various corroborating statements and had myself seen him and other small boys at garden work, that I was convinced that such tiny children actually did make their own gardens. The heavier labour is, of course, done for them by their elders, but they have to work seriously for many hours at cleaning, planting and weeding, and it is by no means a mild amusement to them, but rather a stern duty and a matter for keen ambition.

* A village on the main island [Editors' note].

In gardening, then, we have a big department of tribal life. It has its 17
spiritual depth in magic and in the mystical powers displayed solemnly and
publicly by the hereditary officiating magician of the community. His office
again is backed by a mythology closely connected with native ideas of the
original association between man and the soil from which his ancestors have
sprung (cf. Ch. XII, especially Sec. 1).

THE PRACTICAL TASKS OF THE GOOD GARDENER, *TOKWAYBAGULA*

Let us now pass from our territorial survey and follow the seasonal round of 18
garden work. This falls into four main divisions. First comes the preparing of
the soil by cutting down the scrub and burning it after it has dried.* The
second stage consists in clearing the soil, planting, erecting the yam supports,
and making the fence.† The third stage has for the most part to be left to
nature; the seeds sprout, the vines climb upwards round the supports, the
taro plants develop their big leaves and their roots; while human intervention is confined to weeding, which is done by women, and a preliminary
pruning or thinning out of the tubers and training of vines by the men.‡
Meanwhile the magician is at work, casting spells favourable to growth. Finally, after the crops have matured, we come to the last stage, the harvest.§
Apart from the magic of growth just mentioned, each new type of work is
inaugurated by a magical rite, and these form a series which correspond to
the sequence of practical activities.

Garden work is never done in heavy rain or in windy and what to the 19
natives would be cold weather. During the intolerably hot hours of the day,
at the season of calms, the gardeners usually return home or rest in the shade.
Whether for communal or individual or family work, the farmers generally
go early to the gardens, return between ten and eleven to the village, and
then start out again, perhaps after a light meal and a siesta, to work from
about three or four o'clock till nightfall. Since some of the gardens directly
adjoin the village and the most distant are not more than half an hour's walk

---

* Looking at the Chart of Time-reckoning (Fig. 3) we see in column 7 (main gardens) that the
  first stage falls in the thirteenth moon, and in column 8 (early gardens) in the eleventh.
  Taro gardens are more complicated because the cycles are shorter (cf. Ch. X, Sec. 2) and
  we have two periods of plenty and preparation, falling about the third and fourth moon,
  and about the eighth and ninth [Malinowski's note].

† Column 7 of the chart (main gardens) shows that this stage occupies moons 2, 3, and 4; column
  8 (early gardens) moons 13, 1 and 2; column 9 (taro gardens) moons 4 and 9 [Malinowski's
  note].

‡ Column 7 (main gardens) moons 5 to 8; column 8 (early gardens), moons 3 to 6 or 7. This stage
  is not noted in column 9 (taro gardens), but would fall in moons 6 and 7, and 11 and 12
  [Malinowski's note].

§ Column 7 (main gardens), moons 10 to 12; column 8 (early gardens), moons 8–10; column 9
  (taro gardens), moons 8 and 13. Taro is also harvested on the early gardens in the fourth
  moon, and on the main gardens in the sixth moon [Malinowski's note].

away, there is no difficulty in interrupting and resuming work at the convenience of the moment.

The technical efficiency of the work is great. This is the more remark- 20 able because the outfit of the Trobriand farmer is of the most rudimentary nature. It consists of a digging-stick (*dayma*), an axe (*kema*), an adze (*ligogu*) and, last but not least, of the human hand, which in many of their activities serves as an implement and often comes into actual contact with the soil. The digging-stick is used for turning up the soil at planting and thinning, at harvest and weeding. Axe and adze play an important part in the cutting of the scrub, the thinning out of the tubers and at harvesting. Skill with the hand is important during clearing, planting, weeding, thinning and at harvesting. These then are the tasks and the tools of a "good gardener" (*tokwaybagula*)— one of the proudest titles which a Trobriander can enjoy.

But besides hard work, and a technical skill based on a sound knowl- 21 edge of the soil and its properties, of the weather and its vicissitudes, of the nature of crops and the need of intelligent adaptation to the soil, another element enters into Trobriand gardening which, to the natives, is as essential to success as husbandry. This is magic.

THE MAGIC OF THE GARDEN

It may be said that among the forces and beliefs which bear upon and regu- 22 late gardening, magic is the most important, apart, of course, from the practical work.

Garden magic (*megwa towosi* or simply *towosi*) is in the Trobriands a 23 public and official service. It is performed by the garden magician, also called *towosi*, for the benefit of the community. Everybody has to take part in some of the ceremonial and have the rest performed on his account. Everybody also has to contribute to certain payments for magic. The magic being done for each village community as a whole, every village and at times every subdivision of a village has its own *towosi* (garden magician) and its own system of *towosi* magic, and this is perhaps the main expression of village unity.

Magic and practical work are, in native ideas, inseparable from each 24 other, though they are not confused. Garden magic and garden work run in one intertwined series of consecutive effort, form one continuous story, and must be the subject-matter of one narrative.

To the natives, magic is as indispensable to the success of gardens as 25 competent and effective husbandry. It is essential to the fertility of the soil: "The garden magician utters magic by mouth; the magical virtue enters the soil" (Text 36, Part V, Div. VII, Sec. 2). Magic is to them an almost natural element in the growth of the gardens. I have often been asked: "What is the magic which is done in your country over your gardens—is it like ours or is it different?" They did not seem at all to approve of our ways as I described them, saying that we either do not perform any magic at all, or else let our "misinaris" do the magic wholesale in the *bwala tapwaroro*—the house of the divine service. They doubted whether our yams could "sprout" properly, "rise up in foliage" and "swell." In the course of one such conversation, held in Omarakana with Kayla'i and Gatoyawa, I jotted down the following pointed comment on our method (Text 81, Part V, Div XI, Sec. 9): "The missionaries state: 'We make divine service and because of this the gardens grow.' This is a lie." It should be noted that the native word for "lie" covers anything from a purely accidental mistake, a *bona fide* flight of imagination not pretending to be anything else, to the most blatant lie. The natives do not accuse the missionaries of deception, but rather of a certain feeble-mindedness or, as Professor Lévy-Bruhl would put it, of a prelogical mentality when it comes to gardening magic.

I am afraid that converted natives who act as missionary teachers have *towosi* magic surreptitiously chanted over their gardens. And white traders married to native women have, under the pressure of public opinion and of the wife's influence, to engage the help of the local *towosi* to chant over their gardens; so monstrous did it appear to everybody that a cultivated patch of soil should go without the benefit of magic. 26

The round of gardening opens with a conference, summoned by the chief and held in front of the magician's house, to decide where the gardens are going to be made, who will cultivate such and such a plot, and when the work will be started.* Directly in connexion with this, the magician prepares for the first big ceremony, which is to inaugurate the whole gardening sequence, while the villagers procure a quantity of special food, usually fish, to be offered as a ceremonial payment to the magician. A small portion of this gift is exposed in the evening to the ancestral spirits, sacrificially and with an invocation† the bulk is eaten by the magician and his kinsmen. Then he utters a lengthy spell over certain leaves which will be used on the morrow. Next morning the magician and the men of the village go to the gardens and the inaugural ceremony takes place. The *towosi* strikes the ground and rubs it with the charmed leaves—acts which symbolise in speech and sentiment the garden magic as a whole. This rite officially opens the season's gardening as well as its first stage: the cutting of the scrub. Thereafter each stage of practical work is ushered in by the appropriate ceremony. After the cut scrub is sufficiently dried, he imposes a taboo on garden work, ritually burns the refuse, and introduces the planting of certain minor crops by a series of ceremonies extending over a few days. Later on, a sequence of rites inaugurate successively the main planting of yams, the erection of vine supports, weeding, preliminary thinning out, and finally of harvesting. At the same time in a parallel sequence of rites and spells, the garden magician assists the growth 27

---

* Cf. App. I, Comparative Table of Magic and Work, for the correlation between practical work and magic. [Malinowski's note].
† Cf. Note 8 in App. II, Sec. 4 [Malinowski's note].

of the crops. He helps the plants to sprout, to burst into leaf, to climb; he makes their roots bud, develop and swell; and he produces the rich garlands of exuberant foliage which intertwine among the vine supports.

Each rite is first performed on one of the standard magical plots, the 28 *leywota*. This is important from the practical point of view, because the men who cultivate these plots are bound to keep time with the rhythm of magical ritual and not lag behind. At the same time they must also be worked with special care. They are scrupulously cleared and cleaned, perfect seed tubers are selected, and since they are always made on good soil, they represent not only a very high standard of garden work but also of gardening success. Thus, in punctuality, quality and finish of work, and in perfection of results, these plots set a definite pattern to all the others, and this excellence is mainly attributed to the influence of magic.

THE GARDEN WIZARD

The *towosi* or garden magician is an hereditary official of every village com- 29 munity. As a matter of fact, the position of *towosi* coincides with that of the Chief or the head-man, if not in identity of person, at least in the principle of lineage. In native mythology and legal theory, it is always the head of the kinship group owning a village who is the garden magician. This man, how-ever, frequently delegates his duties to his younger brother, his matrilineal nephew, or his son. Such handing over of the office of garden magician was especially frequent in the lineage of the paramount chiefs of Omarakana, on whom the duties of charming the gardens weighed too heavily.

The mythological system of the Trobrianders establishes a very close 30 connexion between the soil and human beings. The origins of humanity are in the soil; the first ancestors of each local group or sub-clan—for these two are identical—are always said to have emerged from a certain spot, carrying their garden magic with them (cf. Ch. XII, Sec. 1). It is the spot from which they emerged which is usually, though not always, the sub-clan's soil, the territory to which it has an hereditary right.* This hereditary ownership of the soil—mythological, legal, moral and economic—is vested in the head-man; and it is in virtue of these combined claims that he exercises the func-tion of garden magician. "I strike the ground," as I was told by Bagido'u, the proudest garden magician of the island, "because I am the owner of the soil." The first person meant, "I, as the representative of my sub-clan and my lineage."

We shall see in our study of magical texts (Part VII) that the traditional 31 filiation† of garden magic is kept alive by every officiating magician. In some

---

* At times a sub-clan obtains rights of ownership in a district to which they have migrated. Cf. Ch. XII, Sec. 3 [Malinowski's note].
† *Filiation* refers to principles of descent or derivation [Editors' note]. For an account of the principles of inheritance, see Part I, Sec. 9 [Malinowski's note].

of the spells he has to repeat the whole series of the names of those who have wielded the magic before him. At one or two stages of his magic, he offers a ceremonial oblation, consisting of a minute portion of cooked food taken from the substantial present he has received, to the spirits of his predecessor. Such presents from the community are the expression of their gratitude and their submission to him rather than a commercial gift. They are the recognition of his services, and in this spirit they are offered to him and to his forerunners. This ritual offering of food, which is an integral part of the magical proceedings, is called *ula'ula*.

The members of the community, however, usually offer the magician 32 other presents as well. At the beginning of the gardening cycle he is usually given small gifts of food, such as coconuts or bananas; or else he may accept a bunch of betel-nut or such objects of daily use as baskets, axes, mats, spears or cooking-pots. This type of gift, called *sousula*, is meant to repay him for the hardships undergone in the exercise of his calling. As one of my *towosi* friends explained to me, putting it in the concrete form characteristic of native utterance: "When I go about making magic in the gardens, and I hurt my foot, I exclaim: '*Wi! Iwoye kaygegu; gala sene si sousula.*' " "Oh! (the object) has hit my foot; not very much their *sousula* payment (i.e. they don't give me enough to repay me for all my hardships)."

Again from time to time the magician receives a present of valuables 33 called *sibugibogi*: a large ceremonial axe-blade, belts or ornaments of shell-disks or a pair of arm-shells. This gift is usually offered after a bad season to propitiate him, or else at an especially good harvest to express gratitude.

In the carrying out of his duties, the magician is usually helped by some 34 younger men: his younger brothers and his sisters' sons are his natural successors, whom he will have in due course to instruct in magic, teaching them the spells, telling them the substances to be used, advising them how to carry out the ritual and what personal observances they have to keep. Of this instruction, the most difficult is the learning of the formulae. Even this, however, does not require much special training, for garden magic is a public ceremonial, the spells are heard often by everybody, while the ritual is well known and anyone is able to tell you exactly what observances the magician has to keep. Those who have to inherit garden magic and practise it, and are therefore more interested in it, will be acquainted with every detail early in their life. They are the magician's natural help-mates and acolytes.* Whenever the ceremony is cumbersome, they take part in it; or they repeat on other garden plots the rite which the chief magician performs on the standard plots. And they assist him often in the collecting of ingredients or preparing of magical mixtures and structures.

Besides these, he has non-official helpers among the younger people and 35 children, who carry some of his paraphernalia, assist him in putting up certain magical signs and do other such minor services.

---

* One who assists in a religious or magical service [Editors' note].

I have just mentioned the magician's taboos. These consist almost exclu- 36 sively in the abstention from certain foods. In no circumstances may he touch the meat of certain animals and fish, or eat certain vegetables. Generally these are sympathetically connected with the substances which he uses in his ritual or with the aims of his magic. The magician is also not allowed to partake of the new crops until after the performance of a special ceremony, which consists as a rule in an offering to the ancestral spirits. A third type of abstention is the fast which he has to keep on the days on which he performs any ceremony (cf. Ch. II, Sec. 4).

From all this it can be seen that a garden magician's office in the Tro- 37 briands is no sinecure.* Not only does he have to carry out a series of inaugural rites, following closely the practical work of the gardens, not only does he stimulate the growth of the plants in his spells of encouragement; but he also has to observe a system of by no means easy abstentions and fasts, and last, but not least, to carry out a considerable amount of practical work and control.

The garden magician is regarded by the community as the garden ex- 38 pert. He, together perhaps with his elder kinsman, the chief, decides what fields are to be cultivated in a given year. Later on, at each stage, he has to find out how the work in the gardens stands; how the crops are sprouting, budding, ripening, and then he has to give the initiative to the next stage. He must watch the weather and the state of the cut scrub before the burning. He has to see whether the gardens are sufficiently advanced before he performs the planting magic, and so at every stage. And when he finds that people are lagging behind, or that some of them, by neglecting a communal duty, such as the fencing of the garden plots, are endangering the interests of the whole community, it is his function to upbraid the culprits and induce them to mend their ways and to work energetically.

Time after time, as I sat in my tent reading or looking over my notes, 39 or talking to some of my native friends, I would hear the voice of Bagido'u of Omarakana or Navavile of Oburaku or Motago'i of Sinaketa† rising from somewhere in front of his house. In a public harangue, he would accuse such and such a one of not having completed his share of the fence, thus leaving a wide gap in the common enclosure through which the bush-pigs or wallabies could enter; and now that the seeds were in the garden and beginning to sprout, the wild animals would soon be attracted and might do a great deal of damage. Or again he would announce that the cut scrub was practically dry and that the burning would be inaugurated in three or four days. Or again he would impose one of the public taboos on work, saying that as in a few days the large *kamkokola* would be erected, everybody must stop all other work, and bring in the long stout poles necessary for the magical structure and for the final yam supports.

---

* A sinecure is a position that provides an income but requires little work [Editors' note].
† Omarakana, Oburaku, and Sinaketa are Trobriand villages [Editors' note].

Thus the *towosi* exercises not merely an indirect influence on garden 40 work, by giving the initiative and inaugurating the successive stages, by imposing taboos, and by setting the pace, but he also directly supervises a number of activities. In order to do this he has constantly to visit the gardens, survey the work, discover shortcomings, and last but not least, note any special excellencies. For public praise from the *towosi* is a highly appreciated reward and a great stimulus to the perfect gardener, the *tokwaybagula.*

The natives are deeply convinced that through his magic the *towosi* 41 controls the forces of fertility, and in virtue of this they are prepared to admit that he should also control the work of man. And let us remember, his magical power, his expert knowledge and his traditional filiation to his magical ancestors are reinforced by the fact that he is the head-man, or, in a community of rank, a chief of high lineage, or a nephew or younger brother of such. When the office is in the hands of the chief's son, he again only holds it as the delegate of the rightful head of the community (cf. Ch. XII, Secs. 2 and 3). Furthermore, the acts of magic are an organising influence in communal life: firstly because they punctuate the progress of activities at regular intervals and impose a series of taboo days or rest periods; and secondly because each rite must be fully performed on the standard plots, and these plots must be perfectly prepared for it, whereby a model is established for the whole village (cf. App. I). Magic therefore is not merely a mental force, making for a more highly organised attitude of mind in each individual, it is also a social force, closely connected with the economic organisation of garden work. Yet magic and technical activities are very sharply distinguished by the natives in theory and in practice—but to this point we shall have to return presently.

QUESTIONS ABOUT MALINOWSKI'S DISCOURSE COMMUNITY AND HIS CONCERNS IN THIS SELECTION

1. How does Malinowski do his research? How does he seem to gather his information?
2. Do you think that the Trobriand Islanders associate so many activities with the system of gardening primarily because gardening is all they have to do? Or is it because gardening is essential to their survival?
3. The garden wizards seem to be in "no-lose" situations. If the people have a good crop, they give credit to the wizard. If they have a bad crop, they think they have displeased the wizard. What do you think accounts for the wizard's getting into such a position?
4. How does gardening affect the Trobrianders' economy? Social organization? Political power?
5. Why does Malinowski focus so closely on work *and* magic? Why does he choose not to give one more prominence than the other?
6. Why do you think Malinowski pays as much attention as he does to the lan-

guage of the Trobriand Islanders? Why does he cite words from their language in this essay and not just paraphrase them?

7. Does Trobriand society seem to be one in which serious strife could break out? Why or why not?

8. In what specific ways in this selection do you see Malinowski's functional concern for networks, for interconnections between things?

QUESTIONS ABOUT MALINOWSKI'S RHETORICAL STRATEGIES

1. Malinowski addresses the reader quite often, indicating what material he has covered and what he will go on to cover. Do you find this practice helpful or somewhat obtrusive? Why does he use the pronoun *we* so often?

2. Malinowski includes many cross-references in this selection. Does that suggest anything about the nature of his work? About the nature of his primary audience? About the nature of his discourse community?

3. Why do you think Malinowski makes the point that the hands of the islanders often come "into actual contact with the soil"?

4. Examine the last paragraph of section 2. How does Malinowski conclude this section? How effective are his strategies?

5. Where does Malinowski make comparisons to try to make his points about the Trobriand landscape clearer? Do such comparisons reveal anything about his view of his audience?

6. How does Malinowski enliven his general point about the age when boys begin to make their own gardens? Is this a technique that you would recommend to all anthropologists? Why or why not?

7. In his sentences, Malinowski uses many series—of clauses, verbs, direct objects, and the like. Is there anything in his subject matter that would encourage the use of such series? What do the series allow him to accomplish in general?

8. What does Malinowski's attitude toward the Trobriand Islanders seem to be? On what do you base your judgment? Is any part of this attitude reflected in the following comment by Malinowski: "I am afraid that converted natives who act as missionary teachers have *towosi* magic surreptitiously chanted over their gardens"?

WRITING FROM WITHIN AND ABOUT THE SOCIAL SCIENCES: SOCIAL AND CULTURAL ANTHROPOLOGY

Writing for Yourself

1. Explore in your journal how you felt the last time you experienced a culture alien to you.

2. Explore in your journal whether belief in the supernatural is or is not a universal phenomenon.

Writing for Nonacademic Audiences

1. The Trobriand Islanders took joy in a well-cultivated, aesthetically pleasing garden. For your school newspaper, write a humorous column (about 500 words) about how much joy in the well-made product people take today.
2. Contemporary North American gardeners might feel that the magical rites of the Trobriand Islanders are silly and unnecessary. But perhaps it is the case that even North Americans use certain gardening rites: planting and watering under a full moon, putting in tomatoes on Memorial Day and using metal cages rather than stakes to insure good growth, not picking turnips until the first frost, planting a row of marigolds to protect a garden from rabbits. Write a 500-word feature article for a community journal circulated in a rural county near your hometown in which you respond to the question of whether gardeners' rituals are "silly and unnecessary."

Writing for Academic Audiences

1. For the Trobriand Islanders, the title "good gardener" was highly honored. For a course in the sociology of the contemporary United States, write a 500-word expository paper on the titles currently honored in the United States.
2. Explore the origin of the word *human.* Then write a 250-word opinion paper for a course in world mythologies on why various cultures have seen human beings as arising from the soil.
3. For an anthropology course in the cultures of the islands of the South Seas, write a 750-word paper in which you defend a position on whether it was or was not good for the Trobriand Islanders to let children start working the gardens at such a young age.
4. Malinowski shows that in many ways gardening was at the center of the Islanders' lives. For a course in the sociology of contemporary North America, write a 1,000-word analytical paper on what you see as the center of contemporary North American society.
5. Can an anthropologist ever really know what another culture is like? Answer this question in a 1,000-word persuasive paper for a seminar in methods in anthropology.

Harold Dwight Lasswell

(1902–1978)

Harold Lasswell was one of the most prestigious political scientists of the mid-twentieth century. Educated at the universities of Chicago, Geneva, Paris, London, and Berlin, Lasswell focused his attention on investigating the nature of political power, emphasizing especially the relationship between politics and the individual personality. Though he taught at such prestigious schools as the University of Chicago, the City University of New York, Temple University, and Yale University, where he was a fellow at the Center for Advanced Study of the Behavioral Sciences, his fellow political scientists were not quick to accept his ideas. From 1937 to 1950, no political science journal would publish his articles. The importance of his work was not officially recognized by his colleagues until 1955, when he was elected president of the American Political Science Association.

Lasswell was intrigued by the mechanics of the human mind, and he examined the way personality and behavior influenced political power and action. (One practical outcome of this interest was that between 1939 and 1945, when Lasswell was director of war communications research at the Library of Congress, he was able to predict many present-day dictatorships.) His discourse community, then, is behavioral political science, and this suggests his acceptance of many of the assumptions of behaviorists like B. F. Skinner.

During the 1950s particularly, Lasswell's psychoanalytic approach to politics led to innovations in conventional political science. It contributed to a more astute analysis of the study of political roles and political symbols. It contributed to a more technically exact study of the source of public policy, using scientific methods of observation and recording. It contributed to a focus on the individual rather than only on large social groups. In fact, little contemporary North American political theory is uninfluenced by Lasswell's work.

The following essay is from Lasswell's collection The Analysis of Political Behaviour.

THE DEVELOPING SCIENCE
OF DEMOCRACY*

The developing science of democracy is an arsenal of implements for the 1
achievement of democratic ideals. We know enough to know that democracies do not know how to live; they perish through ignorance—ignorance of
how to sustain the will to live and of how to discover the means of life.
Without knowledge, democracy will surely fall. With knowledge, democracy
may succeed.

The significant advances of our time have not been in the discovery of 2
new definitions of moral values or even in the skilful derivation of old definitions from more universal propositions. Our inheritance of brief definitions
has been adequate. The advances of our time have been in the technique of
relating them to reality.

In the process science has clarified morals. This, indeed, is the distinc- 3
tive contribution of science to morality. Science can ascertain the means appropriate to the completion of moral impulse—means at once consistent with
general definitions of morality and compatible with the fulfilment of moral
purpose. The traditional sentences that define and justify morals, in common
with all such sentences, use words of ambiguous reference. Each sentence is
itself part of reality but refers to a larger reality. Standing alone, however,
such a sentence is cryptic and fragmentary. The function of science is to complete it.

General sentences must be made part of a special language composed 4
of postulates, definitions, and operational rules. The rules must specify how
the key terms are to be used by observers who may take up various standpoints for the observation of reality. For artistic and propaganda purposes
we may tolerate dangling sentences of ambiguous reference. But as students
of politics we are seriously concerned with connecting them with the realities
of Cabinet meetings, Congressional inquiries, trade association conventions,
and general staff conferences; hence it is necessary to participate in a long
process of disciplined clarification.

Consider any one-sentence definition of the value that distinguishes 5
democratic societies from other forms of human association. We may affirm
that the democratic value is regard for the dignity of man. Hence society is
democratic when it puts this value into practice; it is then a commonwealth
of mutual deference. Just what do these words mean? How can the observer
of political events decide when to use the term "democratic" in a sense consistent with the definition?

---

*From *The Future of Government in the United States, Essays in Honour of Charles E. Merriam*
[edited by Leonard D. White] (Chicago, 1942) [Lasswell's note].

Are we to determine the truth about a given community by limiting our 6
attention to the government or by examining the structure of business corporations, ecclesiastical organizations, and fraternal orders as well? Are we
to instruct observers to rely upon the clauses of written constitutions or upon
official election returns? Are we to instruct them to look beyond the official
figures to determine to what extent those who vote feel themselves free of
intimidation? Must they go beyond these questions to explore deeper attitudes, such as the degree to which the members of the community have a
lively sense of genuine participation in the determination of democracy?
Without such accompanying specifications, no definition of democracy that
purports to relate to reality can be other than word-mongering.

The friends of democracy who have turned to science have been acutely 7
dissatisfied with the ambiguity of inherited political, social, and philosophical literature. To speak of the movement toward science as a revolt against
philosophy is to fall into error. It was not impatience with democratic morals
that led to the de-emphasizing of general definitions; it was discontent with
the chronic incompleteness of formulation in the traditional literature. The
turning to the specific is more properly understood as a stampede to complete
philosophy, to reconsider every generality for the purpose of relating it to
observable reality.

The mood of impatience was directed as much against speculative sci- 8
ence as against philosophy, whenever speculative science was cultivated far
beyond the limits of available data. This attitude is exemplified in what Wes-
ley Mitchell wrote about his student impressions of philosophy and economic
theory: "Give me premises and I could spin speculations by the yard. Also I
knew my 'deductions' were futile . . . [Veblen] could do no more than make
certain conclusions plausible—like the rest."*

Mitchell, and his American fellow-exponents of the scientific study of 9
society, lived near the end of a long epoch of cultural optimism, in which
democratic values had moved triumphantly toward universal acceptance.
Democratic doctrine was affirmed by both the rulers of society and the most
powerful exponents of revolutionary change. The Marxists did not reject democracy; on the contrary, they declared that the only path to democracy was
the overthrow of capitalism. They acknowledged the historical connection
between free enterprise and free society; but they denied that the capitalistic
method of organizing the productive forces was any longer widening the area
of human freedom. On the contrary, the Marxists suggested that the inexorable march of monopoly spelled the doom of freedom until the inevitable
triumph of the revolutionary proletariat.

There were two replies to the Marxist indictment—to ignore the facts 10
or to restudy them. In America the "individualistic" attitude was to deny the

---

Methods in Social Science; A Case Book [edited by Stuart A. Rice] (Chicago, 1931), pp. 676–7
[Lasswell's note].

facts, to affirm the substantial identity between democratic values and the existing state of affairs. To liberals, and particularly to middle-western liberals, certain facts were all too conspicuous. By assembling them, they hoped to bring reality into closer conformity with doctrine. In intellectual circles hope of reform, not certainty of revolution, was the dominant view of the future.* In such a setting democratic values were not in question.

THE ENLARGING FOCUS OF ATTENTION

The urge for relevance has enormously enlarged the permissible focus of attention among professional students of government in America. Most of those who completed their graduate work during the 'nineties were equipped to study political doctrine, public law, and comparative government (with special reference to Great Britain and the United States). During subsequent decades the leading members of the profession steadily enlarged the scope of their studies to include political parties, pressure groups, and administrative agencies. As they moved from the letter of the law to the significant features of the total context of socio-personal relations, they dealt with progressively more subtle themes connected with public opinion and political leadership, and they enlarged the geographical range of their minds to include the whole panorama of world events.   11

The expanding focus of scholarly attention is aptly exemplified in the publications of Charles E. Merriam, who began his career with *History of the Theory of Sovereignty Since Rousseau* (New York, 1900)—a conventional study of political doctrine. Subsequent books contributed to the discovery of the larger environment; there were studies of parties, public opinion, administration, leadership, world politics (the last being the "Civic Training Series"). Meanwhile, other colleagues were following similar lines of development. Charles A. Beard began with a study in English institutional history, *The Office of Justice of the Peace* (New York, 1904), and went ahead to explore the total economic and cultural setting of American institutions. He studied administrative processes not only in the United States but in Yugoslavia and Tokyo and in recent years dealt with national policy in the light of world movements.   12

NEW PROCEDURES OF OBSERVATION

The expanding focus of attention brought with it the use of new procedures for the observation of reality. By tradition students of government were chiefly collectors, making use of records of events they did not directly see. They depended upon historical documents and court reports. In the new search for the total relevant context, they relied in greater degree on more   13

* Academic figures like Daniel De Leon, Columbia University, were most exceptional [Lasswell's note].

direct methods of observation, like the interview or direct participation. Vigorous personalities, like James Bryce and A. Lawrence Lowell, had always kept alive the more active elements of the tradition that made such men as De Tocqueville possible. There has, of course, always been a struggle within the breast of the scholar between to "wait and read" and to "go and see." When the scholar has a lecture-room the temptation is to narrow his orbit between the library and the podium, resisting the centrifugal lure of the great beyond. In recent times the quest of reality has somewhat neutralized the centripetal forces of desk and rostrum, so that procedures of observation have been more widely utilized.

The repertory of procedures has itself expanded to meet new demands. 14 Random personal contact has been supplemented by the use of carefully prepared questionnaires or polls given to representative groups. Time has been devoted to the preparation of forms for entering and tabulating the primary data of observation. In this connection the methods of the social anthropologist have been particularly stimulating; the observer of non-literate societies has learned to discipline his casual impressions by candid records.*

COLLECTIVE FACT-GATHERING

Significantly enough, fact-gathering operations have become more collective 15 as they became more abundant. Many of the facts contributed to political science have been observed by professors who had the aid of students or research assistants. This is the provenience of most of the material collected under the auspices of the Social Science Research Committee of the University of Chicago, or the Institute of Human Relations at Yale. But special research bureaux, often unconnected with universities, have contributed extensively to recent science. These agencies are more free than teaching departments to adopt strict standards with regard to research personnel and to develop a corps of helots to perform routine operations. Teaching departments are more tolerant of "time out" for courses and seminars, less careful of deadlines and somewhat more impatient with the deserving "mediocrity" than the more professionalized bureau of investigation. Conspicuous among the private bureaux are the National Bureau of Economic Research and the Brookings Institution. However, the government itself is playing a more prominent rôle in reporting on reality, notably through such executive agencies as the National Resources Planning Board and such congressional channels as the Temporary National Economic Committee.

It is significant that when Charles E. Merriam surveyed the state of 16 political research at the end of World War I he emphasized the under-equipment of the college professors of government, who were supposed to contribute to their subject but who were often driven to thresh over old straw through

---

*Bronislaw Malinowski wrote forcefully of method in *Argonauts of the Western Pacific* (London, 1922) [Lasswell's note].

sheer lack of facilities for harvesting new facts.* The idea of a permanent
corps of research assistants comparable with the laboratory technicians of the
physical scientist was all too new. Handicapped by lack of funds for travel
and for advanced study, each successive crop of students was thrown back
upon its parochial frame of reference, destitute of opportunity to explore the
larger world about which they were nominally qualified to speak. Hence the
heavy stress by the fact-gatherers upon the need of ample funds for large-
scale training programmes and upon the advantages of continuous collaboration in the prosecution of research. Hence, too, the institutional form of
the Social Science Research Council, the university social science research
council, and the National Resources Planning Board of the federal government.

NEW IDEAS OF THE SCOPE OF POLITICS

Sweeping changes in the focus of scholarly effort do not fail to bring about a   17
revision of basic concepts, especially with regard to the scope of political
science itself. Many American students had identified their field of investigation with government, but they had failed to distinguish between the
meaning of government as a local institution and government as a function
of society. As a function of society, government is the making of important
decisions. What is locally called government often has very little to do with
this function. We know that what is called government in a mill town may
have but a modicum of influence on important decisions; they may be made
by the board of directors of the mill. If the function of government is the
subject of research, the mill directors are the ones to be investigated, not the
shadowmen locally called government officials.

As the scope of scholarly attention widened, more students of govern-   18
ment became conscious of the difference between government as a social
function and government as a locally named institution. They reached out
after definitions of political science that would clarify their new feeling for
relevance.†

It would be idle to assert that a conceptual or a terminological consen-   19
sus has developed concerning the scope of political science. In terms congenial to the present writer, the function of government is power. (For the
moment we will speak of the function of government or politics interchange-
ably.) Power means the making of important decisions, and the importance
of decisions is measured by their effect on the distribution of values. Values
are such objects of desire as deference, safety, income. The power of individuals and groups is measured by the degree of their participation in the making of important decisions.

---

* *New Aspects of Politics* (Chicago, 1925) [Lasswell's note].
† See Merriam, Charles E., *Political Power; Its Composition and Incidence* (New York, 1934);
　　Catlin, G. E. G., *The Science and Methods of Politics* (New York, 1927) [Lasswell's note].

The definition of government and politics varies according to the nature 20 and variety of values taken into consideration. For certain purposes it is convenient to circumscribe the scope of political science to the study of power. For more comprehensive comparisons the scope may be enlarged to include the study of other forms of deference, such as respect and insight. For certain broad problems of comparative politics it is expedient to conceive of the scope of political science as embracing the distribution of safety and income as well as deference. At this point the subject-matter of political science approaches that of the social sciences as a whole and merges with it. The most inclusive definition of political science thus speaks of it as the study of influence and the influential.*

The enlarged view of the scope of political science just referred to is not 21 confined to the limits of the United States. On the contrary, parallel processes of generalization have gone forward throughout Western European social science. Never officially recognized as a separate university discipline in Europe, none the less the "sociology of politics" has been cultivated by specialists who sought an inclusive frame of reference for their study of changing distributions of value.†

THE SCIENCE OF DEMOCRACY

With the more inclusive science of politics many special sciences are possible. 22 A special science is concerned with the fulfillment and preservation of specific forms of state and society. The science of democracy—one of these special sciences—bears much the same relation to general political science that medicine has to biology. Medicine is a branch of the total field of biology, limiting itself to a single frame of reference, the disease process. Democratic science is restricted to the understanding and possible control of the factors upon which democracy depends.

Suppose we explore in more detail the structure of this developing sci- 23 ence of democracy. A democratic government can be defined in terms of shared power, a democratic society in terms of shared deference (power, respect, insight) or shared influence (deference, safety, income). What are the limits within which sharing may vary in a government or in a society that is entitled to be called "democratic"? With respect to power, we may stipulate that a democratic government authorizes majority participation in the making of important decisions. The majority may express itself directly (direct legislation) or indirectly (elected officials). The majority must participate actively (a large majority—let us specify a two-thirds majority—must qualify to vote and take part in elections). The overwhelming majority must be free

---

* Laswell, Harold D., *Politics: Who Gets What, When, How* (New York, 1936) [Lasswell's note].
† Distinguished European names include Geatano Mosca, Vilfredo Pareto, Max Weber, Robert Michels [Lasswell's note].

of intimidation. Moreover, they must have confidence in their capacity to exert effective control over decisions, whether or not they vote on any given occasion. Communities are democratic if they conform to these specifications, and they are democratic in the degree to which they conform to them.

DEMOCRACY: A PATTERN OF SYMBOL AND PRACTICE

The foregoing definition of democracy refers both to symbol and to practice. 24 The prescription that the majority must be eligible to take part in elections is a reference to symbols—to words combined in sentences accepted as authoritative. A statement is authoritative when it is agreed that it formulates what ought to be done. Whom shall we ask in order to ascertain the state of expectation in a given community? In our society we have authorities, persons who are supposed to know about accepted doctrine. There are lifelong students of constitutional law, and we would not hesitate to include them among our authorities on the state of expectation with regard to "government." They are not authorities, however, upon all of the decision-making rules in our society. We do not expect them to be informed about the rules of trade associations, trade unions, churches, fraternities, producers' or consumers' co-operatives, or monopolistic private business. Hence we must enlarge our jury.

In whatever way we constitute our panel of knowledgeable persons, we 25 must specify the degree of agreement that is necessary to establish a given statement as doctrine. For convenience, let us lay down the rule that eight in ten of our authorities must agree.

What is the degree of conformity between doctrine and practice that is 26 needed before the term "democracy" can be applied? Many clauses in statute books have quietly been allowed to lapse; they are not "law" even though they are in the code. Even if our authorities agree that a given statement is legal doctrine, investigation may reveal that it is largely inoperative. We need to specify a minimum critical frequency of conformity that must be realized before a given doctrine is a "rule." Thus the term "rule" is defined as "doctrine in practice" (within stipulated limits).

How are data-gatherers to proceed in determining the state of practice 27 in a given situation? Official records may show whether elections are held at the time prescribed in the Constitution, and they may report the number of eligible voters who go to the polls. But even if these statements are accepted at face value, they do not reveal the state of intimidation or the degree of public confidence in the genuineness of democratic processes.*

The needed facts can be obtained only by observers who possess skills 28 appropriate to the observation of reality. Such observers must be equipped to establish themselves where they find out what is said and done. They must make reliable and consistent records of what they see. These records must be

---

*See Lasswell, "General Framework: Person, Personality, Group, Culture," in the present volume, Part II. [Laswell's note.]

properly analysed. The observations can aim at completeness (census) or at representativeness (sampling).

Mankind has thrown away most of its experience for lack of competent 29 record-making, and successive generations are left with a more meager social inheritance than need be. If mankind is to adapt civilization to the ideal of human dignity, each generation must be in a position to profit from past errors and to improve upon past achievement.

Men have tried to govern themselves and one another for many gener- 30 ations. In the literatures of ancient China, of East India, of the Mediterranean world, there is no dearth of general principles. But general statements of principle do not suffice. By themselves they do not communicate. We need detailed records of how men tried to put principles into practice—and what came of it. We need the bricks of data no less than the blueprints of precept, if we are to build successfully. To improve the social inheritance of the future, we must transmit generalization plus data.

Every friend of democracy can specify some records that he wishes had 31 been left by preceding generations. There have been great moments when men have detached themselves to some degree from the polemics of their age and have contributed to the reconstruction of knowledge and the redirection of education and public policy. They have withdrawn a step from active combat, yet they have not frozen into the mould of ritualistic scholarship. We need to know how such things can be. A few of the facts we know—how the universities of Leyden (1575), Edinburgh (1583), and Strasbourg (1566 and 1621) emancipated themselves from the religious turmoil of their day and cultivated the sciences and the humanities.* But we do not know the process in helpful detail; adequate records were not made.

There have been great programmes of training for civic life. The system 32 of training for public service that was instituted in China had its effect upon the level of skill and integrity available to the state. Yet the level fluctuated enormously from time to time. At one period the clash of personal, family, fraternal, and regional ambition spelled demoralization. At other times the mills of central administration ground exceeding fine. Proper records would unquestionably enable us to account for many of the astonishing variations in the course of Chinese history—a history that is only changeless in the eye of the uninformed.

Great collections of invaluable data have perished for lack of apprecia- 33 tion of their cumulative significance. For generations the secret agents of the East Indian princes sedulously collected the most intimate obtainable details of the lives of officials and private subjects. These details were not falsified by the needs of literary style. The intellectuals of India left us no compendium of collected data. They relied on the communicative value of the shrewd remark divorced from data.

---

*On the history of universities, see d'Irsay, Stephen, *Histoire des universités* (Paris, 1933–4.) [Laswell's note.]

We are told by the classical writers that men of honesty should be re-   34
cruited to perform certain functions of government. We know that spies were
used to report upon the conduct of officials, often testing them with bribes.
What is lost is the description of who responded how. What were the words
or gestures that enabled the skilful observer to predict who would succumb
to which appeal?

In our own time the observation of human response has advanced by   35
leaps and bounds. Although we are still in the embryonic stage, it is no exaggeration to assert that more advances have been made in the last forty years
than at any time in the history of mankind.

The discovery of ways of studying human response has opened up new   36
potentialities for the removal of obstacles upon the growth of democratic
character and practice. Many of these obstacles have hitherto been unrecog-
nized; one instance is the distortion of human personality during adolescence.
We have popularly thought of adolescent "storm and stress" as a necessary
phase of growth. However, disciplined observation has shown that our civilization itself imposes suicide, schizophrenia, and malformation of personality upon so many of its adolescents. Not human nature, but specific features
of our civilization are responsible—certain ways of rearing children, of in-
corporating the young into the patterns of a rivalrous civilization. How do
we know this to be true? The most convincing demonstration is the discovery
of societies that do not sentence their youth to varying degrees of destructive-
ness.*

We need skilful observers of the total reality of personal and cultural   37
development if we are to know the facts about the prevalence of democracy
and to uncover the factors that condition the survival of free societies.

One long step toward reality is to accept no general sentence as a com-   38
plete communication until we know how it is related to definite observational
standpoints.

EXACT OBSERVATION YIELDS RESULTS NOW

Many students of politics, confronted by the ambiguity of existing language,   39
grow pessimistic about the possibility of science. Perhaps, therefore, it is
worth emphasizing the point that exact methods of observation yield certain
advantages now, quite apart from the contribution they may ultimately make
to a highly systematic science of democracy.†

---

*Note especially the ethnological work of Margaret Mead, beginning with *Coming of Age in
Samoa* (London, 1943). Among psychiatrists, consult Sullivan, Harry Stack, "Conceptions of Modern Psychiatry," *Psychiatry*, vol. 3 (1940). [Laswell's note.]

†Important advances have been made toward a statement of scientific procedure that brings the
data of the social sciences and of the physical sciences into a common universe of events.
We may speak of the manifold of events, and classify events into "movements" and "symbols." A symbol refers; a movement does not. For a long time physicalistic survivals lim-

The democratic ideal includes a decent regard for the opinions and sen- 40
sibilities of our fellows. The moralists who have championed this ideal in the
past have made no progress toward the discovery of methods appropriate to
the understanding of the thoughts and feelings of others. The instrumentation
of morals has had to await reliable methods of observation.

With the best will in the world, we cannot take the attitudes of our 41
fellows into consideration unless we know what they are, and this depends
upon an adequate staff of skilful observers. Lacking these instruments, good
intentions cannot possibly be fulfilled in practice. Knowledge of any kind can
be abused by men of ill will, and men of good will must always choose between their present impotence through lack of knowledge and their possible
weakness through lack of power. In the present state of the organization of
knowledge, the members of the great society cannot live up to democratic
morals; with better organization of knowledge, they may achieve power
without losing their good intentions in the process.

This much, at least, is clear: Whether or not the methods of scientific 42
observation contribute to the eventual completion of a systematic science of
democracy, they are certain to contribute, here and now, to the practice of
democratic morals. Without science, democracy is blind and weak. With
science, democracy will not be blind and may be strong.

QUESTIONS ABOUT LASSWELL'S DISCOURSE COMMUNITY AND HIS CONCERNS IN THIS SELECTION

1. Lasswell assumes that scientific, objective observation of events is possible. Do you accept this assumption? Or is all observation slanted or biased?
2. This essay was first written and published in 1942, during the early stages of America's active involvement in World War II. What in this essay suggests the context of America's entrance into the war?
3. What does Lasswell mean when he suggests that democracies "perish through ignorance" (paragraph 1)?
4. In paragraph 4, Lasswell suggests that the social sciences can be as technically exact in their observations and definitions as any other science. But is such exactness possible when one is dealing with masses of human beings? Would you say that the nature of the social sciences makes such observations and definitions precise or imprecise?
5. Read over Lasswell's brief history of how political science has developed (paragraphs 11 and 12). Does it seem to you that political science has changed from being a prescriptive science to a descriptive science? If so, is this a change that should be deplored or applauded? Why?

---

ited the utility of Rudolf Carnap's logical positivism, but recent formulations have dropped these objectionable features. Even those who accepted a unified-field theory were reluc-tant to admit "words about words" as data of the same standing as "words about move-ments." Hence, the shipwreck of many efforts to apply correct general formulations to socio-personal events, where most of the data sentences are "words about words."

6. Do you agree with Lasswell that "the function of government is power" (paragraph 19)?

7. How does Lasswell define a symbol (paragraph 24)? Which discourse communities might not accept this definition?

8. Is it the case that "mankind has thrown away most of its experience for lack of competent record-making" (paragraph 29)? Or is this merely exaggeration to help make the point of the argument?

QUESTIONS ABOUT LASSWELL'S RHETORICAL STRATEGIES

1. In the introduction and conclusion of this essay, Lasswell uses balanced pairs of sentences to characterize democracies. "Without knowledge, democracy will surely fall. With knowledge, democracy may succeed," he writes in paragraph 1. "Without science, democracy is blind and weak. With science, democracy will not be blind and may be strong," he notes in the final paragraph. Why does Lasswell balance these sentences so? What effect does this balancing have upon the reader?

2. In paragraph 6, Lasswell asks a series of rhetorical questions. How would he expect you to answer those questions? Is this the most effective method of presenting this material?

3. Lasswell divides this essay into rather short sections. What are the purposes of this division? How does Lasswell make transitions between these sections?

4 Several times during the essay Lasswell mentions anthropologists like Margaret Mead and Bronislaw Malinowski. Why does he invoke these writers? Is Lasswell attempting to mix discourse communities? If so, for what purpose?

5. Read over paragraph 20. How does Lasswell connect political science to other social sciences?

6. What different rhetorical modes does Lasswell use in paragraph 22? Which of these modes are central to the overall rhetorical strategies of the essay?

7. Consider the diction of paragraph 23. How is the rhetorical mode of definition suited to the diction? What precisely does this paragraph have to do with the overall purpose of the piece, and why is it placed at this point in the essay?

8. Periodically Lasswell employs very short paragraphs (for example, paragraphs 37 and 38). In general, what is the rhetorical purpose of these paragraphs?

WRITING FROM WITHIN AND ABOUT THE SOCIAL SCIENCES: POLITICAL SCIENCE

Writing for Yourself

1. In your journal, define democracy.
2. In your journal, reflect on those ideals for which any democracy strives.

Writing for Nonacademic Audiences

1. Observe the meeting of a local town government. After attending the meeting, write a 500-word essay describing the workings of democracy in that town, aimed at an audience of your peers.

2. Read Michael Parenti's short book, *Democracy for the Few*, which is a Marxist interpretation of the workings of American democracy. Write a 250-word review of that book for your university's newspaper.
3. Write a 750-word feature article in your university's newspaper detailing how your university is governed. If you have the opportunity, attend one or more sessions of your university's governing bodies and explore in your essay any dichotomy between theory and practice.
4. As a congressional aide, you have been asked to follow a local election that is currently underway. Use whatever methods of political observation you can: personal interviews, media accounts, vote counts, polls, questionnaires, discussions with local analysts. Then for your congressman write a full account of that election, about 2,500 words. Conclude your account with an explanation of why one candidate emerged victorious.

Writing for Academic Audiences

1. For an introductory course in sociology, write a 500-word essay defining the nature of decision-makers in contemporary North America, not limiting yourself to governments alone.
2. For an introductory course in political science, write a 1,000-word paper in which you give your opinion of the source of political power.

B. F. Skinner

(1904–1990)

During his lifetime, B. F. Skinner was the leading exponent of behaviorism, a school of psychology that argues that all human and animal behavior can be explained in terms of responses to stimuli from the environment. The school was introduced by the American psychologist J. B. Watson in 1913, and has been influenced by a deterministic and mechanistic view of humanity. Both Watson and Skinner, proceeding from this view, rejected philosophical speculation about the ethics and sources of behavior, since that behavior was something that was controlled by measurable and observable influences.

Skinner worked at the universities of Minnesota and Indiana, but in 1948 he joined the faculty of Harvard University, becoming the Edgar Pierce Professor of Psychology in 1958. During his time at these institutions he conducted a great deal of research, principally upon rats and pigeons, to demonstrate his belief that behavior could be explained as a pattern of responses to rewards and deprivations that come from outside the organism. He extended this research to include human behavior and had profound effects on American educational theory.

The following essay, "The Steep and Thorny Way to a Science of Behavior," is taken from Skinner's Reflections on Behaviorism and Society (1978), a collection of essays in which Skinner explores the possible implications that a science of behavior might have for a society. In this essay, he explores those "dalliances" that have obstructed the development of such a science, finding that our own proclivity to self-aggrandizement and introspection has hampered our ability to see clearly the sources of our behavior. The essay was first presented as a Herbert Spencer lecture at Oxford University (November, 1973) and later published in American Psychologist (1975, 30, 42–49), and R. Harve's Problems of Scientific Revolution: Progress and Obstacles to Progress in the Sciences (Oxford: Clarendon Press, 1975).

Skinner has been attacked by many critics, particularly those outside his own discourse community. Most frequently he is criticized for his vision of human freedom, as well as for his dismissal of the significance of moral or ethical causes for action. Critics also raise questions about the ethics of deliberately controlling and reprogramming human behavior, as well as about the people who would be doing the programming. Whose vision of proper behavior should be accepted? If behaviorism is to lead us to a world of peace and creativity, who will be the one to describe the nature of that paradise?

THE STEEP AND THORNY WAY TO A SCIENCE OF BEHAVIOR

A critic contends that a recent book of mine* does not contain anything new, 1
that much the same was said more than four centuries ago in theological
terms by John Calvin.† You will not be surprised, then, to find me com-
mending to you the steep and thorny way to that heaven promised by a science of behavior. But I am not one of those ungracious pastors, of whom
Ophelia complained, who "recking not their own rede themselves tread the
primrose path of dalliance." No, I shall rail at dalliance, and in a manner
worthy, I hope, of my distinguished predecessor. If I do not thunder or ful-
minate, it is only because we moderns can more easily portray a truly frightening hell. I shall merely allude to the carcinogenic fallout of a nuclear hol-
ocaust. And no Calvin ever had better reason to fear his hell, for I am
proceeding on the assumption that nothing less than a vast improvement in
our understanding of human behavior will prevent the destruction of our
way of life or of mankind.

Why has it been so difficult to be scientific about human behavior? Why 2
have methods that have been so prodigiously successful almost everywhere
else failed so ignominiously in this one field? Is it because human behavior
presents unusual obstacles to a science? No doubt it does, but I think we are
beginning to see how these obstacles may be overcome. The problem, I submit, is digression. We have been drawn off the straight and narrow path, and
the word *diversion* serves me well by suggesting not only digression but dalliance. In this article I analyze some of the diversions peculiar to the field of
human behavior which seem to have delayed our advance toward the better
understanding we desperately need.

I must begin by saying what I take a science of behavior to be. It is, I 3
assume, part of biology. The organism that behaves is the organism that
breathes, digests, conceives, gestates, and so on. As such, the behaving organism will eventually be described and explained by the anatomist and physiologist. As far as behavior is concerned, they will give us an account of the
genetic endowment of the species and tell how that endowment changes during the lifetime of the individual and why, as a result, the individual then
responds in a given way on a given occasion. Despite remarkable progress,
we are still a long way from a satisfactory account in such terms. We know
something about the chemical and electrical effects of the nervous system and
the location of many of its functions, but the events that actually underlie a

---

* Skinner, B. F. *Beyond freedom and dignity.* New York: Alfred A. Knopf, 1971 [Skinner's note].
† John Calvin (1509–1564) was a famous French Protestant theologian [Editors' note].

single instance of behavior—as a pigeon picks up a stick to build a nest, or a child a block to complete a tower, or a scientist a pen to write a paper—are still far out of reach.

Fortunately, we need not wait for further progress of that sort. We can 4 analyze a given instance of behavior in its relation to the current setting and to antecedent events in the history of the species and of the individual. Thus, we do not need an explicit account of the anatomy and physiology of genetic endowment in order to describe the behavior, or the behavioral processes, characteristic of a species, or to speculate about the contingencies of survival under which they might have evolved, as the ethologists have convincingly demonstrated. Nor do we need to consider anatomy and physiology in order to see how the behavior of the individual is changed by his exposure to contingencies of reinforcement during his lifetime and how as a result he behaves in a given way on a given occasion. I must confess to a predilection here for my own specialty, the experimental analysis of behavior, which is a quite explicit investigation of the effects upon individual organisms of extremely complex and subtle contingencies of reinforcement.

There will be certain temporal gaps in such an analysis. The behavior 5 and the conditions of which it is a function do not occur in close temporal or spatial proximity, and we must wait for physiology to make the connection. When it does so, it will not invalidate the behavioral account (indeed, its assignment could be said to be specified by that account), nor will it make its terms and principles any the less useful. A science of behavior will be needed for both theoretical and practical purposes even when the behaving organism is fully understood at another level, just as much of chemistry remains useful even though a detailed account of a single instance may be given at the level of molecular or atomic forces. Such, then, is the science of behavior from which I suggest we have been diverted—by several kinds of dalliance to which I now turn.

Very little biology is handicapped by the fact that the biologist is him- 6 self a specimen of the thing he is studying, but that part of the science with which we are here concerned has not been so fortunate. We seem to have a kind of inside information about our behavior. It may be true that the environment shapes and controls our behavior as it shapes and controls the behavior of other species—but *we* have feelings about it. And what a diversion they have proved to be. Our loves, our fears, our feelings about war, crime, poverty, and God—these are all basic, if not ultimate, concerns. And we are as much concerned about the feelings of others. Many of the great themes of mythology have been about feelings—of the victim on his way to sacrifice or of the warrior going forth to battle. We read what poets tell us about their feelings, and we share the feelings of characters in plays and novels. We follow regimens and take drugs to alter our feelings. We become sophisticated about them in, say, the manner of La Rochefoucauld,* noting that jealousy thrives on doubt, or that the clemency of a ruler is a mixture of vanity, laziness, and fear. And along with some psychiatrists we may even try to establish an independent science of feelings in the intrapsychic life of the mind or personality.

And do feelings not have some bearing on our formulation of a science   7 of behavior? Do we not strike because we are angry and play music because we feel like listening? And if so, are our feelings not to be added to those antecedent events of which behavior is a function? This is not the place to answer such questions in detail, but I must at least suggest the kind of answer that may be given. William James† questioned the causal order: Perhaps we do not strike because we are angry but feel angry because we strike. That does not bring us back to the environment, however, although James and others were on the right track. What we feel are conditions of our bodies, most of them closely associated with behavior and with the circumstances in which we behave. We both strike *and* feel angry for a common reason, and that reason lies in the environment. In short, the bodily conditions we feel are *collateral products* of our genetic and environmental histories. They have no explanatory force; they are simply additional facts to be taken into account.

Feelings enjoy an enormous advantage over genetic and environmental   8 histories. They are warm, salient, and demanding, where facts about the environment are easily overlooked. Moreover, they are *immediately* related to behavior, being collateral products of the same causes, and have therefore commanded more attention than the causes themselves, which are often rather remote. In doing so, they have proved to be one of the most fascinating attractions along the path of dalliance.

A much more important diversion has, for more than 2,000 years, made   9 any move toward a science of behavior particularly difficult. The environment acts upon an organism at the surface of its body, but when the body is our own, we seem to observe its progress beyond that point; for example, we seem to see the real world become experience, a physical presentation become a sensation or a percept. Indeed, this second stage may be all we see. Reality may be merely an inference and, according to some authorities, a bad one. What is important may not be the physical world on the far side of the skin but what that world means to us on this side.

Not only do we seem to see the environment on its way in, we seem to   10 see behavior on its way out. We observe certain early stages—wishes, intentions, ideas, and acts of will—before they have, as we say, found expression

---

*La Rochefoucauld, Francois duc de (1613–1680) was a French writer who specialized in moral maxims and reflective epigrams [Editors' note].
†William James (1842) was an American psychologist and philosopher [Editors' note].

in behavior. And as for our environmental history, that can also be viewed and reviewed inside the skin, for we have tucked it all away in the storehouse of our memory. Again this is not the place to present an alternative account, but several points need to be made. The behavioristic objection is not primarily to the metaphysical nature of mind stuff. I welcome the view, clearly gaining in favor among psychologists and physiologists and by no means a stranger to philosophy, that what we introspectively observe, as well as feel, are states of our bodies. But I am not willing to give introspection much of a toehold even so, for there are two important reasons why we do not discriminate precisely among our feelings and states of mind and hence why there are many different philosophies and psychologies.

In the first place, the world within the skin is private. Only the person 11 whose skin it is can make certain kinds of contact with it. We might expect that the resulting intimacy should make for greater clarity, but there is a difficulty. The privacy interferes with the very process of coming to know. The verbal community which teaches us to make distinctions among things in the world around us lacks the information it needs to teach us to distinguish events in our private world. For example, it cannot teach us the difference between diffidence and embarrassment as readily or as accurately as that between red and blue or sweet and sour.

Second, the self-observation that leads to introspective knowledge is 12 limited by anatomy. It arose very late in the evolution of the species because it is only when a person begins to be asked about his behavior and about why he behaves as he does that he becomes conscious of himself in this sense. Self-knowledge depends on language and in fact on language of a rather advanced kind, but when questions of this sort first began to be asked, the only nervous systems available in answering them were those that had evolved for entirely different reasons. They had proved useful in the internal economy of the organism, in the coordination of movement, and in operating upon the environment, but there was no reason why they should be suitable in supplying information about those very extensive systems that mediate behavior. To put it crudely, introspection cannot be very relevant or comprehensive because the human organism does not have nerves going to the right places.

One other problem concerns the nature and location of the knower. The 13 organism itself lies, so to speak, between the environment that acts upon it and the environment it acts upon, but what lies between those inner stages— between, for example, experience and will? From what vantage point do we watch stimuli on their way into the storehouse of memory or behavior on its way out to physical expression? The observing agent, the knower, seems to contract to something very small in the middle of things.

In the formulation of a science with which I began, it is the *organism* 14 *as a whole* that behaves. It acts in and upon a physical world, and it can be induced by a verbal environment to respond to some of its own activities. The events observed as the life of the mind, like feelings, are *collateral prod-*

ucts, which have been made the basis of many elaborate metaphors. The philosopher at his desk asking himself what he really knows, about himself or the world, will quite naturally begin with his experiences, his acts of will, and his memory, but the effort to understand the mind from that vantage point, beginning with Plato's supposed discovery, has been one of the great diversions which have delayed an analysis of the role of the environment.

It did not, of course, take inside information to induce people to direct 15 their attention to what is going on inside the behaving organism. We almost instinctively look inside a system to see how it works. We do this with clocks, as with living systems. It is standard practice in much of biology. Some early efforts to understand and explain behavior in this way have been described by Onians in his classic *Origins of European Thought.** It must have been the slaughterhouse and the battlefield that gave man his first knowledge of anatomy and physiology. The various functions assigned to parts of the organism were not usually those that had been observed introspectively. If Onians is right, the *phrénes* were the lungs, intimately associated with breathing and hence, so the Greeks said, with thought and, of course, with life and death. The *phrénes* were the seat of *thumós,* a vital principle whose nature is not now clearly understood, and possibly of ideas, in the active sense of Homeric Greek. (By the time an idea had become an object of quiet contemplation, interest seems to have been lost in its location.) Later, the various fluids of the body, the humors, were associated with dispositions, and the eye and the ear with sense data. I like to imagine the consternation of that pioneer who first analyzed the optics of the eyeball and realized that the image on the retina was upside down!

Observation of a behaving system from within began in earnest with 16 the discovery of reflexes, but the reflex arc was not only not the seat of mental action, it was taken to be a usurper, the spinal reflexes replacing the *Rückenmarkseele* or soul of the spinal cord, for example. The reflex arc was essentially an anatomical concept, and the physiology remained largely imaginary for a long time. Many years ago I suggested that the letters CNS could be said to stand, not for the central nervous system, but for the conceptual nervous system. I had in mind the great physiologists Sir Charles Sherrington and Ivan Petrovich Pavlov. In his epoch-making *Integrative Action of the Nervous System,* Sherrington† had analyzed the role of the synapse, listing perhaps a dozen characteristic properties. I pointed out that he had never seen a synapse in action and that all the properties assigned to it were inferred from the behavior of his preparations. Pavlov had offered his researches as evidence of the activities of the cerebral cortex though he had never observed

---

*Onians, R. D. *The origins of European thought.* Cambridge, England: University Press, 1951 [Skinner's note].

†Sherrington, C. S. *Integrative action of the nervous system.* New Haven, Conn.: Yale University Press, 1906 [Skinner's note].

the cortex in action but had merely inferred its processes from the behavior of his experimental animals. But Sherrington, Pavlov, and many others were moving in the direction of an instrumental approach, and the physiologist is now, of course, studying the nervous system directly.

The conceptual nervous system has been taken over by other disci- 17
plines—by information theory, cybernetics, systems analyses, mathematical models, and cognitive psychology. The hypothetical structures they describe do not depend on confirmation by direct observation of the nervous system, for that lies too far in the future to be of interest. They are to be justified by their internal consistency and the successful prediction of selected facts, presumably not the facts from which the constructions were inferred.

These disciplines are concerned with how the brain or the mind must 18
work if the human organism is to behave as it does. They offer a sort of thermodynamics of behavior without reference to molecular action. The computer with its apparent simulation of Man Thinking supplies the dominant analogy. It is not a question of the physiology of the computer—how it is wired or what type of storage it uses—but of its behavioral characteristics. A computer takes in information as an organism receives stimuli and processes it according to an inbuilt program as an organism is said to do according to its genetic endowment. It encodes the information, converting it to a form it can handle, as the organism converts visual, auditory, and other stimuli into nerve impulses. Like its human analogue it stores the encoded information in a memory, tagged to facilitate retrieval. It uses what it has stored to process information as received, as a person is said to use prior experience to interpret incoming stimuli, and later to perform various operations—in short, to compute. Finally, it makes decisions and behaves: It prints out.

There is nothing new about any of this. The same things were done 19
thousands of years ago with clay tiles. The overseer or tax collector kept a record of bags of grain, the number, quality, and kind being marked appropriately. The tiles were stored in lots as marked, additional tiles were grouped appropriately, the records were eventually retrieved and computations made, and a summary account was issued. The machine is much swifter, and it is so constructed that human participation is needed only before and after the operation. The speed is a clear advantage, but the apparent autonomy has caused trouble. It has seemed to mean that the mode of operation of a computer resembles that of a person. People do make physical records which they store and retrieve and use in solving problems, but it does not follow that they do anything of the sort in the mind. If there were some exclusively subjective achievement, the argument for the so-called higher mental processes would be stronger, but as far as I know, none has been demonstrated. True, we say that the mathematician sometimes intuitively solves a problem and only later, if at all, reduces it to the steps of a proof, and in doing so he seems to differ greatly from those who proceed step by step, but the differences could well be in the evidence of what has happened, and it would not be very satisfactory to define thought simply as unexplained behavior.

Again, it would be foolish of me to try to develop an alternative account   20
in the space available. What I have said about the introspectively observed
mind applies as well to the mind that is constructed from observations of the
behavior of others. The *accessibility* of stored memories, for example, can be
interpreted as the *probability* of acquired behaviors, with no loss in the adequacy of the treatment of the facts, and with a very considerable gain in the
assimilation of this difficult field with other parts of human behavior.

I have said that much of biology looks inside a living system for an   21
explanation of how it works. But that is not true of all of biology. Sir Charles
Bell* could write a book on the hand as evidence of design. The hand was
evidence; the design lay elsewhere. Darwin found the design, too, but in a
different place. He could catalog the creatures he discovered on the voyage
of the *Beagle* in terms of their form or structure, and he could classify bar-
nacles for years in the same way, but he looked beyond structure for the
principle of natural selection. It was *the relation of the organism to the environment* that mattered in evolution. And it is the relation to environment
that is of primary concern in the analysis of behavior. Hence, it is not enough
to confine oneself to organization or structure, even of the most penetrating
kind. That is the mistake of most of phenomenology, existentialism, and the
structuralism of anthropology and linguistics. When the important thing is a
relation to the environment, as in the phylogeny and ontogeny of behavior,
the fascination with an inner system becomes a simple digression.

We have not advanced more rapidly to the methods and instruments   22
needed in the study of behavior precisely because of the diverting preoccupation with a supposed or real inner life. It is true that the introspective
psychologist and the model builder have investigated environments, but they
have done so only to throw some light on the internal events in which they
are interested. They are no doubt well-intentioned helpmates, but they have
often simply misled those who undertake the study of the organism as a behaving system in its own right. Even when helpful, an observed or hypothetical inner determiner is no explanation of behavior until it has itself been
explained, and the fascination with an inner life has allayed curiosity about
the further steps to be taken.

I can hear my critics: "Do you really mean to say that all those who   23
have inquired into the human mind, from Plato and Aristotle through the
Romans and Scholastics, to Bacon and Hobbes, to Locke and the other British
empiricists, to John Stuart Mill,† and to all those who began to call themselves psychologists—that they have all been wasting their time?" Well, not
all of their time, fortunately. Forget their purely psychological speculations,

---

* Sir Charles Bell (1774–1842) was a Scottish anatomist and surgeon [Editors' note].
† Francis Bacon (1561–1626) was an English philosopher, essayist, and statesman. Thomas
    Hobbes (1588–1679) was an English philosopher. John Locke (1632–1704) was an English
    philosopher and founder of empiricism. John Stuart Mill (1806–1873) was an English
    philosopher and economist [Editors' note].

and they were still remarkable people. They would have been even more remarkable, in my opinion, if they could have forgotten that speculation themselves. They were careful observers of human behavior, but the intuitive wisdom they acquired from their contact with real people was flawed by their theories.

It is easier to make the point in the field of medicine. Until the present   24
century very little was known about bodily processes in health and disease from which useful therapeutic practices could be derived. Yet it should have been worthwhile to call in a physician. Physicians saw many ill people and should have acquired a kind of wisdom, unanalyzed perhaps but still of value in prescribing simple treatments. The history of medicine, however, is largely the history of barbaric practices—bloodlettings, cuppings, poultices, purgations, violent emetics—which much of the time must have been harmful. My point is that these measures were not suggested by the intuitive wisdom acquired from familiarity with illness; they were suggested by *theories*, theories about what was going on inside an ill person. Theories of the mind have had a similar effect, less dramatic, perhaps, but quite possibly far more damaging. The men I have mentioned made important contributions in government, religion, ethics, economics, and many other fields. They could do so with an intuitive wisdom acquired from experience. But philosophy and psychology have had their bleedings, cuppings, and purgations too, and they have obscured simple wisdom. They have diverted wise people from a path that would have led more directly to an eventual science of behavior. Plato would have made far more progress toward the good life if he could have forgotten those shadows on the wall of his cave.

Still another kind of concern for the self distracts us from the program   25
I have outlined. It has to do with the individual, not as an object of self-knowledge, but as an agent, an initiator, a creator. I have developed this theme in *Beyond Freedom and Dignity*. We are more likely to give a person credit for what he does if it is not obvious that it can be attributed to his physical or social environment, and we are likely to feel that truly great achievements must be inexplicable. The more derivative a work of art, the less creative; the more conspicuous the personal gain, the less heroic an act of sacrifice. To obey a well-enforced law is not to show civic virtue. We see a concern for the aggrandizement of the individual, for the maximizing of credit due him, in the self-actualization of so-called humanistic psychology, in some versions of existentialism, in Eastern mysticism and certain forms of Christian mysticism in which a person is taught to reject the world in order to free himself for union with a divine principle or with God, as well as in the simple structuralism that looks to the organization of behavior rather than to the antecedent events responsible for that organization. The difficulty is that if the credit due a person is infringed by evidences of the conditions of which his behavior is a function, then a scientific analysis appears to be an attack

on human worth or dignity. Its task is to explain the hitherto inexplicable and hence to reduce any supposed inner contribution which has served in lieu of explanation. Freud moved in this direction in explaining creative art, and it is no longer just the cynic who traces heroism and martyrdom to powerful indoctrination. The culminating achievement of the human species has been said to be the evolution of man as a moral animal, but a simpler view is that it has been the evolution of cultures in which people behave morally although they have undergone no inner change of character.

Even more traumatic has been the supposed attack on freedom. Histor- 26 ically, the struggle for freedom has been an escape from physical restraint and from behavioral restraints exerted through punishment and exploitative measures of other kinds. The individual has been freed from features of his environment arranged by governmental and religious agencies and by those who possess great wealth. The success of that struggle, though it is not yet complete, is one of man's great achievements, and no sensible person would challenge it. Unfortunately, one of its by-products has been the slogan that "all control of human behavior is wrong and must be resisted." Nothing in the circumstances under which man has struggled for freedom justifies this extension of the attack on controlling measures, and we should have to abandon all of the advantages of a well-developed culture if we were to relinquish all practices involving the control of human behavior. Yet new techniques in education, psychotherapy, incentive systems, penology, and the design of daily life are currently subject to attack because they are said to threaten personal freedom, and I can testify that the attack can be fairly violent.

The extent to which a person is free or responsible for his achievements 27 is not an issue to be decided by rigorous proof, but I submit that what we call the behavior of the human organism is no more free than its digestion, gestation, immunization, or any other physiological process. Because it involves the environment in many subtle ways it is much more complex, and its lawfulness is, therefore, much harder to demonstrate. But a scientific analysis moves in that direction, and we can already throw some light on traditional topics, such as free will or creativity, which is more helpful than traditional accounts, and I believe that further progress is imminent.

The issue is, of course, determinism. Slightly more than 100 years ago, 28 in a famous paper, Claude Bernard* raised with respect to physiology the issue which now stands before us in the behavioral sciences. The almost insurmountable obstacle to the application of scientific method in biology was, he said, the belief in "vital spontaneity." His contemporary, Louis Pasteur,† was responsible for a dramatic test of the theory of spontaneous generation, and I suggest that the spontaneous generation of behavior in the guise of ideas

---

* Claude Bernard (1813–1878) was a French physiologist; he is often seen as the founder of experimental medicine [Editors' note].

† Louis Pasteur (1822–1895) was a French chemist. He proposed the germ theory of infection to replace the theory of spontaneous generation [Editors' note].

and acts of will is now at the stage of the spontaneous generation of life in the form of maggots and microorganisms 100 years ago.

The practical problem in continuing the struggle for freedom and dig- 29 nity is not to destroy controlling forces but to change them, to create a world in which people will achieve far more than they have ever achieved before in art, music, literature, science, technology, and above all the enjoyment of life. It could be a world in which people feel freer than they have ever felt before, because they will not be under aversive control. In building such a world, we shall need all the help a science of behavior can give us. To misread the theme of the struggle for freedom and dignity and to relinquish all efforts to control would be a tragic mistake.

But it is a mistake that may very well be made. Our concern for the 30 individual as a creative agent is not dalliance; it is clearly an obstacle rather than a diversion, for ancient fears are not easily allayed. A shift in emphasis from the individual to the environment, particularly to the social environment, is reminiscent of various forms of totalitarian statism. It is easy to turn from what may seem like an inevitable movement in that direction and to take one's chances with libertarianism. But much remains to be analyzed in that position. For example, we may distinguish between liberty and license by holding to the right to do as we please provided we do not infringe upon similar rights of others, but in doing so we conceal or disguise the public sanctions represented by private rights. Rights and duties, like a moral or ethical sense, are examples of hypothetical internalized environmental sanctions.

In the long run, the aggrandizement of the individual jeopardizes the 31 future of the species and the culture. In effect, it infringes the so-called rights of billions of people still to be born, in whose interests only the weakest of sanctions are now maintained. We are beginning to realize the magnitude of the problem of bringing human behavior under the control of a projected future, and we are already suffering from the fact that we have come very late to recognize that mankind will have a future only if it designs a *viable* way of life. I wish I could share the optimism of both Darwin and Herbert Spencer* that the course of evolution is necessarily toward perfection. It appears, on the contrary, that that course must be corrected from time to time. But if the intelligent behavior that corrects it is also a product of evolution, then perhaps they were right after all. But it could be a near thing.

Perhaps it is now clear what I mean by diversions and obstacles. The 32 science I am discussing is the investigation of the relation between behavior and the environment—on the one hand, the environment in which the species evolved and which is responsible for the facts investigated by the etholo-

---

* Herbert Spencer (1820–1903) was an English philosopher who interpreted all phenomena in terms of principles of evolutionary progress [Editors' note].

gists and, on the other hand, the environment in which the individual lives and in response to which at any moment he behaves. We have been diverted from, and blocked in, our inquiries into the relations between behavior and those environments by an absorbing interest in the organism itself. We have been misled by the almost instinctive tendency to look inside any system to see how it works, a tendency doubly powerful in the case of behavior because of the apparent inside information supplied by feelings and introspectively observed states. Our only recourse is to leave that subject to the physiologist, who has, or will have, the only appropriate instruments and methods. We have also been encouraged to move in a centripetal direction because the discovery of controlling forces in the environment has seemed to reduce the credit due us for our achievements and to suggest that the struggle for freedom has not been as fully successful as we had imagined. We are not yet ready to accept the fact that the task is to change, not people, but rather the world in which they live.

We shall be less reluctant to abandon these diversions and to attack these obstacles, as we come to understand the possibility of a different approach. The role of the environment in human affairs has not, of course, gone unnoticed. Historians and biographers have acknowledged influences on human conduct, and literature has made the same point again and again. The Enlightenment advanced the cause of the individual by improving the world in which he lived—the Encyclopedia of Diderot and D'Alembert* was designed to further changes of that sort, and by the nineteenth century the controlling force of the environment was clearly recognized. Bentham† and Marx have been called behaviorists, although for them the environment determined behavior only after first determining consciousness, and this was an unfortunate qualification because the assumption of a mediating state clouded the relation between the terminal events.

The role of the environment has become clearer in the present century. Its selective action in evolution has been examined by the ethologists, and a similar selective action during the life of the individual is the subject of the experimental analysis of behavior. In the current laboratory, very complex environments are constructed and their effects on behavior studied. I believe this work offers consoling reassurance to those who are reluctant to abandon traditional formulations. Unfortunately, it is not well known outside the field. Its practical uses are, however, beginning to attract attention. Techniques derived from the analysis have proved useful in other parts of biology—for example, physiology and psychopharmacology—and have already led to the improved design of cultural practices, in programmed instructional mate-

---

*Completed in 1772, the Encyclopedia championed the rationalism of the Enlightenment [Editors' note].
†Jeremy Bentham (1748–1832) was an English philosopher and political theorist who founded utilitarianism [Editors' note].

rials, contingency management in the classroom, behavioral modification in psychotherapy and penology, and many other fields.

Much remains to be done, and it will be done more rapidly when the 35 role of the environment takes its proper place in competition with the apparent evidences of an inner life. As Diderot put it, nearly 200 years ago, "Unfortunately it is easier and shorter to consult oneself than it is to consult nature. Thus the reason is inclined to dwell within itself." But the problems we face are not to be found in men and women but in the world in which they live, especially in those social environments we call cultures. It is an important and promising shift in emphasis because, unlike the remote fastness of the so-called human spirit, the environment is within reach and we are learning how to change it.

And so I return to the role that has been assigned to me as a kind of 36 twentieth-century Calvin, calling on you to forsake the primrose path of total individualism, of self-actualization, self-adoration, and self-love, and to turn instead to the construction of that heaven on earth which is, I believe, within reach of the methods of science. I wish to testify that, once you are used to it, the way is not so steep or thorny after all.

QUESTIONS ABOUT SKINNER'S DISCOURSE COMMUNITY AND HIS CONCERNS IN THIS ESSAY

1. Skinner writes from within a distinct discourse community within psychology: that of the behaviorists. Based on this essay, what would you say are the behaviorists' major assumptions?

2. Would you agree with Skinner that "human behavior presents unusual obstacles to a science" (paragraph 2)? Why or why not?

3. How do you respond to William James's questioning of the casual order: "Perhaps we do not strike because we are angry but feel angry because we strike" (paragraph 7)? How do you respond to Skinner's reply that "[w]e both strike *and* feel angry for a common reason, and that reason lies in the environment" (paragraph 7)?

4. Skinner asserts that feelings are related to behavior but are not the causes of behavior (paragraph 8). Do you agree?

5. Does it seem logical to you that "introspection cannot be very relevant or comprehensive because the human organism does not have nerves going to the right places" (paragraph 12)? What would Skinner need to use as evidence to support such a claim?

6. Is the analogy between the human brain and the computer a logical, helpful one (see paragraph 18)?

7. What are the implications for one's life if it is true that "it is the relation to environment that is of primary concern in the analysis of behavior" (paragraph 21)? Does this work towards eliminating moral responsibility? Is it the case that we should not become preoccupied "with a supposed or real inner life" (paragraph 22)?

8. Does it seem to you that behaviorism tends to limit human freedom? After

reading paragraphs 26 to 32, how do you think Skinner would respond to this criticism?

9. Read over paragraph 30. What is the connection between behaviorism and the kind of creative world that Skinner envisions? Does this seem to you to be a reasonable connection?

QUESTIONS ABOUT SKINNER'S RHETORICAL STRATEGIES

1. What is Skinner alluding to in the title of this essay, "A Steep and Thorny Way to a Science of Behavior"? What might be the purpose of this allusion?
2. Read over the first two sentences of this essay. Is Skinner agreeing with his critic? What rhetorical purpose does this opening serve?
3. Describe the structure that Skinner uses to order the ideas in this essay. Do you find this structure to be effective? What alternative structures might he have used?
4. What is the nature of the evidence that Skinner uses to support his claims? Based upon this, how do you imagine that the field of behavioristic psychology makes progress?
5. How does Skinner compliment those who are opposed to his views? Why does he do so?
6. What words does Skinner use to indicate that he does not agree with a particular person's or group's viewpoint? Are his practices effective?
7. At times in this essay, Skinner uses the pronoun *we*. Look at the use of this pronoun in paragraphs 32 through 34. To what different rhetorical purposes does Skinner put this pronoun? Should he be more specific about the group he is referring to when he uses *we*?
8. Skinner uses the word *environment* repeatedly. Yet he never defines it. Should he define it? Does his not defining it indicate anything about his original audience?
9. Evaluate the rhetorical strategy of the conclusion. Why might Skinner have seen this as an effective conclusion?

WRITING FROM WITHIN AND ABOUT THE SOCIAL SCIENCES: PSYCHOLOGY

Writing for Yourself

1. In your journal, describe a time when you were controlled by your feelings.
2. In your journal, reflect on when it is appropriate for human freedoms to be curtailed.

Writing for Nonacademic Audiences

1. For your college newspaper, write an opinion article (maximum of 1,000 words) in which you argue your position on whether grading practices in schools are behavioristic or not.
2. After reading Skinner's *Walden II*, write a 750-word review of this novel for your local hometown newspaper.

Writing for Academic Audiences

1. After reading Plato's "Allegory of the Cave" (pp. 316–321), write a response as a disciple of Plato to Skinner's suggestion that "Plato would have made far more progress toward the good life if he could have forgotten those shadows on the wall of his cave" (paragraph 27). Your 500-word response will appear in a collection of readings for an interdisciplinary course in philosophy and psychology.

2. Interview an instructor of psychology at your school, focusing on whether he or she believes it would someday be possible to create a thinking machine, a machine that exactly reproduces the processes of the mind. Write a report of that interview, including relevant quotations, to be printed in the newsletter of the computer science department. You are limited to 750 words.

3. For a class in the psychology of education, write a 750-word description of how behavior modification has been used in North American schools in the twentieth century.

4. Think of a time in history when rigid adherence to a theory or belief has hindered an observer from seeing accurately, observing clearly, or perceiving objectively. For your peers in your writing class, write a 1,000-word narrative in which you chronicle that time.

5. For a class in psychology, write a 1,250-word evaluation of Skinner's positions in "A Steep and Thorny Way to a Science of Behavior," concentrating especially on the implications of his ideas for one of the following: human freedom, the reality or illusion of moral and ethical decisions, human creativity.

Carol Gilligan

(b. 1936)

Carol Gilligan is a professor at the Graduate School of Education, Harvard University. She also works at the Center for the Study of Gender, Education and Human Development, which was founded shortly after the publication in 1982 of Gilligan's In a Different Voice, Psychological Theory and Women's Development. *The purpose of the center is to foster the study of girls, women, and diverse racial and economic groups by developmental psychologists.*

In a Different Voice *shows Gilligan working within a discourse community that brings feminism to bear on the field of developmental psychology—in particular the area of developmental psychology that depends on the life cycle perspective. Psychologists taking this perspective, such as Lawrence Kohlberg, Daniel J. Levinson, and George E. Valiant, among others, have examined how people change as they move from childhood through adolescence into adulthood. The problem with these examinations, according to Gilligan, is that they really do not focus on human development but only on male development. In Gilligan's view, therefore, much of what people take for granted about developmental psychology is true only for men and boys.*

In a Different Voice *develops Gilligan's claim that women are not deficient in moral development, as psychologists such as Freud and Piaget have asserted. Gilligan argues that women have a different way than men of constituting themselves and their vision of morality. They have a different voice or way of talking about what it means to lead a moral life. Only when we study the voice of women, Gilligan goes on, will we understand the full range of possibilities for human moral development.*

The following selection, "Women's Place in Man's Life Cycle," is the first chapter of In a Different Voice.

WOMAN'S PLACE IN MAN'S LIFE CYCLE

In the second act of *The Cherry Orchard*,* Lopahin, a young merchant, 1 describes his life of hard work and success. Failing to convince Madame Ranevskaya to cut down the cherry orchard to save her estate, he will go

---

* *The Cherry Orchard*, by Anton Chekhov, was first presented in 1904.

on in the next act to buy it himself. He is the self-made man who, in purchasing the estate where his father and grandfather were slaves, seeks to eradicate the "awkward, unhappy life" of the past, replacing the cherry orchard with summer cottages where coming generations "will see a new life." In elaborating this developmental vision, he reveals the image of man that underlies and supports his activity: "At times when I can't go to sleep, I think: Lord, thou gavest us immense forests, unbounded fields and the widest horizons, and living in the midst of them we should indeed be giants"—at which point, Madame Ranevskaya interrupts him, saying, "You feel the need for giants—They are good only in fairy tales, anywhere else they only frighten us."

Conceptions of the human life cycle represent attempts to order and 2 make coherent the unfolding experiences and perceptions, the changing wishes and realities of everyday life. But the nature of such conceptions depends in part on the position of the observer. The brief excerpt from Chekhov's play suggests that when the observer is a woman, the perspective may be of a different sort. Different judgments of the image of man as giant imply different ideas about human development, different ways of imagining the human condition, different notions of what is of value in life.

At a time when efforts are being made to eradicate discrimination be- 3 tween the sexes in the search for social equality and justice, the differences between the sexes are being rediscovered in the social sciences. This discovery occurs when theories formerly considered to be sexually neutral in their scientific objectivity are found instead to reflect a consistent observational and evaluative bias. Then the presumed neutrality of science, like that of language itself, gives way to the recognition that the categories of knowledge are human constructions. The fascination with point of view that has informed the fiction of the twentieth century and the corresponding recognition of the relativity of judgment infuse our scientific understanding as well when we begin to notice how accustomed we have become to seeing life through men's eyes.

A recent discovery of this sort pertains to the apparently innocent classic 4 *The Elements of Style* by William Strunk and E. B. White. The Supreme Court ruling on the subject of discrimination in classroom texts led one teacher of English to notice that the elementary rules of English usage were being taught through examples which counterposed the birth of Napoleon, the writings of Coleridge, and statements such as "He was an interesting talker. A man who had traveled all over the world and lived in half a dozen countries," with "Well, Susan, this is a fine mess you are in" or, less drastically, "He saw a woman, accompanied by two children, walking slowly down the road."

Psychological theorists have fallen as innocently as Strunk and White 5 into the same observational bias. Implicitly adopting the male life as the norm, they have tried to fashion women out of a masculine cloth. It all goes back, of course, to Adam and Eve—a story which shows, among other things, that if you make a woman out of a man, you are bound to get into trouble. In the life cycle, as in the Garden of Eden, the woman has been the deviant.

The penchant of developmental theorists to project a masculine image, 6 and one that appears frightening to women, goes back at least to Freud (1905), who built his theory of psychosexual development around the experiences of the male child that culminate in the Oedipus complex. In the 1920s, Freud struggled to resolve the contradictions posed for his theory by the differences in female anatomy and the different configuration of the young girl's early family relationships. After trying to fit women into his masculine conception, seeing them as envying that which they missed, he came instead to acknowledge, in the strength and persistence of women's pre-Oedipal attachments to their mothers, a developmental difference. He considered this difference in women's development to be responsible for what he saw as women's developmental failure.

Having tied the formation of the superego or conscience to castration 7 anxiety, Freud considered women to be deprived by nature of the impetus for a clear-cut Oedipal resolution. Consequently, women's superego—the heir to the Oedipus complex—was compromised: it was never "so inexorable, so impersonal, so independent of its emotional origins as we require it to be in men." From this observation of difference, that "for women the level of what is ethically normal is different from what it is in men," Freud concluded that women "show less sense of justice than men, that they are less ready to submit to the great exigencies of life, that they are more often influenced in their judgements by feelings of affection or hostility" (1925, pp. 257–258).

Thus a problem in theory became cast as a problem in women's devel- 8 opment, and the problem in women's development was located in their experience of relationships. Nancy Chodorow (1974), attempting to account for "the reproduction within each generation of certain general and nearly universal differences that characterize masculine and feminine personality and roles," attributes these differences between the sexes not to anatomy but rather to "the fact that women, universally, are largely responsible for early child care." Because this early social environment differs for and is experienced differently by male and female children, basic sex differences recur in personality development. As a result, *"in any given society*, feminine personality comes to define itself in relation and connection to other people more than masculine personality does" (pp. 43–44).

In her analysis, Chodorow relies primarily on Robert Stoller's studies 9 which indicate that gender identity, the unchanging core of personality formation, is "with rare exception firmly and irreversibly established for both sexes by the time a child is around three." Given that for both sexes the primary caretaker in the first three years of life is typically female, the interpersonal dynamics of gender identity formation are different for boys and girls. Female identity formation takes place in a context of ongoing relationship since "mothers tend to experience their daughters as more like, and continuous with, themselves." Correspondingly, girls, in identifying themselves as female, experience themselves as like their mothers, thus fusing the experience of attachment with the process of identity formation. In contrast, "mothers experience their sons as a male opposite," and boys, in defining themselves as masculine, separate their mothers from themselves, thus curtailing "their primary love and sense of empathic tie." Consequently, male development entails a "more emphatic individuation and a more defensive firming of experienced ego boundaries." For boys, but not girls, "issues of differentiation have become intertwined with sexual issues" (1978, pp. 150, 166–167).

Writing against the masculine bias of psychoanalytic theory, Chodorow 10 argues that the existence of sex differences in the early experiences of individuation and relationship "does not mean that women have 'weaker' ego boundaries than men or are more prone to psychosis." It means instead that "girls emerge from this period with a basis for 'empathy' built into their primary definition of self in a way that boys do not." Chodorow thus replaces Freud's negative and derivative description of female psychology with a positive and direct account of her own: "Girls emerge with a stronger basis for experiencing another's needs or feelings as one's own (or of thinking that one is so experiencing another's needs and feelings). Furthermore, girls do not define themselves in terms of the denial of preoedipal relational modes to the same extent as do boys. Therefore, regression to these modes tends not to feel as much a basic threat to their ego. From very early, then, because they are parented by a person of the same gender . . . girls come to experience themselves as less differentiated than boys, as more continuous with and related to the external object-world, and as differently oriented to their inner object-world as well" (p. 167).

Consequently, relationships, and particularly issues of dependency, are 11 experienced differently by women and men. For boys and men, separation and individuation are critically tied to gender identity since separation from the mother is essential for the development of masculinity. For girls and women, issues of femininity or feminine identity do not depend on the achievement of separation from the mother or on the progress of individuation. Since masculinity is defined through separation while femininity is defined through attachment, male gender identity is threatened by intimacy while female gender identity is threatened by separation. Thus males tend to have difficulty with relationships, while females tend to have problems with individuation. The quality of embeddedness in social interaction and personal relationships that characterizes women's lives in contrast to men's, however, becomes not only a descriptive difference but also a developmental liability when the milestones of childhood and adolescent development in the psychological literature are markers of increasing separation. Women's failure to separate then becomes by definition a failure to develop.

The sex differences in personality formation that Chodorow describes 12 in early childhood appear during the middle childhood years in studies of children's games. Children's games are considered by George Herbert Mead (1934) and Jean Piaget (1932) as the crucible of social development during the school years. In games, children learn to take the role of the other and come to see themselves through another's eyes. In games, they learn respect for rules and come to understand the ways rules can be made and changed.

Janet Lever (1976), considering the peer group to be the agent of so- 13 cialization during the elementary school years and play to be a major activity of socialization at that time, set out to discover whether there are sex differences in the games that children play. Studying 181 fifth-grade, white, middle-class children, ages ten and eleven, she observed the organization and structure of their playtime activities. She watched the children as they played at school during recess and in physical education class, and in addition kept diaries of their accounts as to how they spent their out-of-school time. From this study, Lever reports sex differences: boys play out of doors more often than girls do; boys play more often in large and age-heterogeneous groups; they play competitive games more often, and their games last longer than girls' games. The last is in some ways the most interesting finding. Boys' games appeared to last longer not only because they required a higher level of skill and were thus less likely to become boring, but also because, when disputes arose in the course of a game, boys were able to resolve the disputes more effectively than girls: "During the course of this study, boys were seen quarrelling all the time, but not once was a game terminated because of a quarrel and no game was interrupted for more than seven minutes. In the gravest debates, the final word was always, to 'repeat the play,' generally followed by a chorus of 'cheater's proof'" (p. 482). In fact, it seemed that the boys enjoyed the legal debates as much as they did the game itself, and even marginal players of lesser size or skill participated equally in these recurrent squabbles. In contrast, the eruption of disputes among girls tended to end the game.

Thus Lever extends and corroborates the observations of Piaget in his 14 study of the rules of the game, where he finds boys becoming through childhood increasingly fascinated with the legal elaboration of rules and the development of fair procedures for adjudicating conflicts, a fascination that, he notes, does not hold for girls. Girls, Piaget observes, have a more "pragmatic" attitude toward rules, "regarding a rule as good as long as the game repaid it" (p. 83). Girls are more tolerant in their attitudes toward rules, more willing to make exceptions, and more easily reconciled to innovations. As a result, the legal sense, which Piaget considers essential to moral development, "is far less developed in little girls than in boys" (p. 77).

The bias that leads Piaget to equate male development with child de- 15 velopment also colors Lever's work. The assumption that shapes her discussion of results is that the male model is the better one since it fits the requirements for modern corporate success. In contrast, the sensitivity and care for the feelings of others that girls develop through their play have little market value and can even impede professional success. Lever implies that, given the realities of adult life, if a girl does not want to be left dependent on men, she will have to learn to play like a boy.

To Piaget's argument that children learn the respect for rules necessary 16 for moral development by playing rule-bound games, Lawrence Kohlberg (1969) adds that these lessons are most effectively learned through the opportunities for role-taking that arise in the course of resolving disputes. Consequently, the moral lessons inherent in girls' play appear to be fewer than in boys'. Traditional girls' games like jump rope and hopscotch are turn-taking games, where competition is indirect since one person's success does not necessarily signify another's failure. Consequently, disputes requiring adjudication are less likely to occur. In fact, most of the girls whom Lever interviewed claimed that when a quarrel broke out, they ended the game. Rather than elaborating a system of rules for resolving disputes, girls subordinated the continuation of the game to the continuation of relationships.

Lever concludes that from the games they play, boys learn both the 17 independence and the organizational skills necessary for coordinating the activities of large and diverse groups of people. By participating in controlled and socially approved competitive situations, they learn to deal with competition in a relatively forthright manner—to play with their enemies and to compete with their friends—all in accordance with the rules of the game. In contrast, girls' play tends to occur in smaller, more intimate groups, often the best-friend dyad, and in private places. This play replicates the social pattern of primary human relationships in that its organization is more cooperative. Thus, it points less, in Mead's terms, toward learning to take the role of "the generalized other," less toward the abstraction of human relationships. But it fosters the development of the empathy and sensitivity necessary for taking the role of "the particular other" and points more toward knowing the other as different from the self.

The sex differences in personality formation in early childhood that 18 Chodorow derives from her analysis of the mother-child relationship are thus extended by Lever's observations of sex differences in the play activities of middle childhood. Together these accounts suggest that boys and girls arrive at puberty with a different interpersonal orientation and a different range of social experiences. Yet, since adolescence is considered a crucial time for separation, the period of "the second individuation process" (Blos, 1967), female development has appeared most divergent and thus most problematic at this time.

"Puberty," Freud says, "which brings about so great an accession of 19 libido in boys, is marked in girls by a fresh wave of *repression*," necessary for the transformation of the young girl's "masculine sexuality" into the specifically feminine sexuality of her adulthood (1905, pp. 220–221). Freud posits this transformation on the girl's acknowledgment and acceptance of "the fact of her castration" (1931, p. 229). To the girl, Freud explains, puberty brings a new awareness of "the wound to her narcissism" and leads her to develop, "like a scar, a sense of inferiority" (1925, p. 253). Since in Erik Erikson's expansion of Freud's psychoanalytic account, adolescence is the time when development hinges on identity, the girl arrives at this juncture either psychologically at risk or with a different agenda.

The problem that female adolescence presents for theorists of human [20] development is apparent in Erikson's scheme. Erikson (1950) charts eight stages of psychosocial development, of which adolescence is the fifth. The task at this stage is to forge a coherent sense of self, to verify an identity that can span the discontinuity of puberty and make possible the adult capacity to love and work. The preparation for the successful resolution of the adolescent identity crisis is delineated in Erikson's description of the crises that characterize the preceding four stages. Although the initial crisis in infancy of "trust versus mistrust" anchors development in the experience of relationship, the task then clearly becomes one of individuation. Erikson's second stage centers on the crisis of "autonomy versus shame and doubt," which marks the walking child's emerging sense of separateness and agency. From there, development goes on through the crisis of "initiative versus guilt," successful resolution of which represents a further move in the direction of autonomy. Next, following the inevitable disappointment of the magical wishes of the Oedipal period, children realize that to compete with their parents, they must first join them and learn to do what they do so well. Thus in the middle childhood years, development turns on the crisis of "industry versus inferiority," as the demonstration of competence becomes critical to the child's developing self-esteem. This is the time when children strive to learn and master the technology of their culture, in order to recognize themselves and to be recognized by others as capable of becoming adults. Next comes adolescence, the celebration of the autonomous, initiating, industrious self through the forging of an identity based on an ideology that can support and justify adult commitments. But about whom is Erikson talking?

Once again it turns out to be the male child. For the female, Erikson [21] (1968) says, the sequence is a bit different. She holds her identity in abeyance as she prepares to attract the man by whose name she will be known, by whose status she will be defined, the man who will rescue her from emptiness and loneliness by filling "the inner space." While for men, identity precedes intimacy and generativity in the optimal cycle of human separation and attachment, for women these tasks seem instead to be fused. Intimacy goes along with identity, as the female comes to know herself as she is known, through her relationships with others.

Yet despite Erikson's observation of sex differences, his chart of life- [22] cycle stages remains unchanged: identity continues to precede intimacy as male experience continues to define his life-cycle conception. But in this male life cycle there is little preparation for the intimacy of the first adult stage. Only the initial stage of trust versus mistrust suggests the type of mutuality that Erikson means by intimacy and generativity and Freud means by genitality. The rest is separateness, with the result that development itself comes to be identified with separation, and attachments appear to be developmental impediments, as is repeatedly the case in the assessment of women.

Erikson's description of male identity as forged in relation to the world 23 and of female identity as awakened in a relationship of intimacy with another person is hardly new. In the fairy tales that Bruno Bettelheim (1976) describes an identical portrayal appears. The dynamics of male adolescence are illustrated archetypically by the conflict between father and son in "The Three Languages." Here a son, considered hopelessly stupid by his father, is given one last chance at education and sent for a year to study with a master. But when he returns, all he has learned is "what the dogs bark." After two further attempts of this sort, the father gives up in disgust and orders his servants to take the child into the forest and kill him. But the servants, those perpetual rescuers of disowned and abandoned children, take pity on the child and decide simply to leave him in the forest. From there, his wanderings take him to a land beset by furious dogs whose barking permits nobody to rest and who periodically devour one of the inhabitants. Now it turns out that our hero has learned just the right thing: he can talk with the dogs and is able to quiet them, thus restoring peace to the land. Since the other knowledge he acquires serves him equally well, he emerges triumphant from his adolescent confrontation with his father, a giant of the life-cycle conception.

In contrast, the dynamics of female adolescence are depicted through 24 the telling of a very different story. In the world of the fairy tale, the girl's first bleeding is followed by a period of intense passivity in which nothing seems to be happening. Yet in the deep sleeps of Snow White and Sleeping Beauty, Bettelheim sees that inner concentration which he considers to be the necessary counterpart to the activity of adventure. Since the adolescent heroines awake from their sleep, not to conquer the world, but to marry the prince, their identity is inwardly and interpersonally defined. For women, in Bettelheim's as in Erikson's account, identity and intimacy are intricately conjoined. The sex differences depicted in the world of fairy tales, like the fantasy of the woman warrior in Maxine Hong Kingston's (1977) recent autobiographical novel which echoes the old stories of Troilus and Cressida* and Tancred and Chlorinda,† indicate repeatedly that active adventure is a male activity, and that if a woman is to embark on such endeavors, she must at least dress like a man.

---

*Troilus and Cressida, characters in classical mythology as well as in works by Chaucer and Shakespeare, pledged their love to each other. Later, however, Cressida broke her pledge, and her name has become synonymous with infidelity.
†Tancred, a Christian crusader, fell in love with Chlorinda, a pagan. He unwittingly killed her in a battle at night.

These observations about sex difference support the conclusion reached 25 by David McClelland (1975) that "sex role turns out to be one of the most important determinants of human behavior; psychologists have found sex differences in their studies from the moment they started doing empirical research." But since it is difficult to say "different" without saying "better" or "worse," since there is a tendency to construct a single scale of measurement, and since that scale has generally been derived from and standardized on the basis of men's interpretations of research data drawn predominantly or exclusively from studies of males, psychologists "have tended to regard male behavior as the 'norm' and female behavior as some kind of deviation from that norm" (p. 81). Thus, when women do not conform to the standards of psychological expectation, the conclusion has generally been that something is wrong with the women.

What Matina Horner (1972) found to be wrong with women was the 26 anxiety they showed about competitive achievement. From the beginning, research on human motivation using the Thematic Apperception Test (TAT) was plagued by evidence of sex differences which appeared to confuse and complicate data analysis. The TAT presents for interpretation an ambiguous cue—a picture about which a story is to be written or a segment of a story that is to be completed. Such stories, in reflecting projective imagination, are considered by psychologists to reveal the ways in which people construe what they perceive, that is, the concepts and interpretations they bring to their experience and thus presumably the kind of sense that they make of their lives. Prior to Horner's work it was clear that women made a different kind of sense than men of situations of competitive achievement, that in some way they saw the situations differently or the situations aroused in them some different response.

On the basis of his studies of men, McClelland divided the concept of 27 achievement motivation into what appeared to be its two logical components, a motive to approach success ("hope success") and a motive to avoid failure ("fear failure"). From her studies of women, Horner identified as a third category the unlikely motivation to avoid success ("fear success"). Women appeared to have a problem with competitive achievement, and that problem seemed to emanate from a perceived conflict between femininity and success, the dilemma of the female adolescent who struggles to integrate her feminine aspirations and the identifications of her early childhood with the more masculine competence she has acquired at school. From her analysis of women's completions of a story that began, "after first term finals, Anne finds herself at the top of her medical school class," and from her observation of women's performance in competitive achievement situations, Horner reports that, "when success is likely or possible, threatened by the negative consequences they expect to follow success, young women become anxious and their positive achievement strivings become thwarted" (p. 171). She concludes that this fear "exists because for most women, the anticipation of success in competitive achievement activity, especially against men, produces anticipation of certain negative consequences, for example, threat of social rejection and loss of femininity" (1968, p. 125).

Such conflicts about success, however, may be viewed in a different 28 light. Georgia Sassen (1980) suggests that the conflicts expressed by the women might instead indicate "a heightened perception of the 'other side' of competitive success, that is, the great emotional costs at which success achieved through competition is often gained—an understanding which, though confused, indicates some underlying sense that something is rotten in the state in which success is defined as having better grades than everyone else" (p. 15). Sassen points out that Horner found success anxiety to be present in women only when achievement was directly competitive, that is, when one person's success was at the expense of another's failure.

In his elaboration of the identity crisis, Erikson (1968) cites the life of 29 George Bernard Shaw to illustrate the young person's sense of being co-opted prematurely by success in a career he cannot wholeheartedly endorse. Shaw at seventy, reflecting upon his life, described his crisis at the age of twenty as having been caused not by the lack of success or the absence of recognition, but by too much of both: "I made good in spite of myself, and found, to my dismay, that Business, instead of expelling me as the worthless imposter I was, was fastening upon me with no intention of letting me go. Behold me, therefore, in my twentieth year, with a business training, in an occupation which I detested as cordially as any sane person lets himself detest anything he cannot escape from. In March 1876 I broke loose" (p. 143). At this point Shaw settled down to study and write as he pleased. Hardly interpreted as evidence of neurotic anxiety about achievement and competition, Shaw's refusal suggests to Erikson "the extraordinary workings of an extraordinary personality [coming] to the fore" (p. 144).

We might on these grounds begin to ask, not why women have conflicts 30 about competitive success, but why men show such readiness to adopt and celebrate a rather narrow vision of success. Remembering Piaget's observation, corroborated by Lever, that boys in their games are more concerned with rules while girls are more concerned with relationships, often at the expense of the game itself—and given Chodorow's conclusion that men's social orientation is positional while women's is personal—we begin to understand why, when "Anne" becomes "John" in Horner's tale of competitive success and the story is completed by men, fear of success tends to disappear. John is considered to have played by the rules and won. He has the *right* to feel good about his success. Confirmed in the sense of his own identity as separate from those who, compared to him, are less competent, his positional sense of self is affirmed. For Anne, it is possible that the position she could obtain by being at the top of her medical school class may not, in fact, be what she wants.

"It is obvious," Virginia Woolf says, "that the values of women differ 31 very often from the values which have been made by the other sex" (1929, p. 76). Yet, she adds, "it is the masculine values that prevail." As a result, women come to question the normality of their feelings and to alter their judgments in deference to the opinion of others. In the nineteenth century novels written by women, Woolf sees at work "a mind which was slightly pulled from the straight and made to alter its clear vision in deference to external authority." The same deference to the values and opinions of others can be seen in the judgments of twentieth century women. The difficulty women experience in finding or speaking publicly in their own voices emerges repeatedly in the form of qualification and self-doubt, but also in intimations of a divided judgment, a public assessment and private assessment which are fundamentally at odds.

Yet the deference and confusion that Woolf criticizes in women derive from the values she sees as their strength. Women's deference is rooted not only in their social subordination but also in the substance of their moral concern. Sensitivity to the needs of others and the assumption of responsibility for taking care lead women to attend to voices other than their own and to include in their judgment other points of view. Women's moral weakness, manifest in an apparent diffusion and confusion of judgment, is thus inseparable from women's moral strength, an overriding concern with relationships and responsibilities. The reluctance to judge may itself be indicative of the care and concern for others that infuse the psychology of women's development and are responsible for what is generally seen as problematic in its nature. 32

Thus women not only define themselves in a context of human relationship but also judge themselves in terms of their ability to care. Women's place in man's life cycle has been that of nurturer, caretaker, and helpmate, the weaver of those networks of relationships on which she in turn relies. But while women have thus taken care of men, men have, in their theories of psychological development, as in their economic arrangements, tended to assume or devalue that care. When the focus on individuation and individual achievement extends into adulthood and maturity is equated with personal autonomy, concern with relationships appears as a weakness of women rather than as a human strength (Miller, 1976). 33

The discrepancy between womanhood and adulthood is nowhere more evident than in the studies on sex-role stereotypes reported by Broverman, Vogel, Broverman, Clarkson, and Rosenkrantz (1972). The repeated finding of these studies is that the qualities deemed necessary for adulthood—the capacity for autonomous thinking, clear decision-making, and responsible action—are those associated with masculinity and considered undesirable as attributes of the feminine self. The stereotypes suggest a splitting of love and work that relegates expressive capacities to women while placing instrumental abilities in the masculine domain. Yet looked at from a different perspective, these stereotypes reflect a conception of adulthood that is itself out of 34 balance, favoring the separateness of the individual self over connection to others, and leaning more toward an autonomous life of work than toward the interdependence of love and care.

The discovery now being celebrated by men in mid-life of the impor- 35 tance of intimacy, relationships, and care is something that women have known from the beginning. However, because that knowledge in women has been considered "intuitive" or "instinctive," a function of anatomy coupled with destiny, psychologists have neglected to describe its development. In my research, I have found that women's moral development centers on the elaboration of that knowledge and thus delineates a critical line of psychological development in the lives of both of the sexes. The subject of moral development not only provides the final illustration of the reiterative pattern in the observation and assessment of sex differences in the literature on human development, but also indicates more particularly why the nature and significance of women's development has been for so long obscured and shrouded in mystery.

The criticism that Freud makes of women's sense of justice, seeing it as 36 compromised in its refusal of blind impartiality, reappears not only in the work of Piaget but also in that of Kohlberg. While in Piaget's account (1932) of the moral judgment of the child, girls are an aside, a curiosity to whom he devotes four brief entries in an index that omits "boys" altogether because "the child" is assumed to be male, in the research from which Kohlberg derives his theory, females simply do not exist. Kohlberg's (1958, 1981) six stages that describe the development of moral judgment from childhood to adulthood are based empirically on a study of eighty-four boys whose development Kohlberg has followed for a period of over twenty years. Although Kohlberg claims universality for his stage sequence, those groups not included in his original sample rarely reach his higher stages (Edwards, 1975; Holstein, 1976; Simpson, 1974). Prominent among those who thus appear to be deficient in moral development when measured by Kohlberg's scale are women, whose judgments seem to exemplify the third stage of his six-stage sequence. At this stage morality is conceived in interpersonal terms and goodness is equated with helping and pleasing others. This conception of goodness is considered by Kohlberg and Kramer (1969) to be functional in the lives of mature women insofar as their lives take place in the home. Kohlberg and Kramer imply that only if women enter the traditional arena of male activity will they recognize the inadequacy of this moral perspective and progress like men toward higher stages where relationships are subordinated to rules (stage four) and rules to universal principles of justice (stages five and six).

Yet herein lies a paradox, for the very traits that traditionally have de- 37 fined the "goodness" of women, their care for and sensitivity to the needs of others, are those that mark them as deficient in moral development. In this version of moral development, however, the conception of maturity is derived from the study of men's lives and reflects the importance of individuation in their development. Piaget (1970), challenging the common impression that a developmental theory is built like a pyramid from its base in infancy, points out that a conception of development instead hangs from its vertex of maturity, the point toward which progress is traced. Thus, a change in the definition of maturity does not simply alter the description of the highest stage but recasts the understanding of development, changing the entire account.

When one begins with the study of women and derives developmental 38 constructs from their lives, the outline of a moral conception different from that described by Freud, Piaget, or Kohlberg begins to emerge and informs a different description of development. In this conception, the moral problem arises from conflicting responsibilities rather than from competing rights and requires for its resolution a mode of thinking that is contextual and narrative rather than formal and abstract. This conception of morality as concerned with the activity of care centers moral development around the understanding of responsibility and relationships, just as the conception of morality as fairness ties moral development to the understanding of rights and rules.

This different construction of the moral problem by women may be seen 39 as the critical reason for their failure to develop within the constraints of Kohlberg's system. Regarding all constructions of responsibility as evidence of a conventional moral understanding, Kohlberg defines the highest stages of moral development as deriving from a reflective understanding of human rights. That the morality of rights differs from the morality of responsibility in its emphasis on separation rather than connection, in its consideration of the individual rather than the relationship as primary, is illustrated by two responses to interview questions about the nature of morality. The first comes from a twenty-five-year-old man, one of the participants in Kohlberg's study:

> [*What does the word morality mean to you?*] Nobody in the world knows the 40 answer. I think it is recognizing the right of the individual, the rights of other individuals, not interfering with those rights. Act as fairly as you would have them treat you. I think it is basically to preserve the human being's right to existence. I think that is the most important. Secondly, the human being's right to do as he pleases, again without interfering with somebody else's rights.
>
> [*How have your views on morality changed since the last interview?*] I 41 think I am more aware of an individual's rights now. I used to be looking at it strictly from my point of view, just for me. Now I think I am more aware of what the individual has a right to.

Kohlberg (1973) cites this man's response as illustrative of the principled con- 42 ception of human rights that exemplifies his fifth and sixth stages. Commenting on the response, Kohlberg says: "Moving to a perspective outside of that of his society, he identifies morality with justice (fairness, rights, the Golden Rule), with recognition of the rights of others as these are defined naturally or intrinsically. The human's being right to do as he pleases without interfering with somebody else's rights is a formula defining rights prior to social legislation" (pp. 29–30).

The second response comes from a woman who participated in the rights   43
and responsibilities study. She also was twenty-five and, at the same time, a
third-year law student:

[*Is there really some correct solution to moral problems, or is everybody's opin-*   44
ion equally right?] No, I don't think everybody's opinion is equally right. I
think that in some situations there may be opinions that are equally valid, and
one could conscientiously adopt one of several courses of action. But there are
other situations in which I think there are right and wrong answers, that sort
of inhere in the nature of existence, of all individuals here who need to live with
each other to live. We need to depend on each other, and hopefully it is not
only a physical need but a need of fulfillment in ourselves, that a person's life is
enriched by cooperating with other people and striving to live in harmony with
everybody else, and to that end, there are right and wrong, there are things
which promote that end and that move away from it, and in that way it is
possible to choose in certain cases among different courses of action that obviously promote or harm that goal.

[*Is there a time in the past when you would have thought about these*   45
things differently?] Oh, yeah, I think that I went through a time when I thought
that things were pretty relative, that I can't tell you what to do and you can't
tell me what to do, because you've got your conscience and I've got mine.

[*When was that?*] When I was in high school. I guess that it just sort of   46
dawned on me that my own ideas changed, and because my own judgment
changed, I felt I couldn't judge another person's judgment. But now I think
even when it is only the person himself who is going to be affected, I say it is
wrong to the extent it doesn't cohere with what I know about human nature
and what I know about you, and just from what I think is true about the
operation of the universe, I could say I think you are making a mistake.

[*What led you to change, do you think?*] Just seeing more of life, just   47
recognizing that there are an awful lot of things that are common among people. There are certain things that you come to learn promote a better life and
better relationships and more personal fulfillment than other things that in general tend to do the opposite, and the things that promote these things, you
would call morally right.

This response also represents a personal reconstruction of morality fol-   48
lowing a period of questioning and doubt, but the reconstruction of moral
understanding is based not on the primacy and universality of individual
rights, but rather on what she describes as a "very strong sense of being responsible to the world." Within this construction, the moral dilemma changes
from how to exercise one's rights without interfering with the rights of others
to how "to lead a moral life which includes obligations to myself and my
family and people in general." The problem then becomes one of limiting
responsibilities without abandoning moral concern. When asked to describe
herself, this woman says that she values "having other people that I am tied
to, and also having people that I am responsible to. I have a very strong sense
of being responsible to the world, that I can't just live for my enjoyment, but
just the fact of being in the world gives me an obligation to do what I can to
make the world a better place to live in, no matter how small a scale that
may be on." Thus while Kohlberg's subject worries about people interfering

with each other's rights, this woman worries about "the possibility of omission, of your not helping others when you could help them."

The issue that this woman raises is addressed by Jane Loevinger's fifth 49 "autonomous" stage of ego development, where autonomy, placed in a context of relationships, is defined as modulating an excessive sense of responsibility through the recognition that other people have responsibility for their own destiny. The autonomous stage in Loevinger's account (1970) witnesses a relinquishing of moral dichotomies and their replacement with "a feeling for the complexity and multifaceted character of real people and real situations" (p. 6). Whereas the rights conception of morality that informs Kohlberg's principled level (stages five and six) is geared to arriving at an objectively fair or just resolution to moral dilemmas upon which all rational persons could agree, the responsibility conception focuses instead on the limitations of any particular resolution and describes the conflicts that remain.

Thus it becomes clear why a morality of rights and noninterference may 50 appear frightening to women in its potential justification of indifference and unconcern. At the same time, it becomes clear why, from a male perspective, a morality of responsibility appears inconclusive and diffuse, given its insistent contextual relativism. Women's moral judgments thus elucidate the pattern observed in the description of the developmental differences between the sexes, but they also provide an alternative conception of maturity by which these differences can be assessed and their implications traced. The psychology of women that has consistently been described as distinctive in its greater orientation toward relationships and interdependence implies a more contextual mode of judgment and a different moral understanding. Given the differences in women's conceptions of self and morality, women bring to the life cycle a different point of view and order human experience in terms of different priorities.

The myth of Demeter and Persephone, which McClelland (1975) cites 51 as exemplifying the feminine attitude toward power, was associated with the Eleusinian Mysteries celebrated in ancient Greece for over two thousand years. As told in the Homeric *Hymn to Demeter*, the story of Persephone indicates the strengths of interdependence, building up resources and giving, that McClelland found in his research on power motivation to characterize the mature feminine style. Although, McClelland says, "it is fashionable to conclude that no one knows what went on in the Mysteries, it is known that they were probably the most important religious ceremonies, even partly on the historical record, which were organized by and for women, especially at the onset before men by means of the cult of Dionysos began to take them over." Thus McClelland regards the myth as "a special presentation of feminine psychology" (p. 96). It is, as well, a life-cycle story par excellence.

Persephone, the daughter of Demeter, while playing in a meadow with 52 her girlfriends, sees a beautiful narcissus which she runs to pick. As she does so, the earth opens and she is snatched away by Hades, who takes her to his underworld kingdom. Demeter, goddess of the earth, so mourns the loss of her daughter that she refuses to allow anything to grow. The crops that sustain life on earth shrivel up, killing men and animals alike, until Zeus takes pity on man's suffering and persuades his brother to return Persephone to her mother. But before she leaves, Persephone eats some pomegranate seeds, which ensures that she will spend part of every year with Hades in the underworld.

The elusive mystery of women's development lies in its recognition of 53 the continuing importance of attachment in the human life cycle. Woman's place in man's life cycle is to protect this recognition while the developmental litany intones the celebration of separation, autonomy, individuation, and natural rights. The myth of Persephone speaks directly to the distortion in this view by reminding us that narcissism leads to death, that the fertility of the earth is in some mysterious way tied to the continuation of the mother-daughter relationship, and that the life cycle itself arises from an alternation between the world of women and that of men. Only when life-cycle theorists divide their attention and begin to live with women as they have lived with men will their vision encompass the experience of both sexes and their theories become correspondingly more fertile.

REFERENCES

Bettelheim, Bruno. *The Uses of Enchantment.* New York: Alfred A. Knopf, 1976.

Blos, Peter. "The Second Individuation Process of Adolescence." In A. Freud, Ed. *The Psychoanalytic Study of the Child,* Vol. 22. New York: International Universities Press, 1967.

Broverman, I., Vogel, S., Broverman, D., Clarkson, F., and Rosenkrantz, P. "Sex-role Stereotypes: A Current Appraisal." *Journal of Social Issues* 28 (1972):59–78.

Chodorow, Nancy. "Family Structure and Feminine Personality." In M. Z. Rosaldo and L. Lamphere, Eds. *Woman, Culture and Society.* Stanford: Stanford University Press, 1974.

Edwards, Carolyn P. "Societal Complexity and Moral Development: A Kenyan Study." *Ethos* 3 (1975):505–527.

Erikson, Erik H. *Childhood and Society.* New York: W. W. Norton, 1950.

_____. *Identity: Youth and Crisis.* New York: W. W. Norton, 1968.

Freud, Sigmund. *Three Essays on the Theory of Sexuality,* vol. 7, 1905.

_____. "Some Psychical Consequences of the Anatomical Distinction Between the Sexes," vol. 19, 1925.

_____. "Female Sexuality," vol. 21, 1931.

Holstein, Constance. "Development of Moral Judgment: A Longitudinal Study of Males and Females." *Child Development* 47 (1976):51–61.

Horner, Matina S. "Toward an Understanding of Achievement-related Conflicts in Women." *Journal of Social Issues* 28 (1972):157–175.

Kingston, Maxine Hong. *The Woman Warrior.* New York: Alfred A. Knopf, 1977.

Kohlberg, Lawrence. "The Development of Modes of Thinking and Choices in Years 10 to 16." Ph.D. Dissertation, University of Chicago, 1958.

_____. "Stage and Sequence: The Cognitive-Development Approach to Socialization." In D. A. Goslin, Ed. *Handbook of Socialization Theory and Research.* Chicago: Rand McNally, 1969.

_____. "Continuities and Discontinuities in Childhood and Adult Moral Development Revisited." In *Collected Papers on Moral Development and Moral Education.* Moral Education Research Foundation, Harvard University, 1973.

_____. *The Philosophy of Moral Development.* San Francisco: Harper and Row, 1981.

Kohlberg L., and Kramer, R. "Continuities and Discontinuities in Child and Adult Moral Development." *Human Development* 12 (1969):93–120.

Lever, Janet. "Sex Differences in the Games Children Play." *Social Problems* 23 (1976):478–487.

————. "Sex Differences in the Complexity of Children's Play and Games." *American Sociological Review* 43 (1978):471–483.

Loevinger, Jane, and Wessler, Ruth. *Measuring Ego Development*. San Francisco: Jossey-Bass, 1970.

McClelland, David C. *Power: The Inner Experience*. New York: Irvington, 1975.

Mead, George Herbert. *Mind, Self, and Society*. Chicago: University of Chicago Press, 1934.

Miller, Jean Baker. *Toward a New Psychology of Women*. Boston: Beacon Press, 1976.

Piaget, Jean. *The Moral Judgment of the Child* (1932). New York: The Free Press, 1965.

————. *Structuralism*. New York: Basic Books, 1970.

Sassen, Georgia. "Success Anxiety in Women: A Constructivist Interpretation of Its Sources and Its Significance." *Harvard Educational Review* 50 (1980):13–25.

Simpson, Elizabeth L. "Moral Development Research: A Case Study of Scientific Cultural Bias." *Human Development* 17 (1974):81–106.

Stoller, Robert J. "A Contribution to the Study of Gender Identity." *International Journal of Psycho-Analysis* 45 (1964):220–226.

Woolf, Virginia. *A Room of One's Own*. New York: Harcourt, Brace and World, 1929.

QUESTIONS ABOUT GILLIGAN'S DISCOURSE COMMUNITY AND HER CONCERNS IN THIS SELECTION

1. What is an observational bias? What observational bias does Gilligan say has marked psychological theorists?
2. How does Nancy Chodorow explain the apparent fact that girls emerge from childhood with a greater capacity for empathy than do boys?
3. Do Janet Lever's findings about boys' and girls' games ring true to you?
4. Describe the highest two stages of Kohlberg's theory of moral development. How does Gilligan criticize this theory?
5. Much of Kohlberg's and Gilligan's theorizing about moral development depends on interviewing people. How adequate do you think interviews are in trying to discover someone's conception of morality? What kinds of subjects would you want to see in interviews about conceptions of morality?
6. What does the conception of morality prevalent among women stress? What does the conception of morality prevalent among men, on the other hand, stress?
7. How comfortable are you with the claim that there can be different conceptions of morality?
8. Do you think women's conception of morality could be exploited in the corporate world? How?
9. What does Gilligan say has been "women's place in man's life cycle"?

QUESTIONS ON GILLIGAN'S RHETORICAL STRATEGIES

1. Gilligan begins this selection with descriptions of parts of Chekhov's *The Cherry Orchard*. Do these make her introductory point clearly enough?
2. What are the major steps Gilligan takes in this selection? That is, on its most general level, how is this selection organized? Do you think it is well organized?

3. Gilligan devotes a good deal of space to reporting on Janet Lever's study of children's games. Is the amount of space justified?

4. Gilligan quotes at length from an interview with one of Kohlberg's subjects and from an interview with one of her own subjects (in a rights and responsibilities study). What does she gain by quoting their exact words? Does she gain anything by including such long quotations?

5. Gilligan makes some generalizations without providing much specific evidence. For example, she writes that "the same deference to the values and opinions of others can be seen in the judgments of twentieth century women." She follows this up with little specific evidence. Does she need specific evidence for such a generalization?

6. Do you think Gilligan serves herself well by arguing for a dichotomy between women's conception of morality and men's conception? Do you think she could make a better case for a continuum running between these two conceptions?

7. How effective do you think Gilligan's final three paragraphs are? Why?

8. With what word does this selection end? Why do you think Gilligan chose it?

WRITING FROM WITHIN AND ABOUT THE SOCIAL SCIENCES: PSYCHOLOGY

Writing for Yourself

1. In your journal, write about an incident you have observed in which at least two different conceptions of morality clashed.

2. In your journal, write about what morality means to you.

Writing for Nonacademic Audiences

1. A national news magazine has issued a call for 500-word opinion pieces on how feminism has affected college campuses. You decide to accept this call.

2. You have been elected by your dorm council to write a 500-word brochure on how people should treat each other to make life in your dorm pleasant. This brochure will be sent to all students moving into your dorm at the start of subsequent academic years.

Writing for Academic Audiences

1. For a class in developmental psychology, write a 750-word description of Kohlberg's stages of moral development. This is to be used by your peers in the class to flesh out their knowledge of the life cycle perspective.

2. In a political science class, a young woman claims that the world needs more female leaders in order to ensure a future for the world. Upon hearing this, your instructor assigns all of the rest of the students to write a 750-word paper in which they must evaluate the young woman's claim.

3. How do you think the modern feminist movement will affect the two conceptions of morality that Gilligan describes? Answer this question in a 1,000-word persuasive paper for a modern American sociology course.

4. Use the methods and materials devised by Horner (described in Gilligan's essay) to test for success anxiety among students on your campus. Then write up the results of your test in a standardized research report to be submitted for credit to your instructor in an introductory psychology class.
5. For a class in ethics, argue your position in a 1,000-word paper on whether or not there can be more than one fully formed and acceptable conception of morality.

William G. Ouchi

(b. 1943)

In the early 1970s, as an associate professor of organizational behavior at the Graduate School of Business at Stanford University, William Ouchi became interested in the almost unprecedented economic growth of Japan since World War II. Funded by the National Commission on Productivity, Ouchi began to study Japanese industries, and what he found convinced him that American business firms have much to learn from those of Japan, particularly in regard to personnel management. He saw in the Japanese model of management an approach that developed loyalty between workers and between the company and its workers. He saw an approach that fostered creativity and encouraged the growth of subordinates. He saw an approach that involved the whole life of the individual.

The study of this kind of personnel management is right at the center of Ouchi's discourse community: organizational economics. He sees institutions as social beings and examines the managerial system that helps the individual parts of corporate entities work together smoothly and productively. Writing within such a community, Ouchi frequently personifies the institution; often, for example, he speaks of a business as having a memory. His focus is always on what it is that contributes to the institution's smooth functioning. In Theory Z: How American Business Can Meet the Japanese Challenge *(1981), he examines particularly those cultural elements that contribute to the Japanese style of management and suggests ways in which that style can be adapted to American industries.*

Theory Z *was attacked by some reviewers as being too slanted, too biased towards the Japanese model. Reviewers noted that some elements of the Japanese model, such as participatory decision making and lifetime employment, have long been part of the North American business community. Others implied that his admiration of the Japanese model was culturally biased. Whether or not these assertions are accurate, Ouchi has written a model work in his discourse community, one that is very explicit about the major concerns of the writer.*

In addition to teaching at Stanford University, Ouchi has taught at the Graduate School of Business at the University of Chicago. He now teaches at the Graduate School of Management at UCLA, a post he has held since 1979.

The following selection is the second chapter of Theory Z.

THE WORKINGS OF A JAPANESE CORPORATION

The basic mechanisms of management control in a Japanese company are so 1 subtle, implicit, and internal that they often appear to an outsider not to exist. That conclusion is a mistake. The mechanisms are thorough, highly disciplined and demanding, yet very flexible. Their essence could not be more different from methods of managerial control in Western organizations.

A visit to the United States headquarters of one of the major Japanese 2 banks provided some interesting insights. As expected, the top officers were Japanese expatriates, the middle managers and other employees local Americans (many were Japanese-American). In this case, however, the bank had two vice-presidents who were local Americans, hired away from other banking institutions. Studying this peculiarity brought me an important insight to the managerial control system in a Japanese company. In this hybrid setting the basic differences between Japanese and American approaches clashed, thus illuminating those deeper characteristics not readily apparent among Japanese companies in Japan.

In an interview with the American vice-presidents, I asked how they 3 felt about working for this Japanese bank. "They treat us well, let us in on the decision making, and pay us well. We're satisfied." "You're very fortunate," I continued, "but tell me, if there were something that you could change about this Japanese bank, what would it be?" The response was quick and clearly one that was very much on their minds: "These Japanese just don't understand objectives, and it drives us nuts!"

Next I interviewed the president of this bank, an expatriate Japanese 4 who was on temporary assignment from Tokyo headquarters to run the United States operation, and asked about the two American vice-presidents. "They're hard working, loyal, and professional. We think they're terrific," came the reply. When asked if he would like to change them in any way, the president replied, "These Americans just don't seem to be able to understand objectives."

With each side accusing the other of inability to understand objectives, 5 there was a clear need for further interviewing and for clarification. A second round of interviews probed further into the issue. First the American vice-presidents: "We have a non-stop running battle with the president. We simply cannot get him to specify a performance target for us. We have all the necessary reports and numbers, but we can't get specific targets from him. He won't tell us how large a dollar increase in loan volume or what percent decrease in operating costs he expects us to achieve over the next month, quarter, or even year. How can we know whether we're performing well without specific targets to shoot for?" A point well taken, for every major American company and government bureau devotes a large fraction of its time to the setting of specific, measurable performance targets. Every American business school teaches its students to take global, fuzzy corporate goals and boil them down to measurable performance targets. Management by objective (MBO), program planning and evaluation, and cost-benefit analysis are among the basic tools of control in modern American management.

When I returned to reinterview the Japanese president, he explained, 6 "If only I could get these Americans to understand our philosophy of banking. To understand what the business means to us—how we feel we should deal with our customers and our employees. What our relationship should be to the local communities we serve. How we should deal with our competitors, and what our role should be in the world at large. If they could get that under their skin, then they could figure out for themselves what an appropriate objective would be for any situation, no matter how unusual or new, and I would never have to tell them, never have to give them a target."

This example illustrates that the basic mechanism of control in a Japa- 7 nese company is embodied in a philosophy of management. This philosophy, an implicit theory of the firm, describes the objectives and the procedures to move towards them. These objectives represent the values of the owners, employees, customers, and government regulators. The movement toward objectives is defined by a set of beliefs about what kinds of solutions tend to work well in the industry or in the firm; such beliefs concern, for example, who should make decisions about what kinds of new products the company should or should not consider.

Those who grasp the essence of this philosophy of values and beliefs (or 8 ends and means) can deduce from the general statement an almost limitless number of specific rules or targets to suit changing conditions. Moreover, these specific rules or targets will be consistent between individuals. Two individuals who both understand the underlying theory will derive the same specific rule to deal with a particular situation. Thus the theory provides both control over the ways people respond to problems and coordination between them, so solutions will mesh with one another. This theory, implicit rather than explicit, cannot be set down completely in so many sentences. Rather, the theory is communicated through a common culture shared by key managers and, to some extent, all employees.

The organizational culture consists of a set of symbols, ceremonies, and 9 myths that communicate the underlying values and beliefs of that organization to its employees. These rituals put flesh on what would otherwise be sparse and abstract ideas, bringing them to life in a way that has meaning and impact for a new employee. For example, telling employees that the company is committed to coordinated and unselfish cooperation sounds fine but also produces skepticism about the commitment of others and creates ambiguity over just how a principle might apply in specific situations. When, on the other hand, the value of cooperation is expressed through the ritual of *ringi*, a collective decision making in which a document passes from manager to manager for their official seal of approval, then the neophyte experiences the philosophy of cooperation in a very concrete way. Slowly individual preferences give way to collective consensus. This tangible evidence shows true commitment to what might otherwise be an abstract and ignored value.

Recent research by Professor Alan Wilkins of Brigham Young University 10 indicates that some American organizations have a rich inventory of stories that are told and retold from generation to generation. A value embodied in a specific story rather than stated more abstractly is more believable and better remembered, according to this research. These stories, which form a "corporate memory," may be based on real or partly real events, but they nonetheless form an important part of the culture of an organization.

An organizational culture develops when employees have a broad array 11 of common experiences as touchstones through which to communicate with a great deal of subtlety. In the Japanese company, because managers have passed through many and the same functions over the years, they can refer to a large array of common experiences, tell stories, and remember symbolic events that remind each of them of their common commitment to certain values and beliefs. Moreover, this commonality provides them with a shorthand form of communication. Because the underlying premises or theoretical position from which each person proceeds is held in common with the others, each can assume certain responses or agreements without actually taking the time to negotiate them. Thus the common culture creates a general backdrop of coordination that greatly facilitates decision making and planning over specific issues.

DECISION MAKING

Probably the best known feature of Japanese organizations is their partici- 12 pative approach to decision making. In the typical American organization the department head, division manager, and president typically each feel that "the buck stops here"—that they alone should take the responsibility for making decisions. Recently, some organizations have adopted explicitly participative modes of decision making in which all of the members of a department reach consensus on what decision to adopt. Decision making by consensus has been the subject of a great deal of research in Europe and the United States over the past twenty years, and the evidence strongly suggests that a consensus approach yields more creative decisions and more effective implementation than does individual decision making.*

Western style participative decision making is by now a fairly standard- 13

---

* For a thorough and practical discussion of participative methods of decision making and their use in industry, see Edgar H. Schein, *Process Consultation* (Reading, Mass.: Addison-Wesley, 1969).

ized process. Typically, a small group of not more than eight or ten people will gather around a table, discuss the problem and suggest alternative solutions. During this process, the group should have one or more leaders skilled at managing relationships between people so that underlying disagreements can be dealt with constructively. The group can be said to have achieved a consensus when it finally agrees upon a single alternative and each member of the group can honestly say to each other member three things:

1. I believe that you understand my point of view.   14
2. I believe that I understand your point of view.   15
3. Whether or not I prefer this decision, I will support it, because it was arrived 16
   at in an open and fair manner.

At least a few managers instinctively follow this approach in every com- 17
pany, government office, and church meeting, but the vast majority do not. Some companies have officially instituted this consensual approach throughout, because of its superiority in many cases to individual decision making. However, what occurs in a Japanese organization is a great deal more far reaching and subtle than even this participative approach.

When an important decision needs to be made in a Japanese organiza- 18
tion, everyone who will feel its impact is involved in making it. In the case of a decision where to put a new plant, whether to change a production process, or some other major event, that will often mean sixty to eighty people directly involved in making the decision. A team of three will be assigned the duty of talking to all sixty to eighty people and, each time a significant modification arises, contacting all the people involved again. The team will repeat this process until a true consensus has been achieved. Making a decision this way takes a very long time, but once a decision is reached, everyone affected by it will be likely to support it. Understanding and support may supersede the actual content of the decision, since the five or six competing alternatives may be equally good or bad. What is important is not the decision itself but rather how committed and informed people are. The "best" decisions can be bungled just as "worst" decisions can work just fine.

A friend in one of the major Japanese banks described their process. 19
"When a major decision is to be made, a written proposal lays out one 'best' alternative for consideration. The task of writing the proposal goes to the youngest and newest member of the department involved. Of course, the president or vice-president knows the acceptable alternatives, and the young person tries like heck to figure out what those are. He talks to everyone, soliciting their opinions, paying special attention to those who know the top man best. In so doing he is seeking a common ground. Fortunately, the young person cannot completely figure out from others what the boss wants, and must add his own thoughts. This is how variety enters the decision process in a Japanese company. The company relies so heavily on socializing employees with a common set of values and beliefs that all experienced employees would

be likely to come up with similar ideas. Too much homogeneity would lead to a loss of vitality and change, so the youngest person gets the assignment."

Frequently, according to my informant, this young person will in the process make a number of errors. He will suggest things that are technically impossible or politically unacceptable, and will leave things out. Experienced managers never over-direct the young man, never sit him down and tell him what the proposal should say. Even though errors consume time, effort, and expense, many will turn out to be good ideas. Letting a young person make one error of his own is believed to be worth more than one hundred lectures in his education as a manager and worker. [20]

Ultimately, a formal proposal is written and then circulated from the bottom of the organization to the top. At each stage, the manager in question signifies his agreement by affixing his seal to the document. At the end of this *ringi* process, the proposal is literally covered with the stamps of approval of sixty to eighty people. [21]

American managers are fond of chiding the Japanese by observing that, "If you're going to Japan to make a sale or close a deal and you think it will take two days, allow two weeks and if you're lucky you'll get a 'maybe.' It takes the Japanese forever to make a decision." True enough, but Japanese businesspeople who have experience dealing in the United States will often say, "Americans are quick to sign a contract or make a decision. But try to get them to implement it—it takes them forever!" [22]

Remember that this apparently cumbersome decision process takes place within the framework of an underlying agreement on philosophy, values, and beliefs. These form the basis for common decision premises that make it possible to include a very large number of people in each decision. If, as in some Western organizations, each of the sixty people had a fundamentally different view of goals and procedures, then the participative process would fail. Because the Japanese only debate the suitability of a particular alternative to reach the agreed-upon values, the process can be broadly participatory yet efficient. In Western-style consensual processes, by comparison, often underlying values and beliefs need to be worked out, and for that reason decision making teams are deliberately kept small. [23]

Another key feature of decision making in Japan is the intentional ambiguity of who is responsible for what decisions. In the United States we have job descriptions and negotiations between employees for the purpose of setting crystal clear boundaries on where my decision authority ends and yours begins. Americans expect others to behave just as we do. Many are the unhappy and frustrated American businessmen or lawyers returning from Japan with the complaint that, "If only they would tell me who is really in charge, we could make some progress." The complaint displays a lack of understanding that, in Japan, no one individual carries responsibility for a particular turf. Rather, a group or team of employees assumes joint responsibility for a set of tasks. While we wonder at their comfortableness in not knowing who [24] is responsible for what, they know quite clearly that each of them is completely responsible for all tasks, and they share that responsibility jointly. Obviously this approach sometimes lets things "fall through the cracks" because everyone may think that someone else has a task under control. When working well, however, this approach leads to a naturally participative decision making and problem solving process. But there is another important reason for the collective assignment of decision responsibility.

Many Americans object to the idea of lifetime employment because they fear the consequences of keeping on an ineffective worker. Won't that create bottlenecks and inefficiency? Clearly the Japanese have somehow solved that problem or they couldn't have achieved their great economic success. A partial answer comes from the collective assignment of decision responsibility. In a typical American firm, Jim is assigned sole responsibility for purchasing decisions for office supplies, Mary has sole responsibility for purchasing maintenance services and Fred is solely responsible for purchasing office machines. If Fred develops serious problems of a personal nature, or if he becomes ill or has some other problem that seriously impedes his ability to function at work, a bottleneck will develop. Office machine orders will not be properly processed or perhaps will not be processed at all. The whole company will suffer, and Fred will have to be let go. 25

In a Japanese company, by comparison, Mitsuo, Yoshito, and Nori will comprise a team collectively responsible for purchasing office supplies, maintenance services, and office machines. Each of them participates in all significant decisions in purchasing any of those goods or services. If Nori is unable to work, it is perfectly natural and efficient for Mitsuo and Yoshito to take up his share of the load. When Nori returns to work again, he can step right back in and do his share. This does mean that Mitsuo and Yoshito probably will have to work harder than usual for perhaps six months or a year, and they may also have to draw on Masao, who used to work in purchasing but has now been transferred to the computer section. This flow of people can be accomplished only if Mitsuo and Yoshito are confident that the organization has a memory and know that their extra efforts now will be repaid later. Fairness and equity will be achieved over the long run. It also depends upon the practice of job rotation, so that short-run labor needs can be filled internally without having to hire and fire people as such needs come and go. As with all other characteristics of the Japanese management system, decision making is embedded in a complex of parts that hang together and rely upon trust and subtlety developed through intimacy. 26

COLLECTIVE VALUES

Perhaps the most difficult aspect of the Japanese for Westerners to comprehend is the strong orientation to collective values, particularly a collective sense of responsibility. Let me illustrate with an anecdote about a visit to a 27 new factory in Japan owned and operated by an American electronics company. The American company, a particularly creative firm, frequently attracts attention within the business community for its novel approaches to planning, organizational design, and management systems. As a consequence of this corporate style, the parent company determined to make a thorough study of Japanese workers and to design a plant that would combine the best of East and West. In their study they discovered that Japanese firms almost never make use of individual work incentives, such as piecework or even individual performance appraisal tied to salary increases. They concluded that rewarding individual achievement and individual ability is always a good thing.

In the final assembly area of their new plant long lines of young Japanese women wired together electronic products on a piece-rate system: the more you wired, the more you got paid. About two months after opening, the head foreladies approached the plant manager. "Honorable plant manager," they said humbly as they bowed, "we are embarrassed to be so forward, but we must speak to you because all of the girls have threatened to quit work this Friday." (To have this happen, of course, would be a great disaster for all concerned.) "Why," they wanted to know, "can't our plant have the same compensation system as other Japanese companies? When you hire a new girl, her starting wage should be fixed by her age. An eighteen-year-old should be paid more than a sixteen-year-old. Every year on her birthday, she should receive an automatic increase in pay. The idea that any one of us can be more productive than another must be wrong, because none of us in final assembly could make a thing unless all of the other people in the plant had done their jobs right first. To single one person out as being more productive is wrong and is also personally humiliating to us." The company changed its compensation system to the Japanese model. 28

Another American company in Japan had installed a suggestion system much as we have in the United States. Individual workers were encouraged to place suggestions to improve productivity into special boxes. For an accepted idea the individual received a bonus amounting to some fraction of the productivity savings realized from his or her suggestion. After a period of six months, not a single suggestion had been submitted. The American managers were puzzled. They had heard many stories of the inventiveness, the commitment, and the loyalty of Japanese workers, yet not one suggestion to improve productivity had appeared. 29

The managers approached some of the workers and asked why the suggestion system had not been used. The answer: "No one can come up with a work improvement idea alone. We work together, and any ideas that one of us may have are actually developed by watching others and talking to others. If one of us was singled out for being responsible for such an idea, it would embarrass all of us." The company changed to a group suggestion system, in which workers collectively submitted suggestions. Bonuses were paid to 30 groups which would save bonus money until the end of the year for a party at a restaurant or, if there was enough money, for family vacations together. The suggestions and productivity improvements rained down on the plant.

One can interpret these examples in two quite different ways. Perhaps 31 the Japanese commitment to collective values is an anachronism that does not fit with modern industrialism but brings economic success despite that collectivism. Collectivism seems to be inimical to the kind of maverick creativity exemplified in Benjamin Franklin, Thomas Edison, and John D. Rockefeller. Collectivism does not seem to provide the individual incentive to excel which has made a great success of American enterprise. Entirely apart from its economic effects, collectivism implies a loss of individuality, a loss of the freedom to be different, to hold fundamentally different values from others.

The second interpretation of the examples is that the Japanese collectiv- 32 ism is economically efficient. It causes people to work well together and to encourage one another to better efforts. Industrial life requires interdependence of one person on another. But a less obvious but far-reaching implication of the Japanese collectivism for economic performance has to do with accountability.

In the Japanese mind, collectivism is neither a corporate or individual 33 goal to strive for nor a slogan to pursue. Rather, the nature of things operates so that nothing of consequence occurs as a result of individual effort. Everything important in life happens as a result of teamwork or collective effort. Therefore, to attempt to assign individual credit or blame to results is unfounded. A Japanese professor of accounting, a brilliant scholar trained at Carnegie-Mellon University who teaches now in Tokyo, remarked that the status of accounting systems in Japanese industry is primitive compared to those in the United States. Profit centers, transfer prices, and computerized information systems are barely known even in the largest Japanese companies, whereas they are a commonplace in even small United States organizations. Though not at all surprised at the difference in accounting systems, I was not at all sure that the Japanese were primitive. In fact, I thought their system a good deal more efficient than ours.

Most American companies have basically two accounting systems. One 34 system summarizes the overall financial state to inform stockholders, bankers, and other outsiders. That system is not of interest here. The other system, called the managerial or cost accounting system, exists for an entirely different reason. It measures in detail all of the particulars of transactions between departments, divisions, and key individuals in the organization, for the purpose of untangling the interdependencies between people. When, for example, two departments share one truck for deliveries, the cost accounting system charges each department for part of the cost of maintaining the truck and driver, so that at the end of the year, the performance of each department can be individually assessed, and the better department's manager can receive a larger raise. Of course, all of this information processing costs money, and furthermore may lead to arguments between the departments over whether the costs charged to each are fair.

In a Japanese company a short-run assessment of individual perfor- 35 mance is not wanted, so the company can save the considerable expense of collecting and processing all of that information. Companies still keep track of which department uses a truck how often and for what purposes, but like-minded people can interpret some simple numbers for themselves and adjust their behavior accordingly. Those insisting upon clear and precise measurement for the purpose of advancing individual interests must have an elaborate information system. Industrial life, however, is essentially integrated and interdependent. No one builds an automobile alone, no one carries through a banking transaction alone. In a sense the Japanese value of collectivism fits naturally into an industrial setting, whereas the Western individualism provides constant conflicts. The image that comes to mind is of Chaplin's silent film "Modern Times" in which the apparently insignificant hero played by Chaplin successfully fights against the unfeeling machinery of industry. Modern industrial life can be aggravating, even hostile, or natural: all depends on the fit between our culture and our technology.

WHOLISTIC CONCERN FOR PEOPLE

Anthropologist Thomas Rohlen has described in detail the process of induct- 36 ing young trainees into a Japanese bank.* Training culminates in a formal ceremony held in the company auditorium. The bank president stands at the podium, the training director at his side. The young trainees sit in the front rows with their mothers, fathers, and siblings behind them. The president welcomes the new members into the bank family, challenging them to live up to the expectations of their trainers and leaders. He speaks also to the parents, accepting from them the challenge of providing for their children not only honest work, but also accepting the obligation to see to their complete physical, intellectual, and moral development. A representative of the parents next takes the podium, thanking the bank for offering this opportunity to their offspring and reaffirming the charge to the trainees to be as loyal to their new family as they are to their blood family. Finally, a representative of the trainees rises to speak, thanking both parents and bank for their support and pledging to work hard to meet their expectations.

Most Western organizations practice an attitude of "partial inclusion," 37 an understanding between employee and employer that the connection between them involves only those activities directly connected with the completion of a specific job. Many Western social scientists have argued that partial inclusion maintains the emotional health in individuals. Being partially in-

---

*See Thomas P. Rohlen, *For Harmony and Strength: Japanese White-Collar Organization in Anthropological Perspective* (Berkeley: University of California Press, 1974).

cluded in a number of organizations makes moving from one social domain to another easy, and tensions that have built up in one setting can be released in another. The Japanese organization, by contrast, forms inclusive relationships. A set of mechanisms provide for the social support and emotional release necessary for emotional equilibrium. One such mechanism is the capacity of group members to "change hats" and alter the nature of their relationships to one another for a short time in order to provide this social release and balance. Consider one example: At one American-owned plant in Japan, a golfing day with the manager became a twice yearly tradition. A train ride of four hours each way, plus golf, consumed an entire day for this important event. The American plant manager, to prepare for the outing, made a list of critical issues of strategy and management that he felt were on the minds of his subordinates. As the group approached the first tee, he produced his list and set out the agenda for the next eighteen holes. His subordinates were discouraged and disappointed by this, and the day proceeded in a desultory fashion.

A Japanese manager interpreted the story for me. A Japanese company, 38 he pointed out, is a quite formal and at times even an authoritarian setting. Rarely will an employee disagree openly with a superior or voice complaints. When people anticipate a lifetime of working together, they cannot afford to let deep rifts develop. Thus a stylized pattern of interaction develops. Conflict and refusal would disturb the harmony that must underlie the work relationship. On the other hand, no company can remain healthy with suppressed disagreement, conflict, and complaint. A symbolic change of roles in which different patterns of behavior are acceptable provides one outlet. In the golf outing, for example, the implication was that boss and subordinates were competing as equals. With the physical setting away from the place of work, the acceptable patterns of behavior are also meant to be far removed from the daily norm. At these times subordinates can feel free to ask questions and to raise objections suppressed in the office and expect the boss to respond sympathetically. In a similar manner, office parties with drinks and dinner permit the subordinates to adopt the guise of mild inebriation to tell the boss off and give opinions unspeakable under ordinary conditions. Thus the organization provides the group with a change of venue necessary to healthy social relations.

The wholistic orientation of Japanese organizations stems from both 39 historical accident and underlying social and cultural forces. According to one commonly held view, the historical accident is that industrialism rushed into Japan after having been held out for decades by a feudal political system. Companies were forced to build plants near to the villages where they could recruit workers. With no long and gradual urbanization as Europe had, Japan found itself with a sparsely-distributed rural population faced with the onrush of industrialization. Each plant sent recruiters to village homes asking mothers and fathers to send their offspring to work in the plant twenty or thirty miles away. Village parents who loved their children would simply not release them to go to live and work in a strange place. The companies had to build dormitories, to provide a healthy diet, and to assure parents that their children would receive the moral, intellectual, physical, and domestic training that would prepare them for life. In the case of young women, the company arranged for training in domestic skills needed by a young wife. No partial inclusion, no tentative, tenuous link between company and employee was possible in this setting. Rather, it was a complete and whole relationship which formed between employee and employer.*

Some Japan experts argue that the underlying social patterns developed 40 under feudalism prepared the Japanese for dependent relationship on a paternalistic force to meet their needs and to give their loyalty in return. If such an attitude had existed, it surely would have supported the wholistic work relationship.

When economic and social life are integrated into a single whole, then 41 relationships between individuals become intimate. Rather than a connection through a single work relationship, individuals interconnect through multiple bonds. This one closely-knit relationship makes it impossible to escape the frustrations and tensions by spending time with another, completely unrelated group. Intimacy of this sort discourages selfish or dishonest action in the group, since abused relationships cannot be left behind. People who live in a company dormitory, play on a company baseball team, work together in five different committees, and know the situation will continue for the rest of their lives will develop a unique relationship. Values and beliefs become mutually compatible over a wide range of work and non-work related issues. Each person's true level of effort and of performance stands out, and the close relationship brings about a high level of subtlety in understanding of each other's needs and plans. This mixture of supports and restraints promotes mutual trust, since compatible goals and complete openness remove the fears of or desires for deception. Thus intimacy, trust, and understanding grow where individuals are linked to one another through multiple bonds in a wholistic relationship.

Social scientists have long noted that wholistic relationships develop in 42 "total institutions," but have regarded these as anomalies limited to prisons, mental hospitals, religious orders, and military units. Amitai Etzioni of Columbia University asserts that a wholistic network comprises an effective means of social control, one in which individuals can be free but also capable of a peaceful co-existence.† But Etzioni, like others, has also contended that this form of social control is fundamentally incompatible with modern indus-

---

*Sociologists and anthropologists have offered a great variety of views on the nature and extent of American influence during the post-war era on the structure of Japanese industry. The interpretation which I present here is not definitive, but it is representative.

†See Amitai Etzioni, "Organizational Control Structure," *Handbook of Organizations*, ed. J. G. March (Chicago: Rand McNally, 1965).

trial society, because industrialism inevitably leads to a high degree of specialization of labor, frequent moving between employers, and consequently only a partial inclusion in the group. The Japanese show clear evidence that wholism in industrial life is possible. The final question must address whether wholism and intimacy in industrial life are desirable. In grasping just how we Americans really differ from the Japanese lies the key to what we can learn from them.

QUESTIONS ABOUT OUCHI'S DISCOURSE COMMUNITY AND HIS CONCERNS IN THIS SELECTION

1. Ouchi is most particularly concerned with organizational economics. Based on this selection, what do you think are the major concerns of this particular discourse community?
2. Early in the essay, Ouchi refers to a philosophy of management. He refers to it as a "theory, implicit rather than explicit, [which] cannot be set down completely in so many sentences" (paragraph 8). How would you define this philosophy of management? Does it seem to you that such a philosophy would be transferable to a North American business?
3. If it is the case that the economic success of the Japanese is at least partially based upon the shared assumptions and beliefs of a culture, then does it seem logical to assume that a culture dominated by a multiplicity of beliefs and assumptions would have difficulty in achieving economic success? Explain.
4. Many Japanese firms are committed to the lifetime employment of an individual. What benefits does Ouchi see coming from this practice? Why do you think many North American companies have not accepted this practice?
5. What are the benefits of participatory decision making in a business? What are the potential disadvantages? Does the *ringi* process as Ouchi describes it seem too cumbersome for a North American business? What contributes to its success in a Japanese business?
6. What does Ouchi mean when he writes that "[w]hat is important is not the decision itself but rather how committed and informed people are. The 'best' decisions can be bungled just as 'worst' decision can work just fine" (paragraph 18)?
7. Read over the two anecdotes that begin the section entitled "Collective Values." Can you imagine those same stories being told about North American employees? If not, why not? Is it the case, as Ouchi seems to indicate, that such collectivism is opposed to the rugged individualism North Americans have been taught to honor?
8. Toward the end of the essay, Ouchi mentions the specialization of labor, a practice lauded by Adam Smith. How does Ouchi respond to this specialization?

QUESTIONS ABOUT OUCHI'S RHETORICAL STRATEGIES

1. Much of this selection is developed by anecdotes about Japanese and American businesses. Are there any generalizations that you can make about the anec-

dotes? (Are they all humorous, ironic, bitter, or hostile?) What role(s) do they play in the overall rhetorical strategy of the essay? How adequate do you find these anecdotes as evidence?

2. Is there anything in Ouchi's stance in this selection that suggests his approval or disapproval of the Japanese and American systems? If so, would the piece have been better if Ouchi had maintained a more objective, neutral stance?

3. Does it seem to you that the quotes Ouchi uses are word-for-word, or are they generalized expressions of sentiments and ideas that Ouchi encountered during his interviews? Does knowing the answer to that question affect the meaning of the piece in any way? If not, what might that suggest about the use of quotations in this discourse community?

4. Ouchi divides this selection into several smaller sections, each with an appropriate heading. Clearly this indicates that he is shifting his focus to a new area of concern, but does this division serve *any* other purpose as well?

5. At the beginning of paragraph 23, Ouchi in effect warns his readers: "Remember that this apparently cumbersome process takes place within the framework of an underlying agreement on philosophy, values, and beliefs." How would you describe Ouchi's rhetorical strategy here?

6. In paragraph 24, Ouchi admits that when a group, rather than an individual, has several areas of responsibility, some details may "'fall through the cracks' because everyone may think that someone else has a task under control." But this is all he mentions. Does it seem to you that Ouchi is purposefully mitigating the potential disadvantages through his rhetorical strategies? Or is there simply no more to be said on this subject?

7. Economists, like writers in any academic discourse community, might be prone to use jargon, or words whose meanings are distinct to that discourse community. Is this the case with Ouchi? Based on your response to his diction, how would you describe the audience he is trying to reach?

8. In the preface to *Theory Z*, Ouchi notes that many of the conclusions he presents in the book are based on charts and statistics he has gathered during his research. Why does he not include that material to support the points he makes in this selection?

WRITING FROM WITHIN AND ABOUT THE SOCIAL SCIENCES: ECONOMICS

Writing for Yourself

1. In your journal, reflect on the following: "Modern industrial life can be aggravating, even hostile, or natural: all depends on the fit between our culture and our technology" (paragraph 35).

2. In your journal, reflect on the system of managerial control in Japan's industries. Compare it to the managerial control in a job situation you have encountered. Which seems preferable? Why?

Writing for Nonacademic Audiences

1. Many people separate work life from personal life, but, according to Ouchi, Japanese firms do not accept this kind of dichotomy. Write a 250-word essay

for your peers on your reaction to the Japanese model. You might first wish to read over Ouchi's section entitled "Wholistic Concern for People."

2. In paragraph 35, Ouchi mentions Charlie Chaplin's film *Modern Times*. Your university is presenting an anniversary screening of that film, and a dean has asked you to write a review of it for your university newspaper. You choose to write that review from a Japanese perspective, using Ouchi as your major source. You are limited to 500 words.

3. For your campus newspaper, write a 500-word feature article describing some of the stories glorifying rugged individualism that are prevalent on your campus.

4. Read over Ouchi's description of the *ringi* process. Then research the building of the nuclear plant at Shoreham, Long Island. This plant is currently not operating, and the governor of New York has pledged to keep it inoperative. For the editorial page of the *New York Times*, explain how the process of *ringi* might have helped or hindered in the building of this plant. You are limited to 500 words.

Writing for Academic Audiences

1. Ouchi notes that in Japanese affairs, "the nature of things operates so that nothing of consequence occurs as a result of individual effort. Everything important in life happens as a result of teamwork or collective effort" (paragraph 33). And yet, this stress on the group rather than the individual has been blamed for the economic woes of the Soviet Union and China, both of which are beginning to emphasize individual incentive. For a class in business and management control, write a 1,000-word essay in which you attempt to explain this apparent contradiction.

2. Many Americans have felt hostility toward Japanese business because of the enormous trade imbalance between the two countries. This has led to calls for boycotts of Japanese goods, as well as threats of higher tariffs placed on Japanese products (making them more expensive and therefore less competitive with American products). After researching this situation, write a 750-word essay for your peers explaining your own position on such tariffs.

3. For a class in introductory economics, write a 1,500-word essay explaining the economic factors that have contributed to Japan's economic success since 1945.

Suzanne J. Kessler
(b. 1946)
and
Wendy McKenna
(b. 1945)

Suzanne J. Kessler and Wendy McKenna are psychologists, Kessler at the State University of New York at Purchase and McKenna at Sarah Lawrence College. However, the selection from their work that we anthologize could be classified not only as psychology but also as social psychology, sociology, and anthropology. In this selection they write from within the discourse community of social constructionists.

Social constructionists challenge what is probably the most common traditional view of reality and knowledge. According to this view, reality exists apart from those who perceive and classify it. Humans—the potential perceivers and classifiers—have, as it were, a mental mirror and an inner eye. The mirror reflects reality for us, and the inner eye allows us to contemplate reality. But reality exists apart from our contemplation of it, a universal foundation for our knowledge. Knowledge is valid to the degree that it accords with the nature of reality.

Social constructionists claim that what we normally call reality or truth is a creation or construction of groups of people with similar interests and backgrounds. They do not deny that there are hard, objective things in the world, but they argue that what is important is how different communities classify and respond to these objects as well as to each other. They maintain that different communities classify and respond to the same things differently, no matter how "hard" or "objective" those things may seem. For social constructionists, then, the nature of reality is negotiated in daily interactions among those who use the same language and who respond similarly to the same symbols. These people reach a consensus about what reality is. Reality, therefore, is what people in a community agree that it is.

In Gender, An Ethnomethodological Approach, *Kessler and McKenna take a social constructionist approach to the ways in which people attribute gender to one another. In the preface to* Gender, *they state that their "Theoretical position is that gender is a social construction, that a world of two "sexes" is a result of the socially based, taken-for-granted methods which members use to construct reality" (p. vii). In other words, they argue that the way in which others are male or female is actually a social construction, and that this social construction underlies all research on gender and sexuality. Their claims are all the more striking because most people would say that gender is a basic fact of life, that people are either male or female, that this matter could allow for no social construction whatsoever. Kessler and McKenna would respond by saying that the view of gender as an objective fact has been constructed by people in a large community.*

The following selection is the latter part of "Toward a Theory of Gender," the final chapter in Gender.

TOWARD A THEORY OF GENDER

DOING FEMALE AND MALE

Theory and research on how "normal" people present themselves as either   1
female or male has been almost totally absent from the literature. The most
suggestive is a brief, but important paper by Birdwhistell (1970). Taking it
for granted that there are two genders and that, in order to reproduce, the
two genders must be able to tell each other apart, Birdwhistell raises the
question of what the critical "gender markers" are for human beings. He
rejects genitals as a marker because they are usually hidden and because children do not treat them as a relevant characteristic. He also rejects "secondary
sexual characteristics" as being far from dichotomous, at least when compared to those markers in other species (e.g., plumage in birds). Birdwhistell
believes that "tertiary sexual" characteristics" (nonverbal behaviors such as
facial expression, movement, and body posture) are the predominant gender
markers for humans. Using data and informants from seven cultures, he demonstrates that members can recognize and sketch out, in a rough way, typical
and atypical nonverbal behaviors for females and males. In a study of American "gender markers," Birdwhistell indicates some of the body postures and
facial expressions that differentiate males and females, concentrating on behaviors that convey sexual interest. He emphasizes that no nonverbal behavior ever carries meaning divorced from the context in which it occurs.

   We agree with Birdwhistell on the importance of understanding gender   2
display and recognition, as well as with his assertion that genitals and other
physical characteristics are not the critical signs of gender. It is informative
that people can describe and recognize typical and atypical gender displays,
but if a display can be characterized as typical or atypical, then the gender
of the person who is displaying has already been attributed. Therefore typical
displays are not necessary to make a gender attribution nor are atypical displays grounds for doubting an attribution. A woman is still a woman, regardless of whether she is being (nonverbally) masculine or feminine.

   Birdwhistell's work does not uncover particulars of the gender attribu-   3
tion process. His data on American gender displays was collected in the same
way as every other study on "sex differences." People were sorted *in the first
place* into one of two gender categories, and only then, after an initial gender
attribution was made, were these displays compared. This technique, as we
have stated before, involves assumptions that militate against uncovering the
gender attribution process. By accepting the fact of two genders and precat-
egorizing people as one or the other, the researchers have already (implicitly)
decided that there are differences. Given their ideas of what female and male
mean, certain differences take on importance, while others are seen as irrel-

evant. On the one hand, variables may be chosen for study because they fit the list of differentiating characteristics which researchers already "know" men and women have (e.g., "preening" behavior). On the other hand, some cues may be ignored, either because they seem so obvious that they are not worth studying (e.g., wearing a dress) or because they are not considered relevant; that is, they are not part of the social construction of gender (e.g., the color of the person's hair).

In order to fully understand the role of nonverbal behaviors in the gen- 4 der attribution process, it is necessary to understand that the social construction of gender determines why and how we study certain phenomena. Rather than asking people to notice or describe the typical and atypical behaviors of their own and the other gender (which, as even Birdwhistell notes, can never result in an exhaustive list), information could be gathered on which, if any, nonverbal behaviors are "conditions of failure." In what nonverbal ways could a person behave such that her/his gender is questioned? Although our own interests are theoretical, such concrete knowledge has practical implications for transsexuals and others. If the conditions of failure could be described, then people could be any gender they wanted to be, at any time.

The gender attribution process is an interaction between displayer and 5 attributor, but concrete displays are not informative unless interpreted in light of the rules which the attributor has for deciding what it means to be a female or male. As members of a sociocultural group, the displayer and the attributor share a knowledge of the socially constructed signs of gender. They learn these signs as part of the process of socialization (becoming members). In our culture these signs include genitals, secondary gender characteristics, dress and accessories, and nonverbal and paralinguistic behaviors. As we established in Chapters 2 and 4, these concrete signs of gender are not necessarily universal, nor are they necessarily the same signs used by children.

In learning what the signs of gender are, the displayer can begin to 6 accentuate them, to aid in creating the gender dichotomy. For example, as Haviland (1976) has demonstrated, height of the eyebrow from the center of the pupil differs considerably between adult American women and men, but is virtually identical in male and female infants and young children. The difference in adults is obviously aided, if not caused, by eyebrow tweezing and expressive style.

Along with the displayer learning to accentuate certain signs, the attri- 7 butor contributes to the accentuation of gender cues by selective perception. For example, members of our culture may look for facial hair, while in other cultures this might not be considered something to inspect. In learning to look for facial hair, the attributor perceives in greater detail signs of facial hair than would be the case if facial hair were not a cue. Selective perception occurs in many other contexts. Eskimos differentiate various kinds of snow (Whorf, 1956); people see more or less aggressive behavior in a football game, depending on which side they support (Hastorf and Cantril, 1954).

Although within a positivist framework it is important to delineate spe-   8
cific gender cues and unravel the process involved in learning to accentuate
and selectively perceive these cues, doing so glosses over the deeper structure
of the social construction of gender. Members do not simply learn rules for
telling females from males. They learn how to use the rules in their relation
to the socially shared world of two genders. There is no rule for deciding
"male" or "female" that will always work. Members need to know, for example, when to disregard eyebrows and look for hand size. Gender attributions are made within a particular social context and in relation to all the
routine features of everyday life (Garfinkel, 1967). Among the most important of these features is the basic trust that events are what they appear to be
and not performances or examples of deceit (unless one is viewing a performance; in that case the assumption is that it is a "real" performance which
carries with it other routine features).

Given basic trust regarding gender, successfully passing transsexuals, by   9
virtue of being successful, will be impossible to locate (Sulcov, 1973). To be
successful in one's gender is to prevent any doubt that one's gender is objectively, externally real. We do not live our lives searching for deceit, and, in
fact, classify people who do as paranoid. In contexts where deceit regarding
gender is made salient, everyone's gender may begin to be doubted. For example, Feinbloom (1976) reports that when she speaks on panels that include
"real" transsexuals, she, presenting herself as a "real" woman, is sometimes
asked if she is a transsexual. The context[s] in which persons appear reflexively create the possibility or impossibility of being real or "only" passing.

If there are no concrete cues that will always allow one to make the   10
"correct" gender attribution, how is categorizing a person as either female or
male accomplished in each case? Our answer, based on findings of the over-
lay study, reports from transsexuals, and the treatment of gender in the positivist literature, takes the form of a categorizing *schema*. The schema is not
dependent on any particular gender cue, nor is it offered as a statement of a
rule which people follow like robots. Rather, it is a way of understanding
how it is that members of Western reality can see someone as either female
or male. The schema is: *See someone as female only when you cannot see
them as male.* Earlier in this chapter we stated that in order for a female
gender attribution to be made, there must be an absence of anything which
can be construed as a "male only" characteristic. In order for a "male" gender
attribution to be made, the presence of at least one "male" sign must be
noticed, and one sign may be enough, especially if it is a penis.* It is rare to

---

* Freud was right about the "obvious superiority" of the penis. However, he considered the
    emphasis on the penis as an inevitable psychological consequence of its objective reality.
    We are treating the belief in the penis' objective reality as problematic. Those who read
    Freud as being concerned with (socially real) phalluses, rather than (physically real) pe-
    nises, see psychoanalytic theory as being grounded in meanings that come very close to
    our schema for differentiating females from males: "The alternative (is) between having,

see a person that one thinks is a man and then wonder if one has made a "mistake." However, it is not uncommon to wonder if someone is "really" a woman. The relative ease with which female-to-male transsexuals "pass" as compared to male-to-female transsexuals underscores this point. It is symbolized by the male-to-female transsexual needing to cover or remove her facial hair in order to be seen as a woman and the female-to-male transsexual having the option of growing a beard or being clean shaven. The female may not have any "male" signs.

The schema, see someone as female only when you cannot see them as 11 male, is not a statement of positivist fact. It is *not* that "male" gender characteristics are simply more obvious than "female" ones or that the presence of a male cue is more obvious than its absence. The salience of male characteristics is a social construction. We construct gender so that male characteristics are seen as more obvious. It could be otherwise, but to see that, one must suspend belief in the external reality of "objective facts."

To fail to see someone as a man is to see them as a woman and vice 12 versa, since "male" and "female" are mutually constitutive. However, the conditions of failure are different. The condition of failure for being seen as a woman is to be seen as having a concrete "male" characteristic. The condition of failure for being seen as a man is to be seen as not having any concrete "male" characteristics. In the social construction of gender "male" is the primary construction.*

GENDER ATTRIBUTION AS AN HISTORICAL PROCESS

The gender attribution process is simultaneously an *ahistorical* and an *histor-* 13 *ical* process. It is ahistorical in the sense that we have been discussing; gender attributions are made in the course of a particular, concrete interaction. It is historical in the sense that it creates and sustains the natural attitude toward gender and hence gender as a permanent feature. The historicity of gender is constituted in the course of interaction. In ongoing interactions, once a gender attribution has been made, it is no longer necessary to keep "doing male" or "doing female." What Garfinkel, Agnes, and many others have failed to recognize is that it is not the particular gender which must be sustained, but

---

or not having, the phallus. Castration is not a real 'lack' but a meaning conferred upon the genitals of a woman. . . . The presence or absence of the phallus carries the difference between the two sexual statuses, 'man' and 'woman'" (Rubin, 1975, p. 191) [Kessler and McKenna's note].

* Several features of psychological and biological research and theory on gender seem to have an intriguing relationship to this schema. The specifics of the relationship are unknown and open to speculation, but these features include the precariousness of the development of a male gender identity and male gender role behaviors (as opposed to female), the prevalence of theories of male gender development which cannot explain female gender development, and the scientific fact that, beginning with conception, something (genes, hormones) must be added at every step to make the fetus male [Kessler and McKenna's note].

rather the sense of its "naturalness," the sense that the actor has always been that gender. In sharing the natural attitude, both actor and attributor can assume (and each knows the other assumes) that gender never changes, that people "really" are what they appear to be. As a consequence of holding the natural attitude, the attributor filters *all* of the actor's behaviors through the gender attribution that was made, and the actor's behaviors are made sense of within that context. As we have illustrated in Chapter 5, almost nothing can discredit a gender attribution once it is made. Even the loss of the original criteria used to make the attribution might well become irrelevant. The man might shave his beard; the woman might have a mastectomy. The gender attribution will not change, though, merely because these signs no longer exist.

Since discrediting gender attributions is a matter of discrediting natu- 14 ralness, this can only occur over time through a violation of the gender invariance rule. The person must create a sense of having "changed" genders. She/he must violate the naturalness of the gender (i.e., its historicity) before discrediting occurs and a new gender attribution is made. Even then, a discrediting of the original gender attribution will not necessarily occur. Gender attributions are so impervious to change that the person will be seen as "crazy" long before she/he is seen as being the other gender. For this reason, transsexuals find it most difficult to be seen as their "new" gender by those people who made their acquaintance in their "original" gender. The first impression will not dissipate for a long time (Feinbloom, 1976). If, however, the first impression is made when the transsexual is in his/her "new" gender, it will be most difficult to discredit *that* attribution, regardless of the information given to the attributor. We have had transsexuals lecture in classrooms and have had students question the authenticity of the lecturers' *transsexualism*. These students were unable, after a conscious search, to specify any cues that would unqualifiedly classify the transsexuals' gender as other than that which they appeared to be. The knowledge that these people had admittedly been assigned the other gender at birth and had lived 30 years as that gender became problematic for the students (and fascinating to us) because that information by itself could not be used to discredit the gender attribution.

If transsexuals understood these features of discrediting they would (1) 15 focus on creating decisive first impressions as male or female and (2) then stop worrying about being the perfect man or woman and concentrate on cultivating the naturalness (i.e., the historicity) of their maleness or femaleness.

Just as any concrete cue can be cited as a reason for making a gender 16 attribution, once an attribution has been discredited, anything concrete can be used as a "good reason" for the discrediting. "I knew she was 'really' a woman because of her slight build." In the case of discrediting, just as in the case of original attributions, the "good reasons" given are not necessarily the cues used during the process.

The reason that "normals" do not walk around questioning the gender 17 attributions they make or wondering whether people will see them as they "really" are, is not because gender is a given, but because gender invariance is an incorrigible proposition. Rather than violating invariance, people use what might be seen as discrediting information to reflexively support this proposition. "I know that Greta has a penis, but that's irrelevant, since she's really a woman." All of us, transsexuals and "normals" alike, are in as little or as much danger of not being able to be seen as what we "really" are. It is our method of applying information which maintains our gender, not some intrinsic quality of our gender, itself.

GENDER DIMORPHISM: THE PROCESS AND ITS IMPLICATIONS

Once a gender attribution is made, the dichotomization process is set into 18 motion. The cues involved in the schema which led to the attribution are seen as connected with a myriad of other cues which are consequently also attributed to the person. All of these cues taken together, or any of them separately, can then be used as reasons for having made the attribution in the first place. For example, people might decide that someone is male partly because they notice the presence of a beard which is a socially constructed "male" cue. If asked, "How do you know the person is male?" the attributor might answer, "Because he had narrow hips, a beard, and he walked like a man." The attributor may not have originally noticed the other's hips or walk, and in terms of a measurable distribution, the other might not have narrow hips or a "masculine" kind of walk. Since the other has been dichotomously placed into the gender category "male," and since the attributor "knows" that men have narrower hips than women and walk in a distinctive way, these features come to be seen as having been important in the attribution (see, e.g., Seavey et al., 1975). They are important, however, only because of the way we construct female and male as dichotomous, nonoverlapping categories with male characteristics generally constructed to be more obvious.

It has become increasingly acceptable to assert that the dichotomous 19 behaviors which we attribute to the two genders (i.e., gender roles) are not necessarily the way women and men actually behave. There is growing evidence that the genders behave in very similar ways; and yet many people continue to make differential attributions of motives and behaviors, and to interpret behavior and its consequences in a dichotomous way, depending on whether the actor is female or male (e.g., Deaux, 1976; Rubin et al., 1974). Dichotomous gender role behaviors are overlayed on dichotomous *gender* which has traditionally meant two dimorphically distinct biological *sexes*. In the same way that behavior is dichotomized and overlayed on form, *form is dichotomized and overlayed on social construction*. Given a constitutive belief in two genders, form is dichotomized in the process of gender attribution at least as much as behavior is. As a result we end up with two genders, at least as different physically as they have been traditionally thought to be behaviorally.

The social construction of gender and the gender attribution process are 20 a part of reality construction. No member is exempt, and this construction is the grounding for all scientific work on gender. The natural attitude toward gender and the everyday process of gender attribution are constructions which scientists bring with them when they enter laboratories to "discover" gender characteristics. Gender, as we have described it, consists of members' methods for attributing and constructing gender. Part of members' construction involves seeing gender as consisting of, and being grounded in, objective biological characteristics. Our reality is constructed in such a way that biology is seen as the ultimate truth. This is, of course, not necessary. In other realities, for example, deities replace biology as the ultimate source of final truth. What is difficult to see, however, is that biology is no closer to the truth, in any absolute sense, than a deity; nor is the reality which we have been presenting. What *is* different among different ways of seeing the world are the possibilities stemming from basic assumptions about the way the world works. What must be taken for granted (and what need not be) changes depending on the incorrigible propositions one holds. The questions that should be asked and how they can be answered also differ depending on the reality. We have tried to show, throughout this book, how we can give grounds for what biologists and social scientists do, and how the everyday process of gender attribution is primary. Scientists construct dimophism [dimorphism, *sic*] where there is continuity. Hormones, behavior, physical characteristics, developmental processes, chromosomes, psychological qualities have all been fitted into gender dichotomous categories. Scientific knowledge does not inform the answer to "What makes a person either a man or a woman?" Rather it justifies (and appears to give grounds for) the already existing knowledge that a person is either a woman or a man and that there is no problem in differentiating between the two. Biological, psychological, and social differences do not lead to our seeing two genders. Our seeing of two genders leads to the "discovery" of biological, psychological, and social differences.

In essence we are proposing a paradigm change in the way gender is 21 viewed, a shift to seeing gender attribution as primary and gender as a practical accomplishment. In the remainder of this chapter we outline some of the theoretical and practical implications of such a shift.

One consequence of the shift is a new focus for research. Instead of 22 concentrating on the results of seeing someone as female or male ("sex difference" research), scientists can begin to uncover factors in the gender attribution process. We have offered some suggestions on how this can be done, and will end the book with a few more. However, unless this research is undertaken with a concurrent acceptance of the proposition that gender is a social construction, there will not be, and cannot be, any radical changes in either how science is done or in how gender is viewed in everyday life.

Many of those concerned with sexism and the position of women in 23
society have suggested that what is needed is a change in the concept of, or
even the elimination of, gender roles. The assertion is that, even though the
genders are physically dimorphic, except for a few biological differences related to reproduction, there is no necessary reason for any sort of differentiation. Rubin (1975) has written an excellent article, taking a strong position
on this. She sees gender as a product of social organization, as the process by
which "males" and "females" (the two sexes) become transformed into "men"
and "women" (the two genders). Her analysis demonstrates the possibility of
"the elimination of obligatory sexualities and sex roles . . . of an androgynous* and genderless (though not sexless) society" (p. 204). Rubin's analysis of
gender, while compatible with ours, still is grounded in, and takes for
granted, the objective reality of two biological "sexes." Such a position does
not question the facticity of two genders, as we mean "gender." An "androgynous society," by definition, retains the male/female dichotomy by agreeing to ignore it. Because accepting the facticity of two genders (or sexes; the
former includes the latter) means accepting the assumptions which ground
the gender attribution process, a "simple" elimination of gender role will not
change what it means to be female or male. The social construction of gender
revealed through the gender attribution process creates and sustains androcentric reality. "Male" characteristics are constructed as more obvious; a person is female only in the absence of "male" signs; there is a bias toward making a male gender attribution. In the process of attributing "male" or
"female," dichotomous physical differences are constructed, and once a physical dichotomy has been constructed it is almost impossible to eliminate sociological and psychological dichotomies. Given that the physical dichotomy is
androcentric, it is inevitable that the social one is also.

Whenever science has offered evidence of a biological continuum, but 24
everyday members insist (because of the way reality is constructed) that there
are discrete categories, there have been attempts to legislate against the continuum. Laws in the United States on what constituted a "Negro" and laws
in Nazi Germany on what constituted a Jew are two of the most obvious
examples. These laws did not reject biology, since biology is a crucial part of
the construction of Western reality, but used biology. Race was seen as
grounded in the amount of biological matter ("blood," or genetic material)
of a certain type within a human body. Rulings in sports (see Chapter 3)
which legislate a person's gender are not very different from such laws. As
scientists find fewer biological, psychological, and social dichotomies and
more biological, psychological, and social continua, it is not impossible that
legislators will attempt to legally define "female" and "male," rather than
relying on specific judicial rulings. As long as the categories "female" and

---

*An androgynous person has the characteristics or nature of both male and female [Editors'
note].

"male" present themselves to people in everyday life as external, objective, dichotomous, physical facts, there will be scientific and naive searches for differences, and differences will be found. Where there are dichotomies it is difficult to avoid evaluating one in relation to the other, a firm foundation for discrimination and oppression. Unless and until gender, in all of its manifestations *including the physical*, is seen as a social construction, action that will radically change our incorrigible propositions cannot occur. People must be confronted with the reality of other possibilities, as well as the possibility of other realities.

Scientific studies of gender are ultimately grounded in the biological 25 imperative of reproduction. Dimorphism is seen as necessary for sperm and egg cell carriers to identify one another. Many of those who argue against the blurring of gender roles, against androgyny, against the claim of transsexuals to be a different gender, base their arguments on this "biological imperative." One extreme form of the argument is that if there are not clear roles, functions, and appearances, people will not develop "healthy" gender identities, no one will know how to, or want to, reproduce, and the species will become extinct.

The major premise of such arguments is that "male" and "female" are 26 the same as "sperm carrier" and "egg carrier." However, what we have been demonstrating throughout this book is that they are not. "Male" and "female" are grounded in the gender attribution process and are social constructions. They are more encompassing categories than sperm and egg carrier. Not all egg carriers are female and not all females are egg carriers; not all sperm carriers are male, nor are all males sperm carriers.

The only requirement for the "biological imperative" of reproduction is 27 that sperm and egg carriers must be identifiable to each other for reproductive purposes. However, not every human being can reproduce, nor does every human being who carries reproductive cells want to reproduce. Reproduction is not even a possibility for human beings throughout much of their life cycles. Sperm cell carriers are rarely younger than thirteen or fourteen, and probably have an increasing number of defective sperm cells as they grow older (Evans, 1976). Egg cell carriers are usually no younger than eleven or twelve, and can reproduce for only a few days each month for 30 to 40 years, which totals perhaps 3½ years over their life span when they could be identifiable as capable of reproduction. Thus, for all people, reproduction is not a continuous fact of life. In addition, technologies like artificial insemination, the development of techniques for ovarian and uterine transplants, and genetic engineering may, in the future, change our ideas of what the "biological imperative" for reproduction is.

The argument that certain "suitable sex differences" or stable secondary 28 gender characteristics are necessary in order to make a differentiation between egg and sperm carriers is not an argument for the biological imperative. Rather, it is an argument for the maintenance of gender. Such arguments are based on the social construction of gender, of being female and male, which is much more than reproduction and, in fact, has little to do with reproduction. Gender, in science and in everyday life, is constructed to be dichotomous not only from birth, but even after death. A woman who dies remains a woman forever. If there were cultures whose dead became neuter, then this would suggest very different ideas about gender.

There are alternative ways we can begin to think about gender, new 29 constructions for which "gender" is probably not even the most appropriate word. Some people, at some points in their lives, might wish to be identified as sperm or egg cell carriers. Except for those times, there need be no differentiation among people on *any* of the dichotomies which gender implies. Because the reproductive dichotomy would not be constituted as a lifetime dichotomy, it would not be an essential characteristic of people. Even the reproductive *dichotomy* might someday be eliminated through technology. No technological development related to reproduction, however, is necessary in order for a new social construction to appear.

Our description of this alternative possibility is not meant to be read as 30 a prescription for a new social order, but as a theoretical "blueprint." Perhaps some readers will feel that we are describing myth or science fiction (see LeGuin, 1969, 1976). That is not our purpose here either, although both myth and theory serve important functions. It would be naive to assume that any statement of alternatives could, by fiat, change the way members view reality. We do not expect that there will develop a whole new social construction of gender in everyday life. What we are arguing is that the world we have now is no more or less "real" than any alternative. What we are demonstrating is that through our theoretical framework exciting alternative possibilities for understanding the meaning of gender present themselves.*

As we have reexamined the literature on gender, and as we have ana- 31 lyzed the data we collected on the gender attribution process, we have become convinced of an intriguing possibility. The process of *gender attribution* (deciding whether some one is female or male) and the resultant *gender identification* (assigning the label "female" or "male") may not be the same thing as "*gender*"† *differentiation*—knowing whether the other is similar or different from oneself, perhaps in terms of some basic reproductive criteria.

* The major dilemma of the ethnomethodologist is the problem of infinite regress. If we assert that reality is a social construction, why stop at gender as a social construction? Why not assert that "sperm carriers" and "egg carriers" are as much of a construction as "male" or "female"? We all have to make a decision to take *something* for granted, to stop somewhere; otherwise it would be impossible to get out of bed in the morning. Our decision has been to stop here: others may wish to go on. (See Mehan and Wood (1975) for a discussion of this problem and an explanation of what Garfinkel (1966) meant when he said "Ethnomethodologists know 'tsouris.' ")[Kessler and McKenna's note].

† We have used "gender" as a modifier because no other word exists to convey our meaning. However, we have set it in quotation marks to differentiate it from gender, as the term has been used throughout the book—the socially constructed, dichotomous categories of "male" and "female" with all their layers of implications [Kessler and McKenna's note].

574 *Discourse Communities in the Social Sciences*

Although children are not 100 percent accurate in assigning gender la- 32
bels until they are four or five, and although they cannot give "good reasons"
for their identifications until they are somewhat older (see Chapter 4), Lewis
and Weintraub (1974) reported that infants, before they are a year old, can
make some kind of differentiation between "females" and "males." Male infants looked at pictures of other male infants longer than at pictures of female
infants, and the reverse was true for female infants. What is most interesting
about this study is that Lewis reports (Friedman et al., 1974, p. 191) that
adults could not make accurate gender attributions to the pictures which the
infants differentiated. The adults could not say, beyond a chance level,
whether an infant pictured was female or male. Lewis, however, did not
report whether the adults could differentiate in the same way the infants did,
that is, on the basis of length of eye contact with the picture.

Lewis terms what the infants did "gender differentiation." Both Kohl- 33
berg and Green (Friedman et al., 1974, pp. 192–193) assert that the infants'
behavior has nothing to do with gender and that it is "merely" a self-other
distinction, since the infants were too young to have gender identities and/or
gender concepts. We agree. Gender attribution and gender identification are
not possible before the individual shares members' methods for seeing and
doing gender. It is possible, however, that infants can make "gender" differ-
entiations—the differentiation necessary for the "biological imperative" of
reproduction—a process very different from gender attribution.

Were the infants using cues that adults could not perceive? Their be- 34
havior seems to be related to our finding in the children's drawings study (see
Chapter 4) that preschoolers were better at determining the "gender" of the
other preschoolers' drawings than any other age group. It is also interesting
that several transsexuals have mentioned to us that they have the most difficulty "passing" with young children. Is it possible that there is some ability
which human beings have to differentiate sperm and egg cell carriers which
is then overlayed and superceded by learned members' methods for constructing gender? Obviously a great deal more research on infant and children's
gender attribution and "gender" differentiation processes is needed, as well
as research on how these processes change over time. It is also important to
know more about nonverbal (e.g., eye contact) indicators of "gender" differentiation in adults.

It has become clear to us that within the paradigm of contemporary 35
science we cannot know all that can eventually be uncovered about what it
means to be a woman or a man. All knowledge is now grounded in the everyday social construction of a world of two genders where gender attribution,
rather than "gender" differentiation, is what concerns those who fear change.
With the courage to confront, understand, and redefine our incorrigible
propositions, we can begin to discover new scientific knowledge and to construct new realities in everyday life.

REFERENCES

Birdwhistell, R. "Masculinity and femininity as display." In R. Birdwhistell, *Kinesics and Context.* Philadelphia: University of Pennsylvania Press, 1970.

Deaux, K. *The Behavior of Women and Men.* Monterey: Brooks-Cole, 1976.

Evans, G. "The older the sperm. . . ." *Ms.*, January 1976, 14:7, 48–49.

Feinbloom, D. *Transvestites and Transsexuals: Mixed Views.* New York: Delacorte, 1976.

Friedman, R., Richart, R., and Vande Wiele, R., Eds. *Sex Differences in Behavior.* New York: Wiley, 1974.

Garfinkel, H. *Studies in Ethnomethodology.* Englewood Cliffs, NJ: Prentice-Hall, 1967.

Hastorf, A., and Contril, H. "They saw a game." *Journal of Abnormal and Social Psychology,* 1954, *49,* 129–134.

Haviland, J. M. *Sex-Related Pragmatics in Infants' Nonverbal Communication.* Paper presented at the annual meeting of the Eastern Psychological Association, New York, 1976.

LeGuin, U. "Is gender necessary?" In V. N. McIntyre and S. J. Anderson, Eds. *Aurora: Beyond Equality.* Greenwich, CT: Fawcett, 1976, 130–139.

LeGuin, U. *The Left Hand of Darkness.* New York: Walker, 1969.

Lewis, M., and Weintraub, M. "Sex of parent X Sex of child: Socioemotional development." In R. Friedman et al., Eds. *Sex Differences in Behavior.* New York: Wiley, 1974.

Mehan, H., and Wood, H. *The Reality of Ethnomethodology.* New York: Wiley-Interscience, 1975.

Rubin, G. "The traffic in women: Notes on the 'political economy' of sex." In R. Reiter, Ed. *Toward an Anthropology of Women.* New York: Monthly Review Press, 1975, pp. 157–210.

Rubin, J. Z., Provenzano, F. J., and Luria, Z. "The eye of the beholder: Parents' views on sex of newborns." *American Journal of Orthopsychiatry,* 1974, 4, 512–519.

Seavey, C. A., Katz, P. A., and Zalk, S. R. "Baby X: The effect of gender labels on adult responses to infants." *Sex Roles,* 1, 1975, 103–109.

Sulcov, M. B. *Transsexualism: Its Social Reality.* Unpublished doctoral dissertation, University of Indiana, 1973.

Whorf, B. L. *Language, Thought, and Reality.* New York: The Technology Press and John Wiley and Sons, 1956.

QUESTIONS ABOUT KESSLER AND MCKENNA'S DISCOURSE COMMUNITY AND THEIR CONCERNS IN THIS SELECTION

1. Why do you think Kessler and McKenna use the word *Doing* in their heading for this selection?

2. What are some of the processes for establishing gender that are usually considered scientific?

3. What is usually the first question that parents ask about their newborn babies? In giving answers, what kinds of evidence do doctors and midwives use? How valid do Kessler and McKenna think that evidence is?

4. What would you say is the difference between sexuality and gender?

5. What is Kessler and McKenna's basic charge against those who in the past have done research on gender characteristics?

6. What do Kessler and McKenna mean by "selective perception"? As evidence for their claim that we exhibit selective perception with regard to gender cues, Kessler and McKenna cite Eskimos' perceptions of snow and people's perceptions of aggression in football games. How persuasive do you think this evidence is?

7. What schema for gender attribution do Kessler and McKenna come up with? How valid do you think it is?

8. Kessler and McKenna argue that most manifestations of gender, including the physical, are social constructions. Do you agree? In what senses could this assertion be true?

9. How do you react to Kessler and McKenna's claim that "the world we have now is no more or less 'real' than any alternative" (paragraph 30)?

QUESTIONS ABOUT KESSLER AND MCKENNA'S RHETORICAL STRATEGIES

1. In the first line of this selection, Kessler and McKenna write of normal people, but they enclose the word *normal* in quotation marks. Why?

2. Where in this selection do you find Kessler and McKenna using such words as *perhaps, possibly,* and *might*? Are such words appropriate for social scientists to use? Do these words meet Kessler and McKenna's needs well?

3. At the end of paragraph twenty-four, Kessler and McKenna write the following sentence: "People must be confronted with the reality of other possibilities, as well as the possibility of other realities." How would you characterize the form of this sentence? Is the form effective? What is necessary for it to be effective?

4. Occasionally in this selection, Kessler and McKenna review another researcher's work. Typically they praise that work before finding fault with it from their perspective. Is this strategy consistent with their overall purpose? How does this strategy affect a reader?

5. Kessler and McKenna frequently repeat their claim that gender is a social construction. How effective is this repetition?

6. Kessler and McKenna make some generalizations (such as "we do not live our lives searching for deceit. . . .") without giving specific evidence for them. Do you accept the generalizations? Why or why not?

7. Do Kessler and McKenna provide enough evidence for their claim that biology is no closer to the truth than a deity is?

WRITING IN AND ABOUT THE SOCIAL SCIENCES: PSYCHOLOGY, SOCIAL PSYCHOLOGY, SOCIOLOGY, AND ANTHROPOLOGY

Writing for Yourself

1. In your journal, react to the claim that there may be many different realities.

2. In your journal, explore an incident which involved selective perception on your part or the parts of some of your acquaintances.

Writing for Nonacademic Audiences

1. For a "Life on Campus" column in your school newspaper, interview several students at your institution and write a 500-word essay on the propositions about the world that these students will never cease to believe in.

2. For the Variety section of your hometown newspaper, write a 750-word de-

scription of the methods for determining the sex of participants in the Olympic games.

Writing for Academic Audiences

1. For a class in developmental psychology, write a 500-word definition of Turner's syndrome.
2. For a sociology class on the modern American scene, write a 1,000-word paper classifying the facial expressions, body movements, and body postures that distinguish males from females in modern American society.
3. For a class in the psychology of sexuality, write a 1,000-word paper in which you argue for or against the proposition that sexuality is not a dichotomy (either male or female) but a continuum (running from extreme maleness to extreme femaleness).
4. For a class in the sociology of deviance, write a 1,500-word paper in which you argue your position on whether transsexualism should be considered deviant behavior.
5. For a class in the sociology of sexuality, read Ursula LeGuin's *The Left Hand of Darkness*. Then write a 1,500-word paper in which you describe sexuality as presented in this book and take a position on whether or not you would want to be a natural inhabitant of the planet LeGuin describes.

INTERCONNECTIONS: QUESTIONS FOR WRITING

Writing for Yourself

1. Working within the social sciences requires that one study individuals and groups. One of the difficulties involved, though, is that the observer must be present in some way. This leads to the question of whether the presence of the observer affects the individual or group being observed. Another question is a corollary to the first: Can an outside observer truly enter into the experience of a group of which he or she is not a part?

   In your journal, examine this question as it relates to Malinowski and Ouchi. Afterwards, describe a situation in which your observation has changed someone's behavior.
2. Those social scientists who adhere to the precepts of social Darwinism, whether they accept those precepts uncritically or not, would argue that societies tend to progress. One of the phenomena that such scientists study is the nature of that progression, as well as the effects of that progression on past traditions of the culture.

Examine the presence of social Darwinism in the essays of Smith and Malinowski. Then in your journal, reflect on these writers as you deal with the question of whether society can progress.

Writing for Nonacademic Audiences

1. Though most North Americans would affirm that democracy and capitalism are benevolent governors of the state and the economy, others would find these two problematic. Central to these concerns would be awareness of the situation of the individual set against a group. How does one answer the charges that democracy can establish a powerful majority that can dominate a minority, or a wealthy class that can determine the economic wealth and prosperity of other, less wealthy classes?

   Examine these concerns in the essays of Lasswell and Kessler and McKenna. Then write an open letter of about 250 words to these writers.

2. One area that social scientists examine is the justification for beliefs within a society. One area of intense scrutiny over the last three decades is Western views of women. Such studies have examined social, psychological, communal, cultural, mythic sources of the male domination that has characterized Western history.

   Examine how Gilligan and Kessler and McKenna account for male-dominated history. Then prepare the notes that you will use for a fifteen-minute presentation on that topic to one of the following groups:
   >The local ladies literary club
   >A local chapter of the Veterans of Foreign Wars
   >A fund-raising dinner for one of the local political parties.

3. If a social scientist moves from being descriptive (describing how a group acts) to being prescriptive (showing how a group ought to act), the questions that that social scientist has begun to take up are ethical in nature. The question here is whether the social scientist, in even asking these kinds of questions, is imposing his or her own value system upon another group or culture.

   Examine this question in the work of Smith, Durkheim, and Gilligan. Then in a 750-word editorial to be published in your university's newspaper, examine the ultimate sources of a society's code of values.

Writing for Academic Audiences

1. In that the social sciences involve the study of groups, researchers will at times publish their conclusions in the form of statistical or anecdotal evidence. Not to use that method would be to make generalizations that may be true of a large percentage of the group, but not necessarily of each member of that group. The question here is whether statistics or anecdotes or generalizations can constitute evidence of the kind that a member of another discourse community, such as a historian or natural scientist, would accept.

Examine the nature and validity of the evidence used by Smith, Skinner, and Ouchi in a 1,000-word essay for an introductory interdisciplinary course in the social sciences.

2. At times, social scientists have been accused of reducing the individual to a single element of a mass. That is, the group is the entity that has meaning; the individual merely contributes to that meaning.

   Examine the conception of individuals within a group setting in the essays by Marx and Engels, Durkheim, and Ouchi. For a sophomore-level class engaged in a historical overview of the social sciences, write 100-word definitions of the concept of *group* for each of these writers.

3. One question social scientists must ask is whether the true life of the individual is mirrored in his or her outward actions or in subconscious needs and drives. One, of course, may influence the other, blurring the distinction between the two.

   Examine the work of Freud and Kessler and McKenna, focusing on whether they make distinctions between outward action and the subconscious. Your response should come in the form of a 500-word essay for an introductory course in psychology.

DISCOURSE
COMMUNITIES
IN SCIENCE

INTRODUCTION

In the preface to *The Turning Point*, Fritjof Capra announces his principal subject matter: "What we need . . . is a new 'paradigm'—a new vision of reality; a fundamental change in our thoughts, perceptions, and values" (16). Capra, a physicist, is writing about a new way of understanding the physical universe, and at first glance his subject matter is astonishing. What does hard science have to do with values? Why should our thoughts and perceptions have to be changed when the physical matter of the universe is clearly accessible through the senses? Are we to believe that our senses can deceive us? Or that we allow them to deceive us by our holding to preconceived ideas about what we will find in the real world?

If we are hesitant about Capra's call for a new vision of reality, it might be well to remember that people in a number of ages have experienced this same hesitancy. Scientists of the Middle Ages worked under certain preconceptions about the relationship between the physical world and the spiritual world. When scientists like Galileo—and Leonardo da Vinci and Copernicus and Kepler—challenged those preconceptions, those scientists came under the condemnation of a somewhat intolerant age. But they too were calling for a new vision of reality, a vision culminating in the work of Isaac Newton.

In the nineteenth century, Charles Darwin would also call for a new vision of reality. For his work he would be attacked and condemned, but the new vision that he called for would last. In recent years, theoretical scientists like Stephen Hawking have called for us to see new relationships between time and space. Physicists like James Crutchfield have described systems and patterns in supposedly chaotic systems, lending new understandings of the nature of chaos and randomness. And paleontologists like John Horner have shown that many of our old beliefs about the dinosaurs may be completely wrong.

So perhaps Capra's call for a new vision of reality is not so remarkable. In fact, perhaps a scientist's greatness may lie in his or her ability to see things from a completely new perspective.

Such a call brings into question a belief commonly held in the twentieth century: that scientific beliefs, once established, are permanent. In fact, what the writers in the following section often seem to suggest is that scientific beliefs are never so established as to be beyond question.

Those writers might argue that our understanding varies with our knowledge. Whereas it was once agreed that Saturn was the only planet with rings, since 1988 it has been seen that rings circle other planets as well, notably Uranus. Whereas it was once believed that Mars might support life, now it is believed that life as we know it is not possible there. Understanding changes with knowledge—in this case knowledge gained from the Voyager expeditions.

Understanding also changes as we gain not just knowledge, but avenues of pursuing questions. For example, for decades it was believed that chimpanzees were strict vegetarians; however, in the 1960s and 1970s Jane Goodall used another form of research—field research—to demonstrate that chimpanzees killed and ate monkeys. Her contribution was to suggest an alternative line of research. Others have shown that sometimes our understanding is clouded because we fail to anticipate—or perhaps even to accept—the kinds of answers we may receive. Medieval astronomers before Copernicus and Galileo, for example, were unable to move beyond the assumption that the sun moved around the earth, an assumption seemingly supported by scriptural authority and certainly vigorously supported by European culture. Part of the greatness of Copernicus and Galileo was their ability to accept what must have been the rather surprising results of their experiments and observations.

And, as many scientists have shown, our preconceptions about the nature of reality may cloud our understanding. While some have argued that the quirks and unusual elements of living creatures tend to cast doubt on evolutionary theses, Stephen Jay Gould has argued that just the opposite is true. Others, such as Wayne Frair and Percival Davis, have claimed that a bias towards a certain model—such as an evolutionary model—may distort our interpretation of evidence.

The scientists represented by the following selections have all wrestled with the preceding questions: How is it possible to form a new understanding of the world that will explain certain evidence and phenomena? How to cope with the knowledge that scientific beliefs are subject to change? How to escape those pitfalls that hinder true understanding? These writers have been chosen because they demonstrate within their own disciplines the kind of pioneering vision that has led to new understanding in their fields.

Working within the discourse community of physics, Albert Einstein, Fritjof Capra, and James Crutchfield explore theories that radically alter previously held beliefs about the nature of the physical universe. That energy and matter are related, that the universe is completely interdependent, that chaos has order—all these claims subvert older understandings. In the field of astronomy, Galileo demonstrates that scientific knowledge is based on a series of observations and is not necessarily subject to a faith system. Within the natural sciences, Aristotle shows the significance of orderly classification, a lesson that did not fail to make an impression upon Darwin, who showed that significant conclusions might be drawn from such classifications. Stephen Jay Gould, as a Darwinian, and Wayne Frair and Percival Davis, as Creationists, all come out of discourse communities that some have tried to discredit; at least part of their contribution comes through their articulate expression of the positions of their communities and a defense of those positions.

Each of these writers demonstrates an ability to work with the scientific method, an overall approach that is fairly consistent from one scientific community to another. That process begins with the definition of a problem: How does time relate to space? How does energy relate to matter? How will the element react if it is heated? How is volume on a planetary scale to be measured? What will hinder the rapid growth of cancerous cells? What does the presence of this stratum of rock suggest about the presence of volcanic activity in this region? The nature of the problem varies from one community to another.

The method proceeds with the collection of evidence. For a community like astronomy, the evidence may come through observation. For a chemist or physicist, that evidence may come through experimentation. For a natural biologist, it may come through field research. The methods of gathering evidence will vary as each community defines the nature of the evidence it needs to answer its peculiar problem.

With the evidence gathered, this method calls for the scientist to advance a hypothesis, a theory that may answer the problem. Upon observing that light acted like both a particle and a wave, theorists like Sir James Jeans hypothesized that light is a wavelike particle. A hypothesis such as this is then tested. Does it answer the problem fully? Does it account for all the evidence? If it does not, then the hypothesis is flawed. The evidence must be reexamined—perhaps more needs to be gathered—and a new hypothesis advanced.

Whether the problem is large or small, the scientific method behind its solution remains the same. Archimedes arrived at his hypothesis about how one is to measure the volume of an irregularly shaped object (by measuring the amount of water it displaces when immersed) in much the same way that Stephen J. Hawking is today speculating on the effects of a black hole upon time itself. But at the same time, the kinds of evidence they gather, the methods of such gathering, and the evaluation of the evidence are radically different.

Over and over again, the following writers demonstrate the significance of how one interprets evidence. Like the historian, the scientist gathers evidence, evaluates the meaning of that evidence, and formulates theories based upon those evaluations. In that sense, the discourse communities of these writers are critical, for those communities may inform and affect scientific interpretations in that they govern the nature of evidence, how that evidence is collected, and how that evidence is interpreted and eventually generalized into hypotheses.

In addition, many of the following writers—particularly those after Darwin—have aimed their rhetorical stance at a popular audience as well as at colleagues within their own discourse communities. Such a stance affects their diction, sentence structures, organizational strategies large and small, and even the ways in which they present their evidence. One finds this in the work of writers such as Stephen Jay Gould and Fritjof Capra, who quite consciously avoid the specialized diction of their disciplines and use a kind of narrative voice that effectively conveys their ideas to a wide audience. The suggestion here, then, is that one's discourse community may affect not only how one understands the evidence of one's field, but how one might present that evidence.

Aristotle

384–323 B.C.

Aristotle was born out of the main circles of Greek thought, at a time when the Greeks were settling down after a period of devastating wars. Growing up in remote Stagira, he did not enter into the dominant Athenian culture until 367, when he traveled to Athens to study under Plato. This detachment affected his political and philosophical views, as well as his approach to the sciences.

The study of the natural world by the Greeks was limited by an unwillingness or inability to use what modern scientists would call the scientific method: observation, the collection of evidence, an inductive development of a hypothesis explaining the evidence, and the testing of that hypothesis. Though the Greeks were eliminating superstition and an emphasis on divine causation, in general the scientific community before Aristotle had not yet turned to a systematic observation and evaluation of natural causation.

Aristotle's father was a member of the guild of the Asclepiadae, a medical guild, and perhaps this background contributed to Aristotle's sense of systematic order and careful procedure. A number of documents survive from this guild that observe and record case histories but draw no conclusions or generalizations unwarranted from observations. Aristotle's History of Animals *is marked by this same sense of scientific procedure.*

Aristotle studied under Plato, and upon his teacher's death, Aristotle began to travel, first to Asia Minor and then to the island of Lesbos. It was during these travels that Aristotle began the patient observation and collecting that would mark the History of Animals. *The task he set himself was enormous: To change the nature of scientific exploration, and his later work—and the work of his disciples—suggests his success. Alexander the Great himself offered to send specimens back to Aristotle from the far regions of Asia. However, either he did not keep his promise or Aristotle's comments on them have been lost.*

In the History of Animals, *Aristotle identifies 495 species, many of which were not known again until centuries later. He includes a number of long, learned, accurate passages about specific animals, such as the bee and the cuttlefish. He is able to document animal behavior to a degree that seems surprising, given his primitive research methods: the fact that fish breathe through gills, that dolphins communicate, that insects generate sound through rubbing wings or legs. All such details come from observation. Though this kind of approach to the sciences would lapse for a time, Aristotle's methodology would help define the methodology of later scientific communities.*

The following selection is the first section of book 1 of the History of Animals.

HISTORY OF ANIMALS

Of the parts of animals some are simple: to wit, all such as divide into parts 1
uniform with themselves, as flesh into flesh; others are composite, such as
divide into parts not uniform with themselves, as, for instance, the hand does
not divide into hands nor the face into faces.

And of such as these, some are called not parts merely, but members. 2
Such are those parts that, while entire in themselves, have within themselves
other parts: as, for instance, the head, foot, hand, the arm as a whole, the
chest; for these are all in themselves entire parts, and there are other parts
belonging to them.

All those parts that do not subdivide into parts uniform with themselves 3
are composed of parts that do so subdivide, for instance, hand is composed
of flesh, sinews, and bones.

Of animals, some resemble one another in all their parts, while others 4
have parts wherein they differ. Sometimes the parts are identical in form, as,
for instance, one man's nose or eye resembles another man's nose or eye, flesh
flesh, and bone bone; and in like manner with a horse, and with all other
animals which we reckon to be of one and the same species; for as the whole
is to the whole, so each to each are the parts severally. In other cases the parts
are identical, save only for a difference in the way of excess or defect, as is
the case in such animals as are of one and the same genus. By "genus" I mean,
for instance, Bird or Fish; for each of these is subject to difference in respect
of its genus, and there are many species of fishes and of birds.

Among them, most of the parts as a rule exhibit differences through 5
contrariety of properties, such as colour and shape, in that some are more
and some in a less degree the subject of the same property; and also in the
way of multitude or fewness, magnitude or smallness, in short in the way of
excess or defect. Thus in some the texture of the flesh is soft, in others firm;
some have a long bill, others a short one; some have abundance of feathers,
others have only a small quantity. It happens further that, even in the cases
we are considering, some have parts that others have not: for instance, some
have spurs and others not, some have crests and others not; but as a general
rule, most parts and those that go to make up the bulk of the body are either
identical with one another, or differ from one another in the way of contrariety and of excess and defect. For the more and the less may be represented
as excess and defect.

There are some animals whose parts are neither identical in form nor 6
differing in the way of excess or defect; but they are the same only in the way
of analogy, as, for instance, bone is only analogous to fish-bone, nail to hoof,
hand to claw, and scale to feather; for what the feather is in a bird, the scale
is in a fish.

The parts, then, which animals severally possess are diverse from, or 7 identical with, one another in the fashion above described. And they are so furthermore in the way of local disposition; for many animals have identical parts that differ in position; for instance, some have teats in the breast, others close to the thighs.

Of the substances that are composed of parts uniform with themselves, 8 some are soft and moist, others are dry and solid. The moist are such either absolutely or so long as they are in their natural conditions, as, for instance, blood, serum, lard, suet, marrow, sperm, gall, milk in such as have it, flesh and the like; and also, in a different way, the waste products, as phlegm and the excretions of the belly and the bladder. The dry and solid are such as sinew, skin, vein, hair, bone, gristle, nail, horn (a term which as applied to the part involves an ambiguity, when the whole also by virtue of its form is designated horn), and such parts as present an analogy to these.

Animals differ from one another in their modes of subsistence, in their 9 actions, in their habits, and in their parts. Concerning these differences we shall first speak in broad and general terms, and subsequently we shall treat of the same with close reference to each particular genus.

Differences are manifested in modes of subsistence, in habits, and in 10 actions as follows: some animals live in water and others on land. And of those that live in water some do so in one way, and some in another: that is to say, some live and feed in the water, take in and emit water, and cannot live if deprived of water, as is the case with the great majority of fishes; others get their food and spend their days in the water, but do not take in water but air, nor do they bring forth in the water. Many of these creatures are furnished with feet, as the otter, the beaver, and the crocodile; some are furnished with wings, as the diver and the grebe; some are destitute of feet, as the water-snake. Some creatures get their living in the water and cannot exist outside it: but for all that do not take in either air or water, as, for instance, the sea-anemone and the oyster. And of creatures that live in the water some live in the sea, some in rivers, some in lakes, and some in marshes, as the frog and the newt.

Of animals that live on land some take in air and emit it, which phe- 11 nomena are termed "inhalation" and "exhalation"; as, for instance, man and all such land animals as are furnished with lungs. Others, again, do not inhale air, yet live and find their sustenance on dry land; as, for instance, the wasp, the bee, and all other insects. And by insects I mean such creatures as have notches on their bodies, either on their bellies or on both backs and bellies.

And of land animals many, as has been said, derive their subsistence 12 from the water; but of creatures that live in and inhale water none derives its subsistence from the land.

Some animals at first live in water, and by and by change their shape 13 and live out of water, as is the case with river worms—for out of these the gadfly develops.

Furthermore, some animals are stationary, and some move about. Sta- 14 tionary animals are found in water, but no such creature is found on land. In the water are many creatures that live in close adhesion to an external object, as is the case with several kinds of shellfish. (The sponge actually appears to be endowed with a certain sensibility: as a sign of which it is alleged that the difficulty in detaching it is increased if the movement is not covertly applied.)

Other creatures adhere at one time to an object and detach themselves 15 from it at other times, as is the case with a species of the so-called sea-anemone; for some of these creatures seek their food in the night-time loose and unattached.

Many creatures are unattached but motionless, as is the case with oys- 16 ters and the so-called holothuria. Some can swim, as, for instance, fishes, molluscs, and crustaceans, such as the crayfish. But some move by walking, as the crab, for it is the nature of the creature, though it lives in water, to move by walking.

Of land animals some are furnished with wings, such as birds and bees, 17 and these are so furnished in different ways one from another; others are furnished with feet. Of the animals that are furnished with feet some walk, some creep, and some wriggle. But no creature is able only to move by flying, as the fish is able only to swim; for the animals with leathern wings can walk, the bat has feet, and the seal has imperfect feet.

Some birds have feet of little power, and are therefore called *apodes*. 18 This little bird is powerful on the wing; and, as a rule, birds that resemble it are weak-footed and strong-winged, such as the swallow and the swift; for all these birds resemble one another in their habits and in their wings and look like one another. (The *apous* is to be seen at all seasons, but the swift only after rainy weather in summer; for this is the time when it is seen and captured, though, as a general rule, it is a rare bird.)

Again, many animals move by walking as well as by swimming. 19

Furthermore, the following differences are manifest in their modes of 20 living and in their actions. Some are gregarious, some are solitary, whether they be furnished with feet or wings or be fitted for a life in the water; and some partake of both characters. And of the gregarious, some are social, others independent.

Gregarious creatures are, among birds, such as the pigeon, the crane, 21 and the swan (no bird furnished with crooked talons is gregarious). Of creatures that live in water many kinds of fishes are gregarious, such as the so-called migrants, the tunny, the pelamys, and the bonito.

Man partakes of both characters. 22

Social creatures are such as have some one common object in view; and 23 this property is not common to all creatures that are gregarious. Such social creatures are man, the bee, the wasp, the ant, and the crane.

Again, of these social creatures some submit to a ruler, others are sub- 24 ject to no rule: as, for instance, the crane and the several sorts of bee submit to a ruler, whereas ants and numerous other creatures are subject to no rule.

And again, both of gregarious and of solitary animals, some are at- 25 tached to a fixed home and others are nomadic.

Also, some are carnivorous, some graminivorous, some omnivorous: 26 whilst some feed on a peculiar diet, as for instance the bees and the spiders (for the bee lives on honey and certain other sweets, and the spider lives by catching flies); and some creatures live on fish. Again, some creatures catch their food, others treasure it up, whereas others do not.

Some creatures provide themselves with a dwelling, others go without 27 one: of the former kind are the mole, the mouse, the ant, the bee; of the latter kind are many insects and quadrupeds. Further, in respect to locality of dwelling-place, some creatures dwell under ground, as the lizard and the snake; others live on the surface of the ground, as the horse and the dog. Some make themselves holes, others do not do so.

Some are nocturnal, as the owl and the bat; others live in the daylight. 28

Moreover, some creatures are tame and some are wild: some are at all 29 times tame, as the jennet and the mule; others are at all times wild, as the leopard and the wolf; and some creatures can be rapidly tamed, as the elephant.

Again, we may regard animals in another light. For, whenever a race 30 of animals is found domesticated, the same is always to be found in a wild condition; as we find to be the case with horses, cattle, pigs, donkeys, sheep, goats, and dogs.

Further, some animals emit sound while others are mute, and some are 31 endowed with voice: of these latter some have articulate speech, while others are inarticulate; some are noisy, some are prone to silence; some are musical, and some unmusical; but all animals without exception exercise their power of singing or chattering chiefly in connexion with the intercourse of the sexes.

Again, some creatures live in the fields, as the cushat; some on the 32 mountains, as the hoopoe; some frequent the abodes of men, as the pigeon.

Some, again, are peculiarly salacious, as the partridge and the cockerel; 33 others are inclined to chastity, as the whole tribe of crows, for birds of this kind indulge but rarely in sexual intercourse.

Of marine animals, again, some live in the open seas, some near the 34 shore, some on rocks.

Furthermore, some are combative, others defensive. Of the former kind 35 are such as act as aggressors upon others or retaliate when subjected to ill usage, and of the latter kind are such as have some means of guarding themselves against attack.

Animals also differ from one another in regard to character in the fol- 36 lowing respects. Some are good-tempered, sluggish, and not prone to ferocity, as the ox; others are quick-tempered, ferocious and unteachable, as the wild boar; some are intelligent and timid, as the stag and the hare; others are mean and treacherous, as the snake; others are free and courageous and high-bred, as the lion; others are thorough-bred and wild and treacherous, as the wolf. (An animal is high-bred if it come from a good stock, and an animal is thorough-bred if it does not deflect from its natural characteristics.)

Further, some are crafty and mischievous, as the fox; some are spirited 37 and affectionate and fawning, as the dog; others are easy-tempered and easily domesticated, as the elephant; others are cautious and watchful, as the goose; others are jealous and self-conceited, as the peacock. But of all animals man alone is capable of deliberation.

Many animals have memory, and are capable of instruction; but no 38 other creature except man can recall the past at will.

With regard to the several genera of animals, particulars as to their 39 characters and ways of life will be discussed more precisely later on.

QUESTIONS ABOUT ARISTOTLE'S DISCOURSE COMMUNITY AND HIS CONCERNS IN THIS SELECTION

1. Clearly Aristotle includes human beings in his groupings of animals, but what distinctions does he make between human beings and the other animals? What might these distinctions suggest about Aristotle's views on the nature of human-ity?

2. One distinction Aristotle makes between humans and the other animals is the ability to recall the past at will. Is this an accurate distinction? Another distinc-tion he makes lies in his claim that "of all animals man alone is capable of deliberation" (paragraph 37). Is this an accurate distinction?

3. Aristotle wrote from within a scientific community that was asking basic ques-tions, questions a contemporary scientist might not ask because they would be considered to be foundational premises. Where do such basic questions occur in this passage? Should foundational premises be constantly questioned, or would such questioning lead to a state in which the sciences could not progress?

4. In paragraph 17, Aristotle writes that "of land animals some are furnished with wings, such as birds and bees, and these are so furnished in different ways one from another; others are furnished with feet." What view of causation in the world do you think underlies the use of the word *furnished*?

5. Many classical writers followed Plato in trying to establish a median or mean model, something against which all other like things might be measured. Where does this tendency appear in Aristotle's argument? Does it appear as an assump-tion of the community out of which he writes, or is he questioning the idea of a mean? Do contemporary scientists use models in any similar ways?

6. Aristotle writes that "animals differ from one another in their modes of subsist-ence, in their actions, in their habits, and in their parts" (paragraph 9). What are the advantages of classifying in these ways? Why does Aristotle start classi-fying in terms of parts? What additional ways might a contemporary scientist find to differentiate between two species? What advantages would these ways carry?

7. "No bird furnished with crooked talons is gregarious," notes Aristotle (paragraph 21). What kind of evidence would he need to make this kind of universal statement? Does this generalization seem to contradict Aristotle's careful methods of classification, or is it in keeping with his methodology?

8. Aristotle frequently describes animals in human terms. He writes, for example, that "some animals are inclined to chastity." What are the advantages of Aristotle's technique? Are there any disadvantages?

QUESTIONS ABOUT ARISTOTLE'S RHETORICAL STRATEGIES

1. What kind of audience does Aristotle appear to be addressing? Do they seem receptive or hostile to his ideas? Do they seem to know much or little about animals?

2. In this passage, Aristotle is working from within the rhetorical mode of classification. How does the choice of rhetorical mode affect Aristotle's structure of this section? What principles of classification does he employ? Would such principles be common in the contemporary scientific community?

3. In paragraph 7, Aristotle depends on analogies, claiming, for instance, that what "the feather is in a bird, the scale is in a fish." What does he gain with such analogies? What risks does he run?

4. Why does Aristotle begin with distinctions between composite parts and uniform parts, and between parts and members? What precisely are the distinctions he makes? How do these distinctions set up Aristotle's classifications? Is such a concern with very precise language present in other parts of this passage?

5. Aristotle often uses the following formula: Some animals are this, while other animals are that. "Some creatures provide themselves with a dwelling, others go without one . . ." (paragraph 27). Many of these comments seem axiomatic, too obvious to need stating. Why does Aristotle use this formula so frequently? Is his use of this formula merely a way to state the obvious? Is it an appropriate device in the rhetorical mode of classification? Does it carry any dangers with it? How does it contribute to Aristotle's rhetorical and scientific purposes in this passage?

6. What kinds of supporting examples does Aristotle use to illustrate his classifications? How detailed are the examples? What do the examples add to his classification?

7. On the basis of this essay, how do you think Aristotle would define the word *animal*? How might his definition of this word affect his process of classification?

8. Aristotle notes that "the sponge actually appears to be endowed with a certain sensibility" (paragraph 14). What might Aristotle mean by *sensibility*?

WRITING FROM WITHIN AND ABOUT THE SCIENTIFIC COMMUNITY

Writing for Yourself

1. In your journal, speculate on what separates humanity from the rest of the animal world.

2. Aristotle's desire to classify the animal world led him first to observe, and then to chronicle similarities and differences. At least in this passage he does not seem to rely on any authority other than his own powers of observation. Go to a rural setting—a small woods, a bog, a mature forest—and, after observing its inhabitants (both plant and animal), develop a system of classification for what you have seen. What kinds of basic questions about the natural world are you forced to ask in such an exercise?

Writing for Nonacademic Audiences

1. Create a list of possible analogies between a biological part of one species and those of another (for example, a human being's forearm is comparable to . . .). Does such a process contribute to scientific understanding, or does it promote false connections? Draw up two such lists, one for a biology club in a high school, another for an introductory class in biology. How do these lists differ according to the intended audiences?
2. Today many people protest using animals in scientific experiments. Using what you take to be Aristotle's overall view of animals, write a 500- to 750-word essay responding to these protestors and their position. This will appear on the editorial page of a local newspaper.

Writing for Academic Audiences

1. Aristotle defines insects as "creatures as have notches on their bodies" (paragraph 11). Using several reference sources, write a definition of *insect* that a contemporary scientist would find more acceptable. What kinds of specifics do you need to include in such a definition which Aristotle would either not find important or simply not know?
2. What distinctions, beyond those which Aristotle proposes, might a contemporary scientist establish between human beings and the other animals? Might language help establish such a distinction? Research the question of animal language to decide whether such a distinction is viable, and then write a 1,250-word essay directed toward an audience of scientists and dealing with your findings.
3. Take an excerpt from the essay where you think Aristotle is most clearly wrong. Then write a short essay aimed at elementary-aged people just beginning to learn about science in detail. In this essay explain how Aristotle is wrong and how he came to make the errors.
4. Compare and contrast Aristotelian and modern views of the natural world in a 750-word essay to be included in a reader for a first course in the history of science.

The Book of Secrets

(1550)

At first glance, The Book of Secrets of Albertus Magnus seems to be the product of an age of superstition. Certainly it comes out of a scientific community characterized by a strong need to appeal uncritically to classical authorities, a love of arcane lore, and an intense desire to establish patterns among phenomena observed in the cosmos and in the immediate natural world. When the book was first compiled in the late thirteenth century, probably by a student of Albertus Magnus, perhaps much of its lore was accepted, principally because it was derived from earlier authorities. But by the time of the first English translation in 1550, from which this passage is taken, the lore was questioned. By the seventeenth century it was seen merely as a source of entertainment. The preface to one seventeenth-century edition recommends reading the book "to mitigate and alacrate thy heavy and troublesome mind . . . for believe me, whatsoever is promised . . . is alonely to this end."

Though later generations denied the scientific value of this work, Albertus Magnus himself was seen as a significant figure in the history of science. Though his work depended on authority—he saw his writings as being a lengthy commentary on the work of Aristotle—he also had a reputation for observing the natural world and drawing conclusions from that observation. If that was in fact the case, little evidence of that technique appears in the work attributed to him. Much of what appears in The Book of Secrets is a compilation of simplified comments on plants, minerals, and animals.

Perhaps this uncritical approach represents a regression from the techniques of classical writers like Aristotle. Perhaps writers like the author of The Book of Secrets allowed their search for patterns and their denial of independent evaluation to cloud their scientific inquiries. Perhaps the scientific community from which they worked was too restrictive and credulous, not allowing for the real possibility of unbiased inquiry into the physical world.

But—and here we have one of the reasons why this period is no longer called the Dark Ages—the author of this work is one in a line of encyclopedists who came to the sciences with unbounded faith and hope. Faith in the central fact of orderly structure in the universe, designed by an omnipotent God. Hope in the possibility that people could apprehend that structure and, more importantly, chronicle it.

THE FIRST BOOK OF THE VIRTUES OF CERTAIN HERBS

Aristotle, the Prince of Philosophers, saith in many places that every science 1
is of the kind of good things. But not withstanding, the operation sometimes
is good, sometimes evil, as the science is changed to a good or to an evil end,
to which it worketh. Of the which saying, two things be concluded: the one,
and the first, is that the science of Magic is not evil, for by the knowledge of
it, evil may be eschewed, and good followed. The second thing is also concluded, forasmuch as the effect is praised for the end; and also the end of
science is dispraised, when it is not ordained to good, or to virtue. It follow-
eth then, that every science or operation is sometimes good, sometimes evil.
Therefore, the science of Magic is a good knowledge (as it is presupposed)
and is somewhat evil in beholding of causes and natural things, as I have
considered, and perceived in ancient authors; yea, and I myself, Albert, have
found the truth in many things, and I suppose the truth to be in some part of
the book of *Kiranides*, and of the book of *Alchorath*.

  There be seven herbs that have great virtues, after the mind of Alex- 2
ander the Emperor, and they have these virtues of the influence of the planets.
And therefore, every one of them taketh their virtue from the higher natural
powers.
  The first is the herb of the planet Saturn, which is called *Daffodillus*, 3
Daffodilly. The juice of it is good against the pain of the reins, and legs; let
them that suffer pain of the bladder, eat it, the root of it being a little boiled.
And if men possessed with evil spirits, or mad men, bear it in a clean napkin,
they be delivered from their disease. And it suffereth not a devil in the house.
And if children that breed their teeth, bear it about them, they shall breed
them without pain. And it is good that a man bear with him a root of it in
the night for he shall not fear, nor be hurt of other.
  The second is the herb of the Sun, which is called *Polygonum*, or *Cor-* 4
rigiola. This herb taketh the name of the Sun, for it engendereth greatly, and
so this herb worketh many ways. Other hath called this herb *Alchone*, which
is the house of the Sun. This herb healeth the passions and griefs of the heart
and the stomach. He that toucheth this herb hath a virtue of his sign, or
planet. If any man drink the juice of it, it maketh him to do often the act of
generation. And if any man bear the root of it, it healeth the grief of the eyes.
And if he bear it with him before he have any grief, there shall come to him
no grief of his eyes. It helpeth also them that be vexed with the frenzy, if they
bear it with them in their breast. It helpeth also them that are diseased with

an impostume in the lungs, and maketh them to have a good breath; and it availeth also to the flux of melancholious blood.

The third is the herb of the Moon, which is called *Chynostates*. The juice of it purgeth the pains of the stomach, and breast plates. The virtue of it declareth that it is the herb of the Moon. The flower of this herb purgeth great spleens and healeth them, because this herb increaseth and decreaseth as the Moon. It is good against the sickness of the eyes, and maketh a sharp sight. And it is good against the blood of the eyes. If thou put the root of it brayed upon the eye, it will make the eye marvellous clear, because the light of the eyes has *propinquatum mysticum* [a mystical affinity] with the substance of the Moon. It is also good to them that have an evil stomach or which cannot digest their meat, by drinking the juice of it. Moreover it is good to them that have the swine pox.

The fourth herb is called *Arnoglossus*, Plantain. The root of this herb is marvellous good against the pain of the head, because the sign of the Ram is supposed to be the house of the planet Mars, which is the head of the whole world. It is good also against evil customs of man's stones, and rotten and filthy boils, because his house is the sign *Scorpio*, [and] because a part of it holdeth *Sperma*, that is the seed, which cometh from the stones, whereof all living things be engendered, and formed. Also the juice of it is good to them that be sick of the perilous flux, with excoriation or razing of the bowels, continual torments, and some blood issuing forth. And it purgeth them that drink it from the sickness of the flux of blood, or haemorrhoids, and of the disease of the stomach.

The fifth is the herb of the planet Mercury, which is named *Pentaphyllon*, in English Cinquefoil or the Five-leaved herb; of others *Pentadactylus*, of others *Sepedeclinans*, of certain *Calipendalo*. The root of this herb brayed and made in a plaster, healeth wounds and hardness. Moreover, it putteth away quickly the swine pox, if the juice of it be drunken with water. It healeth also the passions or griefs of the breast, if the juice of it be drunken. It putteth away also the toothache. And if the juice of it be holden in the mouth, it healeth all the griefs of the mouth, and if any man bear it with him, it giveth work and help. Moreover if any man will ask any thing of a king or prince, it giveth abundance of eloquence, if he have it with him, and he shall obtain it that he desireth. It is also good to have the juice of it, for the grief of the stone, and the sickness which letteth a man that [he] can not piss.

The sixth is the herb of the planet Jupiter, and is named *Acharonis*, of certain *Jusquiamus*, Henbane. The root of it, put upon botches, healeth them, and keepeth the place from an inflammation of blood. If any man shall bear it before the grief come upon him he shall never have a botch. The root of it also is profitable against the gout in the feet when it is brayed, and put upon the place that suffereth the pain or grief. And it worketh by virtue of those signs, which have feet, and look upon the feet. And if the juice of it be

Fig. 9.   *Verbena*, vervain.

Fig. 8.   *Jusquiamus*, henbane.
From *Naturalia Alberti Magni* (1548)

drunken with honey, or with wine and honey sodden together, it is profitable against the griefs of the liver, and all his passions, because Jupiter holdeth the liver. Likewise, it is profitable to them that would do often the act of generation; and to them that desire to be loved of women, it is good that they bear it with them, for it maketh the bearers pleasant and delectable.

The seventh is the herb of the planet Venus, and is called *Peristerion*, 9 of some *Hierobotane, id est Herba columbaria*, and *Verbena*, Vervain. The root of this herb put upon the neck healeth the swine pox, impostumes behind the ears, and botches of the neck, and such as can not keep their water. It healeth also cuts, and swelling of the tewel, or fundament, proceeding of an inflammation which groweth in the fundament; and the haemorrhoids. If the juice of it be drunken with honey and water sodden, it dissolveth those things which are in the lungs or lights. And it maketh a good breath, for it saveth and keepeth the lungs and the lights. It is also of great strength in veneral pastimes, that is, the act of generation. If any man put it in his house or vineyard, or in the ground, he shall have abundantly revenues, or yearly profits; moreover the root of it is good to all them which will plant vineyards or trees. And infants bearing it shall be very apt to learn, and loving learning, and they shall be glad and joyous. It is also profitable, being put in purgations, and it putteth aback devils.

Yet this is to be marked, that these herbs be gathered from the twenty- 10
third day of the Moon until the thirtieth day, beginning the gathering of
them from the sign *Mercurius*, by the space of a whole hour, and in gathering
make mention of the passion or grief, and the name of the thing for the which
thou dost gather it. Notwithstanding, lay the same herb upon Wheat, or
Barley, and use if afterward to thy need.

QUESTIONS ABOUT THE DISCOURSE COMMUNITY OF THE AUTHOR OF *THE BOOK OF SECRETS* AND HIS CONCERNS IN THIS SELECTION

1. This work was written during the Middle Ages, a time that many judge to be
   credulous. What assumptions could you make about a society that would produce such a work? What might you infer about the state of the sciences in this
   world?
2. What diseases or afflictions does the writer mention most often? Do they fall
   into general categories? Can we say anything about this society or its concerns
   on the basis of the afflictions or the desired goals listed?
3. The writer of *The Book of Secrets* worked from within a cultural community
   that saw the world of nature as part of an intricately patterned and interdependent structure. Nothing existed in this structure that did not somehow relate to
   everything else. What evidence do you see in this passage for such kinds of
   concerns? What ultimately motivates such concerns? Does it seem that this
   tendency to see a specific kind of pattern might blind a scientist's ability to
   objectively observe the physical world?
4. The opening of this passage questions the ethical nature of science. When, according to the writer, might science become evil? To what extent does the morality of an endeavor depend on its "end"?
5. By citing "Aristotle, the Prince of Philosophers" first in this section, the writer
   indicates that he includes his endeavors within the realm of philosophy. Would
   a modern scientist agree? To what extent do you think philosophy should affect
   the agenda of the sciences?
6. Many of the properties of the various herbs are related to properties that medieval scientists believed the individual planets held. (This list of planets included earth's moon and the sun.) How does the writer work at establishing the
   relationship between the herb and the planet? Does he ever question whether
   such a relationship does indeed exist, or is such a relationship one of his presuppositions?
7. In this section the writer notes the existence of "seven herbs that have great
   virtues." Do you think the number seven would have been significant to him?
   What significance would the medieval world have attached to it?
8. At the end of the fourth paragraph, the writer mentions "the flux of melancholious blood." What view of human character lies behind this reference?

QUESTIONS ABOUT THE AUTHOR'S RHETORICAL STRATEGIES

1. The writer of *The Book of Secrets* is working out of a scientific community that
   was steeped in the tradition of the encyclopedia. All knowledge could be clas-

sified and organized, it was thought, into a single work, representing accumulated understandings of the physical world. How does the encyclopedic tradition affect the structure of this passage? Does the tradition influence the tone of the piece at all?

2. One of the characteristics of scientific writing in the late Middle Ages is an appeal to authority. Where do such appeals occur in this passage? How do such appeals affect the reader's attitude towards the writer? Why, does it seem to you, would a writer in the Middle Ages not be inclined to enter into disputes with accepted authorities?

3. The writer often gives many names by which a particular herb goes. Why does he do this? Does it advance his case or contribute to wordiness?

4. At the beginning of the passage, the writer notes that "Yea, and I myself, Albert, have found the truth in many things" (paragraph 1). Given that Albertus had died before the book was compiled, are we to assume that this is merely a lie designed to give authority to the writer? What other explanations might there be for such a claim? What effect does such a claim have on the reader? The writer later ascribes certain lore to Alexander the Great, mistaking the Macedonian general for the naturalists Alexius Affrious and Flacus Africanus. However, what might such an attribution contribute to his overall rhetorical strategy?

5. Describe the organization of those sections dealing with particular herbs. What patterns do you find in the organization? Are the patterns effective in presenting the material? How so? Would you wish to change them?

6. Frequently, writing students are told not to use the expletive *there* (as in *There are several reasons for Henry's dismissal of the case*) in their sentences. Yet this writer does. Where does he do so? How does he do so? Do you think his use is justified?

7. The writer of *The Book of Secrets* refers to "the science of magic." Using the *Oxford English Dictionary*, examine what the word *magic* meant in the sixteenth century. What does the use of this word suggest about the writer's understanding of the relationship between the physical world and the supernatural world?

8. This passage frequently speaks of the "virtues" of specific herbs. Use the *Oxford English Dictionary* to find the sixteenth-century meaning of this word. Does such a meaning ever appear in contemporary contexts?

WRITING FROM WITHIN AND ABOUT THE SCIENTIFIC COMMUNITY

Writing for Yourself

1. In some ways, the writer of *The Book of Secrets* is a popular scientist, or folk scientist, recounting tales about the physical world that were centuries old and had received no real critical evaluation. Many of his comments have a medical application, dealing with potential cures and preventives. In your journal, generate a list of folk cures that you have encountered. These might range from injunctions against certain foods to advice on which vegetables improve eyesight. Are there any reasonable bases for such cures or preventives?

2. Explore in your journal the influence of the psychosomatic on your friends. When do their minds make them ill? When could a placebo labeled as a certain drug make them well?

Writing for Nonacademic Audiences

1. Take the list of home remedies you have generated in your journal and write a 1,250-word, lightly humorous sketch about them for a magazine like *Reader's Digest*.
2. Browse through the *Foxfire* books, a collection of lore and craftwork from Appalachia. What kinds of herb lore—and other lore relating to the natural world—do you find there? In an essay of comparison and contrast, examine how such scientists as Aristotle and Stephen Jay Gould, who write out of a more academic scientific community, might react to such lore. How do you react to it? Address your essay to a nonscientific audience.
3. In a college course in botany, you decide to explore the nature of the soil in which a particular plant grows. When you tell your parents this, they say that they do not ever recall having seen the plant you will study. Write a 250-word description of the plant for your parents so that they will be able to imagine it accurately.
4. Your grandparents faithfully read *Prevention* magazine. Write them a letter in which you show them how different you think the articles in *Prevention* are from the sections of *The Book of Secrets*.

Writing for Academic Audiences

1. Later editions of *The Book of Secrets* suggested that readers try the various preventives and cures to test their worth. What kinds of evidence would a twentieth-century scientist need to dispel or confirm the lore in this passage? What might the differences between the methods of the medieval scientist and those of the twentieth-century scientist suggest about the contemporary scientific community's vision of the nature and meaning of the physical world? Write this in the form of a report addressed to a scientific discourse community.
2. Write a 250-word report informing your classmates about the discovery of an herb with important uses in medicine.
3. A teacher of introductory courses in literature has asked you to prepare a 500-word report on the theory of the humours, to be used to introduce college sophomores to a theory that affects many medieval and renaissance works of art.
4. Write a 1,250-word paper for the students in an introductory class in ethics. In this paper you should develop your position on the extent to which we should consider an activity's end or goal in deciding how ethical that activity is.
5. You are in a senior-level seminar in the history of science. The group is asked by the dean of the science division to assemble a set of short essays that each underclassman beginning a course in science will be required to read. Your assignment is to write a 500-word report on a case in science in which the scientist's assumptions kept him or her from seeing the true nature of the case.

Galileo Galilei

(1564–1642)

Galileo (1564–1642) was an Italian astronomer, mathematician, physicist, and theoretical scientist. Rejecting the superstition of a past age, Galileo turned to precise observation and experimentation as the basis for his scientific concepts. However, Galileo did what Aristotle had not: He used mathematics to formulate expressions of natural laws. In so doing he laid down the foundations of modern experimental science and paved the way for many of Isaac Newton's experiments and propositions.

As an astronomer, Galileo constructed one of the first useful telescopes, confirming with that instrument the Copernican theory of the solar system. He published this confirmation in 1632 but found that the most powerful discourse community of his age rejected such beliefs, labeling them as blasphemous. Spurred on by Aristotelian professors who felt threatened by Galileo's discoveries, church authorities, particularly Dominican preachers, attacked the supposed impiety of the new mathematicians. Galileo, to forestall a direct attack, wrote a number of letters reminding such authorities—and even the pope—of the time-honored practice of interpreting allegorically those passages of Scripture that did not seem to be supported by scientific discoveries.

But the pope, who was already fighting the rising protestant movement, was not anxious to have yet another controversy to deal with. Eventually Galileo was brought before the Inquisition, where he was forced to deny his beliefs and to affirm that the earth was the center of the universe. Galileo recognized that even his international reputation could not have saved him from the hands of such a fanatical group, and though his retraction might be viewed with some distaste from the perspective of the twentieth century, it is quite another thing to sit on trial, knowing that the fire is already burning in the courtyard outside. After the retraction, he spent the last eight years of his life under house arrest.

The following selection is from De Motu (On Motion), *written between 1589 and 1592, when Galileo was teaching at the University of Pisa. It was not published during his lifetime, though much of this material was incorporated in his* Discourses and Mathematical Demonstrations Concerning Two New Sciences, *published in 1635. The manuscripts of this text were preserved, however, and finally edited and published in 1890 by Antonio Favaro.*

Though much of Galileo's approach to the subject of motion is original, particularly his application of mathematics to the subject, he was part of a discourse community that had long discussed the nature of motion. Francesco Buonamici, a teacher at the University of Pisa while Galileo was a student there, argued against Aristotle's positions as Galileo would in the following selection. Some of Galileo's ideas are derived directly from Buonamici, while others are from classical and medieval science.

*What distinguishes scientists of Galileo's discourse community, however, is their re-
jection of authority and their assumption that no theory was beyond testing. In taking
such a stance, Galileo and other Renaissance scientists stepped onto the threshold of
modern scientific inquiry.*

ON MOTION

BY WHAT AGENCY PROJECTILES ARE MOVED.

Aristotle, as in practically everything that he wrote about locomotion, wrote 1
the opposite of the truth on this question too. And surely this is not strange.
For who can arrive at true conclusions from false assumptions? Aristotle could
not maintain his view that the mover must be in contact with the moving
body, unless he said that projectiles are moved by the air. And he gave testimony of this opinion of his in many passages. And since we must refute this
view, we shall first state it, but only in a summary way, for it is explained at
considerable length by the commentators.

Aristotle holds that the mover, e.g., one who throws a stone, before he 2
lets go of the stone, sets the contiguous parts of the air in motion; that these
parts, similarly, move other parts, and these still others, and so on in succession; that the stone, after being released by the projector, is then moved along
by those portions of air; and that thus the motion of the stone becomes, as it
were, discontinuous, and is not a single motion but several. Aristotle and his
followers, who could not persuade themselves that a body could be moved
by a force impressed upon it, or recognize what that force was, tried to take
refuge in this view. But in order that the other view, the true one, may be
made clear, we shall first seek to demolish completely this view of Aristotle.
Then we shall, so far as we can, explain and illustrate with examples the
other view, which concerns the impressed force.

And so, against Aristotle I argue as follows: Suppose the parts of air 3
which move the body are A, B, C, D, and E, and suppose A is in contact
with the mover. Now either all of these parts are moved at the same time, or
one part is moved after another. If A, B, C, D, and E are all moved at the
same time, then I ask by what they are moved when the mover comes to rest;
and in that case one must come to the notion of an impressed force. If, however, A is moved before B, then again I ask by what B is moved when A
comes to rest. Furthermore, again according to Aristotle, forced motion is
swifter in the middle of the motion than at the beginning. Therefore part C

of the air, under the impulse of B, is moved more swiftly than is B. Hence C will likewise move D more swiftly than A, B, C, D, and E have themselves been moved by B. Hence D will also move E more swiftly than it [D] was moved by C: and so on in succession. Therefore forced motion will always be accelerated.

Secondly, there is the argument of the arrow which is set in motion by   4 the bowstring, even in the face of a strong north wind, and yet flies with great speed. My adversaries have no answer to this argument other than that, however hard the wind blows, air is nevertheless carried against the wind, having received the impetus from the bow. And they are not ashamed to utter such childishness. But what will they say to the following similar argument? Suppose a ship is propelled by oars against the current of a river, and the oars are then taken out of the water, and the ship moves for a considerable distance against the course of the water. Who is so blind as not to see that the water actually flows with very great force in the direction opposite [to that of the ship], and, furthermore, that this water, which is in contact with the ship, does not swerve at all from its natural course because of any impetus of the ship?

Thirdly, if it is the medium that carries moving bodies along, how does   5 it happen that when one shoots an iron ball, and, with the same shot of the cannon, [a ball of] wood, or tow, or something light—the heavy object being the first out—how, I say, does it happen that the iron is flung a very great distance, while the tow, after following the iron for some distance, stops and falls to the ground? If, then, it is the medium that carries along both of them, why does it carry the lead or iron so far, but not the tow? Is it easier for the air to move the very heavy iron than the very light tow, or the wood?

Fourthly, Aristotle does not seem to be self-consistent. For he says (*De*   6 *Caelo* 3.27): "If what is moved is neither heavy nor light, its motion will be by force; and what is moved by force, and offers no resistance of heaviness or lightness, moves without end." And in the next passage he says that projectiles are carried along by the medium. But then, since air has neither weight nor lightness, once it is moved by the projector it will move endlessly and always at the same speed. And it will consequently also carry along projectiles in endless motion, and will never be weakened, since it always moves with the same force. But experience shows that the opposite of this happens.

In the fifth place, consider a marble sphere, perfectly round and smooth,   7 which can rotate on an axis the ends of which rest on two supports. Then suppose a mover comes who twists both ends of the axis with his finger tips. Surely in that case the sphere will rotate for a long time. Yet the air was not set in motion by the mover. Nor can the air act upon the sphere by driving it on, since the sphere never changes its position. And since it is perfectly smooth, it has no cavities into which the air can rush. In fact, the air around the sphere will remain quite motionless. This becomes clear if a flame is brought near the [rotating] sphere, for it will neither be extinguished nor disturbed.

These are the arguments by which we hold that the absurd view is ad- 8
equately, and more than adequately, refuted—a view which those try to
maintain who cannot satisfy themselves as to the nature of impressed force.
But now, in order to explain our own view, let us first ask what is that motive
force which is impressed by the projector upon the projectile. Our answer,
then, is that it is a taking away of heaviness when the body is hurled upward,
and a taking away of lightness, when the body is hurled downward. But if a
person is not surprised that fire can deprive iron of cold by introducing heat,
he will not be surprised that the projector can, by hurling a heavy body
upward, deprive it of heaviness and render it light.

The body, then, is moved upward by the projector so long as it is in his 9
hand and is deprived of its weight; in the same way the iron is moved, in an
alterative motion, towards heat, so long as the iron is in the fire and is deprived by it of its coldness. Motive force, that is to say lightness, is preserved
in the stone, when the mover is no longer in contact; heat is preserved in the
iron after the iron is removed from the fire. The impressed force gradually
diminishes in the projectile when it is no longer in contact with the projector;
the heat diminishes in the iron, when the fire is not present. The stone finally
comes to rest; the iron similarly returns to its natural coldness. Motion is more
strongly impressed by the same given force in a body that is more resistant
than in one that is less resistant, e.g., in the stone, more than in light pumice;
and, similarly, heat is more strongly impressed by the same fire upon very
hard, cold iron, than upon weak and less cold wood.

It would be ridiculous to say that the air previously heated by the fire 10
preserved the heat in the iron after the fire was extinguished or removed to a
distance, for iron glows with heat even in the coldest air. And it is even more
ridiculous to believe that motion is preserved in the projectile by air which is
motionless or which even blows in the opposite direction. But who will not
say that the iron is cooled more quickly in cold air by reason of the coldness
of the air? And who of sound mind will not say that air impedes motion when
it is either at rest or blows in the opposite direction?

But let me give another more beautiful example. Do you wonder what 11
it is that passes from the hand of the projector and is impressed upon the
projectile? Yet you do not wonder what passes from the hammer and is transferred to the bell of the clock, and how it happens that so loud a sound is
carried over from the silent hammer to the silent bell, and is preserved in the
bell when the hammer which struck it is no longer in contact. The bell is
struck by the striking object; the stone is moved by the mover. The bell
is deprived of its silence; the stone of its state of rest. A sonorous quality
is imparted to the bell contrary to its natural silence; a motive quality is
imparted to the stone contrary to its state of rest. The sound is preserved in
the bell, when the striking object is no longer in contact; motion is preserved
in the stone when the mover is no longer in contact. The sonorous quality
gradually diminishes in the bell; the motive quality gradually diminishes in
the stone. But who of sound mind will say that it is the air that continues to

strike the bell? For, in the first place, only one small portion of air is moved by the hammer. But if someone puts his hand on the bell, even on the side opposite the hammer, he will immediately feel a sharp, stinging, and numbing action that runs through all the metal. Secondly, if it is the air that strikes the bell and causes the sound in it, why is the bell silent even if the strongest wind is blowing? Can it be that the strong south wind, which churns up the whole sea and topples towers and walls, strikes [the bell] more gently than does the hammer, which hardly moves. In the third place, if it were the air that caused the sound in the bronze, rather than the bronze that caused the sound in the air, all bells of the same shape would emit the same sound; indeed, even a wooden bell, or at least a leaden or marble one, would produce as much sound as a bronze one. But, finally, let those be still who keep saying that it is the air which causes the sound or carries the sound [to the bell]. For the bell vibrates as it emits the sound, and the vibration and sound remain in it and are preserved even when the striking agent is no longer in contact. But to ascribe to the air the setting in motion of such a great mass [i.e., the bell], when it [the air] has scarcely been moved itself by the hammer, exceeds all reason. To return, then, to our point, why are they puzzled that a motive quality can be impressed in a body by a mover, but not that a sound and a certain motion of vibration can be impressed in a bell by a hammer?

But, what is more, they say that they cannot conceive that a heavy stone 12 should be able to become light by receiving a motive force from a projector. But this force, since it is lightness, will indeed render the body in motion light by inhering in it. Yet these same people say that it is utterly ridiculous to suppose that a stone has become light after its upward motion and weighs less than before. But their judgment of things is not based on a sober and reasonable consideration. For I too would not say that a stone, after its [upward] motion, has become [permanently] light. I would say rather that it retains its natural weight, just as the hot glowing iron is devoid of coldness but, after the heat [is used up], it resumes the same coldness that is its own. And there is no reason for us to be surprised that the stone, so long as it is moving [upward], is light. Indeed, between a stone in that act of motion [upward] and any other light body it will not be possible to assign any difference. For since we call light that which moves upward, and the [projected] stone does move upward, the stone is therefore light so long as it moves upward.

But you will say that that is light which moves upward *naturally*, not 13 that which does so by force. But I say that that is naturally light which moves upward naturally. And I say that that is light preternaturally, or accidentally, or by force, whose upward motion is contrary to nature, accidental, and by force: and such is the stone which is set in motion by force. And in the case of this stone its natural and intrinsic weight is lost in the same way as when it is placed in media heavier than itself. For a stone which floats, let us say, in mercury and does not sink, loses all its weight; indeed, it loses weight and assumes lightness to such an extent that it promptly resists even a great deal of weight that comes to it externally—e.g., if one tries to press it down. Wood, too, becomes so light in water that it cannot be kept down except by force. And yet, neither the stone nor the wood loses its natural weight, but, on being taken from those heavier media, they both resume their proper weight. In the same way, a projectile, when freed from the projecting force, manifests, by descending, its true and intrinsic weight.

Furthermore, those who oppose our views, ask skeptically in what part 14 of the [projected] body the force I speak of is received, on the surface, in the center, or in some other part. My brief answer to them is this. Let them first tell me in what part of the iron the heat is received, and I shall then tell them where the motive force is received. And I shall place it where they place the heat. If the heat is received only on the surface, then I shall say that the force is received only on the surface; and if in the center, then in the center. And if they say that the heat is received where previously there was cold, I shall say that extrinsic lightness entered those parts in which intrinsic heaviness previously resided.

Finally, my opponents express wonder that the same hand has the abil- 15 ity of impressing now lightness, now heaviness, and now even that which seems to be neither heavy nor light. But why don't they express wonder in- stead that they now want a certain thing, and a little later they don't want that same thing; that they sometimes believe something, sometimes have hes- itation and doubt about it, and sometimes even disbelieve it? But if, as in these cases, it depends on the will that we can now lift our arm, then lower it, then move it in various directions, and if the arm, thus governed by our will, has the power now to press down, and now to lift, why need we wonder that that which is pressed down by the arm receives weight while that which is lifted is cloaked with lightness?

But, since it is not foreign to my subject, let me not pass over in silence 16 a certain quite common error. Some people believe that, since air and water are fluids, they can be very easily and swiftly moved, particularly air. And because of this, these people have held that the projector moves the air more than he does the projectile, and that the air carries along the projectile. But the facts are quite different, as those people themselves sometimes admit. For, with their leader Aristotle, they sometimes say that the air, in order to be able to carry along the projectiles, moves very swiftly by reason of its lightness, since it offers practically no resistance. But at other times they say that that which has neither heaviness nor lightness cannot be moved, because that which is moved must offer resistance. In these statements they affirm and deny the same propositions according to what suits their purpose better. But the fact is that the lighter the body is, the more is it moved while it is in contact with the mover, but, on being released by the mover, it retains for only a short time the impetus it has received. This is clear if someone throws a feather, using as much force as if one had to throw a pound of lead. For he will more easily move the feather than the lead, but the impressed force will be retained in the lead for a longer time than in the feather, and he will throw the lead much farther. But if it were the air that carried the projectile along, who would ever believe that the air could carry the lead more easily than the feather? We see therefore that the lighter a thing is, the more easily is it moved; but the less does it retain the impetus it has received. And so, since the air, as was shown above, has no weight in its own proper place, it will be moved very easily, but will not at all retain the impetus it has received. And we shall show below why light bodies do not retain this impetus.

Nor is there any force in the example they give of the pebble thrown 17 into the lake—the pebble by which, they tell us, the water is moved in a [widening] circle over great distances. For, in the first place, it is false to say that the water is moved. This is clear if there are pieces of wood or straw floating on the water; for they will not at all be moved from their position by the eddies of water, but will be lifted only a little by the wavelets and will not follow the circumference of the [widening] circles. Secondly, the analogy does not hold good in the case of air, for the surface of the air is not moved by the projector, while it is only the surface of the water that is moved by the pebble. And this topmost surface of the water is raised and lowered only for the reason that it offers resistance to keep it from being raised and carried into the place of air. But the motive force cannot be impressed in the middle of the air, because in that case the air offers no resistance, since it is not being thrust from its place into the place of another medium. This would also be the case in the middle of the water, which would not retain the impetus it had received, since its motion would have no tendency. It would not have the tendency of natural motion, because it would not be moving toward its own place, since it was already there; nor would it have the tendency of forced motion, since it would not be thrust into the place of another medium.

This was the common error of those who said that projectiles were 18 moved by the medium. And it sometimes happens that certain opinions, however false they may be, attain long-standing currency among men, because at first sight they offer some appearance of truth, and no one bothers to examine whether they are worthy of belief. An instance of this sort of thing is the belief about things that are under the water. Common opinion asserts that these objects appear larger than they really are. But when I could not discover a reason for such an effect, I finally had recourse to experiment and found that a denarius coin at rest in deep water did not at all appear larger [than actual size], but rather appeared smaller. And so, I believe that the one who first put forth this [mistaken] opinion, was led to it in the summertime when plums or other fruits are sometimes placed in a glass vessel full of water, the shape of which vessel resembles the surface of a conoid. These pieces of fruit would appear far larger than they really are to those who view them in such a way that the visual rays pass through the [curved] glass. But the shape of the vessel, not the water, is the cause of this effect, as we have explained in our commentaries on the *Almagest* of Ptolemy, which, with God's help, will be published in a short time. And an indication of this is the fact that if the eye is placed above the water in such a way that the plum can be seen without the interference of the glass medium, it does not appear larger.

Let us, therefore, conclude finally that projectiles can in no way be 19 moved by the medium, but only by a motive force impressed by the projector. And let us now go on to show that this force is gradually diminished, and that in a case of forced motion no two points can be assigned in which the motive force is the same.

QUESTIONS ABOUT GALILEO'S DISCOURSE COMMUNITY AND HIS CONCERNS IN THIS SELECTION

1. Galileo begins this selection with a comment about Aristotle: "Aristotle, as in practically everything that he wrote about locomotion, wrote the opposite of the truth on this question too." How would you describe Galileo's stance at this point? What might it suggest about the scientific discourse community of Galileo's day as opposed to that of the author of *The Book of Secrets*?

2. In this section, Galileo displays much scorn for others' errors. Yet he makes errors of definition and logic in this passage too. What are they? Does his own attitude towards others' errors affect the way you view his errors?

3. What evidence would have led to Aristotle's theory of motion as outlined in paragraph 2? What kinds of evidence would a contemporary scientist gather to refute that theory? Is the contemporary scientist's evidence different in kind from that of Galileo, or are there similarities between these two bodies of evidence?

4. How would you describe the discourse community that Galileo is writing to? Does it seem that this discourse community is open or hostile to his ideas? What clues in this selection might suggest Galileo's continuing battle with the scientific community of his time?

5. How does Galileo define the nature of the force that imparts motion to an object? Would a contemporary scientist agree with this explanation?

6. To advance his case, Galileo proposes an analogy between a bell struck by a hammer and a stone set in motion by force. What might Galileo's dependence on such analogies and examples suggest about the nature of his discourse community and the research techniques of the sciences of his day? Would a contemporary scientist make such an analogy?

7. In paragraph 16, Galileo asserts the following: "We see therefore that the lighter a thing is, the more easily is it moved; but the less does it retain the impetus it has received." Upon what evidence does Galileo base this conclusion? Would you judge this to be sufficient evidence to arrive at a general law?

8. In paragraph 18, Galileo notes that "it sometimes happens that certain opinions, however false they may be, attain long-standing currency among men, because at first sight they offer some appearance of truth, and no one bothers to examine whether they are worthy of belief." Is it possible to tell, given the

context of the essay, whether Galileo holds this to be generally true or if he is using this notion against those who support Aristotle? What conditions would give rise to a situation in which science did not examine accepted truths?

QUESTIONS ABOUT GALILEO'S RHETORICAL STRATEGIES

1. Characterize Galileo's tone in this piece. Do you think it is the most effective tone that he could have used?
2. Read over the first paragraph of this selection. How does Galileo go about announcing the major topics he will consider here? Is there any rhetorical strategy to Galileo's use of the first-person plural pronoun *we*, when he is in fact writing only about himself? Or is he not writing only about himself here?
3. Galileo uses a series of examples to argue against the theory of Aristotle, using the flight of an arrow, the motion of a ship, and the course of an iron bell to demonstrate that there must be some agency other than air that causes motion. Are these logical examples that contribute to Galileo's point? In general, is the use of example an effective method by which to argue a case? What pitfalls lie in such a method?
4. Almost wherever you read in this essay, references to Galileo's opponents are present. Was he wise to keep their presence so steadily before his readers' eyes?
5. At times, Galileo seems to use language to denigrate those who might oppose his ideas. "Are they not ashamed to utter such childishness?" he asks. "Who is so blind as not to see that . . ." he asserts. Does such language suggest that this is a writer out of control, or is there a rhetorical strategy working here? Are there ethical considerations in the use of such language?
6. Read over paragraph 11. How does the sentence structure in this paragraph mirror the argument that Galileo is making? Do you find this to be an effective rhetorical technique? Why or why not?
7. In paragraph 14, Galileo accepts the challenge of responding about where the motive force is placed in physical objects. However, his response is not so much an answer as a challenge to those who would oppose his viewpoints. Is Galileo unable to answer the questions so he is merely using aggressive rhetoric to hide his inability? Or is there another explanation?
8. In some of Galileo's paragraphs, he uses many logical connectives. Find one or two of these connectives. What does he typically do with them? Are these connectives necessary?

WRITING FROM WITHIN AND ABOUT THE SCIENTIFIC COMMUNITY

Writing for Yourself

1. In a brief journal entry, write an informal explanation of Aristotle's theory of motion as described in paragraph 2.
2. Explore in your journal a time in your life when you retracted one of your beliefs or acted in a way contrary to your beliefs. What kind of pressure made you act that way? How did you feel afterwards?

Writing for Nonacademic Audiences

1. Find a church or a religious denomination in which science and religion have had some series confrontations. For a discussion group within that denomination, write a 1,250-word paper in which you delineate the causes for the confrontations and the actual or likely outcomes. If you wish, add comments about how you think science and religion should interact with each other.

Writing for Academic Audiences

1. In an introductory class in physics, you are asked to describe the forces that lead to motion in a stationary object. Write a 250- to 500-word report explaining the nature of those forces.
2. For a history of science course, write a 500-word paper that explains how an actual scientific theory was the result of faulty assumptions.
3. Galileo discusses the notion that an object appears larger when under water, citing two different conditions in which he examined this notion. Repeat Galileo's experiment, using the same two conditions. Write up your hypothesis, materials, procedures, observations, results, and conclusions in a lab report format.
4. Interview several scientists about their views of proper tone in scientific writing. Then prepare a 500-word summary of these views that will be used by the science division of your university to guide students as they do their first pieces of writing for a science class.
5. In this essay, Galileo attacks those who are not willing to examine accepted truths, who are satisfied with a community's assumptions about the nature of the physical universe. Research the trial of Galileo and his recantation of his beliefs about the Copernican system of the solar system, which held that the earth revolved around the sun. Write a 750- to 1,000-word essay in which you discuss whether this retraction hurts Galileo's credibility as a scientist.
6. Have you ever known people who seem to question all that they are told about the natural world? If so, write a 750-word analysis of their character in which you examine why they question statements about the natural world and how their questioning makes their peers and those in authority over them feel. This paper is for a psychology class on personality.
7. Galileo called experimentation *cimento*, an ordeal. In a 1,000-word paper for students majoring in the humanities, examine how experimentation is or is not an ordeal.
8. After reading the following text of Galileo's retraction, write a 750-word essay in which you compare the language of that retraction to the language of *De Motu*. What generalizations could you make about the language of the retraction? Does it seem as sincere and honest as the penultimate paragraph would suggest? How does the audience for the retraction differ from that of *De Motu*? How do those differences affect the language of the retraction?

I, Galileo Galilei, son of the late Vincenzo Galilei, Florentine, aged seventy 1 years, arraigned personally before this tribunal, and kneeling before you, most Eminent and Reverend Lord Cardinals, Inquisitors general against heretical depravity throughout the whole Christian Republic, having before my eyes and touching with my hands, the holy Gospels—swear that I have always believed, do now believe, and by God's help will for the future believe, all that is held, preached, and taught by the Holy Catholic and Apostolic Roman Church. But whereas—after an injunction had been judicially intimated to me by this Holy Office, to the effect that I must altogether abandon the false opinion that the sun is the centre of the [universe] and immovable, and that the earth is not the centre of the [universe], and moves, and that I must not hold, defend, or teach in any way whatsoever, verbally or in writing, the said doctrine, and after it had been notified to me that the said doctrine was contrary to Holy Scripture—I wrote and printed a book in which I discuss this doctrine already condemned, and adduce arguments of great cogency in its favour, without presenting any solution of these; and for this cause I have been pronounced by the Holy Office to be vehemently suspected of heresy, that is to say, of having held and believed that the sun is the centre of the [universe] and immovable, and that the earth is not the centre and moves:—

Therefore, desiring to remove from the minds of your Eminences, and 2 of all faithful Christians, this strong suspicion, reasonably conceived against me, with sincere heart and unfeigned faith I abjure, curse, and detest the aforesaid errors and heresies, and generally every other error and sect whatsoever contrary to the said Holy Church; and I swear that in future I will never again say or assert, verbally or in writing, anything that might furnish occasion for a similar suspicion regarding me; but that should I know any heretic, or person suspected of heresy, I will denounce him to this Holy Office, or to the Inquisitor and ordinary of the place where I may be. Further, I swear and promise to fulfil and observe in their integrity all penances that have been, or that shall be, imposed upon me by this Holy Office. And, in the event of my contravening, (which God forbid!) any of these my promises, protestations, and oaths, I submit myself to all the pains and penalties imposed and promulgated in the sacred canons and other constitutions, general and particular, against such delinquents. So help me God, and these His holy Gospels, which I touch with my hands.

I, the said Galileo Galilei, have abjured, sworn, promised, and bound 3 myself as above; and in witness of the truth thereof I have with my own hand subscribed the present document of my abjuration, and recited it word for word at Rome, in the Convent of Minerva, this twenty-second day of June, 1633.

I, Galileo Galilei, have abjured as above with my own hand.   4

Charles Darwin

(1809–1882)

Like Aristotle, Charles Darwin (1809–1882) came from a family of physicians. His father was a doctor, and his grandfather, Erasmus Darwin, was one of the most famous physicians in Great Britain, as well as an amateur naturalist and poet. Darwin himself was trained in medicine and the strict procedures that that discipline called for, but his horror at the operations performed on children before the use of anesthesia led him away from medical practice and towards the ministry. He spent three years working towards that goal but graduated from Christ College, Oxford, without making any definite commitment to the church.

When he was offered the position of naturalist-assistant to the captain of the H.M.S. Beagle, he accepted and embarked on a five-year voyage around South America that would revolutionize his own life and the character of the natural sciences. He kept a lengthy journal describing unusual plant and animal life, and this he published as The Voyage of the Beagle *(1839); it was the observations made during this time on the variations within the same species that led to his theory of natural selection. Those ideas would later be developed in* The Origin of Species *(1859) and* The Descent of Man *(1871).*

Perhaps because of the controversy these books engendered, Darwin is best remembered today as the father of evolutionary theory, though in fact that theory had already been articulated by others, including Erasmus Darwin. However, Darwin is also the writer of numerous books on the natural world. All of these works are characterized by the same strict adherence to hypothesis-making and observation, methods that received particular emphasis in the Victorian period as the boundaries of science expanded. Darwin's common procedure was to collect observations, measure them against currently accepted theories, evaluate the theories and establish a new hypothesis if necessary, and test that new hypothesis with further observation.

Though Darwin lived in an optimistic age that hailed the growth of science, he also lived in an age of skepticism. The result is that Darwin frequently gathered an enormous number of examples to support his theories, often suggesting that it was unlikely that another naturalist could find a different theory that matched the observations as adequately as his own. Scientists of his own time were not unacquainted with evolutionary theory, given that it had been practiced already in the breeding of horses, pigeons, plants, dogs, and farm animals, but they were reluctant to accept the possibility that the human race itself could have undergone evolutionary changes wrought by nature. Darwin knew he had to struggle against such reluctance, and molded his rhetoric accordingly.

The following passage is taken from The Voyage of the Beagle.

KEELING ISLANDS: CORAL FORMATIONS

I will now give a very brief account of the three great classes of coral-reefs;   1
namely, Atolls, Barrier, and Fringing-reefs, and will explain my views* on
their formation. Almost every voyager who has crossed the Pacific has expressed his unbounded astonishment at the lagoon-islands, or as I shall for
the future call them by their Indian name of atolls, and has attempted some
explanation. Even as long ago as the year 1605, Pyrard de Laval well ex-
claimed, "C'est une meruille de voir chacun de ces atollons, enuironné d'un
grand banc de pierre tout autour, n'y ayant point d'artifice humain."† The
accompanying sketch of Whitsunday Island in the Pacific, copied from Capt.
Beechey's admirable Voyage, gives but a faint idea of the singular aspect of
an atoll: it is one of the smallest size, and has its narrow islets united together
in a ring. The immensity of the ocean, the fury of the breakers, contrasted
with the lowness of the land and the smoothness of the bright green water
within the lagoon, can hardly be imagined without having been seen.

The earlier voyagers fancied that the coral-building animals instinc-   2
tively built up their great circles to afford themselves protection in the inner
parts; but so far is this from the truth, that those massive kinds, to whose
growth on the exposed outer shores the very existence of the reef depends,

---

* These were first read before the Geological Society in May, 1837, and have since been devel-
    oped in a separate volume on the "Structure and Distribution of Coral Reefs." [Darwin's
    note].
† It is a marvel to see each of these atolls, surrounded all around by a great bank of stone, not
    touched at all by human artifice. [Darwin's note].

cannot live within the lagoon, where other delicately-branching kinds flourish. Moreover, on this view, many species of distinct genera and families are supposed to combine for one end; and of such a combination, not a single instance can be found in the whole of nature. The theory that has been most generally received is that atolls are based on submarine craters; but when we consider the form and size of some, the number, proximity, and relative positions of others, this idea loses its plausible character: thus, Suadiva atoll is 44 geographical miles in diameter in one line, by 34 miles in another line; Rimsky is 54 by 20 miles across, and it has a strangely sinuous margin; Bow atoll is 30 miles long, and on an average only 6 in width; Menchicoff atoll consists of three atolls united or tied together. This theory, moreover, is totally inapplicable to the northern Maldiva atolls in the Indian Ocean (one of which is 88 miles in length, and between 10 and 20 in breadth), for they are not bounded like ordinary atolls by narrow reefs, but by a vast number of separate little atolls; other little atolls rising out of the great central lagoon-like spaces. A third and better theory was advanced by Chamisso, who thought that from the corals growing more vigorously where exposed to the open sea, as undoubtedly is the case, the outer edges would grow up from the general foundation before any other part, and that this would account for the ring or cup-shaped structure. But we shall immediately see, that in this, as well as in the crater-theory, a most important consideration has been overlooked, namely, on what have the reef-building corals, which cannot live at a great depth, based their massive structures?

Numerous soundings were carefully taken by Captain Fitz Roy on the 3 steep outside of Keeling atoll, and it was found that within ten fathoms, the prepared tallow at the bottom of the lead, invariably came up marked with the impressions of living corals, but as perfectly clean as if it had been dropped on a carpet of turf; as the depth increased, the impressions became less numerous, but the adhering particles of sand more and more numerous, until at last it was evident that the bottom consisted of a smooth sandy layer: to carry on the analogy of the turf, the blades of grass grew thinner and thinner, till at last the soil was so sterile, that nothing sprang from it. From these observations, confirmed by many others, it may be safely inferred that the utmost depth at which corals can construct reefs is between 20 and 30 fathoms. Now there are enormous areas in the Pacific and Indian Oceans, in which every single island is of coral formation, and is raised only to that height to which the waves can throw up fragments, and the winds pile up sand. Thus the Radack group of atolls is an irregular square, 520 miles long and 420 broad; the Low archipelago is elliptic-formed, 840 miles in its longer, and 420 in its shorter axis: there are other small groups and single low islands between these two archipelagoes, making a linear space of ocean actually more than 4000 miles in length, in which not one single island rises above the specified height. Again, in the Indian Ocean there is a space of ocean 1500 miles in length, including three archipelagoes, in which every island is low and of coral formation. From the fact of the reef-building corals not living at great depths, it is absolutely certain that throughout these vast areas, wherever there is now an atoll, a foundation must have originally existed within a depth of from 20 to 30 fathoms from the surface. It is improbable in the highest degree that broad, lofty, isolated, steep-sided banks of sediment, arranged in groups and lines hundreds of leagues in length, could have been deposited in the central and profoundest parts of the Pacific and Indian Oceans, at an immense distance from any continent, and where the water is perfectly limpid. It is equally improbable that the elevatory forces should have uplifted throughout the above vast areas, innumerable great rocky banks within 20 to 30 fathoms, or 120 to 180 feet, of the surface of the sea, and not one single point above that level; for where on the whole face of the globe can we find a single chain of mountains, even a few hundred miles in length, with their many summits rising within a few feet of a given level, and not one pinnacle above it? If then the foundations, whence the atoll-building corals sprang, were not formed of sediment, and if they were not lifted up to the required level, they must of necessity have subsided into it; and this at once solves the difficulty. For as mountain after mountain, and island after island, slowly sank beneath the water, fresh bases would be successively afforded for the growth of the corals. It is impossible here to enter into all the necessary details, but I venture to defy* any one to explain in any other manner, how it is possible that numerous islands should be distributed throughout vast areas—all the islands being low—all being built of corals, absolutely requiring a foundation within a limited depth from the surface.

Before explaining how atoll-formed reefs acquire their peculiar struc- 4 ture, we must turn to the second great class, namely, Barrier-reefs. These either extend in straight lines in front of the shores of a continent or of a large island, or they encircle smaller islands; in both cases, being separated from the land by a broad and rather deep channel of water, analogous to the lagoon within an atoll. It is remarkable how little attention has been paid to encircling barrier-reefs; yet they are truly wonderful structures. The illustration below represents part of the barrier encircling the island of Bolabola in the Pacific, as seen from one of the central peaks. In this instance the whole line of reef has been converted into land; but usually a snow-white line of great breakers, with only here and there a single low islet crowned with cocoa-nut trees, divides the dark heaving waters of the ocean from the light-green expanse of the lagoon-channel. And the quiet waters of this channel generally bathe a fringe of low alluvial soil, loaded with the most beautiful productions of the tropics, and lying at the foot of the wild, abrupt, central mountains.

---

* It is remarkable that Mr. Lyell, even in the first edition of his "Principles of Geology," inferred that the amount of subsidence in the Pacific must have exceeded that of elevation, from the area of land being very small relatively to the agents there tending to form it, namely, the growth of coral and volcanic action. [Darwin's note].

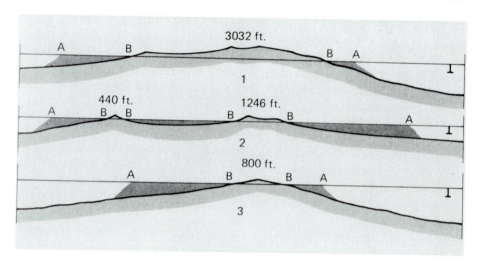

The horizontal shading shows the barrier-reefs and lagoon-channels. The inclined shading above the level of the sea (AA) shows the actual form of the land; the inclined shading below this line shows its probable prolongation under water.

Encircling barrier-reefs are of all sizes, from three miles to no less than forty-four miles in diameter; and that which fronts one side, and encircles both ends, of New Caledonia, is 400 miles long. Each reef includes one, two, or several rocky islands of various heights; and in one instance, even as many as twelve separate islands. The reef runs at a greater or less distance from the included land; in the Society archipelago generally from one to three or four miles; but at Hogoleu the reef is 20 miles on the southern side, and 14 miles on the opposite or northern side, from the included islands. The depth within the lagoon-channel also varies much; from 10 to 30 fathoms may be taken as an average; but at Vanikoro there are spaces no less than 56 fathoms or 336 feet deep. Internally the reef either slopes gently into the lagoon-channel, or ends in a perpendicular wall sometimes between two and three hundred feet under water in height: externally the reef rises, like an atoll, with extreme abruptness out of the profound depths of the ocean. What can be more singular than these structures? We see an island, which may be compared to a castle situated on the summit of a lofty submarine mountain, protected by a great wall of coral-rock, always steep externally and sometimes internally, with a broad level summit, here and there breached by narrow gateways, through which the largest ships can enter the wide and deep encircling moat.

As far as the actual reef of coral is concerned, there is not the smallest difference, in general size, outline, grouping, and even in quite trifling details of structure, between a barrier and an atoll. The geographer Balbi has well remarked, that an encircled island is an atoll with high land rising out of its lagoon; remove the land from within, and a perfect atoll is left.

But what has caused these reefs to spring up at such great distances from the shores of the included islands? It cannot be that the corals will not grow close to the land; for the shores within the lagoon-channel, when not surrounded by alluvial soil, are often fringed by living reefs; and we shall presently see that there is a whole class, which I have called Fringing-reefs from their close attachment to the shores both of continents and of islands. Again, on what have the reef-building corals, which cannot live at great depths, based their encircling structures? This is a great apparent difficulty, analogous to that in the case of atolls, which has generally been overlooked. It will be perceived more clearly by inspecting the following sections, which are real ones, taken in north and south lines, through the islands with their barrier-reefs, of Vanikoro, Gambier, and Maurua; and they are laid down, both vertically and horizontally, on the same scale of a quarter of an inch to a mile.

It should be observed that the sections might have been taken in any 8 direction through these islands, or through many other encircled islands, and the general features would have been the same. Now bearing in mind that reef-building coral cannot live at a greater depth than from 20 to 30 fathoms, and that the scale is so small that the plummets on the right hand show a depth of 200 fathoms, on what are these barrier-reefs based? Are we to suppose that each island is surrounded by a collar-like submarine ledge of rock, or by a great bank of sediment, ending abruptly where the reef ends? If the sea had formerly eaten deeply into the islands, before they were protected by the reefs, thus having left a shallow ledge round them under water, the present shores would have been invariably bounded by great precipices; but this is most rarely the case. Moreover, on this notion, it is not possible to explain why the corals should have sprung up, like a wall, from the extreme outer margin of the ledge, often leaving a broad space of water within, too deep for the growth of corals. The accumulation of a wide bank of sediment all round these islands, and generally widest where the included islands are smallest, is highly improbable, considering their exposed positions in the central and deepest parts of the ocean. In the case of the barrier-reef of New Caledonia, which extends for 150 miles beyond the northern point of the island, in the same straight line with which it fronts the west coast, it is hardly possible to believe, that a bank of sediment could thus have been straightly deposited in front of a lofty island, and so far beyond its termination in the open sea. Finally, if we look to other oceanic islands of about the same height and of similar geological constitution, but not encircled by coral-reefs, we may in vain search for so trifling a circumambient depth as 30 fathoms, except quite near to their shores; for usually land that rises abruptly out of water, as do most of the encircled and non-encircled oceanic islands, plunges abruptly under it. On what then, I repeat, are these barrier-reefs based? Why, with their wide and deep moat-like channels, do they stand so far from the included land? We shall soon see how easily these difficulties disappear.

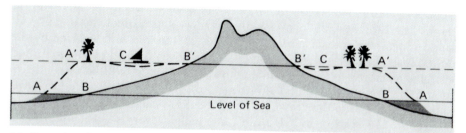

AA: Outer edges of the fringing-reef, at the level of the sea. **BB:** The shores of the fringed island. **A′A′:** Outer edges of the reef, after its upward growth during a period of subsidence, now converted into a barrier, with islets on it. **B′B′:** The shores of the now encircled island. **CC:** Lagoon-channel. **NB:** In this and the following illustration, the subsidence of the land could be represented only by an apparent rise in the level of the sea.

We come now to our third class of Fringing-reefs, which will require a   9
very short notice. Where the land slopes abruptly under water, these reefs are only a few yards in width, forming a mere ribbon or fringe round the shores: where the land slopes gently under the water the reef extends further, sometimes even as much as a mile from the land; but in such cases the soundings outside the reef always show that the submarine prolongation of the land is gently inclined. In fact the reefs extend only to that distance from the shore, at which a foundation within the requisite depth from 20 to 30 fathoms is found. As far as the actual reef is concerned, there is no essential difference between it and that forming a barrier or an atoll: it is, however, generally of less width, and consequently few islets have been formed on it. From the corals growing more vigorously on the outside, and from the noxious effect of the sediment washed inwards, the outer edge of the reef is the highest part, and between it and the land there is generally a shallow sandy channel a few feet in depth. Where banks of sediment have accumulated near to the surface, as in parts of the West Indies, they sometimes become fringed with corals, and hence in some degree resemble lagoon-islands or atolls; in the same manner as fringing-reefs, surrounding gently-sloping islands, in some degree resemble barrier-reefs.

No theory on the formation of coral-reefs can be considered satisfactory   10
which does not include the three great classes. We have seen that we are driven to believe in the subsidence of these vast areas, interspersed with low islands, of which not one rises above the height to which the wind and waves can throw up matter, and yet are constructed by animals requiring a foundation, and that foundation to lie at no great depth. Let us then take an island surrounded by fringing-reefs, which offer no difficulty in their structure; and let this island with its reef, represented by the unbroken lines in the [illustration above] slowly subside. Now as the island sinks down, either a few feet at a time or quite insensibly, we may safely infer, from what is known of the conditions favourable to the growth of coral, that the living masses, bathed by the surf on the margin of the reef, will soon regain the surface. The water, however, will encroach little by little on the shore, the

island becoming lower and smaller, and the space between the inner edge of the reef and the beach proportionally broader. A section of the reef and island in this state, after a subsidence of several hundred feet, is given by the dotted lines. Coral islets are supposed to have been formed on the reef; and a ship is anchored in the lagoon-channel. This channel will be more or less deep, according to the rate of subsidence, to the amount of sediment accumulated in it, and to the growth of the delicately branched corals which can live there. The section in this state resembles in every respect one drawn through an encircled island: in fact, it is a real section (on the scale of .517 of an inch to a mile) through Bolabola in the Pacific. We can now at once see why encircling barrier-reefs stand so far from the shores which they front. We can also perceive, that a line drawn perpendicularly down from the outer edge of the new reef, to the foundation of solid rock beneath the old fringing-reef, will exceed by as many feet as there have been feet of subsidence, that small limit of depth at which the effective corals can live:—the little architects having built up their great wall-like mass, as the whole sank down, upon a basis formed of other corals and their consolidated fragments. Thus the difficulty on this head, which appeared so great, disappears.

If, instead of an island, we had taken the shore of a continent fringed 11 with reefs, and had imagined it to have subsided, a great straight barrier, like that of Australia or New Caledonia, separated from the land by a wide and deep channel, would evidently have been the result.

Let us take our new encircling barrier-reef, of which the section is now 12 represented by unbroken lines, and which, as I have said, is a real section through Bolabola, and let it go on subsiding. As the barrier-reef slowly sinks down, the corals will go on vigorously growing upwards; but as the island sinks, the water will gain inch by inch on the shore—the separate mountains first forming separate islands within one great reef—and finally, the last and highest pinnacle disappearing. The instant this takes place, a perfect atoll is formed: I have said, remove the high land from within an encircling barrier-reef, and an atoll is left, and the land has been removed. We can now perceive how it comes that atolls, having sprung from encircling barrier-reefs, resemble them in general size, form, in the manner in which they are grouped together, and in their arrangement in single or double lines; for they may be called rude outline charts of the sunken islands over which they stand. We can further see how it arises that the atolls in the Pacific and Indian oceans extend in lines parallel to the generally prevailing strike of the high islands and the great coast-lines of those oceans. I venture, therefore, to affirm, that on the theory of the upward growth of the corals during the sinking of the land,* all the leading features in those wonderful structures, the lagoon-

---

* It has been highly satisfactory to me to find the following passage in a pamphlet by Mr. Couthouy, one of the naturalists in the great Antarctic Expedition of the United States:—"Having personally examined a large number of coral islands, and resided eight months among

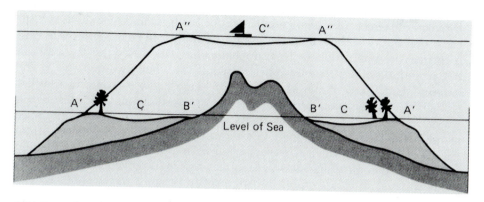

A′A′: Outer edges of the barrier-reef at the level of the sea, with islets on it. **B′B′:** The shores of the included island. **CC:** The lagoon-channel. **A′ A′ :** Outer edges of the reef, now converted into an atoll. **C′:** The lagoon of the new atoll. **NB:** According to the true scale, the depths of the lagoon-channel and lagoon are much exaggerated.

islands or atolls, which have so long excited the attention of voyagers, as well as in the no less wonderful barrier-reefs, whether encircling small islands or stretching for hundreds of miles along the shore of a continent, are simply explained.

It may be asked whether I can offer any direct evidence of the subsid- 13 ence of barrier-reefs or atolls; but it must be borne in mind how difficult it must ever be to detect a movement, the tendency of which is to hide under water the part affected. Nevertheless, at Keeling atoll I observed on all sides of the lagoon old cocoa-nut trees undermined and falling; and in one place the foundation-posts of a shed, which the inhabitants asserted had stood seven years before just above high-water mark, but now was daily washed by every tide: on inquiry I found that three earthquakes, one of them severe, had been felt here during the last ten years. At Vanikoro, the lagoon-channel is remarkably deep, scarcely any alluvial soil has accumulated at the foot of the lofty included mountains, and remarkably few islets have been formed by the heaping of fragments and sand on the wall-like barrier-reef; these facts, and some analogous ones, led me to believe that this island must lately have subsided and the reef grown upwards: here again earthquakes are frequent and very severe. In the Society archipelago, on the other hand, where the lagoon-channels are almost choked up, where much low alluvial land has accumulated, and where in some cases long islets have been formed on the barrier-reefs—facts all showing that the islands have not very lately subsided—only feeble shocks are most rarely felt. In these coral formations, where the land and water seem struggling for mastery, it must be ever difficult to decide

---

the volcanic class having shore and partially encircling reefs. I may be permitted to state that my own observations have impressed a conviction of correctness of the theory of Mr. Darwin."—The naturalists, however, of this expedition differ with me on some points respecting coral formations. [Darwin's note].

between the effects of a change in the set of the tides and of a slight subsidence: that many of these reefs and atolls are subject to changes of some kind is certain; on some atolls the islets appear to have increased greatly within a late period; on others they have been partially or wholly washed away. The inhabitants of parts of the Maldiva archipelago know the date of the first formation of some islets; in other parts, the corals are now flourishing on water-washed reefs, where holes made for graves attest the former existence of inhabited land. It is difficult to believe in frequent changes in the tidal currents of an open ocean; whereas, we have in the earthquakes recorded by the natives on some atolls, and in the great fissures observed on other atolls, plain evidence of changes and disturbances in progress in the subterranean regions.

It is evident, on our theory, that coasts merely fringed by reefs cannot 14
have subsided to any perceptible amount; and therefore they must, since the growth of their corals, either have remained stationary or have been upheaved. Now it is remarkable how generally it can be shown, by the presence of upraised organic remains, that the fringed islands have been elevated: and so far, this is indirect evidence in favour of our theory. I was particularly struck with this fact, when I found to my surprise, that the descriptions given by M.M. Quoy and Gaimard were applicable, not to reefs in general as implied by them, but only to those of the fringing-class; my surprise, however, ceased when I afterwards found that, by a strange chance, all the several islands visited by these eminent naturalists, could be shown by their own statements to have been elevated within a recent geological era.

Not only the grand features in the structure of barrier-reefs and of atolls, 15
and of their likeness to each other in form, size, and other characters, are explained on the theory of subsidence—which theory we are independently forced to admit in the very areas in question, from the necessity of finding bases for the corals within the requisite depth—but many details in structure and exceptional cases can thus also be simply explained. I will give only a few instances. In barrier-reefs it has long been remarked with surprise, that the passages through the reef exactly face valleys in the included land, even in cases where the reef is separated from the land by a lagoon-channel so wide and so much deeper than the actual passage itself, that it seems hardly possible that the very small quantity of water or sediment brought down could injure the corals on the reef. Now, every reef of the fringing-class is breached by a narrow gateway in front of the smallest rivulet, even if dry during the greater part of the year, for the mud, sand, or gravel, occasionally washed down, kills the corals on which it is deposited. Consequently, when an island thus fringed subsides, though most of the narrow gateways will probably become closed by the outward and upward growth of the corals, yet any that are not closed (and some must always be kept open by the sediment and impure water flowing out of the lagoon-channel) will still continue to front exactly the upper parts of those valleys, at the mouths of which the original basal fringing-reef was breached.

We can easily see how an island fronted only on one side, or on one side with one end or both ends encircled by barrier-reefs, might after long-continued subsidence be converted either into a single wall-like reef, or into an atoll with a great straight spur projecting from it, or into two or three atolls tied together by straight reefs—all of which exceptional cases actually occur. As the reef-building corals require food, are preyed upon by other animals, are killed by sediment, cannot adhere to a loose bottom, and may be easily carried down to a depth whence they cannot spring up again, we need feel no surprise at the reefs both of atolls and barriers becoming in parts imperfect. The great barrier of New Caledonia is thus imperfect and broken in many parts; hence, after long subsidence, this great reef would not produce one great atoll 400 miles in length, but a chain or archipelago of atolls, of very nearly the same dimensions with those in the Maldiva archipelago. Moreover, in an atoll once breached on opposite sides, from the likelihood of the oceanic and tidal currents passing straight through the breaches, it is extremely improbable that the corals, especially during continued subsidence, would ever be able again to unite the rim; if they did not, as the whole sank downwards, one atoll would be divided into two or more. In the Maldiva archipelago there are distinct atolls so related to each other in position, and separated by channels either unfathomable or very deep (the channel between Ross and Ari atolls is 150 fathoms, and that between the north and south Nillamdoo atolls is 200 fathoms in depth), that it is impossible to look at a map of them without believing that they were once more intimately related. And in this same archipelago, Mahlos-Mahdoo atoll is divided by a bifurcating channel from 100 to 132 fathoms in depth, in such a manner, that it is scarcely possible to say whether it ought strictly to be called three separate atolls, or one great atoll not yet finally divided.

I will not enter on many more details; but I must remark that the curious structure of the northern Maldiva atolls receives (taking into consideration the free entrance of the sea through their broken margins) a simple explanation in the upward and outward growth of the corals, originally based both on small detached reefs in their lagoons, such as occur in common atolls, and on broken portions of the linear marginal reef, such as bounds every atoll of the ordinary form. I cannot refrain from once again remarking on the singularity of these complex structures—a great sandy and generally concave disk rises abruptly from the unfathomable ocean, with its central expanse studded, and its edge symmetrically bordered with oval basins of coral-rock just lipping the surface of the sea, sometimes clothed with vegetation, and each containing a lake of clear water!

One more point in detail: as in two neighbouring archipelagoes corals flourish in one and not in the other, and as so many conditions before enumerated must affect their existence, it would be an inexplicable fact if, during the changes to which earth, air, and water are subjected, the reef-building corals were to keep alive for perpetuity on any one spot or area. And as by our theory the areas including atolls and barrier-reefs are subsiding, we ought occasionally to find reefs both dead and submerged. In all reefs, owing to the sediment being washed out of the lagoon or lagoon-channel to leeward, that side is least favourable to the long-continued vigorous growth of the corals; hence dead portions of reef not unfrequently occur on the leeward side; and these, though still retaining their proper wall-like form, are now in several instances sunk several fathoms beneath the surface. The Chagos group appears from some cause, possibly from the subsidence having been too rapid, at present to be much less favourably circumstanced for the growth of reefs than formerly: one atoll has a portion of its marginal reef, nine miles in length, dead and submerged; a second has only a few quite small living points which rise to the surface; a third and fourth are entirely dead and submerged; a fifth is a mere wreck, with its structure almost obliterated. It is remarkable that in all these cases, the dead reefs and portions of reef lie at nearly the same depth, namely, from six to eight fathoms beneath the surface, as if they had been carried down by one uniform movement. One of these "half-drowned atolls," so called by Capt. Moresby (to whom I am indebted for much invaluable information), is of vast size, namely, ninety nautical miles across in one direction, and seventy miles in another line; and is in many respects eminently curious. As by our theory it follows that new atolls will generally be formed in each new area of subsidence, two weighty objections might have been raised, namely, that atolls must be increasing indefinitely in number; and secondly, that in old areas of subsidence each separate atoll must be increasing indefinitely in thickness, if proofs of their occasional destruction could not have been adduced. Thus have we traced the history of these great rings of coral-rock, from their first origin through their normal changes, and through the occasional accidents of their existence, to their death and final obliteration.

QUESTIONS ABOUT DARWIN'S DISCOURSE COMMUNITY AND HIS CONCERNS IN THIS ESSAY

1. In the twentieth century, Darwin is principally known as the most articulate spokesman for the theory of organic evolution by means of natural selection. But in the nineteenth century he was known also as an eminent naturalist. What might you infer about Darwin's scientific methodology from this essay? In his line of reasoning convincing?

2. How is Darwin's methodology similar to that of other naturalists represented in this section? Are the differences in their procedures due to differing purposes, or to their different discourse communities? Does Darwin's final use of classification and definition differ in significant ways from that of Aristotle?

3. Darwin appears to work by making careful observations and moving from them to a hypothesis that can be refuted or confirmed. Do you think that this process was actually the one he used? Or do you think he perceived in the light of a hypothesis he had already formed?

4. From the evidence in this essay, what might you surmise about the nature of

Darwin's audience? How might he structure his material to fit the needs of that audience? Does the essay suggest any prejudices that might be characteristic of that audience?

5. What constitutes evidence for Darwin? Some of the same observations Darwin makes are used by others mentioned early in the essay to support alternative theories of atoll formation. How does Darwin reinterpret that information to support his own theory? Might there be still other ways of interpreting that same information?

6. What is Darwin's theory of fringing reef formation? Of submerged reef formation? Of atoll formation? Of barrier reef formation? Darwin arrives at these theories only after careful observations and seems to conclude that no other theory could be deduced from these observations. Is this mere arrogance, or is Darwin correct?

7. Toward the end of this essay, Darwin writes that we must keep "in mind how difficult it must ever be to detect a movement, the tendency of which is to hide under water the part affected." What similar difficulty did he face in arguing for organic evolution?

8. One of the assumptions behind Darwin's work is that the world is not static, that history implies change. How does this assumption manifest itself in this essay?

QUESTIONS ABOUT DARWIN'S RHETORICAL STRATEGIES

1. Like Aristotle, Darwin is, at least in part, going about the task of classification and definition. How important are those rhetorical modes to the structure of the essay? How important are those modes to the context and meaning of the essay?

2. Why does Darwin begin and conclude with a paragraph extolling the beauty of the atoll? Does that suggest a lack of scientific objectivity? Or is Darwin simply being a good stylist? Does the introductory section draw the reader in?

3. At one point, Darwin compares an island to a castle, its reef to a wall with gateways, and its surrounding water to a moat. What does Darwin gain with this extended comparison? What does he lose?

4. "Keeling Islands: Coral Formations" is taken from *The Voyage of the Beagle*, a journal that Darwin edited and then published in 1839. Three years later Darwin published *The Structure and Distribution of Coral Reefs*, in which he further developed his theories on atoll formation. After a very brief opening paragraph describing the purpose of the *Coral Reefs*, he writes:

Without any distinct intention to classify coral-reefs, most voyagers have spoken of them under the following heads: "lagoon-islands" or "atolls," "barrier" or "encircling reefs," and "fringing" or "shore reefs." The lagoon-islands have received much the most attention; and it is not surprising, for everyone must be struck with astonishment, when he first beholds one of these vast rings of coral-rock, often many leagues in diameter, here and there surmounted by a low verdant island with dazzling white shores, bathed on the outside by the foaming breakers of the ocean, and on the inside surrounding a calm expanse of water, which, from reflection, is generally of a bright but pale green colour.

The naturalist will feel this astonishment more deeply after having examined the soft and almost gelatinous bodies of these apparently insignificant coral-polypifers, and when he knows that the solid reef increases only on the outer edge, which day and night is lashed by the breakers of an ocean never at rest. Well did Francois Pyrard de Laval, in the year 1605, exclaim, "C'est une merveille de voir chacun de ces atollons, enuironne d'un grand bane de pierre tout autour, n'y ayant point d'artifice humain." The above sketch of Whitsunday Island, in the S. Pacific, taken from Capt. Beechey's admirable Voyage, although excellent of its kind, gives but a faint idea of the singular aspect of one of these lagoon-islands. Whitsunday Island is of small size, and the whole circle has been converted into land, which is a comparatively rare circumstance. As the reef of a lagoon-island generally supports many separate small islands, the word "island," applied to the whole, is often the cause of confusion; hence, I have invariably used in this volume the term "atoll," which is the name given to these circular coral formations by their inhabitants in the Indian Ocean, and is synonymous with "lagoon-island."

Compare this opening to that of the essay. Are there any distinctions which might suggest different purposes? Why might he have rearranged the order of some of his points in the later version?

5. The conclusion of the essay is enormously confident: "Thus have we traced the history of these great rings of coral-rock, from their first origin through their normal changes, and through the occasional accident of their existence, to their death and final obliteration." However, the corresponding chapter in the later version ends with a series of questions:

But further to test its truth, a crowd of questions may be asked. Do the different kinds of reefs which have been produced by the same kind of movement, generally lie within the same or closely adjoining areas? How are such reefs related to each other in form and position,—for instance, do neighbouring groups of atolls, and the separate atolls in each group, bear the same relation to each other as do ordinary islands? Although coral-reefs which have just begun to re-grow, after having been killed by too rapid a subsidence, would at first belong to the fringing class, yet, as a general rule, reefs of this class indicate that the land has either long remained at a stationary level, or has been upraised. Of a stationary level it is hardly possible to find any evidence except of a negative kind; but of recent elevation, upraised marine remains afford a sure proof: it may therefore be asked do fringed coasts often afford such evidence? Do the areas which have subsided, as shown by the presence of atolls and barrier-reefs, and the areas which have either remained stationary or have been upraised, as indicated by fringing-reefs, bear any determinate relation to each other? Is there any relation between the areas of recent subsidence or elevation, and the presence of active volcanic vents? These several questions will be considered in the following chapter.

Why would Darwin have made such a dramatic change in his conclusion? What might such a change suggest about differing purposes between the essay and the book? What might such a change suggest about Darwin's perception of his audience? Do any of these questions throw doubt on the earlier theories, or are these relatively nonthreatening questions?

6. Near the end of the essay, Darwin predicts some questions that might be asked

of him as well as objections that might be raised against him. Is this a good strategy? Why or why not?

7. Darwin begins by citing other naturalists and their theories on atoll formation. What is the purpose of this strategy? Does it strengthen or weaken his case? What does his use of earlier observations and theories say about science as an endeavor? Why does he not include such references toward the end of the essay?

8. How does Darwin use diction and sentence structure in the following sentence to suggest contrast and to generate in the reader the same kind of awe and delight which an atoll might generate to an observer: "The immensity of the ocean, the fury of the breakers, contrasted with the lowness of the land and the smoothness of the bright green water within the lagoon, can hardly be imagined without having been seen" (paragraph 1).

WRITING FROM WITHIN AND ABOUT THE SCIENTIFIC COMMUNITY

Writing for Yourself

1. Coral reefs clearly left Darwin with a sense of wonder, perhaps even awe. Explore in your journal what inspires awe or wonder in you.

Writing for Nonacademic Audiences

1. One of Darwin's assumptions is that the natural world is always in a state of change, and though those changes are imperceptively slow, we still can see signs of the various stages. The evidence he uses to bolster this assumption comes through direct observation. Examine the world around you. Where might you see evidence for permanent changes? Write a 750-word essay for a popular audience in which you chronicle your observations, pose possible reasons for the changes you observe, and choose the most reasonable theory for the change. You might also wish to predict the possible long-term effects of such a change.

2. Interview several people on your campus and then write up a script for a two-minute report on your college radio station about "what Darwin means to today's college student."

3. Write a 500-word reflective essay for your college newspaper in which you explore the question of whether or not modern college students generally have lost a sense of awe or wonder.

Writing for Academic Audiences

1. Before publishing his material on coral formations, Darwin read a paper to the Geological Society in which he expressed his theories. Using Darwin's own evidence, write a response to this essay suggesting any possible flaws, any omissions in the list of observations, any alternative ways of explaining the growth of the atolls. You will be reading this response to the same Society that has recently heard Darwin's speech.

2. Write a 1,500- to 2,000-word research paper on the formation of atolls. Are contemporary naturalists indebted to Darwin at all? Where might a contemporary naturalist disagree with Darwin's theory? Does it seem that the scientific

methodology of the contemporary naturalist is the same as that of the nineteenth-century naturalist? Where might those methods differ?

3. Interview one of your older relatives about what Darwin's ideas have meant to him or her. Then report on and evaluate this interview for a class on the contemporary religious scene.

4. For a senior seminar on "man as a religious being," write a 1,250-word argument on whether or not God could have and would have used evolutionary processes in creating the world.

5. For a class in scientific and technical writing, write a 750-word argument on whether or not hedges (such as "It is possible that") have any place in scientific writing.

6. For an introductory class in the history of science, write a 750-word report on the principal controversies swirling around Darwin's ideas in the current scientific community.

7. Your biology professor is writing a textbook on science to be used in middle schools. He or she has asked you to write a section on why corals grow on the seaward side of reefs. You have a 500-word limit. You accept.

8. The last sentence of Darwin's *On the Origin of Species* is as follows: "There is grandeur in this view of life, with its several powers, having been originally breathed by the Creator into a few forms or into one; and that, whist this planet has gone cycling on according to the fixed law of gravity, from so simple a beginning endless forms most beautiful and most wonderful have been, and are being evolved." Do some research on Darwin's religious beliefs. Why do you think he refers to a "Creator"? Was he just trying to soothe potentially agitated readers? For a class in science and religion, write a 750-word essay in which you explore answers to these questions.

Albert Einstein

(1879–1955)

While Albert Einstein is recognized as one of the greatest theoretical physicists of all time, his earliest pronouncement of the theory of relativity while he was a doctoral student at the University of Zurich was generally ignored. Regarded as untestable, the theory did not gain wide acceptance until ten years later, when he became professor of physics and director of theoretical physics at Kaiser Wilhelm Physical Institute in Berlin. There he was to remain for almost twenty years, during which time he received the 1921 Nobel Prize. In 1934, with the rise of the Nazi political party, Einstein was stripped of his German citizenship and his property was confiscated.

The year before (1933), Einstein had been awarded a post at the Institute for Advanced Study at Princeton University. He moved there and remained at the post until 1945, becoming an American citizen in 1940. From that position he helped a number of eminent scientists enter the United States during World War II and, encouraged by Niels Bohr, he wrote to President Franklin Roosevelt to urge him to investigate the potential use of atomic energy in bombs, though he himself was an ardent pacifist. Dismayed by the destruction the nuclear bombs that were dropped on Japan did cause, Einstein spent much of his later life campaigning for world peace and disarmament.

Einstein looked for simplicity and beauty in his theories, and for that reason he rejected much of the work in quantum physics that developed in his field late in his career. He found that simplicity in the theory of relativity, a theory he formulated but left to others to prove. Perhaps it is partially because of that simplicity that he was so adept at explaining the theory to an audience of nonspecialists.

The following essay is taken from Out of My Later Years, *a collection of essays by Einstein, most of which are aimed outside of his own primary discourse community of theoretical physicists. This essay was first published in the April, 1946, issue of* Science Illustrated.

$E = MC^2$

In order to understand the law of the equivalence of mass and energy, we   1
must go back to two conservation or "balance" principles which, independent of each other, held a high place in pre-relativity physics. These were the

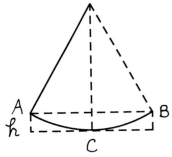

Drawing from Dr. Einstein's manuscript.

dent of each other, held a high place in pre-relativity physics. These were the principle of the conservation of energy and the principle of the conservation of mass. The first of these, advanced by Leibnitz* as long ago as the seventeenth century, was developed in the nineteenth century essentially as a corollary of a principle of mechanics.

Consider, for example, a pendulum whose mass swings back and forth 2 between the points A and B. At these points the mass m is higher by the amount h than it is at C, the lowest point of the path (see drawing). At C, on the other hand, the lifting height has disappeared and instead of it the mass has a velocity v. It is as though the lifting height could be converted entirely into velocity, and vice versa. The exact relation would be expressed as $mgh = (m/2)\,v^2$, with g representing the acceleration of gravity. What is interesting here is that this relation is independent of both the length of the pendulum and the form of the path through which the mass moves.

The significance is that something remains constant throughout the pro- 3 cess, and that something is energy. At A and at B it is an energy of position, or "potential" energy; at C it is an energy of motion, or "kinetic" energy. If this concept is correct, then the sum $mgh + m\,(v^2/2)$ must have the same value for any position of the pendulum, if h is understood to represent the height above C, and v the velocity at that point in the pendulum's path. And such is found to be actually the case. The generalization of this principle gives us the law of the conservation of mechanical energy. But what happens when friction stops the pendulum?

The answer to that was found in the study of heat phenomena. This 4 study, based on the assumption that heat is an indestructible substance which flows from a warmer to a colder object, seemed to give us a principle of the "conservation of heat." On the other hand, from time immemorial it has been known that heat could be produced by friction, as in the firemaking drills of the Indians. The physicists were for long unable to account for this kind of heat "production." Their difficulties were overcome only when it was successfully established that, for any given amount of heat produced by friction, an exactly proportional amount of energy had to be expended. Thus did we

---

*Gottfried Wilhelm, Baron von Leibnitz (1646–1716) was a German philosopher and mathematician [Editors' note].

arrive at a principle of the "equivalence of work and heat." With our pendulum, for example, mechanical energy is gradually converted by friction into heat.

In such fashion the principles of the conservation of mechanical and thermal energies were merged into one. The physicists were thereupon persuaded that the conservation principle could be further extended to take in chemical and electromagnetic processes—in short, could be applied to all fields. It appeared that in our physical system there was a sum total of energies that remained constant through all changes that might occur.

Now for the principle of the conservation of mass. Mass is defined by the resistance that a body opposes to its acceleration (inert mass). It is also measured by the weight of the body (heavy mass). That these two radically different definitions lead to the same value for the mass of a body is, in itself, an astonishing fact. According to the principle—namely, that masses remain unchanged under any physical or chemical changes—the mass appeared to be the essential (because unvarying) quality of matter. Heating, melting, vaporization, or combining into chemical compounds would not change the total mass.

Physicists accepted this principle up to a few decades ago. But it proved inadequate in the face of the special theory of relativity. It was therefore merged with the energy principle—just as, about sixty years before, the principle of the conservation of mechanical energy had been combined with the principle of the conservation of heat. We might say that the principle of the conservation of energy, having previously swallowed up that of the conservation of heat, now proceeded to swallow that of the conservation of mass—and holds the field alone.

It is customary to express the equivalence of mass and energy (though somewhat inexactly) by the formula $E = mc^2$, in which c represents the velocity of light, about 186,000 miles per second. E is the energy that is contained in a stationary body; m is its mass. The energy that belongs to the mass m is equal to this mass, multiplied by the square of the enormous speed of light—which is to say, a vast amount of energy for every unit of mass.

But if every gram of material contains this tremendous energy, why did it go so long unnoticed? The answer is simple enough: so long as none of the energy is given off externally, it cannot be observed. It is as though a man who is fabulously rich should never spend or give away a cent; no one could tell how rich he was.

Now we can reverse the relation and say that an increase of E in the amount of energy must be accompanied by an increase of E/c^2 in the mass. I can easily supply energy to the mass—for instance, if I heat it by ten degrees. So why not measure the mass increase, or weight increase, connected with this change? The trouble here is that in the mass increase the enormous factor c^2 occurs in the denominator of the fraction. In such a case the increase is too small to be measured directly; even with the most sensitive balance.

For a mass increase to be measurable, the change of energy per mass   11
unit must be enormously large. We know of only one sphere in which such
amounts of energy per mass unit are released: namely, radioactive disintegration. Schematically, the process goes like this: An atom of the mass M splits
into two atoms of the mass M' and M'', which separate with tremendous
kinetic energy. If we imagine these two masses as brought to rest—that is, if
we take this energy of motion from them—then, considered together, they
are essentially poorer in energy than was the original atom. According to the
equivalence principle, the mass sum $M' + M''$ of the disintegration products
must also be somewhat smaller than the original mass M of the disintegrating
atom—in contradiction to the old principle of the conservation of mass. The
relative difference of the two is on the order of one-tenth of one percent.

Now, we cannot actually weigh the atoms individually. However, there   12
are indirect methods for measuring their weights exactly. We can likewise
determine the kinetic energies that are transferred to the disintegration products M' and M''. Thus it has become possible to test and confirm the equivalence formula. Also, the law permits us to calculate in advance, from precisely determined atomic weights, just how much energy will be released
with any atomic disintegration we have in mind. The law says nothing, of
course, as to whether—or how—the disintegration reaction can be brought
about.

What takes place can be illustrated with the help of our rich man. The   13
atom M is a rich miser who, during his life, gives away no money (*energy*).
But in his will he bequeaths his fortune to his sons M' and M'', on condition
that they give to the community a small amount, less than one-thousandth of
the whole estate (*energy or mass*). The sons together have somewhat less than
the father had (*the mass sum $M' + M''$ is somewhat smaller than the mass
M of the radioactive atom*). But the part given to the community, though
relatively small, is still so enormously large (*considered as kinetic energy*) that
it brings with it a great threat of evil. Averting that threat has become the
most urgent problem of our time.

QUESTIONS ABOUT EINSTEIN'S DISCOURSE COMMUNITY AND HIS CONCERNS IN THIS ESSAY

1. What is the difference between potential and kinetic energy, as Einstein explains it in paragraph 3? Is "potential energy" something real that exists in the
   physical world, or is it only a linguistic sleight of hand, a way of asserting that
   something has energy even though any observer can see that it is at rest?
2. Einstein writes that "heat is an indestructible substance" (paragraph four).
   What does he mean by this definition? Do you agree with it?
3. In paragraph five, Einstein writes that "it appeared that in our physical system
   there was a sum total of energies that remained constant through all changes
   that might occur." Does such a statement seem believable? What kind of evidence would be needed to prove such a hypothesis?

4. Read over paragraphs six and seven. What assumptions does Einstein hold about the way that science makes progress?
5. In paragraph eight, Einstein introduces his well-known formula. How does he include the velocity of light here? He has not mentioned it before in the essay, nor does he show any of the reasoning which led him to this particular velocity. Is this a flaw in his essay? Could it be explained in terms of the audience for this essay? Should he have explained the presence of that velocity?
6. What is the purpose of the final paragraph? Why does Einstein conclude on such a grim note?

QUESTIONS ABOUT EINSTEIN'S RHETORICAL STRATEGIES

1. Einstein often writes of "physicists" or "the physicists," appearing thereby to distance himself from them. Why does he do this?
2. Einstein poses several questions to the reader. Where does he use them? What does he use them to do? How effective are they?
3. Why would Einstein choose a mathematical formula for the title of this essay? What does that choice announce to the reader?
4. In paragraph three, Einstein writes, "If this concept is correct. . . ." Later in that same paragraph, he notes, "And such is found to be actually the case." Why does he adopt the stance of doubt in the first quoted phrase, when he knows that that doubt will be eliminated later? Could he be accused of manipulating the reader here?
5. Evaluate the effectiveness of the transition in paragraph six, where Einstein is moving from the conservation of energy to the conservation of mass. What alternative methods of transition might he have used?
6. Is the analogy with the rich man (paragraph 9) logical and effective? Does the use of this analogy suggest anything about the audience for this essay?
7. Describe the rhetorical strategy that Einstein is using in paragraph eleven. How does this strategy clarify and explain his major point?
8. Is the conclusion of this essay rhetorically sound? Does it seem to flow logically and reasonably from the rest of the essay? What rhetorical strategies is he using in writing this conclusion?

WRITING FROM WITHIN AND ABOUT THE SCIENTIFIC COMMUNITY

Writing for Yourself

1. In your journal, explore your reactions to the use of atomic bombs at the end of World War II.
2. Some people say that one of the ways human consciousness is different in the modern world is that it is burdened with the threat of the annihilation of civilization through atomic war. In your journal, explore how you cope (in your own consciousness) with this threat.

Writing for Nonacademic Audiences

1. You have been asked to talk to a community adult education class for twenty minutes on the potential for producing energy through fusion, not fission. Write up a draft of this talk.
2. For the Perspective section of your hometown newspaper, write a 750-word description of the first controlled atomic reaction, which took place under the stands at Stagg Field at the University of Chicago.

Writing for Academic Audiences

1. Einstein writes that the law he describes "says nothing, of course, as to whether—or how—the disintegration reaction can be brought about." Write up a 500-word description of how disintegration reactions are triggered in atomic bombs. This description will be used in high school physics classes.
2. Design and write up a lab experiment for a high school physics class in which you illustrate the principle of the "equivalence of work and heat."
3. You are part of a group that is to make an hour-long presentation to your classmates in a history of science class. The general topic is how science makes progress, and your particular task is to write three discussion questions that will generate dialogue when you break the class into small groups. Using Einstein's essay as a resource, write those discussion questions, giving particular attention to the law of the conservation of mass.
4. Write a 1,250-word research paper for a general academic audience in which you analyze Einstein's attitudes toward the nuclear bomb. Have any of those attitudes shaped today's thought?

Rita Levi-Montalcini
(b. 1909)

Rita Levi-Montalcini, born in Torino, Italy, is one of the world's foremost neurologists. She received her education at the University of Turin, though hampered by anti-Semitic laws enacted during the 1930s. Continuing her research during the war on the development of the nervous system of a chick embryo, she eventually published a paper that captured the attention of Viktor Hamburger, a neurologist at Washington University in Saint Louis. Hamburger invited her to spend several months at the university, and in fact, after the war, she moved there and remained until 1981. During that time, she wrote Nerve Cells, Transmitters, and Behavior *(1980). In 1981, she returned to Italy, where she continues her research at the Lab di Biologice Cellulaire in Rome.*

Levi-Montalcini's In Praise of Imperfection *is both a personal narrative of life in Italy during World War II and an account of her scientific experiments. Forced to work under enormously difficult conditions and faced with the kind of fear and persecution that Jews faced under a Fascist and later a Nazi regime, she nevertheless continued her study and began to make significant contributions to the neurological sciences. She herself claims that her drive to continue her research was in some ways an antidote to the horror and despair that continually pressed at her family's door.*

The following selection is the tenth chapter of In Praise of Imperfection.

A PRIVATE LABORATORY À LA ROBINSON CRUSOE

Since I could no longer attend any university institutes, I decided at the end 1
of December 1939 to practice medicine—in clandestine fashion, since this, too, was forbidden. I would look after those patients I had had in my care in past years when they were hospitalized in the university's Medical Clinic. These poor people, who lived in the attics of houses in old Turin, did not care about the laws and were glad of my visits and the help I could offer within

the limits of my scarce finances. The constraint of having to turn to Aryan*
doctors to have prescriptions signed, however, forced me in spite of myself to
reduce and then abandon this activity. I took refuge in reading and cultivated
relationships with the many friends who scorned the danger of being accused
of pietism.

On 10 June 1940, a dear friend and I were hard at work writing her 2
doctoral thesis when, alarmed by the unusual activity in the streets, we
opened the windows. It was six o'clock in the evening. From the loudspeakers
set up in the piazzas and main thoroughfares came the loud voice of the
Duce:† "Fighting men of the army, of the sea and of the air. Blackshirts of
the revolution and of the legions. . . . Attention! A fateful hour is striking in
the sky of our Fatherland. The hour of irrevocable decisions. A declaration
of war has already been presented to the ambassadors." From the Piazza
Venezia, where an immense crowd had been assembled, the listeners still
ignorant of the ambassadors in question roared their enthusiastic approval.
Once the patriotic fervor orchestrated by the Fascist leaders had died down,
he continued, stressing each word: ". . . to the ambassadors of Great Britain
and France."

Italy's ignoble attack on France, by then already in extremis,‡ started 3
the next day. The "Battle of the Alps" cost the French an exiguous number of
casualties, the Italians about two thousand, and many cases of frostbite because the summer equipment of the latter proved inadequate to a sudden
onslaught of winter cold. In the months that followed, Italy's lack of military
preparation was revealed in all its tragedy on the Greek and East African
fronts, while Naples and Sicily were bombed intensively by the British air
force.

A few months after the beginning of the war, in the fall of 1940, Ro- 4
dolfo Amprino, recently returned from the States, came to visit me. I was
surprised when he asked me, in a brusque, "Piedmontese" manner, about my
projects, it not having occurred to me, in that wartime climate, that my
personal problems would be anything but irrelevant to others. My surprise
was even greater in that my relations with Rodolfo, since our meeting eight
years before at the Anatomy Institute, had been limited to laconic exchanges
of information on histological techniques. Or rather, to be more precise, on
the basis of his mastery in the field he would tell me things and I would
clumsily follow his instructions.

My silence in response to his question provoked a sudden and somewhat 5
irritated reaction: "One doesn't lose heart in the face of the first difficulties.
Set up a small laboratory and take up your interrupted research. Remember

---

* Aryan is a term once used to designate the Indo-European race. In Nazi racist literature, Ger-
man descent was traced back to the Aryans.
† Literally, the leader. This is the title used by Benito Mussolini, Italian dictator in World War
II.
‡ In extreme circumstances, near destruction.

Ramón y Cajal who in a poorly equipped institute, in the sleepy city that Valencia must have been in the middle of the last century, did the fundamental work that established the basis of all we know about the nervous system of vertebrates." Rodolfo could not have sown his suggestion on more fertile ground. At that moment he seemed to me Ulysses as Dante* immortalizes him in the twenty-sixth canto of the *Inferno*, when the Greek hero encourages his fellow voyagers not to lose heart but to continue on their course toward the unknown: "My companions I made so eager for the road with these brief words that then I could hardly have held them back."

Rodolfo had, in fact, touched a chord that had been vibrating in me 6 since earliest childhood: the desire to undertake a voyage of adventure to unknown lands. Even more appealing than virgin forest was the jungle lying before me at that moment: the nervous system, with its billions of cells gathered in populations each different from the other and all locked into the apparently inextricable nets of the nervous circuits which intersect in all directions along the cerebrospinal axis. The pleasure I was already savoring in anticipation was enhanced by the prospect of carrying out the project under the conditions contingent on the prohibitive racial laws. If Ramón y Cajal, with his giant's step and exceptional intuition, had dared foray into that jungle, why should I not venture along the path he had opened for me? My first experience with Visintini had been encouraging. Though unable to continue the same line of research, lacking both space (I only had my small bedroom to work in) and competence in electrophysiology, I could nonetheless analyze other aspects of the developing nervous system by relying on my expertise in the selective coloring of nervous tissues with the silver-impregnation technique and on my ability in microsurgery. Ramón y Cajal's success—as well as the much more modest one of Visintini and myself in studying the function and structure of the nervous system of chick embryos—was the result of the tactic of studying the system in its *statu nascendi*,† when it is made up of only some thousand cells interconnected by a still moderate number of neuronal circuits. Chick embryos were ideal material also because they could be easily procured and incubated at home.

I submitted my intention to Mother, Gino, and Paola and received their 7 approval. Mother, in fact, would have been willing to accept any sacrifice rather than face another separation. Gino and Paola, who had been against our moving to the United States because they were both strongly bound to Italy and confident that Nazi-Fascism would be defeated, understood my need to resume the work so suddenly interrupted by my return from Belgium.

The instruments necessary for the realization of this project were few. 8 The need for an incubator was met by a small thermostat which worked very well for the purpose. Another, high-temperature one served to seal the em-

---

*Dante Alighieri (1265–1321) was a famous Italian poet.
†Developing state, prebirth state.

bryos in paraffin. The embryos were then silver-stained and cut into series using a microtomer. The most expensive items were a stereomicroscope, needed for operating on the embryos, and a binocular Zeiss microscope with all the eyepieces and photographic apparatus. The equipment was completed by a series of watchmaker's forceps, ophthalmic microscissors and surgical instruments consisting of common sewing needles which, with a very fine-grained grindstone, I transformed into extremely sharp microscalpels and spatulae. The collection of instruments, glassware, and chemical reagents was like what one of my nineteenth-century predecessors would have found necessary. Gino built me a glass thermoregulated box with two circular openings on the front. Through these I could insert my arms and operate on the embryos under the microscope in an environment of 38°C., protected against possible infection: a point of caution that revealed itself to be entirely unnecessary but had the advantage of surrounding me with a religious sort of respect. My mother also saw to the maintaining of the latter by forbidding my room to curious visitors, telling them that I was operating and could not be disturbed. The "tour de force" of fitting so much apparatus in the small space available to me added to the pleasure of managing to work under prohibitive conditions. The most cumbersome piece was undoubtedly dear old Levi himself who, with his great corporeal mass and meager agility, threatened to destroy all the carefully laid out histological sections with a mere swinging of his large hands each time he moved. "Excuse me, I'll be more careful" he would mutter, without, however, giving too much weight to these accidents on the job.

I spent the winter and spring of 1941 busy with preparations and the 9 first experiments, which turned out well. The worsening of the military situation and the defeat of the Italians in northern Africa, with the English occupation of Ethiopia in April and the loss of eastern Africa, caused the campaign against the Jews to become even more bitter: they were now enemies to be fought on the home front to make up for losses suffered beyond the country's borders. Articles in the newspapers were matched by anti-Semitic graffiti and posters pasted on walls all over the city. On 16 October, Gino came home proud of an honor paid to him. "They've put me in Einstein's company," he told us. On the poster whose contents the partisan Emanuele Artom reproduced in his diary, Gino's name is listed immediately in front of Einstein's, along with other eminent persons belonging to the "Jewish race," such as Franklin Delano Roosevelt, La Pasionaria, Haile Selassie, and Lenin. After listing the horrible crimes committed by these "Jews," the manifesto urged their punishment: "Are we going to put an end to it once and for all, then? Not to the concentration camps, but up against the wall and then at them with a flame thrower! Long live the Duce! Long live Hitler!" The following day, vaguely aware of the fact that they had included in their list the names of persons who did not belong to the Jewish race, the authors urged the citizenry to fire upon Jews at the slightest suspicion, entrusting the Creator with the posthumous task of discriminating any errors. Artom comments in his diary: "To read posters in which one is threatened with death, accused of many crimes, is an experience it is not given to everybody to endure." He was to endure it to the last drop. Revealed early in 1944 as the political commissar of the Action Party, a Jew, and a partisan, he was subjected to horrible tortures at the hands of the SS and killed without his torturers being able to get a single name or complaint out of him. All this his mother learned from Oscar, another partisan who witnessed Emanuele's death.

In 1941, and up to the time of the Nazi invasion of the country, insults 10 and threats were not followed by acts of actual persecution. Thus, from the spring of 1941, I was able to carry on, in the calm of a minuscule laboratory not unlike a convent cell, a research problem that absorbed all of my time from then until the invasion. My aim was to analyze how excision of still non-innervated tissues in the peripheral territories, or limbs, affects the differentiation and subsequent development both of motor cells in the spinal cord and of sensory cells in the dorsal root ganglia at a very early stage of embryonic life. Previously, this problem, one of the first to be tackled experimentally by researchers into the development of the nervous system in the first two decades of the century, had scarcely interested me. Amphibian tadpoles had been the subject of these experiments, but the results obtained seemed to me too vague to lend themselves to satisfactory interpretation. These findings suddenly appeared in a different light one summer day of 1940, shortly after Italy had entered the war on Germany's side.

My conversion, if such it can be called, occurred while I was riding on 11 a train used before the war for the transportation of livestock. After war had been declared, civilian trains were taken over for troop transportation, and these livestock trains, or cattle cars, were used for civilians, for short journeys in the provinces. The wagons, which lacked seats, doors, and windows, offered great panoramic views through the windowless open sides. I was traveling on one, along with my friend Guido, the formidable whistler of classical arias, on our way to a small mountain village. I sat down in what was considered to be one of the best places—the floor of the wagon—with my legs dangling over the side in the open air. The slow progress of the train, the vertical bars that offered firm support and, in my case, Guido's vigilant hand, ensured against possible falls and allowed me to see the fields in their full summer's growth. While enjoying the view and the air which smelled of hay, I was distractedly reading an article Levi had given to me two years before. Published in 1934 in an American periodical, it was the work of a pupil of Hans Spemann, the German biologist who was awarded the Nobel Prize in 1935 for his discovery of a factor (or of factors, which even today have not been precisely identified) called the "organizer" because of its property of inducing the differentiation of organs and of whole embryos that come into direct contact with the tissues releasing it. The author of the article, Viktor Hamburger, had not analyzed this phenomenon, but his interpretation of the effect he described was clearly influenced by the same concept of an inductive reaction of certain tissues on others during the early stages of embryonic development. Hamburger had studied how the ablation* of chick embryo limb buds affected the sensory and motor neurons responsible for their innervation.† The author observed that, one week after such an operation, the motor column and the sensory spinal ganglia responsible for the innervation of the limbs were greatly reduced in volume. Hamburger interpreted these findings as pointing to the absence of an inductive factor,‡ otherwise normally released by the innervated tissues and necessary for the differentiation of motor and sensory nerve cells; without the factor, these cells could not undergo differentiation. For me, Hamburger's limpid style and the rigor of his analysis—in sharp contrast with those of previous authors who had described the same phenomenon in amphibian larvae—cast new light on the problem. I don't know how far the idyllic circumstances in which I read the article contributed to my desire to delve into this phenomenon, but in memory my decision is indissolubly bound up with that summer afternoon and the smell of hay wafting into the wagon. I did not imagine at the time, however, that this interest and my subsequent research would determine my future.

The summer of 1941 was overshadowed by the anguish caused by the news of the triumphant advance of Hitler's troops into Russia and of their successes on all fronts. We were, furthermore, deprived of all news of Levi whom we feared had fallen into Nazi hands since his refusal to leave Belgium after the German occupation. It was with immense joy that, at summer's end, we welcomed him back—shockingly thin and pale after a dangerous trip across Germany. It turned out that, after a year in Nazi-controlled Liège, meeting his friends secretly in a little café outside of town, he had been unable to endure any longer the hunger, loneliness, and boredom, and had set out for home. I was especially happy to see him, and asked him to join me in my new research. He accepted with great pleasure, and thus it was that from that autumn till a year later when we were both forced to leave the city, his imperious voice resounded in my bedroom-laboratory from morning to night. Work would be interrupted when his loyal pupils arrived, and the topic of conversation would shift from chick embryos to the madmen and criminals who were running our country.

In the winter and spring of 1942, our research yielded unhoped-for successes. The examination of embryos whose budding limbs had been excised in three-day specimens, and impregnated using the silver technique, revealed with extraordinary clarity the nerve cells and the fibers that sprang both out of the motor neurons of the spinal column and out of the sensory ganglia in embryos sacrificed at brief intervals from the time of the excision to the end

12

13

---

*Removal.
†Their spreading into the appropriate areas and excitation so that they function properly.
‡A causative factor or inducer.

of the twenty-day incubation period. These findings suggested a different explanation from the one advanced by Hamburger to explain the almost-complete disappearance of the motor cells in the spinal ganglia that innervated the limbs in embryos not subjected to such destructive treatment. It was a question of the absence not of an inductive factor necessary to their differentiation, but of a trophic factor* that is released by innervated tissues and that, under normal conditions, the nerve fibers convey toward the cellular bodies. In fact, in embryos with excised limbs, the differentiation of nerve cells proceeds normally, but a degenerative process followed by the death of the cells begins to occur as soon as the fibers springing out of the cord and from the ganglia reach the stump of the amputated limb. Their death appeared to be caused by the absence of a trophic factor and not, as Hamburger had hypothesized, by an inductive one belonging to the category of those known as "organizers."

Many years later, I often asked myself how we could have dedicated 14 ourselves with such enthusiasm to solving this small neuroembryological problem while German armies were advancing throughout Europe, spreading destruction and death wherever they went and threatening the very survival of Western civilization. The answer lies in the desperate and partially unconscious desire of human beings to ignore what is happening in situations where full awareness might lead one to self-destruction.

In the second half of 1942, with the Allies' systematic bombing of the 15 cities in northern Italy and of Turin in particular, a favorite target because of its great industries, life in the city became every day more dangerous. Almost every night, the lugubrious whine of sirens, warning of British planes overhead, forced us to go down into the basement in spite of the risk—which became tragic reality for hundreds of people—of being buried under the ruins of bombed buildings. Every time the alarm sounded, I would carry down to the precarious safety of the cellars the Zeiss binocular microscope and my most precious silver-stained embryonic sections. These vigils usually dragged on for hours, amid the murmurs of women praying, until the sirens announced that the danger had, for the time being, come to an end. Very often, however, a squeal announcing a new series of planes forced us to rush down again.

When autumn was well under way, we decided, like the majority of 16 the people of Turin, to move out of town. Thus, in a small house in the hilly Astigiano highlands, an hour away from Turin, I set up my laboratory on a small table in the corner of a room that served also as dining area and family sitting room. Since eggs had become extremely scarce, I cycled from one hill to another begging farmers to sell me some "for my babies." Casually I inquired whether there were roosters in the chicken coop because, as I explained, "fertilized eggs are more nutritious." A unforeseen difficulty arose

---

* A nutritional factor.

when my activities in the common room fell under Gino's eyes. He noticed how I used spatulae and ophthalmic scissors to extract from the eggs five-day-old embryos that had been operated on, and how then, instead of throwing the eggs away, I carried them into the kitchen and used them to fix our meals. From that day on, he categorically refused to eat the scrambled eggs and omelets, which up until then he had thought excellent.

Levi lived in a different locality outside of Turin but returned every 17 day. On alternate days, and always after heavy bombings, which my family and I would witness in dismay from the top of the hill, gazing at the sky lit by the glare of fires, I also returned to Turin to meet him. With other friends, we warmed ourselves by a stove in the kitchen of my home, the only warm room in the freezing apartment, and ate the steaming cornmeal that an old housekeeper poured us from the pot while recounting the night's events. With a smiling, rubicund face, he expressed the pride he took in his work, saying, "I do everything on my own"—though doing nothing but stir the cornmeal. These were the most serene moments of those wintry days in the city devastated by night bombing raids. The ruins of bombed buildings, broken pipelines, damaged electrical and telephone plants were swept aside and repaired with unbelievable speed, but hopelessness and despair were written on everybody's face. At dusk began the assault on the overcrowded trains carrying people back to the shelters scattered about in the hills.

In spite of the almost prohibitive conditions—the difficulty of procuring 18 fertilized eggs, and the repeated failure of the power supply upon which depended the functioning of my incubator and the development of the embryos—I completed some projects which I was to carry further a few years later in the United States. Their central theme was the study of the interaction of genetic and environmental factors in the regulation of the differentiation processes of the nervous system during the early stages of its development. At the beginning of spring, from the window of my small room in our cottage, I contemplated the ducklings following their mother in single file, diving from time to time as she did into the ditches that, after rain, flowed down the sides of the little road I used to cycle along every day. In specific areas of the embryonic nervous system, cells in the first stages of differentiation detach themselves from cellular clusters of cephalic nuclei and move singularly, one after the other like the little ducklings, toward distant locations along rigidly programmed routes, as is demonstrated by the fact that the spatial and temporal modalities of these migrations are identical in different embryos. In other sectors of the developing nervous system, thousands of cells move about like colonies of migrating birds or insects—like the Biblical locusts that I was to see many years later in Ecuador. The fact that I was for the first time observing natural phenomena unknown to those who live in cities, such as the springtime awakening of nature, cheered me and stimulated my interest in studying the developing nervous system. Now the nervous system appeared to me in a different light from its description in textbooks of neuroanatomy, where its structure is described as rigid and un-changeable. Only by following, from hour to hour in different specimens, as in a cinematographic sequence, the development of nerve centers and cir-cuits, did I come to realize how dynamic these processes are; how individual cells behave in a way similar to that of living beings; how plastic and malle-able is the entire nervous system. This system, which more than any other must adapt its structure and functions to environmental requirements, was to remain the main object of my research in the years that followed. Its anal-ysis came into focus and grew in that country milieu probably much better than it would have in an academic institution.

In the summer of 1943 occurred the event marking the end of an era for   19 Italy and the beginning of a most dramatic period. On the evening of 25 July, at 10:45 P.M., while we were listening to the radio, the program was inter-rupted by an announcer reading out the following news:

> Attention, Attention! His Majesty the King Emperor has accepted the resigna-   20 tion from the offices of Head of the Government presented by the Prime Min-ister and Secretary of State His Excellency Cavalier Benito Mussolini, and has nominated Head of the Government, Prime Minister and Secretary of State, His Excellency, the Marshal of Italy, Pietro Badoglio.

The news was received in my home, as throughout the entire peninsula, with   21 immense jubilation. The demonstrations of enthusiasm were profoundly gen-uine yet, at the same time, indicative of a collective irresponsibility—or, to describe it in less severe terms, a lack of awareness of the danger looming over us, with German troops stationed in Italy and more massing on its fron-tiers.

The following morning, I went into Turin as usual. On the train, peo-   22 ple were hugging each other, crying and laughing. At the station, from trains that until the previous day had spilled onto the platforms a gloomy and silent crowd, now descended passengers who behaved as if they were intoxicated. They began to cast off Fascist insignia—until the previous day, the precious symbols of support for the regime, and now objects of derision and shame. Leading fascists stayed shut up in their houses that day and the following ones; less important party members mixed in with the crowd who accepted them good-naturedly. Everybody, for that matter, felt somewhat guilty.

If optimism among the "Aryans" was to some extent justified, as they   23 were not directly in the Nazis' gunsights, it was, on the contrary, completely absurd in the small Jewish population, ourselves included. Even though we were only partly aware of what had happened and was still happening in the European countries invaded by the Germans, it was folly not to have taken immediate precautions to save ourselves after 25 July. Faith in the Italians who welcomed us back among them, a common hatred for Nazism, and the absurd conviction that what happened in other countries could not happen in Italy were the source of this irresponsible attitude, an attitude which was to cause thousands of people untold suffering and death.

QUESTIONS ABOUT LEVI-MONTALCINI'S DISCOURSE COMMUNITY AND HER CONCERNS IN THIS SELECTION

1. In this chapter, Levi-Montalcini recounts some events of World War II, narrates a personal story, and describes her scientific experiments. Does the combination of these three suggest that she is not clear about the nature of her audience? Or if you think she is clear, how would you describe the audience she has in mind?

2. How did Ramón y Cajal become a model for Levi-Montalcini? What does her choice of that scientist as a model suggest about the nature of her discourse community at the time when she was beginning her medical research?

3. How would you describe the conditions under which Levi-Montalcini worked? It is a cliché in literary studies that great authors must first starve themselves in attic garrets, writing for the muses rather than for money. Would such hardships also be inspirational to a scientist?

4. Consider the fourteenth paragraph, where Levi-Montalcini explains why she could commit herself so thoroughly to her work during this turbulent time. Does this seem to be a reasonable explanation?

5. Why does Gino refuse to continue to eat eggs (paragraph 16)? Does this represent merely a silly squeamishness on his part, or is there some deeper motive?

6. Levi-Montalcini writes that her analysis of the nervous system "came into focus and grew in that country milieu probably much better than it would have in an academic institution" (paragraph 18). Why might this have been so?

7. After the resignation of Mussolini, Levi-Montalcini writes, people seemed overjoyed and even accepted some of the party members who had supported Mussolini. But then she writes that "everybody, for that matter, felt somewhat guilty" (paragraph 22). Why would this have been so? Does Levi-Montalcini mean to include herself in this "everybody"?

8. Levi-Montalcini writes of successes in her experiments, but she never mentions publishing reports of the experiments. What do you think is more important to the true scientist—discovering things or letting others know about the discoveries?

9. Toward the end of this chapter, Levi-Montalcini writes about the dynamic and plastic qualities of developing nerve systems. Do you think she intends these comments to have significance beyond the realm of nerve development?

QUESTIONS ABOUT LEVI-MONTALCINI'S RHETORICAL STRATEGIES

1. Does the title of this selection adequately describe or introduce the contents of the essay? What connotations is the author trying to establish?

2. Read over the first three paragraphs of this selection. Much of this material focuses on large-scale events: the movement to war and the first battles. Why does Levi-Montalcini begin with this material? How does it prepare the reader for the rest of the essay? In the fourth paragraph, how does Levi-Montalcini make the transition back to a focus on the individual?

3. Levi-Montalcini links Rodolfo Amprino to Dante's portrayal of Ulysses, who

made his men eager to face hardships. What she does not make clear, however, is that Dante put Ulysses in hell for the illegitimate use of his powers of persuasion. Does this withholding of information seem purposeful and deliberate, merely an unconscious omission, or not worthy of mention?

4. At the end of paragraph 8, Levi-Montalcini notes that huge old Levi would mutter "Excuse me, I'll be more careful" without "giving too much weight to these accidents on the job." Is she being too obviously clever in using the words *too much weight?*

5. Speaking of her research, Levi-Montalcini writes in paragraph 10: "These findings suddenly appeared in a different light one summer day of 1940, shortly after Italy had entered the war on Germany's side." Why does Levi-Montalcini link her personal research with this historical event? Where else do you find such linkages in this essay? Would you say that generally she is successful in these linkages?

6. In general, Levi-Montalcini uses very lengthy paragraphs. Do you discern any rhetorical strategy behind the paragraph length? Consider paragraph 11. Would it be possible to divide this into two or more paragraphs, or is it unified as it stands?

7. Describing the differentiation of the cells of the nervous system, Levi-Montalcini uses comparisons (paragraph 18). How do these contribute to the clarity of her explanation? What might these comparisons suggest about the audience she has in mind?

8. How would you evaluate the effectiveness of the conclusion? How does it affect the reader? Why might the author have chosen to conclude in this manner rather than with a note about the success of her research?

WRITING FROM WITHIN AND ABOUT THE SCIENTIFIC COMMUNITY

Writing for Yourself

1. In your journal, explore the nature of a serene moment you have enjoyed in the midst of chaos or distraction.

2. One question that Levi-Montalcini never brings up is the ethics of animal research. In your journal, explore your reactions to a scientist's destruction of a chick embryo. Are those reactions the same as those elicited by the death of, for example, a dog or a monkey? Why or why not?

Writing for Nonacademic Audiences

1. Some instances of racial or ethnic persecution have surfaced recently on your campus. Write a letter to the editor of your campus newspaper; in this letter you should state your reactions to the recent persecution.

2. Representatives of the Society for Prevention of Cruelty to Animals have started to picket the labs in which you are pursuing some undergraduate projects. They are protesting using any animals in research projects. Write them a letter in which you react to their protest.

Writing for Academic Audiences

1. Prepare a 500-word description of the general nature of the nervous system in human beings; this description will be presented to an introductory biology class. Use a single controlling metaphor to help clarify your presentation.
2. Research the conditions under which one other scientist mentioned in this section worked. Write a 750-word essay for a history of science class that explains how those conditions affected the scientist's research.
3. Write a 1,250-word paper for a course in modern European history analyzing why people chose not to flee in the face of the Nazis and Fascists.
4. Write a 2,000- to 2,500-word research paper on the persecution of the Jewish population in Italy during the 1930s and 1940s. What influences led to that persecution? Did non-Jews resist that persecution in any way?

Fritjof Capra
(b. 1939)

In The Tao of Physics *(1975) and* The Turning Point: Science, Society, and the Rising Culture *(1982), Fritjof Capra argues from within a discourse community that many scientists do not recognize as legitimate. Applying Eastern mysticism to quantum physics, Fritjof finds a correlation between modern scientific theory and Taoist philosophy. His basic assumption as he approaches questions of atomic structure and the nature of matter is philosophical: Before everything else, scientists project a worldview that inevitably affects their perceptions of the universe. There is no such thing as complete objectivity in trying to describe reality. To some scientists such a vision would deny the validity of all scientific observation and measurement.*

Capra argues for a holistic approach to understanding the universe. Instead of isolated pockets of matter, he claims, the universe consists of a web of connections. Nothing exists in complete isolation; everything exists in relationships. This, he notes, is a new way of looking at the universe and leads to a profoundly different view of the meaning of matter and energy. Classical models of physical reality are, according to this view, radically altered or eclipsed, since such models are limited by a fundamental misconception about how the universe is constructed.

Many of Capra's assertions are accepted by only a few physicists, but unorthodoxy in a given field is not necessarily to be dismissed. Capra has gained a significant number of readers who accept the union of mysticism and science and who find in it an appropriate means for seeing the nature of reality.

The following selection is chapter 3 of The Turning Point: Science, Society, and the Rising Culture.

THE NEW PHYSICS

At the beginning of modern physics stands the extraordinary intellectual feat 1 of one man—Albert Einstein. In two articles, both published in 1905, Einstein initiated two revolutionary trends in scientific thought. One was his special theory of relativity; the other was a new way of looking at electromagnetic radiation which was to become characteristic of quantum theory, the theory of atomic phenomena. The complete quantum theory was worked out twenty years later by a whole team of physicists. Relativity theory, however, was constructed in its complete form almost entirely by Einstein himself. Einstein's scientific papers are intellectual monuments that mark the beginning of twentieth-century thought.

Einstein strongly believed in nature's inherent harmony, and through-   2 out his scientific life his deepest concern was to find a unified foundation of physics. He began to move toward this goal by constructing a common framework for electrodynamics and mechanics, the two separate theories of classical physics. This framework is known as the special theory of relativity. It unified and completed the structure of classical physics, but at the same time it involved radical changes in the traditional concepts of space and time and thus undermined one of the foundations of the Newtonian world view. Ten years later Einstein proposed his general theory of relativity, in which the framework of the special theory is extended to include gravity. This is achieved by further drastic modifications of the concepts of space and time.

The other major development in twentieth-century physics was a con-   3 sequence of the experimental investigation of atoms. At the turn of the century physicists discovered several phenomena connected with the structure of atoms, such as X-rays and radioactivity, which were inexplicable in terms of classical physics. Besides being objects of intense study, these phenomena were used, in most ingenious ways, as new tools to probe deeper into matter than had ever been possible before. For example, the so-called alpha particles emanating from radioactive substances were perceived to be high-speed projectiles of subatomic size that could be used to explore the interior of the atom. They could be fired at atoms, and from the way they were deflected one could draw conclusions about the atoms' structure.

This exploration of the atomic and subatomic world brought scientists   4 in contact with a strange and unexpected reality that shattered the foundations of their world view and forced them to think in entirely new ways. Nothing like that had ever happened before in science. Revolutions like those of Copernicus* and Darwin† had introduced profound changes in the general conception of the universe, changes that were shocking to many people, but the new concepts themselves were not difficult to grasp. In the twentieth century, however, physicists faced, for the first time, a serious challenge to their ability to understand the universe. Every time they asked nature a question in an atomic experiment, nature answered with a paradox, and the more they tried to clarify the situation, the sharper the paradoxes became. In their struggle to grasp this new reality, scientists became painfully aware that their basic concepts, their language, and their whole way of thinking were inadequate to describe atomic phenomena. Their problem was not only intellec-

---

*Nicholas Copernicus (1473–1543) proposed the first model of planetary motion that had the sun in the middle of the solar system.
†Charles Darwin (1809–1882) proposed the theory of organic evolution through natural selection.

tual but involved an intense emotional and existential experience, as vividly described by Werner Heisenberg:* "I remember discussions with Bohr† which went through many hours till very late at night and ended almost in despair; and when at the end of the discussion I went alone for a walk in the neighboring park I repeated to myself again and again the question: Can nature possibly be so absurd as it seemed to us in these atomic experiments?"‡

It took these physicists a long time to accept the fact that the paradoxes 5 they encountered are an essential aspect of atomic physics, and to realize that they arise whenever one tries to describe atomic phenomena in terms of classical concepts. Once this was perceived, the physicists began to learn to ask the right questions and to avoid contradictions. As Heisenberg says, "They somehow got into the spirit of the quantum theory,"§ and finally they found the precise and consistent mathematical formulation of that theory. Quantum theory, or quantum mechanics as it is also called, was formulated during the first three decades of the century by an international group of physicists including Max Planck, Albert Einstein, Niels Bohr, Louis De Broglie, Erwin Schrödinger, Wolfgang Pauli, Werner Heisenberg, and Paul Dirac. These men joined forces across national borders to shape one of the most exciting periods of modern science, one that saw not only brilliant intellectual exchanges but also dramatic human conflicts, as well as deep personal friendships, among the scientists.

Even after the mathematical formulation of quantum theory was completed, its conceptual framework was by no means easy to accept. Its effect 6 on the physicists' view of reality was truly shattering. The new physics necessitated profound changes in concepts of space, time, matter, object, and cause and effect; and because these concepts are so fundamental to our way of experiencing the world, their transformation came as a great shock. To quote Heisenberg again, "The violent reaction to the recent development of modern physics can only be understood when one realizes that here the foundations of physics have started moving; and that this motion has caused the feeling that the ground would be cut from science."‖

Einstein experienced the same shock when he was confronted with the 7 new concepts of physics, and he described his feelings in terms very similar to Heisenberg's: "All my attempts to adapt the theoretical foundation of physics to this [new type of] knowledge failed completely. It was as if the ground had been pulled out from under one, with no firm foundation to be seen anywhere, upon which one could have built."¶

Out of the revolutionary changes in our concepts of reality that were 8

---

*Werner Heisenberg (1901–1976) was a German physicist.
†Niels Bohr (1885–1962) was a Danish physicist.
‡W. Heisenberg, quoted in Capra (1975), p. 50 [Capra's note].
§W. Heisenberg, quoted *ibid.*, p. 67 [Capra's note].
‖W. Heisenberg, quoted *ibid.*, p. 53 [Capra's note].
¶A. Einstein, quoted *ibid.*, p. 42 [Capra's note].

brought about by modern physics, a consistent world view is now emerging. This view is not shared by the entire physics community, but is being discussed and elaborated by many leading physicists whose interest in their science goes beyond the technical aspects of their research. These scientists are deeply interested in the philosophical implications of modern physics and are trying in an open-minded way to improve their understanding of the nature of reality.

In contrast to the mechanistic Cartesian view of the world,* the world   9 view emerging from modern physics can be characterized by words like organic, holistic, and ecological. It might also be called a systems view, in the sense of general systems theory.† The universe is no longer seen as a machine, made up of a multitude of objects, but has to be pictured as one indivisible, dynamic whole whose parts are essentially interrelated and can be understood only as patterns of a cosmic process.

The basic concepts underlying this world view of modern physics are   10 discussed in the following pages. I described this world view in detail in *The Tao of Physics*, showing how it is related to the views held in mystical traditions, especially those of Eastern mysticism. Many physicists, brought up, as I was, in a tradition that associates mysticism with things vague, mysterious, and highly unscientific, were shocked at having their ideas compared to those of mystics.‡ Fortunately, this attitude is now changing. As Eastern thought has begun to interest a significant number of people, and meditation is no longer viewed with ridicule or suspicion, mysticism is being taken seriously even within the scientific community. An increasing number of scientists are aware that mystical thought provides a consistent and relevant philosophical background to the theories of contemporary science, a conception of the world in which the scientific discoveries of men and women can be in perfect harmony with their spiritual aims and religious beliefs.

The experimental investigation of atoms at the beginning of the century   11 yielded sensational and totally unexpected results. Far from being the hard, solid particles of time-honored theory, atoms turned out to consist of vast regions of space in which extremely small particles—the electrons—moved around the nucleus. A few years later quantum theory made it clear that even the subatomic particles—the electrons and the protons and neutrons in the nucleus—were nothing like the solid objects of classical physics. These subatomic units of matter are very abstract entities which have a dual aspect. Depending on how we look at them, they appear sometimes as particles, sometimes as waves; and this dual nature is also exhibited by light, which can take the form of electromagnetic waves or particles. The particles of light

* As derived from René Descartes (1596–1650), French philosopher and scientist.
† See Chapter 9 [Capra's note].
‡ For a definition and concise description of mysticism, see Stace (1960), Chapter 1 [Capra's note].

were first called "quanta" by Einstein—hence the origin of the term "quantum theory"—and are now known as photons.

This dual nature of matter and of light is very strange. It seems impos- 12 sible to accept that something can be, at the same time, a particle, an entity confined to a very small volume, and a wave, which is spread out over a large region of space. And yet this is exactly what physicists had to accept. The situation seemed hopelessly paradoxical until it was realized that the terms "particle" and "wave" refer to classical concepts which are not fully adequate to describe atomic phenomena. An electron is neither a particle nor a wave, but it may show particle-like aspects in some situations and wave-like aspects in others. While it acts like a particle, it is capable of developing its wave nature at the expense of its particle nature, and vice versa, thus undergoing continual transformations from particle to wave and from wave to particle. This means that neither the electron nor any other atomic "object" has any intrinsic properties independent of its environment. The properties it shows— particle-like or wave-like—will depend on the experimental situation, that is, on the apparatus it is forced to interact with.*

It was Heisenberg's great achievement to express the limitations of clas- 13 sical concepts in a precise mathematical form, which is known as the uncertainty principle. It consists of a set of mathematical relations that determine the extent to which classical concepts can be applied to atomic phenomena; these relations stake out the limits of human imagination in the atomic world. Whenever we use classical terms—particle, wave, position, velocity—to describe atomic phenomena, we find that there are pairs of concepts, or aspects, which are interrelated and cannot be defined simultaneously in a precise way. The more we emphasize one aspect in our description the more the other aspect becomes uncertain, and the precise relation between the two is given by the uncertainty principle.

For a better understanding of this relation between pairs of classical 14 concepts, Niels Bohr introduced the notion of complementarity. He considered the particle picture and the wave picture two complementary descriptions of the same reality, each of them only partly correct and having a limited range of application. Both pictures are needed to give a full account of the atomic reality, and both are to be applied within the limitations set by the uncertainty principle. The notion of complementarity has become an essential part of the way physicists think about nature, and Bohr has often suggested that it might also be a useful concept outside the field of physics. Indeed, this seems to be true, and we shall come back to it in discussions of biological and psychological phenomena. Complementarity has already been used extensively in our survey of the Chinese yin/yang terminology, since the

---

* At present some properties of subatomic particles, like electric charge or magnetic movement, seem to be independent of the experimental situation. However, recent developments in particle physics, to be discussed below, indicate that these properties too may well depend on our framework of observation and measurement [Capra's note].

yin and yang opposites are interrelated in a polar, or complementary, way. Clearly the modern concept of complementarity is reflected in ancient Chinese thought, a fact that made a deep impression on Niels Bohr.*

The resolution of the particle/wave paradox forced physicists to accept 15 an aspect of reality that called into question the very foundation of the mechanistic world view—the concept of the reality of matter. At the subatomic level, matter does not exist with certainty at definite places, but rather shows "tendencies to exist," and atomic events do not occur with certainty at definite times and in definite ways, but rather show "tendencies to occur." In the formalism of quantum mechanics, these tendencies are expressed as probabilities and are associated with quantities that take the form of waves; they are similar to the mathematical forms used to describe, say, a vibrating guitar string, or sound wave. This is how particles can be waves at the same time. They are not "real" three-dimensional waves like water waves or sound waves. They are "probability waves"—abstract mathematical quantities with all the characteristic properties of waves—that are related to the probabilities of finding the particles at particular points in space and at particular times. All the laws of atomic physics are expressed in terms of these probabilities. We can never predict an atomic event with certainty; we can only predict the likelihood of its happening.

The discovery of the dual aspect of matter and of the fundamental role 16 of probability has demolished the classical notion of solid objects. At the subatomic level, the solid material objects of classical physics dissolve into wavelike patterns of probabilities. These patterns, furthermore, do not represent probabilities of things, but rather probabilities of interconnections. A careful analysis of the process of observation in atomic physics shows that the subatomic particles have no meaning as isolated entities but can be understood only as interconnections, or correlations, between various processes of observation and measurement. As Niels Bohr wrote, "Isolated material particles are abstractions, their properties being definable and observable only through their interaction with other systems."†

Subatomic particles, then, are not "things" but are interconnections be- 17 tween "things," and these "things," in turn, are interconnections between other "things," and so on. In quantum theory you never end up with "things"; you always deal with interconnections.

This is how modern physics reveals the basic oneness of the universe. It 18 shows that we cannot decompose the world into independently existing smallest units. As we penetrate into matter, nature does not show us any isolated basic building blocks, but rather appears as a complicated web of relations between the various parts of a unified whole. As Heisenberg ex-

---

*See Capra (1975), p. 160 [Capra's note].
†N. Bohr, quoted *ibid.*, p. 137 [Capra's note].

presses it, "The world thus appears as a complicated tissue of events, in which connections of different kinds alternate or overlap or combine and thereby determine the texture of the whole."*

The universe, then, is a unified whole that can to some extent be divided 19 into separate parts, into objects made of molecules and atoms, themselves made of particles. But here, at the level of particles, the notion of separate parts breaks down. The subatomic particles—and therefore, ultimately, all parts of the universe—cannot be understood as isolated entities but must be defined through their interrelations. Henry Stapp, of the University of California, writes, "An elementary particle is not an independently existing unanalyzable entity. It is, in essence, a set of relationships that reach outward to other things."†

This shift from objects to relationships has far-reaching implications for 20 science as a whole. Gregory Bateson even argued that relationships should be used as a basis for *all* definitions, and that this should be taught to our children in elementary school.‡ Any thing, he believed, should be defined not by what it is in itself, but by its relations to other things.

In quantum theory the fact that atomic phenomena are determined by 21 their connections to the whole is closely related to the fundamental role of probability.§ In classical physics, probability is used whenever the mechanical details involved in an event are unknown. For example, when we throw a die, we could—in principle—predict the outcome if we knew all the details of the objects involved: the exact composition of the die, of the surface on which it falls, and so on. These details are called local variables because they reside within the objects involved. Local variables are important in atomic and subatomic physics too. Here they are represented by connections between spatially separated events through signals—particles and networks of particles—that respect the usual laws of spatial separation. For example, no signal can be transmitted faster than the speed of light. But beyond these local connections are other, nonlocal connections that are instantaneous and cannot be predicted, at present, in a precise mathematical way. These nonlocal connections are the essence of quantum reality. Each event is influenced by the whole universe, and although we cannot describe this influence in detail, we recognize some order that can be expressed in terms of statistical laws.

Thus probability is used in classical and quantum physics for similar 22 reasons. In both cases there are "hidden" variables, unknown to us, and this ignorance prevents us from making exact predictions. There is a crucial difference, however. Whereas the hidden variables in classical physics are local

---

*W. Heisenberg, quoted *ibid.*, p. 139 [Capra's note].
†Stapp, 1971 [Capra's note].
‡Bateson, (1979), p. 17 [Capra's note].
§I am indebted to Henry Stapp for a discussion of this point; see also Stapp (1972) [Capra's note].

mechanisms, those in quantum physics are nonlocal; they are instantaneous connections to the universe as a whole. In the ordinary, macroscopic world nonlocal connections are relatively unimportant, and thus we can speak of separate objects and formulate the laws of physics in terms of certainties. But as we go to smaller dimensions, the influence of nonlocal connections becomes stronger; here the laws of physics can be formulated only in terms of probabilities, and it becomes more and more difficult to separate any part of the universe from the whole.

Einstein could never accept the existence of nonlocal connections and   23
the resulting fundamental nature of probability. This was the subject of the historic debate in the 1920s with Bohr, in which Einstein expressed his opposition to Bohr's interpretation of quantum theory in the famous metaphor "God does not play dice."* At the end of the debate, Einstein had to admit that quantum theory, as interpreted by Bohr and Heisenberg, formed a consistent system of thought, but he remained convinced that a deterministic interpretation in terms of local hidden variables would be found some time in the future.

Einstein's unwillingness to accept the consequences of the theory that   24
his earlier work had helped to establish is one of the most fascinating episodes in the history of science. The essence of his disagreement with Bohr was his firm belief in some external reality, consisting of independent spatially separated elements. This shows that Einstein's philosophy was essentially Cartesian. Although he initiated the revolution of twentieth-century science and went far beyond Newton in his theory of relativity, it seems that Einstein, somehow, could not bring himself to go beyond Descartes. This kinship between Einstein and Descartes is even more intriguing in view of Einstein's attempts, toward the end of his life, to construct a unified field theory by geometrizing physics along the lines of his general theory of relativity. Had these attempts been successful, Einstein could well have said, like Descartes, that his entire physics was nothing other than geometry.

In his attempt to show that Bohr's interpretation of quantum theory   25
was inconsistent, Einstein devised a thought experiment that has become known as the Einstein-Podolsky-Rosen (EPR) experiment.† Three decades later John Bell derived a theorem, based on the EPR experiment, which proves that the existence of local hidden variables is inconsistent with the statistical predictions of quantum mechanics.‡ Bell's theorem dealt a shattering blow to Einstein's position by showing that the Cartesian conception of reality as consisting of separate parts, joined by local connections, is incompatible with quantum theory.

The EPR experiment provides a fine example of a situation in which a   26

---

*See Schilpp (1951); see also Stapp (1972) [Capra's note].
†See Bohm (1951), pp. 614ff. [Capra's note].
‡See Stapp (1971); for a discussion of the implications of Bell's theorem in relation to the philosophy of A. N. Whitehead, see Stapp (1979) [Capra's note].

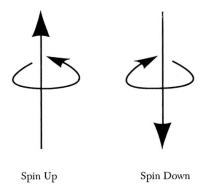

Spin Up   Spin Down

quantum phenomenon clashes with our deepest intuition of reality. It is thus ideally suited to show the difference between classical and quantum concepts. A simplified version of the experiment involves two spinning electrons, and, if we are to grasp the essence of the situation, it is necessary to understand some properties of electron spin.* The classical image of a spinning tennis ball is not fully adequate to describe a spinning subatomic particle. Particle spin is in a sense a rotation about the particle's own axis, but, as always in subatomic physics, this classical concept is limited. In the case of an electron, the particle's spin is restricted to two values: the amount of spin is always the same, but the particle can spin in one or the other direction, for a given axis of rotation. Physicists often denote these two values of spin by "up" and "down," assuming the electron's axis of rotation, in this case, to be vertical.

The crucial property of a spinning electron, which cannot be understood in terms of classical ideas, is the fact that its axis of rotation cannot always be defined with certainty. Just as electrons show tendencies to exist in certain places, they also show tendencies to spin about certain axes. Yet whenever a measurement is performed for any axis of rotation, the electron will be found to spin in one or the other direction about that axis. In other words, the particle acquires a definite axis of rotation in the process of measurement, but before the measurement is taken, it cannot generally be said to spin about a definite axis; it merely has a certain tendency, or potentiality, to do so. 27

With this understanding of electron spin we can now examine the EPR experiment and Bell's theorem. To set up the experiment, any one of several methods is used to put two electrons in a state in which their total spin is zero, that is, they are spinning in opposite directions. Now suppose the two particles in this system of total spin zero are made to drift apart by some process that does not affect their spins. As they go off in opposite directions, 28

---

* The following presentation is based on the comprehensive discussion of the EPR experiment given by David Bohm (1951), pp. 614ff. [Capra's note].

their combined spin will still be zero, and once they are separated by a large distance, their individual spins are measured. An important aspect of the experiment is the fact that the distance between the two particles at the time of the measurement is macroscopic. It can be arbitrarily large; one particle may be in Los Angeles and the other in New York, or one on the earth and the other on the moon.

Suppose now that the spin of particle 1 is measured along a vertical axis 29 and is found to be "up." Because the combined spin of the two particles is zero, this measurement tells us that the spin of particle 2 must be "down." Similarly, if we choose to measure the spin of particle 1 along a horizontal axis and find it to be "right," we know that in that case the spin of particle 2 must be "left." Quantum theory tells us that in a system of two particles having total spin zero, the spins of the particles about any axis will always be correlated—will be opposite—even though they exist only as tendencies, or potentialities, before the measurement is taken. This correlation means that the measurement of the spin of particle 1, along any axis, provides an indirect measurement of the spin of particle 2 without in any way disturbing that particle.

The paradoxical aspect of the EPR experiment arises from the fact that 30 the observer is free to choose the axis of measurement. Once this choice is made, the measurement transforms the tendencies of the particles to spin about various axes into certainties. The crucial point is that we can choose our axis of measurement at the last minute, when the particles are already far apart. At the instant we perform our measurement on particle 1, particle 2, which may be thousands of miles away, will acquire a definite spin—"up" or "down" if we have chosen a vertical axis, "left" or "right" if we have chosen a horizontal axis. How does particle 2 know which axis we have chosen? There is no time for it to receive that information by any conventional signal.

This is the crux of the EPR experiment, and this is where Einstein dis- 31 agreed with Bohr. According to Einstein, since no signal can travel faster than the speed of light, it is therefore impossible that the measurement performed on one particle will instantly determine the direction of the other particle's spin, thousands of miles away. According to Bohr, the two-particle system is an indivisible whole, even if the particles are separated by a great distance; the system cannot be analyzed in terms of independent parts. In other words, the Cartesian view of reality cannot be applied to the two electrons. Even though they are far apart in space, they are nevertheless linked by instantaneous, nonlocal connections. These connections are not signals in the Einsteinian sense; they transcend our conventional notions of information transfer. Bell's theorem supports Bohr's interpretation of the two particles as an indivisible whole and proves rigorously that Einstein's Cartesian view is incompatible with the laws of quantum theory. As Stapp sums up the situation, "The theorem of Bell proves, in effect, the profound truth that the world is either fundamentally lawless or fundamentally inseparable."*

The fundamental role of nonlocal connections and of probability in atomic physics implies a new notion of causality that is likely to have profound implications for all fields of science. Classical science was constructed by the Cartesian method of analyzing the world into parts and arranging those parts according to causal laws. The resulting deterministic picture of the universe was closely related to the image of nature as a clockwork. In atomic physics, such a mechanical and deterministic picture is no longer possible. Quantum theory has shown us that the world cannot be analyzed into independently existing isolated elements. The notion of separate parts—like atoms, or subatomic particles—is an idealization with only approximate validity; these parts are not connected by causal laws in the classical sense.   32

In quantum theory individual events do not always have a well-defined cause. For example, the jump of an electron from one atomic orbit to another, or the disintegration of a subatomic particle, may occur spontaneously without any single event causing it. We can never predict when and how such a phenomenon is going to happen; we can only predict its probability. This does not mean that atomic events occur in completely arbitrary fashion; it means only that they are not brought about by local causes. The behavior of any part is determined by its nonlocal connections to the whole, and since we do not know these connections precisely, we have to replace the narrow classical notion of cause and effect by the wider concept of statistical causality. The laws of atomic physics are statistical laws, according to which the probabilities for atomic events are determined by the dynamics of the whole system. Whereas in classical mechanics the properties and behavior of the parts determine those of the whole, the situation is reversed in quantum mechanics: it is the whole that determines the behavior of the parts.   33

The concepts of nonlocality and statistical causality imply quite clearly that the structure of matter is not mechanical. Hence the term "quantum mechanics" is very much a misnomer, as David Bohm has pointed out.† In his 1951 textbook on quantum theory Bohm offered some interesting speculations on the analogies between quantum processes and thought processes,‡ thus carrying further the celebrated statement made by James Jeans two decades earlier: "Today there is a wide measure of agreement . . . that the stream of knowledge is heading towards a non-mechanical reality; the universe begins to look more like a great thought than like a great machine."§   34

The apparent similarities between the structure of matter and the struc-   35

*Stapp, 1971 [Capra's note].
† See Bohm (1951), p. 167 [Capra's note].
‡ Bohm (1951), pp. 169ff. [Capra's note].
§ Jeans (1930) [Capra's note].

ture of mind should not surprise us too much, since human consciousness plays a crucial role in the process of observation, and in atomic physics determines to a large extent the properties of the observed phenomena. This is another important insight of quantum theory that is likely to have far-reaching consequences. In atomic physics the observed phenomena can be understood only as correlations between various processes of observation and measurement, and the end of this chain of processes lies always in the consciousness of the human observer. The crucial feature of quantum theory is that the observer is not only necessary to observe the properties of an atomic phenomenon, but is necessary even to bring about these properties. My conscious decision about how to observe, say, an electron will determine the electron's properties to some extent. If I ask it a particle question, it will give me a particle answer; if I ask it a wave question, it will give me a wave answer. The electron does not *have* objective properties independent of my mind. In atomic physics the sharp Cartesian division between mind and matter, between the observer and the observed, can no longer be maintained. We can never speak about nature without, at the same time, speaking about ourselves.

36   In transcending the Cartesian division, modern physics has not only invalidated the classical ideal of an objective description of nature but has also challenged the myth of a value-free science. The patterns scientists observe in nature are intimately connected with the patterns of their minds; with their concepts, thoughts, and values. Thus the scientific results they obtain and the technological applications they investigate will be conditioned by their frame of mind. Although much of their detailed research will not depend explicitly on their value system, the larger paradigm within which this research is pursued will never be value-free. Scientists, therefore, are responsible for their research not only intellectually but also morally. This responsibility has become an important issue in many of today's sciences, but especially so in physics, in which the results of quantum mechanics and relativity theory have opened up two very different paths for physicists to pursue. They may lead us—to put it in extreme terms—to the Buddha or to the Bomb, and it is up to each of us to decide which path to take.

37   The conception of the universe as an interconnected web of relations is one of two major themes that recur throughout modern physics. The other theme is the realization that the cosmic web is intrinsically dynamic. The dynamic aspect of matter arises in quantum theory as a consequence of the wave nature of subatomic particles, and is even more central in relativity theory, which has shown us that the being of matter cannot be separated from its activity. The properties of its basic patterns, the subatomic particles, can be understood only in a dynamic context, in terms of movement, interaction, and transformation.

38   The fact that particles are not isolated entities but wave-like probability patterns implies that they behave in a very peculiar way. Whenever a sub-

atomic particle is confined to a small region of space, it reacts to this confinement by moving around. The smaller the region of confinement, the faster the particle will "jiggle" around in it. This behavior is a typical "quantum effect," a feature of the subatomic world which has no analogy in macroscopic physics: the more a particle is confined, the faster it will move around. *
This tendency of particles to react to confinement with motion implies a fundamental "restlessness" of matter which is characteristic of the subatomic world. In this world most of the material particles *are* confined; they are bound to the molecular, atomic, and nuclear structures, and therefore are not at rest but have an inherent tendency to move about. According to quantum theory, matter is always restless, never quiescent. To the extent that things can be pictured to be made of smaller constituents—molecules, atoms, and particles—these constituents are in a state of continual motion. Macroscopically, the material objects around us may seem passive and inert, but when we magnify such a "dead" piece of stone or metal, we see that it is full of activity. The closer we look at it, the more alive it appears. All the material objects in our environment are made of atoms that link up with each other in various ways to form an enormous variety of molecular structures which are not rigid and motionless but vibrate according to their temperature and in harmony with the thermal vibrations of their environment. Inside the vibrating atoms the electrons are bound to the atomic nuclei by electric forces that try to keep them as close as possible, and they respond to this confinement by whirling around extremely fast. In the nuclei, finally, protons and neutrons are pressed into a minute volume by the strong nuclear forces, and consequently race about at unimaginable velocities.

Modern physics thus pictures matter not at all as passive and inert but as being in a continuous dancing and vibrating motion whose rhythmic patterns are determined by the molecular, atomic, and nuclear configurations. We have come to realize that there are no static structures in nature. There is stability, but this stability is one of dynamic balance, and the further we penetrate into matter the more we need to understand its dynamic nature to understand its patterns. 39

In this penetration into the world of submicroscopic dimensions, a decisive point is reached in the study of atomic nuclei in which the velocities of protons and neutrons are often so high that they come close to the speed of light. This fact is crucial for the description of their interactions, because any description of natural phenomena involving such high velocities has to take the theory of relativity into account. To understand the properties and interactions of subatomic particles we need a framework that incorporates not only quantum theory but also relativity theory; and it is relativity theory that reveals the dynamic nature of matter to its fullest extent. 40

Einstein's theory of relativity has brought about a drastic change in our 41

---

* For a more detailed discussion of this phenomenon and its relation to the uncertainty principle, see Capra (1975), p. 192 [Capra's note].

concepts of space and time. It has forced us to abandon the classical ideas of an absolute space as the stage of physical phenomena and absolute time as a dimension separate from space. According to Einstein's theory, both space and time are relative concepts, reduced to the subjective role of elements of the language a particular observer uses to describe natural phenomena. To provide an accurate description of phenomena involving velocities close to the speed of light, a "relativistic" framework has to be used, one that incorporates time with the three space coordinates, making it a fourth coordinate to be specified relative to the observer. In such a framework space and time are intimately and inseparably connected and form a four-dimensional continuum called "space-time." In relativistic physics, we can never talk about space without talking about time, and vice versa.

Physicists have now lived with relativity theory for many years and have become thoroughly familiar with its mathematical formalism. Nevertheless, this has not helped our intuition very much. We have no direct sensory experience of the four-dimensional space-time, and whenever this relativistic reality manifests itself—that is, in all situations where high velocities are involved—we find it very hard to deal with it at the level of intuition and ordinary language. An extreme example of such a situation occurs in quantum electrodynamics, one of the most successful relativistic theories of particle physics, in which antiparticles may be interpreted as particles moving backward in time. According to this theory, the same mathematical expression describes either a positron—the antiparticle of the electron—moving from the past to the future, or an electron moving from the future to the past. Particle interactions can stretch in any direction of four-dimensional space-time, moving backward and forward in time just as they move left and right in space. To picture these interactions we need four-dimensional maps covering the whole span of time as well as the whole region of space. These maps, known as space-time diagrams, have no definite direction of time attached to them. Consequently there is no "before" and "after" in the processes they picture, and thus no linear relation of cause and effect. All events are interconnected, but the connections are not causal in the classical sense. 42

Mathematically there are no problems with this interpretation of particle interactions, but when we want to express it in ordinary language we run into serious difficulties, since all our words refer to the conventional notions of time and are inappropriate to describe relativistic phenomena. Thus relativity theory has taught us the same lesson as quantum mechanics. It has shown us that our common notions of reality are limited to our ordinary experience of the physical world and have to be abandoned whenever we extend this experience. 43

The concepts of space and time are so basic for our description of natural phenomena that their radical modification in relativity theory entailed a modification of the whole framework we use in physics to describe nature. 44

The most important consequence of the new relativistic framework has been the realization that mass is nothing but a form of energy. Even an object at rest has energy stored in its mass, and the relation between the two is given by Einstein's famous equation $E = mc^2$, c being the speed of light.

Once it is seen to be a form of energy, mass is no longer required to be 45 indestructible, but can be transformed into other forms of energy. This happens continually in the collision processes of high-energy physics, in which material particles are created and destroyed, their masses being transformed into energy of motion and vice versa. The collisions of subatomic particles are our main tool for studying their properties, and the relation between mass and energy is essential for their description. The equivalence of mass and energy has been verified innumerable times and physicists have become completely familiar with it—so familiar, in fact, that they measure the masses of particles in the corresponding energy units.

The discovery that mass is a form of energy has had a profound influ- 46 ence on our picture of matter and has forced us to modify our concept of a particle in an essential way. In modern physics, mass is no longer associated with a material substance, and hence particles are not seen as consisting of any basic "stuff," but as bundles of energy. Energy, however, is associated with activity, with processes, and this implies that the nature of subatomic particles is intrinsically dynamic. To understand this better we must remember that these particles can be conceived only in relativistic terms, that is, in terms of a framework where space and time are fused into a four-dimensional continuum. In such a framework the particles can no longer be pictured as small billiard balls, or small grains of sand. These images are inappropriate not only because they represent particles as separate objects, but also because they are static, three-dimensional images. Subatomic particles must be conceived as four-dimensional entities in space-time. Their forms have to be understood dynamically, as forms in space and time. Particles are dynamic patterns, patterns of activity which have a space aspect and a time aspect. Their space aspect makes them appear as objects with a certain mass, their time aspect as processes involving the equivalent energy. Thus the being of matter and its activity cannot be separated; they are but different aspects of the same space-time reality.

The relativistic view of matter has drastically affected not only our con- 47 ception of particles, but also our picture of the forces between these particles. In a relativistic description of particle interactions, the forces between the particles—their mutual attraction or repulsion—are pictured as the exchange of other particles. This concept is very difficult to visualize, but it is needed for an understanding of subatomic phenomena. It links the forces between constituents of matter to the properties of other constituents of matter, and thus unifies the two concepts, force and matter, which had seemed to be fundamentally different in Newtonian physics. Both force and matter are now seen to have their common origin in the dynamic patterns that we call particles. These energy patterns of the subatomic world form the stable nuclear, atomic, and molecular structures which build up matter and give it its macroscopic solid aspect, thus making us believe that it is made of some material substance. At the macroscopic level this notion of substance is a useful approximation, but at the atomic level it no longer makes sense. Atoms consist of particles, and these particles are not made of any material stuff. When we observe them we never see any substance; what we observe are dynamic patterns continually changing into one another—the continuous dance of energy.

The two basic theories of modern physics have thus transcended the   48 principal aspects of the Cartesian world view and of Newtonian physics. Quantum theory has shown that subatomic particles are not isolated grains of matter but are probability patterns, interconnections in an inseparable cosmic web that includes the human observer and her* consciousness. Relativity theory has made the cosmic web come alive, so to speak, by revealing its intrinsically dynamic character; by showing that its activity is the very essence of its being. In modern physics, the image of the universe as a machine has been transcended by a view of it as one indivisible, dynamic whole whose parts are essentially interrelated and can be understood only as patterns of a cosmic process. At the subatomic level the interrelations and interactions between the parts of the whole are more fundamental than the parts themselves. There is motion but there are, ultimately, no moving objects; there is activity but there are no actors; there are no dancers, there is only the dance.

Current research in physics aims at unifying quantum mechanics and   49 relativity theory in a complete theory of subatomic particles. We have not yet been able to formulate such a complete theory, but we do have several partial theories, or models, which describe certain aspects of subatomic phenomena very well. At present there are two different kinds of "quantum-relativistic" theories in particle physics that have been successful in different areas. The first are a group of quantum field theories which apply to electromagnetic and weak interactions; the second is the theory known as S-matrix theory, which has been successful in describing the strong interactions.† Of

---

* The feminine pronoun is used here as a general reference to a person who may be a woman or a man. Similarly, I shall occasionally use the masculine pronoun as a general reference, including both men and women. I think this the best way to avoid being either sexist or awkward.

† The interactions between subatomic particles fall into four basic categories with markedly different interaction strengths: the strong, electromagnetic, weak, and gravitational interactions; see Capra (1975), pp. 228ff [Capra's note].

these two approaches, S-matrix theory is more relevant to the theme of this book, since it has deep implications for science as a whole.*

The philosophical foundation of S-matrix theory is known as the boot- 50 strap approach. Geoffrey Chew proposed it in the early 1960s, and he and other physicists have used it to develop a comprehensive theory of strongly interacting particles, together with a more general philosophy of nature. According to this bootstrap philosophy, nature cannot be reduced to fundamental entities, like fundamental building blocks of matter, but has to be understood entirely through self-consistency. All of physics has to follow uniquely from the requirement that its components be consistent with one another and with themselves. This idea constitutes a radical departure from the traditional spirit of basic research in physics which had always been bent on finding the fundamental constituents of matter. At the same time it is the culmination of the conception of the material world as an interconnected web of relations that emerged from quantum theory. The bootstrap philosophy not only abandons the idea of fundamental building blocks of matter, but accepts no fundamental entities whatsoever—no fundamental constants, laws, or equations. The universe is seen as a dynamic web of interrelated events. None of the properties of any part of this web is fundamental; they all follow from the properties of the other parts, and the overall consistency of their interrelations determines the structure of the entire web.

The fact that the bootstrap approach does not accept any fundamental 51 entities makes it, in my opinion, one of the most profound systems of Western thought, raising it to the level of Buddhist or Taoist philosophy.† At the same time it is a very difficult approach to physics, one that has been pursued by only a small minority of physicists. The bootstrap philosophy is too foreign to traditional ways of thinking to be seriously appreciated yet, and this lack of appreciation extends also to S-matrix theory. It is curious that although the basic concepts of the theory are used by all particle physicists whenever they analyze the results of particle collisions and compare them to their theoretical predictions, not a single Nobel prize has so far been awarded to any of the outstanding physicists who contributed to the development of S-matrix theory over the past two decades.

In the framework of S-matrix theory, the bootstrap approach attempts 52 to derive all properties of particles and their interactions uniquely from the requirement of self-consistency. The only "fundamental" laws accepted are a few very general principles that are required by the methods of observation and are essential parts of the scientific framework. All other aspects of particle physics are expected to emerge as a necessary consequence of self-consistency. If this approach can be carried out successfully, the philosophical im-

---

*See Capra (1975) for a more detailed discussion of both quantum field theory and S-matrix theory [Capra's note].

† *Ibid.*, pp. 286ff [Capra's note].

plications will be very profound. The fact that all the properties of particles are determined by principles closely related to the methods of observation would mean that the basic structures of the material world are determined, ultimately, by the way we look at this world; that the observed patterns of matter are reflections of patterns of mind.

The phenomena of the subatomic world are so complex that it is by no 53 means certain whether a complete, self-consistent theory will ever be constructed, but one can envisage a series of partly successful models of smaller scope. Each of them would be intended to cover only a part of the observed phenomena and would contain some unexplained aspects, or parameters, but the parameters of one model might be explained by another. Thus more and more phenomena could gradually be covered with ever increasing accuracy by a mosaic of interlocking models whose net number of unexplained parameters keeps decreasing. The adjective "bootstrap" is thus never appropriate for any individual model, but can be applied only to a combination of mutually consistent models, none of which is any more fundamental than the others. Chew explains succinctly: "A physicist who is able to view any number of different partially successful models without favoritism is automatically a bootstrapper."*

Progress in S-matrix theory was steady but slow until several important 54 developments of recent years resulted in a major breakthrough, which made it quite likely that the bootstrap program for the strong interactions will be completed in the near future, and that it may also be extended successfully to the electromagnetic and weak interactions.† These results have generated great enthusiasm among S-matrix theorists and are likely to force the rest of the physics community to reevaluate its attitudes toward the bootstrap approach.

The key element of the new bootstrap theory of subatomic particles is 55 the notion of order as a new and important aspect of particle physics. Order, in this context, means order in the interconnectedness of subatomic processes. Since there are various ways in which subatomic events can interconnect, one can define various categories of order. The language of topology—well known to mathematicians but never before applied to particle physics—is used to classify these categories of order. When this concept of order is incorporated into the mathematical framework of S-matrix theory, only a few special categories of ordered relationships turn out to be consistent with that framework. The resulting patterns of particle interactions are precisely those observed in nature.

The picture of subatomic particles that emerges from the bootstrap 56 theory can be summed up in the provocative phrase "Every particle consists of all other particles." It must not be imagined, however, that each of them

* G. F. Chew, quoted *ibid.*, p. 295 [Capra's note].
† See Capra (1979) [Capra's note].

contains all the others in a classical, static sense. Subatomic particles are not separate entities but interrelated energy patterns in an ongoing dynamic process. These patterns do not "contain" one another but rather "involve" one another in a way that can be given a precise mathematical meaning but cannot easily be expressed in words.

The emergence of order as a new and central concept in particle physics 57 has not only led to a major breakthrough in S-matrix theory, but may well have great implications for science as a whole. The significance of order in subatomic physics is still obscure, and the extent to which it can be incorporated into the S-matrix framework is not yet fully known, but it is intriguing to remind ourselves that the notion of order plays a very basic role in the scientific approach to reality and is a crucial aspect of all methods of observation. The ability to recognize order seems to be an essential aspect of the rational mind; every perception of a pattern is, in a sense, a perception of order. The clarification of the concept of order in a field of research where patterns of matter and patterns of mind are increasingly being recognized as reflections of one another promises to open fascinating frontiers of knowledge.

Further extensions of the bootstrap approach in subatomic physics will 58 eventually have to go beyond the present framework of S-matrix theory, which has been developed specifically to describe the strong interactions. To enlarge the bootstrap program a more general framework will have to be found, in which some of the concepts that are now accepted without explanation will have to be "bootstrapped," derived from overall self-consistency. These may include our conception of macroscopic space-time and, perhaps, even our conception of human consciousness. Increased use of the bootstrap approach opens up the unprecedented possibility of being forced to include the study of human consciousness explicitly in future theories of matter. The question of consciousness has already arisen in quantum theory in connection with the problem of observation and measurement, but the pragmatic formulation of the theory scientists use in their research does not refer to consciousness explicitly. Some physicists argue that consciousness may be an essential aspect of the universe, and that we may be blocked from further understanding of natural phenomena if we insist on excluding it.

At present there are two approaches in physics that come very close to 59 dealing with consciousness explicitly. One is the notion of order in Chew's S-matrix theory; the other is a theory developed by David Bohm, who follows a much more general and more ambitious approach.* Bohm's starting point is the notion of "unbroken wholeness," and his aim is to explore the order he believes to be inherent in the cosmic web of relations at a deeper, "nonmanifest" level. He calls this order "implicate," or "enfolded," and describes it with the analogy of a hologram, in which each part, in some sense, contains

---

* Bohm (1980) [Capra's note].

the whole.* If any part of a hologram is illuminated, the entire image will be reconstructed, although it will show less detail than the image obtained from the complete hologram. In Bohm's view the real world is structured according to the same general principles, with the whole enfolded in each of its parts.

Bohm realizes that the hologram is too static to be used as a scientific 60 model for the implicate order at the subatomic level. To express the essentially dynamic nature of reality at this level he has coined the term "holomovement." In his view the holomovement is a dynamic phenomenon out of which all forms of the material universe flow. The aim of his approach is to study the order enfolded in this holomovement, not by dealing with the structure of objects, but rather with the structure of movement, thus taking into account both the unity and the dynamic nature of the universe. To understand the implicate order Bohm has found it necessary to regard consciousness as an essential feature of the holomovement and to take it into account explicitly in his theory. He sees mind and matter as being interdependent and correlated, but not causally connected. They are mutually enfolding projections of a higher reality which is neither matter nor consciousness.

Bohm's theory is still tentative, but there seems to be an intriguing kin- 61 ship, even at this preliminary stage, between his theory of the implicate order and Chew's S-matrix theory. Both approaches are based on a view of the world as a dynamic web of relations; both attribute a central role to the notion of order; both use matrices to represent change and transformation, and topology to classify categories of order. Finally, both theories recognize that consciousness may well be an essential aspect of the universe that will have to be included in a future theory of physical phenomena. Such a future theory may well arise from the merging of Bohm's and Chew's theories, which represent two of the most imaginative and philosophically profound contemporary approaches to physical reality.

My presentation of modern physics in this chapter has been influenced 62 by my personal beliefs and allegiances. I have emphasized certain concepts and theories that are not yet accepted by the majority of physicists, but that I consider significant philosophically, of great importance for the other sciences and for our culture as a whole. Every contemporary physicist, however, will accept the main theme of the presentation—that modern physics has transcended the mechanistic Cartesian view of the world and is leading us to a holistic and intrinsically dynamic conception of the universe.

This world view of modern physics is a systems view, and it is consistent 63 with the systems approaches that are now emerging in other fields, although

* Holography is a technique of lenseless photography based on the interference property of light waves. The resulting "picture" is called a hologram; see Collier (1968). For a comprehensive nontechnical introduction to the subject, see Outwater and Van Hamersveld (1974) [Capra's note].

the phenomena studied by these disciplines are generally of a different nature and require different concepts. In transcending the metaphor of the world as a machine, we also have to abandon the idea of physics as the basis of all science. According to the bootstrap or systems view of the world, different but mutually consistent concepts may be used to describe different aspects and levels of reality, without the need to reduce the phenomena of any level to those of another.

Before I describe the conceptual framework for such a multidiscipli- 64 nary, holistic approach to reality, we may find it useful to see how the other sciences have adopted the Cartesian world view and have modeled their concepts and theories after those of classical physics. The limitations of the Cartesian paradigm in the natural and social sciences can also be brought to light, and their exposure is intended to help scientists and nonscientists change their underlying philosophies in order to participate in the current cultural transformation.

REFERENCES

Bateson, Gregory. 1972. *Mind and Nature*. New York: Dutton.
Bohm, David. 1951. *Quantum Theory*. New York: Prentice-Hall.
_____. 1980. *Wholeness and the Implicate Order*. London: Routledge & Kegan Paul.
Capra, Fritjof. 1975. *The Tao of Physics*. Berkeley: Shambhala.
Collier, Robert J. 1968. "Holography and Integral Photography." *Physics Today*, July.
Heisenberg, Werner. 1962. *Physics and Philosophy*. New York: Harper and Row.
Jeans, James. 1930. *The Mysterious Universe*. New York: Macmillan.
Outwater, Christopher, and van Hamersveld, Eric. 1974. *Practical Holography*. Beverly Hills, CA: Pentangle Press.
Schilpp, Paul Arthur, Ed. 1951. *Albert Einstein: Philosopher-Scientist*. New York: Tudor.
Stace, Walter T. 1960. *The Teachings of the Mystics*. New York: New American Library.
Stapp, Henry Pierce. 1971. "S-Matrix Interpretation of Quantum Theory." *Physical Review D*, March 15.
_____. 1972. "The Copenhagen Interpretation." *American Journal of Physics*, August.
_____. 1979. "Whiteheadian Approach to Quantum Theory and the Generalized Bell's Theorem." *Foundations of Physics*, February.

QUESTIONS ABOUT CAPRA'S DISCOURSE COMMUNITY AND HIS CONCERNS IN THIS SELECTION

1. Capra asserts that "Einstein strongly believed in nature's inherent harmony, and throughout his scientific life his deepest concern was to find a unified foundation of physics" (paragraph 2). What does it mean to have an "inherent harmony"? Could Capra be accused here of using language so as to slant an argument towards a specific philosophical viewpoint?
2. According to Capra, what are the two major developments of physics in the twentieth century? How did they influence the philosophical underpinnings of physics? What might the choice of these two developments suggest about Capra's discourse community?
3. Capra notes that in the current century, "physicists faced, for the first time, a

serious challenge to their ability to understand the universe" (paragraph 4). How is this challenge different from those of earlier scientists? What might this challenge suggest about future kinds of research?

4. In paragraph nine, Capra writes that "the universe is no longer seen as a machine, made up of a multitude of objects, but has to be pictured as one indivisible, dynamic whole whose parts are essentially interrelated and can be understood only as patterns of a cosmic process." Is Capra overstating the case here? What kind of evidence would Capra need to support this assertion?

5. In paragraph fifteen, Capra speaks of matter at the subatomic level as showing "tendencies to exist." What does Capra mean by this description? Does it seem here that his philosophical concerns are overriding his scientific objectivity? Can something have a "tendency to exist"?

6. Read over the explanation of the EPR experiment (paragraphs 25 ff.). What, according to Capra, does this experiment demonstrate? Does Capra seem to be pressing here, or does the experiment logically demonstrate what he claims? Does it hurt or help his case that he never goes into detail on Bell's Theorem?

7. In paragraphs 41 to 43, Capra notes that one of the difficulties in dealing with a universe of four dimensions comes in the limitations of language. Though mathematics can deal with such a reality, natural language cannot because it is bound by concepts of time. Is Capra correct in suggesting that language establishes the boundaries of thought? Can we think of concepts without having an appropriate language for these concepts?

8. Capra mentions that modern physicists have to choose between the Buddha and the bomb. Do you think it will be more or less difficult to think of morality in a universe such as Capra believes in than in one as most people today see it?

QUESTIONS ABOUT CAPRA'S RHETORICAL STRATEGIES

1. At times, Capra includes quotations from prominent physicists who helped to usher in what Capra calls the "new physics." In general, how do these quotes contribute to his argument?

2. The eighth paragraph functions as a transitional paragraph and leads into Capra's main thrust in this selection. How does this paragraph move the reader from the historical discussion to the philosophical discussion?

3. In paragraph nine, Capra notes that the new vision of the universe can be described as "organic, holistic, and ecological." What are the current connotations of these words? Do they suggest a specific discourse community?

4. What is the rhetorical purpose of paragraph ten? How would you describe Capra's stance in this paragraph? Does the paragraph seem to suggest that many would disagree with Capra's uniting of physics and Eastern mysticism? If so, was Capra wise to include such a paragraph?

5. Capra at times advances his own case by setting it against that of another scientist. Where does Capra use this technique? Do you find this to be a successful rhetorical strategy?

6. Why do you think Capra gives no evidence for the dual nature of subatomic particles? Would his intended audience need to see no such evidence?

7. Capra occasionally uses the metaphor of dance to describe the nature of matter.

What has to be true if a metaphor is accurately to describe the thing or concept the writer is envisioning? Is dance an appropriate metaphor for matter, given Capra's argument?

8. Speaking of scientists, Capra notes that "they may lead us—to put it in extreme terms—to the Buddha or to the Bomb, and it is up to each of us to decide which path to take" (paragraph 36). Evaluate the word choice in this paragraph. Is he using diction to manipulate his audience at all?

WRITING FROM WITHIN AND ABOUT THE SCIENTIFIC COMMUNITY

Writing for Yourself

1. Explore in your journal how you react to the view of matter that Capra puts forth.

2. Capra notes the importance of accepting paradoxes in the natural world. Specifically he speaks of light acting as both a wave and a particle. What other paradoxes come to mind as you think of the natural world? Make a listing of such paradoxes in your journal and explore whether such paradoxes exist because we do not properly understand the phenomena or because of limitations of language.

Writing for Nonacademic Audiences

1. One of your best friends has dropped out of college to live in a community of people studying and meditating on the interrelatedness of all. Write to your friend, explaining why you will or cannot join him or her.

2. After rereading paragraphs 22–25 of Capra's essay, write a short definition for a popular audience of Descartes's vision of reality. Try to avoid all terms that might not be understood by such a popular audience.

Writing for Academic Audiences

1. Interview some physicists and write a brief report for your classmates in your writing class about what those physicists think of Capra's ideas.

2. Capra quotes James Jeans's well-known comment, "the universe begins to look more like a great thought than like a great machine" (paragraph 34). Generate a list of comparisons between the universe, a machine, and a thought. Then write a 100-word selection to be included in a pamphlet put out by your university's astronomy department in which you argue which alternative—the universe as a machine or the universe as a thought—seems more reasonable.

3. Write a 500-word description of thought experiments for a history of science class. What are they? In what areas of science are they used? What makes them necessary?

4. If a systems view of the world is correct, how should we go about the process of education? Write a 1,000-word persuasive essay in response to this question; the essay will be used as a device to stimulate discussion in a philosophy of education class.

5. Read Madeleine L'Engle's *Many Waters*, a novel that uses the new physics as a

basis for certain elements of its plot. Based on your reading of Capra, does it seem to you that L'Engle has a firm grasp of the notion of something showing a "tendency to exist"? Write a 1,250-word essay for a class in literature and science in which you evaluate L'Engle's success in weaving this scientific concept into a work of fiction.

Stephen Jay Gould

(b. 1941)

Stephen Jay Gould is a professor of Geology and Curator of Invertebrate Paleontology and Alexander Agassiz Professor of Zoology in the Museum of Comparative Zoology of Harvard University. His publications focus on special evolutionary problems and the evidence such problems present for a Darwinian view of the world. Though Gould is well known as a writer within his specialized discourse community, he is better known as a writer who has attempted to enlarge his discourse community by writing for a popular audience. Such works as Ever Since Darwin *(1977),* The Panda's Thumb *(1980),* Hen's Teeth and Horse's Toes *(1983), and* The Flamingo's Smile *(1985), collect essays aimed at this popular audience; many of these first appeared in the journal* Natural History. *His* The Mismeasured Man *(1981) argues against many practices in the measurement of human intelligence, and his* Time's Arrow, Time's Cycle *(1987) explores metaphors that scientific writers have used to understand the nature of time. His* Wonderful Life: The Burgess Shale and the Nature of History *(1989), deals with one of the strangest geological formations in the world.*

Gould's interest in paleontology began with a childhood visit to the dinosaur skeletons at the American Museum of Natural History. The interest led him eventually to study Darwin, and it is Darwin's vision of natural selection and his theory of evolution that inform many of Gould's works. Gould argues that for Darwin, the evidence for natural selection came not from perfectly adapted models (these could also be used as evidence for creationism), but instead from imperfectly adapted models, cases where biological parts took on unusual functions—functions that differed from their primary function—in cases of need. The panda, for example, uses an extended bone in its wrist as an effective thumb.

Gould writes from within a community that embraces the scientific method. This includes collecting physical evidence from which hypotheses may be advanced. Such hypotheses are valid only insofar as they explain the evidence and as they are not contradicted by later evidence. Gould adheres to this methodology in "Only His Wings Remained." At the same time, he implicitly attacks those who have made assertions based on insufficient evidence.

To broaden his writing community by appealing to a general audience, Gould shapes his language and rhetoric to make clear and accessible what is possibly murky or technical. To attempt to enlarge a writing community risks leaving it at times—or being abandoned by it, as is the case with some popularizers of technical fields. But Gould is not seen as a mere popularizer, and the success of his essays is evidenced by his ability to address both general and specialized audiences and to bring both to conclusions that, though arguable, are worthy of study. Those within the natural sciences—and Gould's fellow paleontologists—admire his work not only because of

his prose, but also because of his ability to bring subdisciplines into play in meaningful ways. Those outside Gould's technical discourse community are accorded a glimpse
into an area of research that would be forever closed to them were it not for the
rhetorical abilities of writers like Gould.

ONLY HIS WINGS REMAINED

The conventional prose of twentieth-century science is lean and spare. But   1
our Victorian predecessors delighted in leisurely detail, in keeping perhaps
with the gingerbread on their houses and the shelves of bric-a-brac inside.
Consider, for example, this extended (but most entertaining) description of
sex and death in praying mantises, published by L.O. Howard in 1886:

> A few days since, I brought a male of *Mantis carolina* to a friend who had been   2
> keeping a solitary female as a pet. Placing them in the same jar, the male, in
> alarm, endeavored to escape. In a few minutes, the female succeeded in grasp-
> ing him. She first bit off his left front tarsus, and consumed the tibia and femur.
> Next she gnawed out his left eye. At this the male seemed to realize his prox-
> imity to one of the opposite sex, and began to make vain endeavors to mate.
> The female next ate up his right front leg, and then entirely decapitated him,
> devouring his head and gnawing into his thorax. Not until she had eaten all of
> his thorax except 3 millimeters did she stop to rest. All this while the male had
> continued his vain attempts to obtain entrance at the valvules, and he now
> succeeded, as she voluntarily spread the parts open, and union took place. She
> remained quiet for 4 hours, and the remnant of the male gave occasional signs
> of life by a movement of one of the remaining tarsi for 3 hours. The next morn-
> ing she had entirely rid herself of her spouse, and nothing but his wings re-
> mained.

I cite this passage not merely for its style, but primarily for its sub-   3
stance—since it represents the first account I know of an all-time favorite
among nature's curious facts. We have all heard that some animals can live
after losing large portions of themselves, but we think of them as just scraping
by in such a limited state, not as improving their skills. Our cliché about
"running around like a chicken with its head cut off" underscores this reasonable assumption that reduced anatomy entails diminished competence. Yet
male mantises, beheaded by a rapacious mate, not only continue their act of
courtship and copulation but actually perform more persistently and successfully.

I want, as usual, to discuss the larger message behind this paramount   4
oddity, but adequate treatment requires a long digression right back to Darwin himself. So bear with me, and we'll eventually get back to mantises and
much more of what the biological literature calls "sexual cannibalism."

The *Descent of Man* is, without doubt, Darwin's most misunderstood 5 book. Many people suppose that it represents Darwin's attempt to fit the facts of human evolution into his evolutionary perspective. But no direct facts existed when he published in 1871, for besides Neanderthal (a race of our own species, not an ancestor or any form of "missing link") no human fossils were discovered until the 1890s. Rather, the *Descent of Man* is an extended essay on the close biological relationship of humans with great apes and the possible modes of our physical and mental evolution from this common ancestry. But Darwin abhorred speculation; he never wrote a purely theoretical treatise. Even the *Origin of Species* is a compendium of facts pointing to a powerful conclusion. He would not have written a naked account of how it might have been, no matter how much he yearned to extend his evolutionary perspective to what he once called "the citadel itself"—the human mind.

The key to the *Descent of Man* is its situation as a relatively short pre- 6 face to a large, two-volume work, *The Descent of Man and Selection in Relation to Sex*. Darwin could weave wonderful and extensive tapestries about central themes—so much so that his readers often lose the core in its extensive mantling. But all his books are solutions to specific puzzles; the rest, for all its brilliance, is superstructure. The coral reef book is about historical inference from contemporary results, the orchid book about imperfect adaptation based on parts available, the worm book about large effects accumulated by successive small changes (see essay 9 in *Hen's Teeth and Horse's Toes*). But because he loved detail, Darwin tells you more than you want to know about how insects fertilize orchids or how worms pull objects into their burrows— and you easily lose the kernel, the paradox, the gem of a problem that started the whole edifice.

The *Descent of Man* is a preface to such a problem. By 1871, twelve 7 years after the *Origin of Species*, Darwin no longer needed to convince people of good will and mental flexibility that evolution had occurred; that battle had been won. But how does evolution work, what kind of world do we inhabit, and how can we know? Darwin's radical message lay in his claim that the beauties and harmony of nature are all byproducts of one primary process called natural selection: organisms struggle to achieve greater personal reproductive success—in modern parlance, to pass more of their genes into future generations (since they cannot preserve their bodies)—and that is all. No overarching laws about the good of species or ecosystems, no wise and watchful regulator in the skies—just organisms struggling.

But how can we know that the world is regulated by selection and not 8 by some other evolutionary principle? Darwin's answer is brilliant, paradoxical, and usually misunderstood. Do not, he cautions, rest your case on what might seem to be the most elegant expression of selection—the beautiful, optimally designed adaptations of organisms to their environments: the aerodynamic perfection of a bird's wing or the streamlined beauty of a marlin. For good design is the expectation of most evolutionary theories (and of creationism as well, for that matter). There is nothing distinctively Darwinian about perfection. Instead, look for the oddities and imperfections that only occur if selection based on the reproductive success of individuals—and not on some other evolutionary mechanism—shapes the path of evolution.

The largest class of such oddities includes those structures and habits 9 that plainly compromise the good design of organisms (and the ultimate success of species) but just as clearly increase the reproductive prowess of individuals bearing them. (My favorite examples are the tail feathers of peacocks and the huge, encumbering antlers of Irish elks, both adaptations in the struggle among males for access to, or acceptance by, females, but certainly not contributions to good design in the biomechanical sense.) Our world overflows with peculiar, otherwise senseless shapes and behaviors that function only to promote victory in the great game of mating and reproduction. No other world but Darwin's would fill nature with such curiosities that weaken species and hinder good design but bring success where it really matters in Darwin's universe alone—passing more genes to future generations.

Darwin realized that natural selection in its usual sense—increasing ad- 10 aptation to changing local environments—would not explain this large class of features evolved to secure purely reproductive benefits for individuals. So he christened a parallel process, sexual selection, to explain this crucial evidence. He argued that sexual selection might work by combat among males or choice by females: the first to produce overblown weapons and instruments of display; the second to encourage those adornments and elaborate posturings that impel notice and acceptance (the nightingale does not sing for our delectation).

Humans enter the story at this point. Why did Darwin choose his long 11 and detailed treatise on sexual selection as a home for his much shorter preface on the *Descent of Man*? The answer again lies in Darwin's fascination with specific puzzles and the contribution made by their solution to his larger goal. The *Descent of Man* has its anchor in a particular problem of human racial variation; it is not a waffling treatise on generalities. We can, Darwin argues, understand some racial differences, skin colors for example, as conventional adaptations to local environments (dark skin evolved several times independently and always in tropical climates). But surely we cannot argue that all the small, subtle differences among peoples—minor but consistent variations in the shape and form of noses and ears or the texture of hair— have their origin in what local environments ordain. It would be a vulgar caricature of natural selection to argue, by clever invention, that each insignificant nuance of design is really an optimal configuration for local circumstances (although many overzealous votaries continue to promote this view. A prominent evolutionist once seriously proposed to me that Slavic languages are full of consonants because mouths are best kept closed in cold weather, while Hawaiian has little but vowels because the salutary air of oceanic islands should be savored and imbibed). How then, if not by ordinary natural selection, did these small and subtle, but pervasive, racial differences originate?

Darwin proposes—and I suspect he was largely right—that different   12
standards of beauty arise for capricious reasons among the various and formerly isolated groups of humans that people the far corners of our earth. These differences—a twist of the nose here, slimmer legs there, a curl in the hair somewhere else—are then accumulated and intensified by sexual selection, since those individuals accidentally endowed with favored features are more sought and therefore more successful in reproduction.

Look at the organization of the *Descent of Man* and you will see that   13
this argument, not the generalities, provides its focus. The book begins with an overview of some 250 pages, all leading to a final chapter on human races and a presentation of the central paradox on the last page.

> We have thus far been baffled in all our attempts to account for the differences   14
> between the races of man; but there remains one important agency, namely
> Sexual Selection, which appears to have acted powerfully on man, as on many
> other animals. . . . In order to treat this subject properly, I have found it nec-
> essary to pass the whole animal kingdom in review.

Darwin now has his handle for the real meat of his book, and he spends   15
more than twice as much space, the next 500 pages, on a detailed account of sexual selection in group after group of organisms. Finally, in three closing chapters, he returns to human racial variation and completes his solution of the paradox by ascribing our differences primarily to sexual selection.

Sexual selection has sometimes been cast as a contrast or conflict with   16
natural selection, but such an interpretation misunderstands Darwin's vision. Sexual selection is our most elegant confirmation of his central tenet that the struggle of individuals for reproductive success drives evolution—a notion that natural selection cannot adequately confirm because its products are also the predictions of other evolutionary theories (and also, for optimal design, of creationism itself). The proof that our world is Darwinian lies in the large set of adaptations arising *only* because they enhance reproductive success but otherwise both hinder organisms and harm species. Darwinian selection for reproductive success must be extraordinarily powerful if it can so often overwhelm other levels and modes of advantage.

We may now return to the blood meal of the mating mantis. W.H.   17
Auden once wrote, with great understanding of our lives, that love and death are the only subjects worth the attention of literature. They are indeed the foci of Darwin's world, a universe of struggle for survival and continuity. But should they be conjoined? At first sight, nothing seems more absurd, less in keeping with any notion of order or advantage, than the sacrifice of life for a copulation. Should a male, in Darwin's world, not survive to mate again? Not necessarily, if he is destined for a short life and unlikely to mate again in any case, and if his "precious bodily fluids" (to cite the immortal line from

Dr. Strangelove) will make a big difference in nourishing the eggs fertilized by his sperm within his erstwhile partner and current executioner.

After all, his body is so much Darwinian baggage. It cannot be passed   18
to the next generation; his patrimony lies, quite literally, in the DNA of his sperm. Thus, sexual cannibalism should be a premier example of why we live in a Darwinian world—a classic curiosity, an apparent absurdity, made sensible by the proposition that evolution is fundamentally about struggle among organisms for genetic continuity. But how good is the evidence? (And now I must warn you—since this essay may be the most convoluted I have ever written—that this eminently reasonable argument for Darwinism has, in my assessment, very little going for it at present. Yet an alternative interpretation, for a different reason, affirms something even more fundamental about Darwinism and about the nature of history itself. Frankly, while I'm at the confessional, I began research for this essay on the assumption that such a lovely and reasonable argument for sexual selection would hold, and found myself quite surprised at the paucity of evidence. I also steadfastly refuse to avoid a subject because it is difficult. The world is not uncomplicated, and a restriction of general writing to the clear and uncontroversial gives a false view of how science operates and how our world works.)

A recent issue of the *American Naturalist*, one of America's three lead-   19
ing journals of evolutionary biology, featured an article by R.E. Buskirk, C. Frohlich, and K.G. Ross, "The Natural Selection of Sexual Cannibalism" (see bibliography). They develop a mathematical model to show that willing sacrifice of life to an impregnated partner will be to a male's Darwinian advantage if he can expect little subsequent success in mating and if the food value of his body will make a substantial difference to the successful development and rearing of his offspring. The model makes good sense, but nature will match it only if we can show that such males actively promote their own consumption. If they are trying like hell to escape after mating, and occasionally get caught and eaten by a rapacious female, then we cannot argue that sexual selection has directly promoted this strategy of ultimate sacrifice for genetic continuity.

Buskirk, Frohlich, and Ross are frank in stating that sexual cannibalism   20
is not only rare in general but also much less common than other styles of consuming close relatives (as in sibling by sibling, or mothers by offspring; see essay 10 in *Ever Since Darwin* and essay 6 in *The Panda's Thumb*). Documented examples exist only for arthropods (insects and their kin), and only thirty species or so have been implicated (though the phenomenon may be quite common in spiders). They cite three examples as best cases.

1. The female praying mantis (*Mantis religiosa*, and several related species) will   21
   attack anything smaller than itself that moves. Since males are smaller than females in almost all insects, and since mating requires proximity, male mantises become a premier target. In his classic paper of 1935 (see bibliography), K. Roeder writes: "All accounts agree as to the ferocity of the female, and her tendency to capture and devour the male at any time, whether it be during the

courtship or after copulation. . . . The female may seize and eat the male as she would any other insect."

A male therefore approaches mating with the punch line of that terrible 22 old joke about how porcupines do it: very carefully. He creeps up slowly, trying at all costs to keep out of the female's sight line. If the female turns in his direction, he freezes—for mantises ignore anything that doesn't move. Roeder writes: "So extreme is this immobility that if a male is in the act of raising a leg when first the female is detected, it will be kept poised in the air for some time, and many curious positions may be observed." Thus, the male continues to approach like a child playing the street game of "red light"—drawing near while his adversary and potential mate averts her eyes, freezing instantly when she looks around (although the penalty for apprehended motion is death, not a return to the starting line). If the male succeeds in creeping up within springing distance, he makes a fateful leap to the female's back. If he misses, he's mantis fodder; if he succeeds, he achieves the Darwinian *summum bonum* of potential representation in the next generation. After mating, he falls off as far away as he can and then skedaddles with dispatch.

So far, the story sounds little like a tale of active male conspiracy in his 23 own demise—the requirement, please remember, for an argument that males are directly selected for sexual cannibalism. Perhaps males are simply trying their darndest to get away, but don't always make it. The strong argument inheres in that great curiosity mentioned at the outset of this essay: decapitated males perform *better* sexually than their intact brothers. Roeder has even discovered the neurological basis for this peculiar situation. Much of insect behavior is "hard wired," so unlike the flexibility of our own actions (and a primary reason why sociobiological models for ants work so poorly for humans). Copulatory movements are controlled by nerves in the last abdominal ganglion (near the back end). Since it would be inconsistent with normal function (and unseemly as well) for males to perform these copulatory motions continually, they are suppressed by inhibitory centers located in the subesophageal ganglion (near the head). When a female eats her mate's head, she ingests the subesophageal ganglion, and nothing remains to inhibit copulatory movements. What remains of the male now operates as a nonstop mating machine. It will try to mount anything—pencils, for example—of even vaguely appropriate size or shape. Often it finds the female and succeeds in making of its coming death the Darwinian antithesis of what Socrates called "a state of nothingness."

2. A hungry female black widow spider is also a formidable eating machine, and 24 courting males must exercise great circumspection. On entering a female's web, the male taps and tweaks some of her silk lines. If the female charges, the male either beats a hasty retreat or sails quickly away on his own gossamer. If the female does not respond, the male approaches slowly and cautiously, finally cutting the female's web at several strategic points, thereby reducing her routes of escape or attack. The male often throws several lines of silk about the female, called, inevitably I suppose, the "bridal veil." They are not strong, and the larger female could surely break them, but she generally does not, and copulation, as they like to say in the technical literature, "then ensues." The male, blessed with paired organs for transferring sperm, inserts one palp, then, if not yet attacked by the female, the other. Hungry females may then gobble up their mates, completing the double-entendre of a consummation devoutly to be wished.

The argument for direct selection of sexual cannibalism rests upon two 25 intriguing phenomena of courtship. First, the tip of the male's palp usually breaks off during copulation and remains behind in the female. Males, thus rendered incomplete, may not be able to mate again; if so, they have become

Darwinian ciphers, ripe for removal. (An interesting speculation identifies this broken tip as a "mating plug" selected to prevent the entry of any subsequent male's sperm. Such natural *post factum* chastity belts are common, and of diverse construction, in the world of insects and would make a fine subject for a future essay on the same issue of why sexual selection identifies our evolutionary world as Darwinian.) Second, males show far less avidity and caution in scramming after the fact than they did in approaching before. K. Ross and R.L. Smith write (see bibliography): "Males that succeeded in insemination lingered in the vicinity of their mates or wandered leisurely away. This was in marked contrast with the initial cautious approach and escape strategies characteristic of males prior to insemination."

3. Females of the desert scorpion *Paruroctonus mesaensis* are extremely rapacious   26 and will eat anything small enough that they can detect. "Any moving object in the proper size range is attacked without apparent discrimination" (G.A. Polis and R.D. Farley, see bibliography). Since males are smaller than females, they become prime targets and are consumed with avidity. This indiscriminate rapacity presents quite a problem for mating, which, as usual, requires some spatial intimacy. Males have therefore evolved an elaborate courtship ritual, in part to suppress the female's ordinary appetite.

The male initiates a series of grasping and kneading movements with his   27 chelicerae (minor claws), then grabs the female's chela (major claw) with his own and performs the celebrated *promenade à deux*, a reciprocal and symmetrical "dance," pretty as anything you'll see at Arthur Murray's. These scorpions do not inseminate females directly by inserting a penis, but rather deposit a spermatophore (a packet of sperm) that the female must then place into her body. Thus, the male leads the female in the *promenade* until he finds an appropriate spot. He deposits the spermatophore, usually on a stick or twig, then bats or even stings her, disengages, and runs for his life. If good fortune smiles, the female will let him go and pay proper attention to inserting his spermatophore. But, in two cases out of more than twenty, Polis and Farley found the female munching away on her mate while his spermatophore remained on a nearby stick, presumably for later ingestion through a different aperture.

What evidence, then, do these cases provide for selection of sexual can-   28 nibalism among males? Do males, for the sake of their genetic continuity, actively elicit (or even passively submit to) the care and feeding of their fertilized eggs with their own bodies? I find little persuasive evidence for such a phenomenon in these cases, and I wonder if it exists at all—although the argument would provide an excellent illustration of a curiosity that makes little sense unless the evolutionary world works for reproductive success of individuals, as Darwinism argues.

The scorpion story, despite its citation among best cases, provides no   29 evidence at all. As I read Polis and Farley, I note only that males try their best to escape after copulation and succeed in a great majority of cases (only two failed). Indeed, their mating behavior, both before and after, seems designed to avoid destruction, not to court it. Before, they turn off the female's aggressive instincts by marching and stroking. After, they hit and run. That a few fail and get eaten reflects the inevitable odds of any dangerous game that must be played.

Black widow spiders and praying mantises offer more to the theory of   30 direct selection for destruction among males. The spiders seem to be as cautious as scorpions before, but quite lackadaisical after, making little if any attempt to escape from the female's web. In addition, if the mating plug that they leave in the female debars them from any future patrimony, then they have fully served their Darwinian purpose. As for mantises, the better performance of a headless male might indicate that sex and death have been actively conjoined by selection. Yet, in both these cases, other observations render more than a bit ambiguous any evidence for active selection on males.

As a major problem for both mantises and spiders, we have no good 31 evidence about the frequency of sexual cannibalism. If it occurred always or even often and if the male clearly stopped and just let it happen, then I would be satisfied that this reasonable phenomenon exists. But if it occurs rarely and represents a simple failure to escape, rather than an active offering, then it is a byproduct of other phenomena, not a selected trait in itself. I can find no quantitative data on the percentage of eating after mating either in nature or even in the more unsatisfactory and artificial conditions of a laboratory.

For mantises, I find no evidence for the male's complicity in his demise. 32 Males are cautious beforehand and zealous to escape thereafter. But the female is big and rapacious; she makes no distinction between a smaller mantis and any other moving prey. As for the curious fact of better performance in decapitated males, I simply don't know. It could be a direct adaptation for combining sex with consumption, but other interpretations fare just as well in our absence of evidence. Hard-wired behavior must be programmed in some way. Perhaps the system of inhibition by a ganglion in the head and activation by one near the tail evolved in an ancestral lineage long before sexual cannibalism ever arose among mantises. Perhaps it was already in place when female mantises evolved their indiscriminate rapacity. It would then be co-opted, not actively selected, for its useful role in sexual cannibalism. After all, the same system works for females too, although their behavior serves no known evolutionary function. Decapitate a female mantis and you also unleash sexual behavior, including egg laying. If one wishes to argue that the system must have been actively evolved because the female tends to eat first just that portion of the male that unleashes sexuality, I reply with a bit of biology at its most basic: heads are in front and females encounter them first as the male approaches.

The black widow story is also shaky. Males may not try to escape after 33 mating, but is this an active adaptation for consumption or an automatic response to the real adaptation—breaking of the sexual organ and deposition of a mating plug in the female (for such an injury might weaken the male and explain his subsequent lassitude)? Also, male black widows are tiny compared with their mates—only 2 percent or so of the female's weight. Will such a small meal make enough of a difference? Finally, and most importantly, how often does the female partake of this available meal? If she always ate the exhausted male after mating, I would be more persuaded. But some studies indicate that sexual cannibalism may be rare, even though clearly available as an option for females. Curiously, several articles report that males often stay on the female's web until they die, often for two weeks or more, and that females leave them alone. Ross and Smith, for example, noticed only one case of sexual cannibalism and wrote: "Only one male of those we observed to succeed in inseminating a female was eaten by its mate immediately after mating. However, several were later found dead in their mates' webs."

Why then, in this disturbing absence of evidence, does our literature 34 abound with comments on the obvious evolutionary good sense of sexual cannibalism? For example: "Under some conditions selection should favor the consumption of males by their mates. His probability of being cannibalized should be directly proportional to the male's future expectation of reproduction." Or, "Successful males would best serve their biological interests by presenting themselves to their mates as a post-nuptial meal."

In this hiatus between reasonable hope and actual evidence, we come 35 face to face with a common bias of modern Darwinism. Darwinian theory is fundamentally about natural selection. I do not challenge this emphasis, but believe that we have become overzealous about the power and range of selection by trying to attribute every significant form and behavior to its direct action. In this Darwinian game, no prize is sweeter than a successful selectionist interpretation for phenomena that strike our intuition as senseless. How could a male become a blood meal after mating if selection rules our world? Because, in certain situations, he increases his own reproductive success thereby, our devoted selectionist responds.

But another overarching, yet often forgotten, evolutionary principle 36 usually intervenes and prevents any optimal match between organism and immediate environment—the curious, tortuous, constraining pathways of history. Organisms are not putty before a molding environment or billiard balls before the pool cue of natural selection. Their inherited forms and behaviors constrain and push back; they cannot be quickly transformed to new optimality every time the environment alters.

Every adaptive change brings scores of consequences in its wake, some 37 luckily co-opted for later advantage, others not. Some large females evolve indiscriminate rapacity for their own reasons, and some males suffer the consequences despite their own evolutionary race to escape. Designs evolved for one reason (or no reason) have other consequences, some fortuitously useful. Male mantises can become headless wonders; male black widows remain on the female's web. Both behaviors may be useful, but we have no evidence that either arose by active selection for male sacrifice. Sexual cannibalism with active male complicity should be favored in many groups (for the conditions of limited opportunity after mating and useful fodder are often met), but it has evolved rarely, if ever. Ask why we don't see it where it should occur; don't simply marvel about the wisdom of selection in a few possible cases. History often precludes useful opportunity; you cannot always get there from here. Females may not be sufficiently rapacious, or they may be smaller than males, or so limited in behavioral flexibility that they cannot evolve a system to turn off a general inhibition against cannibalism only after mating and only toward a male.

Our world is not an optimal place, fine tuned by omnipotent forces of 38 selection. It is a quirky mass of imperfections, working well enough (often admirably); a jury-rigged set of adaptations built of curious parts made available by past histories in different contexts. Darwin, who was a keen student of history, not just a devotee of selection, understood this principle as the primary proof of evolution itself. A world optimally adapted to current environments is a world without history, and a world without history might have been created as we find it. History matters; it confounds perfection and proves that current life transformed its own past. In his famous disquisition on the ages of man—"All the world's a stage"—Jaques, in *As You Like It*, speaks of "this strange eventful history." Respect the past and inform the present.

POSTSCRIPT

In the light of my ever-growing doubts about the existence of sexual canni- 39 balism (despite its plausibility in theory)—as prominently displayed in the personal odyssey of the essay itself—I was delighted by a report from the 1984 annual meeting of the Society for Neuroscience. E. Liske of West Germany and W.J. Davis of the University of California at Santa Cruz videotaped and analyzed courtship behavior for dozens of matings in Chinese praying mantises. No female ever decapitated or ate a male. Instead, frame-by-frame analysis revealed a complex series of behaviors, seemingly directed (at least in part) towards suppressing the natural rapacity of females. Male behavior includes visual fixation, antennal oscillation, slow approach, repetitive flexing of the abdomen, and a final flying leap towards the female's back. Liske and Davis suggest that previous reports of decapitation may represent aberrant behavior of captive specimens (though sexual cannibalism may still be normal behavior in strains or species other than those studied by Liske and Davis. There is no such thing as *the* praying mantis, given nature's propensity for diversity.). In any case, I am even more persuaded that sexual cannibalism is a phenomenon without proven examples, and that the reasons for its rarity (or non-existence) form a far more interesting subject (and an appropriate shift of emphasis) than the one that first inspired my research for the essay—reasons for the presumed (and now dubious) existence itself.

I often argue that the best test for legends is the extent of their seepage 40 into popular culture. In *Sherlock Holmes and the Spider Woman* (1944), one of the innumerable, yet wonderful, Rathbone-Bruce anachronisms that pit Holmes against Hitler and assorted enemies, Holmes unmasks an entomologist *poseur* (and murderer of the true scientist) by catching several subtle fallacies in his speech. The phony calls terraria "glass cages," but then really gives himself away when he says of black widow spiders: "They eat their mates, I'm told." Holmes responds: "You said you were told the black widows eat their mates. Any scientist would know it." I shall be waiting for the next update (who is playing Charlie Chan these days?).

REFERENCES

Buskirk, R. E., Frohlich, C., and Ross, K. G. 1984. "The natural selection of sexual cannibalism." *American Naturalist.* 123:617–625.

Darwin, Charles. 1871. *The descent of man and selection in relation to sex.* London: John Murray.

Gould, Stephen Jay. 1977. *Ontogeny and phlogeny.* Cambridge, MA: Belknap Press of Harvard University Press.

Howard, L. O. 1886. "The excessive voracity of the female mantis." *Science* 8:326.

Polis, G. A., and Farley, R. D. 1979. Behavior and ecology of mating in the cannibalistic scorpion, *Paruroctonus mesaensis stahnke* (Scorionida: Vaejocidae). *Journal of Arachnology.* 7:33–46.

Roeder, K. D. 1935. An experimental analysis of the sexual behavior of the praying mantis mantis religiosa L.). *Biological Bulletin.* 69:203–220.

Ross, K., and Smith, R. L. 1979. Aspects of the courtship behavior of the black widow spider, *Laterodectus hesperus* (Araneae: Theridiidae), with evidence for the existence of a contact sex pheromone. *Journal of Arachnology.* 7:69–77.

QUESTIONS ABOUT GOULD'S DISCOURSE COMMUNITY AND HIS CONCERNS IN THIS ESSAY

1. Read over Darwin's "Keeling Islands: Coral Formations." Based on Darwin's essay, would you agree with Gould's claim that "Darwin abhorred speculation; he never wrote a purely theoretical treatise. Even the *Origin of Species* is a compendium of facts pointing to a powerful conclusion" (paragraph 5)? Is this a process that Gould himself uses in this essay: gathering together a set of facts and reaching a theoretical conclusion?

2. In what kind of society would Darwin's explanation for small and subtle racial differences not hold? Are any human societies like that?

3. Gould argues that the model of sexual cannibalism will work in the scheme of natural selection only if the males actively promote their own consumption. Or might there be other options to explain this behavior? Is Gould, in stating such a premise, too easily willing to ascribe conscious motivation to lower orders of life based upon observations of behavior?

4. How does Gould respond to the examples of sexual cannibalism proposed by other naturalists? Are his responses reasonable? Can his objections be traced back to any central assumption or premise?

5. How would you describe the scientific method? Does Gould follow that method in this essay? What specific conclusions does Gould draw from the scarcity of evidence for sexual cannibalism?

6. Based on the somewhat limited evidence of this one essay, is it accurate to state that Gould's description of a world governed by natural selection is a world

where ethical questions are irrelevant? Or is it a world with one ethic: survival? Is survival—of a species or of an individual—the greatest good?

7. Gould asserts that scientists are not bound simply by the assumptions of their discourse communities, but also by all the other communities in which they participate. The result is that what scientists propose is usually affected strongly by philosophical positions. Do you think that he is correct in this, or do you feel that scientists, as they interpret data, are not affected by philosophies about life? What examples could you give for the position you hold? Do you think that Gould himself is affected by a philosophical position? If so, what is that position?

QUESTIONS ABOUT GOULD'S RHETORICAL STRATEGIES

1. Gould includes a long quote from the Victorian biologist L. O. Howard at the beginning of the essay, in which Howard describes an act of what he views as sexual cannibalism. Since one of Gould's major points is to challenge the existence of such cannibalism, why does he allow Howard's account to stand unchallenged? Is he creating suspense? Is he trying to hook the reader? Is he simply unable to account for this incident other than to say that it is an oddity and not the normal practice? Or is he trying to demonstrate one of his principal themes: that a person's subjective view of the world influences how that person interprets behavior that has been observed?

2. Given the technical nature of the discourse community in which Gould generally works, he might easily have used language in this essay that would have confused and put off the general reader. How does Gould mediate the language of advanced biology so that its meaning is available to the general reader? Where does such mediation occur? What does it suggest about Gould's commitments?

3. Periodically Gould includes some comical notes. Writing of the praying mantis, Gould observes that "Since it would be inconsistent with normal functions (and unseemly as well) for males to perform these copulatory motions continually, they are suppressed by inhibitory centers" (paragraph 23). Of female scorpions Gould notes that their "indiscriminate rapacity presents quite a problem for mating, which, as usual, requires some spatial intimacy" (paragraph 26). What is the role of these comic asides? How do they affect the tone of the essay? Would you say that comic asides are necessary in writing about science for a general audience?

4. Occasionally Gould uses an entire sentence to mark a transition ("We may now return to the blood meal of the mating mantis," (paragraph 17). Are such transitional sentences necessary in a relatively short essay? Why or why not?

5. Gould also sometimes uses questions to connect parts of his essay ("Why did Darwin choose his long and detailed treatise on sexual selection as a home for his much shorter preface on the *Descent of Man*?" paragraph 11). Do such connecting questions work well? What is necessary for them to work well?

6. Examine the metaphors in paragraph 5. Do they work together well, or do they clash with each other?

7. Examine how Gould orders the evidence about mantises, spiders, and scorpions

with an eye to how well this evidence supports the hypothesis of sexual cannibalism. What principle of ordering does he use? Is it a good one?

8. Gould breaks off his discussion of sexual cannibalism to discuss Darwin's *Descent of Man*. "So bear with me," he writes, "and we'll eventually get back to mantises and much more of what the biological literature calls 'sexual cannibalism'" (paragraph 4). Later he suggests that "this essay may be the most convoluted I have ever written" (paragraph 18). Would you agree that his essay is convoluted? If Gould recognized that his essay had a difficult structure, why did he choose to retain that structure? What is the effect of Gould's disclaimers on the reader?

9. Why is it that Gould refers to other areas of culture as he presents his arguments? He cites the poet and essayist W. H. Auden, Shakespeare's *As You Like It*, Stanley Kubrick's *Dr. Strangelove*, the Arthur Murray dance studio, and the Basil Rathbone film versions of the stories of Sherlock Holmes. How strong a part do these play in advancing the argument? Are these references mere decorations?

WRITING FROM WITHIN AND ABOUT THE SCIENTIFIC COMMUNITY

Writing for Yourself

1. In your journal explore how you react to the Darwinian view of the world as explained in this essay.

2. To explain consistent physical differences between the human races, Gould proposes the process of sexual selection, in which process certain characteristics were seen as beautiful and sexually appealing, with the result that those characteristics were passed on to succeeding generations. In your journal, explore this explanation. Does it seem to be logical and reasonable? What difficulties might you find in it?

Writing for Nonacademic Audiences

1. Write a letter to your grandparents in which you explain the nature of the world according to Darwin.

2. The Museum of Natural History on your campus has commissioned you to write an explanatory pamphlet to be distributed to patrons about features in the animal kingdom that enhance reproductive success but are otherwise liabilities. You have a limit of 750 words.

Writing for Academic Audiences

1. Write a 500-word explanatory report for an introductory class in biology about what Gould calls "mating plugs."

2. Gould argues against the existence of sexual cannibalism because of the scarcity of supporting evidence. Is this the only conclusion that can be drawn from Gould's claims? Can you conceive of any other conclusions that might be drawn from the scarce evidence? Does Gould himself adequately address the possibility of alternate conclusions? Address yourself to these questions in a 500-word

review of this essay, to be presented to a group of biology instructors in your university.

3. Research contemporary scientific thought on the significance of the colorful feathers of male birds. What role might those feathers play in terms of the survival of the species? Present your findings in a 1,000-word exploratory essay for your peers in a rhetoric class.

4. Gould writes that "our world overflows with peculiar, otherwise senseless shapes and behaviors that function only to promote victory in the great game of mating and reproduction" (paragraph 9), and he cites the tails of peacocks and the antlers of Irish elk as examples. Are the elk and the peacock sufficient? Should Gould cite additional evidence in order to convince the reader? Might there be other explanations for these "peculiar, otherwise senseless shapes"? Respond to these questions in a 1,000-word persuasive essay designed for a course in science and religion.

5. One of the goals of Gould's essay is to call into question a belief long held in the scientific community and in a large segment of society at large. Scientists have long had to deal with such beliefs: that life can spontaneously spring from non-life, that base metals can be changed into gold, that acquired characteristics (such as the loss of a finger or tail through accident, or stretching one's neck to promote longer necks in one's offspring) can be passed on to the next generation. Write a 1,250-word essay in which you analyze similar beliefs that contemporary scientists should call into question. Would the beliefs in the existence of UFOs or a so-called Bermuda Triangle qualify as such questionable beliefs?

Wayne Frair and Percival Davis

(b. 1926)   (b. 1936)

One of the continuing debates in contemporary science is between those who argue that evolution and natural selection have led to the current state of humankind and those who argue that humanity was created in its current state by a Creator. Reputable scientists on both sides have supported their arguments with what they identify as facts, while they all recognize that such facts are susceptible to interpretation. Perhaps it is not unusual that there has been a certain degree of antagonism between the two sides.

In the following selection, the first chapter of Wayne Frair and Percival Davis's A Case for Creation, *the authors agree that evolutionary theory is subject to the scientific method, suggesting that by using that methodology, they will show that the evolutionary theory is an error. They also suggest that creationism is subject to that same kind of inquiry, but that both visions are also based upon a kind of assumed belief that is not subject to such inquiry.*

Frair and Davis, the first a professor of biology and the second a professor of life science, represent a very specific discourse community: one that affirms the doctrine of creation as being consistent with scientific principles. This discourse community rejects alternate theories of human development such as natural selection. It is, though, a scientific discourse community with a strong philosophical underpinning— something many discourse communities have but may not recognize as consciously as the community represented by Frair and Davis.

EVOLUTION AND SCIENCE

Every age has possessed certain unquestioned presuppositions that served as 1 foundations for its most popular philosophies. Such a presupposition in our day is the theory of evolution. This concept has become the basis of much scientific and political theory, formal philosophy, and even theology. Evolutionary thought appears to be a cornerstone of modern civilization. If this is the case, surely we ought to examine such a cornerstone with care. If it is defective, the consequences one day could be disastrous. Disturbing evidence is accumulating that it has been unwise for us to allow this doctrine of evolution to become so foundational—it may be partially or wholly untrue.

In many high schools and colleges today evolution is nevertheless treated 2 as fact. The evolutionary theory is indeed the product of men of genius and is the result of more than a century of intense and serious intellectual effort. Its very bulk and elaborateness is intellectually intimidating. To the beginning student it seems an impregnable structure, for he is without the knowledge and experience to criticize it. This book is written to show that evolutionary doctrine is wrong. An alternative position is presented in order to challenge concerned individuals to discover more adequate explanations for the origins of living things.

The prevalent feeling in Western culture in recent centuries has been 3 that the general growth and positive progress of things was inevitable. To be sure, we do see all kinds of human activities and organizations starting from small and humble origins and increasing in complexity. We have the feeling, perhaps unconsciously, that there is development and evolution in our world, for one meaning of the word *evolution* is "systematic development from the simple to the complex." *Biological evolution*, therefore, usually refers to a progression in organisms from simple to relatively complex. Living organisms and extinct fossil forms are thought to be descendants of a relatively simple, self-reproducing chemical or protoplasmic substance.

DARWINISM

When Charles Darwin more than a century ago published his book *The Or-* 4 *igin of Species*, people were in the mood to hail it as what seemed to be the first totally acceptable explanation for the origin and development of living things. However, Darwin's theory of biological evolution was not completely original. There are rather ambiguous traces of the beginnings of evolutionary thought in writings of Greeks such as Thales, Anaximander, Empedocles, and Aristotle, hundreds of years before Christ. Nevertheless, it was not until the revival of classical and scientific learning in the seventeenth and eighteenth centuries that new ideas were added to the ancient concepts. This paved the way for the acceptance of Darwinism, supported as it was by a vast array of original observations that had been largely lacking in previous works.

The Origin of Species went through five revisions at Darwin's hand. 5 Darwin presented in it and in other writings his conclusions regarding the development of life. In reading Darwin, one receives a distinct impression that he was almost compulsive in his endeavor to keep abreast of the latest discoveries and generally to face scientific issues fairly. His writings contain good scientific data, much of which is still acceptable today. However, some of his writings have been shown to be incorrect or at least open to considerable question in the light of modern knowledge. Products of their era, his

works lack information on cytology (study of cells), physiology (study of function), and, of course, the newer sciences of biochemistry, biophysics, and
biomathematics. For this reason the works cannot be accepted as valid in all
modern scientific aspects.

Some of Darwin's embryological beliefs are now known to be untrue. 6
Many of his anthropological ideas, such as those regarding the development
of religion and language, have been shown to be incorrect. His ideas on the
relationship between intelligence and sex are rejected today by competent
psychologists. (Although some males still cling to them tenaciously!) He
stated, for example, that "the average of mental power in man must be above
that of woman," and that through sexual selection "man has ultimately become superior to woman."*

Many of those strange ideas were related to his erroneous concepts re- 7
garding heredity. He invented bodies known as *gemmules* in order to account
(as he thought) for observed hereditary data. Understandably, modern concepts of heredity involving genetic ratios, chromosome studies, deoxyribonu-
cleic acid (DNA), and many other new concepts are very different from anything Darwin could have proposed.

Darwin's evolutionary ideas were accepted by many scientists of his 8
day, but a considerable number of great scientists, including Owen, von Baer,
Wigand, Mivart, Agassiz, and Sedgwick, rejected his theories. Today no informed scientist believes exactly as Darwin did, but the most popular current
evolutionary views are still Darwinian in essence. It is undeniable that the
major features of Darwin's evolutionary thought have endured.

Although the doctrine of evolution was presented to account for changes 9
among living things, its implications have been extended into the sociological, political, and religious realms. For example, Darwin's teachings have
been extended to justify taking unfair advantage of others. Known as Social
Darwinism, this idea was expounded by Herbert Spencer† even before Darwin published his ideas. Spencer imagined an evolutionary struggle at all
levels, in which the greatest advancement was secured by ruthless and unethical competition. In this way, by analogy with animal competition and "survival of the fittest," many unscrupulous activities were justified. Teachings of
such leaders as Nietzsche and Hitler have contained ideas consistent with
Social Darwinism and apparently derived from it. Fortunately, this viewpoint is not currently popular in the Western world.

Another popular belief that grew out of Darwin's writings held "wild" 10
tribes to be composed of people who were intermediate between apes and
civilized man. Many people thought culture (including religion) had evolved
through a series of patterns that were all evident among living peoples. Ac-

---

* Charles Darwin, *The Origin of Species and the Descent of Man* (New York: Random House,
    1971), 2:873–74. [Frair and Davis's note].
† Herbert Spencer (1820–1903) was an English philosopher who in *Synthetic Philosophy* inter-
    preted all phenomena in terms of evolutionary progress [Editors' note].

cording to this teaching, lineal cultural evolution began with the savages. But recent studies in cultural anthropology have indicated that regardless of the degree of civilization, members of the human race possess a basic physiological, psychological, and spiritual unity.

For instance, whereas the popular nineteenth-century view held so- 11 called primitive or Stone Age men to be intermediate between apes and modern Europeans with regard to language, arts, and intelligence, it is now recognized that their languages are often more intricate and expressive than our own. Great skill is evidenced in much of their drawing, carving, weaving, and pottery. Their music is often of complex and subtle rhythmic structure, though we may not appreciate it because our ears are attuned to our own concepts of melody and harmony. The culture of Stone Age men living 7,000 years ago was at least as sophisticated as that of many "primitive" tribes of today. In these tribes, as in all cultures of living men, there is belief in the supernatural and in life after death. When adequate testing procedures are used, the intelligence of "primitive" peoples approximates our own. This presence of intelligence and human culture practically and readily distinguishes man from all animals.

Do modern scientific advances depend on the theory of evolution and 12 require an acceptance of its tenets? There seems to be no good reason to insist that biological studies always be informed by evolutionary considerations. What recent important biological achievement could not have been accomplished just as well without a belief in evolution on the investigator's part?

During the twentieth century many of the erroneous early presupposi- 13 tions of evolutionary anthropology have been corrected. So the chief scientific quest in anthropology today is certainly not the determination of which human race is most like the apes, but rather the main area of study is the current diversified patterns of human culture and physique. The most fruitful scientific endeavors in anthropology have been those conducted *within* the family of man.

Similarly, in recent years there has been a growing tendency in many 14 areas (e.g., taxonomy) to use other than evolutionary approaches to scientific data. This has happened because of the misapplication of Darwinism as it spread, and because many exceptions to evolutionary generalizations have been found.

Such scientific studies of current, specific groups of animals are, for the 15 most part, scientifically valid because the results may be verified much more objectively than those studies that have attempted to relate diverse kinds of organisms.

On the other hand, general similarities that exist among members of 16 different groups such as dogs and rabbits, or cats and mice are certainly important. We acknowledge this every time experimental drugs are tested on laboratory rats, mice, or monkeys. Why not perform such tests on lizards or spiders? Because it is obvious that animals most similar to us in a variety of ways can be expected to be most similar to us also in their response to medication. Such similarities can be explained as originating in basic design given by the Creator. Evolution is not necessary to account for the similarities.

There are many reasons for Darwinism's widespread misapplication and 17
its present unfortunate position of prominence in the scientific world. One of the important reasons for this situation is that the methods and techniques of science are not well understood—in many cases, not even by practicing scientists themselves. Until recently the prestige of science has been nearly absolute, and often a statement that something is "scientific" has been taken by the layman to mean it is *certain*. Scientific "facts" of the last twenty years, for instance, held that burns were to be treated with butter or salve (never water) and that Jupiter was a cold planet. These and countless other widely held "facts" are believed by no one today.

Science itself differs from the products of science. Most of the technolog- 18
ical differences between today and the past are because of improved scientific methods for exploiting the environment. The products of science are, from a practical point of view, *tools*. The use of most of these tools, such as bulldozers or airplanes, is obvious. A theory also can be considered a useful tool, a key to nature that opens up new roads to knowledge. However, because it *is* a tool, any theory has certain limitations. It must be used intelligently, it should be improved as knowledge accumulates, and it should fall into disuse when a more effective tool is invented. Let us consider the origin of theories and their use, for these are the most basic tools of science.

THE SCIENTIFIC METHOD

What is it that makes science "scientific"? Dictionary definitions center on 19
the idea of systematic classification and careful collection of data, which is usually assembled into coherent wholes. All these are important aspects of science, but by no means give the essentials of science. Most scientists would insist that an acceptable definition would have to include the concept of the *scientific method*. But such a definition is circular. What is the scientific method?

The scientific method is a hybrid of two main forms of thought—*de-* 20
duction and *induction*. Deduction is probably the most common form of inferential logic in which the necessary consequences of a fact are determined. Induction is the means by which we interpret observations and assess their significance. It is the process of forming generalizations. The drawback of induction is that it can be used too subjectively. It is easy to make erroneous generalizations, especially when they are drawn from insufficient data. Yet who is to say that he is in possession of all relevant data? Since the answer is obviously "No one," it follows that induction is inherently fallible.

Yet induction is a cornerstone of the scientific method. We *must* employ 21
induction, for deduction is parasitic upon it. The only way we obtain the raw

material of reason is to make observations and generalize upon them. The scholastic philosophers of the high Middle Ages appreciated this dilemma and proposed a partial solution. Why not combine the two, they reasoned. One could propose a tentative generalization called a *hypothesis*. The logical consequences of that hypothesis could then be inferred deductively, and those consequences could be tested against reality by further observation. If the consequences were true, the hypothesis could be tentatively accepted; if false, the hypothesis could be rejected.

This method has survived and has become the basis for all modern science. All science must involve the proposal of a testable hypothesis, the inference of its consequences, and the attempt to match those consequences with the real universe by observation. Thus a hypothesis is a proposed explanation for some problem or phenomenon that catches the attention of the scientist, and a prediction is one of the logical consequences of that hypothesis. Predictions are confirmed, or not, by attempted observation. To generate the necessary observations, scientists usually design controlled experiments. 22

Perhaps the characteristics of a genuine hypothesis that most distinguish it from dogma on the one hand and speculation on the other are that a hypothesis is *tentative* and *falsifiable*. That is, a hypothesis must be explicitly understood to be uncertain when it is proposed, and it should suggest predictions that will be observed not only if it is true, *but also if it is false*. 23

One of the chief difficulties of the scientific method is that false hypotheses often appear true because by coincidence they sometimes suggest true predictions. In the early days of the germ theory of disease, for instance, it was suggested that the microbes found in infected wounds did not cause the infection but were permitted to develop there as a consequence of the inflammation. The hypothesis that the microbes are a consequence of the disease did suggest the prediction that they would usually be found in disease states, and so it is. Despite this true prediction, the hypothesis was shown to be false when experimental injuries were inflicted under sterile conditions. When that was done, the microbes and inflammation both failed to appear. That is exactly what one would predict if the hypothesis was false. 24

One cannot know whether a hypothesis is false except by inferring its logical consequences in the foregoing way. If they are demonstrably false, then the hypothesis is necessarily false. But oddly enough, as we have seen, the reverse cannot be said. A false hypothesis can suggest true predictions by coincidence, but a true hypothesis cannot suggest false predictions. That means that the falsification of a hypothesis can be trusted, but not its verification. This leads us to the conclusion that the scientific method is basically negative. It can be used to attempt to prune away some of the untruths we propose, but it cannot assure us of the validity of the remainder. 25

What makes the scientific method work despite this is that if a false hypothesis should suggest a true conclusion, it *must* be by coincidence. By definition, a *coincidence* is an unlikely chance occurrence. Such an occur- 26 rence is even less likely to occur twice or several times. Thus, if we observe a prediction that is consistent with a hypothesis, we should consider that as encouraging, but not as indicating the hypothesis is true. We must try to make other kinds of predictions and test them in their turn. If several such predictions come to pass as expected, the hypothesis is probably (but not certainly) true. Note, however, that because the essence of a scientific hypothesis is its falsifiability, a hypothesis that is proposed in such a way that it *cannot* possibly or practically be discredited, *even if it is untrue*, lies outside the scope of the scientific method. It could be true in fact, but it is scientifically undemonstrable; and it is thus not really a hypothesis at all. Such proposals are usually called *unfalsifiable hypotheses*.

PREDICTION AND RETRODICTION

Must predictions be observed in future time? The ordinary meaning of the word would suggest it, but there is a variety of "prediction" that is a consequential event observable as a *past* occurrence. We shall call such a reverse prediction a *retrodiction*. 27

Past events have had consequences in time that was future time for the events, but past or present for us. The American Revolution led to the War of 1812, which otherwise would not have taken place as it did. If someone were to doubt that the American Revolution took place, but could be convinced that the War of 1812 did take place, he could perhaps be convinced on that basis that the American Revolution was a historic fact. In principle, then, it should be possible to erect testable hypotheses about events that may have occurred in the past. Then one could deduce the consequences and search for evidence that they had occurred. 28

Of the two methods, prediction has much greater falsifying power than retrodiction for two reasons: (1) it is always possible to claim that failure to find evidence of a retrodiction has resulted from chance loss, and (2) it is possible to claim that an unavailable class of evidence is needed to discredit the hypothesis. The upshot is that historic hypotheses are likely to become unfalsifiable hypotheses. Put differently, it is often possible to choose predictions to test the most crucial aspects of a hypothesis, but with retrodictions one is stuck with events that have already occurred, and among those, only the ones whose remains can be detected today. Needless to say, the past has not been designed as a logical instrument for our use. It is certainly not open to experimentation. 29

DIFFICULTIES WITH RETRODICTION

Let us consider an example. One of the great chestnuts of paleontology has been what caused the dinosaurs to become extinct. The really odd aspects of the situation are supposed to be the suddenness with which extinction took place, its thoroughness, and other widespread, simultaneous extinctions, such 30 as that of the trilobites. According to conventional paleontology, the dinosaurs lasted for about 100 million years; according to more recent and less conventional paleontology, they may have become extinct in a period as short as ten years, or even less. If that were true, it would be difficult to name a catastrophe that could have eliminated them so quickly and so thoroughly.

Numerous ones have nevertheless been suggested, some quite sensational: (1) a nearby supernova, for instance, could have saturated the earth with lethal radiation; (2) the Arctic Ocean, if initially landlocked, could have been released by geological events, spreading over the more saline water of the warmer seas and producing drastic climatic changes, including a ten-year, near-absolute drought; (3) an asteroid or comet might have collided with the earth, producing (in addition to tidal waves and earthquakes) atmospheric dust that would have obscured the sun. By interfering with photosynthesis, this would have killed all but a few plants, although presumably seeds would have survived. With the resultant collapse of all terrestrial and aquatic food chains upon which dinosaurs and other organisms were dependent, the dinosaurs would have become extinct.   31

Noncatastrophic explanations have also been advanced, such as flowering plants displacing the gymnosperms that dinosaurs were specially adapted to eat. One version of that theory holds that the gymnosperms contained a cathartic substance without which the dinosaurs died of massive constipation! Each of this plethora of proposals has its advocates and detractors. How can one hope to distinguish among them?   32

A June 6, 1980 article in *Science* magazine, "Extraterrestrial Cause for the Cretaceous-Tertiary Extinction," by Luis Alvarez, Walter Alvarez, Frank Asaro, and Helen V. Michel proposed that a key to the extinction problem is that rocks formed at the time have abnormally high concentrations of platinum-like metals, especially iridium. This metal, rare in earthly surface rocks, is much more richly concentrated in meteorites and presumably in asteroids also. This fact suggested to Alvarez and his colleagues that the high concentrations of iridium in the late Cretaceous rocks may have resulted from the collision of the earth with an asteroid. This collision also would have resulted in the extinctions because of reduced photosynthesis, as already mentioned. Could the iridium have another explanation? Could it have come from the exploding supernova, as rival theorists might suggest? No, for if that were the case, calculations should show that the iridium is accompanied by comparable quantities of a plutonium isotope, and such is not the case.   33

Alvarez and his colleagues seemed to have made a good case for their asteroidal bomb, until a series of letters appeared in subsequent issues of *Science* (as February 13, 1981). In one of those, Dennis V. Kent pointed out that iridium concentrations such as Alvarez et al. found so remarkable are not all that uncommon in rocks of varying ages and locales. Recall that Alvarez et al. believed an asteroid collision released dust that interfered with photosynthesis. Many sedimentary rocks are dependent on living organisms for their   34 formation and hence are directly or indirectly dependent on photosynthesis. Kent reversed this causality and suggested that reduced sediment deposition, resulting perhaps from something else entirely, would have the effect of concentrating iridium in a smaller total volume of rock, in these thinner layers, thus increasing its concentration. As a final blow, Kent referred to "fossil" volcanic eruptions, some of whose craters are known to approach a size of 35 kilometers by 100 kilometers, completely dwarfing that of Krakatoa, to say nothing of Mt. St. Helens. One of those, the Toba caldera in Sumatra, probably ejected some 2,000 cubic kilometers of material into the atmosphere, an amount more than sufficient to suppress earthly photosynthesis. That eruption is supposed to have occurred about 25,000 years B.P. (before present times), a time that paleontologists have not named as a time of massive extinctions.

To these points another correspondent, George C. Reid, added that 35 "Under these extreme conditions [such as those posited by Alvarez] the problem becomes not one of explaining the extinction of half the genera living at the time, but one of explaining the survival of the other half."

Consider how Alvarez's hypothesis was proposed and tested in this typ- 36 ical example of retrodiction, and consider the results, if any. The problem was to account for the apparent massive extinction of late Cretaceous life, which extinction had never been satisfactorily explained. The hypothesis was that dust injected into the atmosphere by an asteroidal collision produced the extinctions by interfering with photosynthesis, thus cutting off all food chains at the source. This hypothesis suggested a family of retrodictions and Alvarez produced one: iridium would be deposited in a particular concentration in the sediments of that time. That retrodiction is indeed true, at least apparently, and Alvarez takes that truth as confirmation of his hypothesis.

Kent, however, infers two other less happy retrodictions. First, he points 37 out that if high iridium concentrations are to be taken as evidence of asteroidal collision, they should occur only in conjunction with catastrophes. But that does not seem to be the case, because such concentrations are widely distributed throughout the geological record. So there is no reason to associate the Cretaceous case examined by Alvarez with an asteroidal collision. It could easily have been produced by a coincidental occurrence of some kind. Second, Kent says if Alvarez's hypothetical asteroid killed the dinosaurs by turning off the light, so should massive volcanic eruptions. But there is no evidence that light ever was cut off, despite clear indications that such eruptions have occurred in the past. Reid adds another contradictory retrodiction: such a horrific event should have nearly wiped out late Cretaceous life, but that does not seem to have occurred either.

Have we then been able to rule out conclusively the asteroid collision 38 hypothesis? Not at all. Quite undiscouraged, Alvarez replied to these criticisms in a familiar vein—further research is needed. Perhaps it is, but for the moment it appears that this attempted application of the scientific method to past events has produced a classic unfalsifiable hypothesis that, although *perhaps* it could be true, cannot be dealt with by means of the scientific method. The final word may have been spoken by yet another correspondent, whose letter to *Science* suggested that the issue had already been examined in a more enjoyable way—in the aptly-named Walt Disney film *Fantasia*.

Despite all this, the asteroid collision hypothesis seems well on its way 39 to becoming an accepted scientific dogma. Articles in periodicals ranging from *The New York State Conservationist* to *Scientific American* have burst into print, most without a hint of the afore-mentioned objections. It has even made prime-time television.

So it is hard to know what data could be used (or whether any still 40 survive) that would enable us to decide which, if any, of the hypotheses is correct. In fact, it could have been caused by a flood! But one would be rash indeed who would suggest that a flood could be demonstrated by retrodiction.

From the foregoing discussion it should be clear that the scientific 41 method is a practical device for resolving questions in "real time." It is far less effective when applied to the past, and for that reason it is doubtful that the general concept of biological evolution is falsifiable by the scientific method. Certain aspects of the theory *can* be studied in real time in the laboratory or field, but as we shall see, those studies have not demonstrated that evolution is true in the general sense, that is, that it has produced the world of life as we know it today. To the extent that it can be demonstrated to be true at all, evolution can be shown to be only trivially true.

IS CREATIONISM SCIENTIFIC?

What of creationism? Is it "scientific," or can it be made so? Strictly speaking, 42 the answer is no. Despite the insistence by proponents that evolution is firmly established as scientific, its dependence on retrodiction greatly weakens that claim. By criticizing evolution as unscientific, however, one does not thereby establish creationism as scientific—*and this should not bother us!* Science is a practical tool for approximating truth. Though there is probably no influence more pervasive in our society than science, and though it has produced a revolution in human thought unprecedented in history, science is not infallible. Truth, in fact, takes precedence over science. Let creationists frankly acknowledge that their commitment to creation depends at least as much on faith* as on science. The evolutionists are no better off. We can and should exceed them in honesty.

THEORY AND TRUTH

When sufficient information on a topic accumulates, the scientist attempts to 43 make a *generalization*. A generalization is a statement encompassing all ob-

---

* As Hebrews 11:3 puts it, "*By faith* [not scientific data] we understand that the worlds were prepared by the word of God" (italics added) [Frair and Davis's note].

served data in summary form. The earliest form of a generalization is termed a *hypothesis*. When observations confirming a hypothesis accumulate, the hypothesis becomes a *theory*. A theory unchallenged and consistently supported by facts is called a *law* after a considerable lapse of time.

This process of moving from generalization to law does not necessarily 44 mean the generalization has become fact; the likelihood of its being correct merely increases, or, as it is commonly stated, it has a higher statistical probability of being right. If any observation (even though seemingly trivial) conflicts with the generalization or hypothesis, the scientist is left with two major alternatives: (1) discard the hypothesis and search for another, or (2) attempt to find some plausible explanation for the observation in accord with the hypothesis. There is no major scientific hypothesis of any age that has not been affected by either one or both of these fates.

The history of science is replete with discarded and amended theories. 45 Those that have been amended so often as to lose their original identity become like the proverbial pair of pants with more patch than pants. When an involved "patching process" raises serious doubt regarding the validity of the basic concept involved, theories are sometimes abandoned entirely. Often a theory seems so well-grounded that it is unchallenged for generations, only to be upset by the uncovering of new data inconsistent with the old. Neither hypothesis, theory, nor law is in the same realm as absolute truth. All three rest upon a perennially shaky foundation, and all are vulnerable to uncomfortable facts.*

As Christians we believe that only God can know the universe as it 46 *really is*. We are limited by our senses and our minds, and we know the universe only as it *appears* to us. In science we do not believe in generalizations because we know them to be *true*; we believe in them only because they are *credible* to us. Several competing explanations for the same phenomenon may be equally attractive, and often none of them can be proved false. Who can say which, if any, reflects reality? Usually we apply the principle of logic called "Ockham's razor" and accept the simplest explanation, but for all we know this may not be the best answer. And even when no alternative explanation exists, does that mean that no alternative is possible? Thus we are forever uncertain in our understanding of the universe; our most assured conclusions are still tentative if we depend only on our own rational faculties.

Truth as God sees it has been revealed in the pages of Scripture, and 47 that revelation is therefore more certainly true than any mere human rationalism. For the creationist, revealed truth controls his view of the universe to at least as great a degree as anything that has been advanced using the scientific method.

---

*An interesting and humorous example concerns one investigator who persuaded a slime mold organism to crawl through a pinhole and hang threadlike from it. This thread of protoplasm twisted in a clockwise direction nineteen times. The experimenter felt he was on the track of a fundamental biological law. Unfortunately, on the twentieth trial, the slime mold twisted in a counterclockwise direction! [Frair and Davis's note].

The purpose of this excursus has been to show that no scientific state- 48 ment is unassailable or final. The theory of evolution, like other theories, depends on the interpretation of observations. Because of its basic nature, it is subject to experimental test or confirmation only in a limited sense.

Evolutionists often differentiate between what they consider the "fact" 49 of evolution and the "theories" of evolution. The fact supposedly consists of observed changes in animal and plant fossils over a period of time, whereas theories of evolution attempt to explain how the changes have occurred. The theories deal with mechanisms, such as natural selection and genetics. Bearing this distinction in mind, we shall see that reliable conclusions are difficult to draw from the fossil record, or from any other kind of evidence. There seems to be little justification for the popular practice of presenting unrestricted evolution as fact or law, because it cannot be proved as such.

A final word is in order for both creationists and evolutionists. The most 50 important part of science is not its method, but the attitude of those who practice it. The scientific attitude may be described as one of honesty and open-minded skepticism—toward one's own views, as well as toward the views of others. Such balance has often been notably absent from the attitudes of evolutionists, who in their strident advocacy and bias sometimes sound like the worst of the theologians they claim to despise.*

But it is also extremely important that creationists, who claim to rep- 51 resent biblical truth and the Lord Jesus Christ, not lose sight of their obligation to treat the opposition fairly. Let us be both cautious and humble in presenting *our* "facts" when they go beyond the bounds of Scripture. How sad that even Christians are often shoddy in scholarship, not checking out facts but merely passing them on in the form of misinformation. In some cases they even create or suppress data in order to support their position most favorably. If creationists are to show themselves conspicuously superior to evolutionists, let it first be in the areas of enlightenment, decency, and courtesy. Second Corinthians 8:20–21 states this principle well: "Taking precaution that no one should discredit us . . . for we have regard for what is honorable, not only in the sight of the Lord, but also in the sight of men."

QUESTIONS ABOUT THE DISCOURSE COMMUNITY OF FRAIR AND DAVIS AND THEIR CONCERNS IN THIS SELECTION

1. How would you define the readers for whom Wayne Frair and Percival Davis write? What clues in the argument, in the language, in the authors' assumptions and stance suggest the nature of these readers?

---

*Here is an example: In *The Monkey Business*, by Niles Eldredge, one finds the statement (p. 83) "A relatively small number of creation scientists have produced the vast bulk of the articles and books that have appeared. *None of them have contributed a single article to any reputable scientific journal*" (italics added). This statement is an egregious falsehood, as anyone who wishes to consult the caption of Figure 3.1 in this book can see for himself [Frair and Davis's note].

2. How do the authors define the concept of evolution? How do they see this concept as extending beyond the realm of the natural sciences? Do you think their definition of Darwinism is full enough?

3. In paragraph four, the authors claim that "When Charles Darwin more than a century ago published his book *The Origin of Species*, people were in the mood to hail it as what seemed to be the first totally acceptable explanation for the origin and development of living things." In fact, though, Darwin was severely criticized from within the scientific community and vigorously attacked by the religious community. What "people," then, are the authors referring to?

4. Frair and Davis appear to acknowledge that the earth is older than 6,000 years and that dinosaurs lived here at one time. In so doing, how do they differ from some creationists?

5. Frair and Davis write that "the purpose of this excursus has been to show that no scientific statement is unassailable or final. The theory of evolution, like other theories, depends on the interpretation of observations. Because of its basic nature, it is subject to experimental test or confirmation only in a limited sense." Would all scientific discourse communities agree with this?

6. Do you agree with Frair and Davis that no one can ever have sufficient data to make generalizations that are certain?

7. Why do Frair and Davis say the evolutionists are no better off than the creationists when it comes to having to depend on faith?

QUESTIONS ABOUT FRAIR AND DAVIS'S RHETORICAL STRATEGIES

1. At least part of the purpose of this essay is to discredit the theory of evolution, and one way that Frair and Davis go about this is through a careful choice of words. Read over the first two paragraphs. What words or phrases do the authors use here to suggest that the concept of evolution is invalid?

2. In the second paragraph, Frair and Davis note that "the evolutionary theory is indeed the product of men of genius and is the result of more than a century of intense and serious intellectual effort." Several sentences later, in that same paragraph, they write that "this book is written to show that evolutionary doctrine is wrong." Do these two sentences seem to be contradictory? Why would the authors use both and place them in the same paragraph?

3. Why do you think Frair and Davis, in pointing out some of Darwin's mistaken beliefs, quote him about women's intelligence?

4. Read over the first five paragraphs of the section entitled "Darwinism." What is the purpose of these paragraphs? What might the inclusion of these paragraphs suggest about the authors' rhetorical strategy? Would it be fair to say that the use of such a strategy weakens the argument and is, in some ways, not scientific?

5. Examine paragraphs nine through eleven. What is the rhetorical strategy of these paragraphs? Is it fair for two scientists to use arguments from outside their own discourse community to argue a case from within their community? In general, should writers who want to argue forcefully and conclusively stay within their own discourse communities, or is that putting too narrow a restriction on them?

6. Why do Frair and Davis include the long section on retrodiction? How does it contribute to the case they make about evolution? Is it a convincing argument or merely an intrusion in the structure of the argument?

WRITING FROM WITHIN AND ABOUT THE SCIENTIFIC COMMUNITY

Writing for Yourself

1. In your journal, explore precisely what you think about the origin and development of the human species.
2. In your journal, write about some people you have encountered who have acted with false assumptions, with disastrous results.

Writing for Nonacademic Audiences

1. Pick one of your friends who you know has a different position than you do on the origin and development of humankind. Write a letter to this friend, explaining why you cannot see things as he or she does.
2. An editor of a local newspaper has asked you to write a 500-word article for the Opinion section of the newspaper, drawing only on your own experience as evidence, on whether or not "members of the human race possess a basic physiological, psychological, and spiritual unity."

Writing for Academic Audiences

1. Do some research on Darwin's hypothesized "gemmules." Write a 500-word description that will be used as a handout in introductory genetics classes to show what in Darwin's view of gemmules is a foreshadowing of ideas in modern genetic theory.
2. After researching the concept of evolution in several recent scientific encyclopedias, write a single paragraph defining the nature of evolution as it is currently understood. How is it to be distinguished from natural selection? You will be discussing this paragraph in an introductory biology class.
3. In paragraph sixteen, Frair and Davis present an old argument: Similar structures imply a single creator. After reading over Stephen Jay Gould's essay in this volume, write a brief essay with Frair and Davis as the intended audience in which you answer this argument from Gould's standpoint. You might also wish to write a response to your essay from the standpoint of Frair and Davis.
4. Under great debate in the last ten years have been the reasons for the extinction of the dinosaurs. Frair and Davis touch upon this controversy. Research this controversy, evaluating the various theories. Write a 2,000- to 2,500-word persuasive essay in which you argue for the theory that seems most credible.

James P. Crutchfield,
(b. 1955)

J. Doyne Farmer,
(b. 1952)

Norman H. Packard,
(b. 1954)

and Robert S. Shaw
(b. 1946)

As graduate students in physics at the University of California at Santa Cruz in the early 1980s, the authors of the following essay formed a study group that they called the Dynamical Systems Collective. Crutchfield is now at the University of California at Berkeley, Farmer at the Los Alamos National Laboratory, Packard at the University of Illinois at Champaign-Urbana, and Shaw has turned to classical and improvisational music, in addition to his scientific interests. At Santa Cruz the group began to study the nature of random systems, a study that led to their study of chaos.

In the prologue to his Chaos: Making a New Science (1987), *James Gleick notes the following:*

> *Where chaos begins, science stops. For as long as the world has had physicists inquiring into the laws of nature, it has suffered a special ignorance about disorder in the atmosphere, in the turbulent sea, in the fluctuations of wildlife populations, in the oscillations of the heart and the brain. The irregular side of nature, the discontinuous and erratic side—these have been puzzles to science, or worse, monstrosities.*

Gleick goes on to show that since 1970, the attitudes among scientists towards randomness and chaos have changed, so that many areas of science and mathematics— physics, meteorology, biology, ecology—have begun to consider the importance of understanding the roles and the pattern of chaos.

Gleick's book, written for a popular audience, comes out of this growing interest in chaos, and articles like that of James Crutchfield and his associates, reprinted here, are appearing in some of the more prestigious journals in the various fields of science; the following article was first printed in Scientific American. *Crutchfield argues that the study of chaos can radically redefine many areas of the sciences, and the authors of this article set themselves against the determinists on the one hand and, on the other hand, against those who argue that chaos can never be measured.*

CHAOS

There is order in chaos: randomness has an underlying geometric form. Chaos imposes fundamental limits on prediction, but it also suggests causal relationships where none were previously suspected.

The great power of science lies in the ability to relate cause and effect. On 1 the basis of the laws of gravitation, for example, eclipses can be predicted thousands of years in advance. There are other natural phenomena that are not as predictable. Although the movements of the atmosphere obey the laws of physics just as much as the movements of the planets do, weather forecasts are still stated in terms of probabilities. The weather, the flow of a mountain stream, the roll of the dice all have unpredictable aspects. Since there is no clear relation between cause and effect, such phenomena are said to have random elements. Yet until recently there was little reason to doubt that precise predictability could in principle be achieved. It was assumed that it was only necessary to gather and process a sufficient amount of information.

Such a viewpoint has been altered by a striking discovery: simple deter- 2 ministic systems with only a few elements can generate random behavior. The randomness is fundamental; gathering more information does not make it go away. Randomness generated in this way has come to be called chaos.

A seeming paradox is that chaos is deterministic, generated by fixed 3 rules that do not themselves involve any elements of chance. In principle the future is completely determined by the past, but in practice small uncertainties are amplified, so that even though the behavior is predictable in the short term, it is unpredictable in the long term. There is order in chaos: underlying chaotic behavior there are elegant geometric forms that create randomness in the same way as a card dealer shuffles a deck of cards or a blender mixes cake batter.

The discovery of chaos has created a new paradigm in scientific mod- 4 eling. On one hand, it implies new fundamental limits on the ability to make predictions. On the other hand, the determinism inherent in chaos implies that many random phenomena are more predictable than had been thought. Random-looking information gathered in the past—and shelved because it was assumed to be too complicated—can now be explained in terms of simple laws. Chaos allows order to be found in such diverse systems as the atmosphere, dripping faucets and the heart. The result is a revolution that is affecting many different branches of science.

What are the origins of random behavior? Brownian motion provides a clas- 5 sic example of randomness. A speck of dust observed through a microscope is seen to move in a continuous and erratic jiggle. This is owing to the bom-

CHAOS results from the geometric operation of stretching. The effect is illustrated for a painting of the French mathematician Henri Poincaré, the originator of dynamical systems theory. The initial image (*top left*) was digitized so that a computer could perform the stretching operation. A simple mathematical transformation stretches the image diagonally as though it were painted on a sheet of rubber. Where the sheet leaves the box it is cut and reinserted on the other side, as is shown in panel *1*. (The number above each panel indicates how many times the transformation has been made.) Applying the transformation repeatedly has the effect of scrambling the face (*panels*

bardment of the dust particle by the surrounding water molecules in thermal motion. Because the water molecules are unseen and exist in great number, the detailed motion of the dust particle is thoroughly unpredictable. Here the web of causal influences among the subunits can become so tangled that the resulting pattern of behavior becomes quite random.

The chaos to be discussed here requires no large number of subunits or 6 unseen influences. The existence of random behavior in very simple systems motivates a reexamination of the sources of randomness even in large systems such as weather.

What makes the motion of the atmosphere so much harder to anticipate 7 than the motion of the solar system? Both are made up of many parts, and both are governed by Newton's second law, $F = ma$, which can be viewed as a simple prescription for predicting the future. If the forces F acting on a given mass m are known, then so is the acceleration a. It then follows from the rules of calculus that if the position and velocity of an object can be measured at a given instant, they are determined forever. This is such a powerful idea that the 18th-century French mathematician Pierre Simon de Laplace once boasted that given the position and velocity of every particle in the universe, he could predict the future for the rest of time. Although there are several obvious practical difficulties to achieving Laplace's goal, for more than 100 years there seemed to be no reason for his not being right, at least in principle. The literal application of Laplace's dictum to human behavior led to the philosophical conclusion that human behavior was completely predetermined: free will did not exist.

Twentieth-century science has seen the downfall of Laplacian deter- 8 minism, for two very different reasons. The first reason is quantum mechanics. A central dogma of that theory is the Heisenberg uncertainty principle, which states that there is a fundamental limitation to the accuracy with which the position and velocity of a particle can be measured. Such uncertainty gives a good explanation for some random phenomena, such as radioactive decay. A nucleus is so small that the uncertainty principle puts a fundamental limit on the knowledge of its motion, and so it is impossible to gather enough information to predict when it will disintegrate.

The source of unpredictability on a large scale must be sought else- 9 where, however. Some large-scale phenomena are predictable and others are not. The distinction has nothing to do with quantum mechanics. The trajectory of a baseball, for example, is inherently predictable; a fielder intuitively

---

2–4). The net effect is a random combination of colors, producing a homogeneous field of green (*panels* 10 *and* 18). Sometimes it happens that some of the points come back near their initial locations, causing a brief appearance of the original image (*panels* 47–48, 239–241). The transformation shown here is special in that the phenomenon of "Poincaré recurrence" (as it is called in statistical mechanics) happens much more often than usual; in a typical chaotic transformation recurrence is exceedingly rare, occurring perhaps only once in the lifetime of the universe. In the presence of any amount of background fluctuations the time between recurrences is usually so long that all information about the original image is lost.

Laplace, 1776

"The present state of the system of nature is evidently a consequence of what it was in the preceding moment, and if we conceive of an intelligence which at a given instant comprehends all the relations of the entities of this universe, it could state the respective positions, motions, and general affects of all these entities at any time in the past or future.

"Physical astronomy, the branch of knowledge which does the greatest honor to the human mind, gives us an idea, albeit imperfect, of what such an intelligence would be. The simplicity of the law by which the celestial bodies move, and the relations of their masses and distances, permit analysis to follow their motions up to a certain point; and in order to determine the state of the system of these great bodies in past or future centuries, it suffices for the mathematician that their position and their velocity be given by observation for any moment in time. Man owes that advantage to the power of the instrument he employs, and to the small number of relations that it embraces in its calculations. But ignorance of the different causes involved in the production of events, as well as their complexity, taken together with the imperfection of analysis, prevents our reaching the same certainty about the vast majority of phenomena. Thus there are things that are uncertain for us, things more or less probable, and we seek to compensate for the impossibility of knowing them by determining their different degrees of likelihood. So it is that we owe to the weakness of the human mind one of the most delicate and ingenious of mathematical theories, the science of chance or probability."

Poincaré, 1903

"A very small cause which escapes our notice determines a considerable effect that we cannot fail to see, and then we say that the effect is due to chance. If we knew exactly the laws of nature and the situation of the universe at the initial moment, we could predict exactly the situation of that same universe at a succeeding moment. But even if it were the case that the natural laws had no longer any secret for us, we could still only know the initial situation *approximately*. If that enabled us to predict the succeeding situation with *the same approximation*, that is all we require, and we should say that the phenomenon had been predicted, that it is governed by laws. But it is not always so; it may happen that small differences in the initial conditions produce very great ones in the final phenomena. A small error in the former will produce an enormous error in the latter. Prediction becomes impossible, and we have the fortuitous phenomenon."

OUTLOOKS OF TWO LUMINARIES on chance and probability are contrasted. The French mathematician Pierre Simon de Laplace proposed that the laws of nature imply strict determination and complete predictability, although imperfections in observations make the introduction of probabilistic theory necessary. The quotation from Poincaré foreshadows the contemporary view that arbitrarily small uncertainties in the state of a system may be amplified in time and so predictions of the distant future cannot be made.

makes use of the fact every time he or she catches the ball. The trajectory of a flying balloon with the air rushing out of it, in contrast, is not predictable; the balloon lurches and turns erratically at times and places that are impossible to predict. The balloon obeys Newton's laws just as much as the baseball does; then why is its behavior so much harder to predict than that of the ball?

The classic example of such a dichotomy is fluid motion. Under some 10
circumstances the motion of a fluid is laminar—even, steady and regular—
and easily predicted from equations. Under other circumstances fluid motion
is turbulent—uneven, unsteady and irregular—and difficult to predict. The
transition from laminar to turbulent behavior is familiar to anyone who has
been in an airplane in calm weather and then suddenly encountered a thun-
derstorm. What causes the essential difference between laminar and turbulent motion?

To understand fully why that is such a riddle, imagine sitting by a mountain 11
stream. The water swirls and splashes as though it had a mind of its own,
moving first one way and then another. Nevertheless, the rocks in the stream
bed are firmly fixed in place, and the tributaries enter at a nearly constant
rate of flow. Where, then, does the random motion of the water come from?

The late Soviet physicist Lev D. Landau is credited with an explanation 12
of random fluid motion that held sway for many years, namely that the motion of a turbulent fluid contains many different, independent oscillations. As
the fluid is made to move faster, causing it to become more turbulent, the
oscillations enter the motion one at a time. Although each separate oscillation
may be simple, the complicated combined motion renders the flow impossible to predict.

Landau's theory has been disproved, however. Random behavior oc- 13
curs even in very simple systems, without any need for complication or in-
determinacy. The French mathematician Henri Poincaré realized this at the
turn of the century when he noted that unpredictable, "fortuitous" phenomena may occur in systems where a small change in the present causes a much
larger change in the future. The notion is clear if one thinks of a rock poised
at the top of a hill. A tiny push one way or another is enough to send it
tumbling down widely differing paths. Although the rock is sensitive to small
influences only at the top of the hill, chaotic systems are sensitive at every
point in their motion.

A simple example serves to illustrate just how sensitive some physical 14
systems can be to external influences. Imagine a game of billiards, somewhat
idealized so that the balls move across the table and collide with a negligible
loss of energy. With a single shot the billiard player sends the collection of
balls into a protracted sequence of collisions. The player naturally wants to
know the effects of the shot. For how long could a player with perfect control
over his or her stroke predict the que ball's trajectory? If the player ignored
an effect even as minuscule as the gravitational attraction of an electron at
the edge of the galaxy, the prediction would become wrong after one minute!

The large growth in uncertainty comes about because the balls are 15
curved, and small differences at the point of impact are amplified with each
collision. The amplification is exponential: it is compounded at every collision, like the successive reproduction of bacteria with unlimited space and

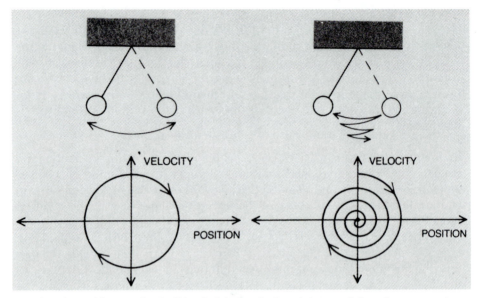

State Space is a useful concept for visualizing the behavior of a dynamical system. It is an abstract space whose coordinates are the degrees of freedom of the system's motion. The motion of a pendulum (*top*), for example, is completely determined by its initial position and velocity. Its state is thus a point in a plane whose coordinates are position and velocity (*bottom*). As the pendulum swings back and forth it follows an "orbit," or path, through the state space. For an ideal, frictionless pendulum the orbit is a closed curve (*bottom left*); otherwise, with friction, the orbit spirals to a point (*bottom right*).

food. Any effect, no matter how small, quickly reaches macroscopic proportions. That is one of the basic properties of chaos.

It is the exponential amplification of errors due to chaotic dynamics that 16 provides the second reason for Laplace's undoing. Quantum mechanics implies that initial measurements are always uncertain, and chaos ensures that the uncertainties will quickly overwhelm the ability to make predictions. Without chaos Laplace might have hoped that errors would remain founded, or at least grow slowly enough to allow him to make predictions over a long period. With chaos, predictions are rapidly doomed to gross inaccuracy.

The larger framework that chaos emerges from is the so-called theory of dy- 17 namical systems. A dynamical system consists of two parts: the notions of a state (the essential information about a system) and a dynamic (a rule that describes how the state evolves with time). The evolution can be visualized in a state space, an abstract construct whose coordinates are the components of the state. In general the coordinates of the state space vary with the context; for a mechanical system they might be position and velocity, but for an ecological model they might be the populations of different species.

A good example of a dynamical system is found in the simple pendulum. 18 All that is needed to determine its motion are two variables: position and velocity. The state is thus a point in a plane, whose coordinates are position and velocity. Newton's laws provide a rule, expressed mathematically as a differential equation, that describes how the state evolves. As the pendulum swings back and forth the state moves along an "orbit," or path, in the plane. In the ideal case of a frictionless pendulum the orbit is a loop; failing that, the orbit spirals to a point as the pendulum comes to rest.

A dynamical system's temporal evolution may happen in either contin- 19 uous time or in discrete time. The former is called a flow, the latter a mapping. A pendulum moves continuously from one state to another, and so it is described by a continuous-time flow. The number of insects born each year in a specific area and the time interval between drops from a dripping faucet are more naturally described by a discrete-time mapping.

To find how a system evolves from a given initial state one can employ 20 the dynamic (equations of motion) to move incrementally along an orbit. This method of deducing the system's behavior requires computational effort proportional to the desired length of time to follow the orbit. For simple systems such as a frictionless pendulum the equations of motion may occasionally have a closed-form solution, which is a formula that expresses any future state in terms of the initial state. A closed-form solution provides a short cut, a simpler algorithm that needs only the initial state and the final time to predict the future without stepping through intermediate states. With such a solution the algorithmic effort required to follow the motion of the system is roughly independent of the time desired. Given the equations of planetary and lunar motion and the earth's and moon's positions and velocities, for instance, eclipses may be predicted years in advance.

Success in finding closed-form solutions for a variety of simple systems 21 during the early development of physics led to the hope that such solutions exist for any mechanical system. Unfortunately, it is now known that this is not true in general. The unpredictable behavior of chaotic dynamical systems cannot be expressed in a closed-form solution. Consequently there are no possible short cuts to predicting their behavior.

The state space nonetheless provides a powerful tool for describing the be- 22 havior of chaotic systems. The usefulness of the state-space picture lies in the ability to represent behavior in geometric form. For example, a pendulum that moves with friction eventually comes to a halt, which in the state space means the orbit approaches a point. The point does not move—it is a fixed point—and since it attracts nearby orbits, it is known as an attractor. If the pendulum is given a small push, it returns to the same fixed-point attractor. Any system that comes to rest with the passage of time can be characterized by a fixed point in state space. This is an example of a very general phenomenon, where losses due to friction or viscosity, for example, cause orbits to be attracted to a smaller region of the state space with lower dimension. Any such region is called an attractor. Roughly speaking, an attractor is what the behavior of a system settles down to, or is attracted to.

Some systems do not come to rest in the long term but instead cycle 23 periodically through a sequence of states. An example is the pendulum clock, in which energy lost to friction is replaced by a mainspring or weights. The pendulum repeats the same motion over and over again. In the state space such a motion corresponds to a cycle, or periodic orbit. No matter how the pendulum is set swinging, the cycle approached in the long-term limit is the same. Such attractors are therefore called limit cycles. Another familiar system with a limit-cycle attractor is the heart.

A system may have several attractors. If that is the case, different initial 24 conditions may evolve to different attractors. The set of points that evolve to an attractor is called its basin of attraction. The pendulum clock has two such basins: small displacements of the pendulum from its rest position result in a return to rest; with large displacements, however, the clock begins to tick as the pendulum executes a stable oscillation.

The next most complicated form of attractor is a torus, which resembles 25 the surface of a doughnut. This shape describes motion made up of two independent oscillations, sometimes called quasi-periodic motion. (Physical examples can be constructed from driven electrical oscillators.) The orbit winds around the torus in state space, one frequently determined by how fast the orbit circles the doughnut in the short direction, the other regulated by how fast the orbit circles the long way around. Attractors may also be higher-dimensional tori, since they represent the combination of more than two oscillations.

The important feature of quasi-periodic motion is that in spite of its 26 complexity it is predictable. Even though the orbit may never exactly repeat itself, if the frequencies that make up the motion have no common divisor, the motion remains regular. Orbits that start on the torus near one another remain near one another, and long-term predictability is guaranteed.

Until fairly recently, fixed points, limit cycles and tori were the only known 27 attractors. In 1963 Edward N. Lorenz of the Massachusetts Institute of Technology discovered a concrete example of a low-dimensional system that displayed complex behavior. Motivated by the desire to understand the unpredictability of the weather, he began with the equations of motion for fluid flow (the atmosphere can be considered a fluid), and by simplifying them he obtained a system that had just three degrees of freedom. Nevertheless, the system behaved in an apparently random fashion that could not be adequately characterized by any of the three attractors then known. The attractor he observed, which is now known as the Lorenz attractor, was the first example of a chaotic, or strange, attractor.

Employing a digital computer to simulate his simple model, Lorenz 28 elucidated the basic mechanism responsible for the randomness he observed:

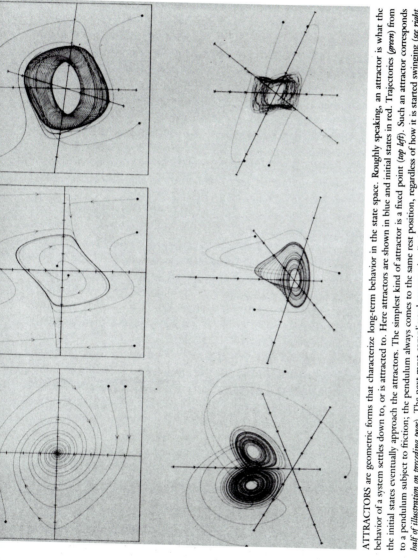

ATTRACTORS are geometric forms that characterize long-term behavior in the state space. Roughly speaking, an attractor is what the behavior of a system settles down to, or is attracted to. Here attractors are shown in blue and initial states in red. Trajectories (*green*) from the initial states eventually approach the attractors. The simplest kind of attractor is a fixed point (*top left*). Such an attractor corresponds to a pendulum subject to friction; the pendulum always comes to the same rest position, regardless of how it is started swinging (*see right half of illustration on preceding page*). The next most complicated attractor is a limit cycle (*top middle*), which forms a closed loop in the state space. A limit cycle describes stable oscillations, such as the motion of a pendulum clock and the beating of a heart. Compound oscillations, or quasi-periodic behavior, correspond to a torus attractor (*top right*). All three attractors are predictable: their behavior can be forecast as accurately as desired. Chaotic attractors, on the other hand, correspond to unpredictable motions and have a more complicated geometric form. Three examples of chaotic attractors are shown in the bottom row; from left to right they are the work of Edward N. Lorenz, Otto E. Rössler and one of the authors (Shaw) respectively. The images were prepared by using simple systems of differential equations having a three-dimensional state space.

707

microscopic perturbations are amplified to affect macroscopic behavior. Two orbits with nearby initial conditions diverge exponentially fast and so stay close together for only a short time. The situation is qualitatively different for nonchaotic attractors. For these, nearby orbits stay close to one another, small errors remain bounded and the behavior is predictable.

The key to understanding chaotic behavior lies in understanding a sim-   29 ple stretching and folding operation, which takes place in the state space. Exponential divergence is a local feature: because attractors have finite size, two orbits on a chaotic attractor cannot diverge exponentially forever. Consequently the attractor must fold over onto itself. Although orbits diverge and follow increasingly different paths, they eventually must pass close to one another again. The orbits on a chaotic attractor are shuffled by this process, much as a deck of cards is shuffled by a dealer. The randomness of the chaotic orbits is the result of the shuffling process. The process of stretching and folding happens repeatedly, creating folds within folds ad infinitum. A chaotic attractor is, in other words, a fractal: an object that reveals more detail as it is increasingly magnified [*see illustration on page 711*].

Chaos mixes the orbits in state space in precisely the same way as a   30 baker mixes bread dough by kneading it. One can imagine what happens to nearby trajectories on a chaotic attractor by placing a drop of blue food coloring in the dough. The kneading is a combination of two actions: rolling out the dough, in which the food coloring is spread out, and folding the dough over. At first the blob of food coloring simply gets longer, but eventually it is folded, and after considerable time the blob is stretched and refolded many times. On close inspection the dough consists of many layers of alternating blue and white. After only 20 steps the initial blob has been stretched to more than a million times its original length, and its thickness has shrunk to the molecular level. The blue dye is thoroughly mixed with the dough. Chaos works the same way, except that instead of mixing dough it mixes the state space. Inspired by this picture of mixing, Otto E. Rössler of the University of Tübingen created the simplest example of a chaotic attractor in a flow [*see illustration on page 709*].

When observations are made on a physical system, it is impossible to   31 specify the state of the system exactly owing to the inevitable errors in measurement. Instead the state of the system is located not at a single point but rather within a small region of state space. Although quantum uncertainty sets the ultimate size of the region, in practice different kinds of noise limit measurement precision by introducing substantially larger errors. The small region specified by a measurement is analogous to the blob of blue dye in the dough.

Locating the system in a small region of state space by carrying out a mea-   32 surement yields a certain amount of information about the system. The more accurate the measurement is, the more knowledge an observer gains about

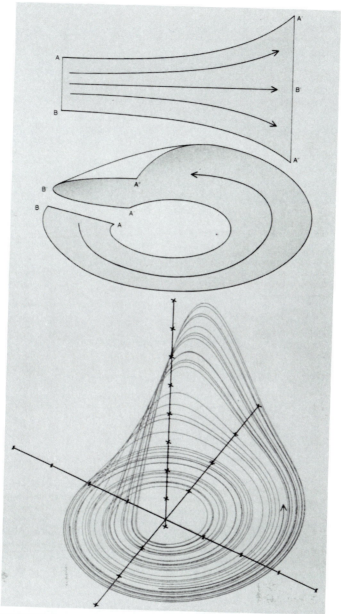

CHAOTIC ATTRACTOR has a much more complicated structure than a predictable attractor such as a point, a limit cycle or a torus. Observed at large scales, a chaotic attractor is not a smooth surface but one with folds in it. The illustration shows the steps in making a chaotic attractor for the simplest case: the Rössler attractor (*bottom*). First, nearby trajectories on the object must "stretch," or diverge, exponentially (*top*); here the distance between neighboring trajectories roughly doubles. Second, to keep the object compact, it must "fold" back onto itself (*middle*): the surface bends onto itself so that the two ends meet. The Rössler attractor has been observed in many systems, from fluid flows to chemical reactions, illustrating Einstein's maxim that nature prefers simple forms.

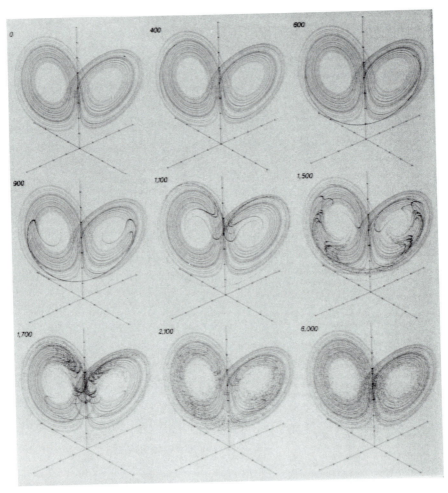

DIVERGENCE of nearby trajectories is the underlying reason chaos leads to unpredictability. A perfect measurement would correspond to a point in the state space, but any real measurement is inaccurate, generating a cloud of uncertainty. The true state might be anywhere inside the cloud. As shown here for the Lorenz attractor, the uncertainty of the initial measurement is represented by 10,000 red dots, initially so close together that they are indistinguishable. As each point moves under the action of the equations, the cloud is stretched into a long, thin thread, which then folds over onto itself many times, until the points are spread over the entire attractor. Prediction has now become impossible: the final state can be anywhere on the attractor. For a predictable attractor, in contrast, all the final states remain close together. The numbers above the illustrations are in units of 1/200 second.

the system's state. Conversely, the larger the region, the more uncertain the observer. Since nearby points in nonchaotic systems stay close as they evolve in time, a measurement provides a certain amount of information that is preserved with time. This is exactly the sense in which such systems are predictable: initial measurements contain information that can be used to predict future behavior. In other words, predictable dynamical systems are not particularly sensitive to measurement errors.

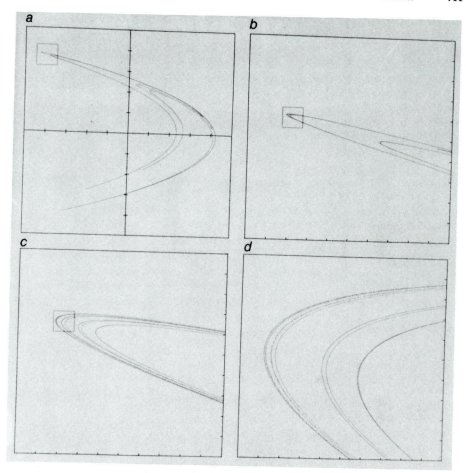

CHAOTIC ATTRACTORS are fractals: objects that reveal more detail as they are increasingly magnified. Chaos naturally produces fractals. As nearby trajectories expand they must eventually fold over close to one another for the motion to remain finite. This is repeated again and again, generating folds within folds, ad infinitum. As a result chaotic attractors have a beautiful microscopic structure. Michel Hénon of the Nice Observatory in France discovered a simple rule that stretches and folds the plane, moving each point to a new location. Starting from a single initial point, each successive point obtained by repeatedly applying Hénon's rule is plotted. The resulting geometric form (*a*) provides a simple example of a chaotic attractor. The small box is magnified by a factor of 10 in *b*. By repeating the process (*c*, *d*) the microscopic structure of the attractor is revealed in detail. The bottom illustration depicts another part of the Hénon attractor.

The stretching and folding operation of a chaotic attractor systemati-   33
cally removes the initial information and replaces it with new information: the stretch makes small-scale uncertainties larger, the fold brings widely separated trajectories together and erases large-scale information. Thus chaotic attractors act as a kind of pump bringing microscopic fluctuations up to a macroscopic expression. In this light it is clear that no exact solution, no short cut to tell the future, can exist. After a brief time interval the uncertainty specified by the initial measurement covers the entire attractor and all

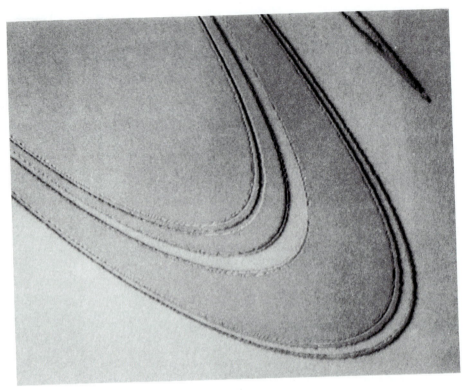

CHAOTIC ATTRACTORS *(cont.)*

predictive power is lost: there is simply no causal connection between past and future.

Chaotic attractors function locally as noise amplifiers. A small fluctua- 34 tion due perhaps to thermal noise will cause a large deflection in the orbit position soon afterward. But there is an important sense in which chaotic attractors differ from simple noise amplifiers. Because the stretching and folding operation is assumed to be repetitive and continuous, any tiny fluctuation will eventually dominate the motion, and the qualitative behavior is independent of noise level. Hence chaotic systems cannot directly be "quieted," by lowering the temperature, for example. Chaotic systems generate randomness on their own without the need for any external random inputs. Random behavior comes from more than just the amplification of errors and the loss of the ability to predict; it is due to the complex orbits generated by stretching and folding.

It should be noted that chaotic as well as nonchaotic behavior can occur 35 in dissipationless, energy-conserving systems. Here orbits do not relax onto an attractor but instead are confined to an energy surface. Dissipation is, however, important in many if not most real-world systems, and one can expect the concept of attractor to be generally useful.

EXPERIMENTAL EVIDENCE supports the hypothesis that chaotic attractors underlie some kinds of random motion in fluid flow. Shown here are successive pictures of water in a Couette cell, which consists of two nested cylinders. The space between the cylinders is filled with water and the inner cylinder is rotated with a certain angular velocity (*a*). As the angular velocity is increased, the fluid shows a progressively more complex flow pattern (*b*), which becomes irregular (*c*) and then chaotic (*d*).

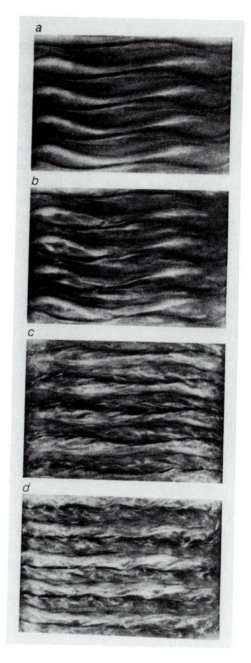

Low-dimensional chaotic attractors open a new realm of dynamical systems 36
theory, but the question remains of whether they are relevant to randomness
observed in physical systems. The first experimental evidence supporting the
hypothesis that chaotic attractors underlie random motion in fluid flow was
rather indirect. The experiment was done in 1974 by Jerry P. Gollub of Hav-
erford College and Harry L. Swinney of the University of Texas at Austin.
The evidence was indirect because the investigators focused not on the attractor itself but rather on statistical properties characterizing the attractor.

The system they examined was a Couette cell, which consists of two 37
concentric cylinders. The space between the cylinders is filled with a fluid,
and one or both cylinders are rotated with a fixed angular velocity. As the
angular velocity increases, the fluid shows progressively more complex flow
patterns, with a complicated time dependence [*see illustration on page 713*].
Gollub and Swinney essentially measured the velocity of the fluid at a given
spot. As they increased the rotation rate, they observed transitions from a
velocity that is constant in time to a periodically varying velocity and finally
to an aperiodically varying velocity. The transition to aperiodic motion was
the focus of the experiment.

The experiment was designed to distinguish between two theoretical 38
pictures that predicted different scenarios for the behavior of the fluid as the
rotation rate of the fluid was varied. The Landau picture of random fluid
motion predicted that an ever higher number of independent fluid oscillations should be excited as the rotation rate is increased. The associated attractor would be a high-dimensional torus. The Landau picture had been challenged by David Ruelle of the Institut des Hautes Études Scientifiques near
Paris and Floris Takens of the University of Groningen in the Netherlands.
They gave mathematical arguments suggesting that the attractor associated
with the Landau picture would not be likely to occur in fluid motion. Instead
their results suggested that any possible high-dimensional tori might give way
to a chaotic attractor, as originally postulated by Lorenz.

Gollub and Swinney found that for low rates of rotation the flow of the 39
fluid did not change in time: the underlying attractor was a fixed point. As
the rotation was increased the water began to oscillate with one independent
frequency, corresponding to a limit-cycle attractor (a periodic orbit), and as
the rotation was increased still further the oscillation took on two independent frequencies, corresponding to a two-dimensional torus attractor. Landau's theory predicted that as the rotation rate was further increased the
pattern would continue: more distinct frequencies would gradually appear.
Instead, at a critical rotation rate a continuous range of frequencies suddenly
appeared. Such an observation was consistent with Lorenz' "deterministic
nonperiodic flow," lending credence to his idea that chaotic attractors underlie fluid turbulence.

Although the analysis of Gollub and Swinney bolstered the notion that cha- 40
otic attractors might underlie some random motion in fluid flow, their work

was by no means conclusive. One would like to explicitly demonstrate the existence in experimental data of a simple chaotic attractor. Typically, however, an experiment does not record all facets of a system but only a few. Gollub and Swinney could not record, for example, the entire Couette flow but only the fluid velocity at a single point. The task of the investigator is to "reconstruct" the attractor from the limited data. Clearly that cannot always be done; if the attractor is too complicated, something will be lost. In some cases, however, it is possible to reconstruct the dynamics on the basis of limited data.

A technique introduced by us and put on a firm mathematical founda-   41
tion by Takens made it possible to reconstruct a state space and look for chaotic attractors. The basic idea is that the evolution of any single component of a system is determined by the other components with which it interacts. Information about the relevant components is thus implicitly contained in the history of any single component. To reconstruct an "equivalent" state space, one simply looks at a single component and treats the measured values at fixed time delays (one second ago, two seconds ago and so on, for example) as though they were new dimensions.

The delayed values can be viewed as new coordinates, defining a single   42
point in a multidimensional state space. Repeating the procedure and taking delays relative to different times generates many such points. One can then use other techniques to test whether or not these points lie on a chaotic attractor. Although this representation is in many respects arbitrary, it turns out that the important properties of an attractor are preserved by it and do not depend on the details of how the reconstruction is done.

The example we shall use to illustrate the technique has the advantage   43
of being familiar and accessible to nearly everyone. Most people are aware of the periodic pattern of drops emerging from a dripping faucet. The time between successive drops can be quite regular, and more than one insomniac has been kept awake waiting for the next drop to fall. Less familiar is the behavior of a faucet at a somewhat higher flow rate. One can often find a regime where the drops, while still falling separately, fall in a never repeating patter, like an infinitely inventive drummer. (This is an experiment easily carried out personally; the faucets without the little screens work best.) The changes between periodic and random-seeming patterns are reminiscent of the transition between laminar and turbulent fluid flow. Could a simple chaotic attractor underlie this randomness?

The experimental study of a dripping faucet was done at the University   44
of California at Santa Cruz by one of us (Shaw) in collaboration with Peter L. Scott, Stephen C. Pope and Philip J. Martein. The first form of the experiment consisted in allowing the drops from an ordinary faucet to fall on a microphone and measuring the time intervals between the resulting sound pulses. Typical results from a somewhat more refined experiment are shown on the [following] page. By plotting the time intervals between drops in pairs, one effectively takes a cross section of the underlying attractor. In the

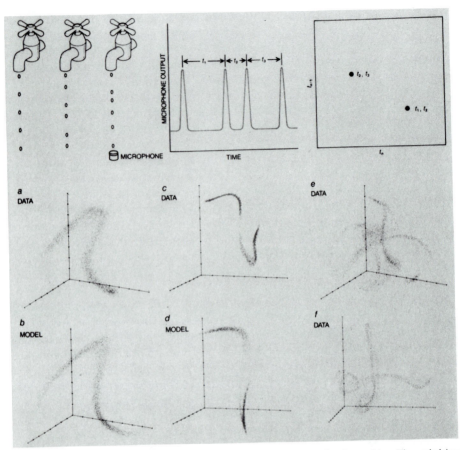

DRIPPING FAUCET is an example of a common system that can undergo a chaotic transition. The underlying attractor is reconstructed by plotting the time intervals between successive drops in pairs, as is shown at the top of the illustration. Attractors reconstructed from an actual dripping faucet (*a*, *c*) compare favorably with attractors generated by following variants of Hénon's rule (*b*, *d*). (The entire Hénon attractor is shown on page 45.) Illustrations *e* and *f* were reconstructed from high rates of water flow and presumably represent the cross sections of hitherto unseen chaotic attractors. Time-delay coordinates were employed in each of the plots. The horizontal coordinate is t_n, the time interval between drop n and drop $n - 1$. The vertical coordinate is the next time interval, t_{n+1}, and the third coordinate, visualized as coming out of the page, is t_{n+2}. Each point is thus determined by a triplex of numbers (t_n, t_{n+1}, t_{n+2}) that have been plotted for a set of 4,094 data samples. Simulated noise was added to illustrations *b* and *d*.

periodic regime, for example, the meniscus where the drops are detaching is moving in a smooth, repetitive manner, which could be represented by a limit cycle in the state space. But this smooth motion is inaccessible in the actual experiment; all that is recorded is the time intervals between the breaking off of the individual drops. This is like applying a stroboscopic light to regular motion around a loop. If the timing is right, one sees only a fixed point.

The exciting result of the experiment was that chaotic attractors were   45 indeed found in the nonperiodic regime of the dripping faucet. It could have been the case that the randomness of the drops was due to unseen influences, such as small vibrations or air currents. If that was so, there would be no particular relation between one interval and the next, and the plot of the data taken in pairs would have shown only a featureless blob. The fact that any structure at all appears in the plots shows the randomness has a deterministic underpinning. In particular, many data sets show the horseshoelike shape that is the signature of the simple stretching and folding process discussed above. The characteristic shape can be thought of as a "snapshot" of a fold in progress, for example, a cross section partway around the Rössler attractor shown on page [709]. Other data sets seem more complicated; these may be cross sections of higher-dimensional attractors. The geometry of attractors above three dimensions is almost completely unknown at this time.

If a system is chaotic, how chaotic is it? A measure of chaos is the "entropy" 46 of the motion, which roughly speaking is the average rate of stretching and folding, or the average rate at which information is produced. Another statistic is the "dimension" of the attractor. If a system is simple, its behavior should be described by a low-dimensional attractor in the state space, such as the examples given in this article. Several numbers may be required to specify the state of a more complicated system, and its corresponding attractor would therefore be higher-dimensional.

The technique of reconstruction, combined with measurements of en- 47 tropy and dimension, makes it possible to reexamine the fluid flow originally studied by Gollub and Swinney. This was done by members of Swinney's group in collaboration with two of us (Crutchfield and Farmer). The reconstruction technique enabled us to make images of the underlying attractor. The images do not give the striking demonstration of a low-dimensional attractor that studies of other systems, such as the dripping faucet, do. Measurements of the entropy and dimension reveal, however, that irregular fluid motion near the transition in Couette flow can be described by chaotic attractors. As the rotation rate of the Couette cell increases so do the entropy and dimension of the underlying attractors.

In the past few years a growing number of systems have been shown to 48 exhibit randomness due to a simple chaotic attractor. Among them are the convection pattern of fluid heated in a small box, oscillating concentration levels in a stirred-chemical reaction, the beating of chicken-heart cells and a large number of electrical and mechanical oscillators. In addition computer models of phenomena ranging from epidemics to the electrical activity of a nerve cell to stellar oscillations have been shown to possess this simple type of randomness. There are even experiments now under way that are searching for chaos in areas as disparate as brain waves and economics.

It should be emphasized, however, that chaos theory is far from a pan- 49 acea. Many degrees of freedom can also make for complicated motions that are effectively random. Even though a given system may be known to be chaotic, the fact alone does not reveal very much. A good example is molecules bouncing off one another in a gas. Although such a system is known to be chaotic, that in itself does not make prediction of its behavior easier. So many particles are involved that all that can be hoped for is a statistical description, and the essential statistical properties can be derived without taking chaos into account.

There are other uncharted questions for which the role of chaos is un- 50 known. What of constantly changing patterns that are spatially extended, such as the dunes of the Sahara and fully developed turbulence? It is not clear whether complex spatial patterns can be usefully described by a single attractor in a single state space. Perhaps, though, experience with the simplest attractors can serve as a guide to a more advanced picture, which may involve entire assemblages of spatially mobile deterministic forms akin to chaotic attractors.

The existence of chaos affects the scientific method itself. The classic ap- 51 proach to verifying a theory is to make predictions and test them against experimental data. If the phenomena are chaotic, however, long-term predictions are intrinsically impossible. This has to be taken into account in judging the merits of the theory. The process of verifying a theory thus becomes a much more delicate operation, relying on statistical and geometric properties rather than on detailed prediction.

Chaos brings a new challenge to the reductionist view that a system can 52 be understood by breaking it down and studying each piece. This view has been prevalent in science in part because there are so many systems for which the behavior of the whole is indeed the sum of its parts. Chaos demonstrates, however, that a system can have complicated behavior that emerges as a consequence of simple, nonlinear interaction of only a few components.

The problem is becoming acute in a wide range of scientific disciplines, 53 from describing microscopic physics to modeling macroscopic behavior of biological organisms. The ability to obtain detailed knowledge of a system's structure has undergone a tremendous advance in recent years, but the ability to integrate this knowledge has been stymied by the lack of a proper conceptual framework within which to describe qualitative behavior. For example, even with a complete map of the nervous system of a simple organism, such as the nematode studied by Sidney Brenner of the University of Cambridge, the organism's behavior cannot be deduced. Similarly, the hope that physics could be complete with an increasingly detailed understanding of fundamental physical forces and constituents is unfounded. The interaction of components on one scale can lead to complex global behavior on a larger scale that in general cannot be deduced from knowledge of the individual components.

Chaos is often seen in terms of the limitations it implies, such as lack of 54 predictability. Nature may, however, employ chaos constructively. Through amplification of small fluctuations it can provide natural systems with access to novelty. A prey escaping a predator's attack could use chaotic flight control as an element of surprise to evade capture. Biological evolution demands genetic variability; chaos provides a means of structuring random changes, thereby providing the possibility of putting variability under evolutionary control.

Even the process of intellectual progress relies on the injection of new 55 ideas and on new ways of connecting old ideas. Innate creativity may have an underlying chaotic process that selectively amplifies small fluctuations and molds them into macroscopic coherent mental states that are experienced as thoughts. In some cases the thoughts may be decisions, or what are perceived to be the exercise of will. In this light, chaos provides a mechanism that allows for free will within a world governed by deterministic laws.

QUESTIONS ABOUT THE AUTHORS' DISCOURSE COMMUNITY AND THEIR CONCERNS IN THIS ESSAY

1. Does the central argument of this essay suggest that there really is no such thing as chaos? Would the authors of this essay assert that? Or would they assert that most people need to understand chaos in a new way?
2. The authors assert that "random-looking information gathered in the past—and shelved because it was assumed to be too complicated—can now be explained in terms of simple laws" (paragraph 4). Does this sound too optimistic to be credible? Is it the case that science usually makes advances by resorting to "simple laws"?
3. What is scientific determinism? Why has this doctrine not survived into the late twentieth century?
4. Consider the example of the billiard balls and the single electron at the edge of the universe. Does it seem to you that in the real world, such an electron would have any effect at all on a billiard ball? If not, can parts of this essay then be dismissed as dealing only with a theoretical universe, having no connection to the world that lies about us?
5. The authors frequently refer to the uncertainty of measurement. What is the origin of this uncertainty? Do the authors seem to indicate whether or not they believe such uncertainty may eventually be overcome?
6. Toward the end of the essay, the authors warn that chaos theory is not a solution for everything. Speaking of the action of molecules in a gas, they note that "Although such a system is known to be chaotic, that in itself does not make prediction of its behavior easier. So many particles are involved that all that can be hoped for is a statistical description, and the essential statistical properties can be derived without taking chaos into account." So what, in the end, is the significance of this new science?
7. Toward the end of this essay, the authors assert that "Biological evolution demands genetic variability. . . ." Why do they claim this?

TRANSITION TO CHAOS is depicted schematically by means of a bifurcation diagram: a plot of a family of attractors (*vertical axis*) versus a control parameter (*horizontal axis*). The diagram was generated by a simple dynamical system that maps one number to another. The dynamical system used here is called a circle map, which is specified by the iterative equation $x_{n+1} = \omega + x_n + k/2\pi \cdot \sin(2\pi x_n)$. For each chosen value of the control parameter k a computer plotted the corresponding attractor. The colors encode the probability of finding points on the attractors: red corresponds to regions that are visited frequently, green to regions that are visited less frequently and blue to regions that are rarely visited. As k is increased from 0 to 2 (*see drawing at left*), the diagram shows two paths to chaos: a quasi-periodic route (from $k = 0$ to $k = 1$, which corresponds to the green region above) and a "period doubling" route (from $k = 1.4$ to $k = 2$). The quasi-periodic route is mathematically equivalent to a path that passes through a torus attractor. In the period-doubling route, which is based on the limit-cycle attractor, branches appear in pairs, following the geometric series 2, 4, 8, 16, 32 and so on. The iterates oscillate among the pairs of branches. (At a particular value of k—1.6, for instance—the iterates visit only two values.) Ultimately the branch structure becomes so fine that a continuous band structure emerges: a threshold is reached beyond which chaos appears.

8. Is it reasonable to compare mental processes with physical processes, as the authors do toward the conclusion of the essay?

QUESTIONS ABOUT THE AUTHORS' RHETORICAL STRATEGIES

1. The first paragraph of this essay is mostly background information about predictability versus randomness. Why not begin with the second paragraph, which

might capture a reader's attention with its announcement of a "striking discovery"? What do the authors gain rhetorically by beginning as they do?

2. The authors use some questions as transitions. Find some of these. Where do they usually occur? What is necessary for a question to provide a good transition?

3. The authors use many specific examples to illustrate their points. Are such examples necessary? What does their use suggest about the intended audience for this essay?

4. What is an "attractor"? What rhetorical strategies do the authors use to define this term? How do the authors subdivide the definition?

5. How important to the argument of the essay are the illustrations? Are there any distinctions between the prose describing the illustrations and the prose of the essay itself?

6. At times, the authors seem to change their level of formality in the essay. Writing of the randomness of a dripping faucet, they note that "this is an experiment easily carried out personally; the faucets without the little screens work best." What is the purpose of changing levels of formality?

7. Describe the rhetorical strategy of the conclusion of the essay.

8. Many scientists rigorously omit any references to those who did experiments or analyzed them, all on the assumption that the experiments and analyses could be repeated by anyone. In this essay, the authors seem careful to include the

names of those who performed experiments or analyzed them. Why do you think they do this?

WRITING FROM WITHIN AND ABOUT THE SCIENTIFIC COMMUNITY

Writing for Yourself

1. In your journal explore the connotations of the word *chaos*.
2. In your journal explore the characteristics of a time when you had some excellent ideas arise out of connections from within what seemed to be chaotic material.

Writing for Nonacademic Audiences

1. The editor of your local newspaper, upon hearing that you have done some reading about chaos theory, has asked you to write a short piece (150 words) for the paper, in which you explain the essence of chaos theory and some of its implications.
2. The Boston Museum of Science is surveying college campuses to find likely candidates for positions at the museum. Your affinity for science has attracted the attention of the museum's directors, and you are asked to show your skills in oral communication by presenting a 20-minute description of the new vision of chaos to the trustees of that museum. Remembering that one of the principal goals of the museum is to interest young students in science, you write up the script for that presentation.
3. Your college or university has established a small science museum, especially for children. One of its displays includes a pendulum, at the end of which children can attach a pen, and which they can then set swinging from different directions with different amounts of force over the surface of some drawing paper. The pendulum draws some marvelously intricate patterns on the paper. The director of the institute, hearing that you know something of chaos theory, asks you to write one hundred words for a placard to be placed near the pendulum. The placard is to explain what principles of chaos theory the pendulum demonstrates, and it will be read by the parents whose children play with this display.

Writing for Academic Audiences

1. Write a description of an experiment that a high school class could conduct that would demonstrate some of the new understandings of chaos.
2. Read over the introductory chapters of James Gleick's *Chaos: Making a New Science*. Write a 750-word essay for a college rhetoric class in which you compare and contrast the intended audiences of the book and of the essay included here. What factors contribute to the differences between the audiences?
3. Write a 2,000- to 2,500-word research paper for a history of science class in which you argue that the growth of the science of chaos is or is not a classic example of the way that the field of science makes progress.

INTERCONNECTIONS: QUESTIONS FOR WRITING

Writing for Yourself

1. Do scientists observe and then postulate hypotheses, or do hypotheses determine what the scientists are predisposed to see? How influential are the scientists' predispositions? One way to understand the science of the Middle Ages and the Renaissance is to see those periods as times within which scientists were expected to hold to certain assumptions: that the earth was flat, that the earth moved around the sun, that the stars were fixed, that man himself was at the center of a great chain of being. To attack these assumptions was to challenge—in addition to many other formidable institutions—the scientific community. The rationalists sought to free science from set assumptions—or sets of assumptions—which are just as steely and fixed, which predispose scientists to specific interpretations.

   Examine this situation as it relates to Galileo, Darwin, and Gould. In each case, would you say that the writer begins with a hypothesis or a set of observations? Is it possible to tell whether observation has been influenced by what the scientist expected to find? Deal with these questions in your journal.

2. Under what conditions does the practice of scientific investigation become ethically wrong? Does the question of ethics enter into the conditions that surround the research or into the nature of the research itself?

   In your journal, explore how the author of *The Book of Secrets* and Levi-Montalcini stand on this issue.

Writing for Nonacademic Audiences

1. One of the large questions in a discipline centers on how that discipline makes progress. Pursuing this question involves dealing with the nature of evidence, wrestling with the possibility—or impossibility—of objectivity in interpreting that evidence, and questioning the permanence and reliability of established theories. If scientific discourse communities make progress only through continued reevaluation of accepted ideas, then one might legitimately ask whether any explanation in the sciences can be judged to be conclusive. And if nothing is conclusive, then one might ask, first, whether the sciences can ever teach us anything that affects real life in ways beyond the obviously practical, and second, whether the message of contemporary scientific discourse communities is that it is not possible to know anything.

   Examine this situation as it relates to Darwin and Crutchfield. For a government pamphlet to be used to encourage more high school students to enter the sciences, write a 500-word essay dealing with questions such as the following:

   How might each of these writers explain the way science makes progress?
   How might their discourse communities affect the ways in which they understand the nature of the progress?
   Is scientific progress itself a laudable goal?

2. The history of science records many instances in which scientific understanding of a natural phenomenon has changed over time. Perhaps this suggests that no phenomenon is ever fully explained. Or perhaps it demonstrates that even apparently simple phenomena are involved in complex and interconnected processes.

Examine the different conceptions of the nature of the physical universe in Darwin, Capra, and Crutchfield et al. How do their specific discourse communities affect these conceptions? Do these conceptions affect the rhetorical strategies of these writers? Your 500-word response will be part of an application for a summer internship at Brookhaven National Laboratory, a facility known for its research on nuclear technology.

Examine the different understandings of the motivations for animal behavior in Aristotle and Gould. How does each writer conceive of animal behavior? How might you explain their different understandings of the motives for that behavior? Your 500-word response will be part of an application for a summer internship at Toronto's public zoo.

3. Is it the case that a particular view of the nature of human beings will influence a scientist's perception of evidence? Or will slant that scientist's interpretation of that evidence? Think about the author of *The Book of Secrets*, Frair and Davis, and Stephen Jay Gould in considering this question. Then write a 750-word open letter to either Frair and Davis or Gould showing the writer or writers how their perceptions have slanted their interpretation of the evidence.

Writing for Academic Audiences

1. Every writer, we have argued, writes out of a particular discourse community and to a specific audience. Most discourse communities have a world-view that a particular writer might share completely, might share partially, or might be in tension with. In any case, a writer's own world-view—and the writer's reaction to and stance toward other world-views—affects that writer's positions, stances, and rhetorical strategies. In scientific discourse communities, this means that a writer's world-view affects the way the writer observes phenomena, interprets phenomena, and organizes observations into meaningful statements on the nature of the universe. This may mean, therefore, that preconceived viewpoints strongly influence a writer, perhaps shaping the writer's understanding of phenomena in ways that would be quite alien to another writer who holds a different set of preconceptions.

Examine this situation as it relates to the author of *The Book of Secrets*, Frair and Davis, and Fritjof Capra. Then draft a 750-word essay, to be presented as a final project for a course on the history of the sciences, in which you deal with the following questions:

What are the principal characteristics of these writers' world-views?
How do they affect the ways in which these writers approach their subjects?
Do the world-views influence rhetorical strategies in any way?

2. Most scientific work is based upon observation of one kind or another. The nature of that observation varies with the discipline, as do the methods of interpreting the observations. One of the questions that the twentieth century in particular has posed is whether scientific theorizing must be limited by some kind of direct observation. Is it legitimate to set forth theories about such phenomena as infinitely small particles, incomprehensibly vast distances, black holes that defy observation?

For an introductory course in one of the sciences, write a 750-word essay in which you examine the ways in which Aristotle, Capra, and Crutchfield et al. use observation to form their hypotheses. Is a hypothesis that is not testable a legitimate hypothesis? Or are direct observations central to the validity of a hypothesis?

INTERCONNECTIONS: QUESTIONS FOR DISCUSSION AND WRITING ABOUT AND FROM WITHIN ALL THE REPRESENTED DISCOURSE COMMUNITIES

Writing for Yourself

1. In your journal, reflect on why some majors do not appeal to you.
2. In your journal, reflect on the reasons for your choice of a major. Alternately, reflect on the reasons why you might not yet have chosen a major.
3. In a journal entry, compare the ways in which information is conveyed to you in several courses you are currently taking. Are the differences due to the instructor or to the nature of the discipline itself?
4. In a journal entry, reflect on the reading you have done in this text. In which discipline did you find the essays most accessible? Is this due to the nature of the subject matter? The quality of the writers? Your own interest in the field?
5. Many of the writers represented in this collection call into question the establishment of fact—whether it be scientific fact, historic fact, or "aesthetic" facts. In your journal, react to this state of unsettledness.
6. In your journal, reflect on which writer represented in this collection you would most like to meet. What about that writer attracts your interest?
7. In your journal, consider what shocked you the most in your reading in this collection.

Writing for Nonacademic Audiences

1. During the 1970s, Steve Allen hosted a series of roundtable discussions in which famous historical figures appeared to assert and debate their points of view. As a scriptwriter for that series, now newly revived, you have been asked to bring together three of the writers represented in this collection—each from a different discourse community—to address the following questions:

   Is it possible for a discipline to make progress?
   If so, then how is progress to be measured in a discipline?

   Choose the figures and write the script for this thirty-minute presentation.
2. Leaders of your local faith community have challenged your decision to attend college, arguing that the studies of various disciplines—except perhaps medical science—do not really benefit or serve either humanity or the individual. They inquire whether your studies actually encourage an individual's moral growth or a community's prosperity and happiness. Defend your decision in a 750-word letter to the head of this community, referring to representative writers from three discourse communities in this collection.
3. The administration of your college is trying to encourage the development of interdisciplinary courses within the curriculum. The academic dean has invited students to react to such a push in a concise 500-word letter. You decide to write such a letter, drawing from the work of two writers from different discourse communities included in this collection.
4. Certain discourse communities, such as the Marxist and Freudian and Feminist communities, cross over several disciplines. Using examples from two writers

included in this collection, write a 750-word explanation to the provost of your college explaining why you feel one of these discourse communities should be better represented in your school's departments.

5. Write a 750-word letter to the academic vice principal of your high school concerning the quality of the high school curriculum which you have recently completed.

6. In an era when cases of scholarly fraud and cheating are not uncommon, your college has added the following question to its application for admission: "Does your area of concentration ask a researcher to make any kinds of ethical decisions in the course of conducting investigations?" Write a 750-word response to that question, showing how your concerns cut across disciplines.

Writing for Academic Audiences

1. For a senior-level course in research methodology, write a 750-word essay in which you examine the different kinds of evidence to which different discourse communities appeal. How does the selection of evidence affect the construction and development of arguments within the field? Draw your examples from three discourse communities represented in this collection.

2. The stance of a writer is defined as the relationship between the writer, the reader, and the subject matter. For a class in rhetoric, write a 750-word essay in which you examine whether certain discourse communities may be characterized by the stance that they take. Or does stance vary from author to author within a discourse community? Choose four representative writers from this collection to illustrate your argument.

3. For a course in rhetoric, choose the author whose tone you found to be particularly attractive and write a 500-word analysis of why that tone works well and how it contributes to the overall effect of the essay.

4. Prepare a 1,000-word essay to be read at an interdisciplinary academic conference in which you attack or defend popularizers—those writers within a discipline who write not only for colleagues in a given specialty, but for the popular audience as well. Use three examples from this collection.

5. Choose the discourse community among those included in this collection that is closest to your major. In a 1,000-word essay for a sophomore-level introduction to your area of concentration, show how at least two other discourse communities might contribute to research within your own discipline. Use examples from this collection to illustrate your argument.

6. As part of an academic conference within the discourse community closest to your major, you have been chosen as a student respondent to one of the pieces included in this collection. From within the appropriate discourse community, choose the piece that you thought was most clearly wrong, and write your 1,000-word response to it.

COPYRIGHT ACKNOWLEDGMENTS

INDEX

A

"Aesthetics of Eskimo Dance"
(Damerow and Luttmann), 298–
310
"American Indian Model of the
Universe" (Whorf), 369–77
"Analysis of Political Behavior"
(Lasswell), 501–13
Apology for Poetry (Sidney), 194–206
Aristotle, *History of Animals*, 585–92
Aristotle, *Poetics*, 183–93
Augustine, *The Confessions*, 322–32

B

Bede, *History of the English Church
and People*, 62–71
Bettelheim, Bruno, *The Uses of
Enchantment*, 254–69
Book of Secrets of Albertus Magnus,
593–99
Bradford, William, *History of Plymouth
Plantation*, 72–84
Braudel, Fernand, *The Mediterranean
and the Mediterranean World in
the Age of Philip II*, 109–27

C

Capra, Fritjof, *The Turning Point*,
645–68
Case for Creation (Frair and Davis),
684–97
"Chaos" (Crutchfield *et al.*), 698–725
Communist Manifesto (Marx and
Engels), 444–56
Confessions (Augustine), 322–32

Coral Gardens and Their Magic
(Malinowski), 483–500
Creation of Patriarchy (Lerner), 137–54
Crutchfield, James *et al.*, "Chaos," 698–725

D

Damerow, Gail, "Aesthetics of Eskimo
Dance," 298–310
Darwin, Charles, *The Voyage of the
Beagle*, 611–26
Davis, Percival, *Case for Creation*,
684–97
De Motu (On Motion) (Galilei), 600–10
Decline and Fall of the Roman Empire
(Gibbon), 85–92
Descartes, René, *Meditations on First
Philosophy*, 342–54
Discoveries of a Critic (Rosenfeld),
230–38
"Dualism of Human Nature and Its
Social Conditions" (Durkheim),
469–82
Durkheim, Émile, "The Dualism of
Human Nature and Its Social
Conditions," 469–82

E

"E = MC^2," (Einstein), 627–32
Einstein, Albert, "E = MC^2," 627–32
Engels, Friedrich, *Communist
Manifesto*, 444–56
*Essay Concerning Human
Understanding* (Locke), 355–68
"Essay in Aesthetics" (Fry), 216–29
Essene, Virginia, *Secret Truths*, 420–28
"Existentialism" (Sartre), 378–89

F

Fatal Shore (Hughes), 167–76
Frair, Wayne, *A Case for Creation*,
    684–97
Freud, Sigmund, *Studies in Hysteria*,
    457–68
Fry, Roger, "An Essay in Aesthetics,"
    216–29

G

Galilei, Galileo, *De Motu* (*On Motion*),
    600–10
*Gender, An Ethnomethodological
    Approach* (Kessler and McKenna),
    563–76
Genovese, Eugene D., *Roll, Jordan,
    Roll*, 155–66
Gibbon, Edward, *The Decline and Fall
    of the Roman Empire*, 85–92
Gilligan, Carol, *In a Different Voice*,
    529–47
Gould, Stephen Jay, "Only His Wings
    Remained," 669–83
Graves, Robert, "Was Benedict Arnold
    a Traitor?" 93–108

H

History of Animals (Aristotle), 585–92
*History of the English Church and
    People* (Bede), 62–71
History of the Peloponnesian War
    (Thucydides), 50–61
History of Plymouth Plantation
    (Bradford), 72–84
Hughes, Robert, *The Fatal Shore*,
    167–76

I

In a Different Voice (Gilligan), 529–47
In Praise of Imperfection (Levi-
    Montalcini), 633–44

J

Julian of Norwich, *Revelations of Divine
    Love*, 333–41

K

Kessler, Suzanne, *Gender, An
    Ethnomethodological Approach*,
    563–76
Kuhn, Thomas S., *The Structure of
    Scientific Revolutions*, 408–19

L

Lamb, Charles, "On the Artificial
    Comedy of the Last Century,"
    207–15
Lasswell, Harold Dwight, *The Analysis
    of Political Behavior*, 501–13
Lerner, Gerda, *The Creation of
    Patriarchy*, 137–54
Levi-Montalcini, Rita, *In Praise of
    Imperfection*, 633–44
Locke, John, *An Essay Concerning
    Human Understanding*, 355–68
Luttmann, Rick, "Aesthetics of Eskimo
    Dance," 298–310

M

Malinowski, Bronislaw, *Coral Gardens
    and Their Magic*, 483–500
Marx, Karl, *Communist Manifesto*,
    444–56
McKenna, Wendy, *Gender, An
    Ethnomethodological Approach*,
    563–76
Meditations on First Philosophy
    (Descartes), 342–54
*Mediterranean and the Mediterranean
    World in the Age of Philip II*
    (Braudel), 109–27
Merton, Thomas, "Zen Buddhist
    Monasticism," 390–407
Modleski, Tania, *The Women Who
    Knew Too Much*, 281–97

O

"On the Artificial Comedy of the Last
    Century" (Lamb), 207–215
"Only His Wings Remained" (Gould),
    669–83
Ouchi, William G., *Theory Z: How
    American Business Can Meet the
    Japanese Challenge*, 548–62

P

Plato, *The Republic*, 316–21
Poetics (Aristotle), 183–93
Poetics of Prose (Todorov), 270–80
Psychopathic God (Waite), 128–36

R

Reflections on Behaviorism and Society
(Skinner), 514–28
Republic (Plato), 316–21
Revelations of Divine Love (Julian of
Norwich), 333–41
Roll, Jordan, Roll (Genovese), 155–66
Rosenfeld, Paul, *Discoveries of a Critic*,
230–38

S

Sartre, Jean-Paul, "Existentialism,"
378–89
Secret Truths (Essene), 420–28
Sidney, Sir Philip, *Apology for Poetry*,
194–206
Skinner, B. F., *Reflections on
Behaviorism and Society*, 514–28
Smith, Adam, *The Wealth of Nations*,
434–43
Structure of Scientific Revolutions
(Kuhn), 408–19
Studies in Hysteria (Freud), 457–68

T

"Talks at the Yenan Forum on Art and
Literature" (Zedong), 239–53
*Theory Z: How American Business Can
Meet the Japanese Challenge*
(Ouchi), 548–62

U

Thucydides, *History of the
Peloponnesian War*, 50–61
Todorov, Tzvetan, *The Poetics of Prose*,
270–80
Turning Point (Capra), 645–68

U

Uses of Enchantment (Bettelheim),
254–69

V

Voyage of the Beagle (Darwin),
611–26

W

Waite, Roert G. L., *The Psychopathic
God*, 128–36
"Was Benedict Arnold a Traitor?"
(Graves), 93–108
Wealth of Nations (Smith), 434–43
Whorf, Benjamin Lee, "An American
Indian Model of the Universe,"
369–77
Women Who Knew Too Much
(Modleski), 287–97

Z

Zedong, Mao, "Talks at the Yenan
Forum on Art and Literature,"
239–53
"Zen Buddhist Monasticism" (Merton),
390–407